To anyone who has heard Pete Seeger in person—and by now that must add up to over a million—the thing that sets him apart from most folksingers is the way he gets his audiences to join in. That is the way you will feel about *The Incompleat Folksinger*. You'll find yourself joining in with some memories and thoughts of your own as Pete rambles over the folk scene of the last twenty-five years—and points beyond.

Here are talk and songs about those who sailed, mined, farmed, loafed, organized unions, spent time in jail, and traveled down many roads. Here are portraits from memory of Woody Guthrie and Leadbelly. Here are the stories and music of people wanting to be free—from the political songs of medieval minstrels to South African freedom songs.

Here, too, are Pete's thoughts on the folk music of the world—British, American, Asian, African—how it came about, how to sing it, play it, appreciate it. *The Incompleat Folksinger* is also a folk song collection—words, music, guitar chords—with songs of the people and places he is talking about.

The Incompleat Folksinger is a wonderful mixture covering just about everything Pete feels is important in the folk scene—and outside it. And whether he is telling us how to compose by ear, choose the right musical instrument, make up our own songs, enjoy the art of unaccompanied singing, or speaking out on the meaning of Americanism (with special reference to the days when the House Un-American Activities Committee was a power in the land), the voice is unmistakably in the American grain: fine, and loud, and clear.

THE INCOMPLEAT

A Footnote to the Title

In 1653 a self-educated ironmonger published a guide and companion for amateur fishermen which became one of the permanent treasures of English literature. The author of the pocket-size volume—durably bound in sheepskin—states in the preface his belief that fellow anglers "may here learn something that may be worth their money, if they be not poor and needy men; and in case they be, I then wish them to forbear to buy it."

This blend of practicality and humaneness is characteristic; later he tells us so vividly how to catch, clean and cook a fish that we can hardly wait to get started—then immediately reminds us that whatever we do not need for supper will of course be passed along "to some poor body." (He sharply condemns destructive wholesale methods of fish catching.) Izaak Walton took the Royalist side in the upheavals of his day (he disliked Puritanical "money-getting men" who frowned on idle pursuits like angling), but obviously he was not insensitive to everyday hardships among his countrymen.

The Compleat Angler was a superb tutor of fishing skills. But it lives today because it brings to life an enthusiastic, honest human being "of mild, and sweet, and peaceable spirits" who loves the beauty of the world around him and wishes to be of service to his fellow man.

We don't aspire to literary immortality; we do admire the spirit in which Izaak approached his subject.

J.M.S.

FOLKSINGER

BY PETE SEEGER

Edited by Jo Metcalf Schwartz

SIMON AND SCHUSTER·NEW YORK

Special mention must be made of *Sing Out* magazine, Moe Asch of Folkways Records, and Oak Publications—sources of much of the material in this book. It is thanks to *Sing Out* and Folkways Records that the folk revival was kept alive when no one else was interested.

We thank the song copyright holders, and especially The Richmond Organization and Sanga Music, Inc., for their generosity in enabling us to include abundant musical examples. We thank also the makers and collectors of the pictures we've used (see p. 583).

We thank Harold Leventhal, Billie Green, and Joy Graeme for the many hours of hard work they devoted to helping us try to trace and communicate with the true sources of all music, words and illustrations herein. Despite our efforts, it is in the nature of folk and folk-related material that we have not in every instance succeeded. Perhaps the book itself will put us in touch with those we failed to reach, so that a future edition may include correct credit.

The Law says we have to print the following statement:

First printing

SBN 671–20954–X
Library of Congress Catalog Card Number: 73–156161
Designed by Eve Metz
Manufactured in the United States of America
Music autographed by Maxwell Weaner

We are grateful to the following additional firms and individuals for use of previously published material:

From *The Newport Folk Festival Song Book,* ed. Jean Ritchie, copyright 1964 by the Alfred Music Co.: parts of Preface, pp. 276–77.

From Jones, Mary, *Autobiography of Mother Jones*, Arno Press Edition 1969: "Mother Jones and the Singing Miners' Wives," pp. 85–86.

From *Chanteying Aboard American Ships*, by Frederick P. Harlow, © 1962 by Barre Publishing Company, Inc.: the song "Santy," pp. 64–65, and text quotations on p. 65.

From *Broadside* No. 30, © 1963 by *Broadside Magazine:* "Report from Greenwood, Miss.: a Singing Movement," pp. 247–48;

from *Broadside* No. 57, © 1965: "The March from Selma to Montgomery," pp. 104–11.

From *Caravan* magazine, October 1968: "Too Many People Listen to Me," p. 575.

From *Tin Horns and Calico,* by Henry Christman, Henry Holt & Co., 1945, used by permission of Henry Christman: "The End of Bill Snyder," pp. 92–93.

From *The Daily World,* July 4, 1968: "This Paleface Does a Double Take," pp. 425–28.

From *Dialog* magazine, Fall, 1967: "Singing in Lebanon and Israel," pp. 431–37.

From the book *Bound for Glory* by Woody

Continued on page 584

1719585

ACKNOWLEDGMENTS: Many parts of this book have been borrowed shamelessly from people with whom I've worked over the years —Lee Hays, Irwin Silber, Moe Asch, Woody Guthrie, Charles Seeger, and many, many more. I guess the best thing is to quote Woody:

"Aw, he just stole from me.
But I steal from everybody.
Why, I'm the biggest song stealer there ever was."

Contents

Special Note for beginning musicians: the tablature method of guitar and banjo notation is explained on page 370.

I CALL THEM ALL LOVE SONGS

THEY TELL OF LOVE of man and woman, and parents and children, love of country, freedom, beauty, mankind, the world, love of searching for truth and other unknowns. But, of course, love alone is not enough.

Love without courage and wisdom is sentimentality, as with the ordinary church member. Courage without love and wisdom is foolhardiness, as with the ordinary soldier. Wisdom without love and courage is cowardice, as with the ordinary intellectual.   —Ammon Hennacy

It's well known that men of thought and action are often out of patience with music: "Why do people waste so much time with this treacherous substitute for worthwhile activity?"

Here's a typical quote:

Let us trace jazz back to its origin. The Negroes were hopelessly enslaved. . . . In their extremity the Negroes discovered song, which likewise answered the needs of faith. . . . Marx's celebrated remark that 19th century religion was the opiate of the European masses is equally applicable to the jazz of the Negro slaves. In jazz they created a true art form. But with it they also shut every door to freedom. Jazz imprisoned the Negroes more and more in their slavery; from then on they drew a morose relish from it. It is highly significant that this slave music has become the music of the modern world. . . . The reason is . . . clear: it is the music of men who are satisfied with the illusion of freedom provoked by its sounds, while chains of iron wind around them ever tighter.   —Jacques Ellul in *The Technological Society*

(Have a good time arguing; don't be misled by his inclusion of all Afro-American music, even spirituals, under the term "jazz." The author is French.)

Scientists and philosophers have often accused singers of not using their heads:

Speech lies halfway between thought and action, and often substitutes for both. . . .   —John Andrew Holmes

And he might have said the same thing about song, which is a heightened form of speech.

Carl Sandburg says there should be an eleventh commandment:

Thou shalt not commit nincompoopery.

How about this one:

Don't start vast projects with half-vast plans.   —Anonymous

Even the angry songs are love songs:

Humanity is outraged in me and with me. We must not dissimulate nor try to forget this indignation which is one of the most passionate forms of love. . . .   —George Sand

If you object to reading all these short quotes, you need read no further. For years I've collected them, pinned them on the wall over my desk, put them in scrapbooks. Some of them seem to contradict each other, but I think of them as supplementing each other. They flit through my head sometimes when I'm singing. I like to sing for kids, but am often reminded:

Every society faces the task of civilizing an onrushing horde of barbarians —its own children. . . .   —Source unknown

But Woody Guthrie said:

I don't want to make kids more like grown-ups; I want to make grown-ups more like kids.

An editorial in rhyme rarely makes a good song. The most long-lasting ballads tell a story and let the listener draw the moral. But just as the newspaper owner uses his editorial opinion to select what stories to print, every singer shows his opinion in the songs he selects to sing.

Some say "Wrap your troubles in dreams and dream your troubles away." But I think that if songs can help us explore our past and our present, and even speculate about our future, then you and I have a better chance of going out and doing something about our troubles.

A last quote:

An open mind is a great idea, but if you make it your primary aim in life, what you'll end up with will more resemble a cave of winds. —Heywood Broun

Introduction

WHAT CAN A SONG DO?

"Songs have overthrown kings and empires," exuberated Anatole France, probably recalling "La Marseillaise."

He was oversimplifying. Some songs mainly help people forget their troubles. Other songs help people understand their troubles. Some few songs inspire people to do something about their troubles. Occasionally these different roles are present in one song. The following pages give one man's attempt to explore the situation in mid-twentieth century, mainly in the U.S.A.

The term "folk music" was invented by nineteenth-century scholars to describe the music of the peasantry, age-old and anonymous. Nowadays it covers such a multitude of sins as to be almost meaningless. To me it means homemade-type music played mainly by ear, arising out of older traditions but with a meaning for today. I use it only for lack of a better word. Similarly I have had to accept the label "folksinger," although "a professional singer of amateur music" would be more accurate in my own case.

No matter. Just remember that words are slippery things.

I was born in New York City in 1919. As a child I was allowed to bang or tootle on any musical instrument that struck my fancy. Age eight I got a ukulele; my roommate and I gave a performance of sea shanties for the rest of the school. We especially liked the one about the drunken sailor. My brother and I would harmonize on Christmas carols, school and camp songs, anything. I can sing you the pop songs from 1928 to 1934:

He's just a sentimental gentleman from Georgia, Georgia,
Gentle to the ladies all the time!*

But it never occurred to me to try and make a living from music.

When I dropped out of college in my sophomore year I wanted to be

---

* Copyright 1932, Mills Music, Inc. Copyright renewed © 1960, Mills Music, Inc. Used by permission of Belwin-Mills Publishing Corp.

a journalist, but months of knocking on doors brought no job. It was the Dirty Thirties; there was lots of unemployment. A schoolteacher relative said she could pay me all of five dollars for coming to sing for the children. It seemed like stealing, to take money for something I'd always done for fun. It still does.

One thing led to another. I never did get that job on a newspaper, but over a period of years, and between singing for a good many thousand kinds of audiences, I wrote a number of articles for small folk-music magazines.

This book started as a compendium of magazine articles and columns written for *Sing Out* and other journals over the past two decades. We hoped it would add up to Helpful Hints for the Frustrated Banjo Picker, Guitar Picker, Song Leader, and Soul Searcher.

But in reading it over and trying to improve the grammar, I winced at too much archaic slang and too many opinions disproved by history. Furthermore, a stage performer repeats himself a lot. We ended up trying to blue-pencil and rewrite a good deal. As it stands now, this book is neither a true record of all the mistakes I've committed to paper in twenty years, nor is it a true record of all the mistakes I'm making right now. Just a bramble patch you must wade through in hopes of plucking some sweet berries.

The book has no story line. It has no plot, not even the Communist Plot (see Chapter 12). If you are one of the several millions who recently bought a guitar, or fell in love with some kind of homemade music, you may be able to glean a little useful information here, but don't feel you have to slog through it all. Leaf through lightly; settle on some part that interests you; use the index to locate paragraphs on specific subjects.

Sorry the book has to cost so much. For many people this represents a good day's pay or more—which is what books used to cost before the paperback revolution.

In any case, please don't accept any of the volume as gospel. Assume each paragraph to be prefaced by the phrase, "It seems to me that . . ." One of the best things about this kind of music is that there is no high priest who knows all the answers. Everyone has to make up his or her mind: What is right? What is wrong? It's a job, but maybe the most necessary job of all, for every modern man or woman.

Hoping to be of help,

Sincerely,

PETER SEEGER

EDITOR'S NOTE

APPROXIMATELY three-fifths of the contents of this book have been in print before, but I doubt that even the most avid Seeger fan has seen all the periodicals, books, and record liners in which they appeared. They are here brought together—supplemented from letters and other manuscript material—in the shape suggested by their inherent continuity; Pete has provided new writing to fill gaps and to share some of his current preoccupations and experiences.

We offer the compilation as a convenience for old friends and a friendly companion for those just beginning to enjoy folk music. ("Old Songs and New People" explores the meaning of the American folk revival, with an account of Pete's share in its beginnings and an examination of a few kinds of folk music. "A Folk Revival in the Atom Age" chronicles many of the Revival's later ramifications, satisfactions, and problems. "Making Homemade Music" focuses on practical information about singing and playing. "The World That Music Lives In" evaluates several aspects of Pete's experience with the—often controversial—interaction between folk creativity and twentieth-century institutions.) This is not a folklore textbook, nor an autobiography, nor a full history of the folk revival, nor yet a systematic preformers' manual; but a reader desiring any of these will find a good deal of what he is looking for, and a number of guideposts for further exploring.

He will find, also, fascinating insights which fall into none of these categories. Pete's thinking, in fact, does not fit a strict outline, just as his life defies any philosophical pigeonhole. These writings (produced, over a quarter-century, mainly to meet current needs of his audience) contain quirks and ambiguities, and multiple interlocking trains of thought. Nevertheless there is logic and unity here, of a highly individual kind (just as there is unique, unmistakable integrity in his life).

One theme is recurrent: the gaiety—the tenderness—the improbable gallantry and fortitude—with which, by singing, our human family has infused its long struggle to possess its future.

Clearly Pete Seeger ranks among our major creative artists; but this man is cherished in a way that transcends the usual criteria of success. His extra dimension is readily perceived; it is less easy to define. These pages, however, exemplify what is perhaps the mainspring of his crowded work-life: an urge to infect all whom he can reach with the irresistible, deeply humanizing itch to make music together.

J.M.S.

No alert person will look through this volume and fail to notice the abiding, indispensable presence of Toshi—to whom I, also, am indebted in far too many ways to enumerate. It would be out of the question to edit a Pete Seeger book without her wise and generous help.

PART I

Old Songs
and
New People

1·A Revival of Interest in Folk Music?

IN THE EARLY 1960s the guitar became the favorite instrument of many a college campus: books and LPs of "folk songs" gathered on every shelf. Why should these songs catch on in many a school and summer camp, not to speak of coffee houses, and Washington Square Park of a summer Sunday?

Five possible reasons:

One: Since World War II there has been evidence on many sides that Americans were curious to rediscover their roots, to learn about their own country's heritage. I'm thinking of the numerous historical re-creations dotted around the United States, of the magazines such as *American Heritage,* the movies and novels of American life.

Two: A general increase in a great variety of do-it-yourself activities during these same years. Skiers, bowlers, boaters, Sunday painters, potters, weavers, furniture builders, gardeners, camera bugs, hot rodders— all these and many more wanted to be more than passive spectators. And the millions of guitar pickers are one more sign that not all Americans are satisfied to simply sit and watch TV.

Three: We were handed on a silver platter some of the world's best songs, by the folklorists who dug the gold out of the hills and presented it to us. Our country is rich in many different traditions, with variety to suit almost any taste, from the old classic ballads to rough work songs and raucous fun songs. LP records made it possible to hear this music performed by people who knew it well.

Four: It takes a certain sophistication to sing an old hillbilly song without being worried that someone will call you an old hillbilly. Or to sing an old spiritual without wondering if someone will call you an Uncle Tom. Maybe we had to wait a few years till we were far enough away from our past to be able to pick and choose the good from the bad.

Five: Young people found that here was a way to make social comments about events in present-day America—comments they had been unable to make any other way.

Every industrialized country in the world has seen some sort of revival of interest in music of the countrysides or traditional music played by ear in the cities. The revival of interest in folk music which mushroomed in the 60s actually started in the nineteenth century. Collectors such as John Lomax of Texas, and England's Cecil Sharp, spent years going from one section of the country to another, painstakingly locating songs and singers. Of course, their efforts were scoffed at, especially in the regions richest in music. Lomax went to a cattlemen's convention, trying to trace some of the old cowboy ballads. A rancher stood up and said: "There's a man named Lomax here who wants to know if anyone knows some of the old cowboy songs. Why everybody knows those damn-fool songs, and only a bigger damn fool would try to collect them. I vote we adjourn to the bar." And they did. But thanks to the persistence of Lomax we know songs like "Whoopee-ty-yi-yo, Get Along Little Dogies" and "Streets of Laredo," not to mention "Home on the Range."

Lomax's Texas professors also scoffed at his efforts. He did get encouragement from Professor Kittredge of Harvard; Kittredge was interested in carrying on the work of Francis James Child, who had made the classic compilation of British ballads.

The problem was, as another Texan, J. Frank Dobie, once observed, that many collectors "dug up dead bones from one graveyard only to bury them in another." The songs, having been dug up in the hills, were now buried in libraries.

In the 1930s came a younger breed of folklorist, who said, in effect, "Let's give folk music back to the folks." They started taking the folk songs out of their collections and giving them to the popularizers. (Carl Sandburg's 1927 collection, *The American Songbag*, had made an impression; and Sandburg used to end his poetry recitations with some songs.) In particular, one man should get credit: Alan Lomax, son of John. In 1938 Alan persuaded a young actor named Burl Ives that he should sing folk songs professionally; he taught Burl some of his most successful songs, like "Blue Tailed Fly." Alan showed Leadbelly, Woody Guthrie, and Josh White that there were new audiences up north for their southern songs.

And he got me started. I was just one of the first Yankee college students who discovered there were more different kinds of native American music than what Tin Pan Alley gave out over the radio. By the 1960s there were millions of us.

Perhaps a few personal recollections can illustrate what these successive generations of young people were looking for.

In 1935 I was sixteen years old, playing tenor banjo in the school jazz band. I was less interested in studying the classical music that my parents taught at Juilliard. But my father is a musicologist, and it was through him that I first got interested in American folk music and became conscious of the immensity of the field. In 1935 a good deal of song collecting was being done under the auspices of different government agencies such as the Resettlement Administration. Such work was called boondoggling* at the time, but through the work of these agencies, the famous Library of Congress collection was first built up.

My father, as an expert in several branches of musical scholarship, was involved in these projects. And I accompanied him on one field trip to North Carolina. We wound down through the narrow valleys with so many turns in the road that I got seasick. We passed wretched little cabins with half-naked children peering out the door; we passed exhibits of patchwork quilts and other handicrafts which often were the main source of income. I first became acquainted with a side of America that I had never known before.

At the Asheville square dance and ballad festival I fell in love with the old-fashioned five-string banjo, rippling out a rhythm to one fascinating song after another. I liked the rhythms. I liked the melodies, time-tested by generations of singers. I liked the words.

Compared to the trivialities of the popular songs my brothers and I formerly harmonized, the words of these songs had all the meat of human life in them. They sang of heroes, outlaws, murderers, fools. They weren't afraid of being tragic instead of just sentimental. They weren't afraid of being scandalous instead of giggly or cute. Above all, they seemed frank, straightforward, honest. By comparison, it seemed to me that too many art songs were concerned with being elegant and too many pop songs were concerned with being clever.

In 1935 I tried learning some of this style of music. Thirty-seven years later I'm still learning. I've found out that some of the simplest music is some of the most difficult to do.

Wisht I had a nickel,	'Round and 'round, old Joe Clarke
Wisht I had a dime.	'Round and 'round, I say
Wisht I had a pretty girl,	'Round and 'round, old Joe Clarke
I'd kiss her all the time.	I'm a-going away.

---

* An enormously popular word among 1935 anti-New Dealers. My dictionary says a boondoggle is "any unnecessary and wasteful project," or—of all things—a leathercraft project popular among Boy Scouts.

At that time I still didn't know much about America; I really had a rather snobbish attitude. I thought there wasn't anything west of the Hudson River worth seeing. Woody Guthrie taught me different. "Pete, you ought to see what a big country it is."

"How do you do it if you don't have money to travel?"

"Well," he said, "use the rule of the thumb—if you can't hitchhike, ride a freight train."

In 1940 he took me with him for a ways. I kept on going by myself— as far north as the copper mines of Butte, Montana, and as far south as the steel mills of Birmingham, Alabama.

The first train I ever hitched a ride on was in St. Joe, Missouri. Up until that time I'd only thumbed along the highways. Some professional hoboes assured me, however, that the only sensible way to travel was by freight. After lurking around the yards all night, I finally jumped on what I thought was the right train. After an hour of switching back and forth, I found I had been shunted onto a siding.

Later on I got the right train, but I was warned that I'd have to jump off before the yard bulls came around to check the cars. When we finally pulled into Lincoln, Nebraska, I broke my banjo when jumping off. Inexperience. This put me in a spot. It was the only way I had to make a living.

I hocked a small camera I had for a five-dollar guitar and started playing in saloons. In three days I was able to get the camera out of hock and continued west exploring one new city after another.

I was singing in a bar in Montana when an old fellow came up and asked, "Shay, do you know all the vershes to 'Shtrawberry Roan'?" When I admitted I didn't he sat right down then and there and insisted upon dictating them to me—some twenty-three verses; it took us nearly as many bottles of beer to complete the job.

In Butte, Montana, I told members of the local miners' union that I knew some miners' songs, and they asked me to sing at the next union meeting. I had planned to catch a freight train east at nine o'clock, and as the agenda grew long I became afraid I wouldn't be able to make it. I heard the train whistle down at the foot of a hill and told the chairman that I would have to go on then or not at all, so he put me on. I sang a few songs, and he then gave me a check for five dollars.

I looked at it in dismay; it was of absolutely no use to me, since I didn't know where I could cash it. "Oh," says he, "the bar downstairs will take care of this for you." Down I run. What did they give me but five silver dollars. I started running downhill and the damn things kept falling out of my jeans pockets, rolling down the sidewalk, and me trying to find them in the grass—and all the time that train whistling down at the bottom of the hill, just like it's ready to start.

Finally, I never did find one of the silver dollars and ran on without it. It was 20 percent of my total capital, but I really wanted to catch that train.

One bunch of boys I stayed with in Alabama, a coal-mining family, were so broke I would have felt embarrassed to be their guest if I hadn't been just as broke myself. We had cornbread and beans three times a day, with what they called "bulldog gravy" to force it down. The three sons in this family made up a crackerjack fiddle band, and the only time we got good meals was when we visited some neighbors, who would feed us up in return for an evening's music.

Back in New York, in 1941, I met Lee Hays. He, Mill Lampell, and myself started singing together, calling ourselves the Almanac Singers. ("In the country," said Lee, "a farmhouse would have two books in the house, a Bible and an Almanac. One helped us to the next world, the other helped us make it through this one.")

We recorded some peace songs and some union songs* with the help of friends.

Woody Guthrie arrived in June, having just ridden freights and hitch-hiked from the Pacific Northwest, where he'd recently completed writing a batch of songs for the Bonneville Power Administration. He no sooner set foot in our apartment when we said, "Woody, how would you like to go west?" He scratched his head. "I just came from the West, but I don't guess I mind if I join up with you." We had bought a nine-year-old Buick for $125, a terrible eater of gas and oil.

Within the next few days, we made a few extra dollars recording some records, *Sod Buster Ballads*† and *Deep Sea Shanties.*† Then, with a little gasoline money in our pockets, we took off. We sang for automobile workers in Detroit, half a dozen varieties of CIO union people in Chicago, Milwaukee and Denver, and then we got to San Francisco.

---

* See *Talking Union*, Folkways FH 5285.
† Now combined as *The Soil and the Sea*, Mainstream 56005.

When we walked down the aisle of a room where one thousand local members of the longshoremen's union were meeting, we could see some of them turning around in surprise and even disapproval. "What the hell is a bunch of hillbilly singers coming in here for? We got work to do."

But when we finished singing for them "Union Maid," "Talking Union," "Which Side Are You On?," and especially "The Ballad of Harry Bridges," their applause was deafening. We walked down that same aisle on our way out and they slapped Woody on the back so hard they nearly knocked him over.

The Almanac Singers went down to Los Angeles, temporarily lost a couple members, then zigzagged back up to the San Joaquin Valley. Woody and I went up the coast to Oregon and Washington, then zigzagged east, stopping at Butte, Montana, and then Duluth, Minnesota. An organizer for the lumberjacks' union asked us if we would be willing to go around and sing in some of the camps, and we said sure.

He was on a routine inspection tour to make sure that the union contract was being obeyed by the bosses. In the old days lumberjacks used to get lousy food (beans, beans and more beans), and their bedding was often dirty and the bunkhouse full of bugs. Now these matters were all attended to in the union contract. The workers still lived in one big bunkhouse, but it was roomy, clean and warm. And as for food, I never saw such a groaning board. For breakfast they had on the table (no fooling!) ham, sausage, bacon, chops, they had scrambled eggs, fried eggs, boiled eggs. They had applesauce, prunes, figs, oranges, grapefruit, tomato juice, grape juice, milk, coffee, tea, fried potatoes, pancakes, biscuits, toast.

When the cook rang the bell fifty husky men clumped into the cook shack, and sat down and started shoveling in the food. There was no conversation, no talking whatsoever, except maybe "pass the butter, please." This was an old country custom, an inflexible rule: no conversation at mealtimes. If anybody had tried to start talking about the weather or anything else, he would have been looked upon as a boor.

The men were mostly of Scandinavian background. The nineteenth-century logging camps had been full of Irish and French Canadians. The twentieth-century camps were full of Finns and Swedes. They were a taciturn lot. The organizer had told us the previous day, "Don't expect these workers to make a big fuss over your songs, they are Scandahoovians. But I know they will be glad to hear you."

In the evening, around the big stove in the center of the bunkhouse, the organizer spoke briefly to the men and answered a few questions, and then he introduced Woody and me. We walked up to the center, sang a song. There was dead silence. We sang another song; there was still dead silence. We looked at each other and said, "Suppose we ought to sing another?" Well, we sang one more. There was still dead silence. We thanked the men for listening to us, and walked over to the side. One of the men said quietly, "Aren't you going to sing any more, boys?" A little reluctantly we went back and sang a couple more songs, again to complete dead silence, and then we figured we better not push our luck any more and said good night.

The next morning one of the men said to us, "Boy, that music sure was wonderful. Wish you had sang a lot more; we could have listened to it all night."

In the fall of '41, we settled in Greenwich Village, in a cooperative apartment known as Almanac House. People came and went all the time. The cuisine was erratic but interesting, the furniture and decorations almost nonexistent, the sleeping done at odd hours. The output of songs was phenomenal.

We got bookings on the subway circuit: five dollars here and ten dollars there. By working hard we just managed to keep body and soul together. On Sunday afternoons we'd hold open house. Thirty-five cents was charged at the door, and we and friends would sing all afternoon. We called 'em "Hootenannies."

In early '42 our beat-Hitler songs ("Reuben James," "Round and Round Hitler's Grave," etc.) actually got us a radio job or two. An agent working for the William Morris Agency got interested in us.

He took us around to the Rainbow Room, which was at that time a top New York nightclub at Rockefeller Center. We sang a few songs over the mike that afternoon while the bored manager sat in the empty nightclub. He said he might have us work there, but we had to "make the act look better." The men should all wear one-suspender overalls and the women members of the Almanacs wear sunbonnets and gunnysack dresses.

We didn't take too kindly to that suggestion and started improvising verses, which Woody mentioned in *Bound for Glory:*

> At the Rainbow Room the soup's on to boil,
> They're stirring the salad with Standard Oil.

And:

> The Rainbow Room it's mighty high;
> You can see John D. a-flyin' by.

Oh, and this one:

> It's sixty stories high, they say,
> A long way back to the U.S.A.

We walked out of there not expecting that he'd want to hire us, and not really wanting to work there on his terms. Furthermore, right after that we were red-baited in one of the New York papers, and the agent quit trying to get us any work.

The first day I was in the Army (in 1942), I won an amateur contest with "Round and Round Hitler's Grave." I was inducted in Alabama, and the nickname they immediately gave me was "New York." They were amazed that anyone coming from north of the Mason-Dixon line could know how to play a five-string banjo. I got used to singing every imaginable kind of song, from barbershop harmony and hillbilly, to jazz, sweet and hot.

Some of the best singing I ever heard in the Army was in the latrines. In 1943 I was studying aircraft mechanics in Keesler Field, Mississippi. One warm evening I was sitting with a banjo on the steps of the barracks picking a few tunes to myself, when a small group gathered. One man steps forward and asks, "Could you bring that thing over to my barracks for a spell? I got a mandolin, and there's a buddy of mine plays a good fiddle."

Over at his quarters we found also a couple guitar players, and we sat on the beds and started playing up a storm. Just about that time the sergeant hollers that it's time for the lights to go out. "Hell, we're just gitting warmed up." So we adjourned to the latrine, at the end of the building, and started going again.

The latrine was about twelve by eighteen in size, as I remember. A dozen or more soldiers followed us into it. The echoing walls made us sound so great, we didn't want it to ever stop. From neighboring barracks they heard us and drifted in to join the party. The latrine soon had twenty, then thirty, and finally almost forty people in it, standing in the shower stalls, seated on sinks and toilet seats.

The four or five stringed instruments were going it hot and strong, and then we hit some songs that everyone wanted to sing. Some New York fellow had a good bass, and a couple southerners knew how to hit that high harmony. The fiddle screeched and soared. The mandolin twanged, the guitars whomped all around those bass strings.

After half an hour a noncom came back and said we were supposed to quiet down, but, as I remember, we didn't pay him any mind. Half an hour later, after several attempts to halt us, a lieutenant squeezes into the room.

"Okay, men, break it up. You sound pretty good, but it's eleven-thirty. Everybody back to their own outfits."

And that was that. I never met the mandolin player again. I can't remember exactly what tunes we played outside "Wabash Cannonball" and "Steel Guitar Rag." It wasn't a very lengthy music session, as sessions go. But if anyone ever asks me where it was I made some of the best music I ever made in my life, I'm liable to reply: "In a latrine."

On the boat going overseas, we held a half-hour song session almost every evening. Just for the hell of it, I decided to try and not repeat a single song until we absolutely had to. I had never realized that I knew so many different songs. One night I sat down and wrote down titles, and before I finished I'd found about 300 songs that I knew all the way through and about an equal number that I knew enough to start off and then let the other people carry the main burden of singing.

On Saipan I became acquainted with four different groups of people— the Chamorros, Japanese, Koreans and Kanakas (natives of other islands to the south). They all had their own distinctive music, and we organized troupes of them to travel through hospital wards. From the Koreans I got school children who sang their own folk songs and also Protestant hymns and hillbilly songs which they had picked up from missionaries or soldiers. "You Are My Sunshine" was a hit song among all the islanders, and they all had versions written in their own languages.

At this time I played with a string band called the Rainbow Boys over the local GI radio station WXLD on their daily program, "Calico Jamboree." I still keep running into people who heard us at that time. The band would get invited out to ships in the harbor to put on a personal-appearance show. On shore most of us were privates and treated as such;

aboard ship we were guests and ate steak and ice cream with the officers.

The Rainbow Boys also played for tips down at a big Navy beer barn called the Chief's Club—nothing but a big Quonset hut with a couple hundred drunken chiefs guzzling away. The afternoon would consist of the following, several hundred times over: a big drunken chief staggering out and saying, "Shay, will ya play 'My Wild Irish Rose,' and dedicate it to all the chiefs on the U.S.S. _____?" So we played "My Wild Irish Rose," "San Antonio Rose," "Last Rose of Summer," "Rose of Tralee," "The One Rose"—I didn't know so many songs could be written about one flower. Then, of course, some rebel would come up and ask us to play "Dixie" and then demand that everybody stand at attention.

In 1945 Americans came home from the war. We dived enthusiastically into long-deferred projects. A number of us who loved to sing folk songs and union songs thought it the most natural thing in the world to start an organization that could keep us all in touch with one another, that could promote new and old songs and singers, and in general bring closer the broad revival of interest in folk music and topical songs that we felt sure would sooner or later take place. We called our organization People's Songs, to distinguish it from the scholarly folklore societies, and started a bulletin. I wanted it to be a weekly; others persuaded me to be more conservative and make it a monthly.

The *People's Songs Bulletin* started off in 1946, a new kind of magazine. Each issue carried old songs, new songs, plus articles and reviews about singers, books and records.

It was strictly a shoestring operation. The first issue was mimeographed. When we had to start paying a salary to at least one person ($25 a week) we felt we were being wildly extravagant. Monthly hootenannies paid the office rent.

We held normal commercial musical endeavors in contempt. We were convinced that the revival of interest in folk music would come through the trade unions. Union educational departments had already put out many fine songbooks. There was the singing tradition of the old IWW to build on. We envisioned a singing labor movement spearheading a nationwide folk song revival, just as the Scottish progressives sparked a folk song revival at the time of Robert Burns, and the Czech progressives sparked another at the time of Dvořák.

How our theories went astray! Most union leaders could not see any connection between music and pork chops. As the cold war deepened in '47 and '48 the split in the labor movement deepened. "Which Side Are

You On?" was known in Greenwich Village but not in a single miner's union local.

We worked our way up to a huge circulation of 2,000 before the shoestring ran out and we still hadn't learned how to tie on another.

The organization People's Songs closed its doors for lack of funds in early 1949. We couldn't raise the (for us) huge sum of $3,000 to pay printers and landlords.

But the singers and songs carried on. The revival of interest in folk music and topical songs did come about, and the existence of People's Songs helped to do it. The very banishment of singers such as myself from labor-union work forced us to make a living in commercial ways, such as nightclub appearances, or giving concerts for schools and colleges. Basically ours were good songs, as any fool could plainly hear. And our theory about singing them in an informal way was correct.

When I look over the pages of the little mimeographed bulletin* of 1946 I am at times appalled by its amateurishness, and at other times filled with a flush of pride for bravery and honesty. Maybe fools walk in where angels fear to tread, but here's to the young and foolish, and may the world have more of them.

In 1950 we started publishing again, in the form of *Sing Out* magazine. For a few years, it barely stayed alive, but with the hope and faith of a few, and the sweat of one or two, it staggered to its feet, and now has a worldwide circulation of 15,000. Magazines like it started up in England and on the Continent, in Australia, New Zealand and Japan, and several North American cities. The basic idea is sound: to combine songs and criticism. The printed page is a handy device, and there is value in being able to count on a certain number of pages appearing regularly with up-to-date information on a certain subject.

The basic idea would be better if we could afford to include a phonograph record with every issue. Or a roll of video tape you could play through your TV set. But this will come in time. The scientists will come to our aid if they don't blow us up first.

The 1941–42 Almanac Singers had been undisciplined ("the only group that rehearses on the stage," said Woody). In November 1948 Lee Hays and I discussed the possibility of forming a more organized singing group, to see if we could get a solid sound on such songs as "The Saints

---

* See *Reprints from the People's Songs Bulletin* (Oak Publications, New York, 1961), $1.95.

Go Marching In." Originally we had thought of three men plus three women, but it simmered down to a quartet.

I had met Fred Hellerman right after World War II. He and Ronnie Gilbert had both started singing folk songs before the war, as counsellors at the same summer camp. (In 1951, when "Kisses Sweeter Than Wine" was in the jukeboxes, an interviewer asked whether Ronnie and I were really married. "Yes," says I, "she is married to her husband and I am married to my wife.")

So now Ronnie, with her exciting contralto, and Fred, a gifted guitarist who could sing either high or low,* joined their voices with my split tenor and Lee's big gospel bass. To our delight we found we could give a big solid warmth to the songs of Leadbelly and to many songs which had seemed ineffectual with one voice. After long discussions we finally named ourselves: the Weavers.

We helped put on some of the world's best little hootenannies, but in late '49 we were ready to break up. We had never intended to be a commercial group. We were dead broke and about to go our separate ways. As a last desperate gasp we decided to do the unthinkable: get a job in a nightclub.

Six months later we had a manager, a recording contract with Decca, and a record selling almost two million copies ("Goodnight Irene" with "Tzena Tzena" on the flip side). The Weavers sang on vaudeville stages and in some high-priced saloons. "So Long," "On Top of Old Smoky," and "Wimoweh" made the top of the Hit Parade. People coming up to me in the street said, "Pete, isn't it wonderful finally to be a success?"

I thought to myself, we were just as successful in 1941 when we sang "Union Maid" for 10,000 striking transport workers. But those months of early 1950 were an interesting experience. And at that time millions of teen-agers first heard the words "folk song."

In midsummer of 1950 we were offered a weekly network TV show, but a couple of days later the red-baiting publication *Red Channels* came out with a blast against us. The TV contract was torn up.

We kept on with personal appearances, but it got to be more and more of a drag. Our then manager would not let me sing for the hootenannies and workers' groups. Decca—hungry for more hits—insisted on teaming us with a big band; predictably, the result was almost the opposite of how we wanted to sound.†

---

* In recent years he has been a composer, producing "Healing River" and other fine songs.
† Whatever we recorded became Decca property, of course. Eleven years later several "takes" which had been rejected during those 1951 sessions made a sudden appearance

One night Lee and I found ourselves in a Reno nightclub discussing the theory of our poet friend Walter Lowenfels that everything in the world is grist for the writer's mill.

"Grist," says I, looking about me.

"Yeah, but where do you start shoveling when it's up to your neck?" says Lee.

In '53 we took a "sabbatical." As Lee says, it turned into a Mondical and a Tuesdical. Ronnie took time to raise a baby. Lee started to concentrate on being a writer. Fred became the arranger-accompanist of several successful singers.

Moe Asch's new Folkways company made some records of me. (Moe had already lost a shirt or two in the record business but was still obstinately determined to get more folk music into the hands of more people.) I gradually found audiences at colleges and camps for my solo programs. And I sang gratis whenever I felt like it. Toshi organized my bookings and benefits; at first, the job didn't keep her very busy. I had time to work on our unfinished log cabin and watch the kids grow—and was thankful that there wasn't any rent to pay.

Then in 1955 the Weavers got a new manager and producer, Harold Leventhal. Although that was the year the House Un-American Activities Committee turned its beady eye in my direction, the overall climate had brightened a little.* We decided to hold a reunion at Carnegie Hall just before Christmas.

This concert was received so well that the Weavers were in business again. With Harold's cooperation we now made freer choices about where and how we wanted to sing; and audiences responded to the informal give-and-take which we ourselves enjoyed. (Lee's vein of satire, which had been a highlight of the *People's Songs Bulletin*, spiced every performance.) Our Vanguard LPs were for the most part recorded at live

---

in the record shops. Somebody had decided that in 1962 any commodity that could be labeled FOLK MUSIC could be turned into cash.

* In our present uneasy times it may be interesting to recall a few examples of what, during the Weavers' (and *Sing Out*'s) early years, could fairly be called encouraging developments:

1953: The Korean war ended with a compromise.

1954: President Eisenhower decided not to send American bombers against the Communist-led independence fighters who were crushing France's elite army in Vietnam. . . . The Supreme Court finally outlawed Jim Crow education; the movement to challenge all racist institutions was slowly beginning to gather strength. . . . And Senator Joseph McCarthy—whose "lists" of alleged subversives had demoralized a series of civilian agencies—took on the U.S. Army and lost.

1955: In Geneva, the American and Russian heads of state talked "at the summit" for the first time since World War II.

concerts—the first one by Harold himself—and controlled by our own concepts.

The TV industry wasn't noticing us; but we seldom looked at them either.

By this time, though, I was singing pretty regularly on my own; all sorts of people were getting excited about homemade music. To coordinate my schedule with that of the Weavers, and still leave time to see my family, proved impossible. I asked if Eric Darling (already well known to banjo enthusiasts) couldn't become a Weaver in my place. Later, Eric was succeeded as banjo picker by Frank Hamilton (of Chicago's Old Town School of Folk Music), and Frank in turn by Bernie Krause of Boston. The Weavers continued to tour for another half dozen years.

Meanwhile, their example encouraged first the Kingston Trio, and then hundreds of young strummers, to become professional folk music interpreters. Some saw fit to parody and belittle the country people whose lifework they were looting for the sake of a fast buck. At their best, though, some of the groups introduced a commercial public to music which ignored worn-out formulas and said something about people's real lives. The commercial folk boom died down before long, but many of these performers—and new ones every year—still search out treasures of tradition to introduce to a wider audience. (In a number of instances they have also smoothed the path to worthwhile bookings for authentic country musicians.) Other alumni of the folk groups have moved into rock music and helped to widen its horizons.

The Weavers proved that a good singing group needn't have the conventional soprano-alto-tenor-bass lineup. Our work was a little like what Benny Goodman did for jazz: well-rehearsed arrangements but still folk-rooted, and allowing room for improvisation. In 1968 I noticed that groups of singers on rock records also made better music than soloists merely accompanied by some sidemen.

Just one disadvantage to singing with a group: one loses flexibility and can't as easily adapt on stage to the needs of various audiences. So nowadays I do the next best thing: I try and get an audience singing with me. If we have a good echoing auditorium, and a gang of young people with strong lungs, and we can really raise the roof—then I don't mind if I sing myself hoarse and drip with sweat. It's great.

In the thirties many of us thought the folk music revival would come through the trade-union movement. We couldn't have been more wrong.

It came through the camps and colleges. But it came anyway. It was a logical development of pop music.

Look at it historically. In ancient times, when people lived in tribes, there was only one kind of music. All the men knew the same hunting songs and the same war dances. All the women knew the same lullabies.

Then man became smarter, learned how to herd sheep and store grain. An aristocracy developed that could afford to hire musicians to perform *for* them. Thus started the first art music. In Europe it eventually led to symphony orchestras in the castles. The first pop music came about when cities developed and some musicians found they could make a good living playing for tips in the marketplace.

American popular music, like popular music in Europe for several hundred years since the rise of the cities in the Middle Ages, always maintained a position midway between country music and the music of the aristocracy, or "classical" music. It has borrowed ideas and techniques from both of them. Thus a composer like W. C. Handy leaned more to the folk, and a composer like Victor Herbert more to the other side.

In America there have always been many idioms to borrow from. In the early nineteenth century most dance music was based on ancient traditions of fiddle playing in Ireland and Scotland. Then, during the 1840s, the country was swept by a wave of minstrel music and "plantation" songs.

In the twentieth century the waves of enthusiasm for this or that idiom have come and gone more suddenly, perhaps because of quicker transcontinental communication. Thus one year it was the tango, another year the rhumba, another year the mambo or the calypso song. The weakness of all these fads was that Tin Pan Alley was only interested in exploiting the superficial or sensational characteristics. The subtleties were ignored.

Carmen Miranda came from Brazil in the thirties, bringing her favorite guitarists with her. They knew some magnificent Brazilian music. But after a few years the guitarists went home because Hollywood was only interested in having Carmen Miranda swing her hips and roll her eyes.

The calypso boom of 1956 ignored the real meat of calypso music, which is its powerful sense of social satire.

The "folk revival" was different in some interesting ways. For one thing, Tin Pan Alley was in a weaker position than ever before in its career, and the folk music revival came about not so much because of it as in spite of it. The Hit Parades dropped from 80 percent of the music business to less than 30 percent of all recordings. The LP changed the whole picture in the recording industry, allowing hundreds of minority tastes to be satisfied as never before.

Another difference was that the folk revival involved not simply a lot of people listening to music but also an army of amateurs playing in schools and camps, at beach parties and beer parties, and often on lonesome evenings all by themselves.

Finally, the term "folk music" became so broad that it now covers an indigestible variety. Among the thousands who attend Newport Folk Festivals are devotees of Elizabethan ballads, honky-tonk blues, southern mountain banjo and fiddle playing, and songs in many different languages. The range of subject matter covers nearly all walks of life and aspects of human experience.

Today—just as before the 1963 "folk boom"—one seldom hears folk music on the "top forty" stations, but nearly every major city has FM stations with one or more folk programs playing to a devoted band of listeners. The wide range of folk music played indicates that here is a new kind of cosmopolitan citizen: one who can listen to an Israeli hora one minute, and the next minute an unaccompanied English sea chanty or a gutty Deep South blues.

Everyone is more free than ever to decide what they like best, what they think is most meaningful and honest. Perhaps we no longer need to think in terms of Folk Music, Pop Music, or Classical Music. The same person might like to dance to a good band, listen to a symphony, hum an old lullaby to put his kid to sleep, or sing almost any song in the world on a Saturday night with his friends.

2•Two American Musicians

WHO SHOWED US
HOW TO COMBINE OLD AND NEW

*American singers are fortunate that two of our greatest folk artists have
lived in our own times, one from each of the two great traditions that
make up the main fabric of our folk music.*

LEADBELLY

> *The best and loudest singer that I ever run onto his name
> was Huddie Ledbetter and we all called him Leadbelly,
> his arms was like big stove pipes, and his face was
> powerful and he picked the twelve-string guitar.*
> —Woody Guthrie

HUDDIE LEDBETTER, nicknamed Leadbelly, died in December
1949, age sixty-three, just six months before his song "Goodnight Irene"
was to sell two million copies and make Hit Parade history. Until the last
three years of his life, he had recorded barely more than a few dozen
songs, never made any Hollywood movie appearances, and only occasional radio appearances. Today, through his recordings, he is world-
famous as one of the great singers of folk songs of this century. Songs
he composed, or helped put together out of the fragments of older tunes,
or adapted into the form in which we all know them now, have sold in
the tens of millions: "Goodnight Irene," "Bring Me a Little Water, Silvy,"
"Midnight Special," "Rock Island Line," "Kisses Sweeter Than Wine" (the
tune), "Old Cotton Fields at Home," and many others.

Leadbelly came out of the Deep South. John and Alan Lomax, on one of their folk song collecting trips in 1933, met him in prison, and arranged for him to tour northern colleges with them the following year, demonstrating Negro folk music. He made an explosive impact on everyone he met.

But John Lomax was a conservative Texan. Leadbelly, finding a freedom up north which he had not known before, declared his independence, and settled down with his wife Martha in New York. He never wanted to live in the South again.

Woody and I first met Huddie when he was in his fifties. He was gray-haired, not tall—perhaps five feet ten—but compactly built, and he moved with the soft grace of an athlete. He had a powerful ringing voice, and his muscular hands moved like a dancer over the strings of his huge twelve-stringed guitar.

Leadbelly and Martha had a little flat in New York's lower East Side. Woody and I visited him often there and made music together with him till the neighbors complained of the noise.

He was determined to build a successful career as a musician. If he could have lived ten more years he would have seen all his dreams come true—young people by the millions learning and singing his songs. But there was not such interest in folk music then. In the 30's and 40's the Hit Parade was dominated by the big bands, and all entertainment, to be successful, had to be geared to Hollywood standards.

Huddie got occasional jobs singing for schools and colleges, or at little parties where they were raising money for some cause, like helping Loyalist Spain. We loved him, but I wish we hadn't been his only audience.

Too bad he was never in movies. He was an expert at country-style buck-and-wing dancing. In one number he would imitate the gait of all the women of Shreveport, Louisiana, high and low. And another dance accompanied the story of a duck hunter. His guitar became the gun. Pow!

He was wonderful with children.* He'd get them singing with him, clapping their hands and swaying their bodies.

He'd sometimes get on a rhyming kick. For a couple hours on end, every sentence that came out of his mouth was rhymed. Sitting in the car, on our way to bookings, he'd go on fanciful flights of poetry and imagination.

One year he started having to use a cane to go on stage. His voice, always soft and husky when speaking, still rang out high on the melodies, but his hands grew stiffer and less certain on the guitar. Then one day

---

* Listen to his charming explanations on the play song record, Stinson SLPX 39.

he was gone, and we were left with regrets that we had not treasured him more.

Perhaps this modern age will not produce again such a combination of genuine folk artist and virtuoso. Nowadays when the artist becomes a virtuoso, there is a greater tendency to cease being "folk." When Leadbelly rearranged a folk melody he had come across—he often did—he did it in line with his own great folk traditions.

A disservice is done him by songbook editors who claim "Words and music by Huddie Ledbetter" for songs which he did not write—like "In the Evening," written by Leroy Carr in the 1920's, and "Meeting at the Building," an old spiritual. The claim that Leadbelly wrote all these confuses the fact that he actually *did* write some songs: "Bourgeois Blues," "Fannin' Street," "Old Cotton Fields at Home" and others.

It should be possible for the various publishers involved to simply say "Words and music adapted, arranged, and added to by Huddie Ledbetter." For this is exactly what this immensely talented man did do, to every song he sang, old or new. He would not have claimed more. Leadbelly was an honest man.

For example: Alan Lomax and I figure that "Old Riley Walked the Water, on Them Long Hot Summer Days" is really two separate work songs that Leadbelly combined together to make a fine performance piece.

OLD RILEY   As transcribed by Hally Wood from Leadbelly's record (In Dem Long Hot Summer Days). Words and music by Huddie Ledbetter. Collected and adapted by John A. and Alan Lomax. TRO-© copyright 1951, Folkways Music Publishers, Inc., New York, New York. Used by permission.

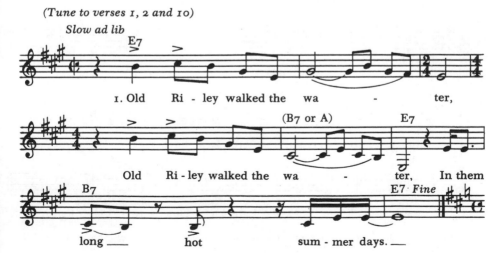

(Tune to verses 3, 7 and 8) a tempo

3. Ri -ley walked the wa - ter; Here, Ratt - ler,* here. Old

Ri - ley walked the wa - ter; Here, Ratt - ler, here

(Tune to verses 4 and 5)

4. Ri - ley's gone like a tur - key through the corn;

Here, Ratt - ler, here. Old

Ri - ley's gone like a tur - key through the corn;

Here, Ratt - ler, here.

6. Toot, toot, toot; Here, Ratt - ler, here.

Toot, toot, toot; Here, Ratt - ler, here.

9. Here, Ratt - ler, here, Ratt - ler, here, Ratt - ler, here.

Here, Ratt - ler, here, Ratt ler, here, Ratt - ler, here.

---

* "Rattler" is the traditional name for a bloodhound used to help recapture escaped convicts.

2. Old Riley he is gone,
   Old Riley he is gone,
   In them long hot summer days.

5. Rattler come when I blow my horn,
   Here, Rattler, here.
   Old Rattler come when I blow my horn,
   Here, Rattler, here.

7. Old Rattler's got him a marrow bone,
   Here, Rattler, here.
   Old Rattler's got him a marrow bone,
   Here, Rattler, here.

8. Old Riley's gone like a turkey through the corn,
   Here, Rattler, here.
   Old Riley's gone like a turkey through the corn,
   Here, Rattler, here.

10. Old Riley walked the water,
    Old Riley walked the water,
    In them long hot summer days.

In 1939 in New York he learned a modal, minor melody from an Irish singer named Sam Kennedy. Sam's tune was kind of like this:

One of these lonesome Irish songs. Leadbelly wanted to sing it, but he wanted to change it to his own style. One evening he met Sam at a crowded New York fund-raising party in somebody's apartment. They went into the bathroom, the only quiet place. Huddie said, "Sam, I'd like to sing your song, but this is how I'd like to do it." And sitting there on the edge of the bathtub, he played that same melody:

You'll probably recognize the tune now. Years later, after Huddie had died, the Weavers put new words to it, and it even got on the Hit Parade.

Oh, kisses sweeter than wine
Oh, kisses sweeter than wine

* Words by Paul Campbell (The Weavers), music by Joel Newman (Huddie Ledbetter). TRO-© copyright 1951, Folkways Music Publishers, Inc., New York, New York. Used by permission.

Another song which reached the Hit Parade was "Old Cotton Fields at Home." Odetta revived it, and Harry Belafonte learned it from her. I confess that when I first heard Huddie sing it, back around 1941, I thought it was one of his lesser efforts. Shows you how wrong you can be.

I'm still convinced he tossed it off in a hurry. Probably he was at a party once and some rich drunk said, "Come on, now, Leadbelly, sing us about those old cotton fields" (meaning a song like Stephen Foster's phony weeping for "old Massa"). Huddie, being quick at rhyming, perhaps improvised the song on the spot.

He used what I call the Great American Folk Melody (because in various forms it is used for so many different songs). By repeating the same couplet twice for each verse, and using the same refrain after each couplet, he managed to string out a whole song by writing only about eight lines.

What makes the song great (aside from a good tune) is the powerful rhythmic effect the words give it, and the solid workingman's outlook which strengthens the old clichés.

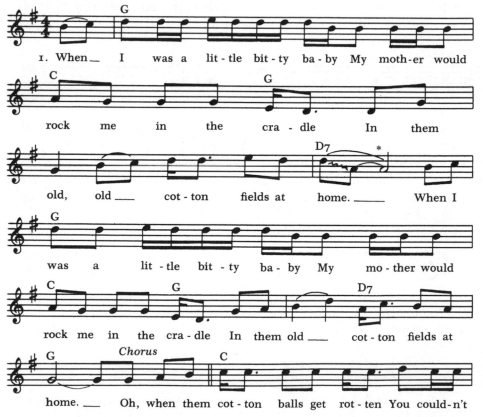

_____

* A typical Leadbelly slur.

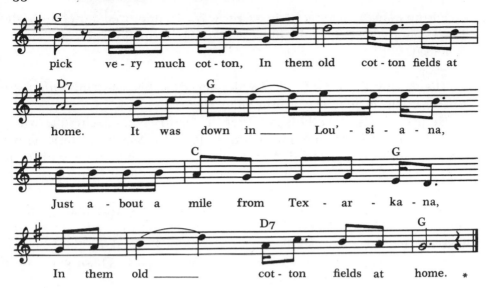

pick   ve - ry   much   cot - ton,   In   them   old   cot - ton   fields   at

home.   It   was   down   in ____   Lou' - si - a - na,

Just   a - bout   a   mile   from   Tex - ar - ka - na,

In   them   old ____   cot - ton   fields   at   home. *

2. It may sound a little bit funny,
   But you didn't make very much money
   In them old cotton fields at home.
   It may sound a little bit funny,
   But you didn't make very much money
   In them old cotton fields at home.   (*Chorus*)

3. I was over in Arkansas,
   People ask me, what you come here for
   In them old cotton fields at home.
   I was over in Arkansas,
   People ask me, what you come here for
   In them old cotton fields at home.   (*Chorus*)

Huddie made up "Bourgeois Blues"† in 1938, out of an experience he had in Washington, D.C. He and some white friends were told to leave first one hotel and then another, because the management didn't want an interracial party on the premises.

> Me and my sweet wife Martha was standing upstairs;
> Heard a white man say I don't want no Negroes up there.
>   He was a bourgeois man,
>   Hoo! Living in a bourgeois town . . .
> Listen here, people, listen to me:
> Don't try to buy no home in Washington, D.C.
>   Cause it's a bourgeois town,
>   Ooh! It's a bourgeois town.
>   I got the bourgeois blues, I'm gonna
>   Spread the news all around.

---

* Words and music by Huddie Ledbetter. TRO-© copyright 1962, Folkways Music Publishers, Inc., New York, New York. Used by permission.
† Words and music by Huddie Ledbetter; edited with additional material by Alan Lomax. TRO-© copyright 1959, Folkways Music Publishers, Inc., New York, New York. Used by permission.

Fortunately, Washington in some ways is improved now, and who knows but that this song might have helped in a small way? Yes, I'm sure it helped.

The driving rhythms Leadbelly developed on his 12-string guitar are unforgettable to anyone who ever heard them.

He played basically the same type of country-blues technique which we have heard from such musicians as Brownie McGhee, Merle Travis and Big Bill Broonzy. The thumb plays bass notes and chords with regularity. The fingers take the top strings with as much syncopation as necessary.

Where Leadbelly's style differed from the others' was mainly in his emphasis of the bass line, to which the double strings give power and body. Instead of a flat pick he used a thumb pick—making the bass line even more impressive—and a long steel finger pick. These got a deep thump and drive out of the instrument.

He was not the cleverest guitar player; he didn't try and play the fanciest chords, the trickiest progressions, or the fastest number of notes. (For example, the "Salty Dog" progression—four chords, over and over again: C, A⁷, D, G—was used for several songs.) The notes he played were powerful and meaningful. But perhaps his genius was not so much in the notes he played as in the notes he didn't play. Often he accompanied a song with single big notes and practically no full chords—for example, "Good Morning Blues"—all done with his thumb, in a walking bass pattern. Or he would use single bass notes and occasional single top strings.

When he put together the "Fannin' Street"* guitar part, I think he composed as great an opening line as that in Beethoven's Fifth Symphony— you know, the one that goes "dit-dit-dit-*dah!*" Well, those notes of Leadbelly's twelve-stringer are just as emphatic.

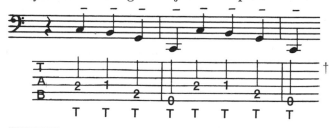

* (Mister Tom Hughes' Town) Words and music by Huddie Ledbetter. Collected and adapted by John A. and Alan Lomax. TRO-© copyright 1936, renewed 1964, Folkways Music Publishers, Inc., New York, New York. Used by permission.
† Two tones lower on the 12-string guitar than standard 6-string tuning.

1719585

He used it for half a dozen other blues as well.

Sometimes he played melody right along with the voice. Other times he echoed the melody after the phrase. Sometimes he answered the melody with another phrase.

Usually the guitar was more than just accompaniment. It was actually a part of his song. After the guitar introduction of his "Hitler Song"* you hear him say, "Do that again; I didn't understand you that time. Take it easy." The guitar repeats the whole introduction; then Leadbelly's voice says "Yes, yes" and starts singing:

> Hitler started out in nineteen hundred and thirty-two;
> Hitler started out in nineteen hundred and thirty-two;
> When he started out, he took the home from the Jew.
>
> We're gonna tear Hitler down . . .

"All right, get out where you can talk to me," he says before a guitar break in "T.B. Blues."† The guitar sound in this great blues is a prodigious champing, munching, like a big locomotive that won't be stopped or slowed!

> Too late— too late— too late, too late, too late . . .

Oh, Huddie! How we miss you. Sometimes audiences couldn't understand your Louisiana accent. Sometimes young people thought your style of music was old-fashioned. But you were always honestly yourself, never trying to pretend you were someone else, never trying to be a chameleon for the fashions of the day.

Nowadays we try and recall Leadbelly by singing his songs. But I wish people would stop trying to imitate his accent, and rather learn his subtle simplicity and his powerful pride.

Listen to the endings of his songs: straightforward, abrupt. He usually kept steady, even tempos, avoiding cute accelerandos and ritards, pianissimos and crescendos. While he sang some songs louder, others softer, he never crooned a song, lingering over "pear-shaped tones." He usually

---

* (Mr. Hitler) Words and music by Huddie Ledbetter; edited with additional material by Alan Lomax. TRO-© copyright 1959, Folkways Music Publishers, Inc., New York, New York. Used by permission.

† Copyright by Victoria Spivey.

placed songs in as high a key as conveniently possible for him. I don't need to describe his vocal tone; you can hear it on his records. I, for one, admire it tremendously. I used to say that if there was ever a voice teacher who could teach me how to sing like Leadbelly, that would be one worth studying with.

A teen-age girl imitates her favorite movie actress by copying her hairdo. A would-be singer imitates the very accents of his idol. But if you would learn from Leadbelly, you should look deeper to find his greatest qualities. In other words, don't just try to imitate him note for note. Learn his straightforward honesty, vigor and strength.

Hobo and train songs have always been popular with young people. You want to travel, you want to see people, learn things. And maybe all of us are hitchhikers in one way or another. When you go into a big library you hitch a ride with the experience of every writer of every book there.

Through his records, we can all take a hitchhike trip with old Huddie Ledbetter, who was a wonderful man and a wonderful musician and who bequeathed to us a couple hundred of the best songs any of us will ever know. We'll never see his exact like again, never.

But if he could see us now, trying to master his songs and the instrument that he knew and loved so well, he might say:

"Now, just take it easy. Relax your mind and take your time. Play it like you feel it and soon you believe it. You're doin' all right. Just be yourself. There now, we're fine as wine in summertime."

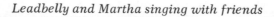

Leadbelly and Martha singing with friends

A short bibliography*:

John A. and Alan Lomax, *Negro Folk Songs as Sung by Lead Belly*, The Macmillan Co., New York, 1936.
(Melodies transcribed from recordings by the musicologist George Herzog. He tried to reproduce Leadbelly's exact rhythms and pitches, using standard notation plus some extra symbols—and pointing out that complete accuracy is really impossible. The result is extremely difficult reading for singers—but an interesting demonstration of how much, in an authentic folk performance, is left out by the usual written versions.)

John A. and Alan Lomax, eds., *Leadbelly, a Collection of World-Famous Songs by Huddie Ledbetter* (music ed. Hally Wood), Folkways Music Publishers, Inc., New York, 1959.

Moses Asch and Alan Lomax, *The Leadbelly Songbook*, Oak Publications, New York, 1962, $1.95.
(with 14 pages of reminiscences about Leadbelly)

Julius Lester and Pete Seeger, *The 12-String Guitar as Played by Leadbelly*, an Instruction Manual. Oak Publications, New York, 1965, $2.95.

Frederic Ramsey, Jr., "Leadbelly: a Great Long Time," *Sing Out*, Vol. 15, No. 1, 1965.

Leadbelly on records†:

ELEKTRA

Leadbelly Library of Congress Recordings (made by John and Alan Lomax 1933–42, songs and talk), EKL 301/302: three LPs

Mr. Tom Hughes' Town, De Kalb Blues, Take a Whiff on Me, The Medicine Man, I'm Sorry Mama, Po' Howard (*discussion of dance steps*), Gwine Dig a Hole, Tight Like That, Green Corn, Becky Dean (*discussion of prison singing*), Midnight Special, I Ain't Gonna Ring Them Yellow Women's Door Bells, Rock Island Line, Governor Pat Neff, Irene, Governor O.K. Allen, Git on Board, Hallelujah, Backslider Fare You Well, Amazing Grace, Must I Be Carried to the Sky on Flowered Beds of Ease?, Down in the Valley to Pray, Let It Shine on Me, Run Sinners, Ride On, Thirty Days in the Workhouse, Four Day Worry Blues, Match Box Blues, You Don't Know My Mind, Got a Gal in Town with Her Mouth Chock Full of Gold, Alberta, Take Me Back, Henry Ford Blues, Ella Speed, Billy the Weaver, Frankie and Albert, If It Wasn't for Dicky, Mama Did You Bring Me Any Silver?, The Bourgeois Blues, Howard Hughes, Scottsboro Boys, The Hindenburg Disaster, Turn Your Radio On, The Roosevelt Song

FOLKWAYS

Take This Hammer (Leadbelly Legacy Vol. 1), FA 2004

Green Corn, Yellow Gal, You Can't Lose Me Cholly, Laura, Good Morning Blues, Leaving Blues, Big Fat Woman, Take This Hammer, Grey Goose, Pick a Bale

---

* Don't believe everything you read in these publications. Some of them overemphasize Leadbelly's rough-tough youth. I have purposely ignored it here, to write about him as I knew him.

† This list is fairly complete as of 1970. It does not, however, include every recorded performance in which Leadbelly participated as part of a group—nor, of course, the many performances of Leadbelly songs by other artists, some of which are excellent.

of Cotton, Bring Me a Little Water Silvy, Moaning, Meeting at the Building, We Shall Walk Through the Valley, Irene

Rock Island Line (Leadbelly Legacy Vol. 2), FA 2014
Cotton Song, Ha Ha Thisaway, Sukey Jump, Black Girl, Rock Island Line, Blind Lemon, Bottle Up and Go, On a Monday (Almost Gone), Shorty George, Duncan and Brady, Old Riley, Leavin' Blues, Pigmeat

Leadbelly Legacy, Vol. 3, FA 2024
Fort Worth and Dallas Blues, Black Snake, Roberta, Driving Song, Daddy I'm Coming Back to You, See See Rider, Pigmeat

Easy Rider (Leadbelly Legacy Vol. 4), FA 2034
There's a Man Going Round Taking Names, Easy Rider, Red Bird, Line 'Em, T.B. Blues, Jim Crow Blues, Bourgeois Blues, Army Life, Mr. Hitler

Leadbelly Sings Folk Songs (with Woody Guthrie, Cisco Houston, Sonny Terry, Brownie McGhee), FA 2488
There's a Man Going Round Taking Names, Stewball, Keep Your Hands Off Her, Good Good Good, We Shall Walk in the Valley, Lining Track, Outskirts of Town, We Shall Be Free, The Blood Done Sign My Name, On a Monday, Jean Harlow, Alabama Bound, Corn Bread Dough, Defense Blues, Children's Blues, Fiddler's Dram, Meeting at the ⌐uilding

Negro Folk Songs for Young People, FC 7533
Irene Goodnight, John Henry, Boll Weevil, When a Man's a Long Way from Home, Good Morning Blues, Every Time I Feel the Spirit, They Hung Him on the Cross, Swing Low Sweet Chariot, By and By When the Morning Comes, Rock Island Line, Julie Ann Johnson, Haul Away Joe, Christmas Is Coming, We're in the Same Boat Brother

Leadbelly's Last Sessions, Vol. 1, FA 2941; two LPs (conversation and songs)
I Was Standing in the Bottom, Yes I'm Goin' Down in Louisiana, I Ain't Goin' Down to the Well No More, Dick Ligger's Holler, Miss Liza Jane, Dog-Latin Song, Leaving Blues, Go Down Old Hannah, Blue Tail Fly, Nobody in the World Is Better Than Us, We're in the Same Boat Brother, Looky Looky Yonder, Jelly O' the Ransom, Ship of Zion, Bring Me a Little Water Silvy, Mistreatin' Mama, Black Betty, Ain't Going Down to the Well No More, I'm Going Back Down in Louisiana, I Don't Know You, What Have I Done, Rock Island Line, Old Man Will Your Dog Catch a Rabbit, Shorty George, Stewball, Bottle Up and Go, You Know I Got to Do It, Ain't It a Shame to Go Fishin' on Sunday, I Ain't Going to Drink No More, My Lindy Lou, I'm Thinking of a Friend, He Never Said a Mumblin' Word, I Don't Want No More Army Life, In the World, I Want to Go Home, New Iberia, Dancing with Tears in My Eyes, John Henry, Salty Dog, National Defense Blues, Easy Mr. Tom, Relax Your Mind, Polly Polly Wee, Pig Latin Song, Hawaiian Song, Drinking Lum Y A Alla, The Grey Goose, Silver City Bound, The Titanic, Death Letter Blues, Mary Don't You Weep

Leadbelly's Last Sessions, Vol. 2, FA 2942: two LPs
Midnight Special, Boll Weevil Blues, Careless Love, Easy Rider, Cry for Me, Ain't Goin' Drink No More, Birmingham Jail, Old Riley, Julie Ann Johnson, It's Tight Like That, 4 5 and 9, Good Morning Babe, Jail House Blues, Well You Know I Had to Do It, Irene, Story of the 25¢ Dude, How Come You Do Me Like You Do Do Do, Hello Central Give Me Long Distance Please, The Hesitation Blues, I'll Be Down on the Last Bread Wagon, Springtime in the Rockies, Chinatown, Rock Island Line, Backwater Blues, Sweet Mary, Irene, Easy Mr.

Tom, In the Evening When the Sun Goes Down, I'm Alone Because I Love You, House of the Rising Sun, Mary Don't You Weep and Don't You Moan, Fannin' Street, Sugared Beer, Didn't Old John Cross the Water, Nobody Knows You When You're Down and Out, Bully of the Town, Sweet Jenny Lee, Yellow Gal, He Was the Man, We're in the Same Boat Brother, Leaving Blues

The 12-String Guitar as Played by Leadbelly (instruction by Pete Seeger, with excerpts from Leadbelly's playing) FI 8371: two LPs

STINSON

Play-Party Songs, SLPX 39
Skip to My Lou, You Can't Lose-a Me Cholly, Little Sally Walker, Red Bird, Ha Ha This-a Way, It's Almost Day, More Yet, How Old Are You, Green Grass Growing Around, All For You, What Are Little Boys Made Of, Polly Polly Wee, Don't Mind the Weather, How Do You Know, Little Children's Blues

Leadbelly Memorial, Vol. 1, SLP 17
Good Night Irene, Good Morning Blues, On a Monday, Old Riley, John Henry, Rock Island Line, Ain't You Glad, How Long, T.B. Blues, Pigmeat, Man Going Around Taking Names, See See Rider

Leadbelly Memorial, Vol. 2, SLP 19
Meeting at the Building, Yellow Gal, Talking Preacher, We Shall Walk Through the Valley, Cow Cow Yicky Yicky Yea, Out on the Western Plains, Green Corn, Big Fat Woman, Fiddler's Dream, Noted Rider, Borrow Love and Go, Linc 'Em, Bring Me Li'l Water Silvy, Julie Ann Johnson, John Hardy, Whoa Back Buck

Leadbelly Memorial, Vol. 3, SLP 48
The Grey Goose, Red Cross Store Blues, Ham and Eggs, Red River, Black Girl, You Don't Miss Your Water Blues, Blind Lemon, Leadbelly's Dance, Alberta, In the Evening When the Sun Goes Down, Digging My Potatoes, In the Pines

Leadbelly Memorial, Vol. 4, SLP 51
The Boll Weevil, Ain't Going Down to the Well No Mo', Go Down Old Hannah, Frankie and Albert, Fannin' Street, The Bourgeois Blues, Looky Looky Yonder, Black Betty, Yellow Woman's Door Bells, Poor Howard, Green Corn, The Gallis Pole, De Kalb Woman

ALLEGRO

Good Night Irene, LEG 9025
Good Night Irene, When the Boys Were on the Western Plains, Roberta, John Hardy, Where Did You Sleep Last Night?, In New Orleans, Pretty Flower in Your Back Yard, Bill Brady, I've a Pretty Flower, Good Morning Blues, How Long?

CAPITOL

Ledbetter's Best, T 1821
Goodnight Irene, Grasshoppers in My Pillow, The Eagle Rocks, Rock Island Line, Ella Speed, Backwater Blues, Take This Hammer, Tell Me Baby, Eagle Rock Rag, Western Plain, Sweet Mary Blues, On a Christmas Day

RCA VICTOR

The Midnight Special, LPV 505
Easy Rider, Good Morning Blues, Pick a Bale of Cotton, Sail On Little Girl Sail

On, New York City, Rock Island Line, Roberta, Grey Goose, The Midnight Special, Alberta, You Can't Lose-a Me Cholly, T.B. Blues, Red Cross Store Blues, Whoa Back Buck, Don't You Love Your Daddy No More, I'm on My Last Go-Round

EVEREST
Leadbelly ("Archive of Folk Music"*), FS 202

---

* No connection with Library of Congress.

WOODY

I hate a song that makes you think you're not any good! I hate a song that makes you think that you are just born to lose. Bound to lose. No good to nobody. No good for nothing. Because you are either too old or too young or too fat or too thin or too this or too that. Songs that run you down or songs that poke fun at you on account of your bad luck or your hard traveling.

I am out to fight those kind of songs to my very last breath of air and my last drop of blood.

I am out to sing songs that will prove to you that this is your world, and that if it has hit you pretty hard and knocked you for a dozen loops, no matter how hard it's run you down and rolled over you, no matter what color, what size you are, how you are built, I am out to sing the songs that make you take pride in yourself and in your work. And the songs I sing are made up for the most part by all sorts of folks just about like you.

W.W.G.

WOODROW WILSON GUTHRIE, one of the great folk song ballad makers of this century, wrote more than a thousand songs between 1932 and 1952. Some may never be worth singing. Others may stand the test of time and become world classics.

Born 1912 in Okemah, Oklahoma. Childhood in an oil-boom town. In 1935 he drifted to California, along with thousands of other Okies forced by dust storms and depression woes to leave their homes. Made a living singing in saloons, occasional fly-by-night radio programs and later on for union meetings, parties, political rallies, dance and theater groups, the Library of Congress Folksong Archives. Dozens of restless trips across the U.S.A. Three marriages and many children.

And over one thousand songs.

Woody has described his musical education pretty well. The lonesome old ballads sung by his mother, the honky-tonk blues, and the wild hollers that he heard from his father and the other men in town. And it is worth emphasizing that his style of guitar picking he picked straight off the recordings of the Carter Family, which were popular around 1931, when Woody was 18 years old. He also learned some of his favorite songs directly off their recordings.

Another favorite of his, of course, was Jimmie Rodgers, "the yodeling brakeman." Woody also used to accompany his uncle Jeff, who was a fiddler, and they played on the radio occasionally. And so you see he fits right into the usual "country music" category of a small town in Oklahoma in the '20s and '30s. So much so, that some people in New York when they first heard him would say, "Why, he's just a hillbilly singer, isn't he?"

Like most country musicians, Woody was also interested in topical material. As Jimmie Rodgers made up songs about his TB, Woody naturally made up songs about the dust storms.

After he had gone to California and was singing for a dollar a day on a Los Angeles radio station, he attracted the attention of Ed Robbin, who was a news commentator on the same station for a radical newspaper, the *People's World*. Robbin got interested in Woody and Woody's ideas, and Woody got interested in him and his ideas. The year was 1938.

Woody was introduced to Will Geer, the actor, who was doing benefits to raise money for the migratory labor camps. Woody came along and dived into the struggle. He became a close friend of Will Geer and his family. Through Will, Woody started to make a living singing at fund-raising parties around Los Angeles.

Will sent me a copy of Woody's mimeographed songbook, *On a Slow Train Through California*, and told me I sure ought to meet Woody when he came to New York. I did meet him in March of 1940 at a midnight folk song session held on the stage of a Broadway theater. It was again a benefit for the California migratory workers. *The Grapes of Wrath* had been published a year before, and in New York many of us felt that we wanted to learn more.

Will Geer was MC of the show. Burl Ives was on it, also Leadbelly, Josh White, and there was Woody. A little, short fellow with a western hat and boots, in blue jeans and needing a shave, spinning out stories and singing songs that he had made up himself. His manner was laconic, offhand, as though he didn't much care if the audience was listening or not.

I just naturally wanted to learn more about him. I became a friend of his, and he was a big piece of my education.

Soon after, in 1940, he had a job paying $200 a week—which was a lot of money then—to sing one or two songs per week for the Model Tobacco network radio program. If he'd been willing to play along with them and sing the songs they wanted him to sing (and not sing the songs they didn't want him to sing) and quit doing left-wing bookings on the side, he could have stayed with them and had a successful commercial career. But he quit after a month or so.

I was working for Alan Lomax down in the Library of Congress in Washington, D.C. Woody came down several times, usually on some kind of booking or other. We hit it off pretty well together. Around May 1940, he came down driving a car which he hadn't finished paying for, and asked me if I'd like to come with him to Oklahoma.

I quit my job—such as it was—and we "hitchhiked on credit" down through Virginia and Tennessee, on to Oklahoma, and then to Pampa, Texas, where Woody's wife and children were staying with her parents. I don't think we stayed in Pampa more than a week or two, and then we went back to Oklahoma City.

There Bob Wood, the Communist organizer, asked Woody and me to sing for a small meeting of oil workers, who were out on strike. Hardly fifty or sixty people were present, but it included women (who evidently couldn't get babysitters) and children. It also included some strange men, who walked in and lined up along the back of the hall without sitting down. Bob Wood leaned over and said, "I'm not sure if these guys are going to try and break up this meeting or not. It's an open meeting and we can't kick them out. See if you can get the whole crowd singing." So Woody and I did just that. You know, those guys never did break up the meeting. We found out later they had rather intended to. Perhaps it was the presence of so many women and children that deterred them, perhaps it was the singing. Next morning I found the first two verses of "Union Maid" stuck in a typewriter. The third verse was written by Mill Lampell of the Almanac Singers when we were going to record it and found it a little too short.

(Years later, in 1947, I got a job singing in a little Greenwich Village nightclub. Woody came down to see how I was doing and in his honor I sang "Union Maid." Some young drunk at a table near Woody started joining in on the chorus but with his own variation. "Oh, you can't scare me, I'm a capitalist, I'm a capitalist, I'm a capitalist." Woody started waving an empty beer bottle around in the air, trying to bean him, and shouting, "It's bastards like you who stayed home making millions while we was out fighting the fascists.")

In Oklahoma City the finance company came and took Woody's car, as I remember it. We went back east with Bob Wood, and were learning things all the way.

I spent the rest of 1940 hitchhiking by myself. Woody rejoined his family on the west coast and went to work writing songs for the Bonneville Power Administration.

Anything worth discussing was worth a song to Woody: news of the front page, sights and sounds of the countryside he traveled through, thoughts brought to mind by reading anything from Rabelais to Will Rogers.

I remember the night he wrote the song "Tom Joad." He said, "Pete, do you know where I can get a typewriter?"

I said, "I'm staying with someone who has one."

"Well, I got to write a ballad," he said. "I don't usually write ballads to order, but Victor wants me to do a whole album of Dust Bowl songs, and they say they want one about Tom Joad in *The Grapes of Wrath*."

I asked him if he had read the book and he said, "No, but I saw the movie. Good movie."

He went along to the place I was staying—six flights walking up—on East Fourth Street. The friend I was staying with said, "Sure, you can use my typewriter."

Woody had a half-gallon jug of wine with him, sat down and started typing away. He would stand up every few seconds and test out a verse on his guitar and sit down and type some more. About one o'clock my friend and I got so sleepy we couldn't stay awake. In the morning we found Woody curled up on the floor under the table; the half gallon of wine was almost empty and the completed ballad was sitting near the typewriter.

And it is one of his masterpieces. It's a long song—about six minutes—and it compresses the whole novel into about twenty verses. It doesn't cover every detail, but it gets an awful lot of them.

TOM JOAD

Words and music by Woody Guthrie. TRO-© copyright 1960, 1963, Ludlow Music, Inc., New York, New York. Used by permission.

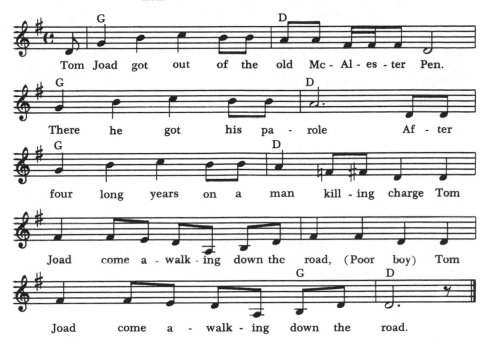

Tom Joad got out of the old Mc - Al - es - ter Pen. There he got his pa - role Af - ter four long years on a man kill - ing charge Tom Joad come a - walk - ing down the road, (Poor boy) Tom Joad come a - walk - ing down the road.

2. It was there that he found him a truck driving man;
   It was there that he caught him a ride,
   Said, "I just got a-loose from McAlester's Pen
   On a charge called homicide. Great God,
   A charge called homicide."

3. That truck rolled away in a big cloud of dust
   And Tommy turned his face towards home.
   He met Preacher Casey and they had a little drink
   And he found that his family they had gone, Tom Joad;
   He found that his family they was gone.

4. He found his mother's old fashion shoe
   And he found his daddy's hat;
   He found Little Muley and Muley said,
   "They been tractored out by th' cats, Tom,
   They been tractored out by th' cats."

5. Well, Tom he walked over to the neighboring farm
   And he found his family,
   And they took Preacher Casey and they loaded in a car
   And his mammy said, "We got to git away, Tom,"
   His mammy said, "We got to git away."

6. The twelve of the Joads made a mighty heavy load
   And Grandpa Joad he cried;
   He picked up a handful of land in his hand
   And said, "I'm stickin' with my farm till I die.
   I'm stickin' with my farm till I die."

7. They fed him spare ribs and coffee and soothing syrup,
   And Grandpa Joad he died.
   We buried Grandpa Joad on the Oklahoma road
   And Grandma on the California side,
   And Grandma on the California side.

8. We stood on a mountain and we looked to the west
   And it looked like the Promised Land;
   Was a big green valley with a river running through
   And there was work for every single hand, We thought,
   There was work for every single hand.

9. Now the Joads rolled into a jungle camp;
   It was there that they cooked them a stew,
   And the hungry little kids in the jungle camp
   Said, "We'd like to have some too. *Yes.*
   We'd like to have some too."

10. A deputy sheriff fired loose at a man
    And he shot a woman in the back,
    But before he could take his aim again
    It was Preacher Casey dropped him in his tracks, Good boy,
    Preacher Casey dropped him in his tracks.

11. Well, they handcuffed Casey and they took him to jail
    And then he got away,
    And he met Tom Joad by the old river bridge
    And these few words he did say, Preacher Casey,
    These few words he did say.

12. "Well, I preached for the Lord a mighty long time.
    I preached about the rich and the poor.
    But us workin' folks has got to stick together
    Or we ain't got a chance anymore, God knows,
    We ain't got a chance any more."

13. Then the deputies come and Tom and Casey run
    To a place where the water run down,
    And a vigilante thug hit Casey with a club
    And he laid Preacher Casey on the ground,
    And he laid Preacher Casey on the ground.

14. Tom Joad he grabbed that deputy's club
    And he brung it down on his head.
    When Tommy took flight that dark and rainy night
    Was a preacher and a deputy lying dead, Two men,
    A preacher and a deputy lying dead.

15. Tommy ran back where his mama was asleep
    And he woke her up out of bed,
    And he kissed goodbye to the mother that he loved
    And he said what Preacher Casey said, Tom Joad,
    He said what Preacher Casey said.

16. "Ever'body might be just one big soul,
    Well, it looks that-a-way to me,
    So everywhere you look in th' day or th' night
    That's where I'm a-gonna be, Ma,
    That's where I'm a-gonna be.

17. "Wherever little kids are hungry and cry,
    Wherever people ain't free,
    Wherever men are fightin' for their rights,
    That's where I'm a-gonna be, Ma,
    That's where I'm a-gonna be."

Later, at Almanac House, I saw him compose other songs over a period of months. He'd have an idea and fool around with it a little bit, wouldn't be satisfied with it, and then maybe he'd come back to it a month or two later and fool around with it some more.

One thing the Model Tobacco people wanted Woody to do in 1940 was quit writing columns for his favorite newspaper, which he euphemistically called the *Sabbath Employee*.* Those columns of his are classics. (Some are reprinted in *Born to Win*.) Every day, a few paragraphs. He got the idea from the columns that Will Rogers used to do for *The New York Times*. Just a few sharp comments on the news of the day.

He went down to Washington in the spring of 1940 and wrote: "I'm down here looking at the Potomac River; they say that George Washington threw a silver dollar across it once. It looks a little bit too far for me to do that trick, but maybe he could. After all, a dollar went further in those days."

Here's a true story about how Woody got around to writing his autobiographical book, *Bound for Glory*. It starts with the fact that I had a job as a cook in 1938 when I was a Harvard student. The man I was cooking for was a bachelor living on Beacon Hill. And one night we had some Harvard instructors in for dinner.

One of these instructors was active in the Teacher's Union in Harvard; his name was Charles Olson. I understand he became a well-known critic and poet. Big tall man.

---

* *The Sunday Worker*, weekend edition of the Communist *Daily Worker*.

Anyway, in Greenwich Village in 1942, four years later, I meet him on the street and invite him up to supper at Almanac House. I can still cook. He meets Woody and is fascinated, and asks him to write an article for a little magazine called *Common Ground*. The article was called "Ear Music" and was a beautiful piece of Woody's genius. "A definition of folk music by one of the folks." The article was so well received that a number of people suggested that Woody write a book. And before we knew it, he'd started work on *Bound for Glory*.

When World War II came along, I went into the Army and he went into the Merchant Marine. He's written about his experiences there

Woody and Pete in 1944

better than anybody else could tell them. He got torpedoed, visited half a dozen countries—or at least saw their ports—and kept writing verses every day, unconcerned who thought he was what kind of a character by the way he dressed or acted.

After he got out, he had a new family and had to take care of them; I also had a family I was starting, so we saw each other only at occasional hootenannies.

In 1952, at a party in California, I heard him sing for the last time. He'd come out west hoping to start a new life, not realizing that his occasional dizzy spells were soon going to get worse and send him to the hospital forever. He sang one or two of his old songs. Then somehow he and I got started making up verses to "Acres of Clams." Woody improvised an unforgettable couple.

The first describes how he was sitting at home one day and the doorbell rings, and there's a man who says he's from the FBI and would like to ask a few questions. Woody's following verse:

> He asked, "Will you carry a gun for your country?"
> I answered the Effbee-eye "Yay!"
> "I *will* point a gun for my country,
> But I won't guarantee you which way!
>
> "I won't guarantee you which wayyyyy,
> I won't guarantee you which way!
> I will point a gun for my country,
> But I won't guarantee you which way!"

When Woody went to the hospital in 1952 with a wasting illness, Huntington's Disease, young people with their guitars and banjos were already singing his songs and making them famous around the world. I think that, of his thousands of verses, a large number are going to outlive this century.

This is a rare thing for a songwriter. Stephen Foster only had a handful of his many songs that outlived his own lifetime. The same is true of many other great songwriters. They're lucky if they get four or five songs which are sung by a future generation. But I think that maybe several dozen of Woody's songs are going to be sung by my grandchildren and their grandchildren.

Alan Lomax calls him "our best contemporary ballad composer." Others say, "a rusty-voiced Homer," and "the greatest folk poet we've had."

Why are the songs great? Look through his songbooks.

Yes, the words show a fine sense of poetry, of reaching out for exactly the right word at exactly the right place. He used some fine time-tested tunes. The songs are honest; they say things that need to be said.

But above all else, Woody's songs show the genius of simplicity. Any damn fool can get complicated, but it takes genius to attain simplicity. Some of his greatest songs are so deceptively simple that your eye will pass right over them and you will comment to yourself, "Well, I guess this was one of his lesser efforts." Years later you will find the song has grown on you and become part of your life.

Woody took his tunes mostly from different kinds of American folk songs and ballads. He had a deep respect for the ballad form. He knew enough about other song forms to choose many others, but he felt that the old four-line stanza, which told a story and slowly unfolded a moral, was as good as any he could use.

Woody said, "I'm not saying some of your tunes from other countries aren't good. But I wasn't raised to them, and neither are the people I'm trying to sing to. So I'm going to use the kind of tunes we understand."

You know the old "Ballad of the Butcher Boy"?

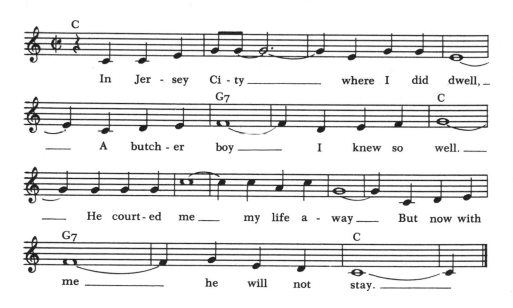

Oh, dig my grave both wide and deep,
Place a marble stone at my head and feet,
And on my breast, a turtle dove,
To show the world I died for love.

He used that tune for five or ten songs. One of his best children's songs is "Cleano."

Ma - ma, oh   Ma - ma, ___   come wash my   face.

Come wash my   face;   come wash my   face

Ma - ma, oh   Ma - ma, ___   come wash my   face, ___

and   make   it   nice ____   and   clean - o.

Woody wrote that song, and a lot of others, for his little girl Kathy. Kathy died tragically, aged four. Burned in a household accident. But she'll live forever in the songs he wrote for her.

He put another famous verse to this tune in 1942, when the CIO Ladies Auxiliaries asked him to write a theme song for them. "What's wrong with 'Union Maid'?" he asked. "We wrote that for you." They said it was a good song, but it wasn't dignified enough, and besides, it didn't have the words "Ladies Auxiliary" in the chorus. So Woody, off the top of his head, sang:

Oh, the La - dies Au - xil - ia - ry   is   a   good au -

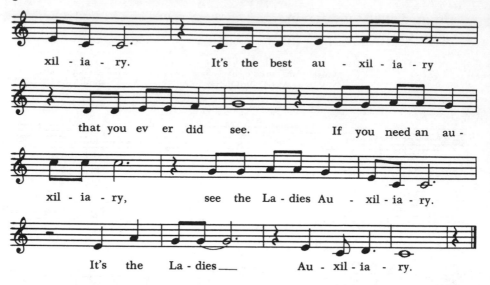

xil - ia - ry.   It's the best   au - xil - ia - ry

that you ev - er did   see.   If   you need an   au -

xil - ia - ry,   see the La - dies Au - xil - ia - ry.

It's   the   La - dies___   Au - xil - ia - ry.

"Philadelphia Lawyer" used the tune of "The Jealous Lover of Lone Green Valley."

PHILADELPHIA LAWYER

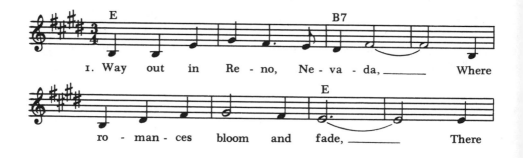

1. Way   out   in   Re - no,   Ne - va - da, _____   Where

ro - man - ces   bloom   and   fade, _____   There

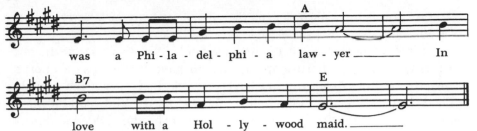

was   a Phi - la - del - phi - a   law - yer ⸺⸺   In

love   with a   Hol - ly - wood maid. ⸺⸺

2. Come love and we will wander,
   Out where the lights are so bright,
   I'll win you a divorce from your husband,
   And we can get married tonight.

3. Now Bill was a gun-toting cowboy,
   Six notches carved on his gun;
   And all of the boys around Reno
   Left Bill's Hollywood darling alone.

4. One night when Bill was returning
   From riding the range in the cold,
   He thought of his Hollywood darling,
   Her love was as lasting as gold.

5. As Bill drew near to her window,
   Two shadows he saw on the shade,
   It was the great Philadelphia lawyer
   Making love to Bill's Hollywood maid.

6. The night was as still as the desert,
   The moon hanging high overhead,
   Bill listened awhile at the window,
   He could hear every word that they said.

7. Your face is so pretty and lovely,
   Your form so fair and divine;
   Come, go back with me to Philadelphia,
   And leave this wild cowboy behind.

8. Now tonight back in old Pennsylvania
   Beneath those beautiful pines,
   There's one less Philadelphia lawyer
   In old Philadelphia tonight.

"Pastures of Plenty" used one of the many versions of "Pretty Polly," and "Tom Joad" used the tune of "John Hardy."

Sometimes Woody would get a melody and make up verses to it, but then feel he needed a chorus. And he would have to compose a chorus because the original melody didn't have one. "So Long" used the melody of "The Ballad of Billy the Kid"; "Reuben James" used "Wildwood Flower," a tune recorded by the Carter Family. To each of these he added a chorus worthy of any good composer. He fiddled around with the melody of the verse, until he compounded and developed elements of it into a singable refrain.

So Woody was a music composer as well as a poet.

As a prose writer, too, I think him a genius. All of a piece. He wasn't pretending to be anybody else—he was just himself. He wrote fairly fast, and his big problem was that he had not learned how to rewrite and boil down later on.

He learned from everybody, and from everything. He learned from the King James Bible; he learned from the left-wing newspapers and publications; he had a devouring curiosity. I'll never forget the week he discovered Rabelais and read through a two-inch-thick volume, a relatively unexpurgated edition, in a couple of days. During the following weeks I could see him experimenting with some of the techniques of style that Rabelais used, such as paragraphs full of images, adjective after adjective, getting more and more fantastic.

At the same time he was highly selective. He once wrote, "I must remember to steer clear of Walt Whitman's swimmy waters."

(What does he mean here? Perhaps his disapproval of Whitman's unrhymed, unmetered free verse. Woody tended to stick to traditional rhymed quatrains. I think rather, he suspected that he himself, like Whitman, had a weakness for undisciplined rambling on. Emerson, who early praised Whitman, later wrote, "I thought he would write a nation's songs, but he seems content to take its inventory." Woody's prose also does this occasionally—but of course I like it!)

Woody fought to retain his own identity as a representative of Oklahoma and the Dust Bowl. People thought he was being consciously bohemian, wearing blue jeans in New York City, shaving only when it was convenient. But he was just being like Popeye: "I yam what I yam what I yam."

He was an erratic performer. If he felt like telling stories, he might get up on the stage and talk most of the time:

"You know, my home state of Oklahoma is really a rich state. If you want some oil, just go down in a hole in the ground and get you some oil. We got lots of it. You want coal, we got coal, just go down in a hole in the ground and get you some coal. Do you want lead, zinc, we got them, just go down in a hole and get it. And if you want clothes or groceries or any thing else, you go in the hole and stay there."

I once bumped into Woody in Boston. "What you doing tonight, Pete? Come along with me. I got to sing for a big fund-raising dinner party in some hotel here." The dinner really was in one of the swankiest Boston hotels and Woody and I must have looked like two characters, in our boots and cowboy hats. Whether it was drinking a little too much wine or his general feelings on the subject of hotel dinner parties, I don't know, but Woody got on the platform and started talking. Twenty-five minutes later the chairman was whispering to me, "Won't you get him to sing a song please? We haven't got much time and all he's done so far is talk." I don't know how I managed it exactly, but I got out on the stage, and since he was talking about Jesse James and outlaws in general, we both sang "The Ballad of Jesse James" and walked off the stage.

> *Arlo Guthrie tells that when his father went into the hospital he was asked what religion he was, so it could be entered on the correct form.*
> *"All," replied Woody firmly.*
> *"Mr. Guthrie, we must know under which religion to list you."*
> *"All."*
> *"I'm sorry, Mr. Guthrie, it must be one or another."*
> *"All or none," said Woody.*

Once he was hired for twenty dollars to sing for a lawn party given by a wealthy lady in Bucks County, Pennsylvania. He sang one song amid all the cocktail chatter. He sang another, but the chatter still didn't subside.

In the middle of the third song he stopped and quietly slung his guitar on his back. On his way out he grabbed up a whiskey bottle in each hand in lieu of pay. Without saying a word he strolled out the door while the hostess stood openmouthed. I understand she has still not gotten over it.

"That man!" she said.

She assumed that he'd be like any cocktail pianist, I suppose, and just make a pleasant rattle in the background.

Burl Ives told me how Woody visited him right after Burl had gotten a new apartment on Riverside Drive in New York. Burl was proud of his furnishings. He had a guest room and said, "Woody, stay overnight with me."

Woody said, "Sure, don't mind if I do."

And he never took off his boots all night long. He was a restless sleeper; Burl told me that the next day he found his brand new sheets torn to ribbons by the heels of Woody's cowboy boots.

Well, that's Woody for you. He didn't always pay his bills, and he made life hard for his family and friends sometimes—always traveling, itching heels, ants in his pants. I guess I first learned what an undependable husband Woody must have been when we visited his family in Pampa in 1940. His first wife, Mary, gave up on him when he called it quits on his job with the Bonneville Power Administration. She went back to Texas.

Is that the price of genius? Is it worth paying? Maybe it's easy for me to ask that. It wouldn't be as easy for poor Mary, who was trying to build a home and a family.

But Lord, Lord, he turned out song after song after song!

Some creative people have created by staying in one place. Cézanne never traveled. Thoreau once said, "I have traveled widely in Concord." There are other creative people who must travel a great deal and continually make it hard on friends and family. Like Robert Burns, Gauguin, Hemingway, and others.

Robert Burns was much like Woody in many respects, a man from a small town whose natural genius brought him to the attention of the big city, but who also refused to fit into the polite mold that the big city wanted him to fit into. Robert Burns went back to his small town; Woody just kept on traveling. Never really stopped traveling.

Woody was not averse to having his songs sung on the Hit Parade, but to my knowledge he never wrote a song with the Hit Parade in mind. He considered most commercial music men as slick people who didn't really know what folks wanted, but who foisted their own ideas of music upon the country. He thought of them the way an Oklahoma farmer thought of Wall Street bankers. So Woody put out of his head the idea of making a lot of money from his songs. He'd write and sing them himself, and mimeograph copies for friends from time to time, and trust that if he put together a song that hit the spot, people would take it up as their own.

While he didn't chase after commercial work, he'd be perfectly willing to accept a commercial job, not only because it brought him some money but because it helped him reach people. He would quit the job if it started to interfere with anything else he wanted to do.

The Model Tobacco Company tried and failed to force Woody into a respectable mold. There were other attempts. John Greenway's *American Folk Songs of Protest,* published in McCarthy-ridden 1953, contains the following:

"Once more in New York, Guthrie became associated with the Almanac Singers, and through them with People's Songs, an organization in which his individuality was quickly submerged. Before any harm was done to his style, however . . . he gradually dissociated himself from the group."

The best person to answer this is Woody himself. In 1951—just after he signed a contract with a major recording company—Woody wrote to *Sing Out* (founded by People's Artists, the successor to People's Songs):

Dear Editor:

When some super-reactionary friend of mine looked through several issues of *Sing Out* and failed to find any songs of my own making, he wrote me and said: "Thank God you're not having anything to do with that bunch."

I've read just about every word of every issue of *Sing Out* and I just want to say right now before any more of you write in to thank me that I could not agree any more or any plainer nor any stronger with *Sing Out* if I had wrote every single word of it, and every song my own self by my own hand.

I know everybody on this *Sing Out* staff just as good as I know any of the members of my own family, or any of my sisters and my brothers. I believe in peace and *Sing Out* believes in peace; I do my best to fight against war and *Sing Out* fights just as hard to stop wars as I do; I make ballad-songs about the news of every day and show you how Jim Crow and race hate . . . hurts and stings and kills off a good part of my country every minute that flies by; and *Sing Out* sings out with songs to teach, to show, to prove to you these same terrible things; *Sing Out* sings out, too, to tell you about every little inch we gain in our fight against all of this reaction of hate.

One little issue of *Sing Out* is worth more to this humanly race than any thousand tons of other dreamy, dopey junk dished out from the trees of our forest along every Broadway in this world. I don't know of a magazine big or little that comes within a thousand million miles of *Sing Out* when it comes to doing good around this world.

More of my songs, my latest peace pieces and my later and older ballads too, will be printed in the pages of *Sing Outs* to come. I don't want your

Tommy Glazzeye Mackarthurish* cold bloody handshake nor your word of thanks nor your anything else. Whichever side Mac ain't on, I'm on, whichever side MacCarran ain't on, I am, whichever side Taft-Hartley's not on, I'm on double watch.

Let this be the end of those remarks that I will use my record contract to fall in love with my bellybutton and forget all of the Peekskills that I've been through with Pete Seeger, Lee Hays, and Earl Robinson, and lots of others. If I do fall into ten percent ownership of this Record Co. in the morning soon, that will not change one little word of this letter as to which side of things I am and am not on.

Your Buddy,
WOODY GUTHRIE

I learned so many different things from Woody that I can hardly count them. His ability to identify with the ordinary man and woman, speak their own language without using the fancy words, and never be afraid—no matter where you were: just diving into some situation, trying it out. When he and I used to go around singing together, we hit all kinds of places: CIO unions, churches, saloons, meetings, parties.

I learned from him how just plain orneriness has a kind of wonderful honesty to it that is unbeatable. He was going to cuss, he was going to speak bad language, he was going to shock people, but he was going to stay the way he was. He wasn't going to let New York make him slick and sleek and contented. He was going to stay a rebel to the end.

On most days of the week, he was always ready with a joke. But if he felt mad about something, he would come out and say it. He wasn't polite at all. And that kind of honesty—boy, you have to take off your hat to. It cost him a lot of jobs.

He scattered his genius so, it will never be all collected. Rhymes, letters, notes to himself. In 1960 I came across a notebook from 1941, when he and I were singing for our supper in the Pacific Northwest. On one page were some memos from me. On the next page was his own memo to himself.

---

* Tom Glazer had just written a song glorifying General MacArthur, who wanted to extend the Korean war into China.

The worst thing that can happen to you is to cut yourself loose from people. And the best thing is to sort of vaccinate yourself right into the the big streams and blood of the people.

To feel like you know the best and the worst of folks that you see everywhere and never to feel weak, or lost, or even lonesome anywhere.

There is just one thing that can cut you to drifting from the people, and that's any brand or style of greed.

There is just one way to save yourself, and that's to get together and work and fight for everybody.

I have traveled around the country and around the world singing his songs, and although Woody was in a hospital for years before his death in 1967, I have always felt he was very much with me, very much alive. I sing his songs with thousands of people, and Woody is right beside me, strumming along. His life is in the words sung from our lips.

I know his songs will go on traveling around the world and will be translated into many languages during the coming centuries and will be sung by many people who never heard his name.

What better kind of immortality could a man want?

A short bibliography:

Woody Guthrie, *Bound for Glory*. New York, E. P. Dutton & Co., Inc., 1943; paperback reprint Dolphin Books, Garden City, N.Y., Doubleday Co., Inc., *n.d.*
———, *Born to Win*. Robert Shelton, ed. New York, The Macmillan Co., 1965. (selected writings and drawings)
———, *American Folksong*. Moses Asch, ed., New York, Disc Co. of America, 1947; reprinted by Oak Publications, New York, 1961, $1.95.
———, *California to the New York Island* (a Cantata for Folksingers). Woody Guthrie Children's Trust Fund, Oak Publications, New York, 1958, $1.95. (29 songs with a script arranged from Woody's writings by Millard Lampell)
———, *Ballads of Sacco and Vanzetti*. New York, Oak Publications, 1960, $1.50.
———, *The Nearly Complete Collection of Woody Guthrie Folk Songs*. New York, Ludlow Music, Inc., 1963.
———, Alan Lomax and Pete Seeger, eds., *Hard-Hitting Songs for Hard-Hit People*. Oak Publications, 1967, $12.50.
Peter Seeger, Phil Ochs, Gordon Friesen and Josh Dunson, *Mainstream* (Woody Guthrie Issue), Vol. 16, No. 8, New York, August 1963; reprinted as *Woody Guthrie, A Tribute*, New York, Woody Guthrie Children's Trust Fund.

(Dick Reuss has compiled a complete Woody bibliography of about 500 items, including magazine and newspaper articles. It is available in mimeographed form from Woody Guthrie Children's Trust Fund, 200 W. 57th St., New York 10019, Room 1304, $5.00.)

Woody on records*:

ELEKTRA
Woody Guthrie Library of Congress Recordings (songs and conversation recorded by Alan Lomax in 1940), EKL 271/272: three LPs
Lost Train Blues, Railroad Blues, Rye Whiskey, Old Joe Clark, Beaumont Rag, Greenback Dollar, Boll Weevil Song, So Long It's Been Good to Know You, Talking Dust Bowl Blues, Do-Re-Mi, Hard Times, Pretty Boy Floyd, They Laid Jesus Christ in His Grave, Jolly Banker, I Ain't Got No Home, Dirty Overalls, Chain Around My Leg, Worried Man Blues, Lonesome Valley, Walkin' Down That Railroad Line, Goin' Down That Road Feeling Bad, Dust Storm Disaster,

---

* The footnote to Leadbelly's discography (p. 37) applies also to this one.

Foggy Mountain Top, Dust Pneumonia Blues, California Blues, Dust Bowl Refugee, Will Rogers Highway, Los Angeles New Year's Flood

FOLKWAYS

Dust Bowl Ballads, FH 5212

Talkin' Dust Bowl Blues, Blowin' Down This Road, Do Re Mi, Dust Cain't Kill Me, Tom Joad, The Great Dust Storm, So Long It's Been Good to Know You, Dust Bowl Refugee, Dust Pneumonia Blues, I Ain't Got No Home in This World Anymore, Vigilante Man

Bound for Glory (with Millard Lampell script read by Will Geer; see *California to the New York Island* in Bibliography), FA 2481

Stagolee, Vigilante Man, Do Re Mi, Pastures of Plenty, Grand Coulee Dam, This Land Is Your Land, Fishing, Reuben James, Jesus Christ, There's a Better World A-Coming, *and others*

Ballads of Sacco and Vanzetti, FH 5485

I Just Want to Sing Your Name, Red Wine, You Souls of Boston, Suassos Lane, The Flood and the Storm, Vanzetti's Rock, Root Hog and Die, Old Judge Thayer, We Welcome to Heaven, Vanzetti's Letter, Two Good Men. (Also, Sacco's Letter to His Son *by P. Seeger*)

Songs to Grow on for Mother and Child (Vol. 0), FC 7015

Grassy Grass Grass, Swimmy Swim Swim, Little Sack of Sugar, Rattle My Rattle, I Want My Milk, Grow Grow Grow, 1 2 3 4 5 6 7 8, One Day Two Days Three Days Old, Washy Wash Wash, I'll Eat You and I'll Drink You, Make a Bubble, Who's My Pretty Baby?, Write a Word

Songs to Grow On, Nursery Days (Vol. 1), FC 7005

Put Your Finger in the Air, Come See, Race You Down the Mountain, Car Song, Don't You Push Me Down, My Dolly, How Doo Do, Pick It Up, Merry Go Round, Sleepy Eyes, Wake Up, Clean-O

RCA VICTOR
Dust Bowl Ballads, LPV 502

TRADITION
The Legendary Woody Guthrie, TLP 2058

EVEREST
Woody Guthrie ("Archive of Folk Music"*), FS 204

Some records of Woody singing and playing with other folk musicians:

American Folksay, Stinson SLPX 5, SLPX 9, SLPX 12: three LPs
(with Leadbelly, Cisco Houston, Sonny Terry, Josh White, Gary Davis and others)

Chain Gang, Stinson SLPX 7
(with Sonny Terry and Alek Stewart)

Woody Guthrie Sings Folksongs, Vol. 1, Folkways FA 2483; Vol. 2, FA 2484
(with Leadbelly, Cisco Houston, Sonny Terry and Bess Hawes)

Woody Guthrie and Cisco Houston, Stinson SLP 32, SLP 44, SLP 53: three LPs

---

* No connection with Library of Congress.

3·Some Folk Roots and Protest Traditions

Folk singing is not new at all, for it has been going on since there were folks on earth to sing.
—*The Weavers Sing*, 1951

"THAT'S NICE, BUT IS IT A FOLK SONG?"

No TWO PEOPLE, not even the professors, have been able to agree completely on a definition of folk music. The Funk & Wagnalls *Dictionary of Folklore* lists many, which only partly overlap each other.

One definition says: "A folk song must be old, carried on for generations by people who have had no contact with urban arts and influence. A folk song must show no trace of individual authorship."

At the other end is the definition of the late Big Bill Broonzy, the blues singer. He was asked if a certain blues he sang was a folk song. "It must be," he replied. "I never heard horses sing it."

Face it: folk traditions will change as the folks who inhabit this earth change. The real traditional folk singer, who lived in past centuries and learned and sang his songs within a small folk community, sang a song because he thought it was a good song, not because he thought it was old.

Likewise, most sensible guitar pickers and singers today sing a song because they feel it is a good song, not because they have previously screened it to be sure it is traditional. The person who beats his breast and says "I will sing nothing but a folk song" is either fooling himself or trying to fool someone else.

If a conscientious anthropologist needs to hear an accurate presentation of Kentucky mountain banjo picking, he should go and get a good field recording, and not chide a Washington Square musician for failing to give him an exact imitation.

Nevertheless, I feel that the more young musicians strive to master the finest folk traditions of the past, the better music they will make in the future. It took thousands of years to develop these traditions; let us not lightly think we can improve upon them without considerable artistry.

In the following pages let's explore some of the different musical traditions that came to this country and how they mixed when they got here.

SOME AMERICAN TRADITIONS

Work Songs

WORK SONGS are a participative art form, not a performance form like narrative ballads. When work songs are arranged into performance songs, they are usually so drastically changed as to be useless.

In earlier centuries, people on every continent knew work songs as a normal accompaniment of living. Herdsmen and peddlers had their lonesome cries, and there were the group chants of diggers, pushers, lifters, hammerers, and haulers. Domestic tasks, such as spinning, milking, or rocking the cradle, had their own songs. (A lullaby is a work song, and should be sung by the luller. "Four and twenty trained singers caroling in harmony are not so effective as one mother's voice, however out-of-tune.")

Singing Under Sail*

THERE HAVE BEEN a number of books of sailor songs; it's nice to find one written by a sailor. Frederick Pease Harlow shipped before the mast in the 1870s and put together his manuscript when he was an old man. Besides some literary doggerel and trash, the book includes some

---

* Written in 1963 (review of *Chanteying Aboard American Ships* [Barre Publishing Co., Barre, Mass., 1962, $8.50]). The standard collections in this field are Joanna Colcord, *Songs of American Sailormen* (W. W. Norton, New York, 1938, reprinted by Oak Publications, N.Y., 1964), $4.95; and William Doerflnger, *Shanty Men and Shanty Boys* (Macmillan, New York, 1951). On *Sea Songs and Shanties,* Library of Congress AAFS L 26, you can hear the singing of actual old sailors. The best modern reconstruction is probably *Blow Boys Blow,* sung by A. L. Lloyd and Ewan MacColl, Tradition TLP 1026.

great new versions of old songs, some full-page photographs of sailors at work in those days, and firsthand reports of experiences. (Less valuable are his attempts to theorize outside his experiences, such as when he attributes Negro origin to a song clearly Yankee or Scottish in character. You will also find in his book the casual insulting words for other races and nations which were common among white sailors then. And a typically anti-women attitude.)

SANTY*

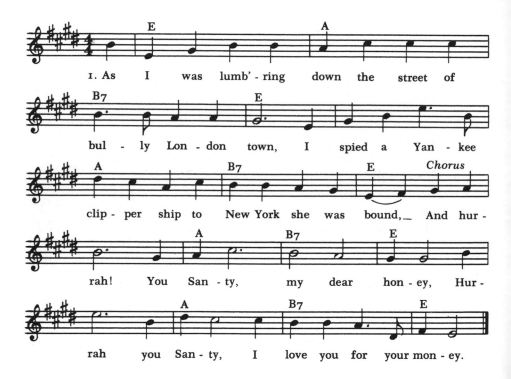

2. She had the finest clipper rig, now you must understand.
   She did not sail the rolling deep, but cruised upon dry land.   (*Chorus*)

3. She was a trim old fire ship and rigged out in disguise,
   To burn up sailor boys like me and others, damn her eyes.   (*Chorus*)

4. But when her hawser she stuck out, I made fast to her a tow;
   She squared away to a nearby dive and had me on the go.   (*Chorus*)

---

* Reprinted from *Chanteying Aboard American Ships.*

5. She filled me full of whiskey red and, drunk, I fell asleep;
   She rifled all my pockets, boys, and ruined me complete.   (*Chorus*)

Here are some of Harlow's comments on chantying:

Sailors were so accustomed to singing out when there was a pull to be made, that I have actually heard an old sailor give a "Yo-Ho-Hip" when pulling on his sea boots.

A good chanteyman . . . was often paid more than the common sailor, for his ability to get work out of the men; which was sometimes very much needed in ports where the crew was obliged to work the cargo.

. . . instead of confining themselves to the old verses and rhymes, sailors were privileged to sing any words that would rhyme. Consequently the riffraff of creation felt at liberty to use words of their own choice, rhyme or no rhyme, with the result that they frequently had vulgar songs so vile and rotten . . .

When the whale is alongside and the great dripping blanket piece is being cut in, every pound of which represents so much gold, the sweating, oil-soaked, greasy crew would burst into some such song as:

> My father's a hedger and ditcher
> My mother does nothing but spin
> While we hunt whales for a living
> Good Lord how the money comes in.

'Badian Negroes took great delight in singing the words in many variations and when once started would sing one after another, changing the air to suit their mood.

. . . usually the chorus was sung in unison by the (white) crew. The southern Negroes . . . employed their harmonious faculties on the chantey.

Singing Over the Oars

"MICHAEL, ROW THE BOAT ASHORE" comes from a section of America rich in Negro folk song, the Georgia Sea Islands. For over a hundred miles these low flat islands decorate the Atlantic Coast. Here slaves were brought fresh from Africa and spent their lives out of touch with mainland life. Only in recent years have bridges been built.

In olden days the only transportation was provided by small boats and strong arms to row them. The boat crews from different plantations prided themselves on their singing, each making up new songs, which no other boat would ever sing.

The lead oarsman on one of these boats might have been a man named Michael. (But, of course, the song also refers to the archangel.)

"Pay Me My Money Down," another Sea Island song, has been heard more recently, sung by stevedores loading produce on the island docks. If you listen carefully, you'll notice that the melody is a reworking of "Blow the Man Down." The words, with the exception of the word "down," are new.

Here's the principle: Every folk song was a topical song at its birth, a comment upon the life and times of the singers and listeners.

PAY ME MY MONEY DOWN

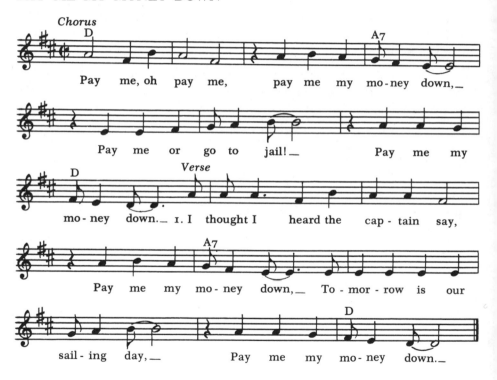

(Chorus)

2. The very next day we cleared the bar,
    Pay me my money down,
    He knocked me down with the end of a spar,
    Pay me my money down.   (Chorus)

3. I wish I was Mr. Howard's son,
    Pay me my money down,
    Sit in the house and drink good rum,
    Pay me my money down.   (Chorus)

4. I wish I was Mr. Steven's son,
    Pay me my money down,
    Sit on the bank and watch the work done,
    Pay me my money down.   (*Chorus*)

Singing in Prison Work Gangs

TODAY in mechanized North America one can only rarely hear work songs. Certain scattered ethnic groups, such as the Gaelic-speaking Cape Breton Islanders of eastern Canada, still preserve a few. Among southern Afro-Americans a tradition of work song has lasted into our own times. Songs have accompanied road building and railroad building, fishing, and other occupations that required coordinated muscular effort of a gang of men. In the segregated prisons of the South, where older prisoners pass on songs to younger men, some of the oldest and most traditional are still sung.

In 1951 my wife and I, with John Lomax, Jr., and some others, got permission to take a tape-recording machine down to one of the prison farms about fifty miles south of Houston, Texas. The warden let us set up the microphone in the kitchen. Some prisoners were allowed to stay up late and sing for us.* (All the singers were Negro; white prisoners in Texas were then segregated into separate prisons, where work songs were rarely, if ever, sung.)

We had a regular party amongst the pots and pans. But one very young man stepped up to the microphone and said: "Well, gentlemen, this is Andrew B. Crane, serving a lifetime sentence on Retrieve State Farm. This is a song I sing with the boys when I get worried."

And this is what he sang, and what I will never forget as long as I live:

GO DOWN, OLD HANNAH

1. Won't you go down, old Han - nah?_ Well, *well, well.* ___ Don't you

---

* *Negro Prison Camp Work Songs*, Folkways FE 4475.

rise   no   more!__   *Don't you rise   no   more!__*   Won't you go down,old

Han - nah? _____   Don't you rise   no __   more!

Sample variation in melody

Ju - lie's _____   tell 'er   I   won't   *be*   home. __

(Old Hannah is their nickname for the sun; the only thing Crane wanted was that sun never to come up unless it brought Judgment Day. Think of it next time you read headlines that the cities are burning.)

(Italicized words sung by gang)

2. If you rise in the morning, *well, well, well,*
Bring Judgment Day, *bring Judgment Day;*
If you go up, come up in the *morning,*
Bring Judg*ment Day.*

3. Well, I looked at old Hannah, *well, well, well,*
She was turning red, *she was turning red;*
Well, I looked at old *Hannah,*
She was tur*ning red.*

4. Well, I looked at my partner; *well, well, well,*
He was almost dead, *he was almost dead;*
Well, I looked at my *partner,*
He was *almost dead.*

5. Well, wake up, old dead man, *well, well, well,*
Help me carry my row, *help me carry my row;*
Why'n't you wake up, old *dead man,*
Help me *carry my row.*

6. Well, my partner looked around, *well, well, well,*
This is what he said, *this is what he said;*
Well, my partner looked a*round,*
This is *what he said:*

7. Well, I'm sorry, man, *well, well, well,*
   They done drove me down, *they done drove me down;*
   Well, I'm *sorry, man,*
   They done *drove me down.*

8. Well, if you get lucky, *well, well, well,*
   And make it back home, *and make it back home;*
   If you get *lucky*
   And make it *back home,*

9. Well, go down by Julie's, *well, well, well,*
   Tell her I won't be home, *tell her I won't be home;*
   Go down by *Julie's,*
   Tell her I won't *be home.*

10. Well, I was a good man, *well, well, well,*
    But they drove me down, *but they drove me down;*
    I was a good *man,*
    But they *drove me down.*

11. Well, look-a-here, partner, *well, well, well,*
    What I done done, *what I done done;*
    Look-a-here, *partner,*
    What I *done done:*

12. Well, I drove so hard, *well, well, well,*
    Couldn't see a whole turn row, *couldn't see a whole turn row;*
    Well, I drove so *hard,*
    Couldn't see a *whole turn row.*

13. Well, I shook my head, *well, well, well,*
    I began to moan, *I began to moan;*
    Well, I shook my *head,*
    And began *to moan.*

14. Well, it looks like everything, *well, well, well,*
    Everything I do, *everything I do,*
    Well, it looks like *everything*
    I do *is wrong.*

15. Well, I made up my mind, *well, well, well,*
    I'm gon' head home, *I'm gon' head home;*
    Well, I made up my *mind*
    I'm gon' *head home.*

Where do the songs come from?

Prison inmates have often composed songs, but one melody ("Long John") has been traced to West African origin. Another well-known Negro work song, "Stewball," has been traced to an eighteenth-century

British ballad about a racehorse, but the words are greatly changed and the tune is a world away from the earlier narrative ballad. "Gray Goose" refers often in the lyrics to "Master" and "Missus" and "white house," indicating that the song was probably a product of slavery days.

"Take This Hammer" uses the same basic melodic and harmonic structure of "Goodnight Irene" and the spiritual "I'm on My Way to Canaan Land." It should be pointed out that while some of these prison work songs have specific prison references and perhaps local origins, many of the songs would be known to black laborers and singers of folk songs elsewhere in the South. Inasmuch as new verses and variant melodies are continually being created, it would be unusual to hear any song sung twice the same way.

Musically, there are several points worth noting. Like most Afro-American work songs (and most spirituals, too) these use antiphony, that is, one voice answering another—solo balanced against chorus, for example. Antiphony is used by many work songs the world over, but it is almost a basic principle of African music tradition.

Harmony does not figure as importantly in this music as in spirituals sung in church. The lack of accompaniment did not bother the singers, of course; they had probably never heard the songs sung except in the fields, accompanied only by the sound of tools. Harmonically, most of the songs rarely leave the tonic chord. Only a few have an occasional dominant or subdominant feeling.

However, any singer able to would sing a high tenor part, or bass.

The melody will often change as the song progresses. The first few verses will generally be sung "straight"—as a jazz musician might "set" the conventional melody before enlarging upon it. Later verses, whether sung by the original soloist or another stepping in to relieve him, will tend to embody melodic variations.

Rhythmically, any work song must be appropriate to the work. Even slow songs, such as "Go Down, Old Hannah," would fit when each man was hoeing around plants with short, irregular strokes. Only with such a long "surgelike" song could a group of men find common rhythm.

The more rhythmically regular songs would be more likely to accompany such work as axe chopping. If all strokes came in unison, they would occur normally on the third beat of each four-beat measure. If two groups alternated strokes, the stroke would come on the first beat as well.

GRIZZELY BEAR

(Melody for first verse only; it must be varied as the song progresses.)

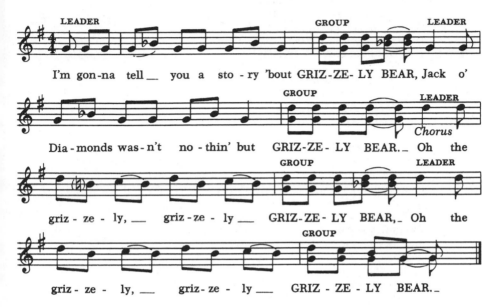

The words GRIZZELY BEAR are sung by the group after every line sung by the solo leader throughout the entire song.

Leader:
Tell me, who was that grizzely
Tell me, who was that grizzely
Oh, Jack o' Diamonds was that grizzely
Oh, Jack o' Diamonds was the grizzely
He had great long tushes like a
He had great long tushes like a
He made a track in the bottom like a
He made a track in the bottom like a
 Well, that grizzely, grizzely
 Oh, that grizzely, grizzely
Tell me, who was the grizzely
Tell, a-who was the grizzely
Jack o' Diamonds was the grizzely
Jack o' Diamonds was the grizzely
He made a noise in the bottom like a
He made a noise in the bottom like a
Well, my mama was scared of that
Well, my mama was scared of that

Well, my papa went a-hunting for the
Well, my papa went a-hunting for the
Well, my brother wasn't scared of that
Well, my brother wasn't scared of that
    Oh, the grizzely, grizzely
    Oh, the grizzely, grizzely
Well-a, I'm gonna kill that
Well-a, I'm gonna kill that
    Well, the grizzely, grizzely
    Oh, that grizzely, grizzely
Well, I looked in Louisiana for the
Well, I looked in Louisiana for the
    Well, the grizzely, grizzely
    Well, that grizzely, grizzely

(Another soloist might take over the lead, with a slightly different style.)

I'm gonna tell you a story 'bout the
Jack o' Diamonds wasn't nothing but a
He come a-huffing and a-blowing like a
He had great long tushes like a
He come a-wobbling and a-squabbling like a
And Jack o' Diamonds was the great big
He was a great big grizzely
He was the great big grizzely
Everybody was scared of that
Everybody was scared of that
    Oh, the grizzely, grizzely
    Oh, the grizzely, the grizzely
Jack o' Diamonds was the great big
He come a-wobbling and a-squabbling like a
He come a-huffing and a-blowing like a
He come a-walking and a-talking like a
He had great long tushes like a
He had big blue eyes like a
He had great long hair like a
    Oh, the grizzely, grizzely
    Oh, the grizzely, grizzely
I'm gonna tell you people 'bout the
I'm gonna warn you and gonna tell you 'bout the
You better watch that grizzely
You better watch that grizzely
Well, the bear's gonna get you now
    Oh, the grizzely, grizzely
    Oh, the great big grizzely
Well, Jack o' Diamonds wasn't nothing but a

(And so on!)

This brings us to a much-disputed point. What was the real purpose
and function of work songs? Was it mainly distraction and entertain-

ment, such as music over a PA system gives a line of workers on a monotonous beltline? One could not categorically state that work songs were essential, since so often labor was accomplished without their assistance. Captain Alan Villiers was once asked if he ever heard sailors sing chanteys. "No!" he replied decisively. "We were too busy working." But Dana, in *Two Years Before the Mast,* disagrees.

I asked one of the Texas prisoners why they sang them. "Oh, it makes the work go easier."

I feel sure that one function of work songs has been to help secure a steady, even pace of work. This pace might be faster than some would like, slower than others could achieve if necessary, but it would be a workable average. Leadbelly told me that he purposely held out the last note of the third line of every stanza of a certain song so that men could rest their hammers on their shoulders for a moment before coming down on the next stroke.

The lyrics of the prison chants have a strong and agile imagery. One word might mean several things at the same time. Who is the Grizzely Bear? Undoubtedly some white overseer. The hammer of the song "Hammer Ring" means several things before the last verse is sung.

Probably work songs, like other art forms, have fulfilled several functions. A people that traditionally loved to sing would logically fit the rhythm of a song to the rhythm of work being done at the time, as hikers sing songs in march tempo. Occasionally the song could notify all the gang to bring concerted muscular effort at a certain point.

And the poetry of a song might lift a worker's mind out of the rut of a monotonous job, or at least relate it to the larger necessities and drama of life.

Music and Organized Labor

LIKE HYMNS and patriotic songs, union songs are songs with a message. Put together, the ballads, anthems, and ditties composed by American union members would tell the best part of the history of the American labor movement.

Unlike most hymns and patriotic songs, union songs are usually composed by amateurs to suit a particular occasion, and have a short life. More often than not, they are simply new words to an older melody.

A few of such songs, however, prove worthwhile enough in melody and lyrics to warrant being passed on by one generation of workers to the next.

Whatever Happened to Singing in the Unions?

EXCEPT IN A FEW UNIONS, there was not as much singing as some people now suppose. From listening to the *Talking Union* record and reading a couple of novels about early labor struggles, some jump to the conclusion that the United States was full of class-conscious harmonizing in those days. 'Tain't true.

The singingest union America ever had was the old Wobblies. Their official name was the Industrial Workers of the World, started in Chicago in June of 1905 by Big Bill Haywood, of the Western Federation of Miners, and others who were dissatisfied with the lack of progress of the little old craft unions under Sam Gompers' American Federation of Labor. The IWW quickly grew to 150,000 before World War I. It was put down then by the government because of its opposition to the war, made an upsurge after the war, and then in the 1920s dwindled to a fraction of its old strength.

They were a defiantly radical group, mostly anarchist-syndicalists of a sort, and they argued bitterly with socialists as to the value of trying to elect working-class congressmen. Their idea was to ultimately sign up all the workers in One Big Union, improve their conditions, and eventually call a general strike to decide who was going to run the world—the workers or the bosses.

With every new union card, they also handed out a little red songbook.* The cover carried a motto: "To Fan the Flames of Discontent." Inside were the words to about fifty songs, usually parodies of well-known melodies—pop songs of the day, hymns, or older tunes commonly sung. Their best-known songwriters were Joe Hill and Ralph Chaplin, both of whom rose from the ranks to become full-time organizers for the IWW. (The latter's song, "Solidarity Forever," is still officially sung at many a labor-union convention, but I'll bet Joe Hill's "Casey Jones" becomes a more permanent part of American folklore.)

The songs were roared out by Wobblies at meetings, on picket lines, in jails (where IWW men were often put by the dozens and hundreds), on freight trains through South Dakota (filled with migrant harvest hands

---

* *IWW Songs* (*Songs of the Workers*), 50th Anniversary Edition (Industrial Workers of the World, Chicago, 1956, $.25).

for the wheat fields), or wherever Wobblies happened to meet. If the Salvation Army was preaching against them from one street corner, they might set up a soapbox on the opposite corner. When the Salvation Army band started up "In the Sweet Bye and Bye," Wobblies would use it to accompany their own singing of Joe Hill's parody, "Pie in the Sky."

Prior to the IWW, labor songs were not unknown, but they were by no means common (the eight-hour-day movement of the 1880s had some). By researching old union records and newspapers, one could probably compile a list of thousands of songs made up during this or that strike. But when the strike was over, usually the songs were forgotten, as might be the songs of some war after the armistice is signed.

The music of these songs often reflected the folk background of the workers involved. Thus, the anthracite miners of Pennsylvania might have Irish or Slavic tunes for their strike songs. In the southern states, one could find old English ballad melodies or hymn tunes, with new words made up by the country people who came down to work in the textile mills.

During the 1920s and '30s, some of the northern city unions, such as the International Ladies Garment Workers, also printed songbooks. They had many immigrant members who had an Old World love of singing; often, they joined choruses which rehearsed to perform at rallies and May Day parades. In 1935, the CIO was formed, again to try to do the job not being done by the conservative old craft unions. There was a wave of organizing drives throughout the country that produced a flood of parodies to pop melodies. The Flint sit-down strikers who took over the General Motors plant there in 1935 sang:

> When we walked out on you,
>   we set you back on your heels,
> Goody goody!
> So you lost some money and now
>   you know how it feels
> Goody goody!

And they had many more songs like it.

But again, when the strikes were over, the songs were usually forgotten. In 1940, I learned the song "Which Side Are You On?" from a folklorist who had been researching in eastern Kentucky in 1932. Later, I met Mrs. Reece, who wrote the song. At that time, it was unknown except in the memories of her family and a few miners of Harlan County who heard her daughters sing it at the 1932 union meetings.

In the 1930s, as in the 1960s, it was the Negro people of the South, with their fine traditions of church singing, who provided some of the best songs picked up throughout the country. "We Shall Not Be Moved" is supposed to have come out of one of the organizing drives of the Southern Tenant Farmers Union in the early thirties. It was originally "Jesus Is My Captain, I Shall Not Be Moved." But, significantly, the new words were not antireligious, as were the Wobbly parodies. They simply emphasized a militancy that was always present in the older spirituals.

"It's That Union Train A-Coming" was once "The Old Ship of Zion." "Roll the Union On" recalls "Roll the Chariot Along," and also came out of the 1935 sharecropper struggles. This and a number of other songs were put together by union people studying at Commonwealth College, Arkansas, a union school of the thirties.

The 1941 *Talking Union* recording (now available on Folkways FH 5285) represented an attempt to carry on this tradition and spread it through the North and West. But then the war came, and union drives were shelved until Hitler was beaten. In 1946, the former Almanac Singers and others joined to form the People's Songs organization, with the idea of reviving folk and labor songs through the unions of the nation. But now the Cold War came along and American labor unions kicked out most of the militants and radicals, the very ones who had always been the enthusiastic singers and songwriters. Even unions with left-wing leadership felt they had to concentrate on pork chops to the exclusion of songbooks and choruses. A west-coast longshoreman told me that at the 1952 ILWU* Seattle convention, a group of newly organized Hawaiian workers marched enthusiastically into the convention hall singing union songs. "Why! all our mainland delegates turned around in surprise. They hadn't seen anything like that in a long time!"

Today, a few unions still publish songbooks, and a few even have choruses. But an average of only 3 percent of American union members attend union meetings, except during crises, and the songbooks are by and large unused. In 1968, "Wallace for President" buttons sprouted on the lapels of officials of local unions; and "Union Maid" is far better known on college campuses than it is in the average union hall.

And this is what happened to singing in the unions.

If all this is disillusioning, let me add one thing: History shows that there is a hidden heritage of militancy which comes and goes, but never completely dies. It undergoes transformations and permutations from

---

* International Longshoremen's and Warehousemen's Union.

century to century, but the lessons learned by one generation, even though through defeat, are passed on to the next. In the 1960s many of the song traditions of the 1930s have seen new life as never before—in the freedom songs of the South and in the topical songs of many a campus.

Mrs. Florence Reece, wife of a rank-and-file organizer for the old National Miners' Union in Harlan County, Kentucky, was at home one day in 1931 when High Sheriff J. H. Blair and his "deputies" ("they were really company gun thugs," she said) came to her house. One of her little girls started to cry. "What you crying for?" said a deputy. "We ain't after you, we're after your old man." They poked their rifles into closets, under beds, even into piles of dirty clothes, and finally left. Mrs. Reece tore an old calendar off the wall and wrote these now famous verses. She fitted them to an old hymn tune, and her little girls used to sing it at the union hall.

WHICH SIDE ARE YOU ON?

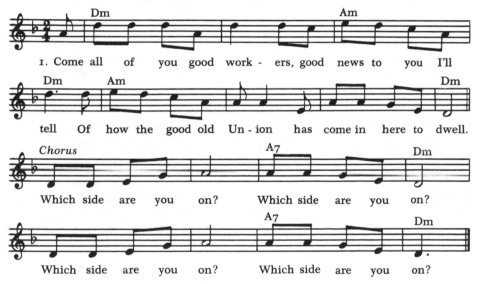

1. Come all of you good work - ers, good news to you I'll
tell Of how the good old Un - ion has come in here to dwell.

Chorus
Which side are you on? Which side are you on?

Which side are you on? Which side are you on?

2. My daddy was a miner,
   He's now in the air and sun,*
   And he'll stick with the Union
   'Til every battle's won.   (*Chorus*)

3. They say in Harlan County
   There are no neutrals there;
   You'll either be a Union man
   Or a thug for J. H. Blair.   (*Chorus*)

* Blacklisted from the mines. More recently this line has been sung: "And I'm a miner's son."

4. Oh workers can you stand it?
   Oh tell me how you can.
   Will you be a lousy scab
   Or will you be a man?   (*Chorus*)

5. Don't scab for the bosses,
   Don't listen to their lies.
   Us poor folks haven't got a chance
   Unless we organize.   (*Chorus*)

In 1961:

"I rewrote the old labor song by Florence Reece, 'Which Side Are You On?,' on the spur of the moment in the Hinds County Jail after the Freedom Riders who were imprisoned there had been discussing and speculating about the attitude of local Negroes regarding the Freedom Rides. We had learned through trustees in the jail that most local Negroes were with us, but afraid to do anything because of fear of reprisals. They told us that, of course, there were a lot of Uncle Toms around and it was hard to tell who was and who was not."*

New words by James Farmer. Copyright © 1946, 1963, Sing Out, Inc.

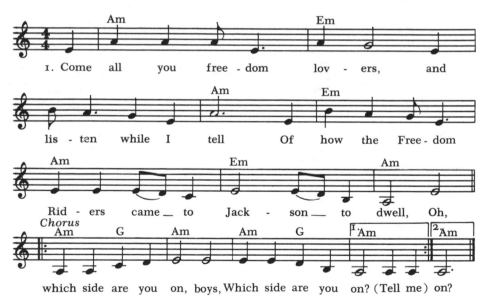

1. Come all you free-dom lov-ers, and lis-ten while I tell Of how the Free-dom Rid-ers came to Jack-son to dwell, Oh,

Chorus

which side are you on, boys, Which side are you on? (Tell me) on?

2. My daddy was a freedom fighter and
   I'm a freedom son;
   I'll stick right with this struggle until
   the battle's won.

---

* James Farmer of CORE. The quote and this version of the song are from *We Shall Overcome, Songs of the Southern Freedom Movement* (Oak Publications, New York, 1963).

3. Don't "tom" for Uncle Charlie, don't listen to
     his lies,
   'Cause black folks haven't got a chance until
     they organize.

4. They say in Hinds County no neutrals have they
     met;
   You're either for the Freedom Ride or you "tom"
     for Ross Barnett.

5. Oh people can you stand it, tell me how you can.
   Will you be an Uncle Tom or will you be a man?

6. Captain Ray will holler "move on," but the Freedom
     Riders won't budge;
   They'll stand there in the terminals and even before
     the judge.

The Coal Creek Rebellion

PAY DAY AT COAL CREEK

Collected, adapted and arranged by John A. Lomax and Alan
Lomax, TRO-© copyright 1941, renewed 1969, Ludlow Music,
Inc., New York, New York. Used by permission.

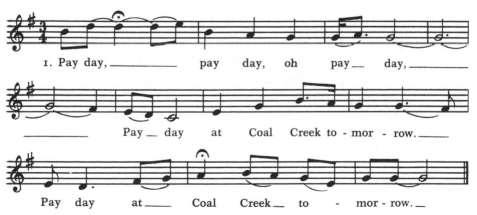

1. Pay day, _____ pay day, oh pay__ day, _____
   _____ Pay __ day at Coal Creek to - mor - row. _____
   Pay day at __ Coal Creek __ to - mor - row. _

2. Pay day, pay day, oh, pay day,
   Pay day don't come at Coal Creek no more,
   Pay day don't come no more.

3. Bye-bye, bye-bye, oh, bye-bye,
   Bye-bye, my woman, I'm gone,
   Bye-bye, my woman, I'm gone.

4. You'll miss me, you'll miss me, you'll miss me,
   You'll miss me when I'm gone,
   You'll miss me when I'm gone.

5. I'm a poor boy, I'm a poor boy, I'm a poor boy,
   I'm a poor boy and a long ways from home,
   I'm a poor boy and a long ways from home.

6. He's a rider, he's a rider, he's a rider,
   Oh, he's a rider, but he'll leave that rail some time.
   He's a rider, but he'll leave that rail some time.

In the 1890s black and white coal miners in Tennessee banded together to oppose the convict-labor system which threatened their livelihood. They called it the "Coal Creek Rebellion." It was marked by a series of armed skirmishes, during three years. The state militia eventually had to muster several thousand soldiers to quell the revolt. An old miner told me, "For several years the state of Tennessee couldn't collect taxes from those eastern counties."

During the 1880s Tennessee miners had tried to organize in the Knights of Labor. Their efforts were thwarted by the presence in the mines of thousands of convicts, leased at $60 a head by the Tennessee state government to the companies, who thus had convenient scabs ready to break any strike. Petitions to the governor had no effect. He seemed to care more for the interests of the Tennessee Coal and Iron Corporation, then and now a Yankee-owned colossus astride the South.

On July 4, 1891, a group of desperate miners marched to the prison stockade. At gunpoint they freed the prisoners and burned the stockade. The state retaliated by building a new stockade and guarding it with a detachment of militia. The miners now organized and burned down several stockades and defeated the militia in several pitched battles.

To prevent the state from simply rounding up the convicts and putting them to work again, the miners finally hid prisoners in their homes, gave them clothing, and helped them escape across state borders. If one realizes that most of the miners were white, and most of the convicts were black, the significance of the affair emerges.

Eventually the miners were starved into submission and defeated in battle, their leaders sentenced to prison. To all appearances their struggle had been in vain. But, following a classic American pattern one can see recurring throughout our history,* their struggle *did* succeed. Their attacks made the convict-labor system less profitable for both the state and the companies. By focusing the attention of the whole state on the shabby and immoral setup of convict labor, the miners gained public sympathy. The next election brought a new state administration, which abolished the system and pardoned the union leaders. (Nearby Alabama coal miners, without such a struggle, had to wait another twenty years for the system to be abolished.)

Today, Coal Creek, near Norris Dam, is renamed Lake City. Few miners alive can remember those brave years. Conventional school histories ignore the events, as they ignore the rent wars of New York State, the Dorr Rebellion of Rhode Island, slave revolts, and early labor struggles.

But as always happens, many topical folk songs were composed by local balladeers. The best of these have survived and been collected into archives by serious-minded professors who don't always know what the words are all about.

"The Coal Creek March," it appears, was a famous banjo solo around the turn of the century. It has been superlatively performed by Pete Steele, carpenter, of Hamilton, Ohio.† His version is a folk fragment. Doc Hopkins, whose string band, the Bucklebusters, was well known on the country-music hit parade during the early 1930s, plays an extended version.

Doc's banjo plays bugle calls ("That's the Tennessee militia lining up; they're off to put down the miners"). The banjo gives a train imitation ("They're off for Coal Creek"). The banjo head is struck sharply ("Rifle shots. The miners are firing on the train from the hillsides"). The banjo imitates dogs barking ("That's the dogs yapping at the soldiers when they get off the train at Coal Creek"). And so on.

"Roll Down the Line" is a miner's version of a song made up by Negro convicts working in the mines. As given here, it is from the singing of the late Uncle Dave Macon,** long a star on Nashville's Grand Ole Opry radio program. Uncle Dave was a young man at the time of the Coal Creek Rebellion, and probably learned the song first-hand.

---

* A pattern successful for light-skinned Americans. See Chapter 10.
† Library of Congress AAFS L2. (A tablature transcription of the way I play it is included in *The Goofing Off Suite*, Hargail Music Press; also in record notes, Folkways FA 2412.)
** Folkways *Anthology of American Folk Music*, Vol. III, FA 2953; originally issued by Brunswick in 1930.

Uncle Dave Macon

ROLL DOWN THE LINE

1. Way back yon-der in Ten-nes-see, They leased the con-victs

out.   Put   them   work - ing   in   the   mine __   A -

gainst free lab - or   stout.   Free lab - or   re - belled a -

gainst it;   To   win   it   took   some   time.   But

while the lease was   in ef - fect, They made 'em   rise and shine.

Chorus

Bud - dy, won't you roll   down   the   line?   Bud - dy, won't you

roll   down   the   line?   Yon - der comes   my   dar - lin',

com - ing down   the   line.   Bud - dy, won't you roll down   the

line?   Bud - dy, won't you   roll   down   the   line?

Yon - der comes   my   dar - lin',   com - ing   down the   line.

2. Early Monday morning
   They get you up on time,
   Send you down to Lone Rock
   Just to look into that mine;

Send you down to Lone Rock
Just to look into that hole,
Very next thing the captain says,
"You better get your pole."   (*Chorus*)

3. The beans they are half done,
The bread is not so well;
The meat it is all burnt up
And the coffee's black as heck!*
But when you get your task done,
And it's on the floor you fall,
Anything you get to eat
It 'ud taste good, done or raw.   (*Chorus*)

4. The bank boss, he's a hard man,
A man you all know well;
And if you don't get your task done
He's gonna give you hallelujah!
Carry you to the stockade,
And it's on the floor you fall,
Very next word you hear,
"You better get your pole."   (*Chorus*)

Mother Jones and the Singing Miners' Wives

One of the most colorful figures in the history of the American labor movement was a demure little old lady, usually dressed in prim black, known to millions by the simple name of Mother Jones. She died in 1931, aged one hundred and one. She could harangue a large crowd as well as any man, and was not afraid to sprinkle her speeches with a few unladylike "hells" and "damns." Absolutely fearless, she often risked death, and was in jail scores of times. She first became interested in the labor movement during the 1870s, and for fifty years, until 1923, was an active free-lance organizer, mainly among miners and steelworkers. The following is a chapter from her autobiography.† The event she describes took place shortly before the First World War.

---

* As sung by Uncle Dave Macon.
† *Autobiography of Mother Jones*, ed. Mary Field Parton (Charles H. Kerr & Co., Chicago, 1925).

The miners in Greensburg, Pennsylvania, went on strike for more wages. Their pay was pitifully low. In answer to the cry for bread, the Irish—that is, the Pennsylvania—constabulary were sent into the district.

One day a group of angry women were standing in front of the mine, hooting at the scabs that were taking the bread from their children's mouths. The sheriff came and arrested all the women "for disturbing the peace." Of course, he should have arrested the scabs, for they were the ones who really disturbed it.

I told them to take their babies and tiny children along with them when their case came up in court. They did this, and while the judge was sentencing them to pay thirty dollars or serve thirty days in jail, the babies set up a terrible wail so that you could hardly hear the old judge. He scowled and asked the women if they had some one to leave the children with.

I whispered to the women to tell the judge that miners' wives didn't keep nurse girls; that God gave the children to their mothers and He held them responsible for their care.

Two mounted police were called to take the women to the jail, some ten miles away. They were put on an interurban car with two policemen to keep them from running away. The car stopped and took on some scabs. As soon as the car started the women began cleaning up the scabs. The two policemen were too nervous to do anything. The scabs, who were pretty much scratched up, begged the motorman to stop and let them off, but the motorman said it was against the law to stop except at the station. That gave the women a little more time to trim the fellows. When they got to the station those scabs looked as if they had been sleeping in the tiger cat's cage at the zoo.

When they got to Greensburg, the women sang as the car went through the town. A great crowd followed the car, singing with them. As the women, carrying their babies, got off the car before the jail the crowd cheered and cheered them. The police officers handed the prisoners over to the sheriff and both of them looked relieved.

The sheriff said to me, "Mother, I would rather you brought me a hundred men than those women. Women are fierce!"

"I didn't bring them to you, Sheriff," said I, " 'twas the mining company's judge sent them to you for a present."

The sheriff took them upstairs, put them all in a room and let me stay with them for a long while. I told them women:

"You sing the whole night long. You can spell one another if you get tired and hoarse. Sleep all day and sing all night and don't stop for anyone. Say you're singing to the babies. I will bring the little ones milk and fruit. Just you all sing and sing."

The sheriff's wife was an irritable little cat. She used to go and try to stop them because she couldn't sleep. Then the sheriff sent for me and asked me to stop them.

"I can't stop them," said I. "They are singing to their little ones. You telephone the judge to order them loose."

Complaints came in by the dozens; from hotels and lodging houses and private homes.

"Those women howl like cats," said a hotel keeper to me.

"That's no way to speak of women who are singing patriotic songs and lullabies to their little ones," said I.

Finally after five days in which everyone in town had been kept awake, the judge ordered their release. He was a narrow-minded, irritable, savage-looking old animal and hated to do it, but no one could muzzle those women!

Mother Jones

Joe Hill

The Man Who Never Died

IT TOOK NEARLY FORTY YEARS for the first book to be published which gave the true facts on the life and death of Joe Hill, legendary songwriter and organizer for the Wobblies between 1911 and 1915.*

Half of Barrie Stavis' book is an absorbing play. The other half is a documentary preface quoting letters and newspaper articles of the time. If you read it through, you will feel that for the first time you really know Joe as a friend and as a person.

For a wonderful person he was, brave, generous, lighthearted and gay, single-mindedly dedicated to his cause, thoughtful toward others, and always militant.

He arrived in the United States from Sweden in 1900, nineteen years old, and took the name of Joseph Hillstrom. Eleven years of miscellaneous jobs followed—harvesting wheat in the Dakotas, shipping out to Honolulu. He wrote his first well-known union song in 1912 while in-

---

* Barrie Stavis, *The Man Who Never Died* (Haven Press, New York, 1954, $3.00).

volved in a longshore strike in San Pedro, California. Within a few short years hundreds of thousands of copies of the little red Wobbly song-books had carried his parodies of popular songs of the day, hymns and folk tunes. He wrote ballads to order for lumberjacks in the Northwest and textile workers of New England.

In 1914, he was framed in Salt Lake City on a murder charge, and in spite of pleas from around the world, including attempted intervention by President Wilson and the Swedish Government, he was shot by a Utah firing squad on November 19, 1915.

An immense job of research faced Barrie Stavis when he undertook this book in 1948. To begin with, the complete court records of Joe's trial had mysteriously "disappeared" from the county clerk's office in Salt Lake. In addition, all the records in the office of the IWW, which Joe himself counted on to ultimately vindicate him, were either seized by Federal agents during World War I, or burned in a disastrous fire that gutted the Chicago headquarters of the organization a few years later.

Nevertheless, using newspaper accounts which quoted verbatim from the trial, and other sources such as the large collection of Joe's letters to Elizabeth Gurley Flynn (then twenty-five years old), who helped to or-ganize his defense, a completely creditable reconstruction has been made. Stavis points out at several points that a definitive biography is still to be written. Within his space limitations he could give little more than an extended essay. But his documentation is sufficient to give the lie to several slanderous writings on Joe Hill.

These writings are a novel, *The Preacher and the Slave*, by Wallace Stegner, an article in the *Industrial and Labor Relations Review*, "The Legend of Joe Hill," by Vernon Jensen, and a chapter in *American Folk-songs of Protest* by John Greenway. One or more of the following points were made in these three pieces: 1) He was guilty. 2) His songs were no good. 3) He was just a hobo and had no influence.

Well, Joe Hill's parody* of a Salvation Army hymn added "pie in the sky" to nearly everyone's vocabulary. We also owe him the union version of "Casey Jones" and probably "Hallelujah, I'm a Bum." Others well worth remembering include "Tramp, Tramp, Tramp, Keep on A-tramping," "Rebel Girl," "There Is Power," and "Mister Block."

He himself would be the last to claim great credit as a musician. He liked to "rattle the ivories" on pianos in the union halls, and knew how to notate his songs, but little more. But he had a real flair for lyrics. All his

---

* Originally titled "The Preacher and the Slave."

life he had "scribbled," as he called it. Probably hundreds of parodies of popular songs were made up by him which will never be known. Only two of his songs, "Casey Jones" and "Pie in the Sky," have been on the all-time union hit parade, it is true. Others have fallen into disuse because the very qualities that made them so timely and acute in 1913 make them now as obsolete as yesterday's newspapers. Some of his finest efforts are rarely sung simply because the melodies have been forgotten or are never reprinted because of copyright restrictions.

From time to time in recent years, the November 19 anniversary of Joe's execution has been memorialized with a program of his songs. They bring his presence close. To the singers it must seem as though he peered over their shoulders occasionally, with a grin creasing his features as though to say, " 'Pears to me you're making a lot too much fuss over me, personally. But if it helps organize the OBU,* go to it, Brother!"

CASEY JONES—THE UNION SCAB

1. The work-ers on the S. P. Line to strike sent out a call; But Ca-sey Jones, the en-gi-neer, he would-n't strike at all; His boil-er it was leak-ing, and its driv-ers on the bum, And his en-gine and its bear-ings, they were

---

* One Big Union.

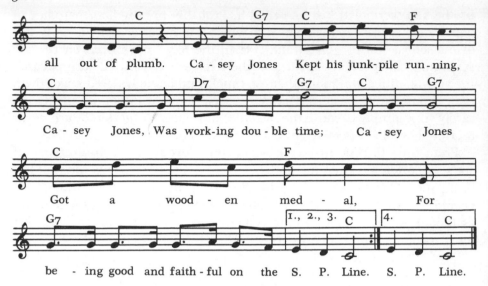

all out of plumb. Ca - sey Jones Kept his junk-pile run - ning,

Ca - sey Jones, Was work-ing dou - ble time; Ca - sey Jones

Got a wood - en med - al, For

be - ing good and faith - ful on the S. P. Line. S. P. Line.

2. The workers said to Casey, "Won't you help us win this strike?"
   But Casey said, "Let me alone, you'd better take a hike."
   Then Casey's wheezy engine ran right off the worn-out track,
   And Casey hit the river with an awful crack.

   > Casey Jones hit the river bottom,
   > Casey Jones broke his blooming spine,
   > Casey Jones became an angeleno,
   > He took a trip to heaven on the S.P. Line.

3. When Casey Jones got up to heaven to the Pearly Gate,
   He said, "I'm Casey Jones, the guy that pulled the S.P. freight."
   "You're just the man," said Peter, "our musicians are on strike;
   You can get a job a-scabbing anytime you like."

   > Casey Jones got a job in heaven;
   > Casey Jones was doing mighty fine;
   > Casey Jones went scabbing on the angels,
   > Just like he did to workers on the S.P. Line.

4. The angels got together, and they said it wasn't fair
   For Casey Jones to go around a-scabbing everywhere.
   The Angels Union No. 23, they sure were there,
   And they promptly fired Casey down the Golden Stair.

   > Casey Jones went to Hell a-flying.
   > "Casey Jones," the Devil said, "Oh fine,
   > Casey Jones, get busy shoveling sulphur—
   > That's what you get for scabbing on the S.P. Line."

For other union songs, see:

The Songs of Joe Hill, ed. Barrie Stavis and Frank Harmon (People's Artists Inc., New York, 1955; Oak Publications, New York, 1960, $1.95).

Edith Fowke and Joe Glazer, eds., *Songs of Work and Freedom*. Roosevelt University, Chicago, 1960, $5.00 cloth, $2.50 paper.

Waldemar Hille, ed., *The People's Song Book*. Boni and Gaer, New York, 1948; reprinted by Oak Publications, New York, $1.95.

George Korson, ed., *Minstrels of the Mine Patch*. University of Pennsylvania Press, Philadelphia, 1938.

———, ed., *Coaldust on the Fiddle*. University of Pennsylvania Press, Philadelphia, 1943.

(Both Korson books deal with songs of Pennsylvania coal miners.)

Irwin Silber, ed., *Lift Every Voice* (The Second People's Songbook). People's Artists, Inc., New York, 1953; Oak Publications, New York, $1.95.

Protest songs? Even the singer of dirty songs is protesting— sanctimoniousness. Aunt Molly Jackson said, "Propaganda or proper goose; the truth is what matters."

Aunt Molly Jackson

Songs of Some American Experiences

The Hudson Valley Rent Rebellion

IN THE 1840s most of the Hudson Valley was still owned by a few large landlords. One man had 2,000,000 acres. Tenant farmers formed an illegal organization; when a sheriff tried to evict some family for refusing to pay rent, they waylaid him at gunpoint, tarred and feathered him, and burned his writs of eviction.

For several years the "Down Rent Wars" went on. Hundreds of farmers were jailed. Their main leader was convicted and sentenced to be hung. But because they put up a struggle they got some publicity. The next governor was elected with a plank in his platform to force the breaking up of the huge estates. The Hudson Valley farmers won that battle.

THE END OF BILL SNYDER
(*Tune: "Old Dan Tucker"*)

The moon was shining silver bright,
The sheriff came in the dead of night;
High on a hill an Indian* true,
And on his horn this blast he blew—

Chorus:
Keep out of the way, Big Bill Snyder,
We'll tar your coat and feather your hide, sir.

The Indians gathered at the sound,
Bill cocked his pistol, looked around;
Their painted faces, by the moon
He saw, and heard that same old tune—   (*Chorus*)

Says Bill, "The music's not so sweet
As I have heard; I think my feet
Had better be used," and he started to run;
But the tin horn still kept sounding on—   (*Chorus*)

---

* The calico "Indian" costumes in which antirenters disguised their identity were reminiscent of the Boston Tea Party. They signaled each other with the tin horns commonly used to call farm families to dinner. The full story is told in Henry Christman's *Tin Horns and Calico* (Henry Holt & Co., New York, 1945). The book includes several dozen songs.

"Legs, do your duty now," says Bill,
"There's a thousand Indians on the hill,
When they catch Tories they tar their coats,
And feather their hides; and I hear the notes—"   (*Chorus*)

Bill ran and ran 'til he reached the wood,
And there, with horror still he stood,
For he saw a savage, tall and grim,
And he heard a horn, not a rod from him;   (*Chorus*)

Bill thought he heard the sound of a gun,
And he cried in fright, "My race is run;
Better that I had never been born
Than to come within the sound of that tin horn."   (*Chorus*)

And the news flew around and gained belief
That Bill was murdered by an Indian Chief;
And no one mourned that Bill was slain;
But the tin horn sounded again and again.   (*Chorus*)

Next day the body of Bill was found;
His writs were scattered on the ground,
And by his side a jug of rum
Told how he to his end had come.   (*Chorus*)

American Songs Not in English

"THE TROUBLE with your People's Songs organization, it's not American enough." Frank Ilchuk, leader of a Ukrainian chorus, looked me square in the eye. "Where are the Italian songs," says he, "the Polish songs, the Greek songs? We're American too."

I decided he was right, and from time to time have learned a song from this or that ethnic group I've sung for, even though it's in a foreign language. Translations are difficult, but not impossible.

Here's an Italian favorite which has had many a barroom workout. Of all the songs brought to America by these music-loving people, it is the best known. However, it has never been printed in any school song-book, or in any collection of Italian songs that I have seen. Reason: it is not exactly a polite and proper song. Neither, however, is it a dirty song. It is just full of fun. Read it for yourself.

If you want to learn it, get some Italian to help you out. Nine chances out of ten he will say that the words are given here incorrectly. This is because every dialect in Italy has a different version and different spelling and pronunciation.

Some people know the song in a 1932 pop version known as "The Butcher Boy." Rudy Vallee had a hit record of it. But the words were bowdlerized in translation.

In its own way it is a protest song. "Mama, the moon is on the water, I want to get married. Who do you have in mind?" The mother cautions the daughter against rushing too hastily into childbearing. The verses, which are more or less bawdy, tell how a man of each occupation (butcher, fruit seller, fisherman, plumber, etc.) treats his wife.

C'E 'NA LUNA

A. C'e 'na lu - na mez - zo ma - re, Ma- ma I' vo - glio mar - i -
ta - re.   Fi - glia mi - a, chi da da - re.
Ma - ma mi - a, pen - za - to   tu.
1. Si   ti   don - no   lu   pis - ci - au - lo,   Is - so va,
Is - so ve - ne,   Sem - pre   lo   pis - cia ma - na
te - ne.   Si   li   pi - glia 'na

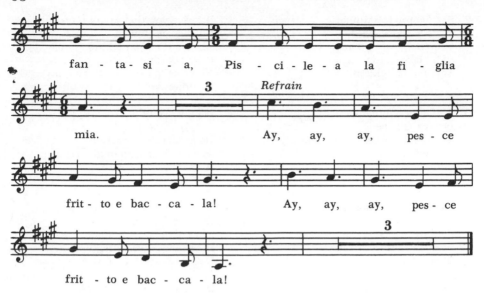

fan - ta - si - a, Pis - ci - le - a la fi - glia

mia. Ay, ay, ay, pes - ce

frit - to e bac - ca - la! Ay, ay, ay, pes - ce

frit - to e bac - ca - la!

Normally it is sung in a high key, and loudly. In between phrases the accompanying instrument should put in some runs such as this:

	Literal translation (not for singing):
A. C'e 'na luna mezzo mare, Mama I' voglio maritare. Figlia mia, chi da dare. Mama mia, penzato tu.	A. There is a moon over the sea; Mother, I want to get married. Daughter, whom shall I give you? Mother, you think about it.
1. Si ti donno lu pisciaulo, Isso va, isso vene, Sempre lo piscia mana tene. Si li piglia 'na fantasia, Piscilea la figlia mia.	1. If I give you the fisherman, He goes, he comes, Always the fish in his hands. If he takes the desire, He'll use the fish on you, my daughter.
Refrain: Ay, ay, ay, pesce fritto e baccala! Ay, ay, ay, pesce fritto e baccala!	*Refrain:* Ay, ay, ay, fried fish stinks! Ay, ay, ay, fried fish stinks!
(Repeat A. before each verse and refrain, with appropriate phrase for each verse, afterward.)	

2. Si ti donno lu salumeria,
   Isso va, isso vene,
   Sempre la salama mana tene.
   Si li piglia 'na fantasia,
   Salamia la figlia mia.

2. If I give you the salami merchant,
   He goes, he comes,
   Always the salami in his hand.
   If he takes the desire,
   He'll use the salami on you, my
      daughter.

3. Si ti donno lu pompero,
   Isso va, isso vene,
   Sempre la pompe mana tene.
   Si li piglia 'na fantasia,
   Pompelea la figlia mia.

3. If I give you the fireman [the
      [pumper],
   He goes, he comes,
   Always the pump in his hands.
   If he takes the desire,
   He'll pump on you.

4. Si ti donno lu polizzio,
   Iso va, isso vene,
   Sempre la bastone mana tene.
   Si li piglia 'na fantasia,
   Bastonea la figlia mia.

4. If I give you the policeman,
   He goes, he comes,
   Always the club in his hand.
   If he takes the desire,
   He'll use the club on you.

5. Si ti donno lu scarparo,
   Isso va, isso vene,
   Sempre scarpe mana tene.
   Si li piglia 'na fantasia,
   La scarpa in testa, figlia mia.

5. If I give you the shoemaker,
   He goes, he comes,
   Always the shoe in his hand.
   If he takes the desire,
   He'll use the shoe on you.

6. Si ti donno lu sartore,
   Isso va, isso vene,
   Sempre l'ago in mana tene.
   Si li piglia 'na fantasia,
   Con l'ago punge la figlia mia.

6. If I give you the tailor,
   He goes, he comes,
   Always the needle in his hand.
   If he takes the desire,
   With the needle on you, my daughter.

7. Si ti donno lo panetiero,
   Isso va, isso vene,
   Sempre lo pala mana tene.
   Si li piglia 'na fantasia,
   Ti palolea la figlia mia.

7. ?

8. Si ti donno lo scupino,
   Isso va, isso vene,
   Sempre lo scapa mana tene.
   Si li piglia 'na fantasia,
   Ti scapulia la figlia mia.
   Etc.

8. ?

Needless to say, the song can go on as long as someone can think of a new occupation and phallic symbol.

Over a hundred years ago, the great Norwegian violinist, Ole Bull, was touring in America, and was seized with the grand idea to start a Norwegian colony in Pennsylvania. But some sharpers sold him a lot of poor land—rocks and trees—and the first colonists nearly starved to death before the project was abandoned. It would all be forgotten now, but that someone in Norway wrote what became a tremendously popular song on both sides of the Atlantic, satirizing the unrealistic dreams of Norwegians who had "America fever."

OLEANNA English lyrics by Pete Seeger, based on a traditional Norwegian song. TRO-© copyright 1958, 1960, Ludlow Music, Inc., New York, New York. Used by permission.

Oh, to be in O - le - an - na! That's where I'd
like to be, Than be bound in Nor - way, and
drag the chains of slav - er - y. O - le, O - le,
an - na. O - le, O - le, a - an - na.
O - le, O - le, O - le, O - le, O - le, O - le a- an- na.

In Oleanna land is free; the wheat and corn just plant themselves,
Then grow a good four feet a day, while on your bed you rest yourself. (*Chorus*)

Beer as sweet as Münchener* springs from the ground and flows away.
The cows all like to milk themselves and hens lay eggs ten times a day. (*Chorus*)

Little roasted piggies rush about the city streets,
Inquiring so politely if a slice of ham you'd like to eat. (*Chorus*)

---
* Munich.

Say, if you'd begin to live, to Oleanna you must go;
The poorest wretch in Norway becomes a Duke in a year or so.   (*Chorus*)

Oh, to be in Oleanna, that's where I'd like to be;
Than be bound in Norway and drag the chains of slavery.   (*Chorus*)

The 22 Norwegian stanzas (with literal translation*):

1. I Oleana der er det godt at være,
   i Norge vil jeg inte Slavenlæken
   bære!
   Ole—Ole—Ole oh! Oleana!
   Ole—Ole—Ole oh! Oleana!

1. In Oleana, that's where I'd like to
   be, and not drag the chains of
   slavery in Norway.
   Ole—Ole—Ole—oh! Oleana!
   Ole—Ole—Ole—oh! Oleana!

2. I Oleana der faar jeg Jord for Intet,
   af Jorden voxer Kornet,—og det gaar
   gesvint det.
   Ole—Ole—Ole oh! Oleana!

2. In Oleana they give you land for
   nothing, and the grain just pops
   out of the ground. Golly, that's
   easy.
   Ole—Ole—Ole—oh! etc.

3. Aa Kornet det tærsker sig selv oppaa
   Laaven,
   imens ligger jeg aa hviler mig i
   Koven.

3. The grain threshes itself in the
   granary while I stretch out at
   ease in my bunk.
   Ole—Ole—Ole—oh! etc.

4. Hej Markedsgang! Poteterne skulde
   Du se, Du.
   Der brændes mindst en Pot af hver-
   eneste en Du.

4. And the markets! You just ought to
   see the potatoes! You can dis-
   still at least a quart of whiskey
   from every one of them.
   Ole—Ole—Ole—oh! etc.

5. Ja Bayerøl saa godt, som han Ẏtte-
   borg kan brygge,
   det risler i Bækkene til Fattigmand-
   ens Hygge.

5. And Münchener beer, as sweet as
   Ytteborg's, runs in the creeks
   for the poor man's delectation.
   Ole—Ole—Ole—oh! etc.

6. Aa Laxene dem springer saa lystig i
   Bække,
   dem hopper selv i Gryden aa roper:
   dem ska' dække!

6. And the salmon, they leap like mad
   in the rivers, and hop into the
   kettles, and cry out for a cover.
   Ole—Ole—Ole—oh! etc.

7. Aa brunstegte Griser de løber om saa
   flinke
   aa forespør sig høfligt, om Nogen
   vil ha' Skinke.

7. And little roasted piggies rush about
   the streets, politely inquiring if
   you wish for ham.
   Ole—Ole—Ole—oh! etc.

---

* From *Norwegian Emigrant Songs and Ballads,* ed. and trans. Theodore C. Blegen and
Martin B. Rund (The University of Minnesota Press, Minneapolis, 1936).

8. Aa Kjørene dem melker aa kjærner
   aa yster
   liksaa naturlig som Else, mi Syster.

8. And the cows, they milk and churn
   and make cheese just as skill-
   fully as Else my sister.
   Ole—Ole—Ole—oh! etc.

9. Aa Storstuten sjelve staar inte og
   hænger,
   han banker sine Kalve, fordi de gaar
   og slænger.

9. And the bull himself doesn't stand
   around idle; he beats his calves
   for loafing and shirking.
   Ole—Ole—Ole—oh! etc.

10. Aa Kalvene de slagter sig hurtig og
    flaar sig
    aa stejker sig fortere end man tar en
    Taar sig!

10. And the calves, they kill and flay
    themselves and turn to veal
    roast faster than you can take a
    drink.
    Ole—Ole—Ole—oh! etc.

11. Aa Høna værper Æg saa svære som
    Stabur,
    mens Hanen angir Tiden som et
    ottedags Slaguhr.

11. And the hens lay eggs as big as a
    storehouse, and the cocks strike
    the hour like an eight-day clock.
    Ole—Ole—Ole—oh! etc.

12. Fra Skyerne det regner med Kolera-
    kaker.
    Aa Gubevare Dere vel for dejlige
    Saker!

12. And cakes fairly rain from the skies
    above you. Good Lord, what
    wondrous tidbits!
    Ole—Ole—Ole—oh! etc.

13. Aa Sola hu skinner saa trufast hele
    Natta
    saa atte man kan se i Mørke liksom
    Katta!

13. The sun shines faithfully all night
    long, so that you can see in the
    dark just like a cat.
    Ole—Ole—Ole—oh! etc.

14. Aa Maanen hver Aften er fuld—det
    er sikkert.
    Jeg ligger just aa ser paa'n med
    Flaska tel Kjikkert.

14. The moon is full every night, that is
    certain: I am observing it now
    with a bottle for a telescope.
    Ole—Ole—Ole—oh! etc.

15. Ja to Daler Dagen det faar Du for
    at svire,
    aa er Du rektig doven, saa kanske
    Du faar fire.

15. You bet, they give you two dollars a
    day for carousing; and if you
    are good and lazy, they'll prob-
    ably give you four.
    Ole—Ole—Ole—oh! etc.

16. Aa Kjærringa og Unger dem falder
    paa Kommynen.
    Betaler dem ikke, saa faar dem paa
    Trynen!

16. The old woman and the kids, why,
    they go on the township; if the
    authorities don't pay they get
    it on the snout.
    Ole—Ole—Ole—oh! etc.

17. Kronarbejde findes ej—nej det var
    saa ligt da!
    jeg sad nok ikke ellersen saa frisk
    her aa digta.

17. You don't have to work to support
    your bastards; if you did, I
    shouldn't be sitting here spin-
    ning verses.
    Ole—Ole—Ole—oh! etc.

18. Vi gaar i Fløjelsklæder besat med Sølverknapper,
Aa ryker af Merskum, som Kjærringa strapper.

18. And we all stalk about in velvet suits with silver buttons, smoking meerschaum pipes which the old woman fills for us.
Ole—Ole—Ole—oh! etc.

19. Aa Kjærringa maa brase aa styre aa stelle—
aa blir hu sint, saa banker hu sig sjelv—skal jeg fortælle.

19. And she has to sweat and toil and struggle; and if she doesn't do it, she gives herself a beating.*
Ole—Ole—Ole—oh! etc.

20. Aa Fiolin det speller vi Allesammen —hejsan!
Aa Danser en Polskdans, aa den er'nte lejsan.

20. And every last one of us plays upon the fiddle, and dances a merry polka; and that's not so bad!
Ole—Ole—Ole—oh! etc.

21. Ja rejs til Oleana, saa skal Du vel leve,
den fattigste Stymper herover er Greve!

21. Aye, go to Oleana, there you'll begin to live! The poorest wretch in Norway is a count over there.
Ole—Ole—Ole—oh! etc.

22. I Oleana langt heller vil jeg være, end længer i Norg min Slavelænke bære!
Ole—Ole—Ole oh! Oleana!
Ole—Ole—Ole oh! Oleana!

22. Oh, I'd much rather live in Oleana than drag the chains of slavery over there in Norway.
Ole—Ole—Ole—oh! Oleana!
Ole—Ole—Ole—oh! Oleana!

"He Lies in the American Land" was composed about 35 years ago by a Slovakian steel worker of Pittsburgh. In his own words: "I was a young foreman in a Bessemer mill here in McKeesport. A very good friend of mine, a member of my crew, had saved enough money to send to Slovakia for his family. While they were on their way to America he was killed before my eyes, under an ingot buggy. I tried to grab him, but it was too late. It was terrible. I felt so bad that when I met his wife and little children at the railroad station I hardly knew how to break the sad news to them. Then I made this song. My friend was very proud of America, and it was with pride and happiness that he had looked forward to raising his children as Americans. The song made me feel better, and also my friend's wife. But she cried very hard. I have never forgotten it!"

---

* This song was obviously composed by a man.—P.S.

HE LIES IN THE AMERICAN LAND*

Words and music by Andrew Kovaly; English lyrics adapted by
P. Seeger.

A very free narrative style

1. Ah, my God, what is this land of A - me - ri - ca?

So _____ man - y peo - ple trav - el - ling there!

I will go ___ too, for I am still young. ___

God, the Lord, will grant me ___ good luck there. _____

The Slovak words:

ODPOčÍAM V AMERICKEJ PÔDE

1. Ej Bożemoj cotej Ameriki!
   Idze doňej narod preveliki,
   Ija pojdzem, šak som mladi ešče.
   Dami Panboh tam dajake sčesce.

2. Jaše vracim kecme nezabije,
   lem ti čekaj odomňe novinu.
   Jak ot domňe novinu dostaneš,
   sama šedneš navraneho koňa,
   atak pridzeš draha dušo moja.

2. You, my wife, stay here till you hear
   from me.
   When you get my letter, put everything in order.
   Mount a raven-black steed, a horse
   like the wind.
   Fly across the ocean to join me here.

---

* From the chapter "Folk Songs of an Industrial City," by Jacob A. Evanson, in *Pennsylvania Songs and Legends,* ed. George Korson (University of Pennsylvania Press, Philadelphia, 1949).

3. Ajak vona do McKeesport prišla,
   to uš muža živoho nenašla;
   lem totu krev co znoho kapkala
   atak nadnu, prehorko plakala.

3. Ah, but when she arrived in this
   strange land,
   Here to McKeesport, this valley of fire,
   Only his grave, his grave, did she
   find;
   Over it bitterly she cried.

4. Ej mužumoj co žeši učinil,
   žesi tote dzeci osirocil!
   Povic ženo tej mojej siroce,
   žeja ležim utej Americe;
   povic ženo najme nečekaju,
   boja ležim v Americkim kraju.

4. Ah, my husband, what have you done
   to this family of yours?
   What can you say to these children
   you've orphaned?
   Tell them, my wife, not to wait for
   me;
   Tell them I lie here in the American
   land.

A Contemporary Ballad Maker in the Hudson Valley*

SOME FOLKLORE AUTHORITIES feel that the day of the true
folk ballad maker is irretrievably over. Universal literacy, changing music
tastes, canned entertainment, have all combined to make him obsolete,
they say.

Yet the interest in folklore and folk music, though a revival, not a sur-
vival, has produced not only collectors and listeners. Performers, though
they may not fit neatly into any of the old categories of folk singers,
nevertheless have more often than not learned their songs by ear, and
produced their own variants. In many places one finds singers composing
whole new ballads, often without bothering to write them down. And
their songwriting method is the same as that of the ballad makers of old:
First, they borrow an old melody, using it either note for note, or making
slight changes. Second, their verses often start with the words of the
older song, changing them to localize the story and make it more meaningful for friends and neighbors who may be listening.

The Hudson Valley can boast one of the finest of these present-day
ballad makers in the person of Les Rice, a farmer living a few miles
north of Newburgh. In 1947 Mr. Rice heard a friend sing folk songs
at a gathering of the local Farmers' Union. He borrowed a guitar himself,
and since then has turned out a string of first-rate ditties, mostly concerning the life and problems of a small farmer. They have been picked
up by his friends, passed from hand to hand on small scraps of paper,
and from time to time amended or added to, quite in the folk tradition.

---

* Written for *New York Folklore Quarterly* (Summer 1954).

Perhaps we might steal a march on folklorists of the twenty-first century, who may collect a variant of one of his ballads and use it to illuminate a study of life and times in New York State, 1954. Here is one of his best ones, "Acres of Apples."* He used the famous old Irish melody, "Men of the West," as he had heard it in one of its countless New World versions, "Acres of Clams," from Washington State pioneer days. Les Rice's lyrics remind one of the tenant-farmer songs of the 1840s, which also had an axe to grind.

ACRES OF APPLES

(Tune: "Acres of Clams," known also as
"Rosin the Bow" or "Men of the West")

I came to the mid-Hudson Valley
A-many a long year ago.
I have spent all my time in the orchard,
A-making those red apples grow.
    A-making those red apples grow,
    A-making those red apples grow,
    And thinking each year as I labored
    That someday I would make me some dough.

I sprayed them and sprayed them and sprayed them
From early in April till fall;
Those trees were so loaded with apples
You couldn't see green leaves at all.
    You couldn't see green leaves at all,
    You couldn't see green leaves at all.
    And what did I get for those apples?
    A penny a pound for them all.

I have raised in my time enough apples
To feed the whole state of New York,
But I have never had enough money
To buy me a good roast of pork.
    To buy me a good roast of pork,
    To buy me a good roast of pork.
    The apples are raised in the Valley,
    But the money is made in New York.

NOTE: In 1954, the above verses were all the folklore magazine dared

---

* Other songs by Les Rice include "Banks of Marble," "I Can See a New Day," and "I've Raised a Lot of Sweat in Days Gone By."

print, and even so, it was attacked in the New York *Herald Tribune* for "allowing Communists to infiltrate the folklore field." Here's the rest of Les Rice's song:

> But now I am joining a union,
> A union of farmers like me.
> I'm tired of paying the broker
> His hundred and ten percent fee.
> > His hundred and ten percent fee,
> > His hundred and ten percent fee.
> > I'd like just a little left over,
> > A little left over for me.

> And now that we're all in the Union,
> Some fellows had better get wise.
> They've stolen our left and our right arms,
> But we're damned if we'll give them our eyes.
> > But we're damned if we'll give them our eyes,
> > But we're damned if we'll give them our eyes.
> > The next time they come to the Valley
> > We'll cut down those bastards to size.

The March from Selma to Montgomery*

March 24, 1965

HEREWITH are a few songs heard during the past day and a half, sung by a wonderful group of people. Yesterday their numbers were limited to 300. Today they grew each hour till by midafternoon they were well over 5,000. Len Chandler was on the march for the full five days. Guy Carawan was also there, and a fine young guitar picker and singer from Chicago, Jimmy Collier. All of us wish we'd had tape recorders—the young singers and songwriters of Selma were creating one great song after another, right before our eyes. One woman saw me trying to notate a melody and said with a smile, "Don't you know you can't write down freedom songs?"—which has been said by everyone who

---

* From *Broadside* No. 57, April 10, 1965. On March 25, 1965, 25,000 black and white Americans entered Montgomery, the state capital, to protest the obstacles (including murder) to voter registration in Selma and other Alabama cities. But before the day was over, Mrs. Viola Liuzzo of Detroit was shot to death while driving some friends home to Selma.

In 1966 Julius Lester quoted a SNCC veteran: "Man, the people are too busy getting ready to fight to bother with singing anymore." For some more afterthoughts, see p. 484 below. (The Selma songs were recorded on Folkways FH 5595, *WNEW's Story of Selma*, and FH 5594, *Freedom Songs: Selma, Ala.*)

ever tried to capture Negro folk music with European music notation. All I can do is repeat what my father once told me: "A folk song in a book is like a photograph of a bird in flight."

One of the most popular new songs uses a melody, I'm told, similar to a rock-and-roll song called "Kidnapped." Since I've not heard the record, I can't tell you how much it's been changed. The refrain "Dadat, dadat, *dat*" may be a vocalization of notes once played by instruments. In any case, though the syncopation is difficult, anyone can join in on the refrain. It's catchy. You won't be able to get it out of your head. And the first line of the chorus I think is truly great and triumphant.

OH, WALLACE!

Chorus Dm

Oh, — Wal-lace!   You nev-er can jail us all! —

Oh, — Wal-lace!   Seg-re-

ga-tion is bound to fall, —   da da - da da-

dat, Da-da da - da da-da-dat, da da da-da-

Verse

dat I I read in the pa-pers (da-da da-da

dat) Just the oth-er day (da-da da-da

dat)   That the free-dom _____   fight-ers (da - da   da - da

(into chorus)

dat) Were on   their   way (da - da   da - da   dat)   Oh, __

2. They're coming by bus (dadat dadat dat)
   And airplane too,   ("   "   ")
   They'll even walk   ("   "   ")
   If you ask them to.   ("   "   ")   *(Chorus)*

3. I don't want no mess,   (dadat dadat dat)
   I don't want no jive,   ("   "   ")
   And I want my freedom ("   "   ")
   In 'sixty-five.   ("   "   ")   *(Chorus)*

When I asked people, "What are the words to 'Oh, Wallace!'" they were perplexed. "There are no words," I was told. I found out my error was to ask for "the" words. I finally asked for "some" words, and found that the above three verses were the most common. But each singer had several favorite others and had heard dozens more. Few of them are high-class poetry, but tune and rhythms are so catchy and the chorus is so great that it doesn't matter. Here are a few of the other verses I was able to write down:

4. Tell Al Lingo
   And Jim Clark too
   We want our freedom
   And want it now.

5. The ocean is deep,
   The river is wide.
   I'll find my freedom
   On the other side.

6. Don't worry about
   Going to jail,
   Cause Martin King
   Will go your bail.

7. He'll get you out
   Right on time,
   Put you back
   On the picket line.

If the song is going well it can go on for ten or twenty more verses, depending on how many can be remembered or improvised. If it only lasts for three or four verses, that means the spirit isn't moving the singers. Which reminds me of another song that, I'm told, also comes from Selma:

WE'RE GONNA MARCH WHEN THE SPIRIT SAY "MARCH"

Copyright © 1965, SNCC and Folkways Records.

Other verses: "You got to *move*," etc.; "You got to *sing*," etc.; "You got to *pray*," etc.

And again, the song leader can repeat and ad-lib verses at will. When I say "the song leader," I am, of course, not speaking about any official person. In the march any person who felt like singing could start off a song, and it could continue as long as anyone within earshot wanted to keep it going. Toshi and I were fortunate to have for several hours a group of teen-age girls walking in the row behind us. They had good voices and "h'isted" one song after another. (I use the old folk term comparing starting a song to hoisting a sail or a flag, to see if the wind catches it.) This group of girls helped me get down on paper most of the songs I give here. They sang many others I failed to write down. They also would occasionally break into a standard tune that they might have sung in high school, such as "America the Beautiful," or the theme song from the movie *Exodus*.

For the convenience of you guitarists I have indicated chords and harmony, but you must realize that the accompaniment for these songs (if any) was handclapping on the second and fourth beats of the measure. If you do accompany the songs, remember one of the characteristics of so much Afro-American folk music: You can sing in minor and play in major. The next song is typical. Sung alone, it sounds in the key of E minor. But I guarantee you, better not accompany it in E minor. Play E major, and it will come out just right.

I LOVE EVERYBODY

Copyright © 1965, SNCC and Folkways Records.

I love ev' - ry - bo - dy in my heart,

I love ev' - ry - bo - dy in my heart. _____

I love ev' - ry - bo - dy,   I love ev' - ry - bo -

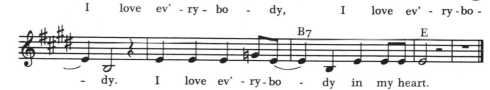

- dy.   I love ev' - ry - bo - dy in my heart.

Other verses: "You can't make me doubt it in my heart"; "I love Governor Wallace* in my heart"; etc.

This is another song obviously easy to add verses to. The first and second verses return from time to time almost as a refrain.

Many of the freedom songs that have become well known in the last five years were sung on the march. I especially heard "Ain't Gonna Let Nobody Turn Me Around," "Which Side Are You On?," "Hold On," "Woke Up This Morning," and, of course, "We Shall Overcome." Sometimes the local version of the tune was slightly different from the way I had known it. For example, "We Shall Not Be Moved" was usually sung with the

---

* Believe it or not, this was sung—in 1965.

melody below. The verse given here was one of the most popular, along with the usual "Black and white together," etc.

WE SHALL NOT BE MOVED

Copyright © 1965, SNCC and Folkways Records.

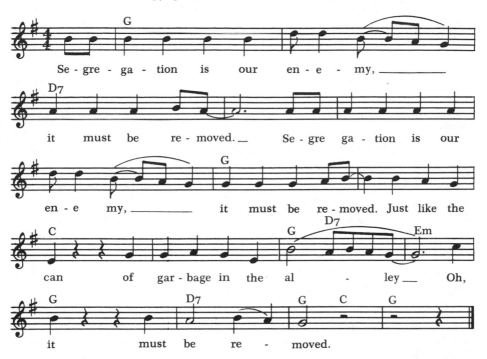

Se - gre - ga - tion is our en - e - my, ___ it must be re - moved. __ Se - gre ga - tion is our en - e my, ___ it must be re - moved. Just like the can of gar - bage in the al - ley __ Oh, it must be re - moved.

Here's one I'd not heard before. Juvenile as it may look on paper, it was a welcome relief and gave nonsingers a chance to participate, as well as some rest for the throats of those who were hoarse. I trust you all know the tune ("She'll Be Coming Round the Mountain").

Copyright © 1965, SNCC and Folkways Records.

1. If you want to get your freedom clap your hands
    (clap-clap-clap)
   If you want to get your freedom clap your hands
    (clap-clap-clap)
   If you want to get your freedom
   If you want to get your freedom
   If you want to get your freedom clap your hands.
    (clap-clap-clap)

2. If you want to get your freedom stamp your feet
   (stamp-stamp-stamp)

3. If you want to get your freedom jump and shout
   (everyone jumps in air)

4. Repeat and improvise at will—this same thing
   could be said for almost every song.

Altogether, any folklorist would have found the day a fascinating experience in living folk music. I've read arguments about how folk songs of the past must have been created. For me, there's no argument any more. One talented person may start a song off (using traditional elements), and others add to his creation and change it. I'm positive in my mind that this is how "The Old Chizzum Trail" and "Blow the Man Down" were made up.

Maybe some of the chants should be given as well. The most common one (which is not new at Selma) is a short, crisp one. Some one person will holler out, "What do we want?"—and all within earshot shout back, "FREEDOM!" "When do we want it?" "NOW!" "Who do we want it for?" "ALL OF US!" Sometimes if the leader feels the first response is not loud enough, he repeats the first question two or three times before going on to the second and third questions.

The 300 marchers were mostly younger people, but I saw a woman of sixty or so with a sign tied across a small, cheap suitcase that read: "If you don't vote, don't squawk—REGISTER!" Probably two-thirds of the 300 were Selma Negroes, and the other third were Negro and white from other parts of Alabama and from all over the U.S.A., including Hawaii. About 10 percent, it seemed to me, were clergy. I've never been surrounded by such an ecumenical group: Catholic priests, Jewish rabbis, and ministers from a dozen Protestant denominations. Two young men had beautiful, flowing beards, like John the Baptist, and were continually photographed by that section of the southern press which wants to show that all the out-of-state participants were "Communists and beatniks."

Next month I hope *Broadside* can carry some more of the songs which came out of Selma. There's another sassy, syncopated one Len Chandler told me about:

Copyright © 1965, SNCC.

Last night and the night before,
    (Jump back, Wallace, jump back!)
Twenty-five troopers at my door,
    (Jump back, Wallace, jump back!)
I got up and let 'em in . . .

. . . and I didn't get down more. There's also a lyrical song, "Can't You Hear Them Freedom Bells Tolling?" by young Fred Moss of Selma. (One case where we know the author.)

We Shall Overcome*

"WE SHALL OVERCOME" has become famous around the world. To hundreds of thousands of freedom-loving Americans it was in 1963 no longer just "a" song, but "the" song. They locked arms and stood swaying as they sang, one song leader calling out the short phrases that constituted the next verse.

The history of the song is another beautiful example of the constant interchange between Negro and white musicians in creating American music. In 1946 Zilphia Horton of the Highlander Folk School, helping to organize a tobacco workers' union, heard some Negro union members singing on a picket line. It was a cold winter day, and they were singing to keep their spirits up.

* Written in 1965.

Zilphia Horton

One of the old songs was "I Will Overcome"—but they had made a significant change in the words, to "*We* Will Overcome."

Zilphia added some extra verses, and it was occasionally sung as a union song then. In 1947 she taught it to me, and I sang it up north, adding still more verses which gave it a more general flavor (such as "We'll walk hand in hand").

Guy Carawan took it south again in 1960 and sang it to the Negro college students who started the sit-in movement—going into restaurants and refusing to leave until they were served. Within a few months the song in its new version spread through the South, and had many more verses added to it.

People sometimes ask me what exactly do the words mean. Who do we intend to overcome?

Well, you know, a song is not a speech. It is a work of art. It reflects new meanings as life shines new lights upon it. Thus this song undoubtedly has many meanings to many people.

In Selma, Alabama, they were probably thinking about overcoming Sheriff Jim Clark. But others, with more experience, were thinking about overcoming the whole system of segregation which makes children second-class citizens from the day they are born, simply because their skin is a darker color. Still others think of overcoming all hate and prejudice that divides people.

I have sung the song in twenty-five countries, before people of many races and religions, and I confess that for me the most important word is "We"—and when I sing it, I think of the whole human race, which must stick together if we are going to solve crucial problems that face us all: problems of war and peace, of poverty, ignorance and fear, of health and population.

Those young people of the early 1960s—of Greensboro and Albany, Georgia, of Alabama and Mississippi—taught everybody else a lesson, all the older people who had learned how to compromise, how to take it easy, be polite, get along—and let the status stay quo.

The very best verse was made up in Montgomery, Alabama, the city of the 1956 bus boycott:

"We are not afraid—today!"

You and I—every human being in the world—we *have* been afraid; but still you sing "We are *not* afraid!"

Without this verse, none of the other verses could come true.

A Postscript: In 1964 I overheard an old radical white friend say contemptuously, " 'We Shall Overcome'? They call that a revolutionary song?

What kind of namby-pamby, wishy-washy moaning, always 'some day, so-o-meday'! That's been said for two thousand years."

I relayed the criticism to a black friend in Atlanta. She admitted the drawback, "But still if we said we were going to overcome next week, it would be a little unrealistic. What would we sing the week after next?"

On the 1965 Selma march militant young people tagged the call-and-response chant ("What do we want? Freedom! When do we want it? NOW!") to the end of this song. The chant would be repeated five or ten times till all within earshot were drawn into it.

A few years later, even this was not enough to take away the milky taste of "so-omeday." The disagreement on tactics between militant youngsters and compromising oldsters became too great. The song no longer gave unity to black Americans. It might be sung as a rather official anthem by some groups. To others it was anathema.

In 1972 I occasionally find myself humming it at work when I feel low and pessimistic about the human species.

SOME BRITISH TRADITIONS

*A Contemporary Singer and His Ballad Heritage**

IN THE NINETEENTH CENTURY Professor Francis James Child of Harvard canonized several hundred classic British ballads. For many folklorists today they are the core, the most important part of American folk music. "Here you must start your study," they say.

They're wrong, of course. You can start anywhere you like. You can ignore these ballads if you wish. But they gave to American musicians some great melodies, some great stories, and a meter-and-stanza technique used in later American songs such as "John Henry." They also gave us a style of singing which many think is the greatest.

The most truly classical music that we have, my father once told me, are the great British ballads sung in the classic manner. Most so-called classical music, he went on, is romantic as all get-out. On the other hand, the sustained serenity of the great folk ballad is truly classic. Like a Greek statue, it neither smiles nor frowns. It starts on an even keel and stays

---

* Written in 1955.

there to the end of the song, when it simply stops without any fancy flourishes. It is this sustained serenity (sustained intensity!) that marks the most truly classic art in any age.

Why is Francis James Child so famous? Because he plowed through a hundred years of bowdlerizing and rewriting, sentimentalizing and romanticizing of old ballads to try and establish the "original" song of the people. It was a Herculean task, a cleaning of the Augean stables.

THE HOUSE CARPENTER

(A traditional English ballad; version of Mrs. Texas Gladden of Virginia, plus verses from several other sources.)

1. Well met, well met, my — own true — love! Well met, well met, cried — he. I've just re-turned — from the salt, salt — sea, And it's all for the love of — thee.

2. I could have married a king's daughter there,
   So freely she would to me,
   But I slighted her and all her gold,
   All for the love of thee.

3. If you could have married a king's daughter there
   I'm sure you're much to blame,
   For I've lately been married to a house carpenter,
   And I think he's a nice young man.

4. If you'll forsake your house carpenter
   And come along with me,
   I'll take you where the grass grows green
   By the banks of the bonny blue sea.

5. If I forsake my house carpenter
   And go along with you,
   Why, you'd have nothing to maintain me on;
   Oh then what would I do?

6. I have three ships upon the main
   All sailing for dry land,
   And twenty-five jolly sailor boys
   All at your command.

7. She dressed herself in rich array
   All from her golden store,
   And she glittered and she glistened as on the streets she walked
   Just like a shining star.

8. She called to her, her sweet little babes
   And gave them kisses three,
   Saying, stay at home, my sweet little babes;
   Keep your papa good company.

9. They had not been sailing but a long winter's night,
   I'm sure it was not three,
   When she throwed her arms 'round her true lover's neck,
   Weeping most bitterly.

10. Why do you weep, my fair young maid?
    Do you weep for your golden store?
    Or do you weep for your house carpenter
    That you never shall see any more?

11. I do not weep for my house carpenter
    Nor for my golden store,
    But I do weep for my sweet little babes
    That I never shall see any more.

12. They had not been sailing but a long winter's night,
    I'm sure it was not four,
    When under the decks the ship sprung a leak
    And sunk to rise no more.

13. Once around spun our gallant ship,
    Twice around spun she.
    Three times around spun our gallant ship,
    And sunk in the cold, cold sea.

*Bishop Percy collected English ballads in the eighteenth cen-
tury, and lamented that only a few old people still knew them.
He predicted that the art form would soon die out. A hundred
years later, Child predicted the same thing, as did Cecil Sharp
fifty years ago, and as people do now. It seems reasonably certain that, two hundred years from now, in some corners of the
world, these ballads will still be loved and sung—and critics
will be found predicting their early demise.*

EWAN MACCOLL is a Scotsman who has worked for the English
subsidiary of Anaconda Copper, also as garage hand, builder's laborer,
organizer of the unemployed, reporter on a textile journal, radio script-
writer, actor, playwright, and songwriter.

He is also a crackerjack ballad singer. He inherited more than a hundred songs from his Gaelic-speaking mother and lowland father, including some of the most tragically beautiful and some of the most magnificently bawdy of the age-old ballads.

THE KEACH IN THE CREEL*

From *Last Leaves of Traditional Ballads*, Alexander Keith, ed.,
Aberdeen, 1925; reprinted in Ewan MacColl, *Personal Choice*.

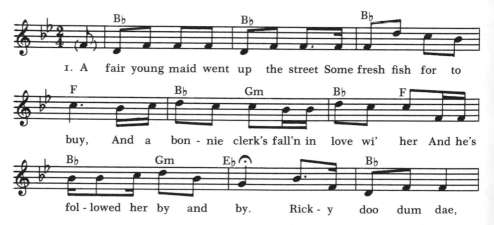

1. A fair young maid went up the street Some fresh fish for to
buy, And a bon - nie clerk's fall'n in love wi' her And he's
fol - lowed her by and by. Rick - y doo dum dae,

---

* From Ewan MacColl, *Personal Choice* (Hargail Music Press, New York, $.75). Among
Ewan's ballad records are *Child Ballads*, Folkways 3509, and *Classic Ballads* (with Peggy
Seeger), Tradition 1015.

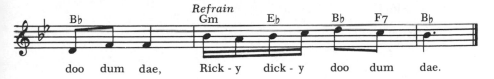

doo dum dae,   Rick - y dick - y doo dum dae.

2. "O where live ye, my bonnie lass?
    I pray ye tell tae me,
And though the nicht were never sae mirk
    I wad try and win in tae thee."   *(Refrain)*

3. "My faither he aye locks the door
    And my mither keeps the key,
And though the nicht were never sae mirk
    Ye couldna win in tae me."   *(Refrain)*

4. Now the clerk he had a true brother,
    And a wily wicht was he,
And he has made a lang ladder
    Wi' thirty steps and three.   *(Refrain)*

5. He has made a pin but and a creel,
    A creel but and a pin,
And he has ga'en to the chimla-top
    To let the bonnie clerk in.   *(Refrain)*

6. Now the old wife she lay wide awake
    Though late, late was the hour;
"I'll lie my life," said the silly old wife,
    "There's a man in our dochter's bower."   *(Refrain)*

7. The old man he gat oot o' the bed
    To see gin the thing was true;
But she's ta'en the bonnie clerk in her airms
    And covered him ower wi' blue.   *(Refrain)*

8. "What are ye daeing, my ain dochter?
    What are ye daein', my doo?"
"I'm praying on the muckle buik
    For my silly old mammie and you."   *(Refrain)*

9. "Pray on, pray on, my ain dochter,
    And see that ye do it richt,
For if ever a woman has tint her reason,
    Your mither has done this nicht."   *(Refrain)*

10. "O wife, o wife, ye silly old wife,
    An ill deith may ye dee;
She's gotten the muckle buik in her airms
    An' she's praying for you and me."   *(Refrain)*

11. The old wife she lay wide awake,
        No' anither word was said,
    Till, "I'll lay my life," said the silly old wife,
        "There's a man in oor dochter's bed."   (*Refrain*)

12. "Get up again, my old guid man,
        And see if the thing be true."
    "Get up yoursel', ye silly old wife,
        I'll no' be fashed wi' you."   (*Refrain*)

13. "Get up yoursel', ye silly old wife,
        And may the deil tak' ye,
    For atween you and your ae dochter
        I havna aince blinkit an ee."   (*Refrain*)

14. The old wife she gat ower the bed
        To see gin the thing be true,
    But she slippit her fit and fell into the creel
        And at the tow he drew.   (*Refrain*)

15. "O help, o help, my old guidman!
        O help me noo, my doo!
    For he that ye wished me wi' this nicht,
        I fear he's gotten me noo!"   (*Refrain*)

16. The man that was at the chimla-top,
        Finding the creel was fu',
    He's wrapt the rope his shouther roond
        And up the tow he drew.   (*Refrain*)

17. "Gin he has got ye, I wish he may haud ye,
        I wish he may haud ye fast,
    For atween you and your ae dochter
        I hanna aince gotten my rest."   (*Refrain*)

18. O, hey the blue and the bonnie, bonnie blue,
        And I wish the blue richt weel,
    And for ilka old wife that wakes at nicht,
        May she get a guid keach in the creel!   (*Refrain*)

Ewan's father was an iron-molder and a militant trade unionist, so frequently blacklisted that the family was always on the move. In *The Shuttle and the Cage** Ewan published 21 of the industrial folk songs he has inherited and collected. His introduction to the book is the best possible description of these songs:

There are no nightingales in these songs, no flowers—and the sun is rarely mentioned; their themes are work, poverty, hunger and exploitation. They

---

* Hargail Music Press, New York, $.55.

should be sung to the accompaniment of pneumatic drills and swinging hammers, they should be bawled above the hum of turbines and the clatter of looms, for they are songs of toil, anthems of the industrial age.

Few of these songs have ever appeared in print before, for they were not made with an eye to quick sales or to catch the song-plugger's ear—but to relieve the intolerable daily grind.

If you have spent your life striving desperately to make ends meet; if you have worked yourself to a standstill and still been unable to feed the kids properly, then you will know why these songs were made. If you have worked in a hot pit, wearing nothing but your boots, and felt that the air you were breathing was liquid fire, then you will know why these songs were made. If you have crouched day after day in a twelve-inch seam of coal with four inches of water in it, and hacked with a small pick until every muscle in your body shrieked in protest—then you will know why these songs were made.

THE BLANTYRE EXPLOSION*

From *Come All Ye Bold Miners*, Lawrence and Wishart, London, 1952.

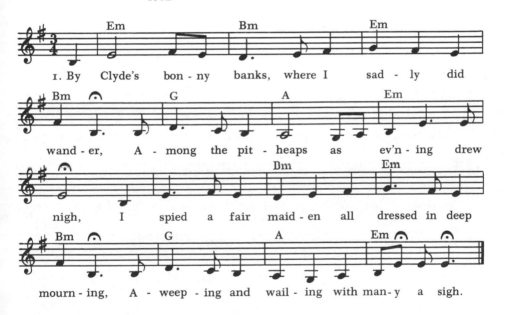

1. By Clyde's bon - ny banks, where I sad - ly did wand - er, A - mong the pit - heaps as ev'n - ing drew nigh, I spied a fair maid - en all dressed in deep mourn - ing, A - weep - ing and wail - ing with man - y a sigh.

2. I stepped up beside her and then I addressed her:
   Pray tell me, fair maid, of your troubles and pain.
   Sobbing and sighing, at last she did answer:
   Johnny Murphy, kind sir, was my true lover's name.

---

* Reprinted from *The Shuttle and the Cage.*

3. Twenty-one years of age, full of youth and good looking,
   To work down the mines from High Blantyre he came.
   The wedding was fixed, all the guests were invited;
   That calm summer evening young Johnny was slain.

4. The explosion was heard; all the women and children,
   With pale anxious faces they haste to the mine.
   When the truth was made known, the hills rang with their meaning;
   Three hundred and ten young miners were slain.

5. Now husbands and wives and sweethearts and brothers,
   That Blantyre explosion they'll never forget;
   And all you young miners that hear my sad story,
   Shed a tear for the victims who're laid to their rest.

Coincidentally, in the same week when I first listened to Ewan's record of these songs* I also heard recordings of the musical *Pajama Game,* whose story also concerns the lives and problems of industrial workers. The clever and fast-paced show songs sounded phony and thin beside Ewan MacColl's slow measured ballads, with their raw strength and beautiful melodies.

THE WORK OF THE WEAVERS

1. We're all met to-geth-er here, to sit and to crack. With our glass-es in our hands and our work up-on our back. And there's not a trade a-mong them all can eith-er mend nor mak'

---

* *Fourpence a Day and Other British Industrial Folk Songs,* Stinson SLP 79; also *British Industrial Ballads,* Vanguard 9090.
  (Ewan has recorded other varieties of folk songs—and songs of his own composition—for Folkways, Stinson, and other companies; check the Folkways catalog, and England and Scotland in the Schwann Supplementary Catalog.)

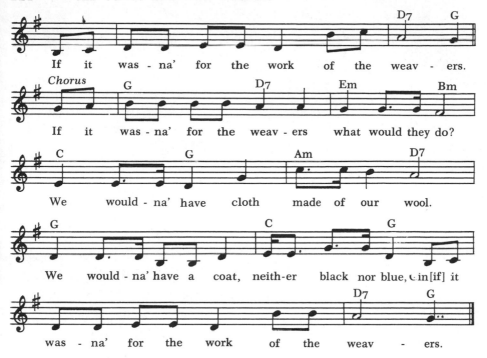

2. The hireman chiels [mill-owners], they mock us and crack aye aboot's,
   They say that we are thin-faced, bleached like cloots [cloths];
   But yet for a' their mockery they canna do wi'oots,
   No! They canna want the work of the weavers.   (*Chorus*)

3. There's our wrights and our slaters and glaziers and a',
   Our doctors and our ministers and them that live by law;
   And our friends in South America, though them we never saw,
   But we know they wear the work of the weavers.   (*Chorus*)

(In this song a partial translation has been made which attempts to retain the original character of the text, while changing occasional words
which are unknown in America. It's a major problem for every singer
who wants to add dialect or foreign songs to his repertoire. Some try to
learn the original from the record—they would imitate Ewan, burr for
burr—and give the baffled listener a spoken translation from time to
time. Beware.)

Ewan MacColl and his mother

The Miller

THERE ARE THOSE who believe that folk songs of social protest are the invention of a few present-day disgruntled radicals. But this traditional song dates back to British broadside balladry of the early eighteenth century—and probably earlier than that. Various American adaptations have been reported and recorded throughout the country. In one version, collected in North Carolina by Cecil Sharp, the youngest son says:

> O dear father, I am your son,
> I'll take three pecks and leave just one.
> And if a good living at that I do lack,
> I'll take the other and swear to the sack.
>
> You are my son, the old man said,
> For you have fairly learned my trade.
> The mill is yours, the old man cried,
> And he closed up his eyes and died.

Our version here, also from North Carolina, was learned from Doris Plenn, whose grandmother taught it to her when she was a little girl. "My grandmother must have been very unorthodox in her choice of lullabies," she writes. "To her mind a baby had the right to be sung to sleep, but the singer had the right to sing whatever pleased her."

THE MILLER

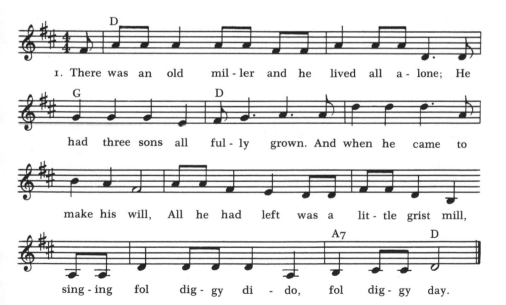

There was an old mil-ler and he lived all a-lone; He had three sons all ful-ly grown. And when he came to make his will, All he had left was a lit-tle grist mill, sing-ing fol dig-gy di-do, fol dig-gy day.

2. He called to him his eldest son,
   Said, "Son, o son, my race is run.
   And if I a miller of you make,
   Pray tell me what toll you'd take."   (*Refrain*)

3. "Father, o father, my name is Bill;
   Out of each bushel I'd take a jill."
   "You fool, you fool!" the old man cries,
   "Out of such a little you'd never make a rise."   (*Refrain*)

4. He called to him his second son;
   "Son, o son, my race is run;
   And if I a miller of you make,
   Pray tell me what toll you'd take."   (*Refrain*)

5. "Father, o father, my name is Alf;
   Out of each bushel I'd take half."
   "You fool, you fool!" the old man cries,
   "Out of such a little you'd never make a rise."   (*Refrain*)

6. He called to him his youngest son;
   "Son, o son, my race is run;
   And if I a miller of you make,
   Pray tell me what toll you'd take."   (*Refrain*)

7. "Father, o father, my name is Jack;
   I'd steal all the corn and swear to the sack."
   "Hallelujah!" the old man cries;
   The old man turns up his toes and dies.   (*Refrain*)

8. They buried him in a little box grave;
   Some do think his soul was saved.
   Where he went no one can say,
   But I rather think he went the other way.   (*Refrain*)

Political Songs of Medieval Minstrels

When I see the fair weather return,
And leaf and flower appear,
Love gives me hardiness
And heart and skill to sing.
Then, since I do not want money,
I will make a stinging song
Which I will send yonder for a present
To King John to make him ashamed.

How's that for a grand opening to a ballad? I quote it from a fascinating collection of minstrel songs of medieval England. The book, given

me by folklorist Herbert Halpert, was privately printed in London in 1839 and is entitled *Political Songs from the Reign of John to That of Edward the Second*. Most of the songs are in Norman French, Latin, or in Middle English (which is equally incomprehensible to most of us). Fortunately, translations are given in the footnotes. One can easily gather that the minstrels, who traveled from castle to castle entertaining, not only sang love songs and comic songs but long polemics in support of this or that baronial faction.

> I am driven to sing,
> My heart wills it, in sorrowful language.
> All with ears was made this song concerning our gentle barons.
> Who, for the peace, so long after, suffered themselves to be destroyed,
> Their bodies to be cut and dismembered to save England.
> Now is slain the precious flower who know so much of war,
> The Earl Simon de Montfort
> His death the land will deeply lament.

Most of the songs are so long that they could not possibly be memorized by anyone except a professional. They are not five or ten stanzas long but twenty, thirty, forty, or fifty. A few of them are shorter: "The following song seems to have been popular soon after the accession of Edward the First. It is written in Latin and in Anglo-Norman in order that it might be sung more generally" (*Political Songs* . . .).

> Charity is wounded, love is sick.
> Perfidy reigns and malice is engendered.
> The fraud of the rulers prevails.
> Peace is trodden underfoot,
> Faith fettered in prison is desolate.
> The sons of iniquity crush those who resist.
> All the land of England is moist with weeping.

As you can see, the bitterness gets pretty wordy and flowery. At other times it can be quite to the point.

> Rich men, ill advised,
> If I knew anything in you worthy of praise
> I would willingly tell you of it.
> But think not to take up my leisure,
> For I desire neither your thanks nor your goods.

It is interesting to see that no matter what insults or praises the minstrel slings around, he usually agrees to start off his song with lovely flourishes alluding to the seasons of the year and the beauties of nature. His song might end with a totally irrelevant aside, such as the following:

> Lady, whom I desire and hold dear,
> And fear and flatter above the best:
> So true is your praise
> That I know not how to say it or relate it.
> That, as gold is more than tin,
> You are worth more than the best hundred.
> And you are better worth to a young man
> Than are the monks of Caen to God.

It is easy to see that some of the ballads took the place of newspapers in those days. As they went on and on, relating exact details of battles and intrigue, they managed to include the names of every man and his brother who were involved. This is, of course, good journalistic tradition.

> It was before St. Bartholomew's Mass that Fraser was taken
> To Sir Thomas de Moulton, a gentle knight and liberal
> And to Sir John Jose he was delivered then.
> They sent him to London with many an armed man.
>
> He came in at Newgate, I tell you faithfully,
> A garland of leaves placed on his head of green.
> Because he should be known both by high and by low as a traitor,
> Fettered were his legs under his horse's belly.
> Both with iron and with steel manacled were his hands.

Altogether it must have been a bloody period and I guess we are well shut of it.

Most of the songs related the battles, or sieges, and were either in praise of or in opposition to some king or bishop or baron. Some songs, however, satirized extravagance in dress, or the "Pride of the Ladies," or were "Against the King's Taxes" or "On the Venality of the Judges."

A fascinating book. It bears out what every historian knows: you can come to understand a nation, its people and its times, through its songs.

Protest in the Nursery

IT IS WELL KNOWN that nursery rhymes are often fragments of political-satirical songs. In sixteenth- and seventeenth-century Europe, young members of the rising artisan and tradesmen classes would meet regularly and (over a convivial glass) compose political rhymes. The repression of the times forced them to caution, and so their deft barbs were full of poetic double-talk:

> Robin the Bobbin, the big bellied Ben
> Ate more meat than three score men.
> He swallowed the church, he swallowed the steeple,
> He swallowed the priest and all the people,
> And still his belly wasn't full.

If one remembers the famous painting of pot-bellied King Henry the Eighth, who took over the churches of England in the sixteenth century, this rhyme springs to life.

A book by Katherine Elwes Thomas, *The Real Personages of Mother Goose,** claimed to trace practically every one of the well-known nursery rhymes to famous figures and events of several centuries ago. Unfortunately, the book was poorly documented, and since many of the rhymes could be interpreted several different ways, many of Mrs. Thomas' identifications were dismissed as being pure conjecture. Iona and Peter Ople, whose mammoth compilations, such as *The Oxford Dictionary of Nursery Rhymes,* have made them recognized authorities in the field, feel that while some of our nursery rhymes are descended from political parodies, others may be fragments of popular ballads or love songs, street rhymes, or even hymns.

Long ago Arthur Stern, former member of the Almanac Singers, promised to write an authoritative article on the subject, but he got sidetracked into painting murals. He did research one rhyme quite thoroughly, and I give his findings here:

> Little Jack Horner sat in a corner
> Eating his Christmas pie.
> He stuck in his thumb and pulled out a plum
> And said "What a good boy am I."

---

* Lothrop Stoddard, England, 1930.

In the late nineteenth century the Horner family, now a titled and wealthy family of England, gave out a bowdlerized version of the rhyme's origin. They claimed that their ancestor Jack Horner was delivering some land deeds, gifts from the wealthy Abbot of Glastonbury to King Henry VIII, circa 1534; the deeds had been put inside a piecrust "after the custom of the period"; the king in thanks gave one deed to the messenger.

Somersetshire folk tradition has it slightly different: they say that Jack Horner stole the deed for himself.

Arthur Stern, after reading a small stack of books, including a detailed and documented biography of Richard Whiting, the last Abbot of Glastonbury, has uncovered what now appears the most accurate version of the story:

King Henry was in the process of taking over the monasteries of England and expropriating their wealth for himself. He could not find a pretext for closing Glastonbury. Then one John Horner, a young man who had been raised since an orphan child by the old abbot, informed the king that not all the monastery's wealth had been reported, as law required. There was, so to speak, some gold and silver stashed away in the attic. This was all the pretext the king needed. The trial took place at Christmastime. The eighty-year-old abbot was tortured, then dragged behind horses around the countryside, and then hanged. His body was quartered and placed on posts. The chief witness for the crown was John Horner. As a reward for having informed on his guardian, he was given a big slice of church property. Now recite out loud to yourself:

> Little Jack Horner sat in a corner
> Eating his Christmas pie.
> He stuck in his thumb and pulled out a plum
> And said "What a good boy am I."

SOME SOUTH AFRICAN TRADITIONS

Choral Folk Songs of the Bantu Villages*

WHAT DOES the average American think of when he hears the word "Africa"? Jungles? Cannibals? Political unrest? Most of us, raised

---

* Written in 1960.

on a diet of Tarzan movies and comic books, actually know little about the traditions of that continent. Great civilizations there were destroyed by centuries of the slave trade and wars of conquest. Over two thousand years ago they were forging iron and casting brass, at a time when men in northern Europe still used stone hatchets. Eight hundred years ago a university flourished in Timbuctoo, drawing scholars from many lands to its halls. Today one can find African cultural expressions which challenge the world to produce their equal for beauty, vigor, subtlety and rich variety. Music is one of these. You don't have to have a degree in anthropology to learn a lot about African music. Folkways* and other recording companies have issued fine field recordings in recent years.

The music of Africa has become justly famous for its complex and exciting drumming, but the great variety of other music indigenous to the continent is not so generally known. In East Africa one can find large xylophone orchestras. In West Africa the predecessor of the American banjo is still played. Flutes, bowed instruments, thumb pianos, trumpets, harps, all can be found, not only playing ancient traditional music but also in contemporary combinations which result from the influence of European music.

Africa also has a highly developed choral tradition. In West Africa this usually takes the form of antiphony—one group of voices answering another. In South Africa, the Zulu and Xhosa people don't think a song is a song unless it has three or more parts in parallel harmony. The bass part is usually very important and helps the whole to achieve a rich sonority.

This tradition existed long before the coming of the Europeans; the first European explorers heard village choruses singing in harmony, with counterpoint and antiphony entirely African in character.

In 1946 Joseph Maselwa, an African student at St. Matthews College, Capetown Province, South Africa, transcribed traditional harmonizations for forty songs of several different Bantu peoples. For bringing this collection to the attention of Americans, thanks are due a gracious lady, Mrs. Frieda Matthews. Her husband, Dr. Z. K. Matthews, a teacher and a courageous leader of the African National Congress, lectured in New York at the Union Theological Seminary in 1952–53.

Mrs. Matthews had heard the recordings made by the Weavers of the popular South African song "Wimoweh," and told me, "Yes, your record of it was quite popular down in Johannesburg. But, you know, you should

---

* Check the Folkways catalog. (One of my favorites is *Music of the Ituri Forest*, FE 4483.) Also valuable is the *Journal of the African Music Society*, P. O. Box 138, Roodeport (near Johannesburg), South Africa.

learn some of our older folk songs, which have been in danger of dying out because of changed conditions in Africa."

She then presented me with *African Folk Songs,** the rare and remarkable volume edited by Mr. Maselwa and Rev. H. C. N. Williams. It contained forty songs: worksongs, wedding songs, lullabies, songs for initiation ceremonies, songs of the witch doctor, drinking songs, children's songs and warrior songs. All were written out in full harmony, with from two to six parts. No accompaniment was indicated.

SOMAGWAZA

At the end of the Abakweta period of initiation, the boys wash off the ceremonial clay from their bodies. They leave their huts on the hillside, and run down to the river to wash, singing this song as they go. This song is usually interrupted by various types of "war cries" of the "question and answer" type.

_____

* St. Matthews College, Capetown Province, 1947. An American edition, *Choral Folksongs of the Bantu* (with introduction and some English lyrics by P. Seeger), was published by G. Schirmer, Inc., New York, in 1960.

No formal notation [wrote the editors] can convey the intricacies of rhythm and suspended syncopation. . . . It must be strongly emphasized that the bars and note values are only intended as a preliminary guide, and every encouragement should be given to freedom of expression to keep the natural rhythmic flow essential to the attractiveness of the songs. . . .

The impossibility of conveying the times of the songs as heard . . . is accounted for largely by the recitative effect of disregarding the normal time for two or three bars to crowd in additional words, while the time is "assumed," and then of returning to strict time values for the completion of the phrase. This is a very characteristic form. A further complication is presented by the fact that in many of the songs as heard the Cantor or "Umhiabeli" adds a flowing descant which often bears no direct relation to the time of the remaining parts.*

----

* As in "Bayeza (Oonomothotholo)" (see Chapter 5, pp. 334–36) or "Wimoweh" in *Bells of Rhymney* (Oak Publications, New York, 1964), p. 73.

These village songs are not of the ancient type, neither are they the jazzy songs now popular in large cities like Johannesburg. In varying degrees they show the influence of over one hundred and fifty years of contact with European missionaries. "Here's to the Couple," for instance, shows a great deal of missionary influence; "Somagwaza" practically none.

Mr. Henry Ramaila, a student at Union Theological Seminary, translated some of the songs for me, but gave up on many. "This song is untranslatable; it is *felt* by Africans," he noted under "Somagwaza." Of another he said, "Don't try to render this song in English. It will make no sense. The idiom has no equivalent to give the exact emotion in English."

The English lyrics of the following song are in no way a translation, but intend rather to carry the spirit of the original.

HERE'S TO THE COUPLE

"This is a wedding 'competition' song, normally sung during the night following the wedding, or during the signing of the register in church."

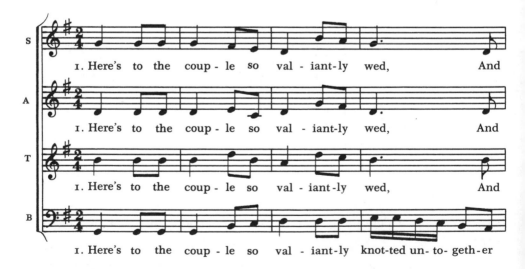

here's to the years that for them lie a - head. We

here's to the years that for them lie a - head.

here's to the years that for them lie a - head.

Here's to the years that for them lie a - head.

wish them good for - tune and health of the best. We

wish them good for - tune and health of the best.

wish them good for - tune and health of the best.

wish them good for - tune and health of the best.

wish them good for - tune and health of the best. Strong

wish them good for - tune and health of the best.

wish them good for - tune and health of the best, and al - so —

wish them good for - tune and health of the best.

2. Here's hoping that they never do part,
   (*Basses:* . . . never have trouble with the baby.)
   And all their quarrels be patched ere they start.
   Let love be the teacher and make all the rules,
   Let love be the teacher and make all the rules.
   (*Tenor:* Remember!)
   Let love be the doctor and cure the fools.
   (*Basses and altos:* Love be the doctor and cure the fools.)

3. They venture now out on life's stormy seas.
   (*Basses:* . . . on the waves and the waters of the ocean.)
   May they hold to their course, be it north, south or east,
   May they hold to their course though the tempests may blow,
   And reach their goal, the goal of us all.
   (*Tenors:* Forever!)
   For them and their children, a world at peace.
   (*Basses and altos:* And for their children, a world at peace.)

4. (Repeat verse 1.)

The original words:

Lo mfan' unesangota
Lo mfan' unesangota
Ha dovale le ma gqibelaka Nkqo yi

Ndi khokele O Yehova
Ndingumhambi nkosi yami
Una mandia a ndi na wo
Ebu tha tha ke ni bami
O msindi si, O msindi si
Nguwe O li khakala me

*South African Freedom Songs**

THOUSANDS OF SONGS are composed and sung in Africa that
treat of contemporary subjects, the most important of which is the struggle to attain first-class citizenship. The songs vary tremendously. Some
are satirical, some are fervent anthems. Some use ancient forms of African folk music, others sound more like Christian hymns or American
jazz, or calypso.

Four of these songs were taught me by Mrs. Mary Louise Hooper when
she returned from Africa in 1959. Mrs. Hooper, a native of San Francisco, spent several years in South Africa and became closely acquainted

---

* These notes were written in 1960 (for Folkways Records) and refer to an earlier stage of
the struggle against Apartheid. These songs are rarely sung now. Black Africa, too, has
given up on passive resistance.

with some of the leaders of the African National Congress. When she left that country at the insistence of the government her friends gave her a going-away party and made a tape recording of their favorite songs.

We do not care if we go to prison; We are determined to get freedom.	Asikatal' nomasiya bozh' Sizimiseli ukululeko.

This load is heavy;
   It needs real men.
	Unzima lomtwalo
	   Ufuna madoda

We, the children of Africa, Are determined to get freedom.	Tina bantwan baseh Afrika Sizimiseli ukululeko

This load is heavy;
   It needs real men.
	Unzima lomtwalo
	   Ufuna madoda.

These two brief verses were sung over and over again on picket lines and at demonstrations. If the singers did go to jail, it meant real hardship—often hunger and starvation—for their families, who were left without support.

For years all nonwhite men in South Africa had been forced to carry pass cards. In 1956, the government of the Orange Free State said women must carry them too. When the women realized that these were the same hated permits that their men were forced to carry, they brought their passes back and burned them. Of course, they were arrested for this. Their song was "Liyashizwa": "It is burned."

Let it be praised, let it be praised—
The name of women should be praised.

One of the favorites of Chief Albert Luthuli, of the African National Congress, was "Tina Sizwe": "We, the brown people." Chief Luthuli was for years a professor at Fort Hare University in Capetown Province. In 1960, he was awarded the Nobel Peace Prize.*

The tune of "Tina Sizwe" is taken from a hymn and sung with rich harmony. One person alone cannot sing the song. The rhythm is carried with a slow, steady pulse. (I first transcribed it in 4/4 time and then later found that 3/4 made some of the phrases easier to learn.) The overlapping of parts is very important.

---

* Dr. Luthuli died in 1967 after being kept under house arrest for several years. His wife believes his death was not accidental.

TINA SIZWE

Pronunciation guide: *e* as in "eggs," *a* as in "father," *u* as in "rule." The *hl* in "abam-hlop'he" and "kumhlaba" is guttural, as in the German *ch* (Bach). All other consonants are pronounced as in English.

ma - bou - ye,   Kum - hla - ba   we - tu   ke —

ma - bou - ye,   Kum - hla - ba   we,   Ma - bou - ye - ke, —

ma - bou - ye,   Kum - hla - ba   we - tu

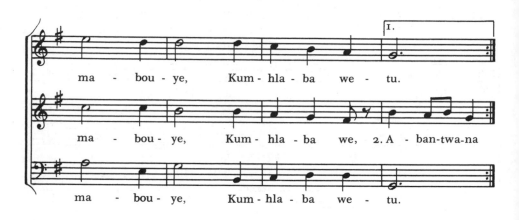

ma - bou - ye,   Kum - hla - ba   we - tu.

ma - bou - ye,   Kum - hla - ba   we,   2. A - ban - twa - na

ma - bou - ye,   Kum - hla - ba   we - tu.

3. Ti - na si - zwe, Ti - na   si - zwe,   e - sin - sun-

3. Ti - na si - zwe, _____ e - sin - sun,

tu.   3. Ti - na — si - zwe,   e - sin - sun-

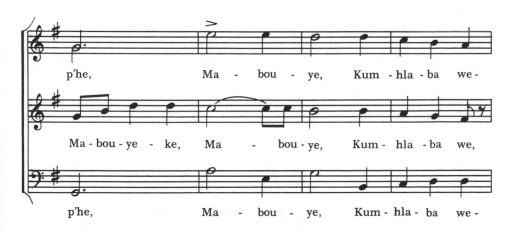

tu.   Ke — Ma - bou - ye,   Kum - hla - ba   we - tu.

ma - bou- ye - ke — Ma - bou - ye,   Kum - hla - ba   we - tu.

tu.   Ma - bou - ye,   Kum - hla - ba   we - tu.

1. We, the brown nation,
   We cry for our country
   That was taken by the white people.

   They must leave our land alone!
   They must leave our land alone!

2. We, the children of Africa,
   Are crying for Africa
   That was taken by the white people.

   They must leave our land alone!
   They must leave our land alone!

3. (Repeat verse 1.)

   While it would be impossible for a solo voice to demonstrate such a
song, it is ideal for an amateur chorus.* The bass line is as important as
the melody. Also needed is a soprano or tenor part a few notes above
the melody.

* The songs discussed here are performed by such an American group on Folkways EP 601;
the liner notes include complete texts and harmonizations. (Some freedom songs current
in 1963, recorded by South African refugees in Tanzania, are available on *This Land Is
Mine,* Folkways 5588.)

African vs. European Style in Music

HUGH TRACEY is a South African of English background who early became enthusiastic about African music. Although he had little formal training either in music or anthropology, by his energy and enthusiasm he became a leader in this field. The African Music Society, which he directed, grew fast and enlisted the support of an extraordinarily wide range of people, from missionaries and scholars to Africans, in various parts of the continent.

Among their many interesting publications my favorite is *Ngoma,* an inexpensive little exposition of African music written by Tracey, published in 1948.* He wrote the book mainly to be read by Africans who were unaware of the tremendous importance of their own musical traditions. They were scorning their own heritage in order to study European music techniques. The book has a number of fine photographs of African instruments, but most important is the way it gets down to the roots of the differences between European and African music.

Thus, he says, "We [meaning Africans] prefer:
1. uneven rhythm
2. in strict time
3. with loose melody which follows the tone of the words.

"They [meaning Europeans] prefer:
1. even rhythm
2. in loose time
3. with strict melody which follows the stress of the words."

By "tone," he was referring to the fact that many African languages are like Chinese in that the same syllable can mean different things, depending on whether it is spoken in a high, medium, or low pitch of voice.

Maselwa and Williams have these further comments about African melody:

Many have heard Africans singing, and have been impressed with the resonance of the harmonies and the attractiveness of the rhythm, but few have

---

* Longmans, Green & Co., Capetown, South Africa.

ever regarded these harmonies and rhythmic effects as songs with a clear melody, and still fewer have felt them to be beautiful music representative of a unique and valuable tradition. Prejudice based on ignorance of the music which these songs exemplify, and an undue exaggeration of the lack of "respectability" in their associations in non-Christian customs have been responsible for their rapid disappearance. . . .

The ancient and original tradition has been characterized by what has been called the Pentatonic scale. No satisfactory theory has been produced to question the validity of that scale as the basis of African traditional music. Non-essential additional notes beyond the scale do not affect the validity of this theory. But a further analysis of these original songs will show that within the Pentatonic scale there is a characteristic melodic phrase peculiar to each tribal group which maintains its traditional song. The phrase always starts on the "dominant" of the Pentatonic scale, and works down the scale, and is then repeated, beginning with the next note down the scale. This similarity of phrasing in African songs is noticeable in the more modern folksongs where the octave scale is used. This makes for similarity of harmonization, which is normally in parallel thirds or fifths, and accounts to a large extent for the ease with which Africans are able to harmonize their songs.

Agreed: the two principal strains of music that have contributed to the early building of American folk song have been from West Africa and from England-Scotland-Ireland. They have in this country borrowed melodies, rhythms, harmonies from each other. But in at least one respect, their basic principles so contradict each other that people familiar with one do not really enthuse over the other.

Here's why: One tradition likes to hear the same melody repeated over and over with different words. The other tradition likes to hear the same words repeated over and over with slightly different melody.

When I sang an old English ballad for an Afro-American audience in a Baptist church down south, one woman leaned over to a friend of mine, Cordell Reagon, and said, "If this is white folks' music, I don't think much of it."

"Shush," says he. "If we expect white folks to understand us, we've got to try and understand them."

There I was, repeating the same unrhythmic melody over and over again, with little or no variation, except for the changing syllables, consonants and vowels of each verse. The story was so ancient, so unfamiliar, as to have little meaning for the listeners. I sang with a deadpan expression, purposely not to detract from the words, and this only made the melody seem more boring to them.

On the other hand, many a European-American has found himself listening to Afro-American music, and wondering why the same words were repeated over and over so often. They don't realize that the melody is being subtly changed with each repetition; the intensity of the attack is being sharpened.

In June 1968, I sat in on a songfest in Resurrection City. Rev. Frederick Douglass Kirkpatrick was handling it; except for a five-minute intermission around suppertime, it ran from 3 P.M. to midnight. Kirk got different members of the audience to lead songs.

A little man of about seventy years came up to the mike, and with a broad smile, started off the well-known hymn, "Leaning on the Everlasting Arm." The first verse was sung with no strong rhythm, but on the refrain the audience joined in and added some offbeat handclapping. Soon the singer was syncopating the melody, moving his body rhythmically. Then he let out a whoop and jumped in the air. The audience sang the two short verses over and over while he was leaping, whirling, arms and legs shooting out in all directions. I thought he'd have a heart attack, but he didn't stop. For ten minutes the song went on, till not a soul present escaped its power.

Finally, with a big grin, the old man flung himself on a chair, out of breath; the song ended. I laughed to see a young white guitar-picking friend; he sat openmouthed, utterly astonished. He had never seen a white hymn Africanized before.

As one Negro friend said to me, "You might as well not sing a song, unless you're going to sing it long enough to really get with it."

> What a fellowship, what a joy we have,
> Leaning on the everlasting arm.

Still, to this writer the most exciting thing about African music is not so much the differences between it and European tradition but the similarities between African musical traditions and those of the U.S.A. Certain African musical principles, such as that of having a solid beat throughout an entire song, with no change of tempo whatsoever, are accepted as standard in American folk and popular music nowadays.

Furthermore, we are increasingly able to trace not only specific rhythms and instruments (such as the banjo) to Africa, but also styles of singing, harmony and even certain melodies. The tune of the work song "Long John" has been recorded by anthropologists in the back hills of West Africa.

It is interesting to note that in present-day Africa many Africans are likewise latching onto American traditions in music. Throughout many of the cities the guitar is being played in a style very similar to American country folk music such as is played by Merle Travis or blues singers such as the late Big Bill Broonzy.

At the same time as we hope that older strains of music are not driven out by modern sophistications, it is nevertheless fascinating to see the combinations of European and African traditions which are being put together by young African musicians.

There is so much of Africa already in American folk traditions that these songs can be learned very quickly by anyone familiar with spirituals, blues and square dances.* Some are like rounds, which may be repeated almost endlessly.

We cannot duplicate exactly the way they are sung in Africa. African scales don't have the exact same pitches as our major and minor scales, and our voices are unused to traditional African inflections, slides and accents.

But we can try to be faithful to the spirit of the songs. There is no reason why African folk songs should not be added to the world's heritage of song. This Yankee song leader has gotten thousands of voices in Moscow and Tokyo to help him sing "Somagwaza," "Bayeza Kusasa (Oonomothotholo)" and "Wimoweh."

THE FOLK PROCESS

THE FOLK SONGS WE LOVE are masterpieces of composition. We can say this even though we know that no one person composed them. In some cases we are able to name the authors of the lyrics, but remember: these authors started on a firm basis of tradition, which guided them at every turn, in choice of words, meter, rhyme and image.

The tunes, harmonies and rhythms may never have been played exactly alike but are the products of centuries of traditions from England, Ireland, Africa, etc., brought to this continent and more or less amalgamated by thousands of singers over a period of several hundred years.

Maybe we should say that folk music is not so much any particular

---

* Several songs from the Maselwa-Williams collection are performed by untrained American voices on *Bantu Choral Folk Songs*, Folkways FW 6912. For additional comments on singing African songs with American audiences, see Chapter 5, pp. 333–36.

group of songs or singers, but rather it is a process, an age-old process of ordinary people making their own music, reshaping old traditions to fit new situations. Some songs have more of this process; others have less. But even old ballads like "Barbara Allen" were probably influenced at some time in their long history by individuals in the music professions. And even the pop song on the radio has been influenced in some way by folk music.

Think of folk music as a process; then the history of any folk song will show continual change, contradictions, action and interaction of opposing influences. Now, this might be called, in the term of my mother-in-law (a wonderful woman), diabolical materialism. But we have support here from scientists, such as the late Alfred North Whitehead, mathematician and philosopher. He said: *"The process is the actuality."*

In other words, if you want to understand any phenomenon, study it in motion. If you could suddenly solidify all the water in a brook, and measure it, would that be the brook? An engineer wishing to throw a bridge across it must study it in motion, its origins and destinations, its fluctuations. He tests its qualities at many places and times. He must study the stream as a process. A pail of its water dipped up would no longer even be part of the brook.

Likewise, a song is ever moving and changing. A folk song in a book is like a picture of a bird in mid-flight printed in a bird book. The bird was moving before the picture was taken, and continued flying afterward. It is valuable for a scientific record to know when and where the picture was taken, but no one is so foolish as to think that the picture *is* the bird.

Thus also, the folk song in the book was changing for many generations before it was collected, and will keep on changing for many generations more, we trust. It is valuable for a scientific record to know when and where it was collected, but the picture of the song is not the song itself.

If you think of folk music as a process, you know that words and melodies may not be so important as the way they are sung, or listened to. The process includes not only the song, but the singer and the listeners, and their situation. In this sense, a mountaineer singing a pop song to some neighbors in his cabin might have more of folk music in it than a concert artist singing to a Carnegie Hall audience an ancient British ballad he learned out of a book.

After defining folk music (as a process, rather than any set repertoire of songs) to a class at the Idyllwild Music School in California, I was still asked by a student: "Just how do you define a folk song, then?" I tried to dodge the issue.

"It's like two geographers arguing the exact boundaries of the Rocky Mountains. One says they run all the way from Mexico to Canada and beyond. The other says no, they are just a few big peaks in Colorado. Perhaps it is necessary for the geographers to be able to draw a line on their maps some place, but for you and me, does the exact name matter that much? We climb a mountain for the view. Likewise, we can sing a song because it is a good song, not because of its classification."

"Not me," says the student. "I am a classroom teacher. My music supervisor says I can teach folk songs to the students, but not pop songs. I have to know."

Ah ha! Here is the source of the trouble, is it not? A phony value judgment: "Folk songs are good. Pop songs are bad."

Isn't this similar to the trouble that racists have in defining the difference between colored and whites races? "White is good; colored is bad." Now, maybe it is important for an anthropologist to analyze physical and cultural differences of peoples. But for you and me the important thing is to accept a man or woman on their individual worth. Only by ignoring phony value judgments based on such trivial aspects as skin coloring and eye slanting can we see our way to a peaceful world.

So can't we agree that there are good and bad folk songs, good and bad pop songs?

"Yes," says the student, "but I still have to be able to define a folk song. My supervisor insists."

All right, let's define our process, and see if we can put it to work. It's an age-old process, of learning and singing mostly by ear, of formally untrained musicians, singing for fun, not for pay, to friends and neighbors, and from time to time changing or creating verses or melodies as events move them to.

"That lets me out," says the student. "I'm a trained music teacher, teaching songs from a book for pay. And my supervisor would chop my head off if he found me changing any of the songs."

Hm.

Hmmmmmmm.

I do believe the only solution is to confound the enemy. If he asks, "Is it a folk song?" tell him "Frankly, no. None of the songs you have ever taught in the schools are strictly folk songs." Back up your claim with copious reference to the experts. You can do it. Be so damn particular in your definition of folk music that even the supervisor will beat a retreat. Show him that a lot of what he has been calling folk music is not really authentic folk music. When he finally throws up his hands and says,

"Well, it may not be folk music, but it's good music to teach the children," then you've got him licked. For if he can say it, you can too.

Sometimes a method of arguing like this is the only way. It's like when a Unitarian friend of mine, a minister, was asked by a fundamentalist, "Do you believe, or not, that Jesus Christ was the son of God?"

"Of course he was," says my friend, looking the other straight in eye, "and so are we all."

A few years ago Dr. Duncan Emrich, then in charge of the Archive of American Folk Song, in the Library of Congress, expressed with heavy finality to me: "In a few years there will be no more folk singers in America." And in the sense in which he was speaking, I had to agree with him. There are only a few of the genuine old country-ballad singers left, who have not been influenced by radio, TV, and book learning. And if a sophisticated urbanite tries to consciously reject these influences, he usually ends up looking and sounding more precious and affected than if he'd gone ahead and been normally jazzy.

But what Emrich didn't figure was that new traditions of folk music will emerge, even though the old ones will have faded. All definitions change with the centuries. What is called a "play" nowadays is far different from what was called a "play" in Shakespeare's time. The definitions of folk songs and folk singers are liable to change also.

Folks will insist on it.

In the 60s there was a flood of good new American songs written by young people who are singers and guitar pickers, who try out their new songs every week on small, informal audiences. They know right away how their song is being received, and if it needs amending.

Are these songs folk songs? They might fit one definition, but certainly would not fit another. The important thing is: are they good songs? Do they sing well? Is the poetry so good you can't get it out of your head? Are the words true, and do they need saying? Does the music move you?

It's worth pointing out obvious differences between these songs and what we usually call "pop" songs:

1) They're often concerned with controversial subjects.

2) They may be short or long, or ignore the Big Beat and other time-honored jukebox requirements.

On the other hand, I'd guess that most of these songwriters are very glad if their songs make the top forty and are sung by all kinds of singers, as long as the songs are not massacred in the process. Whether or not the songs have this brief flash of lucrative notoriety, some of them are picked up by some of the millions of guitar pickers in our country, and the best will be handed on to future generations.

Then some professor can come along and collect them. He can call 'em folk songs then, if he wants. Our dust will not object.

The Flowing Stream of Folk Music: How Fast Should It Flow?

Many people agree that folk music is constantly changing, as people change. Perhaps it is worth pointing out that if it changes too fast, one cannot really get to know it well. Houses change, too, but few would want to move into a new one every month.

Some peoples of the world change traditions very slowly, others much faster. The Eskimos of Greenland have been separated for a thousand years from the Eskimos of Alaska, yet they can understand each other's language. But teen-age slang might be incomprehensible to a group of teen-agers in the same high school ten years later.

A conservatory-trained musician might scoff at the simplicities of a folk tune. Perhaps he doesn't know that you have to live for a while with the subtleties of a tradition before you really get to know them well.

What is it, in a thousand varieties of folk music, that I find I like?

The expertness of someone who has done something many times until he really does it well? But classically trained virtuosos can also do this.

Maybe it's the unpretentious honesty of someone who is doing something because he really loves doing it—not because he's being paid to do it, or hopes to impress someone, or because he thinks it the latest thing to do. But a trained singer might have this also.

Perhaps it's the homogeneity of design, the simplification produced by generations of artists discarding whatever is unnecessary and discordant.

Is it because this simplicity is something that I might be able to learn to do myself?

Maybe it's the song reflecting a whole people, their strength, courage, will to live, desire to stick together?

I confess I don't know for sure. All the above could be true of great art music—or at least some of it. And great pop music.

When is it that I get bored by even the most "authentic" folk music? When it is just too inexpert? When its range is just too limited—such as the melody with three notes? When I am so unfamiliar with a style that it is really not communicating to me what it is supposed to?

Questions, questions.

But here's one more question: When will American TV networks allow the singing of the dozens of songs floating around which tell how Americans really feel about the war in Vietnam?

A minuscule sample of the folk music that exists has been discussed and illustrated in the preceding pages. I hope your curiosity is not satisfied; our planet is full of singing people. In addition to those whom you can meet, or hear in concert, many may nowadays be encountered in recordings and in print. Suggestions about starting your own discoveries are on pp. 573–83.

PART II

A Folk Revival in the Atom Age

4·1954-69 Notes For and About Johnny Appleseed, Jrs.

(MAINLY FROM THE PAGES OF *SING OUT*)

SEVERAL MILLION AMERICANS, of various shapes and sizes, keep a guitar or banjo in the house. The biggest percentage of them are young.

In the 50s and 60s increasing numbers of young people who loved music found that no music school was teaching what they wanted, and so they had to teach themselves. Dissatisfied with the machine-made commercial way, they also were wary of those who, in a feverish search for originality, were forever Blazing New Trails that seemed to lead nowhere. Instead, many of these young folks found a trail used by our great-grandparents. It was still quite usable. In homemade music, well performed, they were able to simply Be Themselves (still quite the most original thing in the world).

Furthermore, this folk music, as it was called (though no two authorities agreed on the limits of the term), proved a fine means of communication between people, drawing them together. And where once it was argued that the pen was mightier than the sword, perhaps now the guitar could be mightier than the Bomb.

1954

(SUPREME COURT DECLARES SCHOOL SEGREGATION UNCONSTITUTIONAL. U.S.-BACKED COUP OVERTHROWS GOVERNMENT OF GUATEMALA. GENEVA ACCORD CONFIRMS INDEPENDENCE OF LAOS, CAMBODIA AND VIETNAM. WEST GERMANY BECOMES SOVEREIGN STATE AND JOINS NATO. JOSEPH MCCARTHY CENSURED BY SENATE AFTER WITCH-HUNT IN ARMY. ATOM SCIENTIST OPPENHEIMER CLEARED OF DISLOYALTY BUT DENIED SECURITY CLEARANCE.
(CLEVELAND DISC JOCKEY ALLAN FREED JOINS N.Y. RADIO STATION TO PROMOTE ROCK & ROLL—NEGRO "RHYTHM & BLUES"—STYLE FOR WHITE AUDIENCES. HARRY BELAFONTE BECOMES STAR WITH CALYPSO AND U.S. FOLK MATERIAL.)

Fall 1954

Johnny Appleseed, Jr.

JOHNNY APPLESEED, the character of American folk history, was a real flesh-and-blood man—John Chapman, born 1776 in Massachusetts; died in Indiana 1847. When hardly out of his teens he got the wanderlust and joined other pioneers with their clumsy wagons lumbering over the rocky forest trails to western Pennsylvania. There he hit upon the scheme of starting an apple nursery to supply farmers with their first orchards. He footed it east to the cider mills, begged for the pressed pulp, separated and dried the seeds, and started back with his precious cargo.

Here his story becomes unique. A deeply religious man (he had joined the Swedenborgian Church when a student, some say, at Harvard), he scorned usual business methods; indeed, they wouldn't have worked on the frontier. For fifty years he traveled back and forth, trading a night's lodging for seeds or seedlings. Many thought him eccentric, thousands loved him, but all recognized the practicality of his system. He refused to carry a gun, became friends with Indians, and transmitted their lore of healing herbs to the new settlers. A letter writer for the illiterate, a librarian who loaned books as he traveled his route, he became also an abolitionist in later years, helping runaway slaves escape to Canada by the Underground Railroad. It is said that he knew Abe Lincoln in Illinois. He never married and early sold the only home he ever had. After he died such a legend sprang up about him that many today think he is pure myth.

This column is dedicated to Johnny Appleseed Jrs.—the thousands of boys and girls who today are using their guitars and their songs to plant the seeds of a better tomorrow in the homes across our land. They are lovers of folk songs and the best of our heritage of the past, and they are creating a new folklore, a basis for a people's culture of tomorrow. For if the radio, the press, and all the large channels of mass communication are closed to their songs of freedom, friendship and peace, they must go from house to house, from school and camp to church and clambake.

This column aims to print news of and for these modern Johnny Appleseeds. I have met them in every state of the union, playing their guitars and building a new folklore out of the best of the old.

1955

(AFRICAN AND ASIAN NATIONS CONFER AT BANDUNG, INDONESIA. S. VIETNAM PRESIDENT DIEM REFUSES NATIONWIDE ELECTION. EMMETT TILL, TEENAGE NEGRO VISITOR FROM CHICAGO, LYNCHED IN MONEY, MISSISSIPPI. PERON DICTATORSHIP OVERTHROWN IN ARGENTINA. AF OF L AND CIO MERGE.
(FIRST FOLK COFFEE HOUSE OPENS IN PHILADELPHIA. UN-AMERICAN ACTIVITIES COMMITTEE SUBPOENAS ENTERTAINERS AFTER BLACKLIST CONTROVERSY IN BROADCAST UNION. "BALLAD OF DAVY CROCKETT" SWEEPS COUNTRY. THE WEAVERS GIVE SUCCESSFUL COMEBACK CONCERT. U.S. GUITAR SALES REACH 500,000.)

Spring 1955

Vive la Compagnie

ONE AND ONE equal four. Two and two equal fifty. How come?
When two people get together their ideas multiply geometrically. Ten ideas plus ten ideas equal not twenty but one hundred.

In traveling this continent I have observed that the greatest music has been in those communities not where a few talented individuals compete for the limelight, but where young people have pooled their repertoire, talent, ideas and energies, and formed folk-singing groups.

They are not choruses or quartets in the strict sense of the terms. They work out their own arrangements and harmonies in their heads, and have no rigid requirements for voices.

The Weavers were a good example. Two low baritones, one brilliant alto, and a split tenor. What more unlikely combination could you have for a quartet? Yet the Weavers produced a solidity of tone that every recording company on Tin Pan Alley tried to copy.

As our knowledge of the folk traditions of the world deepens and broadens, we realize that the best music will come from a group. How can fewer than two sing many songs from Latin America? How can fewer than four really enjoy the harmonies and counterrhythms of a South African choral chant? We need a small chorus to know the full power of some Slavic folk tunes. And a roomful must rock and swell if we are to sing "Saints Go Marching In" or "We Shall Overcome."

How to start? In your family, school, camp, college, or club. Don't demand a large group. Two or three can start. Don't feel you have to have harmony. Start singing all in unison and gradually work out one or two extra parts.

(The Weavers' song arrangements were seldom written down at first. They were what musicians call "head arrangements": one person might scribble out an idea, others would try it, amend it, even swap parts; the song was worked out in rehearsal and ironed out in performance.)

By thus improvising their parts, groups can create the subtle variations in melody, rhythm, tempo, harmony and accompaniment, to bring out the true meaning and purpose of a song.

Set a date to put on a program for your friends. Pool your ideas. Be firm in criticism and self-criticism until you are all happy with the result.

Down with the star system!

Summer 1955

LAST YEAR, in Los Angeles, I stopped by at a little music store to visit Ray Glaser, the songwriter whose death this spring saddened a lot of people. Ray wrote the lyrics of such songs as "Put It on the Ground," "Everything Is Higher," and "The Union Way."

He was feeling discouraged at the time, and when I asked him whether he was writing any new songs, he answered, "Oh, who sings them?"

I told him that I'd heard kids and grown-ups singing his songs in Canada, in the South, East, and other points of the compass. Singing his songs though they never heard his name or knew who wrote the songs they were singing.

We don't give enough encouragement to songwriters. Commercial pop-song composers get used to living the life of gamblers (the curse of all cultural workers in our country), and the royalties from an occasional hit may compensate for the months or years of fruitless knocking on doors.

But people such as Earl Robinson, Lewis Allan, Woody Guthrie, and in the past, Joe Hill and Robert Burns, have never been able to make a full-time living from writing people's songs. And that is a scandal and a shame.

One result is that we, the people, suffer, by not having the songs we need—songs which will echo in poetic form the thoughts and experiences we've had. We need thousands of new songs these days: humor, to poke fun at some of the damn foolishness going on in the world; songs of love and faith in mankind and the future; songs to needle our consciences and stir our indignation and anger.

One thing we can do is write letters of encouragement and appreciation to songwriters, or letters of constructive criticism and suggestions.

More concretely, in many towns we should be able to organize song-writers' concerts or hootenannies to which performers could contribute their services and the proceeds be sent to the songwriter for a change. We might send along a few ideas for songs we would like to have written, and be surprised by receiving a finished song in exchange.

Which leads one to suggest that more often songs should be commissioned. The Oil Workers' Union once commissioned Woody Guthrie and the Almanac Singers to compose and record a song for their organizing drive. They took $100 out of their treasury and got a ballad, "Boomtown Bill," which for years was played in union hall jukeboxes along the Texas coast.

Dear Editor:

The *Sampler* record I made last winter for Folkways Records has been withdrawn and is coming out in a new edition, with "El Dia de Tu

Santo" in it. That's the beautiful birthday song of the Mexican American people that Jenny Vincent has taught to us all. *Not* in the new edition is "Tu Ya No Soplas," taught me by an amiable soldier in the army ten years ago. I found out from Jenny that it is a piece of *double entendre* about as insulting to womankind as any song could be. Not only that, but because the album notes credited Jenny with having taught me the song, she was harmed. For all this, I apologize.

As Jenny wrote in a recent letter to me: ". . . The main lesson to be learned is that when singing songs in foreign languages it is necessary to understand fully the significance of the song. I had a friend once who gave me a wonderful old book of Jewish folk songs which she had picked up in a second-hand store in New York. We sat down and went through them, and she indicated to me which songs I should *not* learn, for they wouldn't be good ones today."

No song is "absolutely good" or "absolutely bad" except in the light of the people who sing and hear it. And many a "folk song" has been sung which has perpetuated slanders of one sort or another.

Sincerely,
PETER SEEGER

Fall 1955

SINCE HARPSICHORDS are difficult to come by these days, why can't we play Bach on our own modern instruments?

In Lenox, Massachusetts, home of the Berkshire Music Festival, I chanced to hear a chamber music program last summer. It's great stuff,* and folk musicians should hear more of it. In between each movement of a suite there is absolute silence, because music is holy, or should be.

I figured, folk musicians should try to write some suites. When it came to choosing a name for my suite I decided on *The Goofing-Off Suite.*†

Here's the reason. If you want to learn a folk instrument, such as guitar, you'll never get around to it if you say, "I'll practice for an hour every Thursday at 5:30." You never get around to it. Unless you know how to goof off.

---

* Some of it.
† Folkways FA 2045.

(I'll admit I'm in a favored position. In my home everybody can be working to beat the band, and I'm lying on the bed, plunking at the banjo. The kids say, "Pop's practicing.")

My Suite has a number of changes of mood in it. After all, barriers are being broken down all over the world, between races, nations, and peoples. We might as well break down a few musical barriers and show that there is nothing heretical in liking several different kinds of music at the same time. I am in favor of folk musicians swiping tunes from symphonies, just as I am in favor of symphony composers continuing to swipe folk tunes. Composers, arrangers and performers, whether amateur or professional, have a vast heritage to draw upon, in the folk and fine-arts music traditions of every continent.

I hope that those who like to fool around with music, picking up tunes by ear, will take hold of my fragments and work them into something really worthwhile. Keep a banjo or guitar hung on the wall, where it's handy. Then if a musical friend drops in, it's no trouble to reach over, and make some sociable noise. Stop goofing off and really create music!

1956

(KHRUSHCHEV DENOUNCES STALIN PURGES. U.S. TESTS HYDROGEN BOMB. 3 MARINES DROWNED IN PARRIS ISLAND TRAINING EXERCISE. SCIENTISTS PREDICT RADIATION DAMAGE TO HUMAN GENE POOL. RUSSIAN TROOPS PUT DOWN HUNGARIAN UPRISING. ISRAEL, BRITAIN, FRANCE INVADE EGYPT AFTER SUEZ CANAL IS NATIONALIZED. YEAR-LONG BOYCOTT WINS DESEGREGATION OF MONTGOMERY, ALA., BUSES.
(ROCK 'N' ROLL STAR PRESLEY RECORDS MULTI-MILLION SELLER "HOUND DOG." SING OUT MAGAZINE REACHES 1500 CIRCULATION.)

Winter 1955–56

"Sixteen Tons"

AT THIS TIME it seems superfluous to review a record which was on the Hit Parade all last fall. But perhaps if you know some recalcitrant musician who pays little attention to radio and the jukebox, you can tell him the story of how one of our best, most hard-hitting miners' songs became the talk of Tin Pan Alley.

The song was written years ago by Merle Travis, son of a Kentucky coal miner. He pulled no punches: "Saint Peter don't you call me, cause I can't go; I owe my soul to the company store." Travis was (and still is) a fine guitar player and singer. He got a job on a hillbilly program and then went to Hollywood, where he now lives and records for Capitol Records. In Los Angeles he got to know Earl Robinson, the composer, and was impressed with Earl's manner of explaining an old folk song to make it come alive to the audience. Merle persuaded Capitol to let him record some older folk songs, instead of the commercialized country music he is usually saddled with. Capitol agreed only reluctantly, never pushed the album, *Folk Songs of the Hills*, and it sold only sparsely. But "Sixteen Tons" and another song in the album, "Dark as a Dungeon," spread through the country.

Last spring, Tennessee Ernie, another star in the country-music field, sang "Sixteen Tons" on his nationwide TV program. To everyone's surprise, he had thousands of requests for it. He sang it again, and last summer his record of it was released.* His version was straight, as Travis wrote it, with a very sparse accompaniment. The words stood out clearly. A strong rocking beat kept it moving throughout.

Surely the New York songwriters, such as Cole Porter, Irving Berlin, and others, must be scratching their heads and wondering what you have to do to get a hit these days. First it was "Goodnight Irene," and now "Sixteen Tons." We've a suggestion for them: take cognizance of the full-scale revival of interest in folk music throughout the 48 states; note

---

* Tennessee Ernie's version (originally issued as a 78-rpm single) is on Capitol T-1380. The Merle Travis album, retitled *Back Home*, is Capitol T-891.

that whereas many a Tin Pan Alley publisher is singing the blues, companies selling collections of folk songs are doing very well. Write a meaningful song, not an ersatz imitation, and if it is not suitable for a plush cocktail lounge, perhaps it will be all the more suitable to millions of music-loving Americans looking for hard-hitting music these days.

Spring 1956

WITHIN THE PAST TEN YEARS there has arisen a new people's-songs movement in India, sparked by the popular new songs written by composers and recording artists of the Indian People's Theater. In the main their principle is to write new words to old folk tunes. Musically as well, however, there is a good deal that is new. For one thing, India has been widely influenced by western music through the movies. The movie industry of India frankly uses many western motion picture techniques.

One of the leading composers of the Indian People's Theater is Harindranath Chattopadhya. He is a Bengali poet, an actor and a member of Parliament. He is also a friend of Nehru's, although his politics are considerably to the left of the Indian Premier. His English-language poem, "The Curd Seller," is performed similarly to the American "Talking Blues." A fast and syncopated drum accompanies the words. This song is in the ancient tradition of the clown saying things that would not be permitted to others.

THE CURD SELLER

by Harindranath Chattopadhya

> The world is full of paddy, and the world is full of wheat;
> The world is full of paddy, and the world is full of wheat;
> Yet there are tens of thousands who have no food to eat!
>   Come—taste these curds,
>   They are white as snow . . . They are . . . Ahahaha . . .
>
> Oh, come with me my children, to the sweet and holy town;   (*Repeat*)
> Where every clown becomes a king, and every king a clown!

The priest performs the marriage, just for your money's worth; (*Repeat*)
All marriages are made in Heaven, and broken on the earth!

I would not call the temple priest a parrot in a cage;   (*Repeat*)
For that might hurt the parrot's pride and put it in a rage!

A gentleman is one who lives a highly cultured life;   (*Repeat*)
He calls on me, but then, you see, he comes to meet my wife!

My wife has got a baby, the baby is divine!   (*Repeat*)
People congratulate me—I hope the child is mine!

Oh I am sure that God above would cease to feel a fool,   (*Repeat*)
If every temple would become a hospital or school.

The hunger of the children is the Holy Book I read;   (*Repeat*)
The World is my religion—and Humanity my creed!

Art has no place in politics, nor politics in art;   (*Repeat*)
Which is as good as saying that the wife and husband part!

Where artists are neglected and mere politicians boomed,   (*Repeat*)
That country's destiny is done, the nation's fate is doomed!

There was a mighty auction in the market-square of life;   (*Repeat*)
One bid was for a neighbor's cow, another for his wife!

Oh, all things are expensive now because of war and strife;   (*Repeat*)
The only thing that's really cheap today is human life!

About my character I hear so many vile complaints;   (*Repeat*)
I am the only sinner in a world of perfect saints!

The doctor's fees are heavy, and the lawyer's fees are high;   (*Repeat*)
But the artist, he is just supposed to entertain and die!

With firm determination, I am going to the goal;   (*Repeat*)
Not all your tempting money could ever buy my soul.

Now, I am a wealthy gentleman, my moneybags are fat;   (*Repeat*)
But, if you scratch me deep enough, you'll find I am a rat!

They starved and killed the poet, and now it makes me laugh;   (*Repeat*)
To see them bring their bags of gold to buy his autograph!

IRISH SONGS OF RESISTANCE*
IRISH REBEL SONGS†

This short, inexpensive book should become a classic. It will be of interest not only to Irish-Americans, but to any who are interested in tracing the manner in which a people's songs reflect their struggles for freedom. Patrick Galvin is an Irishman living in England, where this book was originally published. He writes well and clearly. Too bad the book is so short.

Primarily, it is a book of history of the last two hundred years, and includes songs and fragments of songs as illustrations. The various movements within and fluctuations of the cause of Irish independence are analyzed and placed in perspective. The way the songs were written and used is described.

An interesting analysis is made of "drawing-room sentimentalists," such as Thomas Moore, and the "Oirish" songs of the American music halls, which, through dialect and misrepresentation, are actually often anti-Irish. This reviewer does not wholly agree with Galvin's condemnation of the song "No Irish Need Apply," even though it is allied with this "Oirish" tradition. If it is sung without phony dialect, I believe it can make a worthwhile point in a program of American songs. But he is right when he points out the song's weaknesses. It does nothing to dispel the lie that all Irish workers are "stupid and violent." Perhaps anti-Irish chauvinism is more prevalent on the English than the American stage, where it was largely displaced by humor derogatory of the Negro or Latin American peoples.

This book sets a pattern which could be valuably followed in presenting the topical patriotic songs of many peoples. Song material for such volumes exists in every country of the world. Such volumes would round out the picture of a nation's music which is so often left incomplete in standard collections which present the "pretty" songs—love songs, lullabies, etc.—or comic songs, and ignore songs of struggle and the passion for freedom. We owe a vote of thanks to the newly formed Folklore Press for making this book available to us at a low price. May they be encouraged to issue more like it.

The three LPs are companion pieces to the book. A total of 29 songs

---

* By Patrick Galvin (Folklore Press, New York), paperback, 102 pp., including words and melodies for 48 songs.
† Sung by Patrick Galvin, accompanied by Al Jeffrey, three 10-inch LPs, Stinson SLP 83, 84, and 85.

are sung in a straightforward and traditional manner. Those expecting to hear the smooth rendition of another John McCormack will be disappointed; Mr. Galvin is no trained singer. A number of the songs are sung without accompaniment; this makes for authentic presentation, although those not used to it may find the volumes difficult to listen to. All songs are in English and the words are clear.

Volume I contains songs of the Rebellion of 1798, such as "Men of the West," "The Boys of Wexford," and "Rising of the Moon." Volume II covers the period of the Fenian Brotherhood and the nineteenth century. Volume III carries us up to the twentieth century, the Easter Uprising and the Black and Tan Wars.

Summer 1956

TRINIDAD, B.W.I., is a British crown colony,* an island lying about ten miles off the coast of Venezuela. It is almost as big as the state of Rhode Island—about 65 miles long. The population about 800,000. The majority are descendants of African slaves. One-third are East Indians—Moslem and Hindu—who were brought to work the plantations after slavery was abolished in 1837, and freed Negroes moved to town. The East Indians are in some ways the poorest section of the population now.

There are also descendants of Carib Indians and of early Spanish and French settlers, and a smattering of English and Americans—mostly executives in government or business, as you might expect.

Port of Spain, the one large city, numbers 100,000. Races and languages mix amiably, if competitively. Looming large over the whole scene, economically and culturally, is not England so much as America. Coca-Cola is in every restaurant. Hollywood movies are everywhere. (Second place goes to English or Indian movies.) American Hit Parade tunes come out of the radio. English cars sell better because of better gasoline mileage, but, in general, American products are everywhere.

Think of what this means to a population whose average weekly wage is from two to twenty dollars. And prices are not that much cheaper. Cokes are a nickel, and harmonicas and monkey wrenches cost more

---

* In 1962 it became independent along with the rest of the former British West Indies.

than in New York. Meat is medium high; only fruit is cheap. Were it not for the latter, and plentiful sunlight, the children couldn't grow up, I was told by the Tiger, one of the leading Calypso singers. Personally, I am not proud that my country is rich while others are not.

The island exports petroleum products, foodstuffs, Angostura bitters, and Calypso music. It is the most cosmopolitan island in the West Indies.

I went to Trinidad last winter to try to learn more about the steel drums I had first heard at a recital by the dancer Geoffrey Holder. By great good luck I met Kim Loy Wong, leader of one of the champion steel bands. He and his friend Renwick Walker made six "pans" for me in their backyard, and permitted me to make a film of them.

The steel drum was invented for use in the annual 48-hour spree known as Carnival. As in Brazil and in New Orleans, Carnival is celebrated just prior to Lent, usually late February or early March. It was introduced to Trinidad in the late eighteenth century by French planters fleeing revolutions on other islands of the West Indies. During the early nineteenth century the middle and upper classes of Trinidad celebrated the season with masques, balls, and pageants. The slaves carried on similar parties in their own quarters.

After emancipation in 1837, the lower classes brought their parties out into the open. The upper classes recoiled in horror. "Carnival is desecrated!" They gradually abandoned their own celebrations. By the end of the century Carnival was a bacchanal, an occasion for the unrespectable to poke fun at the respectable. Satiric songs (predecessors of modern Calypsos), fantastic costumes, and dancing shocked the ruling groups, who periodically tried to get the celebrations suppressed by the police.

It was impossible. Carnival was too much fun. A person could put on a mask and abandon propriety anonymously. Finally, in the twentieth century the celebration became a truly national affair, with all classes participating. The most obscene satires were banned. Nowadays there are official contests for the prettiest girl, the best dancer, etc. Imagine Halloween, New Year's, July Fourth, May Day, and Labor Day all rolled into one!

A housewife with sad eyes told me, "Really, the only time of year that I live for is Carnival. Even Christmas does not make me happy. But Carnival!" Her eyes lit up. "Not a woman in this building does any housework. We leave the youngest children with their grandparents. Everybody with legs to dance is in the streets. I don't cook a meal for two days. We just step into one of the sidewalk booths and eat Roti." (Roti is an East Indian delicacy, a thin pancake folded into a cornucopia and filled with curried shrimp, chicken, or goat meat.)

A generation ago, carnival music was made by "bamboo tamboo" bands, composed of hundreds of young people.* Each one carried a bamboo stick as thick as your arm, and four to six feet long. Pounding one end on the ground gave off a deep, muted tone. With careful selection of sizes of bamboo, and rehearsal of counterrhythmic effects, one had a thunderous rhythm orchestra.

In 1937, the stick bands were forbidden by the police, who said that the rival bands were getting into fights too often and using the sticks on each others' heads. (The Duke of Iron—a Calypso singer—also told me that in that year there were riots of the unemployed in the south end of the island, and the sticks had been used on policemen's heads.) This presented a catastrophic situation. How could one celebrate carnival with no rhythm? The young people refused to be discouraged. They raided the junkyards and that year danced in the streets with clanging of tin cans, brake drums from old cars, and other pieces of metal. These were the first steel bands; they had no melody or harmony.

Some genius then discovered that a dent in the bottom of a garbage can gave off a musical note. According to Winston "Spree" Simon, an early steel bandsman, someone threw a rock at the bottom of his garbage can. In hammering out the dent he found he could control the pitch. He purposely put several other dents in the can, and started an impromptu parade about the neighborhood, playing "Mary Had a Little Lamb," while an excited crowd gave him rhythmic accompaniment.

Within a few years the young men worked out, by trial and error, a system of using large and small dents, and learned means of controlling pitch and tone.† Since there is a large oil industry on the island, oil drums replaced the garbage cans. Today the steel drum has grown to be Trinidad's national instrument. They are as proud of it as the Scots are of bagpipes.

At 5 A.M. on the Monday two days before the start of Lent, all the bells start ringing; bands start assembling in the streets. Each band has rehearsed and costumed itself in secret. Some may have fifty or more

---

* There had been for some years restrictions on the use of conga drums, because of the desire of the official church to stamp out religious groups which used drums as part of the ritual.
† For more details see pp. 393–96 below.

Kim Loy Wong teaching a steel band

players, and several hundred similarly costumed friends and neighbors who will dance with them up one street and down the other.

The music that emerges is not what you might expect. It can be subtle, poignant, and haunting. It can also be exciting, with the compulsive drive of the bass booms, the seductive tinkle of the ping pongs, and the bittersweet cello note of the tenors.

Once in the 1940s the police threatened to ban steel drums too, but this time the whole island protested. There are now several hundred bands, totaling many thousand members, on the island. Last February literally the entire population, young and old, rich and poor, crowded the streets of Port of Spain to dance to the music of the steel bands.

In my opinion the instrument will spread around the world. Within the last five years it has gone to the other islands in the British West Indies. Another generation may see it in other parts of South and North America, Africa, Asia, and Europe—wherever there are vigorous and youthful amateurs wanting a rhythmic music.

Fall 1956

I AM GLAD to report partial success in my campaign to lead the younger generation astray by persuading them to spend their college vacations hitchhiking around the country, learning about peoples and regions, instead of spending the summer assiduously earning loot to get through the coming year. One youth I know hitchhiked from the east to the west coast and back, covering some ground by freight out in the desert country. Another managed to land a job as cook's helper on a Great Lakes ore boat. This is OK. It counts as traveling. One girl took herself and camping equipment to the Rocky Mountains and home again in one piece, carrying everything in her Volkswagen, 37 miles to the gallon. Another took a tape recorder with her and set up small hootenannies in country stores, and recorded the singing.

I have been accused of being anti-Tin Pan Alley. I confess it. Deep within me lurks a prejudice against the institution and its Hit Parade. I hesitate to let it be known, since some of my best friends, as they say, work there. They like to think of their jobs as channeling the best popular music of the nation so that it reaches the most people. They think of Tin Pan Alley as a funnel. Some of us think it more of a bottleneck.

I am against the Hit Parade because I am against anything that would make a sheep out of a human being. The world is too big, and its people too varied, to try and make one hit parade suit us all. True, the gods of mass production may proclaim that it is much cheaper, much more efficient, to produce everyone's music at one place and at one time. But which would you rather have—cheap music or good music? (And by good you might mean anything from Calypso to blues to Bach.)

Not only every country, but every region and town, every national group, every age group, every industry, even every school or summer camp should have its own hit parade, refusing to follow slavishly the dictates of Hollywood and New York.

Fortunately, at the same time that TV has concentrated the entertainment business as never before, LPs have enabled hundreds of minority idioms to receive hearings. The so-called Hit Parade is, today, simply the most popular songs of the fourteen-to-eighteen age group, and is supported by them and a few saloon goers who help feed the jukeboxes. There have been many songs which have attained Number One on the Hit Parade, yet 75 percent of the population have never heard of them.

Even so, many popular songs are among my own personal favorites. I don't mind being herded with the sheep a bit if they'll give me occasionally a real patch of green grass.

1957

(GHANA FIRST BRITISH AFRICAN COLONY TO BECOME INDEPENDENT. U.S. AND USSR TEST INTERCONTINENTAL MISSILES. INTERNATIONAL GEOPHYSICAL YEAR, WORLDWIDE COOPERATIVE SCIENTIFIC STUDY OF PLANET EARTH, IS LAUNCHED. USSR ORBITS FIRST MANMADE SATELLITE. U.S. TROOPS PROTECT NEGRO CHILDREN INTEGRATING LITTLE ROCK HIGH SCHOOL.
(JACK KEROUAC'S BOOK "ON THE ROAD" CELEBRATES ANTI-ESTABLISHMENT LIFE STYLE OF SAN FRANCISCO "BEAT" COMMUNITY. "SKIFFLE" CLUBS— DRAWING ON NEGRO FOLK STYLES—SPREAD THROUGHOUT BRITAIN. OLD TOWN SCHOOL OF FOLK MUSIC OPENS IN CHICAGO.)

Spring 1957

LAST YEAR, when the bus boycott in Montgomery, Alabama, was at its height, I got a letter from an old friend in that city.

Dear Pete:

I received the copy of *Sing Out* which I have enjoyed so much. Thanks for sending it to me. I am no musician, but I am so much interested in folk music as the repository of the history of a people, both emotionally and politically and in all other ways. I have always thought it would be fascinating to take a definite period of history and relate the events and the changes that took place to the songs that arose out of it.

The kind of thing I mean is, for instance, the rise of the Blues. No doubt there were and had been some of the Blues for years and years among the Negroes and perhaps among the whites (you say this in the account of "Joe Turner," but I have never heard of any Blues among the whites); but they came to their fruition in the Twenties and, as I was a girl in the Twenties, I was a participant and saw it happen. It is hard to realize how prim we were and how ignorant and how scared—sex was a dirty word and you would go to Hell forever and the Devil would continually roast you over Hell fires if you kissed a boy, and anything more than that meant Eternal Damnation of the deepest kind. But after the First World War there was the throwing off of the inhibitions and the rise of the Blues with their deep throbbing sexual harmonies.

I used to visit in Memphis and the boys would go down on Beale Street and pick up a "two-bit" band just out of any pool room or anywhere. They were called "two-bit bands" because all the boys would pick up or chip in 25¢. The bands would consist of three or four players, piano, saxophone, banjo, drum, maybe more, and they would play all night for three or four dollars—and such music. I am not sure if Handy was there then or not, although I remember dancing to his music at big dances in Alabama, but the music was wonderful and St. Louis Blues, Beale Street Blues, and all the Blues were played and lots of songs and music that I can only remember bits of—"Red Hot Mama, Tree Top Tall, Won't you kindly turn your damper down." Or, "Shake it and Break it and Hang it on the Wall." "I wish I was a Rich Man's Bird Dog." I kissed my first boy in Memphis after one of those dances and—My! It was so much fun!

I always relate the dances in the Twenties to the Blues and while they (the Twenties) were messy in a lot of ways, they did overturn so much that was bad and hypocritical and vicious. I wish I could reproduce for you the excitement of one of the big dances with Handy's band with everybody crowded around the bandstand and swaying with the music and dancing until their feet gave out, except then they never did, in spite of the silver slippers.

Now as for your questions about the music in connection with the Bus Boycott. I called Mrs. King, the wife of the Rev. M. L. King, who is the leader of the boycott and who has just been tried, but you know all that. She is a musician herself and sings very beautifully and knew of you and was glad to give me the information.

Yes, there is a great deal of singing at the mass meetings. Both Hymns and Spirituals. The hymns come mostly out of the standard Hymnals, such as Broadman's Baptist Hymnal, and they sing hymns like Leaning on the Everlasting Arms, What a Friend We have in Jesus, Onward Christian Soldiers, Pass Me Not, O! Gentle Saviour; and then they also sing the spirituals.

She says the ones she remembered as being sung the most are: Steal Away, Old Time Religion, Shine on Me, Study War No More, Swing Low, I Got Shoes (this has been sung a great deal and a lot of people have sent boxes of shoes here for the walkers), I Got a Home in That Rock, and

> Rich Man Dives lived so well,
> When he died he went to Hell.
> Poor Man Lazarus, poor as I,
> When he died he had a home on High.

She says you are absolutely right, that these songs were and are sung as songs of struggle and that even in the time of slavery they were, but had to be allegorical and they had to use symbolic meanings to survive and had to conceal what they wanted to say. The Church has been and is the center of their lives and it was only when the NAACP militants got the Churches behind them that the movement developed into a mass movement.

It is still going strong and looks as though it would keep on. But they need lots of help to keep it going, money for the transport system mainly, and even with that the walkers bear a big burden and with the hot weather coming on it will be heavier. I wish I could write a song about the beauty of these patient Negro women, their heads tied in scarfs, walking morning and night to and fro. It is like some dark, deep silent stream welling up out of the bowels of the earth, and as irresistible and as compelling; some of them old, some of them fat, lots of them with their feet hurting, and walking no matter what—rain, cold, sleet, ice, heat—nothing stops them.

HANNAH JOHNSTON

Fall 1957

ONE OF THE MOST unusual evenings of folk music that I ever participated in was the program of songs by Woody Guthrie, called "Bound for Glory," put on in New York over a year ago. When we first proposed such an evening, some friends said, "Won't all the songs sound alike? Will there be enough variety?"

It is true that most of the songs use the same major tonic, dominant and subdominant harmonies in familiar sequence. Most are in a moderate 2/4 or 4/4 time. But the lyrics cover a wide range of subject matter.

There was plenty of variety. The voices that sang Woody's songs ranged from Ed McCurdy's rich baritone to the Kossoy Sisters' sweet harmonizing, solos, duets, Earl Robinson's children's chorus, and audience participation.

What the evening *did* have, which was so unusual, was homogeneity. The average hootenanny has a rather scattered imagery. Your mind is led off in this direction and then that. There's variety all right, often too much.

But here, in an evening of Woody's songs, we saw the face of America as it was seen by one man. No matter how widely we circled, we kept returning to a center. Furthermore, none of the singers on the stage did any talking themselves. Millard Lampell had done a deft job of selecting certain paragraphs of Woody's to introduce each number. These were read from the side of the stage by bass-voiced Lee Hays. Therefore Woody's prose flowed into Woody's poetry and then back into Woody's prose without a break, and without the contradiction that so often occurs when a song is introduced with one vocabulary and sung in another.

A break in the singing was arranged in the second half of the program, when some children did pantomime dances to the Songs to Grow On which Woody wrote for his daughter Kathy.

Altogether, it made a fascinating evening, and I look forward to the program being put on many times throughout the land. It tells a good story, and would be fun for those who put it on as well as those in the audience.* It would require little rehearsal. No one person would have to learn more than a few songs. The only accompaniment needed would be guitar or banjo.

One ingredient the New York premiere had which no other could duplicate was an ending that almost proved too melodramatic. It couldn't have been planned. The show was over, the performers were taking bows, when the spotlight shifted to the balcony, where sat Woody himself. He'd been let out of the hospital for the occasion. Earl Robinson whispered in my ear: "Sing the last chorus over again." The whole crowd of over one thousand, mostly teen-agers who had never seen Woody before, stood up and sang his song to him, as though to tell him they would carry his music across the land. Tears were in the eyes of many old-timers as they listened to the strong, young voices:

> This land is your land,†
> This land is my land,
> From California to the New York Island.
> From the redwood forests
> To the Gulf Stream waters,
> This land was made for you and me.

1958

(USSR SUSPENDS ATOMIC TESTING. U.S. MARINES LAND IN LEBANON TO PROTECT PRO-WESTERN GOVERNMENT. DE GAULLE BECOMES FIRST PRESIDENT OF FRENCH FIFTH REPUBLIC AFTER UPHEAVALS OVER ALGERIAN WAR.

("DIXIELAND" JAZZ REVIVED—AGAIN—BY MAINLY WHITE BANDS. AMERICAN PIANIST VAN CLIBURN WINS PRIZE IN USSR. FRANK PROFITT'S "TOM DOOLEY" BECOMES KINGSTON TRIO HIT. BORIS PASTERNAK DECLINES NOBEL PRIZE.)

---

* The script and songs are published in *California to the New York Island* (Oak Publications, New York, 1958, $1.95). The Folkways recording of the program is *Bound for Glory*, FA 2481.

† Words and music by Woody Guthrie. TRO-© copyright 1956, 1958, Ludlow Music, Inc., New York, New York. Used by permission.

Winter 1957–58

The Purist vs. the Hybridist

THE PURIST: One of the beauties of a great folk art form is its homogeneity. Each part of it matches and fits with the rest. With a real folk singer, his vocal tone, the accompaniment (or lack of it), the poetry and the subject matter of the lyrics, all are unified with the melody, and the whole fits in with the singer, his clothing, his daily speech, yes, his daily life. And it relates with his whole position in the world.

Now along comes your fresh young upstart. He assumes that because of his education he can do as well, or even improve upon the original. But the ways of the old song do not match the ways of this young fellow's life. And when he tries to "improve" the original, he introduces elements which do not harmonize with the original. It has lost its homogeneity.

You might as well go to a Navaho Indian rug maker and say to him: "Would you please weave a rug for me with this pretty Armenian design right in the center? Thanks. Here's the money."

So you end up with a delicate Armenian rosette in the middle of all those triangles.

If you love folk music, you will value the homogeneity it has built up through thousands of years of tradition. You will not want to add accompaniments to pure Irish balladry, for example.

THE HYBRIDIST: Cultural purity is as much a myth as racial purity. Even your Irish balladry shows influence of Rome and Scandinavia, in addition to the Celtic. And other obvious cultural hybrids are among the greatest achievements of the human race. Take the English language, for example, composed of Celtic, Saxon, Danish, French, and so on. Or Flamenco music, a blend of the East, Europe, and Africa.

Some of the greatest achievements of modern biology have been in the field of hybridization. Look at Henry Wallace's corn. Why refuse to allow experimentation to continue when it may produce some greater music than anything we have known in the past?

I'll grant you that there is such a thing as an unsuccessful hybrid, like your Navaho rug with an Armenian rosette in the center. But unsuccessful hybrids will be forgotten. Good ones will last and be a permanent contribution to human culture.

THE PURIST: I hope you don't think some of the versions of folk songs I hear nowadays on the radio are permanent contributions to human culture.

> THE HYBRIDIST: No, I wince at some of it myself. But I think some of it is good music, even though it may not be folk music in the old sense. And certainly some of America's hybrid music has proved so powerfully popular that it is sweeping the world—jazz, for example.

THE PURIST: Yes, and that's just the trouble. It's like the starling population in some of our cities. This bird, introduced from overseas, soon became like a plague, wiping out many beautiful local varieties of birds.

Thus also, in country after country in this world, local musicians are fighting for the right of their own loved traditions to stay alive at all. They are being swamped by American pop music.

> THE HYBRIDIST: But aren't *you* trying to deny the hybrids the right to exist?

THE PURIST: I guess I would, if I could. I like Irish ballads pure.

> THE HYBRIDIST: Come, now, maybe you like what you think are pure Irish ballads, but I bet you'd be sorry to do without some of the hybrids in other fields. Look at the food we eat. What would America be like with no Italian pizza, or sour cream, or borscht, or garlic, or curry?

THE PURIST: Okay, okay. Just you better not try to sprinkle any curry on my pizza.

> THE HYBRIDIST: Coexistence! Isn't that the answer?

THE PURIST: Coexistence?

> THE HYBRIDIST: Yes. And realize, too, that America's great contribution to world culture in this age may be its hybrids. After all, our people, uprooted from their old cultures in many lands, have come here and have had to put together something new out of many old traditions.

THE PURIST: Contribution, smogtribution! I prefer the "Ballad of Dhrinnin Dhu" to "Kisses Sweeter than Wine," which murdered the beautiful old melody. And come to think of it, I prefer Tchaikovsky played by a symphony, not Freddy Martin's orchestra. And I prefer any folk song sung by someone who has grown up with it, not learned it out of a book.

> THE HYBRIDIST: Remember—coexistence!

THE PURIST: Okay. But would you please tell your radio stations, your jukeboxes, and your publishers about this coexistence theory? After all, it's gotta be reciprocal.

Spring 1958

THE MAIN FUNCTION of my *Sleep-Time* record* will be achieved if parents take to the idea of singing lullabies for their own children, and making up stories for them. Just as we would not want to miss the pleasure of using our legs simply because we have automobiles, we would not want to forget the fun of singing and retelling stories, even though we can agree that the LP record and the printing press were great inventions.

I can sing lullabies only to my youngest child. The older two long ago discovered that lullabies were propaganda songs, and refused to allow them to be sung. They much prefer stories, the longer the better. Two main kinds seem to be most popular: stories out of history, told as truly as possible, and nonsense stories, which can be made up as one goes along. The idea is simply to find an unlikely situation to start with, and follow it to its illogical conclusion. When inspiration fails for either of these two types, one can fall back upon retelling of old stories: only the bare plot need be remembered. Let us look forward to the folk process taking hold and retelling hundreds of the world's great stories. And let us hope not too many of them are written down.

Summer 1958

THE AUTHOR of "The Bells of Rhymney" was Idris Davies, who died while still young, in the nineteen forties. His poem paraphrased the Mother Goose rhyme "Oranges and lemons, say the bells of St. Clemens." It was published in a volume of essays by Dylan Thomas, *Quite Early One Morning.*

According to a Welsh friend: "The places are all in South Wales. Cardiff, my home town, is now the capital of Wales, and is on the Bristol Channel. Swansea is a coastal city. Caerphilly is a pretty town by a mountain of the same name. It gives its name to a delightful cheese that

---

* Folkways FC 7525.

I sorely miss. Rhondda is the name of a valley, and Merthyr is a mining town in the Rhondda, mostly grim and comparatively well fed since the after-war brought small industry. It was despondent throughout the Hungry Thirties. Rhymney* is a town in a tiny valley of the same name. Neath is a market town." (Wye is a more prosperous valley to the east.)

The melody I put together myself. I say "put together" because I sat down and thought it up, and then later realized that the opening phrase is nothing more than "Twinkle Twinkle Little Star."

THE BELLS OF RHYMNEY

Words by Idris Davies, music by Pete Seeger. TRO-© copyright 1959, 1964, Ludlow Music, Inc., New York, New York. Used by permission.

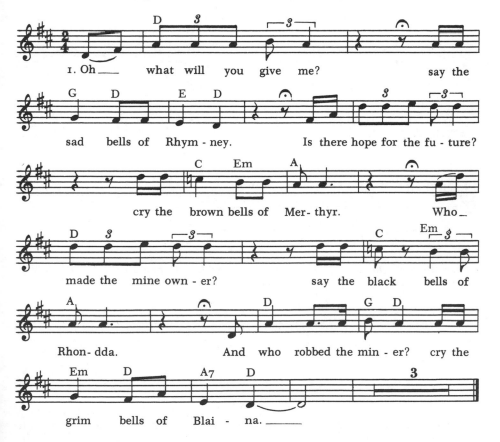

1. Oh___ what will you give me? say the
sad bells of Rhym - ney. Is there hope for the fu - ture?
cry the brown bells of Mer- thyr. Who_
made the mine own - er? say the black bells of
Rhon- dda. And who robbed the min - er? cry the
grim bells of Blai - na. _____

* Pronounced more like "Rh*uh*mney."

2. They will plunder willy-nilly, cry the bells of Caerphilly.
They have fangs, they have teeth, shout the loud bells of Neath.
Even God is uneasy, say the moist bells of Swansea.
And what will you give me, say the sad bells of Rhymney.

3. Throw the van-dals in court say the bells of New-port. All would be well if if if if, cry the green bells of Car-diff. Why so wor-ried, sis-ters, why?__ sang the sil-ver bells of Wye.__ And what will you give me?____ say the sad bells of Rhym-ney.

(*I usually sing the song freely, and then repeat two verses with strong rhythm.
Then I end by whistling the following coda.*)

(WHISTLE)

NOTE FOR GUITARISTS: The accompaniment for "The Bells of Rhymney" was worked out on a twelve-string guitar, which is customarily tuned lower than a six-string. Thus D turned out to be B flat, a comfortable key in which to sing the song. On a six-stringer, you either have to sing in a tenor (or soprano) range, or retune strings, or else capo up five frets or so (to sing it in G, for example). Or else figure out a new accompaniment. The one I use is as follows:

The bass string is tuned down one whole note.   Thus

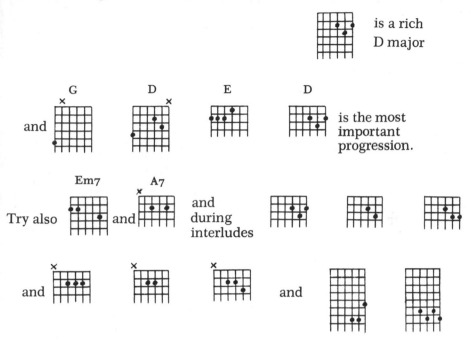

is a rich
D major

and

is the most
important
progression.

Try also   and   and during interludes

and   and

"Beethoven ruined those beautiful melodies," said Shaemas O'Sheel, the old Irish poet. "Beethoven and that metronomic German stamping music of his." Shaemas was referring to a suite of Irish songs to which Beethoven, for a paid commission, once wrote accompaniments.

Another Irish poet and sculptor, Sam Kennedy, said a little wistfully to me, "Americans don't know how to sing Irish songs. They give them rhythm. They are not supposed to have rhythm. They have cadence."

I thought of these comments as I listened to the lovely unaccompanied singing of Sorcha Ni Guarim (Folkways FW 861, *Traditional Irish Songs*). The Irish vocal tradition is really one of free form, like the free-form designs that modern ceramic and furniture designers like to experiment with. One might call it "imperiodic" rhythm, but the most important thing about it is the irregularity, and the completely unexpected time values.

Compared to Irish free form, German folklore tends to be geometrically proportioned; it may be either round, square, or triangular, but in the main, regular. We're not talking about dance music at the moment. In both countries this tends to be regular.

An interesting thing is, though, that in both countries (as in most European countries) there is a tendency for whatever rhythm the song has to be carried by the melody. When the melody stops, the rhythm stops. When the melody is picked up again, the rhythm picks up again. Again we're not talking about dance music, but songs.

How about Africa? There, it seems that any song can be danced to. True, singing and dancing are more closely related there than in Europe. But even in straight narrative singing, love songs, or lullabies, a steady tempo is usually maintained.*

In other words, an African song will have a geometric base, with a free-form overlay of melody on top of it. Not so free as the Irish, though, because it never loses its relationship to the rhythm.

The African song is like a drawing by David Stone Martin, in which he blurs his accurately representational outline by going over it again with another wiggle and a jiggle of a line.

The African melody may be behind the beat, before the beat, under it, over it, all around it, but less frequently right on top of it.

Nowadays we can listen to LP recordings—and appreciate the pure differences in various music idioms. But we can also appreciate the considerable achievement of American folk singers, who, through the generations, have taken the straightforward warmth of German folk songs, added some of the wild subtlety of Celtic vocalizing, and underlaid it all with the rocking African pulse. They have produced new music idioms for the world to hear. Of course, those that know and love the earlier and relatively purer traditions do not appreciate it. And I'm inclined to agree that it would be a pity if the modern hybrids should completely obliterate older strains, as in many countries they threaten to do. We treasure every variety of bird in our forests, and mourn the extinction of a species, such as the passenger pigeon. So also, until we have One World and perhaps one language, let us treasure each of our many languages; and let not a single one die; and let each be proudest of his own.

---

* See also pp. 141–44 above.

Fall 1958

Big Bill Is Gone

BIG BILL is gone. A great guitar picker, a great singer, a composer of over three hundred blues, and above all, a great person. He's gone to join the ranks of other legendary blues singers, such as Blind Lemon Jefferson and Huddie Ledbetter.

We shan't meet his like again. He was long, lean and relaxed. His voice could hit strong, clear, high notes that are usually only possible for far younger singers. He was in his early sixties in 1957 when a friend of his, a doctor in Chicago, told him he had cancer of the lung. He was operated on in July of that year and unfortunately the surgeon had to touch his vocal cords with the knife. Bill was never able to sing again, and could only talk with a hoarse whisper. Friends in Europe and America held concerts to raise money for him. In the spring of 1958 the cancer made its reappearance and during the summer he sank fast. On Friday, August 15, he was in an ambulance with his friend, the singer Win Stracke, when he died.

Bill was born in Mississippi and early knew hard work and poverty and Jim Crow. He used to say, "I am glad to say that I am from Mississippi and I mean *from* Mississippi." With hardly any formal schooling, he left farm life and got odd jobs in manual labor throughout the South. He once described how they used hammers when they were working on the railroad. They would shave the handles so thin that they were as flexible as a polo mallet. Two men would crouch on either side of the steel spike and whirl the hammers around, not over their heads but directly in front of them; right, down, left, up, right, down, left, up. The two hammers would hit the spike alternately, as quickly as five or six times a second.

After serving in World War I Bill came to Chicago, and in the 1920s emerged as one of the leading blues singers of the nation, along with people like Leroy Carr, Tampa Red, and Lonnie Johnson. Right up until the mid-forties his records sold widely in "Rhythm and Blues" catalogues of major recording companies. However, in the 1950s Bill was discouraged. He said that the people who used to buy his blues records were

Big Bill Broonzy and Pete in 1957

all grandparents now, and the young people were going for a different kind of music. Here's when he suddenly discovered a whole new audience of young people who were interested in folk music.

He went abroad and had a series of extraordinarily successful tours throughout Europe. He would usually tour with a traditional jazz band. During the concert, the band would take a break for half an hour while Bill would sing blues. He was on the threshold of a new era in his career when cancer cut him down.

Of course he will live on for many years in the memory of the friends who knew him and those who heard him sing. His records will be reissued and the book *Big Bill Blues** will be read and reread. There is also a fifteen-minute motion picture of him playing in a nightclub in Belgium.

Most of all, he will live on in the songs which he composed. Some of them will be sung for a few years and then forgotten. Others may be changed and added to. But perhaps thousands of years from now some young couple on a routine rocket flight through the galaxy will hum a snatch of some old folk song. In it will be a stanza or a phrase which (though they don't know it) was composed by Big Bill Broonzy. So there will be a little piece of Bill sailing on through the stars, through the ages.

1959

(CASTRO'S GUERRILLAS OVERTHROW CUBAN DICTATORSHIP. 25,000 ENTER TRA-FALGAR SQ., LONDON, AFTER 57-MILE NUCLEAR DISARMAMENT MARCH. U.S. LAUNCHES MISSILE-CARRYING SUBMARINE. KHRUSHCHEV AT UN CALLS FOR TOTAL DISARMAMENT IN 4 YEARS.
(JIMMY DRIFTWOOD'S "BATTLE OF NEW ORLEANS" A TOP HIT. NEW LOST CITY RAMBLERS RECORD PRESENTS CITY-BORN MUSICIANS PLAYING IN MOUNTAIN FOLK STYLE. SHERIFFS RAID INTERRACIAL HIGHLANDER FOLK SCHOOL IN TENNES-SEE. 13,000 ATTEND FOLK FESTIVAL AT NEWPORT. COLLEGE INSTRUCTOR VAN DOREN ADMITS TV QUIZ FAKING.)

Winter 1958–59

Welcome Back, Alan

ALAN LOMAX, considered by many to be America's foremost folklorist, has returned to the United States after nine years in England. He left the U.S.A. as an "enfant terrible," and he returns a legend. It is probably not an easy experience. Thomas Wolfe wrote a book *You Can't*

---

* *Big Bill Blues*, William Broonzy's story as told to Yannick Bruynoghe (Cassell & Co., England, 1955; Oak Publications, New York, 1964). The 1964 edition contains a 20-page discography; but, for a start, Folkways FA 2326 and FG 3586 include some of Bill's greatest songs and some of his comments on them.

Alan Lomax

Go Home Again. Why? Because homes change too, and when you return, home can be unrecognizable.

I welcome back Alan Lomax, not just because he is an old friend but also because, in my opinion, he is more responsible than any other single individual for the whole revival of interest in American folk music.

In the late 1930s Alan was put in charge of the Archive of American Folk Songs in the Library of Congress. He listened to tens of thousands of variants and versions of folk songs. With a keen sense for good melody and good poetry, he began selecting and combining the best of the best.

He taught Burl Ives and Josh White some of the best songs they know. He persuaded recording companies and radio networks to take a hesitant first step toward an idiom which most of America then scorned.

Well, of course the folk song revival did grow, and flourishes now like any happy weed, quite out of control of any person or party, right or left, purist or hybridist, romanticist or scientist. Alan Lomax probably looks about him a little aghast. We wish him well in his many projects and hope that we will be hearing from him. We think we will. He is not averse to speaking his mind.

Spring 1959

MY FRIEND Joe H—— is planning his master's thesis in folk-lore at the University of Indiana. "I plan to trace all known versions of 'Our Goodman,'" says he. This is the song many of us know by the title "Four Nights Drunk":

> I got home the other night, drunk as I could be;
> I spied a horse in the stable, where my horse ought to be.

I supposed that he would be poring through hundreds of different printed collections of folk songs of America, Scotland, England, and the rest of Europe. Who knows but what traces of the plot may show up in Africa or Asia, or among the Eskimos or Patagonians?

"The trouble is, Joe," I protested, "too much folklore research these days is done from paper, in libraries. Aren't you going to do any work out in the field?"

"Why, I may try to collect some versions of the song myself . . ."

"No, Joe, you don't understand what I mean. To really understand the situation whose recurrence prompts the continual re-creation of this ballad, you must set up a scientific experiment, to test the basic validity of the plot. You will have to locate a married man who has a habit of coming home drunk. Then you will have to interest his wife in the research project. The first night you must have your car in the man's garage. The next night your coat must be hanging on his coatrack, and so on. And you must take copious notes."

Joe considered the proposal. He wouldn't give a definite answer, but I could see he felt challenged by the scientific spirit. So if within the next few months you read headlines from Indiana: "Student shot in triangle," you will know that Joe is giving his all to the cause of scholarship.

"The MTA Song" was written in 1948 as a protest against a proposed fare increase in the Boston subway and, at the same time, as a campaign song for Walter F. O'Brien, the Progressive party candidate for mayor. The proposed increase set up a system whereby the passenger paid one fare upon entering the subway and an additional fare on leaving.

In 1957 Will Holt recorded the song almost exactly as Bess Hawes and Jackie Sharpe had written it. He made a real production out of it and the record company was pleased. They were going to make a hit record out of it; advance copies went out to about 10,000 disc jockeys.

Suddenly, after a week, comes word back from Boston.

"Hold on, do you know who this son of a bitch O'Brien is? They say vote for O'Brien."

"No."

"Well, let us tell you . . ."

Will had to redo the record without the fatal words "Vote for Walter O'Brien" in the next-to-last line—and it was distributed all over again.

THE MTA SONG

Words by Jacqueline Steiner Sharpe and Bess Hawes; tune, "The Ship That Never Returned." Copyright © 1956–57, Atlantic Music Corp., New York, New York.

* The chorus is often sung to the verse melody.

streets of Bos - ton, He's the man who nev - er re -

turned.   Char - lie,   turned. ____

2. Charlie handed in his dime at the Kendall Square Station,
   And he changed for Jamaica Plain.
   When he got there, the conductor told him one more nickel,
   Charlie couldn't get off that train.   (*Chorus*)

3. Now all night long, Charlie rides through the tunnel,
   Saying, "What will become of me?
   How can I afford to see my sister in Chelsea,
   Or my cousin in Roxbury?"   (*Chorus*)

4. Charlie's wife goes down to the Scollay Square Station,
   Every day at a quarter past two.
   And through the open window, she hands Charlie a sandwich,
   As the train comes rumblin' through.   (*Chorus*)

5. Now you citizens of Boston, don't you think it is a scandal,
   That the people have to pay and pay?
   Fight the fare increase, vote for Walter O'Brien;
   Get Charlie off the M.T.A.   (*Chorus*)

Fall 1959

Found: A Prolific New Songwriter

ERNIE MARRS is about thirty-one years old, a stonemason by trade. I met him last year in the small mountain town of Idyllwild, California, where he dropped in to see what the Idyllwild Folk Music Workshop was doing; he allowed as how he also liked to pick a guitar a bit and try to put together some rhymes.

In appearance and mannerism he resembled a cross between Woody

Guthrie and Will Rogers (though much more shy). His parents also came from Oklahoma.

Ernie's first love was for the poetry of Robert Burns. Another influence in his life was Jimmie Rodgers, the original Blue Yodeler, who recorded for Victor circa 1928–32. Many an evening Ernie would sit in the little 6′ x 14′ trailer that was his home and play country-music recordings, or read books and poetry, or more likely do some verse writing himself. The songs were on topics of the day, or about people he had known, or parodies of other songs. Occasionally he would follow Robby Burns's example and pen a long letter to a friend, in complete rhyme.

The songs were heard by friends in the local beanery or when Ernie helped entertain at a neighboring square dance. Now his songs may reach a wider audience, since this year he decided to cut out and see what was happening across the United States. *Sing Out* is privileged to be the first to publish a man who, we feel, has a great future as a writer of people's songs, in the tradition of Woody Guthrie, Joe Hill, Jimmie Rodgers, and Robert Burns.

On these pages is a sampling of the hundred-odd efforts turned out by him in the last eighteen months.

PLOP GOES THE MISSILE*

(*Words, E.M.; tune, "Pop Goes the Weasel"*)

This was written in early 1958. The recession was particularly hard on construction workers, and Ernie was out of a job at the time.

> Around and round the weary old world
> The muttnik chased the sputnik
> And Uncle Sam joined in the race,
> Built him a Pfffutnik.
> People came from near and far,
> Cameras did bristle;
> A flash of fire, a cloud of smoke!
> Plop! Goes the missile.
>
> Well, up goes one and up goes two
> And Uncle Sam relaxes
> Until he gets the bill, and then
> Up! Go the taxes.

* Copyright © 1972, Ernie Marrs.

Still he plays the same old tune,
Hopes the world will whistle.
We must have a *bigger* moon!
Plop! Goes the missile.

Unemployment hits the land,
Gone are smiles and cheering;
Beans on a lot of our plates
Are re-appearing.
No more fat, no more lean,
Just bone and gristle . . .
We need bread—but, instead,
"Plop!" Goes the missile.

Ernie says that it was an old tradition in his family to make up verses. His father did it. And he can remember his grandfather, also a man of strong opinions, playing a five-string banjo and singing:

Al Smith holds the bottle,
Raskob pulls the cork.
But they'll not reach the White House
From the sidewalks of New York.

Californians will appreciate a couple of Ernie's verses on one of their most pungent local problems:

TALKING SMOG BOWL*

Down in south Californ-i-ay
There's a town that's called L.A.
Where the smoke boils up and rolls around;
It likes the place so much it sticks around.

Some time back the radio said
The smog was green or the smog was red,
But the colored smog is gone today;
Investigators came this way:
They found it . . . a foreign element.

Standing on the street corner the other night
Watching some kids in a smogball fight,
When someone came from behind my back
And belted me with a smog blackjack,
Then he ran . . . he hadn't packed it quite hard enough.

The best verses on this situation Ernie put to the tune of Woody's "So Long, It's Been Good to Know You."

---

* Copyright © 1972, Ernie Marrs.

SMOGGY OLD SMOG*

> I've sung this song, and I'll sing it again
> Of a place that I wish that I never had been
> In old California, the town of L.A.,
> Here's what all of the people there say:
>
> *Chorus:*
>> So long, it's been good to know you   (*Repeat twice*)
>> The smoggy old smog is a-getting my home
>> And I got to be drifting along.
>
> When I hit town my eyes started to run
> There wasn't no sky and there wasn't no sun,
> Just a big yellow cloud that wandered along,
> And the folks were all coughing and choking this song: (*Chorus*)
>
> I went to a house and I knocked on the door,
> Hunting some folks I had known long before.
> The door it was bolted, the weeds was all dead,
> And the neighbors, they told me the last words they said, it was
>> (*Chorus*)
>
> I went to the depot and looked at the board;
> I wanted a ticket I couldn't afford.
> I talked and the ticket man listened and then
> A grin hit his face and he reached for his pen.
>
> He counted up all of the money he had,
> He wrote out a note which he gave to a lad.
> He made out a ticket, I think it said "Dover,"
> He said "Here's my pen and my job; *you* take over." And it's   (*Chorus*)
>
> A train pulled in with a roar and a shriek,
> Some big shot stepped out on the platform to speak,
> He opened his mouth and he choked on the gas;
> The smog did some good for the people at last, and it's   (*Chorus*)

Lest you think that all Ernie's verses are polemical, here is a sample from the verses he is always adding to songs he knows. The following is to be inserted in "The Frozen Logger":

> And when he went deer hunting
> He never fired a shell.
> He'd just pull off his logging boots
> And kill them with the smell.

---

* Copyright © 1972, Ernie Marrs.

But some of the best ones seem to have been written in a surge of indignation over some headline:

POPLARVILLE JAIL*

(*Words, E.M.; tune, "Cryderville Jail"*)

Poplarville Jail, it's no jail at all,
The sheriff hides out when the Klan comes to call,
And it's hard times in the Poplarville Jail,
Hard times, poor boy.

They caught Mack Parker, and accused him of raping,
Then left the jail open so he could be taken,
And it's hard times . . . , etc.

The law says we're equal, dark face or pale.
Was there ever a Klansman in the Poplarville Jail?
And it's hard times . . . , etc.

[Mack Parker was kidnaped from the Poplarville, Miss., jail, and lynched, in April 1959.]

The above are only fragmentary excerpts from his songs. The next is given complete. I sang it to 5,000 people at about 12:30 A.M. last July 11, near the end of one of the programs of the Newport Folk Festival.

THEY'LL BE PAID FOR BYE AND BYE*

(*Words, E.M.; tune, "What a Friend We Have in Jesus"*)

What a friend we have in Congress
Who will guard our every shore,
Spends three quarters of our taxes
Getting ready for a war,
Guns must make our coastline bristle,
And we have to fill the sky
Full of planes and guided missiles,
They'll be paid for bye and bye.

Have you heard of all the progress
In our mighty airborne fleet?
By the time a plane's adopted
It's already obsolete.
There's no factory profit, brother,
And we have to do or die,

---

* Copyright © 1972, Ernie Marrs.

One improvement, then another,
They'll be paid for bye and bye.

Have we trials, investigations?
There's subversion everywhere.
Careless words make complications;
Jail your thoughts and keep them there.
Listen only to our statesmen,
Close each wicked wondering eye,
Save our old traditional freedoms;
They'll be paid for bye and bye.

Modern bombs are sure to carry
Loads of glory, joy and thrills,
What a privilege to bury
All the dead our money kills,
Never mind the widows weeping,
Disregard the orphan's cry,
When God wakes the dead and sleeping
They'll be paid for bye and bye.

Ernie Marrs

Winter 1959–60

My Favorite Magazine Title of the Century

WHEN A YOUNG science-fiction writer named Lee Shaw became addicted to folk music four years ago, she devoted one of her occasional "fanzines" (fan magazines) to folk music. The response was so tremendous that she gave up everything to edit a folk song fan magazine, and called it *Caravan*. *Caravan* in turn was so popular that she found herself with the burdens of running a full-time office complete with telephone calls and bills to pay. So she cheerfully turned the magazine and its headaches over to Billy Faier and started out again with a mimeographed fanzine, as informal, as unexpected and irregular as she wanted. The name she picked: *Gardyloo*. Thereby hangs a tale.

The title is taken from some French words meaning "Look out for the water," which were shouted in eighteenth-century Scotland when people wanted to empty a bucket of slops out into the street.

Gardyloo! My nomination for the most charming name for a magazine.

I look forward to the day when:
   —It will be most unfashionable to try and be in fashion.
   —It will be considered most unoriginal to strive to be "original."
   —It will be thought rather old-fashioned to attempt to be "modern."

Thanks to the long efforts of Rockwell Kent and Walter Briehl, and the good progressive people who supported them in their two-year fight to force the U.S. State Department to grant them passports, the U.S. Supreme Court handed down a decision last year forbidding the State Department to arbitrarily deny passports to U.S. citizens. So thanks to all this, yours truly went last September to England and Scotland for two weeks. It was a thrilling experience; I met some fine people and learned some good songs. In the course of trying to explain my own country to them, I found I got a deeper insight into the character of our own past and present. Sang for 2,000 people in London, and concerts also in Liverpool, Birmingham and Glasgow.

In Glasgow I was baptized a Scot. Here's how. I wanted to demonstrate an axe-chopping song and bought a good axe (Britain is famous for fine-quality steel). One hour before the concert in Glasgow I needed to find a log, and hailed a cab. "Can you take me to the nearest park?" says I. "Surrrrre," says he, and off we got at a park near Glasgow University. There, near the banks of the small river Kelvin, I thought I saw in the dusk several logs, debris from dead trees which surely no one could miss. I stepped down onto what I thought was some level ground covered with dry leaves, and suddenly found myself chest deep in the river Kelvin. The leaves were simply floating on the surface. The cabdriver was most sympathetic, and hastened me back to the hall; I performed that night with no jacket, and with Jack Elliott's shoes on (I only travel with one pair).

If it is possible to be baptized a Scot, I am now baptized. I'll show them the log-chopping song another year.

In Liverpool I passed Paradise Street, famed in the song "Blow the Man Down" ("As I was a-walking down . . ."). It looked little different from any other street. No girls to be seen. But it was something to place a foot on hallowed ground. Or, as sailors said, the Holy Ground.

1960

(GREENSBORO, N.C., STUDENTS SIT-IN AT SEGREGATED LUNCH COUNTERS. SOUTH AFRICAN POLICE MASSACRE ANTI-APARTHEID DEMONSTRATORS AT SHARPEVILLE. CALIFORNIA STUDENTS HOSED AND BEATEN OUTSIDE HUAC HEARINGS. BELGIAN CONGO BECOMES INDEPENDENT. CHESSMAN CASE STIMULATES ANTI-CAPITAL PUNISHMENT CAMPAIGN.
($117,644 "PAYOLA" PARTY FOR DISC JOCKEYS EXPOSED IN CONGRESSIONAL HEARING. SINGING SCHOOLS HELP SOUTHERN VOTER REGISTRATION DRIVE. "SING OUT" CIRCULATION REACHES 5,000.)

February 1960

A fairy one night in Rangoon
Took a lesbian up to his room.
    They turned out the light,
    But they argued all night
Who'd do what and with which and to whom.

Here's an example of the screwy things that can happen when businessmen get involved with folk songs. In a music store last month I bought a folio published by Leeds Music, Inc., a well-known Broadway firm. It's called *Folklore for Guitar* and has some fine songs in it; I hope it sells well. But on page 35 I see to my surprise: " 'Follow the Drinking Gourd,' words and music by Peter Seeger," etc.

Of course, I had nothing to do with writing the song. I once helped make an arrangement of it for a quartet and accompanying instruments, and helped collect royalties from a record company which used this arrangement. But this arrangement is not the one used in the Leeds folio anyway.

I've written them to ask they reprint the book, or enclose an errata note.

I am proud of some of the songs I did help write; but this ain't one.*

Summer 1960

SUMMER is a-coming in. It looks as though there would be more folk festivals than ever before in the history of the country. East, west, south, north, and overseas as well.

While not wishing their backers any financial bad luck, let's hope there are lots of them, but not necessarily too large in size. In folk music, bigger does not perforce mean better.

Some of the best festivals this writer has seen have been such neighborly gatherings as the Camp Woodland Festival in the Catskill Mountains, where the campers supply half the program and local people supply the other half. No big stars, no outside talent. But the warmest, most neighborly swapping of songs, stories, and dances, and fiddling that one could ask for.

Set up a 50-foot stage, and have 5,000 or more seated in front of it eagerly looking forward to a show—I mean a Show—and you might as well realize that a lot of America's truest folk performers could not appear

---

* See also "The Copyright Hassle," p. 448 below. (The drinking-gourd song, of course, originated long before my time among the brave men and women of the pre-Civil War Underground Railroad, and lived on in black folk tradition.)

successfully. From beyond the tenth row no one would see the twinkle in the old ballad singer's eye, nor the grace of gnarled fingers on the fiddle strings. So who has to take over the show—I mean, Show? The seasoned performer, who with gestures and broad smiles and stage experience can project to the back rows.

This problem was also faced a few years ago when the International Folk Music Council had a huge folk festival in a stadium at Biarritz, France. The Yugoslavian dancers, with stamping and clapping, were the hit of the first day's program. The Balinese dancers were being just as artistic with lifting their little fingers, but to 95 percent of the audience they were just sitting still. Their "act" was a dud. Other performing groups took the hint, and on subsequent days one could see more hand-clapping and stamping thrown in, even where it was not traditional to do so. Folk performers like applause, too.

So this summer, there may be some fine big shows—but some of the finest may not necessarily be the biggest. Unless—and it's a $100,000 unless—somebody takes the gamble of putting it on television. And this is another chapter in the story. For the TV cameras *can* move in close, and can give you the twinkle in the old ballad singer's eye.

As a performer, yours truly does not have much of a voice, and there are plenty of young people who can play rings around me on guitar or banjo. But I'm proud that I've hardly ever met an audience I couldn't get singing. I figure my main function in life is that of a sort of catalyst, bringing some good people together with some good songs.

One of the only audiences I ever really failed with in this respect was, curiously enough, in Kansas City, where I sang a few years ago for the Art Institute. The problem there was that I was facing a lot of talented young people from farms and small towns of the Midwest who were eager to travel to New York and Paris and prove how modern they were.

When I sang "The Ballad of Jesse James" they looked at each other in confusion: "He's from New York? But he's singing what Uncle Jake does on the back porch, and we're ashamed of that."

I didn't get to first base. They refused to sing.

October 1960

The D-Day Dodgers

THE FOREMOST contemporary collector of Scottish ballads and folk songs is Hamish Henderson, of the School of Scottish Studies in Edinburgh. He is also a first-rate songwriter. Elsewhere in this issue is "MacPherson's Lament," a song he collected in Scotland. Scheduled for future publication are Hamish Henderson's wonderful World War II song "Farewell To Sicily" and other songs which he has collected. Below is Henderson's rewrite of a song widely sung by British troops in Italy during World War II. The tune is "Lili Marlene," a melody which seemed to fascinate soldiers on both sides of the line. Concerning the background of the song, a recent letter from Hamish Henderson tells us: "Many of the troops who had fought in Egypt and Libya also took part in the Italian campaign. Others (such as the 51st Highland Division) returned to Britain after the conquest of Sicily, to prepare for the D-Day of the Western Front, the invasion of France. Among the troops who remained in Italy, a curious piece of folklore began to circulate. This was that Lady Astor (bugbear and Aunt Sally of the British swaddies in the Middle East and elsewhere) had said in Parliament that the forces in Italy were 'D-Day Dodgers,' i.e., that they had funked returning home for fear of being carved up in the French invasion. The idea of this, needless to say, infuriated troops who had plenty of D-Days of their own (Sicily, Salerno, Anzio).

"The song of the 'D-Day Dodgers' consequently enjoyed an enormous vogue—with Lili Marlene and Lady Astor, it just couldn't fail!"

D-DAY DODGERS

We're the D-Day Dodgers, way off in Italy—
Always in the vino, always on the spree.
Eighth Army scroungers and our tanks,
We live in Rome, among the Yanks.
We are the D-Day Dodgers, in sunny Italy.   (*Repeat last line in each verse.*)

We landed in Salerno, a holiday with pay,
The Jerries brought the bands out to greet us on the way,
Showed us the sights and gave us tea,
We all sang songs, the beer was free,
To welcome D-Day Dodgers to sunny Italy.

Naples and Casino were taken in our stride,
We didn't go to fight there, we went just for the ride,
Anzio and Sangro were just names,
We only went to look for dames,
The artful D-Day Dodgers way out in Italy.

On the way to Florence we had a lovely time,
We ran a bus to Rimini, right through the Gothic Line;
Soon to Bologna we will go,
And after that we'll cross the Po;
We'll still be D-Day Dodgers way out in Italy.

Once we heard a rumor that we were going home,
Back to dear Old Blighty, never more to roam.
Then someone said, "In France you'll fight!"
We said, "No fear—we'll just sit tight!"
(The windy D-Day Dodgers, way out in Italy.)

We hope the 2nd Army will soon get home on leave;
After six months' service, it's time for their reprieve.
But we can carry on out here
Another two or three more years—
Contented D-Day Dodgers, to stay in Italy.

Dear Lady Astor, you think you're mighty hot,
Standing on the platform talking tommyrot,
You're England's sweetheart and her pride,
We think your mouth's too bleeding wide,
That's from your D-Day Dodgers in sunny Italy.

Look around the mountains in the mud and rain,
You'll find the scattered crosses, there's some which have no name,
Heartbreak and toil and pain all gone,
The boys beneath them slumber on,
Those are the D-Day Dodgers who'll stay in Italy.

More thoughts on the copyright situation: there is nothing really wrong with plagiarism except the dishonest claim to have created something which was really borrowed from another. If human beings didn't plagiarize, we would all still be living in caves.

December 1960

From Aldermaston to London

IRVING BERLIN, composer of "White Christmas" and dozens of other popular songs, was once asked, "What would be a good new subject to write a song about?" Peace, he is reported to have said, but it's a very hard thing to handle.

In England the subject doesn't seem hard to handle at all. As a result of the successful Aldermaston marches a rash of first-rate peace songs have made their appearance.

These four-day-long marches were initiated in 1958 by a few serious-minded intellectuals. They proposed a silent protest march to Aldermaston, the British H-Bomb center, from London—a 57-mile trip. They persuaded a few well-known people, including novelist J. B. Priestley and philosopher Bertrand Russell, to endorse it. Practically no group in the country gave it organized support. Some left-wingers said it was too much a middle-class intellectual affair. Some on the right accused the marchers of being traitors. But over 3,000 people turned out on the last day, mostly young adults. The early plan for a dignified silence was soon shattered by a skiffle band (washboard, washtub, guitar) breaking loose with "Study War No More." And who can walk four days in silence? The British magazine *Sing* offered its services, produced a song sheet and organized 40 singers.

The new hit song of the parade was "The H-Bomb's Thunder," by John Brunner, a young folk song enthusiast. (Early subscribers to *Caravan* magazine may remember his columns in it.) He used the tune "Miner's Lifeguard," which George Korson collected among Pennsylvania miners and which had earlier been a gospel hymn tune in Wales and America. Sing through his three verses and see how they must have struck home as only a direct topical song can.

> Don't you hear the H-Bomb's thunder*
> Echo like the crack of doom?
> While they rend the skies asunder
> Fall-out makes the earth a tomb.

---

* Copyright © 1972, John Brunner.

Do you want your homes to tumble,
Rise in smoke towards the sky?
Will you see your cities crumble?
Will you see your children die?

Chorus:
>Men and women, stand together;
>Do not heed the men of war.
>Make your mind up now or never,
>Ban the bomb forevermore.

Tell the leaders of the nations,
Make the whole wide world take heed,
Poison from the radiations
Strikes at every race and creed.
Must you put mankind in danger,
Murder folk in distant lands?
Will you bring death to a stranger,
Have his blood upon your hands?   (*Chorus*)

Shall we lay the world in ruin?
Only you can make the choice.
Stop and think of what you're doing;
Join the march and raise your voice.
Time is short; we must be speedy.
We can see the hungry filled;
House the homeless, help the needy.
Shall we blast, or shall we build?   (*Chorus*)

Eric Winter told me last fall that the initiators of the march were very leery of the London Youth Choir even participating. They wanted to know what songs would be sung and ruled out some as being "too left." But after the march was over, all agreed that the music and singing gave everyone just the spirit they needed.

John Foreman, another song leader, wrote me of his technique: "My method is to get at the front of the march, dive in, sell a dozen or so song-books in one spot, and then to teach the songs. The fact that I don't sing or play very well is a great help. When that group knows the bulk of the songs, I bail out and wait at the side for the next likely looking lot."

The 1958 march ended with between 3,000 and 4,000 arriving at Aldermaston. (The U.S.A.'s similar 1958 peace walk had 700 arriving at the UN Building.) The next year the organizers of the Aldermaston March purposely sought out song leaders like Winter and Foreman. It became a musical parade: choruses, jazz bands, bagpipers, steel bands. Folk dancers adapted their figures to the line of march. Thousands of song sheets passed from hand to hand till everyone knew by heart "The H-Bomb's Thunder" and other songs. The line of marchers (this time from Aldermaston to London) stretched for miles. Five thousand started. Four days later 25,000 entered Trafalgar Square.

Several new songs caught on in 1959. Again one used an American tune, "Buddy, Won't You Roll Down the Line," with new words by Ewan MacColl and Denise Keir.

> Want to hear the songbird's singing?
> Want to see the sun as well?
> We don't want no fusion bombs
> To blow us all to—hallelujah!
> We don't want our bodies
> Scattered all around
> We'd rather go on living
> With both feet upon the ground.
>
> *Chorus:*
> Brother, won't you join in the line?
> Brother, won't you join in the line? . . .

Among other good songs making their appearance in 1959 were "The Family of Man," "Strontium 90" and "Hey, Little Man" (tune: "Oh Sinner Man"), by Fred Dallas.

The 1960 march, according to the New York newspapers, topped all records. Marchers included Tories and Communists. 15,000 started it; nearly 100,000, including Bertrand Russell, joined it on the last day. Ewan MacColl and Peggy Seeger put new words to an old sea chanty, and literally hundreds of impromptu verses got added to it before the march ended.

> We're marching to Trafalgar Square
> Oh, yes, Oh!
> Today we're marching to declare
> That bomb has got to go!

Too many people think that a peace song needs to be humorless. The Aldermaston marchers certainly didn't appear of that opinion. One group of Quakers carried a large banner inscribed, "For Christ's sake, ban the bomb." And a well-known British poet and pacifist, Dr. Alex Comfort, author of *Letters from an Outpost* and many other books, is responsible for the following bit:

FIRST THINGS FIRST*

Words by Alex Comfort; music by John Hasted and Eric Winter

1. On the night of the Wemb-ley Cup Fin-al, ___ I had a most hor-ri-ble dream.___ I'd just been in-vit-ed to ___ play for U-nit-ed And Matt put me in-to the team. ___ Like a re-gu-lar he-ro I charged down the field, The goal lay wide o-pen a-head.___ The crowd bel-lowed shoot, I'd the ball on me boot, When the ref blew his whis-tle and said: ___ 2."Ban the bomb! It's the high-est pri-or-i-ty. ___

* Reprinted from *Sing* magazine.

(And then follow the first-stanza tune until ...)

... scrag old Mac - mill - stone in - stead." _____

2. ("Ban the bomb! It's the highest priority.)
    Don't stand there kicking that ball!
    If some bloody mutton should sit on the button
    There'll be no more soccer at all.
    O you who think nothing of scragging the ref
    Just get this idea in your head.
    The crowd that turns up when we play for the cup
    Could scrag old Macmillstone* instead."

3. Then I dreamed that I went to the Arctic
    Exploring the wastes on a sledge,
    And whenever some ass fell into a crevasse
    It was I pulled him back from the edge.
    The Queen was so thrilled when I planted the flag
    To the palace I quickly was called.
    She took out her sword to create me a lord
    When in marched a penguin and bawled:

4. "Ban the bomb! It's the highest priority.
    Someone should send for the cops.
    They're all flying sorties in thirties and forties
    Whenever a meteor drops.
    It once was so peaceful up there in the cold;
    Now the bombers are swarming like lice.
    Don't wait for some gupp to blow us all up;
    Let's put all the bastards on ice."

5. Then I dreamed I came home from a party
    To a flat with a beautiful blonde.
    I'd reason to hope and I thought I could cope,
    And her ways were familiar and fond.
    With feverish fingers I undid her hooks
    And bundled her on to the bed
    And I'd just reached the part where the asterisks start
    When she fluttered her eyelids and said:

6. "Ban the bomb! It's the highest priority.
    Then you can sample my charms.
    With those things above I can't settle to love
    And I don't want to die in your arms.

---

* Prime Minister Macmillan.

If anything slips you won't fancy my lips
And I shan't be worth taking to bed.
So don't mess around while we're still above ground
Let's do old Macmillstone instead."

While the above song might shock some peace-loving people, I think in general one could accept the principle that just as peace itself can only be achieved by the participation of many people of differing backgrounds, there will be peace songs of many different sorts. Some may be ardently anti-Wall Street. Others may be ardently religious. There is also the viewpoint to consider of a Quaker friend of mine. He believes that any good song about growing things—pigs, cows, and so on—is basically a peace song. Let's add lullabies to the list.

The lesson would seem to be that good songs grow naturally out of activity. There have been thousands of peace songs written in the U.S.A. during the fifteen years since World War II, but only a few seem to this singer to have hit the mark so squarely as these songs from Britain.

Postscript, Nov. 15, 1969: On this day half a million gathered in Washington, D.C., to protest the war in Vietnam. Songs and speeches alternated. For those present, it was one of the most moving days of their lives. The high point of the afternoon came, if I say so myself, when a short phrase from a record by Beatle John Lennon was started up by Brother Fred Kirkpatrick and me.

All we are say - ing   is   give peace a chance. *

Peter, Paul and Mary joined in, also song leader Mitch Miller, and soon hundreds of thousands were singing it over and over, swaying their bodies, flags, and signs from right to left in massive choreography. It was not as militant or forceful a song as will be needed, but it united that crowd as no speech or song had been able to all afternoon.

But perhaps the limited effectiveness of music was also proved. The President of the United States announced that he had purposely not listened, had watched a telecast football game instead that afternoon. The TV networks, cowed by the Vice-President's attacks, devoted a few minutes' attention to the demonstration, and did not mention it again. The CBS film footage was destroyed on orders from the top, so no more could be shown.

1961

(IMPRISONED EX-PREMIER LUMUMBA OF THE CONGO IS MURDERED. EISEN-HOWER WARNS AGAINST "UNWARRANTED INFLUENCE BY THE MILITARY-INDUS-TRIAL COMPLEX." FREEDOM RIDERS TRAVEL TO DESEGREGATE SOUTHERN BUS STATIONS. REVOLT IN ANGOLA, AFRICA, EXPOSES PORTUGUESE ATROCITIES. OF-FICER REBELLION AGAINST DE GAULLE'S ALGERIAN INDEPENDENCE PLAN FAILS. MASS ARRESTS OF CIVIL RIGHTS DEMONSTRATORS IN ALBANY, GA. EAST GER-MANY BUILDS "BERLIN WALL" TO CURB UNAUTHORIZED TRAVEL.
(FCC COMMISSIONER MINOW CALLS TV A "VAST WASTELAND." BAN ON WASH-INGTON SQ. FOLK SINGING REVERSED AFTER PROTEST DEMONSTRATION. FIRST U. OF CHICAGO FOLK FESTIVAL FEATURES COUNTRY SINGERS.)

January 1961

JIMMIE RODGERS, "The Yodeling Brakeman," sold four million records for Victor between 1928 and 1933, and died of T.B. The day before he died he had a last recording session, resting on a cot between takes.

A man once told me in a Montana saloon, "The reason I like Jimmie Rodgers is everything he sings is true"—the highest praise a folk singer could ever have. "T.B. Blues" is one of the hundreds of yodeling bluesy songs Jimmie wrote. (Others are "All Around the Water Tank Waiting for a Train," "Way Out on the Mountain," "Good Morning, Captain," "T for Texas.")

T. B. BLUES

Words and music by Jimmie Rodgers. Copyright 1931, Peer International Corp. Copyright renewed, Peer International Corp. Used by permission.

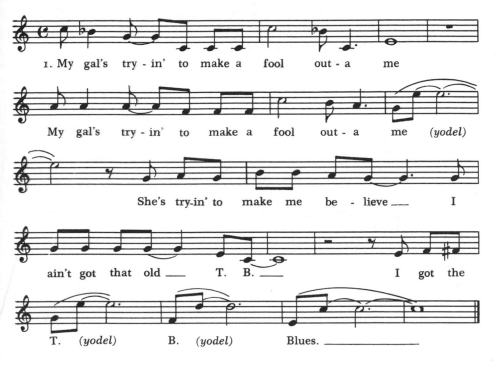

1. My gal's try-in' to make a fool out-a me
My gal's try-in' to make a fool out-a me (yodel)
She's try-in' to make me be - lieve ____ I
ain't got that old ____ T. B. ____ I got the
T. (yodel) B. (yodel) Blues. ____

2. Well, I'm fighting like a lion, but I know I'm bound to lose   (Repeat)
   'Cause there never was a body whipped these old T.B. Blues.
     I got the T.— — B.— — Blues.

3. When it rained down sorrows, it rained all over me   (Repeat)
   'Cause my body rattles like a freight on the old S.P.
     I got the T.— — B.— — Blues.

I've met many a frustrated songwriter who feels that after years of effort hardly any song they've ever written has been used. I try and cheer them up by pointing out that some of the world's greatest songwriters, such as Burns, Shevchenko, Thomas Moore, or Stephen Foster, end up by only having a scant handful of songs which really outlast their generation. "This is encouragement?" they answer.

Songwriters do have a hard row to hoe. Every new song, in a sense, is in competition with all the best old songs that a singer knows already. It's up against the stiffest competition in the world.

A painter once complained to me: "Scientists have it easy. They can build their work upon all the investigations that have been done already in their field. (A dwarf on a giant's shoulders can see farther than the giant.) But an artist is expected to do different or better. There is no sense trying to improve on Michelangelo's muscles, if he's already pictured them better than anyone else can."

He's got a point. But I'm not sure I agree with him all the way. Too many pursue the Great God Originality. In a sense, with our use of folk music, we *are* building on the work of many others.*

The following are the verses to the hymn "Amazing Grace," as sung in Choctaw:

> Shilombish *h*oli *t*opa *ma*
> Isht *minti* pullah *cha*
> Ha*tak* il *busha* pia *ka*
> Isht *pia* yuk *pul* ish *keh*

It was given me by an Oklahoma schoolteacher. The same person told me that the American "O.K." was originally the Choctaw "hokay" meaning "all right." Andrew Jackson was supposed to have been the first person who used it, signing papers with the two letters, O and K.

May 1961

Another Plug for the Songwriting Profession

IN TIMES OF UNREST or repression, the difficulties of getting a play produced, or an opera or symphony performed, seem almost insuperable even for seasoned professionals, not to speak of struggling amateurs. Therefore once again I urge writers and musicians to concentrate on shorter forms—specifically, one song, or a group of songs around a sub-

---

* Cooks are the luckiest artists. Their past efforts do not linger to haunt them.

ject. Songs can be memorized when printing is difficult. Songs can go places and do things and cross borders which people cannot.

Another big advantage of writing songs rather than longer forms: critics don't bother reviewing songs. Thus many a new song has not been snipped in the bud, but has been allowed to grow and grow.

There is a time for criticizing and a time for creating. One of the best writers I know has never gotten a book to press because he was such a good critic. Every time he took a page out of the typewriter he could think of a dozen reasons it should be improved.

Fortunately Love Is Blind, and the human race continues to create new babies—including baby artists and critics.

Atilla

ATILLA THE HUN is in the hospital. Let me explain. If you like Calypso songs, you have probably heard of Atilla the Hun, composer of "The Commissioner's Report," "The Guardian Beauty Contest," and scores of other top-notch satirical songs during the past thirty years. He ran for office in the Trinidad Legislature some years back and was elected and re-elected several times in a row. At one time the colonial government would have liked to jail him, we suspect, for his outspoken songs, but they didn't attempt it. "I could have been re-elected without making one campaign speech," remarked Atilla dryly.

He had a heart attack a couple of years ago, however, and has been in the hospital most of the last year. Now his money is gone. It occurred to me that if those of his admirers who read this paragraph would send a letter—and perhaps something—it would cheer him up a lot. Address: Atilla (Hon. Raymond Quevedo), 121 Eastern Main Road, Barataria, Trinidad, Federation of the West Indies.

Summer 1961

LAST YEAR in my review of *Songs of Work and Freedom,* by Edith Fowke and Joe Glazer, I expressed regret that Maurice Sugar, the Detroit labor attorney, had not been credited with authorship of "The

Soup Song." Since then, investigation has brought to light the person responsible for the error—it is none other than . . . *myself*. In the *People's Songs Bulletin* of 1947 and the *People's Songbook* of 1948 we credited Sugar with writing the song during the sit-down strikes of 1937. But Joe Glazer had a 1934 workers' songbook where authorship of it was credited to "unemployed workers."

The fact is, we now find out, it was written in 1931 by Sugar, who was not an unemployed worker but a much-employed if underpaid young lawyer. Since it is still as good a song as ever, we give the verses once again.

THE SOUP SONG

Words by Maurice Sugar; tune, "My Bonnie Lies Over the Ocean"

I'm spending my nights at the flophouse;
I'm spending my days on the street.
I'm looking for work and I find none;
I wish I had something to eat.

> Sooo-oup, sooo-oup, they give me a bowl of sooo-oup,
> Sooo-oup, sooo-oup, they give me a bowl of soup.

I slaved twenty years in the factory;
I did everything I was told.
They said I was loyal and faithful,
Now, even before I get old,   (*Repeat refrain*)

I saved fifteen bucks with my banker
To buy me a car and a yacht,
I went down to draw out my fortune
And this is the answer I got: (*Repeat refrain*)

I fought in the war for my country;
I went out to bleed and to die.
I thought that my country would help me,
But this was my country's reply: (*Repeat refrain*)

At that time the author withheld from publication another verse "out of consideration for what I felt would be the sensitivities of some workers . . ."

> I went on my knees to my Maker,
> I prayed every night to the Lord,
> I vowed I'd be meek and submissive,
> And now I've received my reward.   (*Repeat refrain*)

October 1961

The Theory of Cultural Guerrilla Tactics

WHEN THE NAZIS overran the other nations of Europe, those who opposed them had several possible choices of action. Some foolhardy young ones said:

"I'm going down and throw a hand grenade at the first Nazi truck I see. I may get killed, but I'll do something. I won't stand by and let them take over our country."

And they did this, and they were killed, and it was the last of their contribution against Nazism. Certain more cautious citizens took the opposite stand:

"The thing to do is get some groceries and hole up somewhere. There is no sense in getting killed yet. When the liberating armies appear, we'll emerge to help them."

But rarely did these live to see liberation either. Because they stayed in the same place, sooner or later they were discovered by the Nazis, captured, and executed.

Those who not only stood the best chance of living to see liberation, as well as consistently doing the most to harass the Nazis, were those who kept *mobility*. It took coolness and self-control. They picked their own battles, and always selected limited engagements which they could win. Since they had no reserves to call upon, they could not capture a town and hold it for more than a short while. But over the country as a whole, these thousands of isolated guerrillas did tremendous damage to the Nazis. In Yugoslavia a whole division of Nazis troops, which Hitler badly needed elsewhere, was tied down.

It may seem a farfetched comparison, but for many years I figured I pursued a theory of cultural guerrilla tactics. I could not hold a steady job on a single radio or TV station. But I could appear as guest on a thousand and one disc jockey shows, say a few words while they played a few records. I could not hold down a job at the average college or university, but I could appear to sing some songs, and then be on my way. I kept as home base this one sector of our society which refused to knuckle under to the witch-hunters: college students. Now, I figure, most of my job is done. The young people who have learned songs from me are taking them to thousands of places where I myself could never expect to go. Though I cannot get on network TV, many of my friends do. Though I cannot get a job in a university, those whom I have helped get interested in folk music are getting them.

But even more important are the literally hundreds of thousands of amateur guitar pickers and banjo pickers—and each has an important job. Like fireflies they light up the night. Or maybe I should compare them to a more potent insect. Once a white politician told Sojourner Truth, the black abolitionist leader:

"Woman, I care no more for you than a mosquito."
"Maybe so," she said, "but, praise God, I'll keep you scratching."

Eight years ago I first fell in love with the music of steel drums. I went to Trinidad and made a short movie on the technique of making them, certain that within a year the drums would be sweeping the U.S.A. in some sort of musical revolution. I was an abortive revolutionist. No one could figure out how to make them and keep them in tune. This year an instruction booklet comes off the press. Let's see what reaction it gets.

Of course, many will not like steel drums. Some will simply want to get to sleep and be willing to wring the neck of the person who spread the idea.

Others feel that the U.S.A. already has enough hybrids in its musical garden. Alan Lomax told me, "Look at the English sparrow! Look at crabgrass!"

1962

(ISRAEL HANGS EICHMANN FOR ORGANIZING NAZI DEATH TRAINS. RACHEL CARSON'S "THE SILENT SPRING" EXPOSES DDT DANGERS. JAMES MEREDITH BECOMES FIRST NEGRO AT U. OF MISSISSIPPI. WAR THREATENS OVER RUSSIAN MISSILES IN CUBA. STUDENTS FOR A DEMOCRATIC SOCIETY, IN PORT HURON STATEMENT, ADVOCATE "PARTICIPATORY DEMOCRACY." CHINESE TROOPS WITHDRAW AFTER BRIEF OFFENSIVE AT DISPUTED INDIAN BORDER. "WOMEN STRIKE FOR PEACE" LEADER QUESTIONED BY UN-AMERICAN ACTIVITIES COMMITTEE.
("THE TWIST" DANCE SWEEPS COUNTRY. JOHN FAULK WINS DAMAGES FROM

RADIO-TV BLACKLISTERS. BROADSIDE MAGAZINE'S FIRST 18 ISSUES PRESENT NEARLY 100 NEW TOPICAL SONGS INCLUDING FIRST PUBLISHED BOB DYLAN SONGS.)

January 1962

Fable

ONCE UPON A TIME there was a young man named Sam. He was poor but ambitious. He announced to the whole town that By God he was going to Get Somewhere and Make Something of Himself. The old, established families in town, that usually controlled things, said, "Well now, if he gets a little culture and education we might admit him to our society." But Sam said, "Bedamn your culture; just because a man is dirty and poor and ignorant is no reason he isn't entitled to as many of the good things of life as anyone else. It's hard work that counts," said Sam, and he rolled up his sleeves and set out to prove it.

As the years passed he did prove it. He got things done, even if he was sometimes a little rough about it, and if someone stood in his way he wasn't gentle about pushing them aside. Came the day when the old, established families not only had to Admit Him to Their Society, but acknowledge that he really was the Top Man in Town. No doubt about it. A good number of townspeople were working for him.

By now he was a few years older, and there were other young ambitious men coming along, like he had been once. Sam didn't like their pushing, and he told 'em so. They started quoting back to him some of the very things he himself had said when he was young. Sam got mad and said, "Don't you start saying those words to me—I'm the man that knew what they mean. You don't even understand 'em." The situation was getting pretty tense, and fighting might have broken out, but some of Sam's own family intervened and said to him, "Uncle, those words you said when you were young *were* right, and unless you act like you believe in them again we're not going to support you."

"Traitors in my own house!" roared Sam, but he found that unless he had people on his own side he was helpless, unless he wanted to blow up the whole town and himself with it. He had enough TNT in his warehouse to do just that, and I think the thought must have passed through his mind. But it was those early words he said when he was young that gave him pause.

Now you know the title of this fable—The Story of Uncle Sam.

March 1962

MY WIFE AND I spent five weeks in Great Britain last fall. We rented a small English car, learned how to drive on the left, and covered 3,000 miles of winding roads. Met thousands of warmhearted people, and heard a lot of good music. We covered expenses by my singing in a variety of places, from small pubs to concert halls with large audiences (2,200 in Glasgow, 4,000 in London's Albert Hall).

Although we didn't have time to do any conventional sightseeing, we found what a tremendously varied country it is, from the crowded Midlands, to the smoky valleys of Wales, through the high wind-swept moorlands, to the rocky coasts of Scotland. And the people, the language, the architecture also were more varied in many ways than in our own much larger land.

There are about sixty* "folk song clubs" in Britain. A typical one would get started when four or five singers and their friends find they need a bigger room and a regular gathering place. They'll rent a room one evening a week, upstairs over a local pub, decide on a name for themselves, and advertise their existence to the general public. Two shillings (28 cents) for a membership card, and two shillings to spend an evening. Add sixpence (7 cents U.S.) for a large glass of strong English beer, sent up from below. The music will vary according to the tastes of the founders. Two years ago there was still a lot of imitation American singing. Nowadays you'll find a lot more appreciation of English, Scottish, and Irish songs.

The most striking thing about the whole English scene, and one that filled this singer with envy, was the large number of really first-rate songs being made up—which seemed to grow so naturally out of their older traditions that there was no sharp break between the newer and older songs. Here in America our new songs are either strictly fly-by-night satirical, or sentimental, or flat-footedly earnest. There, the best songs, like those of Woody Guthrie, seemed to capture glints of humor in the middle of tragedy. Seriousness and banter all rolled into one. They set

* In 1969, over 700.

a high mark for us to aim at, and perhaps we can learn something from them on how to compose a good song.

Mays Landing, N.J.

Dear Editor:

Folk song is all right in its place in the music of Bartók, Shostakovich, Charles Ives, but what is this rage among millions for the songs our forefathers created out of their immediate experience?

And what are city people today thinking of as they go bohemian and twang out cowboy ditties? Hearing these long-drawn-out echoes, I feel as if rural idiocy had been elevated into a national cult.

I grew up thinking Joplin's "Maple Leaf Rag" or Handy's "Beale Street Blues" were on the same level as Schubert's lieder. I participated in the folk-song revival in the days when Woody Guthrie, Josh White, Pete Seeger and the Almanacs were part of a great upsurge among millions of people—in the organizing days of the CIO and the New Deal.

I don't think anyone should be jailed for the yodeling that is now being perpetrated in game cellars, coffee houses and campuses. I will even admit that the current madness for guitars and their dominants and subdominants is superior to other forms of juvenile terrorism.

I do want to dissociate myself from this nostalgic attempt to treat as youthful, avant-garde art—in the Space Age—this musical counterpart of candlelight and whale fishing. I wonder if it isn't an escape from the effort to reflect in contemporary forms, such as modern jazz or verse, the true beat of our own sophisticated and urban shellshock?

Are we going back to Grieg? Or are we going to try and keep up with Bach?

I dread this civilization going to glory singing "Jingle Bells" in unison. Give me Billie Holiday—or give me silence.

WALTER LOWENFELS

The editors of *Sing Out* are always trying to goad the readers into action. Or at least into alarm. But, sadly, no one tried to reply to Walter Lowenfels' stimulating letter. So I'll try:

Walter, would you advise, "Give me Shakespeare or give me a blank piece of paper—"?

I agree: our song sessions should have more contemporary bite. But until you poets write better poetry, we're going to continue mostly singing the old. And often the old song will flash out a new meaning as fresh as today's atomic tragedies.

> "God gave Noah the rainbow sign.
> No more water, but fire next time."

What have you got to beat that, Walter?

One of the surest ways a city singer can betray a tradition is by tacking a fancy ending on the end of a beautifully simple folk song. Putting a music-hall flourish to the last line of an old ballad is like tacking a garish nylon fringe around the edge of a rough Navaho Indian blanket.

Whitman once said, "Great art demands great audiences." The demands of an audience help shape and improve the art. More appreciative eaters make for better cooks. And vice virtue.

Artists can also shape and build audiences, as twenty years of New York hootenannies built up an audience for folk music in New York City. Ideally, there should be a constant interplay, action and reaction, between artist and audience. This is why folk singers are so much luckier than novelists and sculptors.

I used to make the mistake of trying to give long introductions to songs, hoping thus to help everyone understand all the facets of meaning. But more often than not it killed the song. Nowadays I'm more likely just to shoot out a batch of tunes. Some may find them merely diverting melodies. Others may find them incitements to red revolution. And who will say if either, or both, is wrong? Not I.

May 1962

Chicago, Illinois

Dear Editor:

This is written by a lover of music, and one who is somewhat sad and angry at the moment. There are so few good publications these days which deal seriously with the revival and distribution of the wonderful old songs which the people of times past used to sing. The words "something should be done" have been uttered by many people.

Your magazine has been a good example of the attempt to communicate a certain type of music to those of us who are unable to find the time to dig it out ourselves. You refer to this music as the "people's music" or "folk music." The definition of these terms is perhaps more understood than stated, but I think you will agree that it encompasses the music of all the people and not merely that of the laboring groups or of the socialistic party groups. It is to the manifestation of this type of music almost exclusively in your magazine that I object. The dissemination of political ideas and propaganda is one thing, and the printing of folk songs is definitely another. Many times these two fields cross, but not, I believe, with the frequency and intention which you portray in your magazine.

Possibly the magazine market is bigger these days for political ideas than it is for folk music. In this regard I do not condemn what you print. But might I remind you that the historian's point of view, and that of the musicologist, is one of objectivity. The music lover's point of view may be both objective and subjective; it is his realm to decide what music he likes to sing and hear. Therefore, might I kindly ask you to print a more representative cross section of the people's music you are aware exists and not constantly portray your own subjective political feelings.

Sincerely,
PETER GENTLING

Dear Mr. Gentling:

I think it is important that *Sing Out* print various opinions, and if you will examine various issues and compare them with the songs printed in any other magazine, I think you will agree that we have printed a wider range of opinions and music than any other magazine in the country.

We've had religious songs and antireligious songs. We've had songs of different religions—Jewish and Christian, and

Moslem for that matter. Can you think of another magazine which has done this? We have had union songs and we've had songs poking fun at unions and take-offs on people who sing union songs. We've had marching songs and peace songs. We've had songs praising love and songs satirizing love, praising marriage and satirizing marriage, drinking songs and prohibitionist songs. Can you think of a single other magazine which has done this?

I grant you that it's every human being's purpose and duty to try and get at the objective truth, and yet in all honesty I think you would agree that there's no such thing as perfect objectivity. Even if you try to represent all the opinions of the human race, you would still be leaving out the opinions of the animals which most of us eat in order to stay alive. Don't think I'm joking; I'm not. There is no such thing as pure objectivity, not even in a photograph, because, after all, someone had to aim that camera at a certain place instead of another, and when he made the choice he was being subjective, not objective. There is no college textbook in any science I know of which is completely objective. The only fair thing to do is to let everybody know what your opinions are, so that they may know how many grains of salt to use when they listen to you. This I believe *Sing Out* does, and this I believe makes it a much more fair magazine than many other publications which pretend to be objective but are really not.

I suppose if we left out of the magazine some of the various peace songs and union songs (you call them "socialistic") then you would be happier, but frankly it would no longer be such a fair or broad magazine. Our general theory is to throw as many songs as we are possibly able to do out into the public air, so to speak, and let the people choose which they think are good and which they think are bad. What method can you think of which would be any more democratic than that?

Sincerely,

PETER SEEGER

(for the editorial board of *Sing Out*)*

---

* 1969. This was too long a letter. I should have simply answered, "The dissemination of political ideas and the printing of folk songs are *not* two separate things. They overlap and intertwine and have done so for centuries."

It is only in recent years that the Folk Process has been thought to have *improved* songs. For generations the accepted view among folk-lorists was that folk songs were simply degenerated versions of composed songs. Thus by this theory, the older the version, the Better Art. But here is an actual example of how the Folk Process does improve a song. A few years ago in Nevada I met Curly Fletcher, who in 1919 composed the song "Strawberry Roan."* His first verse, the exact words he wrote, started thus:

> I was hanging around town, just spending my time,
> Out of a job without even a dime.

In 1940, in a Montana saloon, I was taught these two lines:

> I was laying 'round town, just spending my time,
> Nothing else to spend, not even a dime.

Somewhere along the line an anonymous folk singer improved the verse. The whole lesson of folk music: the genius of a few is not so important as the genius (and honesty) of the many.

"Why are you guys scared to be serious?" Woody Guthrie once asked some of us who were sitting around trying to make clever parodies for a political campaign.

This same question should be directed to some of the commercially successful "folk song" groups now traveling the country. They have a suspicious inability to sing a song straight. Many of them can actually do a very good job as far as singing goes, but at some point in the song they have to louse it up just to let the audience know they are not so naïve as to take it seriously.

It is like Casanova kissing a girl, and then breaking wind to let her know he is not taking her too seriously.

Quote for the day:

"The expert avoids all the little errors on his way to the big fallacy." (Anon.)

---

* By Fred Howard, Nat Vincent and Curly Fletcher. Copyright 1931 Vincent, Howard, and Preeman. Copyright renewed, Southern Music Co., Inc. Used by permission.

Summer 1962

"*Why Do You Guys Publish So Much Rubbish?*"

I ASKED a Tin Pan Alley friend recently why so much rubbish was published. "You're always prattling about democracy," he needled me back. "And yet you're always running down the Hit Parade. How come? What could be more democratic than the way a hit is selected?—Requests to disc jockeys, sales to ordinary people of discs and sheet music, and nickels in jukeboxes."

"Well," I rejoined, trying to think hastily, "look at the limited type of candidates you put up to be voted on. What kind of an election do you call that, when I can only vote between 'Ibba Bibba Boo' and 'My Rocky Socky Baby'?"

"Aw, come now, do you really think that Beethoven's Ninth would stand a chance of earning nickels in a jukebox? Or even the 'Ballad of Lord Randall'?"

"No, but that's because you've discouraged anyone from voting along that line. Look at your limited electorate. It's not the Hit Parade, it's the Kiddie Parade. You might as well say you have a fair election in Mississippi, with a small fraction of the people voting for a restricted list of candidates. Or in the UN, where a quarter of mankind is not even represented. Or a national election between Tweedledum and Tweedledee."

"So, you really think that Beethoven's Ninth and Lord Randall would be on the Hit Parade if they were only given a chance? How can you kid yourself so? The average man doesn't have the sense to appreciate good music. How many in the U.S. listen to FM stations? They could if they wanted."

"Well, I'll concede that maybe the Hit Parade wouldn't change overnight. But at least it would stand a chance of changing. As a matter of fact, the FM audience is growing and the Hit Parade is shrinking. Tin Pan Alley has been crying the blues for ten years, hasn't it? But my main disagreement with you is when you say that the average man doesn't have the sense to appreciate good music. You rule out the possibility of human nature and taste changing."

"What do you want me to do?"

"Give minority tastes more of a chance. How can you call it democratic when minorities are ruled off the ballot? Even if certain songs never get to be 'Hits' (ugh!), American music would be richer for the variety—just as American politics was once richer for the radicals in it. Give the minorities a chance."

"So you want me to publish and record stuff that won't sell? How do you think I'm going to stay in business?"

"All right, all right. We're back where we started. I guess it's up to people who have no financial interest at stake to improve American music. And politics."

What happens to the promising young girl singers one sees for a while, and then no more? One of two things: either they get married, and despite our much-vaunted equality of the sexes, find it impossible to continue a singing "career" while raising a family, or else they get caught in "The Trap of Sweet Sixteen."

This trap results from the convention that a woman should try not to mature and grow old, but should remain always young, fresh, and girlishly innocent. When the girl really is sweet sixteen, she can often take your breath away by her songs. But if she tries to continue to sing in exactly the same fashion for another ten or twenty years, it will start wearing thin. Eventually her audience won't put up with the sham any more.

Those women who manage to last many years as singers are those who develop a wholesome, full-bodied maturity. Look at Ella Fitzgerald, Mahalia Jackson.

New Songs from Britain

ANY FOOL CAN WRITE a poor song, but it takes considerable truth and skill (and a little luck) to write one good enough for listeners to want to memorize and hand it on to others. Only a handful of songs in each generation outlast their times. These are the songs you can live and grow with, and as you learn more about life they mean more to you.

I present here some new songs which I ran across in England and Scotland when touring there last fall. They all stand up well by themselves as songs; that is, they paint a picture, or tell a story. The humor is not merely flippant, but contains hints of tragedy, as is true of all the world's greatest humor. The sadness is not merely sentimentality, but has a realistic bite. The editorializing or moralizing is never forced, but inserted just to heighten a point already made. In other words, it is a natural part of the song.

Picture now a crowded room upstairs above a pub in Liverpool. The Spinners Club is having its weekly songfest. A hundred voices give out with the chorus of what has practically become their theme song. Tune and verses were written by a Liverpudlian, Stan Kelly:

> I wish I was back in Liverpool,*
> Liverpool town where I was born!
> Where there ain't no trees, no scented breeze,
> No fields of waving corn.
> But there's lots of girls with peroxide curls,
> And the black and tan flows free.
> We're six in the bed by the old pier head,
> And it's Liverpool town for me!

The Spinners, three men and a girl, with guitars and banjo, sing a variety of old and new songs and then introduce some guest singers. One is a man in his fifties, with bushy gray beard, bald head, and twinkling eyes like Santa Claus. His name is Leslie Haworth. I found out later that he is a fruit farmer from Cheshire, and comes in religiously to the Spinners Club every Friday evening; he is famous for long ballads with umpteen verses. I could imagine him striding between his rows of apple and pear trees singing verse after verse to himself. He now sings his own reworking of the old "Froggie Went A-Courting," completely unaccompanied; it has a leisurely pace, and when you get into it, you haven't the slightest desire for it ever to stop.

HERE'S TO CHESHIRE

New words and new music adaptation by Leslie Haworth. TRO-© copyright 1962, 1964, Melody Trails, Inc., New York, New York. Used by permission.

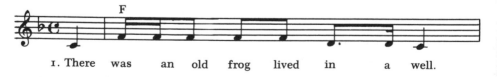

1. There was an old frog lived in a well.

---

* Words by Stan Kelly, tune by Leon Rosselson. Copyright © 1964, Heathside Music.

2. Froggie went a-courting and he did ride.
    Ding, Dang, Dong go the wedding bells.
   Now Miss Mousie you must decide.
    Ding, Dang, Dong go the wedding bells.

   (*Repeat chorus after each verse.*)

3. Oh, I am rich and I am brave.
    Ding, Dang, Dong, etc.
   What better husband could you have?
    Ding, Dang, Dong, etc.

4. Oh I'd never take your word for that . . .
   You'll have to satisfy Uncle Rat . . .

  5. Said Uncle Rat I'm much afraid . . .
     If you don't take froggie you'll die an old maid . . .

  6. The knot was tied secure and fast . . .
     She's off her uncle's hands at last . . .

  7. Tune up the fiddles and let's have a square . . .
     Top couple must be the happy pair . . .

  8. Open the oysters, spill the champagne . . .
     Never will there be such a feast again . . .

  9. But as they were going it hot and strong . . .
     The good gray cat comes prowling along . . .

 10. She sprang through the window right out of the yard . . .
     Didn't bring no invitation card . . .

 11. Uncle Rat like a hero stood . . .
     Puss wet her whiskers in his blood . . .

 12. Miss Mousie made a dive for a crack . . .
     Puss made a bounce and broke her back . . .

 13. And where was the valiant frog the while? . . .
     He just about broke the four-minute mile . . .

 14. He came to a brook and he didn't stop to look . . .
     The old Drake nabbed him in his fluke . . .

 15. This was the end of him and her . . .
     There won't be no tadpoles covered in fur . . .

Some of Leslie Haworth's other songs are "The Ascent of Everest" and various modern translations of old ballads. His "Tiger Gordon" remakes an old border ballad: the fast horse of the lord becomes a jet plane; the magical ring becomes a transistor radio; interclan rivalries become the racial tensions in a modern English city. (*Spin* magazine, 34, Thirlmere Drive, Wallasey, Cheshire, England, is his publisher.)

Next, a song from Ewan MacColl: this has proved itself good enough to be sung by the men on the fishing boats, about whom the song was composed. There could be no higher praise. Ewan has been writing songs now for thirty years. One, which he composed when a member of a teen-age hiking club, has had dozens of new verses written to it, and

is generally thought by this generation of hikers to be simply another
old folk song:

> I'm a rambler, I'm a rambler, from Manchester way;*
> I get all my pleasure the high moorland way.
> I may be a wage slave on Monday,
> But I am a free man on Sunday.

The song we print here was first made up in 1961 for one of the half-
hour BBC radio ballads, a documentary on the herring industry of Britain,
called "Sing the Fishing." The words of many of the verses were taken
right out of the tape-recorded words of an old fisherman named Sam
Larner, who described his career, starting off when he was a cabin boy.

SHOALS OF HERRING

By Ewan MacColl. Copyright © 1962, Stormking Music, Inc. All
rights reserved. Used by permission.

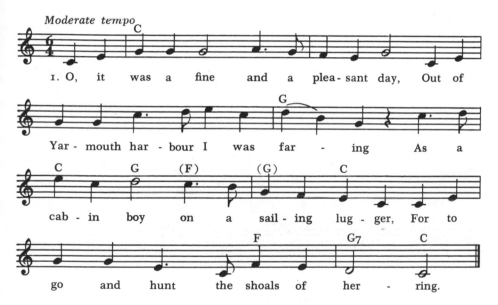

Moderate tempo

1. O, it was a fine and a plea-sant day, Out of
Yar-mouth har-bour I was far - ing As a
cab - in boy on a sail-ing lug - ger, For to
go and hunt the shoals of her - ring.

2. O, the work was hard and the hours were long,
   And the treatment, sure, it took some bearing,
   There was little kindness and the kicks were many
   As we hunted for the shoals of herring.

3. O, we finished the Swarth and the Broken Bank,
   I was cook and I'd a quarter-sharing,
   And I used to sleep, standing on me feet,
   And I'd dream about the shoals of herring.

4. O, we left the home grounds in the month of June,
   And to canny Shiels we soon was bearing,
   With a hundred cran of the silver darlings
   That we'd taken from the shoals of herring.

5. Now you're up on deck, you're a fisherman,
   You can swear and show a manly bearing,
   Take your turn on watch with the other fellows
   While you're searching for the shoals of herring.

6. In the stormy seas and the living gales,
   Just to earn your daily bread you're daring,
   From the Dover Straits to the Faroe Islands,
   As you're following the shoals of herring.

7. O, I earned me keep and I paid me way,
   And I earned the gear that I was wearing,
   Sailed a million miles, caught ten million fishes,
   We were sailing after shoals of herring.

On the original radio ballad, a great introductory verse was used for "Shoals of Herring." The melody is slightly different; it can be used for the last verse also.

Some of the best songs I heard were up in Scotland. The Scots have a sassy tradition of satirical song, going back into ancient times. Rival bards would insult each other in contests of wit. Some of the political songs of the seventeenth- and eighteenth-century wars with England are still among the most popular of the old ballads.

At the present time a considerable argument rages through Scotland about the American atomic submarine base at the Holy Loch. Many Scots say, "Well, we don't particularly like the Yanks, but this will bring in some money—and we can use the money!" The opposing group has been picketing the base, and its songs have spread like wildfire through the country.

DING DONG DOLLAR

From the Glasgow Song Guild. Tune, "She'll Be Coming 'Round the Mountain" (in Glasgow, "Oh You Canna Shove Yer Granny off a Bus")

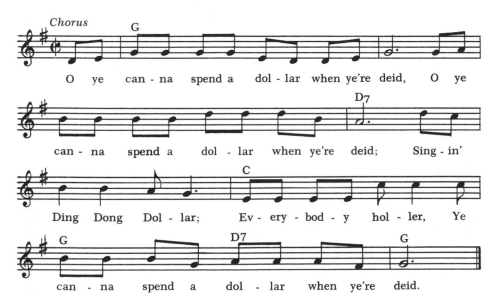

(Verses sung to same melody as chorus.)

1. O the Yanks have juist drapt anchor in Dunoon,
   An' they've had their civic welcome frae the toon,
   As they came up the measured mile,
   Bonnie Mary o'Argyll
   Wis wearin' spangled drawers ablow her goun.   *(Chorus)*

2. An the publicans will aa be daein swell,
   For it's juist the thing that's sure tae ring the bell,
   O the dollars they will jingle,
   They'll be no lassie single,
   Even though they maybe blaw us aa tae hell.   (*Chorus*)

3. But the Glesca Moderator disnae mind;
   In fact, he thinks the Yanks are awfly kind,
   For if it's t' heaven that ye're goin',
   It's a quicker way than rowin',
   An there's sure tae be naebody left behind.

   Final chorus:
   O ye canna spend a dollar when ye're deid,
   Sae tell Kennedy he's got tae keep the heid,
   Singin' Ding Dong Dollar,
   Everybody holler,
   Ye canna spend a dollar when ye're deid.

To round off this little sampler of songs from Britain, here's one more from Dr. Alex Comfort, whose "First Things First" was printed in *Sing Out* last year. Dr. Comfort is a world-famous authority on geriatrics, and an irreverent poet, so prolific in singable ditties that a small songbook of his songs has been published by *Sing* Magazine, and can be ordered from Collet's Record Shop, 70 New Oxford Street, London W.C. 1.

THE YOUNG C.N.D.*

Words by Alex Comfort; tune, "Villikins and His Dinah"
(The way they often sing this tune in Britain is slightly different from the U.S. "Sweet Betsy from Pike," so I print it in full here.)

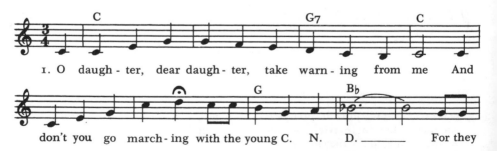

1. O daugh-ter, dear daugh-ter, take warn-ing from me   And don't you go march-ing with the young C. N. D. _____ For they

---

* Committee for Nuclear Disarmament.

rock you and roll you and shove you in - to bed, And if they

steal your nuc - le - ar sec - rets, you'll wish you were dead.

Refrain

Sing - ing Too - ra - li, oo - ra - li, oo - ra - li - ay.

2. O mother, dear mother, I am not afraid,
   For I'll go on that march and I'll come back a maid,
   With a brick in my handbag and a scowl on my face
      And barbed-wire in my underwear to keep off disgrace.   (*Refrain*)

3. But as they were marching a young man came by
   With a beard on his chin and a glint in his eye,
   And before she'd had time to remember her brick
      They were holding a sitdown on a neighbouring rick.   (*Refrain*)

4. Now once at the briefing she'd heard a man say,
   "Go perfectly limp and be carried away."
   So when this chap suggested it was time she was kissed
      She remembered her briefing and did not resist.   (*Refrain*)

5. Oh meeting is pleasure but parting is pain—
   I don't need to sing all that folk stuff again—
   O mother, dear mother, I'm stiff and I'm sore
      From sleeping three nights on a hard classroom floor.   (*Refrain*)

6. Now mother, don't flap, there's no need for distress;
   That marcher has left me his name and address,
   And if we can win, though a baby there be,
      He won't need to march like his dadda and me.   (*Refrain*)

This article leaves out many first-rate songwriters, such as Matt McGinn, Enoch Kent, and others. My apologies! My only excuse is a paraphrase of the traditional 10 P.M. pub announcement: "Space, gentlemen, space."

Lines remembered from long ago:
      FIRST POET: Art is a weapon.
      SECOND POET: But it must first of all be art.
      THIRD POET: A bread knife is a weapon, but it also cuts bread.

October 1962

SOMEONE once asked me: "Don't you ever sing any *anti*union songs?"

To tell you the truth, I only heard one such song in my life. You might say it's the exception that proves the rule. Fleming Brown of Chicago heard it sung by a southern Illinois miner in 1950. I can only remember part of it:

> Come and listen to my song
> The story of a country wronged.
> Idle men in roving bands
> Strike the tools from a miner's hand.
> John L.'s pay is big and fat.
> Wish I had a tenth of that.
> Flag of blue, white and red
> A man's got a right to earn his bread.
> Now I have to sit at home
> Hear the wife and children moan.

Thinking about the revival of interest in folk music, a question occurred: at what other times in history have men reached back into the past to attempt to revive an idiom? The first example that comes to mind is the Greek revival in U.S. architecture, from 1800 to 1850. In fact, many today still think of it as a golden period of American house-building. It ended when the Gothic Revival came, and a flood of imitation this and that. In sculpture, think of the Italian Renaissance, learning from Greece and Rome. The revivals which did not come off were those which failed to be newly creative, which only imitated.

No, that's an oversimplification. A lot of attempted revivals did not come off because the times were not right for them.

Press agents occasionally falsely credit this or that professional performer with having "done research at the Library of Congress." Me, I only worked there as a very amateurish and inefficient assistant to Alan Lomax for three or four months back in 1940. Fifteen dollars a week, and overpaid at that. But it was an ear-opening education for me.

The folk song archives there are now pitifully starved for lack of funds, but they still contain thousands of priceless recordings. Many of the best were recorded by John and Alan Lomax in the 1930s—material unobtainable now from any commercial company whatsoever. It includes instrumental and vocal music, secular and religious, of many regions, races, and languages, from Latin America as well as U.S.A.

Some of the best has been put onto LP records, which can be ordered from the Library of Congress. Write for their catalogue: Folklore Section, Library of Congress, Washington, D.C. (send 40 cents). And if you are a bona fide researcher, not just a "tourist," it is possible to look at a list of other material in the archives and order tape copies of a good deal of it.

"Lady, I don't sing for bad causes."

So said Woody Guthrie, when a woman asked him to sing free of charge "for a good cause."

Moral: If you want young singers to stick around, help 'em eat.

This is quite a different matter, of course, from the astronomical fees demanded by "stars" for their services. Even so, there are different opinions in this field. The German radical songwriter, Hans Eisler, used to say that he always wanted to be able to make a living from commercial work so he could afford to contribute his services "to the workers."

Singer Bill Crofut, who spent some months touring Japan in 1961, found himself on a bus in which the driver started up a hootenanny on the bus's PA system. A microphone was passed around from passenger to passenger, getting a song from every region of Japan possible.

(Bill was also in Korea at the time the students forced a change in the government. Young people commandeered vehicles, and sang songs like "Ariran" and student songs as they drove through the streets.)

In Boston I met an old Army acquaintance who was managing a young pop singer and taking him on a tour of TV dance-band programs to build up his current "hit" record. We stood in the wings while his protégé mouthed the words, and offstage his record played, and the TV audience squealed and clapped on cue. My friend leaned over to me and said, "You know, Pete, this teen-age racket is a tough one to bust into."

Attention songwriters: We need new songs—

—Some songs so funny that even people who disagree will find themselves doubled up with laughter.

—Some so shocking they will chill you to the bone.

—Some so warm they will make you feel like throwing your arms about the nearest person to you.

—Melodies so catchy you'll find yourself whistling them as you walk down the street.

—Songs so strong that even cowards will stop fleeing and turn with a breath of courage.

December 1962

THE FREEDOM SINGERS are six Negro college students who got together this year in Atlanta, Georgia, to embark on a tour of churches and colleges to raise money for the work of the Student Nonviolent Coordinating Committee. This organization (SNCC is colloquially pronounced "snick") was formed as a result of the sit-in demonstrations of 1960, grew during the freedom bus rides of 1961, and as this is written,

Four of the Freedom Singers: Charles Neblett, Bernice Reagon, Cordell Reagon, Rutha Harris

is mobilizing young people to attain the right to vote for all citizens of the South.

One of the group is a former rock-and-roll singer, others got their training by singing in country churches, another was a jazz trumpet player. All of them for various reasons have dedicated their lives to this cause, have faced danger, and have spent time in southern jails for their beliefs.

The songs they sing are a combination of traditional southern gospel music and newly composed songs, which hold closely to old or new folk traditions. In most cases the authors are unknown; often verses have been added by singers in buses or cars who feel the song is going too good to just let it stop.

If your heart is downcast or blue, if you feel discouraged and it seems as though the future is all darkness and uncertainty, take up some of their songs.* Songs have accompanied every liberation movement in history. These songs will reaffirm your faith in the future of mankind.

1963

(POPE JOHN'S "PACEM IN TERRIS" ENCYCLICAL URGES ORGANIZING WORLD FOR PEACE. HAZARD, KY., MINE STRIKE DOCUMENTS POVERTY IN APPALACHIA. MEDGAR EVERS MURDERED IN MISSISSIPPI. USSR-CHINA CONFERENCE ENDS WITHOUT AGREEMENT. U.S. AND USSR AGREE TO END ABOVE-GROUND ATOM TESTING. 250,000 MARCH ON WASHINGTON FOR NEGRO RIGHTS. 4 NEGRO CHILDREN KILLED IN BIRMINGHAM CHURCH BOMBING. COUP OVERTHROWS PRES. DIEM OF S. VIETNAM. PRESIDENT KENNEDY ASSASSINATED IN DALLAS.
(DYLAN'S "BLOWIN' IN THE WIND," SUNG BY PETER, PAUL AND MARY, BECOMES A HIT. ATTENDANCE OF 40,000 AT REVIVED NEWPORT FOLK FESTIVAL. IN SENATE SPEECH, KEATING OF NEW YORK REBUTS REDBAITING OF FOLK SINGERS BY CALIFORNIA FIREMEN.)

---

* The Freedom Singers performed "Ain't Gonna Let Nobody Turn Us Around" in *Broadside*, Vol. I, BR 301, and are also included in *Newport Broadside*, Vanguard 79144, and *Evening Concert at Newport*, Vol. I, Vanguard 9148. Their two Mercury discs (20879 and 20924) are apparently out of print, as is *Freedom in the Air*, the beautiful Albany, Ga., documentary issued by SNCC.

The freedom songs of the early sixties are collected in *We Shall Overcome*, ed. Guy and Candie Carawan (Oak Publications, New York, 1963), $1.95.

January 1963

The Folk Process in Albany, Georgia

SEVERAL SONGS well known to readers of this magazine are widely sung by members of the Southern Freedom Movement, but with changed words. For example:

> If you go to Mississippi,
> No neutrals have we met;
> You'll either be a freedom fighter
> Or a Tom for Ross Barnett.
> > Which side are you on?
> > Which side are you on?
>
> Have you heard about the Paddy wagon
> That Big Red likes to Drive?
> If you stand up for your rights
> He'll take you for a ride.
> > Which side, *etc.*
>
> Have you heard about the laws
> That Chief Pritchett made?
> If you stand up for your rights
> He'll put you in his cage.
>
> Oh, tell me, Mayor Kelly:
> Where is your heart?
> We are all children
> Of the Almighty God.
>
> Come all you freedom lovers,
> It's time to make a stand.
> Will you be an Uncle Tom
> Or will you be a man?

When I sang in October for several Negro churches in Albany,* they were surprised to know that there had ever been union verses written in 1931 by Mrs. Reece of Kentucky.

New verses, and changes in old verses, are constantly being written not only to this song, but others. "Hold On" (which they usually sing in a special minor way) often gets these lines:

---

* During their civil-rights struggle which lasted nearly all year.

The only thing that we did wrong
Was staying in the wilderness too long;
Keep your eyes on the prize, hold on.
Hold on, hold on, *etc.*

The only thing that we did right
Was the day we begun to fight;
Keep your eyes on the prize, hold on.
Hold on, *etc.*

You can talk about me just as much as you please,
But I'll talk about you on bended knees.

When they heard "The Hammer Song" as sung by Peter, Paul and Mary on the Hit Parade their first reaction was "What a crazy way those pop singers are singing our song!" Their way of singing it omits the words "danger" and "warning" and instead goes:

I'll hammer out freedom,
I'll hammer out justice

And extra verses are like as not to be added: "If I had a story, if I had a sit-in, if I had a march, a pray-in," etc.

The song "I'm on My Way" has been picked up essentially as the Almanac Singers adapted it in 1940, but with some fine new verses added:

If you won't go (if you won't go)
Let your children go (let your children go)

and

If you won't go (if you won't go)
Don't hinder me (don't hinder me)

Probably by the time this magazine is on the stands, there will be several dozen new verses current and going the rounds.

One of the best documentary LP recordings in a long time has just been issued by the Student Nonviolent Coordinating Committee in Atlanta, Georgia. It tells the story, so far, of the history-making events in Albany during the first half of 1962. The record was put together by Alan Lomax and Guy Carawan from tape recordings made on the spot by Guy Carawan. You hear preachers and other speakers, extemporaneous prayers outdoors and indoors, and some magnificent singing. On the record are many of the new hymns and gospel songs to which freedom words have been put within the past few months. The record is called *Freedom in the Air*.

A singer in one of the most successful commercial "folk song" groups, frustrated by his schedule, inquired of his RCA Victor A & R man: "Isn't there some way we can make records when we're *ready* to make them?"

"Yes," came the quick answer. "But don't expect to sell them."

"I am an artist," said the composer, "and I do not create for my own times but for posterity, which will appreciate me."

"I, too, am an artist," said a baker, overhearing him. "But should I adopt the same philosophy?"

Hamish Henderson sends in a beautiful poem, an epitaph for the Hamilton Covenanters who were hanged and dismembered in the "Killing Times" of the seventeenth century.

> *Stay, passenger—tak notice what thou reads;*
> *At Edinburgh lie our bodies, here, our heids.*
> *Our right hands stude at Lanark: these we want*
> *Because with them we sware the Covenant.*

There is a story told in Greece about their dance, like the one to "Miserlou," which goes "three steps one way, two the other." Centuries ago, the men of a certain village went out to fight the advancing Turkish army. All were killed. The Greek wives and daughters—all that were left in the town—determined not to be captured alive and started this dance on the edge of a cliff outside their town. Three steps one way, two the other—they inched toward the cliff, until they reached the edge, and fell off. I hope this doesn't spoil the singing or dancing of "Miserlou" for you.

Izzy Young and I are both alumni of Margot Mayo's American Square

Dance Group, and lament the great gap that exists through the country, between lovers of folk songs and lovers of dancing. But even this is not as great as the schism between the folk dancers and the square dancers. The former look down on the latter for "just kindergarten steps," and the latter look down on the former, with all their costumes and dancing to recordings, as hopeless nuts. Then there is the opinion of Al Minns, the great jazz dancer. He says that the real American folk dance of the twentieth century is the Lindy.

One of the most frequent sins of the trained musicians who tried to make use of folk songs in schools was attempting to write choral arrangements for songs that were essentially meant to be sung solo. Thus the song "Old Woman, Are You Fond of Courting," dutifully mouthed by fifty assorted basses, tenors, altos, and sopranos, loses all its subtle humor and becomes inanely "cute." The pop singers of folk songs have never done much worse than this.

Nice quote (from William Dean Howells): "Men are more alike than unlike one another. Let us make them know each other better, that they may be all humbled and strengthened with a concept of their fraternity."

To understand what the old spirituals meant to the people who made them up and sang them, read *Lay My Burden Down*. It is a firsthand narration, taken down from the memories of elderly Negroes who had once been slaves, by the Federal Writers Project (in the 1930s); edited by Ben Botkin, University of Chicago Press, 1945, Phoenix Press paperback, $1.65.

March 1963

New Songs by Woody Guthrie

BACK IN 1951, when the Weavers put "So Long, It's Been Good to Know You" on the Hit Parade, a Broadway publisher asked Woody Guthrie if he had some more songs. Woody replied more or less to the effect that sure, he had lots of 'em, and by God he'd like to find a publisher who'd publish 'em and collect some money for them, too. So they worked out a deal: Woody would get a regular stipend, and would sit down and tape-record all his songs and send them in. The publisher gave Woody a tape machine, and then the flood began. Every day it seemed that a new tape arrived. The publisher didn't have time to listen to them all. He gave an ear to a couple, but didn't at the time see any obvious successors to "So Long," and the tapes were put away "to be listened to later." Then Woody got itching heel again, went west for the umpteenth time, and a year later went into the hospital.

In 1961 the publisher decided to put out a Woody Guthrie songbook, but the tapes were nowhere to be found. He asked me and many others for our nominations for songs which could go in the book. Our suggestions simmered down to a book of about seventy pretty fine songs. A first printing of the book was run off the press in London, but some errors had been made in it, and it was withdrawn. Pending corrections, meanwhile, the publisher's old partner happened to see a copy.

"Hey," said he, "where's all those songs we got on those tapes?"

The tapes are lost, he was told.

"No, they're not. I got 'em home someplace."

"I think," he added.

So the search began. At the bottom of one closet were four tapes; piled on a bookshelf were four more, and so on. Sixteen have been found so far. They believe eighteen are still mislaid. Norman Cazden was set to work transcribing them, and a greatly enlarged Woody Guthrie songbook should come out within this next year. I got a chance last month to look at the blueprint copies, and was thunderstruck to find sixty or seventy songs among them that I had never before seen in my life—and I thought I was acquainted with all of Woody's songs. I felt like a prospector who found that a vein of gold he thought had petered out had unexpectedly widened and led to a new rich lode.

We might add one thing: in fairness to Woody, we're printing the songs exactly as he taped them. But also in fairness to Woody and to yourself, we should add that all of the songs are highly susceptible to the Folk Process. Woody wrote in flashes of inspiration, and later on, as he sang the songs, changed and amended them. This is a job you may have to do. Perhaps you'll find some ideas for verses to add to the first. It is such a honey; it is a pity it is so short.

MAIL MYSELF TO YOU

1. When you see me in your mail box
   Cut the string and let me out;
   Wash the glue off of my fingers,
   Stick some bubblegum in my mouth!   (*Chorus*)

2. Take me out of my wrapping paper,
   Wash the stamps off of my head;
   Pour me full of ice cream sodies,
   Tuck me in my nice warm bed.   (*Chorus*)

ONE LITTLE THING THE ATOM CAN'T DO

Words and music by Woody Guthrie. TRO-© copyright 1963,
Ludlow Music, Inc., New York, New York. Used by permission.

1. In the near - by day to come When we
whip this at - om bomb, And when we
use its pills of pow - er to build
hous - es to the sky; At - om
pow - er is bound to be, But the big - gest
mir - a - cle that you'll see Will be
one lit - tle thing the at - om can't do.

Chorus
One lit - tle thing the at - om can't do.
One lit - tle thing the a - tom can't do: It can't

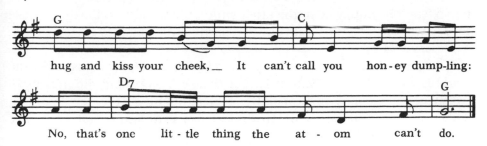

hug and kiss your cheek, __ It can't call you hon - ey dump-ling:

No, that's one lit - tle thing the at - om can't do.

2. You can drop your atom pill
   Down in the gas tank of your car;
   It'll roll you 'round this world and shine your shoes ten times a day;
   It can't show you how to court nor kiss,
   It can't sing songs about your lips:
   No, that's one little thing the atom can't do.   (*Chorus*)

3. Atom wheels can take you rolling
   Down to the shade of lover's lane;
   Atom sody will taste good with atom sandwiches you bring,
   But when love's lips get wet and woozeldy,
   When my love light shines its eyes on you,
   Well, hmm, that's one little thing the atom can't do.   (*Chorus*)

4. Atom bells can ring my wedding;
   Atom songs can fill my home;
   Atom this and atom that, my atom smile I can put on;
   But when mommy an' daddy nature
   Teach you all the tricks they knew,
   That's one little thing the atom can't do.   (*Chorus*)

In traveling around the country, I get a chance to meet some of the hundreds of talented young performers coming up in the folk music field. This year, returning to one city, I found a young fellow I'd especially admired was experimenting with narcotics—the hard stuff, with needles. I felt sick at heart, almost like weeping. This guy was talented. Now his career will be like the brief flare of a match, instead of a fine hearth fire which could have warmed us all, for years.

I felt I'd like to kill the guy who got him on it, if I only knew him, and then realized that, for all I knew, the pusher was helpless himself, and behind him there was a bigger villain—and behind him reached the shadowy world of organized big-money crime. What can you do?

Well, maybe you can't stop the steamroller, but you can snatch someone out from in front of it.

I feel almost as violent about the milder but more common forms of narcotics—the happy dust, the ether sniffs, the tea sticks. Partly because they pave the way for the needle, partly because they're all so unnecessary.

"Okay, okay, trim your beard, patriarch," I hear someone say. "So the world is full of habits." Sure it is, but there's a damn big difference between common ones like smoking, which might cost a few hundred dollars a year, and forms which drain every cent you've got and leave you willing to steal or prostitute to get more.

Furthermore, the need for secrecy opens this field of folk music wide open to some of the most vicious kind of blackmail. Artistic, political and otherwise. So don't tell me that it's none of my affair. That monkey on his back is the concern of us all.

On the two acres of land my family and I cleared on the mountainside by the Hudson, birds occasionally drop seeds of poison ivy. But my father-in-law and I rip it up every time old three-leaves makes his appearance. So, though the plant is common throughout this region, on our two acres friends can roam safely, lie on the grass.

How many other airline passengers besides myself have been driven nuts by the interminable "music" coming out of speakers everywhere at airports, and in planes waiting to take off? I finally found a way to persuade stewardesses and others to turn it off, or at least lower the volume. I offer to bribe them to do it.

At a recent international conference in Africa an Englishman made the statement, "It seems to be true that Africans seemed more peculiarly adapted to slavery than other races."

A tall African slowly stood up. "That statement reminds me of something which Cicero wrote in a letter to his friend Agrippa, the millionaire owner of many slaves. He said that of all his slaves, he felt the English most deserved to be slaves. As a people they seemed best adapted to slavery, and made the best slaves."

Artist vs. Critic

"PAY NO ATTENTION to critics; there has never been a statue erected to a critic," wrote the Finnish composer Sibelius. Of course it's a little unfair; furthermore, at least in this country, most statues are to soldiers and politicians, so that's scant comfort to the artist. But many a performer must at some time feel like paraphrasing G. B. Shaw's cruel phrase: "Those who can, do; those who can't, teach" into: "Those who can, make music; those who can't, criticize."

Yet every great philosopher started out as a critic of the world, and insofar as an artist is a philosopher, he is also a critic, and a fortunate one to be able to couch his criticism in a form which can reach many people. But every artist, also, can learn from more prosaic critics, wise or foolish, just as one can also learn from applause. The important thing is not to depend on them too much. In the end, you have to be your own severest critic, so that whether you are panned or praised, it won't jar you off your course. Paderewski said, "If I don't practice for one day, I know it; if I don't practice for two days, the critics know it; if I don't practice for three days, the audience knows it."

I feel grateful to book reviewers and record reviewers as well, who wade through hundreds of items to let us know what they think is good or bad in 'em. They also put their life into their work, and for far less pay—or no pay at all. And if occasionally they fail to see the cheese for the mold, or to realize that some of the very best cheese has mold as an integral part of it, nevertheless they're performing an invaluable function.

I think I start paying less attention to them when they spend too much effort trying to be clever. Critics, like entertainers, like applause. Some find they can get it (as do pop-music groups) by a wisecrack.

A good working definition of the word "sophomoric": The itch to be clever.

May 1963

I'LL PROBABLY get in dutch with a number of people for writing these paragraphs. I'm relaying information which, while not exactly given me in confidence, was told me by people who thought I was a mere musician, not a journalist. However, the story needs to be told now, not next year or even next month.

It looks as though the much-ballyhooed national TV show, "Hootenanny," will be a bitter disappointment for anyone who loves folk music or who thought the word Hootenanny meant a healthy mixture of the old and new. The ABC network, the talent agency (Ashley), the sponsor (Procter & Gamble) are all charging ahead with the idea of making "a fast-paced show, 26 minutes of screaming kids in the studio audience." All strictly professional performers will be used. Real folk musicians, such as Doc Watson, Horton Barker, or Bessie Jones and the Sea Island Singers, will not stand a chance of being considered. Even the Tarriers were first turned down because they are an interracial group. (All-white or all-Negro groups are allowed.)

Perhaps it's worth while reviewing briefly the history of the situation. After many years in which Alan Lomax and others tried to get the airways interested in folk music, the networks have finally got this sponsored show. How? Because about a year ago the Greenwich Village coffee house The Bitter End let Ed McCurdy start Tuesday-evening jam sessions for new and old talent to drop in on. The term "Hootenanny," developed in the forties by Woody Guthrie and the Almanac Singers (see Chapter 5, p. 326, for the real history), was common property by 1962, and the "Hoots" at The Bitter End became fabulously successful. The directors of the coffee house, two young former advertising men, sold the name and the idea for a show to ABC. Each week the show would be video-taped at a different college. One "star"—a different one each week —would sing three or four songs, and then introduce a couple or three other artists, each to do one or two songs. The students, grouped closely around, would join in on the choruses.

It could be a nice format. The folk song revival on its home grounds. With good performers allowed to ad-lib, with meaningful songs and youthful participation, it could be a breath of fresh air on TV. But with the producers of the show knowing little about folk music besides what they learn from the pages of *Billboard* and *Variety* (listing "top sellers"), and with their usual concern that every song be "socko!"—nothing underplayed, everything overplayed—it will be a miracle if much meaningful music gets to reach the TV screens. How I hope I am wrong. I would love to be proved wrong.

When will the TV producers learn that some of the greatest music in our country is made by unlettered farmers, miners, housewives, people with generations of folk traditions in their veins? The great thing about the old hootenannies was their ability to put together on one stage the old-timer and the new-timer, the citybilly and the hillbilly. The professional and the amateur. But the TV networks have not learned this lesson.

What can you do about it? Two things, it seems to me. First, the way is still wide open for a decent folk music show to be put on the networks. Fight TV with TV. Second, anyone who knows how to use pen and paper can sit down and write a letter to ABC, to the ad agency, and the sponsor, and give a considered opinion of the shows when they're aired in April. Those hucksters have no minds of their own, you know.

Bertolt Brecht was a cheesophile, as am I. He once visited Paris, where friends took him to a restaurant which specialized in good cheese. A waiter brought wine and then a huge tray with dozens of varieties of cheese to choose from. Brecht gazed on it in rapture and exclaimed: "I wish I could take this whole tray, as it is, to Berlin. I would rent the biggest exhibition hall and invite the people in to see it. Then I would say, 'There is civilization.'"

The Newport Folk Festival, after a two-year lapse, is being started up again. George Wein, who also runs the Newport Jazz Festivals, responded to criticism of the '59 and '60 festivals ("too many city professionals, not enough folks") and has asked a committee of performers to take responsibility for choosing the program. The committee, which will change annually, this year consists of Theo Bikel, Jean Ritchie, Pete Seeger, Clarence Cooper, Erik Darling, Bill Clifton and Peter Yarrow. First decision: all performers to get union minimum, no more no less, plus travel and hotel expenses. Aim is to combine on the same program some well-known names with unknown but exciting and genuine folk performers. All profits will be used for the benefit of the field itself, be it in the shape of travel grants, of folklore on tape or film, etc., scholarships, folk library endowments, the support of permanent records.

Summer 1963

LEN HOLT, young Virginia lawyer and a spark plug for the southern freedom movement, called up just before we went to press to describe a new song being sung by teen-agers in Birmingham. It goes to the tune of "The Old Gray Mare."

I ain't scared o' your jail 'cause*
I want my freedom
I want my freedom
I want my freedom

I ain't scared o' your jail 'cause
I want my freedom
I want my freedom now.

It goes along with a new dance step popular these days. "Kind of a hesitation step," says Len. "Starts with a twist, then a step back and a step forward.

"The way it's used is a sight to see. Reverend King is lecturing 'em all in church. Says it's to be a silent demonstration. No songs, no slogans, no replies to any obscenities shouted at them. 'Until you're arrested. Then the singing can begin.'

"So all the young people file out of church, solemn as deacons, quiet as mice. Then the cop comes and shouts, 'You're all under arrest!' That's the cue. Five hundred at once, bodies moving, voices ringing out:

> I ain't scared o' your jail 'cause
> I want my freedom . . ."

Most American Indians had little concept of private property as far as real estate went. Like air and water, land was for the use of all the tribe, for all beings who trod it. But songs could be privately owned. An individual Indian often had a personal song, that no one else could sing.

Which reminds me: when I was a kid I read every single book of the Canadian naturalist Ernest Thompson Seton. Seton held up the Indian as an ideal, for strength and dignity, morality, and selflessness, and in tune with all of nature. Anthropologists call this period of human history "tribal communism." I think next time some character asks me "Are you a communist?" I'll answer, "Oh, about as much as the average American Indian."

Some people prefer songs without words to interfere with the music; but since consonants give better rhythm and definition to melody, one rarely hears them singing just "Ah-ah-ah." Scat singers make up their own ("Boodly ba da") nonsense syllables. Irish singers could fill up a lot of time with "whack-fol-diddles." Art singers, not quite so frank, sing arias in unintelligible German or Italian. Old-time choirs repeat a phrase like "Kyrie eleison" over and over.

Pete LaFarge was turned down by a Chicago "folk music" nightclub. Reason? The manager explained to Pete, "I can't use you. People have to listen while you're singing."

Folk songs run in families, as you soon find out after you hear more than a couple hundred. Thus "Casey Jones" is a distant cousin of "Jay

Gould's Daughter," and "Streets of Laredo" a cousin of "St. James Infirmary." It's not so much that one is descended from the other, but both are descended from a common great-grandpa.

Marvin Bell, red-headed Georgia Tech student, says he has worked out a combination banjo-picking style, half frailing and half Scruggs picking. He calls it Frugging.*

Report from Greenwood, Mississippi: A Singing Movement†

I WAS THREE DAYS in Greenwood this July lending some small support to the Negro voter-registration drive down there. Sang in a small Baptist church, at a large NAACP meeting, and out in an open field. The last was a songfest also attended by Theodore Bikel, Bob Dylan, and several hundred of the most enthusiastic freedom fighters and singers one could imagine. All ages.

Because reporters were present from *Life* Magazine and *The New York Times,* as well as press and television cameramen, the police were on their guard against any rough stuff. They dispersed a crowd of vengeful Dixiecrats who tried to assemble across the highway from the field.

The most popular song by all odds was "This Little Light of Mine—I'm Going to Let It Shine." I must have heard it sung a dozen times a day, and once it was started it would go on for 10 and 15 and 20 minutes with people singing new words and repeating old ones. They sing it slightly differently than the way I've been used to singing it, and end with the line:

Let it shine, let it shine, let it shine.

This is actually the better-known version. They don't put any verses in; but what they do is change the first line of each chorus so the second time through it might go:

I've got the light of freedom,
I'm going to let it shine.
I've got the light of freedom,
I'm going to let it shine.

I've got the light of freedom,
I'm going to let it shine.
Let it shine, let it shine, let it shine.

---

* This predated the Frug dance.
† From *Broadside* Magazine (New York), No. 30, August 1963.

Another popular song is one written by Bertha Gober, a teen-ager in Albany, Georgia, last year, entitled "We'll Never Turn Back." It is a slow and deeply moving song that was sung by thousands at the funeral of Medgar Evers.

"We Shall Overcome" is still, of course, the theme song of the Negro freedom movement. But equally popular down in the South are songs such as "Everybody Wants Freedom" (same tune as "Amen") and "Ain't Goin' to Let Segregation Turn Me Around." Also "Keep Your Eyes on the Prize, Hold On," "I'm Goin' to Walk the Streets of Jackson One of These Days," "Oh, Freedom," "We Shall Not Be Moved," "Wade in the Water," and others.

In each case they keep on putting new words into the old songs, including a lot of names of friends or foes in the integration battle. To hear them singing these songs with hands clapping and bodies swaying and faces lighted up with a fierce joy of the freedom struggle was an experience I'll never forget.

October 1963

CHOPPING FIREWOOD on the hillside one morning, I was humming, then singing loudly to myself and the birds, and to the tree I was massacring. The axe was making music too. Found myself on "Take This Hammer."* Remarkable how a good work song can keep one going at an even pace. Doesn't speed you up so much as it slows you down. Keeps you from getting out of breath. And that long-held note in the third line works just as Leadbelly described it. Gives you a chance to draw a free breath—also varies the regular meter.

> Take this hammer (*whup!*) Carry it to the captain (*whup!*)
> Take this hammer (*whup!*) Carry it to the captain (*whup!*)
> Take this hammer (*whup!*) Carry it to the captain (*Rest here*) . . .
>   (*whup!*)
> Tell him I'm gone (*whup!*) Tell him I'm gone (*whup!*)

Went through all the verses I knew. If he asks you was I running, tell him I'm flying, tell him I'm flying. If he asks you was I laughing, tell him

---

* New words and new music adapted by Huddie Ledbetter. TRO-© copyright 1963, Folkways Music Publishers, Inc., New York, New York. Used by permission.

I was crying. I don't want no cornbread and m'lasses, hurts my pride, hurts my pride. I don't want no cold iron shackles, 'round my leg, 'round my leg.

How times have changed. Only a wastrel would use an axe now for more than occasional cutting. With a portable chain saw, gasoline-powered, noisy and smelly, a man can cut six times the wood. And nowadays who wears cold iron shackles? Instead we are asked to wear a clean white collar and get to work on time. Or else.

Found myself making up new verses—irrelevant, I suppose, to all but me. I don't want no shit-filled river, past my door, no, past my door. I don't want your litterbug highway, through my land, no, through my land. I don't want no damnfool strontium, in my sky, no, in my sky.

Maybe this is the best time for a defense of the double negative. I *don't* want *no* cornbread and molasses. No accredited English teacher would approve it—would say it's illogical. But it's perfectly legal in some other languages—Spanish, for example. Furthermore, the word "any," pronounced "enny," is a prune-pinching, piddling word which doesn't sing well at all. Not compared to that grand, great, two-letter world-shaker: NO.

Alan Lomax has for years used a good device for getting a group of singers started. He will pose to them a certain subject and ask them all to get a song out of it. I can remember an automobile ride when he kept four or five of us going for two hours singing all the animal songs that we could think of—"Blue-tail Fly," "The Fox," "Groundhog." This was twenty-five years ago. More recently he found himself emceeing a group of people in a Greenwich Village nightclub and asked each one to sing a song of Woody Guthrie's. Everybody in the room was surprised how long they kept on going without running out of Woody's songs. One lone folk-nik wandered into the session after it was started and sat entranced, and later in the evening leaned over to ask the actor Will Geer,

"What's the name of that cat who's emcee of this affair?"

"Why, that's Alan Lomax," Will replied.

"Alan Lomax? Holy cow! I thought he was dead."

No, Alan Lomax is just as lively as ever. He's just been working awful hard, becoming an anthropologist.

One of the most charming things that has happened in many a year is the way three small magazines all started 19 months ago, each calling itself *Broadside*. Today each continues to publish, under the same name, undoubtedly confusing many readers.

I can see some serious student trying to determine which is the Authentic *Broadside*. Which is The Original? Which is the Folk and which is the Fake?

All three have honestly individual characters and aims. The Boston *B* reports on coffee-house doings and occasional record reviews and songs and singers in that area. The Los Angeles *B* has more theoretical articles. The New York *B* exists mainly to print up new topical songs, with editorial content at a minimum.

In some other field but folk music they would all be suing each other, or at least sniping. Here they all blithely go on their way. Long live coexistence!

At a recent college jam session I overheard a song leader start off a crowd singing "This Train Is Bound for Glory," followed immediately by a verse of "The Saints Go Marching In," a verse of "Crawdad" and a verse of "Hard Traveling." After he had fixed the melodies and harmonies in everyone's mind he proceeded to start all four of the songs going at the same time with various parts of the audience each singing one of them. It makes a fantastic sound. The chords for each of the four songs are the same.

I think I'm against pay-TV, for a most bass-ackwards reason. At present the average TV fare is so poor that even the most benumbed vidiot sooner or later shakes his head and decides that surely there must be some more interesting way to spend the time. So we have a growing percentage of do-it-yourselfers, book-readers, sports participants, doers and thinkers. If pay-TV really produced good shows, the trend could be reversed, and it could also gobble up everyone's spare cash.

1964

(PRES. JOHNSON ANNOUNCES WAR ON POVERTY. BOYCOTT FOR INTEGRATION CUTS NY SCHOOL ATTENDANCE 44%. FTC ORDERS HEALTH WARNINGS ON CIGARETTE PACKAGES. CIVIL RIGHTS BILL PASSES AFTER 75-DAY FILIBUSTER. 3 CIVIL RIGHTS WORKERS MURDERED DURING "MISSISSIPPI SUMMER." "GULF OF TONKIN" RESOLUTION GIVES PRESIDENT NEW AUTHORITY FOR VIETNAM FIGHTING. 800 U. OF CALIFORNIA STUDENTS ARRESTED IN FREE-SPEECH MOVEMENT.

(MALVINA REYNOLDS' "LITTLE BOXES" BECOMES A HIT. MC LUHAN'S "UNDER-
STANDING MEDIA" ANNOUNCES END OF LINEAR ERA. BEATLES SPARK NEW STAGE
OF ROCK 'N' ROLL POPULARITY.)

January 1964

WELL, SOME DAY this old TV blacklist will be long gone and dead, and those who perpetuated it or put up with it will be forgotten. Right now, the only comment I can think of that is applicable to the situation is in a story Lee Hays told me.

When the restaurants in the District of Columbia were ordered by the courts to desegregate, an old Negro man decided to see if the new ruling was really effective. He dressed up in his best clothes and went to one of the most expensive restaurants in Washington and sat down at a table. Sure enough, the waitress came up with menu in hand. He didn't bother reading it, though. He just looked up at her and said, "Ma'am, do you have chitlins here?"

She said, "No, sir, sorry, we do not have chitlins."

"Well, do you have collard greens?"

"No, sir."

"Well, tell me, do you have black-eyed peas with ham hock?"

"No, sir."

"Well," the old man said, "it appears to me you folks just aren't ready for desegregation."

I don't think I ever do a children's program without doing a couple of what, to children, are the most intensely topical songs—all about the general subject of the war between the young and the old. "Be Kind to Your Parents," "The Younger Generation," "The Housewife's Lament," "The Declaration of Independence" (four-year-old). But they can all be tempered by singing lullabies and game songs to show that cooperation is possible, if difficult.

Parents really are the hardest working section of the working class. The longest hours, and no vacations. But they do it because of the high pay: kisses.

And the fringe benefits, such as Hope of Immortality.

In Rio de Janeiro, I'm told, there is a tough section of town just in back of one of the many mountains. The women make their living as domestic servants working in the homes of the more well-to-do citizens of Rio. The men in this tough section, as a point of honor, do not work at regular jobs. They devote their lives to culture. That is, they spend the entire year preparing for Rio's gigantic and world-famous carnival, which occurs just before Lent. Usually in February or March. It is therefore no accident that the carnival in Rio has such magnificent dancing, costumes, and music. Some of the carnival prize songs have become popular on the U. S. Hit Parade—songs such as "Tico, Tico." I wonder if there is any town in North America which can match these Latin American celebrations. The Mardi Gras in New Orleans? The Calgary Stampede up in Canada? It takes a tradition and a whole population to throw themselves into the spirit of the thing.

Here are some of my own feelings about the current hootenanny craze. I wonder if anyone else feels the same way.

For years I have tried to persuade young people, "Don't fall for the tyranny of the Hit Parade. Like what you like and don't like what you don't like. Be damned whether or not it is fashionable or respectable, or 'the current thing.' "

So now, suddenly, the word "hootenanny" is temporarily the thing. I'm mighty sorry to see a lot of people falling for it, if that is the only reason. I suppose they'll get as much out of it as the American teen-ager found out about Calypso music from the so-called "Calypso boom" of '56, or found out about Tchaikovsky from Freddy Martin's recording of that piano concerto, or found out about real jazz from some of the slick swing bands of the 1940s.

March 1964

JACK ELLIOTT is a self-made man. Some people inherit their riches, others earn them in a slow, painful way, and Jack, in the face of years of discouragement, has slowly made himself into one of the finest pickers and singers and all-around entertainers I've ever seen on a stage.

When some people find that Jack Elliott was born in Brooklyn—he

Jack Elliott

with his cowboy hat and boots, rough lingo and expert guitar playing—their first reaction is, "Oh, he's a fake." They're dead wrong. Jack re-borned himself in Oklahoma. He didn't just learn some new songs. He changed his whole way of living.

We are used to this happening in the opposite direction; a country youth goes off to college and then gets into business in the city. When he goes back to visit the farm, the people back home hardly recognize him with his fancy talk and fancy clothes. But this kind of change happens to so many, nobody calls him abnormal, nobody calls him a phony, at least not usually.

My guess is that there will always be young people who for one reason or another will feel that they have to violently, radically, re-form themselves. A personal revolution. They abandon the old like a hated mask and rebuild on new foundations.

Attention, banjo and guitar pickers: I've discovered how to get stronger fingernails. And it doesn't cost a cent. But the question is, is it worth the cost?

Let me explain the details. I've always been troubled with a weak, thin, splitty nail on my main picking finger—the right index finger. But one frosty morning last winter, I banged it accidentally. A month later the whole fingernail fell off. Three months later, when the new one had grown in, it was nice and thick and strong. It's about twice as strong as any other nail on my whole hand.

Now, my problem is this. Do I dare try the process intentionally on my other fingers? All one needs is a small hammer, courage, and about six months for the nail to grow out again after you've hit it. Is there a doctor in the house who can advise on a thing like this?

This is ancient history, but you might be interested to know that the December 1962 *Time* Magazine article on folk music was actually sparked by the insistence of the fifteen-year-old daughter of one of the staff editors. This daughter finally said, "Mother, if you don't persuade them to have a story on folk music, I'm going to go right down to your office and speak to the top editor myself."

As it so happened, the daughter's parent was taken off the story as it was in preparation. And when the story came out, the daughter was so disgusted with it that she wouldn't speak to her mother for a whole week. Ah, well, I guess fifteen years is not too young to find out how history is made.

Apropos of nothing: The man who won't lie to his wife has no regard for her feelings.

May 1964

SEVEN THOUSAND MILES from home, this occasionally travel-weary family received *Sing Out* by airmail, and pounced on it. Big argument: who reads it first? Bless the hardworking and underpaid people who paste it up, proofread it, and see that it has appeared more or less on time for thirteen years.

The Guitar Improvisations of Mwenda Jean Bosco

Fourteen years ago, the African folklorist Hugh Tracey heard a young man singing and playing the guitar in the streets of a town in Katanga Province. The following morning Tracey recorded him. Some of the recordings were issued commercially and launched the young man, whose name is Mwenda Jean Bosco, on a career as a folk singer famous throughout most of Central and East Africa.

Guitars are being widely played throughout the cities of Africa today. Manufactured models are on sale much as in American cities. The music being played on them is, of course, part European, part African.

Over the past two years, *The Journal of the African Music Society* has printed two fascinating articles by the South African-born Englishman David Rycroft analyzing Bosco's music. Accompanying the articles were 25 pages of transcriptions of Bosco's guitar improvisations.

We hope the readers of *Sing Out* would like to take the trouble to try and explore this piece of music. It's really delightful. Unfortunately, there are no recordings of it currently available in the U.S.A., although once upon a time London Records had a 10″ LP called "African Guitar" which included it. Perhaps one could get a copy of the African recording by sending the necessary dollars to Gallo Records in Johannesburg.

MASANGA—Excerpts from Guitar Improvisations*
By Mwenda Jean Bosco

Bosco capos up five frets so that he plays the G chord but it comes out sounding as though it were in C. This gives the whole piece a delightfully delicate sound.

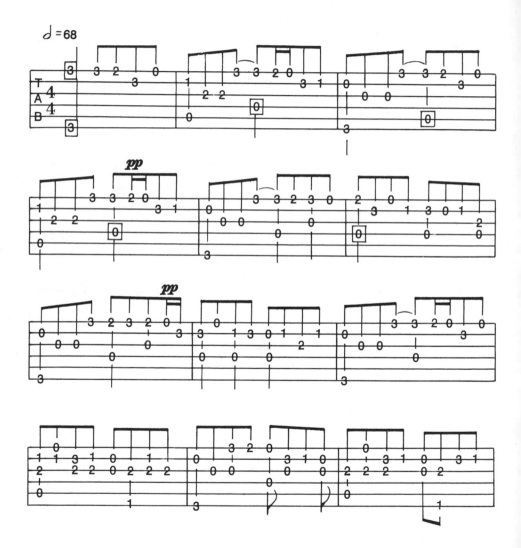

* As recorded on Gallotone GB 1586T. Transcription by David Rycroft (England). Tablature conversion by Bernie Krause (New York). Copyright © International Library of African Music. (For an explanation of tablature notation see p. 370 below.)

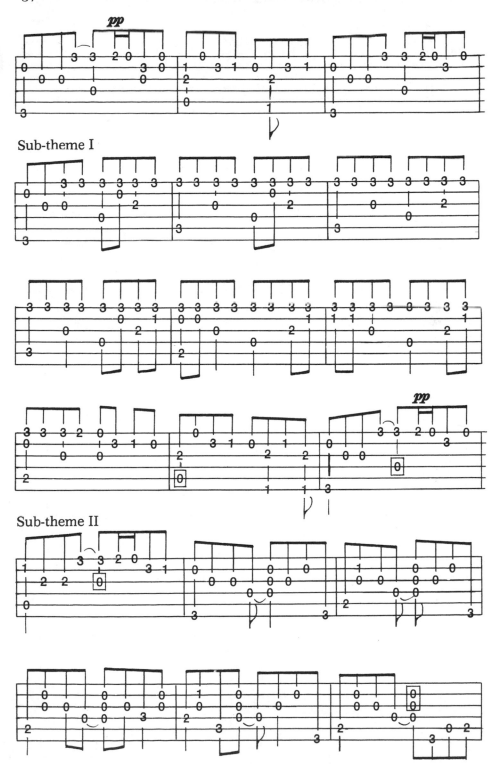

Sub-theme I

Sub-theme II

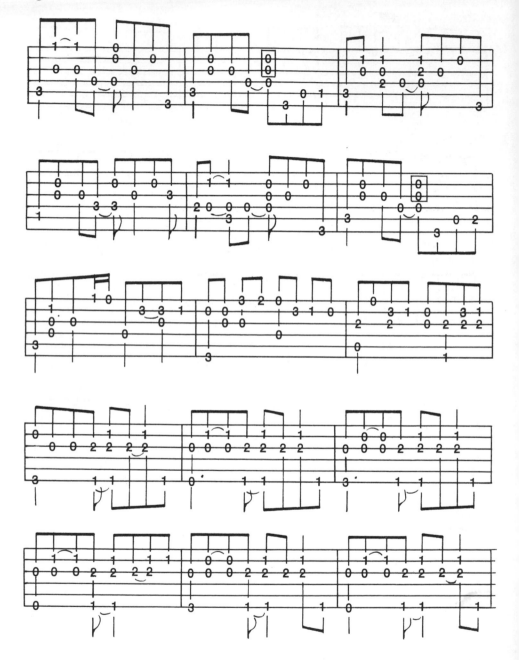

August 5, 1964

Written in Meridian, Mississippi:

FOR A FEW DAYS, I am down here seeing if I can help, in a small way, some very wonderful people bring more democracy to their state.

Everything has been going smoothly. The only discordant note was a man in the Jackson airport. He had overheard me talking with a reporter on the plane. In the airport, he accosted me with blood in his eye. "Are you coming down here to sing for the Ni————rs?"

"I've been asked down here by some friends to sing," says I, trying to be at my most gracious. "I hope that anyone who wants to hear me can come, either Negro or white."

"Well, you just better watch your step. If we hadn't been on the plane when I heard you talking, I would have knocked the s—t out of you." I tried to mollify him, but he wasn't interested in listening.

The friends who picked me up, Bob Cohen and his wife, are two young Yankees who are spending the summer here. They have organized what they call the Music Caravans, and have written hundreds of musicians such as myself, asking us to spend a few days or a week or more here. They give us food and transportation, and the time is spent in giving a number of short programs for what are known as Freedom Workshops.

There are about ninety of these workshops throughout the state. The NAACP, CORE, SNCC, and SCLC have pooled their forces in what is known as COFO (Council of Federated Organizations). They run classes in voter-registration requirements, and now classes are held in history and geography, mathematics, languages, and other subjects. The students are mainly young. Older people are often scared of losing their jobs or being evicted from their homes, but they get the materials through the children.

The teachers are mainly college students, both white and Negro, mainly from the North or West, who are volunteering their summer vacation time. About eight hundred are in the state, I'm told. But not all are young. I met a woman of fifty whom Woody and I stayed with twenty-five years ago when we were singing for the lumberjacks in Minnesota.

Her husband was then a labor lawyer. Now she is a widow and a California schoolteacher.

Most of the classes are held in churches. Since a number of the churches have been bombed (a stick of dynamite thrown from a moving car at night), when they can't get a church they buy or rent some other building. My first concert was held in the backyard of such a building. It had been slightly damaged by a bomb three weeks before, but none of the young people seemed scared. I think, like soldiers in the trenches, they had survived initial nervousness and had learned to live with danger. There are certain safety measures always taken, such as always checking in and checking out, especially when any trip is taken.

My program was essentially not too different from what I always give. A few old songs, hinting at the history of our country. A few songs from other countries, hinting at the different types of people in this big world—but also good songs which will give us a feeling of friendship to them. A few stories or songs for kids, such as "Abiyoyo," the allegory on the power of music. But my audience was happiest when, near the end, I concentrated on what they call "our" songs, the spirituals and gospel songs with freedom verses which have swept through the South in the last few years.

And, when I started one of these songs, did they sing! It was inspiring to me to hear them.

My audience tonight was mostly young—from ten years old to twenty-five years old, plus a few older women. All Negro, except for a handful of white college students. And the town sheriff stood silently in the back during the whole performance. Just two local white people dared to come. I was told that they worked at a local radio station and were students at a nearby college. They'll take some rough questioning when they get home.

And what am I accomplishing? some will ask. Well, I know I'm just one more grain of sand in this world, but I'd rather throw my weight, however small, on the side of what I think is right than selfishly look after my own fortunes and have to live with a bad conscience. The voter-registration campaign is inching forward slowly, and there's no doubt that within a few years Mississippi is going to be a much freer and happier place in general.

No doubt, there's some hurting going on now. There was during the American Revolution, too. And G. B. Shaw once said, "I can no more show a play without causing pain than a dentist can do his job without causing some pain. The morals of the country are in a bad way and of course it hurts to touch them."

The right to vote is the crucial thing. Better schools, jobs, and housing will flow from this. And, if we believe this is one country, the United States, then we must be concerned with a part of it which has for so long lagged behind the rest of the country. How long will it take? It will be easier to predict this after the coming elections. If the Negroes who do vote are able to continue without losing their jobs or homes, tens of thousands will follow their example next year.*

And perhaps this is one of the more peaceful revolutions of history. Last night I had to announce to my audience that the bodies of the three young civil rights workers had just been found. But no one was shouting for revenge. Rather, one felt simply an intense determination to continue this work of love. Afterward, people came up to me to get the words to a new song I've been singing:

> O healing river,
> Send down your water,
> Send down your water
> Upon this land.
> O healing river,
> Send down your water
> And wash the blood
> From off the sand.†

September 1964

A LOT OF the best American songs I know are not in the English language: Spanish from the Southwest, French from Louisiana, German from Pennsylvania, Mohawk from New York State, and so on. Ruth Rubin collected "Tumbalalaika" (Yiddish) not in Europe but in New York City.

I have no degree in folklore (or anything else). I am no linguist. The only reason I try to sing so many different kinds of songs is that I sing for many different kinds of audiences. I want to meet them halfway. If

---

* And in 1969 I start to realize how much I have to learn.
† By Fran Minkoff and Fred Hellerman. Copyright © 1964, Appleseed Music, Inc. All rights reserved. Used by permission.

they are willing to listen to some of my down-home music, at least I can make an attempt to learn some of their own down-home music.

I know that in my well-meaning attempts I have massacred many a song. At least, in all these attempts, I learned. And, they're such good songs that they can even survive my singing them.

When Lee Hays and I wrote "If I Had a Hammer" in 1949, we really doubted that many besides he and I would sing it. But it has gone round the world and is now known in many versions. The most recent changes in it were wrought by a young rock-and-roller who recorded it in '62.

Do I resent the changes he made? I have changed so many other people's songs that I hardly have any right to demand that they not change one of mine. But I also discovered an interesting thing: You can sing the tune as I wrote it simultaneously with the R&R version. They harmonize with each other! Now, isn't that a good moral for the world?

November 1964

WALLY HILLE stopped being choirmaster of a Lutheran church, and got a similar job in a Unitarian church. "Well," he thought, "here, they are so broad-minded we can sing anything." But when he tried "The Seven Blessings of Mary," old-line Unitarians hit the ceiling. "What's all this about 'Father, Son, and Holy Ghost?' We are a *Unitarian* church!"

It's nice to see the art of storytelling make a comeback, along with folk singing. Printing was a great invention, but there are times when one shouldn't have to completely rely on it. Such times are when you're sitting around a campfire, when you're putting your children to bed, or maybe when you're driving along in the car and some members of the party are beginning to get bored or out of temper.

Woody Guthrie was one of the best storytellers I ever heard. Lee Hays is another. Ed McCurdy has put out one of the best LPs for children that has ever been issued. It is called *Children's Stories and Songs.** The stories are told and made up by Ed, for his own children, but they will de-

---

* Folkways FC 7771.

light millions of others. I've already tried retelling them for children's programs.

Vivienne Richman of Pittsburgh has had a fine time for several years song-leading at Duquesne University's annual Festival of Nationalities.

She comes on the stage between the various dance group performances and foreign language choruses and sings some familiar songs in English which, however, are related to non-English songs sung at the Festival. It might be the tune which is similar, or she might have a verse of "Cindy" quoting a Bulgarian folk saying. Or she may get one of the Italian instrumentalists to come up and help her with "Down by the Riverside."

Now It's Folk Music That's Commercial

FROM the *Broadside* of Boston: "The swinging warmth of a muted trumpet, a tenor saxophone vibrant and melodic, a walking rhythmic bass, the comping chord-filling of a sympathetic piano, the spurring insistence of drums providing, accenting a rhythm—that, in essence, is jazz, live jazz; and that is what we don't hear (except for some recordings) in Boston coffee houses.

"Why? Obviously they feel jazz won't sell. There is no room for artistic appreciation; coffee houses in Massachusetts have become crassly commercial, commercial in the sense of pseudo-folksters (three chords and faking) and raucous weird groupings, group sings, and hootenannies. With all of this, they don't have time to explore and sell America's largest contribution to the creative world: Jazz."

1965

(MALCOLM X ASSASSINATED. VOTER REGISTRATION WORKERS MURDERED IN ALABAMA: THOUSANDS MARCH FROM SELMA TO MONTGOMERY. UNIVERSITY TEACH-INS AND LARGE-SCALE DEMONSTRATIONS PROTEST CONTINUOUS BOMBING OF N. VIETNAM AND ESCALATION OF U.S. GROUND TROOPS. SENECA TREATY

LAND TAKEN FOR KINZUA DAM. U.S. MARINES PREVENT LEFT-WING GOVERN-
MENT IN DOMINICAN REPUBLIC. MASSACRE OF HUNDREDS OF THOUSANDS FOL-
LOWS ANTI-COMMUNIST COUP IN INDONESIA.
(FOLK FESTIVALS FLOURISH IN MANY PARTS OF U.S. NASHVILLE COUNTRY
MUSIC STYLE BECOMES COMMERCIAL SUCCESS IN BIG CITIES. BOB DYLAN GOES
ELECTRIC: "FOLK-ROCK" TREND FEATURES REBELLIOUS THEMES. "THE EVE OF
DESTRUCTION" HEADS FALL CHARTS. "SING OUT" CIRCULATION REACHES
25,000.)

January 1965

I WHOOPED when I first saw the song "Plastic Jesus," and often
when driving down the highway, I find myself recalling the phrase with
a grin.* Our Plastic Age molds Everything to its purposes. But, after a
little rethinking, I decided not to sing the song. Why? I realized it was
partly my own Protestant religious background that made me amused.
Prohibition against graven images and all that sort of thing.

If there's one thing we don't need these days, it's sectarian religious
arguments. I'd be glad to table them for a while and try to concentrate
on finding unity for more pressing jobs. Incidentally, the nicest defense
of religious images I know of was that given by a young Russian Orthodox
priest to William Mandel in Moscow, 1963: "If you and your wife had
lost a child in infancy many years ago, and had kept no photograph of
it, it would be increasingly difficult to recall its appearance and what it
meant to you as the years rolled by. But a picture would bring it all
back. . . ."

Ed McCurdy, the composer of "Last Night I Had the Strangest Dream,"
is a tall, handsome singer and storyteller who loves to shock people on
occasion, with profanity or more. Underneath it, he is a sentimental guy,
and a deeply pessimistic one. If you ever want to make him angry, try
changing a line in his song "The Strangest Dream." Someone, in a songbook, once wrote it, "Last Night I Had the Greatest Dream." McCurdy
was livid with rage.

---

*"I don't care if it rains or freezes
  Long as I got my plastic Jesus
  Riding on the dashboard of my car.
  Plastic Jesus! Plastic Jesus!
  Me and plastic Jesus will go far."

Ed McCurdy

What makes this song great? From one angle, it is a mystic song; from another, a sarcastic, ironic song; and from another, a very warm and loving song.

Sometimes a singer will want to emphasize one facet and polish it more brilliantly than the rest. But, if he is not careful, he throws off the balance of the jewel, and this destroys some of its effectiveness as a work of art.

Often the artist who creates a work does not realize all the possible meanings, all the possible facets of light which can be shown by his finished piece. Certainly, Shakespeare never could have thought of all the thousand-and-one meanings which people have read into his plays. "Great art demands great audiences." As people grow in experience, they are able to get more out of even the simplest folk song, such as "Go Tell Aunt Rhody" or "Careless Love."

Incidentally, Ed McCurdy says that his own favorite antimilitarist song is the old jingle printed below. The two short stanzas should be sung over and over again to let the real effect sink in. My guess is that it has been sung by generations of disgusted soldiery and by generations of ribald and drunken satirists. It grows on you.

THE NOBLE DUKE OF YORK

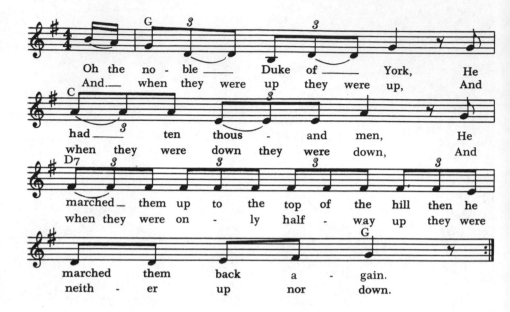

Oh the no-ble ___ Duke of ___ York, He
And.___ when they were up they were up, And

had ___ ten thous - and men, He
when they were down they were down, And

marched ___ them up to the top of the hill then he
when they were on - ly half - way up they were

marched them back a - gain.
neith - er up nor down.

March 1965

OVERSEAS NOTE: Leon Bibb, on tour in the USSR last fall, was swimming at the beach in Yalta, when a middle-aged man stuck his head out of the water, grinned, and said, "Sure beats Florida, don't it?"

The folk process seems to have caught up with Malvina Reynolds' song "It Isn't Nice" sooner than is fair. Before her original melody—printed in the N.Y.C. *Broadside* last year—had a chance to be circulated around much, a rock-and-roll-type melody was put to her lyrics and picked up by Mississippi teen-agers last summer—and last month was printed in *Sing Out*. Malvina's original melody can be found in Broadside #43. It's a great song and just right for these times.

From Rita Weill, visiting in Ireland: "No wonder there are so few Irish painters. How to improve upon the reality of the ever-changing light? I am convinced that a wise hand cast this land in mist and rain most of the time; for the brilliance of all the greens would surely be blinding under the sun! Have spent most of my time among the good people of Connemara (which looks exactly the way its music sounds) and Clare. Isn't it amazing? With all the social diversions that man has invented (cinema, TV, etc.) nothing beats sitting by a turf fire, the wind howling outside, engaged in the art of visiting."

From a friend in South Africa: "You ask what is happening to us down here. Well, at present, and for the past year or so, sabotage and other political trials have been following on, one after the other, without abating. There must be literally thousands of political prisoners in our prisons, as is evidenced by the fact that conditions in the prisons have become seriously overcrowded. I went to Pretoria last Saturday to visit M——, who is due to be released in July after serving a three-year sentence. He has been in solitary most of the time with a minimum of 'privileges,' but fortunately has stood up to it magnificently. You've probably read about the execution of three Africans a week ago which aroused world-wide protest. They were executed in the same prison, and he told me that for a week beforehand they could be heard singing freedom songs, day and night. I know that one man, Mini, had a beautiful baritone voice."

Record Review: Pete Seeger*

PETE SEEGER will be forty-six this year. He has been singing professionally for twenty-five years, and as an amateur for many years before that. His first recording was made in 1941 (with the Almanac Singers). This review is not of any one of his discs, but makes some general comments on all of them—the forty or fifty solo LPs he has done for Folkways, and the five he has done for Columbia in the last three years.

---

* By the early sixties Pete had become a popular success; as a natural consequence he was sharply criticized in some quarters for singing songs which were not folk in the narrow definition of the term. On the other hand, he was extravagantly admired by many who tended to accept him as a completely authentic ethnic singer. He felt that both these opinions were wide of the mark; finally he decided to put in writing his own analysis of the musical intentions, successes and failures of Pete Seeger.—J.M.S.

Taken all together, they form one of the most uneven bodies of re-corded music that any performer could boast of, or perhaps be ashamed of. Now, it is true that some songwriters have written thousands of songs and let posterity decide which few dozen of them were worth singing. But does a performing artist have the same right to spew out thousands of recorded performances to the commercial market, without being judged for the poor ones as well as the good ones?

Some of Seeger's earliest discs, such as *Darling Corey* (1948), have the nearest to traditional folk music on them, although a still earlier one, *Talking Union* (1941), is the most frankly propagandistic.

Scattered throughout the discs, you will occasionally hear some pass-able ballad singing. (Pete's sister Peggy is a much better ballad singer. But if you really like ballads, why not listen to the master balladeer, Horton Barker, on Folkways and Library of Congress LPs?)

As for banjo picking, Pete only occasionally does some good traditional picking. His brother Mike can play rings around him, not only on the banjo, of course, but on guitar and half a dozen other instruments which Pete does not attempt. But much of P.S.'s banjo accompaniment is mere whamming.

If community singing is your meat, you can probably learn a lot from him, since he has been at this game for a long time—according to his own account, since his mother gave him a ukulele at the age of eight. But if you prefer your folk songs less noisy, better performed, and with a smaller number of voices, best steer clear. He also has a disturbing habit of sing-ing harmony to his own songs when the crowd is warmed up. On the stage, perhaps he can get away with it. Over a loudspeaker in one's living room, it can be just plain annoying.

If you like blues, don't even bother listening to him. He doesn't know how to sing or play blues, though he occasionally tries to.

If you like spirituals and gospel songs, he does a little better here—in fact, better than most white musicians. But still his voice tends to get tense and hard, and he rarely achieves that full, relaxed but powerful tone that most good Negro singers have naturally. No, if you like spir-ituals, listen to Vera Hall (Folkways) or Blind Gary Davis, or the Gospel Keys, or to the modern commercial singers such as Mahalia Jackson (her early discs, for Apollo, are some of her best).

Pete Seeger's concerts are a different matter. I will not mention them in this article except to say that while there's hardly a song he sings which couldn't be sung better by someone else, his concerts—most of them deft improvisations upon program themes he has developed through the years—are often masterpieces of programming.

This is probably why his records are rarely criticized properly. People like the guy, and hesitate to slam his discs as they should.

Sometimes the intensity of his performance can pick you up and carry you away, especially if you agree with what he is saying (not all do, of course). Jimmy Durante, the old-time comedian, is supposed to have said once, "When I face a crowd, I give 'em all I got!" and Seeger, when he walks out on a stage, often seems to follow this philosophy. Some people try to recapture the excitement by listening to his records. Others, who know what kind of music they like, will not join in on the chorus, and feel more and more repelled. You're either with it or you're not, baby.

It is probably because of his indefatigable concertizing that he has made so many records. Any recording company knows that sales follow personal appearances. Probably a number of readers of this article were first introduced to folk music through a Seeger concert at some college. They can be a lot of fun, and sometimes a deeply moving experience.

But that doesn't mean one has to like his records. Really, I don't think the guy listens to them himself. In between two pretty good songs is sandwiched a sentimental little piece of nothing. If someone recommends a Pete Seeger record to you, the standing rule should be: Don't buy it sight unseen, or sound unheard. You might like it. You might not be able to stand it. The discs range from children's songs through standard American folk repertoire to modern composed songs by people like Malvina Reynolds and Bob Dylan, and to songs from a dozen different countries. Which prompts one to say that Seeger would probably do a better job generally if he didn't spread himself so thin. Perhaps he has opened up Young America's ears to new sounds and songs, but he has also given them a bad example: "You, too, can sing in sixteen idioms."

It's not true. He can't, and you can't.

He is known to go out on a stage before a thousand people (who have paid hard-earned cash for tickets) and, sticking the words of a song with Scotch tape to the microphone, sing them for the first time in his life. You may be able to get away with it on a stage, but do you have to record it, Peter?

To sum up, if one could dub onto a tape a few songs from here and there on his many LPs, one might have quite a good one-hour tape of Pete Seeger. The trouble is, no two people would make the same selections.

Therein lies his defense.

May 1965

WELL, I GUESS I've got to come clean, especially since I see by the letters column that there's some confusion about the authorship of that record review in the last issue of *Sing Out*. I wrote it for the *Little Sandy Review* about a year ago, feeling that they needed it, but just as I was about to send it off, I saw Jon Pankake's more well-rounded article (in *Sandy* #29), and I tabled mine. It was lying around unused when it was collected, adapted and arranged—and published. It is, I believe, a truthful account, although one-sided. But I regret the implied criticism of Folkways Records.

Folkways Records stands for all time a unique landmark in the history of the recording companies of the world.

Other companies put out records to make money, and when they no longer sell well, withdraw them from the market. Moe Asch set out twenty-five years ago to document the music and sounds of the world. He would issue a record he thought valuable, even though only a few dozen others agreed with him (to the extent of five dollars). Even today, 50 percent of the LPs in his catalogue only sell a few hundred copies a year, but he keeps them in the catalogue.

It's a crazy way to do business. The miracle is that Moe Asch has stayed in business, cutting corners in a hundred little ways, and always surprising his closest friends and competitors by bringing out new and wonderful records they never thought of. I used to describe Folkways as a two-horse company, with Moe Asch and Marian Distler both working like horses to keep it afloat. I'd come in at ten o'clock on a Saturday evening and find them still getting out mail. At nine o'clock the following morning, I could find Moe Asch back in the little office, editing his next LP in the only spare minutes he could find.

Now, the business is bigger, but the problems and the work load have increased tenfold. No matter what happens, I could forgive Folkways any sin, because of what it has accomplished.

Credit Moe Asch with a second big accomplishment: his example has encouraged the starting of numerous other small recording ventures, in the United States and elsewhere, to continue the huge job of documenting the music and sounds of the world, unarranged, unprettified, unadorned . . . or unsatisfied.

Years ago, my father pointed out to me that "there is a constant war going on between different cultural forms. It is not so much a war of thunder and lightning, but more like that constant struggle that goes on unseen beneath the ground, between the roots of plants and trees." And, to carry on the simile, I suppose a battlefield which had become stabilized for years could be set into action again by a climatic change, or a forest fire, or man-made changes. I realize this every time I select one tune over another to sing, whenever any artistic judgment is made, whenever a woman decides to buy one dress rather than another. A skirmish is won or lost.

In 1758, an English force attacked at Brittany. Local militia advancing to battle were astounded to hear a local song. It was Welsh mountaineers, singing an old Celtic melody, older than their estrangement. French officers commanded the militia to fire, but the troops would not.

Richard Chase is one of America's best storytellers and also the best leader of play-party "dances" I've ever heard. He's one of those who wishes the definition of "folk music" hadn't become so broad. "When I hear folk songs advertised, I want to hear folk songs," he says. "When I ask, 'Please pass the potatoes,' I don't want to be handed a bowl of cabbage."

Another quote from somewhere: "We have become a race of librarians, racing along the stream of life but afraid to plunge in." (In Washington Square, you can see the photographers taking pictures of other photographers.)

July 1965

ON ROUTE 80 in Alabama,* I met a friend, the Reverend James Bevel, one of the veterans of the Nashville sit-ins of 1960. "Hello there, Brother Seeger," says he. "We're still down here fighting Sin."

In Montreal, there is a coffee house called the Fifth Amendment. Which reminds me: in England the pubs have more poetic titles than the

---

* See p. 104 above.

folk-singing groups, there or here. We have too many Wayfarers, Ramblers, Wanderers, Travelers. I got called up at 1 A.M. once by a trio in Ohio wanting assistance in choosing a name for their group. Since then, we've had an unlisted phone.

As far as coffee houses go, here's some suggestions, free for the taking: the Bone and Vulture, the Scum and Sediment, the Whiff of Grapeshot, the Scent of Danger, the Universal Depth, the Black Hole, the Womb with a View.

A young man out west writes that an elderly relative of his wrote the original poem "My Get Up and Go" sixty years ago, and has a Kansas City newspaper clipping of those years to prove it. (Other claims, from Nova Scotia and Texas, were less documented.) He says this relative doesn't think much of all this folk music stuff, and would prefer to stay anonymous.

My thanks to him anyway. Generations of folks with creaky joints will chuckle over his lines:

> How do I know my youth is all spent?
> My get up and go has got up and went . . .
> But nevertheless, I'm able to grin
> And think of the places my get-up has been.

A friend writes that he heard a speech by a "California Crusader" in Fresno, California, claim that the Beatles are part of a Communist plot to make our young people's minds sick. Here's the Red Master Plan for music, says he: rhythmic music for children ages two to eleven, "beat" music for teens, and folk music for university students.

I told you in an earlier column about Ed McCurdy. Here's more. He used to work for CBC Radio in Toronto. One day, the lunchroom was so crowded people were standing in line for seats, and Ed only had ten minutes for lunch. He put down his guitar case, took out the guitar, and started singing one of his bawdier songs—loudly. Some women finished their lunch quickly, got up, and left. Ed got a seat.

> The golf links lie so near the mill
> That almost any day
> The laboring children can look out
> And see the men at play.

These four lines, which were reprinted hundreds of times, are given much credit for helping to abolish child labor. Sarah Cleghorn, who wrote them in 1915, must have been a wonderful person. I've met people who knew her. She lived to a ripe old age and died only a few years ago.

I tried several times to set this short poem to a tune, and failed. Came to the conclusion that perhaps it was because the poem looked down on the situation from a high point. It wasn't "inside" the situation. First person singular. One of the best songs about factory life is the one collected years ago by old John Lomax.

> No more shall I work in the factory*
> To greasy up my clothes.
> No more shall I work in the factory
> With splinters in my toes.
> Oh, pity me, my darling,
> Oh, pity me, I say,
> Oh, pity me, my darling,
> And carry me away.

But perhaps I'm wrong. Another favorite poem is in the first person singular, but also fails as a song.

> He called me heretic, rebel, a thing to flout
> And drew a circle that kept me out.
> But Love and I had the wit to win:
> We drew a circle that put him in.†

Speaking of poets, if you occasionally see in *Sing Out* quotations from one Walter Lowenfels and wonder who he is, let me introduce him to you. He is a nimble-witted poet who coauthored with Lee Hays some good songs, such as "Lonesome Traveler," "Wasn't That a Time," and "Lousy Dime." Now sixtyish, he was in his youth an émigré in Paris, acquaintance of Henry Miller, e. e. cummings, and others. Returned and fell in love with his country all over again in the thirties, helped edit a small radical paper (oh, why be coy, it was the Philadelphia edition of *The Worker*), went to jail, had a heart attack, and is now retired in south

---

* (The Factory Girl) Collected, adapted and arranged by John A. and Alan Lomax. TRO-© copyright 1934, renewed 1962, Ludlow Music Inc., New York. Used by permission.
† "Outwitted," by Edwin Markham. (This poem came to me orally—a folk version; for the correct poem as written by Markham, see, for example, Louis Untermeyer's 1919 anthology, *Modern American Poetry.*)

Walter Lowenfels

New Jersey, where he turns out reams and volumes of sparkling poetry and provocative prose—and letters which I can't refrain from quoting occasionally. Here's one:

These are singing times. That is the beginning and the end of everything. But sometimes we get dizzy in between.

The baby starts life howling its melody. And in his last hours Socrates returned to music.

The enemy only wants us to hear the atomic explosions. But we hear and we sing the song of the world as a poem, every atom a brother to every other, and a sister, not a splitter.

Dryden wrote of the "music of the spheres." There is the music of electrons, all whirling around.

Leadbelly's life as a singer, an "opener of doors," is in its infancy. This we shall see as all his children, and all his children's children sing.

Yes, he's a Grey Goose A-Flying, and nobody will ever count the infinite number of singing goslings it was his destiny to let loose.

(*The above was written the day Huddie Ledbetter died.*)

It's nice that *Sing Out* will hold one of its Carnegie Hall hootenannies this coming September. Just because the word "hoot" was prostituted for a while is no reason it has to be ruined forever. It is worth fighting to keep the definitions of things we love from being ruined by foolish and/or avaricious people.

THE PENGUIN BOOK OF AMERICAN FOLKSONGS. Compiled, edited, and with notes by Alan Lomax. Piano arrangements by Elizabeth Poston. Penguin Books, Baltimore, Md., 160 pages, $1.95.

WHAT MAKES John and Alan Lomax the greatest American folk song collectors is not just that they roamed all America, with unmatched perseverance, searching for songs. But whereas most collectors were looking for the *oldest* songs they could find, the Lomaxes were looking for the *best* songs they could find. If they found half a good song in Texas and another half of it in Montana, they combined the versions to make one wholly good song. "Bad folkloristic practice," sneered the scholars. But thanks to the Lomaxes, more than any other two Americans, a nation rediscovered its own music.

This collection, selling for a lovely low price, was put together ten years ago for the English market. Alan Lomax was living in London, and found a crowd of young people unable to buy his books published in America. There is a certain amount of duplication with the more recently compiled *The Folk Songs of North America* (a much larger and more expensive volume), but in any case, if you like American folk music, this volume should be on your shelf, or in your guitar case.

The copyright status of the songs is handled much better than in some of the other Lomax books. Detailed credit is given to other collectors and authors for some songs, and only on the back of the title page is this formal claim:

Unless otherwise stated, the songs in this book are drawn from previously copyrighted sources and, as composite versions, have been adapted and arranged by Alan Lomax, by John A. Lomax, or by other editors. They may not be reprinted, recorded, or used for commercial purposes without the written permission of the authors, through Ludlow Music, Inc., Columbus Circle, New York, or Essex Music Ltd., London.

The key words are "composite version," since the details are never spelled out, of course. What was adapted, what was arranged?

This reviewer has never seen eye-to-eye with Alan Lomax on the matter of copyrighting folk songs, but I have to admit I can see his reasoning. Around 1955, a crew of managers, publishers, and recording companies were making hundreds of thousands of dollars out of Lonnie Donnegan's recording of "Rock Island Line," and Alan Lomax, who collected the song, was unable to raise $3,000 to go on another collecting trip. Not to speak of Kelly Pace and other Arkansas Negroes who sang him the song in the thirties, and Leadbelly, who added the "I got hogs" part. If everybody else is making money from the song, why not the collector and the country person who sang it to him?

But the heck with it. This is a great collection. Go down and buy it. The introduction alone, analyzing main types and styles of American songs and singing, is worth the price.

The Newport Festival has tried to put on one stage as many different varieties of what could be called "folk music" as possible. It's not easy; in our rainbow-patterned country there are many kinds of folks. What is a "good" song in one idiom may be "bad" in another. Nevertheless, we have done this, and year after year capacity audiences of 15,000 have applauded three-and-a-half-hour programs which included knowns and unknowns, commercial and noncommercial, famous and infamous. They have heard lonesome ballads and raucous shouts, satires and sentiments, South-North-East-and-West.

How is it possible for a big audience to applaud such disparate elements?

The audience respects the basic integrity of each performer. No singer is singing a song because it happens to be on the "top forty." Each is making the kind of music he or she thinks is the best in the world, even though only a small corner of the world may agree. Also, all the music shares certain basic qualities: Even the most age-old and anonymous songs once rose out of the lives of hardworking people, and even the newest songs drew upon traditions of music handed down by generations of unknown musicians.

As you know, the singers come to Newport not for riches, because no performer at Newport, but nobody, gets paid more than a small standard fee, slightly above Musicians' Union minimum, plus their traveling expenses and hotel.

Since the Newport Folk Festival is a nonprofit corporation, what happens to all the money? In the first place, there is not always so much left over, after paying $30,000 or more for two hundred artists. And the Newport city police charge an arm and a leg—over $20,000. But sometimes there is $10,000 left over, sometimes more.

The official policy is to plow the money back into the general field of folk music. The John Edwards collection of country music in California has got several thousand. Some collectors have been given tape recorders, some performers have been given instruments. Best of all, to my opinion, is the helping along of a number of small local folk festivals that needed a little cash to get started. For example, the French-speaking Cajun people in Louisiana have a unique style of singing and playing fiddle with accordion and a triangle. One of them wrote these words of thanks:

Mamou, La.
1965

The Newport Folk Foundation has accomplished for Acadian music in one year what more than 20 years of conscious effort by folklorists and lay enthusiasts had not only failed to accomplish, but had "proven" could not be accomplished. . . .

Acadian music had lost all semblance of status. It lay captive, isolated and dying, hedged in by a "sub-tradition" of mediocre imitation of country or western or popular music. Cajun music held itself aloof from the conventional musician, and was rejected as inferior by the current hip generation. Its simple traditional instruments—the accordion, violin, and triangle—were drowned out and outclassed by the steel guitar, drum, and brass horn . . .

Through the sponsorship and encouragement of Newport, the Louisiana Folk Foundation held Acadian music competitions at all major area and state festivals during the last year . . . More important, and also a twentieth-century innovation, the Cajun musician is overcoming his feeling of inferiority and has attracted the attention of his young audience.

September 1965

"WELL, THE FOLK BOOM IS DEAD," I read in *Variety*. This reminds me that twenty years ago there was a big hit record of Freddy Martin's orchestra doing a pop version of a Tchaikovsky piano concerto. Soon, there was a rash of similar attempts to popularize "classical" music. A year later, the fad had passed, and pop music moved on to exploit other idioms. I wonder if one would have said then, "Classical music is dead."

Two Goddard College students got a summer job cutting brush in

Maine. The other workers on the gang were a batch of down-and-outers well intimidated by their bosses. The students taught them "The Banks of Marble," and one afternoon they all came stepping into the office singing it, the whole gang, no longer demoralized, but with heads held high and singing out. The students were fired.

In an argument with someone, it is sometimes necessary to use shock treatment to start them thinking. George Bernard Shaw was famous at this trick. But people got used to being shocked by him. At the end of his life, Shaw thought bitterly: They never take me seriously now. I say something and they react, "Oh, that's just G.B.S."

Kids invent the greatest new words. "Rambustificationjambihoppitidoodan," one said to me. "It's spelled 'pq' and means 'look.'"

I once wrote, "Down with the cult of originality," and a friend brought me up short by remarking that to call anything a cult was to automatically damn it. What's wrong with a cult? "An unthinking, almost religious attitude toward the worshiped object."

Why should writers think that their highest aim in life must be to get published? I once knew a poet who never thought of seeing his work in print. He never made a carbon copy and gave his poems away as fast as he wrote them. They could be birthday presents or unbirthday presents, or maybe he would just leave them on the bureau of somebody he was visiting. His poems had every imaginable theme: one might be a narrative of some funny incident, another would be philosophical. It was his way of expressing himself, just as others express themselves by painting pictures, baking apple pie, or playing banjos.

Some songwriters prefer anonymity and refuse to claim credit for their songs. They remind me of the story about the Anonymous Movement, a group of Paris poets in the 1920s. Some were well known and got book reviews. Others were unknown and could never even get a nod from the literary critics. So, to foil the reviewers, they formed a club which published all their works anonymously. The critics were baffled and furious. Knowing that a few famous poets were members of the club, they did not dare ignore any of its output.

Which further reminds me: In 1946, a tall, awkward man came upstairs to the offices of People's Songs and offered to help with the typing.

The offer was gratefully accepted. Three days later, we asked his name.

"Frank."

But what's your last name?

"Frank."

Just Frank Frank? No middle initial?

"O."

So, Frank O. Frank came to help us, and invaluable help it was, too. A few months later, he said that in his home county, Bexar County, Texas, were some fine songs, and that he had mimeographed a collection of them. Later, it appeared that many were rewritten by him, and some were almost totally original songs, but in any case, they went from hand to hand, and some people sing them now as old folk songs, such as "Get You a Copper Kettle," "See Them Buzzards," and "Quantrell Side." Good songs, folk or Frank.

The following news item got me started writing the song "All Mixed Up":

"Two enterprising Brooklynites, Allan Nussbaum and Jerry Fishman, have organized a fleet of 'Chow Chow Cup' vans to dispense Oriental food to Occidental neighborhoods. A Chinese tune by a Japanese composer played on Swiss chimes heralds the van's arrival. Food is served in a 'Chow Chow Cup' made of tasty noodles."

You want to know one of the most political songs I know? It's an old pop song I think I remember hearing on a Bing Crosby recording. "Wrap Your Troubles in Dreams and Dream Your Troubles Away."

I hear somebody saying, "But that's not political in the slightest. In fact, it's antipolitical."

That's just it. Suppose you were having a school board election in your town. There had been a do-nothing bunch of board members and the aroused parents were determined to vote the rascals out. Then into the community comes a person going from door to door, whispering, "It's no use voting; politics is crooked anyway; you'll just elect somebody worse than the people already on the board. Any person with integrity will stay home on election day."

Supposing somebody accuses this person of trying to keep the old school board in power. He protests, "No. I'm *not* in favor of the old school board; I'm just against *all* politics."

But you all know the logical results of his campaign: the old crew would be left in power. As Edmund Burke said, "The only thing necessary for evil to triumph is for men of good will to do nothing."

So that's why I say that this is one of the most political songs I know. "Wrap Your Troubles in Dreams and Dream Your Troubles Away."

November 1965

When "If I Had a Hammer" was first written, the next-to-last line went ". . . between all of my brothers." But within a year, opponents of male supremacy forced common usage to change it to ". . . my brothers and my sisters." Lee Hays, the author, tried to resist in vain. He even once sang, ". . . between all of my siblings," but this was not appreciated either.

My guess is that language is just going to have to change to take into account the equality of the sexes. The brochure of the Unity Theatre, London, instructing new volunteers about their jobs, includes this paragraph:

"To avoid 'he-or she-ing' in the text, 'he' has been used in most descriptions of jobs to be done, on the time-honored principle that in all times of doubt, the male embraces the female. It must be stressed, however, that almost all jobs at Unity can be done, and are done, equally well and equally badly by women as well as men."

A college student wrote asking how to get copyright permission to reprint songs. Said he wanted to put out a mimeographed collection of several hundred songs. Said he didn't want to be commercial about it, just wanted to pay for the expense of the paper, etc. I wrote him a long letter and tried to answer his questions, but it all boiled down to this: If he kept his project small and just ran off a few hundred copies for friends, he could probably get away with breaking copyright laws. But the moment he officially offered something for sale, he'd be liable to get into trouble. I guess that's the way it is in this world, you're either big or you're small. The middle-sized man is wiped out.

Some kinds of music that I admire but never could listen to for long at a stretch: real flamenco guitar playing, and blues, such as those of the great Robert Johnson. Why? Hard to put it in words. Perhaps the aggressive sound puts me on edge. I just don't feel that aggressive.

In the summer of 1960, folklorist George List met in the Southwest a Hopi Indian musician who had composed (on order) a song for a festival dance, and whose composition was turned down. It happens there, too.

Anyone concerned with the folk-song-star syndrome can take heart from a sentence in last issue's article on the British music hall tradition: "They idolized their stars." Why take heart? Because economic pressure and professionalized music developed stars then as now, almost inevitably. And because now, a hundred years later, the stars have been forgotten, but a handful of great songs has lasted.

I would like to enlist the help of the readers of this column in a little scholarly research: compiling all the various known songs using the melody of "Twinkle, Twinkle, Little Star."

"When I First Came to This Land" uses it. So does "Oleanna." And "Kum Ba Ya" (the third and fourth lines). I've heard German, French, Swedish, Greek, Italian, and Ukrainian versions, but don't have copies. The Ukrainian version is in a minor key and, when slowed down, shows itself to be none other than "Hatikvah," the Israeli national anthem.

Sometimes, the resemblance may be very disguised, but it is still worth noting. A year after I wrote the melody of "Bells of Rhymney," I realized that the first line was clearly "Twinkle." And, if you analyze the melody of "My Darling Clementine," you find that, except for two notes (shown in parentheses below), it also is basically this melody. Accent the italicized syllables and you'll see:

> Oh, my *dar*ling, oh, my *dar*ling,
>   Oh, my *dar*ling (Clementine),
> You are *lost* and gone for*ev*er,
>   Dreadful *sor*ry, Clemen*tine*.

I admit that this is stretching the point, but for the purposes of the research project, it's worth stretching. I'll gratefully accept any contributions. Musicologist Norman Cazden got me started on the whole idea. My thanks to him.

Worth Quoting:

"IN MOST of the songs, we have adhered strictly to the original script, but in a few of the oldest ballads, we thought it best to make some slight alterations to render the text suitable for present-day publication. In our generation, we do not deal so frankly with all subjects as writers formerly did, and certainly we could not sing the original versions of some of the ballads with the unconscious simplicity of James and Mary. They accept these ballads in their entirety and feel in no way obligated to apologize for them, although James will occasionally prepare the hearer with some such remark as 'There ain't nothing bad about this song, so fur ez I can see, 'ceptin' its criminality' " (from the introduction to *Songs from the Hills of Vermont,* collected and edited by Edith Sturgis, 1919).

1966

(GM APOLOGIZES FOR HARASSING SAFE-CAR CRUSADER RALPH NADER. CALIFORNIA GRAPE STRIKERS MARCH 250 MILES TO STATE CAPITOL. JAMES MEREDITH WOUNDED ON MISSISSIPPI MARCH; BLACK POWER SLOGAN POPULAR AMONG MARCHERS. BUDDHIST UPRISING CRUSHED IN S. VIETNAM. SUPREME COURT SETS STANDARDS TO PREVENT COERCED CONFESSIONS. 3 FORT HOOD GI'S REFUSE TO GO TO VIETNAM. CHINESE LEADERS ENDORSE "CULTURAL REVOLUTION" LED BY YOUNG RED GUARDS. BLACK "REBELLION" IN WATTS AREA OF LOS ANGELES.
("GREEN BERETS" SONG A TOP HIT; PATRIOTIC THEMES PROMINENT IN COUNTRY-WESTERN SONGS. NEWARK TV STATION PRESENTS PETE SEEGER WITH AUTHENTIC FOLK MUSICIANS IN "RAINBOW QUEST" SERIES. CUBAN JOSÉ MARTI'S "GUANTANAMERA," SUNG BY THE SANDPIPERS, ON POP CHARTS.)

(In 1966 I took leave of absence from half a dozen committees in order to try and edit some of the folk music movies our family had filmed around the world two years before. I got

friends to write guest Johnny Appleseed, Jr., columns in my place.)

Dear Editor,

I was very sorry to see your well-intentioned international section being exploited for political purposes in your July issue. The not too subtle anti-Israeli comments in Rashed Hussein's otherwise very generalized article on Arab folk music were very unbecoming of a magazine which has consistently tried to further understanding among the peoples of the world. Also why the mystery about Rashed Hussein's identity? He is a disenchanted Israeli Arab, whose nihilistic outlook is contributing nothing to the solution of the problems of the Israeli Arabs, or the breaking down of the barriers between Arabs and Jews. The sour political comments aside, I enjoyed the article and I'm looking forward to many others of its type. I'm also willing to correspond with anyone who is interested in the Israeli folk-scene.

HILLEL SCHENKER
Israel

I agree with the letter of Hillel Schenker, in that Rashed Hussein (author of the article on Arab folk music, *Sing Out*, Vol. 15, No. 3) should have been identified. There my agreement ends. Rashed Hussein is a most remarkable young man, a poet and a journalist. For some time he was the world's only Arab writing for a Jewish newspaper. He told me with a soft smile: "In Egypt they call me a collaborationist. But I said to them, 'Tell me, where in this world is a Jew supposed to live?'" Some of Rashed's most beautiful poems are about peace; would that Israel—and all the world—had more human beings like him.

Here is an excerpt from Hussein's *Sing Out* article, "Arabic Folk Song —a 1,000-Year Legacy":

The authors of most Arabic folk songs are not known. Besides, even if the author is known, the people almost always change the words or add some of their own. At weddings, for instance, the village women spontaneously change the words to express more exactly what they want to say at the time. Changes are made in different countries to fit the political conditions and struggles. For instance, a love song that took on political phrases and names, in the original begins:

> Oh, Gazelle, wrapped in your gown,
> You love me and like to torture me.
> But if I live even two thousand years,
> Other than you I'll never love.

Later an unknown person changed it to:

> Oh, Gazelle, wrapped in your cape,
> You love me and like to torture me.
> Since you are sitting beside me
> Why should I need electricity?

An unknown patriot put it differently:

> Oh, Gazelle, wrapped in your cape,
> Let the breeze of youth blow.
> My country fell in love with a foreigner,
> Although I am in my best years!

1967

(MILITARY COUP IN GREECE. BLACK PANTHER PARTY FOR SELF-DEFENSE FOUNDED IN CALIFORNIA. SPANISH AMERICAN ALIANZA DEMANDS NEW MEXICO LAND UNDER TREATY RIGHTS. ISRAEL AND ARAB COUNTRIES FIGHT "6-DAY WAR." MUHAMMAD ALI, BOXER AND MUSLIM MINISTER, SENTENCED FOR DRAFT REFUSAL. RIOTING OVER POLICE BRUTALITY IN NEWARK AND DETROIT. CHE GUEVARA KILLED IN BOLIVIA. PEACE DEMONSTRATORS BEATEN AND GASSED AT PENTAGON.

(HUMAN BE-IN AT SAN FRANCISCO; "HIPPIE" REJECTION OF MIDDLE-CLASS VALUES PERMEATES YOUTH CULTURE AND ROCK MUSIC. FOLK-STYLE "ODE TO BILLY JOE" A TOP HIT. ARLO GUTHRIE SINGS "ALICE'S RESTAURANT" AT NEWPORT. COFFEE HOUSES NEAR ARMY BASES OFFER MUSIC AND POLITICAL DISCUSSION.)

January 1967

I have com - mit - ted crimes __ a - gainst na - ture!

Staying in - doors ___ on sun - ny days! __

Here's Pete Seeger again, resuming this rambling column, with many thanks to Tom Paxton, Dominic Behan, and the other friends who have filled in for me. I spent much of the year trying to edit some movies, and thereby hangs a tale:

"Sitting at a desk while the sun is shining bright outside is bad enough. Standing at a set of rewinds editing film in a dark room is worse. Okay; somebody has to do it. But I'm getting too old for it."

I was grumbling thus to my wife while we drove in to the city through Bear Mountain State Park. We passed three or four park service employees raking near the highway.

"Now, there's a good job. Lots of fresh air," says I.

"I can give you that any time you like," answers my wife. "You can start in on our lawn as soon as we get home."

It so happens that several months later I did, by inadvertence, find myself with a rake in my hand, and had filled a wheelbarrow, when I heard my wife's voice, cheerful but edged:

"Well, well, WELL! I'll keep track of the hours and give you a paycheck from the Bear Mountain State Park."

"No, this isn't the same. The men there looked so carefree. But I can't get my mind off Vietnam."

"How do you know it's not the same with them?"

She went indoors. I got to thinking how many great songs must have been composed by men at work. Think of the cowboy songs, the sailor songs, the lumberjack ballads, the mining songs. I disagree with Eric Bentley: I doubt that the guy borrowed a pencil from the cook after supper and sat down determined to write a song. I bet that in ninety-nine cases out of a hundred the main lines came to him while his muscles were busy earning a few pennies. His head cheated on the boss and put together stories, meter and rhyme.

So I'll close this little rumination with the resolve to ask my song-writing friends under what conditions they can remember being inspired to write their best songs. And under what conditions they persevered to complete them. You know the saying: the true test of an artist's power is to be able to complete the work of art after the first flush of enthusiasm has passed.

As for me, if "The Ballad of Lizzie Strada" ever gets finished, it'll be thanks to some leaf-raking.

Matt McGinn's "The Pill" is a great song. The division between the sexes is not so serious as the multiplication.

Marc Antony was wrong. Shakespeare quoted him claiming that the bad things people do tend to be remembered, and the good forgotten. But an architect's bad houses are torn down, or fall down. The most beautiful ones are preserved. Good parents are remembered; bad ones forgotten. And most clearly: a songwriter's good songs are remembered, the bad ones forgotten.

Can't we apply the term "artist" to almost anyone who does a job extremely well? A boxer like Muhammad Ali, a good cook, a master carpenter or plasterer or bulldozer driver? I knew an old woman who worked at a blueberry farm and could pick 60 quarts a day. She was an artist; you should have seen her hands fly.

Notes from Many Countries

AMERICAN POPULAR "folk music" is sweeping much of Europe (and Japan) with almost frightening success. When I get letters from overseas, I often ask in reply what do they know about their own folk music. Quite usually the answer is that they do not know too much about it. Here is a typical letter:

"You asked me what I liked best in Swedish folk music and what I liked in American folk music. I'm sorry to say that I don't know very much about Swedish folk music but I know that I like our old, sad songs from the Middle Ages best. We don't have so many styles to choose from. American folk music, however, has a great many different styles. Blues, old-time, mountain songs, blue-grass, ballads, gospels and so on. American music thrills me more because of that.

"You asked me also if I believed one could use American folk instruments with Swedish songs, and vice versa. I must say yes: almost always. It's just that some songs sound deep Swedish to me. I don't think that an old herdsmaid's song and a five-stringer go along very well together. And I don't think a key fiddle from Dalarna would fit very well in a blues. (I may be wrong, but that's what I believe.)"

Sam Bolotin, in Moscow, USSR, is arranging for the publishing of a book of 50 or 60 newly composed songs of the type that are printed in *Broadside* (N.Y.).* He has translated into singable Russian songs of Paxton, Ochs, Dylan, and many others, and plans to call the book, "New American Folk Songs." I wrote and advised him to be prepared to answer the professional folklorists who will claim—with some justification—that he is misusing the term "folk song."

"If I were you, I would say these are not cabaret songs, because they are not meant to be sung in cabarets. They are not pop songs, because—while the authors would not object to their being played on radio and TV—it is not expected that they will be. They are not art songs; often the authors cannot read or write music notation. We can only call them folk songs because the same people who like to sing and play old folk music also like to sing these. If some few of them are good enough to last 100 years, then assuredly they will be collected and called folk songs. Meanwhile, you are to be known as a premature folk song collector."

Jean Murai, who is from a New York Jewish background, was singing for college students in Montreal. She made the effort to rehearse an old French Canadian song, "Voilà le Bon Vent"—and got an ovation. Afterward she asked a student how come. He answered, "Yes, we all know that's a very commonplace song, but you made it sound quite new to us by singing it in a meaningful way."

The French view of things: On a French TV program, I sprawled on

* *Guitars in the Battle,* published early in 1968.

the floor chatting with the announcer while they set up the lights. He learned I was trying to study Russian. "Ah, yes. In France we say it is very reasonable to study Russian . . . and even more reasonable to study Chinese."

In Scotland's best folk song club, run by Arthur Argo and friends in Aberdeen, a fine traditional ballad singer mentioned, "You know what I was listening to last night? Chinese folk music. Yes. On the wireless, short wave. I listen to it quite often. They have announcers in English. I do believe that next to Scottish folk music, I like Chinese folk music best. It has that high lonesome sound."

Believe me. His very words.

A refugee from the land of apartheid writes that in the spring of '65 a dozen friends of hers were in jail, charged by the South African government with some sort of seditious activity. They had learned some songs from a few of my LP records, and sang them together. Gradually the attitude of the other prisoners, and the guards and wardens, changed toward them. By the time of their trials and sentencing (they were found guilty) it was as a sad group of friends that the jailers bid them goodbye. The government of South Africa has become very concerned now, she says, about folk music, has confiscated certain LPs from the music stores, and insists that college folk song clubs abjure political songs.

Concerning Electrified Music:

I LIKE the 1966 electric guitars a lot better than the ones I tried playing in the 1930s. The tone was too bland then. Nowadays the speaker gives out more twang. But even so, I don't think the range of tone, or the flexibility, can beat a good acoustic guitar. And all that equipment to lug around! Ugg. Of course, me, I've been playing electrified music for a long time. Ever since I first started using microphones.

Pete La Farge helped me build a beautiful fireplace and chimney for our cabin, and I'll never look at it without thinking of him. The song of his I'll remember best is a subtle little thing called "Coyote,"* with only

---

* Copyright © 1962, United International Copyright Representatives Ltd., 5 Riverside Drive, New York, N.Y. 10023. Reprinted by permission.

one mournful music phrase repeated over and over. Pete told me that the Indian name for the coyote was "Little Brother." His song used the fate of the coyote to symbolize what modern man was doing to all of nature (whereas the Indian lived in harmony with nature).

> Coyote, coyoteeeeee!
> What have they done?
> My little brother, where . . .
> Where do you runnnnnnnnn?

> > They've poisoned the mesas;
> > They've poisoned the plains;
> > My little brother, the coyote,
> > Won't come back again.

> You can hear them calling,
> The ones that are left;
> He's warning the human race
> Of his death . . .

> > Coyote, coyoteeeeeee! . . .

February 1967

Malvina Reynolds, of Berkeley, California, is the author and composer of such songs as "Little Boxes," "Where Are You Going, My Little One?," "God Bless the Grass," and "What Have They Done to the Rain?" Last fall she breezed over the ocean, and I got the following letter from her:

"Spent September in England, and mostly in London and in central London. It was my first visit, and I did none of the usual things. In fact I was dragged kicking and screaming to the Changing of the Guard at Buckingham Palace—and found it quite charming, with the slim, doll-like soldiers in the nifty uniforms moving with precision to their band, which played U.S. show tunes mostly. A knowledgeable friend took us after the pipe band instead of having us follow the main body of the guard, and you could walk close enough to touch, right into the palace grounds. This is what soldiers should be for—to look handsome, march neatly and play jolly music on pipe and drum.

"For the first few days, the whole thing—England, the English—seemed like one big put-on for my amusement. Everything, the way they talked, the taxis, the buildings (the ordinary business building in London would be set aside as a national antique here). But I soon got used to it all and felt almost at home—I learned to avoid the so-called coffee shops, which look like those in the U. S. but prepare a hamburger that's paper-thin and tastes as though it's been boiled, and cook an omelet by pouring a ladle of beaten egg into a bowl of smoking fat and forgetting it there. There are good eating places in London—you can get an excellent cold-meat sandwich in a pub if you know what hours they are open, and women patronize them as a matter of course—the good restaurants are expensive.

"Our speech is, for them, a dialect, of course. I soon got in the way of speaking what would be for me an affected English accent in order to be understood by waiters, clerks, busmen and telephone operators. And in Birmingham, which has its own way of speaking, a young fellow came up to me after my show there and said some nice things that I could just barely understand, ending with, 'Where did you get that darling accent?'

"I sang at the Jug O' Punch in Birmingham under the aegis of the Ian Campbell Group, who are great. They've never appeared in this country, and that's a shame—the one tour they had planned was messed up by some booking-agent shenanigans. Birmingham is a tremendous industrial city; its folk club meets in a union hall the size of a medium auditorium. When I first went in I thought, 'A folk club here! They'll be lost.' But before it was well under way the seats were filled and the audience was standing three deep around the walls. The singing was great, the audience singing along in fine voice, and talent to burn at the microphone.

"I did some other appearances around London, and on BBC radio and TV. I've never seen such quality TV as they have there—the lighting, the direction, the timing. And the newspapers—people read newspapers in England. The newsstand at the hotel has not two or three but dozens of daily and Sunday papers.

"I got to the John Snow pub in Soho, where Ewan and Peggy MacColl are in charge, and I sang a couple there. Room above a pub crowded to the doors. This seems to be the main problem there—finding rooms big enough for the attendance at folk clubs. Here, too, the quality of the songs and the singing was glorious. The Dolphin pub, near St. Pancras Station (I always find myself saying 'pancreas,' and that's wrong) has altogether free-form singing on Sunday nights—no one in charge, three

Malvina Reynolds

or four at a table will start a song—and soon everyone is singing, often a capella, and with such songs and voices as I never heard before. You could dip a fishnet into the room and pick up a 'quartet' as good as any that are recording here, I believe.

MALVINA."

I only heard the song "Eve of Destruction" once. On a neighbor's car radio. It was interesting to listen to, but after it was over, I got the feeling that to say there is no hope in anything—not in anything at all in the world—is next to saying therefore that you might as well just look out for yourself, let's you and me have a ball, baby. That's what pop music has been saying about as long as I can remember.*

" Middle age: when the narrow waist and broad mind begin to change places." (I keep getting reminded of this, these days.)

Any reader know the French language well? There's a long article on Vietnamese folk music in the current *Journal of the International Folk Music Council,* Vol. XVIII. (The issue also has articles in English and German.) $4.50 from Messrs. Heffer and Sons, Ltd., Cambridge, England.

Manny Greenhill, managing Joan Baez's tour of Europe last year, found himself talking to a young radio announcer in East Berlin. Manny doesn't know German, but spoke Yiddish, and the announcer, who was Jewish, replied in the same language. Manny said,

"You're the first person I've met who realizes I'm speaking Yiddish. I've been speaking to people over in West Berlin for several days, and they understand me, but they all seem to assume I'm speaking some country dialect of German."

"Mr. Greenhill, you must understand. No one there has heard Yiddish for over twenty-five years."

---

* Malvina Reynolds' comments, in the next issue of *Sing Out:*

I can't agree with Pete Seeger about "Eve of Destruction." When Roger Heyne of U.C. first took over as chancellor after a Free Speech fight, he had some very good things to say about this generation of students, in whom he found "an ingredient of emotional muscularity, of fire-and-ice, of cool and critical distance from many of our generation's ways" (this is from an interview in the *SF Chronicle* of 11/13/65). Then he went on (and this is what is pertinent to the song) that the new generation is "absolutely bugged on the subject of hypocrisy. That is why its angry negations—like those of the prophets—are stronger than its affirmations. That is why it is surer of what is wrong with where we are as a society, than of where we ought to go. Prophets are not redeemers."

When you consider this harsh statement—the lyrics of "Eve of Destruction"—against the background of puppy-love pap (even the new *love* songs are "muscular—cool and critical" in many cases) and bathos that was the typical pop song on the charts when this came on the scene and swept the country for a time, we shouldn't underestimate its significance. I'm not saying it was a great song, but in the history of popular song and protest, it was very important.

Too many of the topical songs tend to draw conclusions for the listener, fearful of letting him draw his own. One type of listener might well conclude from "Eve" that there is no use to do anything but live the day. I'd say those wouldn't be the ones who bought the record in the thousands. The ones who did might well be saying, "Thank God, here's somebody who's saying what has been eating me since my first air-raid drill. I'm not alone!" And that is the beginning of action.

A young white fellow from South Africa writes me to the effect that we over here must understand that the African people are only just emerging from tribalism.

I answered, of course, that's true, and so are you and me and the whole damn world.

Richie Havens is one of the few guitar players I know who makes full chords sound rhythmically interesting. With him it's not just "wham wham wham." He uses a flat pick. No single strings, just beautiful chords, but accented with great variety and superb taste.

Iranian girls have a nice courting custom: they tie knots in the living grass. Still rooted and growing together.

April 1967

Random Notes from All Over

I READ in a magazine that Senator Spong wants to propose a bill to prevent pop songs from being pirated by Hong Kong disc outfits. He wants Senator Long (from Louisiana, home of jazz) and Senator Fong (from Hawaii, nearest to Asia) to co-sponsor it, so that it will be known as the Long Fong Spong Hong Kong Song Bill.

Add deathless rhymes (Ogden Nash assures me that it is over 56 years old, and anonymous):

> *The rain it raineth every day*
> *Upon the just and unjust fella,*
> *But more upon the just, because*
> *The unjust steals the just's umbrella.*

You've heard of "Gresham's Law"?—the tendency for the bad to drive out the good. And the person who quotes it need only point to the TV

screens, the neighborhood movie theater, the suburban highway display-
ing the Great American Adscape.

Nevertheless the folklorist in his very profession sees Gresham's Law
refuted in the history of many a ballad. Over the centuries the best verses
have been remembered, the poor ones forgotten. The best songs have
been remembered, the poorest forgotten.*

When is it that Gresham's Law does win out? I'd say it's when the
average person makes a too-hasty choice. That's when the good is abandoned, the bad kept. When do prejudice, fear, ignorance, thoughtlessness,
selfishness, prompt someone to make a wrong decision? When that decision is made in haste.

Here is a good argument for letting the folk process not change things
too swiftly, for not having fads and fashions switch too suddenly. No
wonder the bad drives out the good when the average citizen is forced
to make too many hasty decisions. No wonder, as Oscar Wilde said,
fashion is a form of ugliness so unbearable that it has to be changed
every few months.

An anecdote for folk singers to remember:

A highland Scotsman was once visited by a friend from down in the
city of Aberdeen. In the morning they had a big bowl of oatmeal porridge
for breakfast. At lunchtime, his friend found that again they had porridge. In the evening, still again, porridge was the meal. The friend
asked cautiously, "Don't you ever get tired of porridge?"

The highlander looked up in frank surprise. "Why, mon, how can you
ever get tired of food?"

For disgruntled employers who wonder why there are no anti-union
songs, I hereby present, gratis, a great tag line for an employer's song.
The rest they will have to compose on their own.

Those   bas - tards   ne - ver   had   to   meet   a   pay - roll!

---

* From Bob Bush of Cambridge, Mass. (*Sing Out,* August 1967): ". . . It's not fair to
botch up Gresham's Law like he did. G. says that bad drives good out of *circulation:* that
means just the contrary of people holding onto the bad stuff."

One of the hardest audiences I ever faced: five hundred inmates of a Texas prison. Sang 'em the songs I learned from Leadbelly. They worked. Included "Go Down, Old Hannah," and was mighty proud when a prisoner told me the following day, "You know, I didn't really think of what those words meant till you sang it."

The meaning of a song is nearly always more than the songwriter intended. The meaning of words—any word—grows with experience. The word "house" can mean various things in various countries. A neighbor's kid once looked at our log cabin and said, "That's a house?"

And think of the switches in meanings, when history pulls out the rug from under a style of life. The same words that once meant "brave and new" now mean "quaint and dated."

Almeda Riddle, Ozark ballad singer, was teaching an old song to Bernice Reagon of Atlanta, while sitting in a motel room in Boston after the video-taping of the TV show "Roomful of Music." The hymn "Amazing Grace" was mentioned. "Someone asked me," said Almeda, "is that a folk song? I told 'em, honey, it's a folk song because it's been kept alive because folks like it."

In her own quiet way Almeda is a religious person. But she's reticent about it: "I'm not going to come here with a Bible under one arm and a songbook under the other and say 'Look at God's gift to Boston.' "

Add problems of a nuclear age: an American anthropologist returned safe from a trip into the jungles of New Guinea, visiting people who had never before seen or heard of the outside world. He wanted to thank and reward some local guides who had risked great danger in accompanying him. But what to give them? Money would mean nothing. Food? They didn't like our canned or dehydrated food, and just candy wouldn't do. Clothing? They hardly used it. My friend ended by giving one of them a hatchet.

He came back to the area a year later. That hatchet had completely upset the local economy. The former guide, by loaning out the hatchet, had become the richest man in the village, and now owned slaves. The little tool was a priceless miracle, introduced into a stone-age economy.

June 1967

WHEN WOODY GUTHRIE was singing hillbilly songs on a little Los Angeles radio station in the late 1930s, he used to mail out a small mimeographed songbook to listeners who wanted the words to his songs. On the bottom of one page appeared the following:

> "This song is Copyrighted in U.S., under Seal of Copyright #154085, for a period of 28 years, and anybody caught singin it without our permission, will be mighty good friends of our'n, cause we don't give a dern. Publish it. Write it. Sing it. Swing to it. Yodel it. We wrote it, that's all we wanted to do."

Last fall I asked Clark Kessinger, the great West Virginia fiddler, to be a guest on a program at the University of West Virginia. The people sponsoring the show were not certain how he would be received. "Our students are too sophisticated for this old mountain fiddling."

The fact is that he was the hit of the show. The students stormed and cheered. At the age of seventy Clark has got more life and zing than most people half his age or even a quarter his age. Anybody who would like to have him perform for a long or short time, get in touch with his manager, Ken Davidson, Kanawha Records, 1889 Palm Drive, Charleston, West Virginia 25311.

For some traditional singers, the very style of singing makes every song a protest song: the harsh vocal tone says things that words hardly need add to. But beware trying to fake it. And if any McLuhanites are listening, I challenge them to let me visit their mailboxes every morning for a month and remove the contents of all their letters, presenting them only with the empty envelopes. The envelope is not the message. Just a part of it.

Add unforgettable occasions: when the cloudburst opened up on six thousand people at the Newport Folk Festival, 1965. They were in the middle of listening to Mimi and Dick Farina. Not a soul scurried for shelter. The music kept on, hotter and stronger. Some in the audience started stripping, and dancing in the downpour. The number was over.

Everyone, soaked to the skin, was hollering for more, on their feet, clapping, stamping, dancing, as the dulcimer and guitar started up again.

August 1967

Being interviewed on the David Susskind TV show, I found myself heckled by right-wingers in the audience. "Isn't it true that every time the Communist party line changes, your songs change, too?"

Like a damn fool, I tried to talk politics with him. I should have said, "Yep, between the song 'Irene Goodnight' and 'Kisses Sweeter Than Wine' it is obvious there was a change in the party line on love."

Seen at the Berkeley Folk Festival: a young guitar player whose right arm had been amputated just below the elbow. He expertly plucked the strings with a calloused bony stump.

On the way to sing for a miners' union in Trail, British Columbia, I saw a huge farmhouse along the highway. "That looks big enough for four families!"

"It is," the young labor lawyer replied. "It's a Doukhobor farm. Each family lives on a different floor, but they all work together like a little collective farm. And they are members of one parish church, which sticks together to help out any farm that is having a bad year. They stick very close to each other and hardly ever invite outsiders. Last year a local real-estate speculator inflamed the nearby town against a Doukhobor farm, with the aim of forcing them off their land. The speculator wanted it for himself. I volunteered to defend them in court, and when we won the case, they invited me over for a victory party. I sat around all evening listening to the most glorious choral singing of Russian folk songs and Doukhobor hymns. Most Canadians never hear them."

Ace banjo picker Paul Cadwell uses nylon strings for his banjo, but for years has scorned the expensive store-bought kind. He found that trout-fishing leader, guaranteed for a three-pound fish, was just right for the first string, and much cheaper. Leader guaranteed for a seven-pound fish took care of the second string.

Singing in various countries overseas these days takes on a special poignant quality. I am glad to show them a different side of America than one they may know of. But as much as I personally love the songs I sing, I can't fool my audience and say, "These are songs which 190 millions of North Americans also love to sing." Nor even a majority.

It is interesting to see how the same song will take on new meanings when sung for different audiences. The most nearly universal songs I know are Negro spirituals and freedom songs. But even these can be misinterpreted and argued about.

In January 1967 I sang in Germany. I had sung in every country on its borders, and finally realized that only a psychological block was holding me back. I suppose I was afraid that every time I met someone my age or older I'd be wondering what they were doing in 1938 or 1942. Then I realized this was silly. In future years an American will receive the same glances: what was he doing in 1967? So my wife and I went to Germany. Met some wonderful people. Sang in both West Berlin and East Berlin to some of the warmest audiences I've ever met. Heard "Peat Bog Soldiers" sung out like nowhere else.

Sang "Shtill di Nacht" (written in 1943 by the nineteen-year-old Polish-Jewish partisan, Hirsch Glick). After one concert, a woman pressed into my hand a tiny memento, a six-pointed star the size of my little fingernail. "Please keep this. It was given me by a friend just before they took her away. We were both in the death camp together."

When I sang my ballad about Lisa Kalvelage (the German-American housewife who was jailed in California last spring for picketing a dock where napalm bombs were being loaded) the audience was pin-drop quiet.

Like most would-be poets, I've written my share of blank verse. But I keep coming back to Robert Frost's opinion on free verse vs. rhyme: "I'd as soon play tennis without a net." And Woody Guthrie once penned a memo to himself: "I must steer clear of Walt Whitman's swimmy waters."

Hamish Henderson, lecturing on Scottish folk music to the Aberdeen folk song club: "How does money come into the picture? And how, for Christsake, can we occasionally keep it out of the picture?"

I suppose we must love this frivolous human race in spite of its frivolity, its technical achievements, its earnest pursuit of power. Surely common sense would tell us that the most urgent task for us three billion is to learn to laugh at ourselves and laugh with each other.

October 1967

ABOUT A YEAR AGO a young Spanish disc jockey got a batch of Weavers' records. He was conducting a pop program for a radio station in Madrid. One day he played the Weavers' "Si Mi Quieres Escribir." The next day he was visited by the security police and asked where did he get the record? Why did you play this song? He told them he had no idea that this song was connected with the Spanish Civil War—and he had to assure them that he would not play the song again. Within the next few days, he received well over a thousand letters requesting that he repeat the song on his program. He could not. He only found out about the song's 1937 origin when he spoke to his parents.

When I was at Harvard, I listened to one of the last lectures given by Alfred North Whitehead, the great British philosopher. A little wisp of a guy, with a good sense of humor. A student once spoke to him, feeling that his explanation of a certain point was unnecessarily abstruse.

"Perhaps you're right," he told her. "Why don't you see if you can rephrase it more clearly? Work on it tonight, and we'll talk about it tomorrow."

Next day she showed him her rewriting of several paragraphs. "Why, yes, this is very good; much clearer than I had." Whitehead ruminated a moment, and then added, "I just hope it isn't *too* clear."

He felt this strongly—that words should not be clearer than the truth. He once said that every university should inscribe over its gate: "Strive for simplicity—and learn to mistrust it."

Which phrase keeps coming back to me every time I'm interviewed by journalists these days, asking important questions and hoping to get catchy headline answers.

Whitehead, like some other mathematicians, was really a poet at heart. After all, mathematics starts with a poetical assumption, that one equals one. It's really not true. No two snowflakes are equal, or two raindrops. Another writer described math as like a rope hanging down from a cliff to a pathway cut into the face of the cliff. The path is blocked by a rockslide. But by grasping this rope, swinging out over space, and then back to the path beyond the rockslide, the traveler can proceed. While one is hanging onto the rope, one's feet dangle over thin air. But if you hold on tight, you can get back to solid ground.

Some fine 16-mm folk music films exist, but spend most of their time on library shelves, because people who like folk music prefer to make it themselves, rather than sit in a dark room watching a shadow on a screen. But some of the British folk song clubs have worked out a compromise. They rent a projector and film, but start off the evening with live music, and arrange to have the singers lead up to the kind of music shown in the film. Then the lights go off, and the film comes on. Afterward they take a break, because they found it was too hard for eyes to focus back on live singers after a half hour concentrating on the screen.

I told Lee Hays I needed more optimistic stories. "The thing to be most pessimistic about in this world today is the prevalence of pessimism."

How about this, says he: "A little old lady didn't have but two teeth in her head, one on the top and one on the bottom. But she said, 'Thank God they're hitters!' "

Which reminds me: at a meeting of the woman's suffrage movement in the nineteenth century, the chairman addressed a few earnest words to the delegates. "Ladies! We disperse now to our own communities, where we each have a tremendous task ahead of us. There will be difficulties and disappointments. But remember, in our hours of most urgent need, we can pray to God; *She* will hear our prayers."

(Lord, forgive my many little jokes on thee/And I'll forgive thy one big joke on me.—Housman?)

December 1967

I guess in modern life you have to plan. But there's such a thing as planning too much. There's such a thing as planning too early. Here's what jazz musicians can teach the politicians of the world: we must plan for improvisation.

It's well known that in colonial countries many people thought that the way to be civilized was to ape the ways of the mother country. It happened in New Spain, New France, New England, and also among the Quisling classes of Asia and Africa. Nowadays it happens in many countries that are being Coca-colonized. Young people, claiming they want to be "modern," will follow every new fashion and fad from U.S.A.

If they really wanted to be modern they would learn from *every* country, new and old. A lot of what they learn, they would, after consideration, turn down. Some of it they would adopt, and adapt to fit their own neck of the woods.

Go-go boots are silly in the tropics, bikinis out of place in Greenland. And this goes for musical fashions, too.

Long live great melodies!
But that's an unnecessary hurrah. Great melodies will live a long time without assistance from me or any other individual. That's what makes them great.

I've observed that most music schools can teach their students how to write harmony, counterpoint, rhythms, etc., but none of them knows much about writing melody. Bach, Beethoven and the rest of the gang knew how to write great melodies, but nowadays the job seems to be left up to pop composers.

Composers of most folk songs of past centuries have (wisely, I think) often decided to swipe a great melody to fit their words to, rather than use a half-great new tune.

But what makes a great melody? I wrote half a dozen expert musicologists and asked them this question. They all threw up their hands, saying, in effect, "Beauty is in the ear of the listener." Granted no two people have the same opinions. And obviously no two national traditions agree: a great melody in the Russian tradition would not be a great melody in the Chinese tradition. Some prefer smooth, flowing subtleties; others like staccato jumps.

I think that in the decades to come, great melodies will cross the oceans as never before. They will be borrowed and reborrowed, arranged and disarranged and rearranged. Competition! The best melodies will find a place in our grandchildren's hearts whether or not they bring with them any of their earlier lyrics.

Just as well. Often the early lyrics deserve to be forgotten. The words of Stephen Foster's "Massa's in de Col' Col' Ground" are weak and silly, but the melody is strong and great.

Speaking of great melodies, here's a prediction: centuries from now, people will remember some of the pop tunes and show tunes of the twenties and thirties, because the melodies were great. The words? Eccch. Except for an occasional phrase, maybe. But like seventeenth-century madrigals, these pop songs will be remembered for their music, not their words. I say some of them are great:

Bob Dylan is essentially a writer, not a performer. The writer creates something; his job is done; he restlessly moves on to create something else. The performer re-creates something, and through many performances explores the subtle changes of meanings in a song as he sings it to different audiences and in different times and places.

Meanings?

Meanings!

Last year I got in a long debate with a scholar friend over the meaning of the word "meaning," and whether or not music could be said to have "meaning." He felt that, strictly speaking, it cannot. Not in the sense that words have meaning. "You can translate words from one language to another. But no one, hearing a melody whistled from beyond a wall, would ask that it be translated. When a melody is changed in some way— as is always happening—it is not translation, but an acculturative process." Music does not have meaning; music *is*, says he.

But I felt that while music can't carry the vast range of specific meanings that words can carry (Can a melody describe the shape of a chair?), nevertheless we all, even scientists, use the word "meaning" in the sense of "signify."

"What do those clouds in the west mean? we ask the meteorologist. "Rain," says he.

Astronomers, noting that the faintest distant galaxies which the Mount Palomar telescope could see were more red in color, asked each other, "What is the meaning of the red shift?" And they finally decided that the red shift in the spectrum meant that these distant galaxies are traveling away from us and from each other at fantastic speeds.

The danger is in thinking that you can tell someone in words *the* meaning of a piece of music. Art has many layers of meaning. The medium is only part of the message. A song will mean ten different things to ten different people—and different things to the same person at different times.

1968

(MCCARTHY PEACE CAMPAIGN WINS N. HAMPSHIRE PRESIDENTIAL PRIMARY. "TET" OFFENSIVE HURTS U.S. IN VIETAM. PRES. JOHNSON ANNOUNCES RETIREMENT. MARTIN LUTHER KING ASSASSINATED. DEMONSTRATORS FOR BLACK COMMUNITY RIGHTS AND STUDENT POWER OCCUPY COLUMBIA UNIV. BUILDINGS. STUDENT DEMONSTRATIONS AND INDUSTRIAL STRIKES IN FRANCE. ROBT. KENNEDY ASSASSINATED. POOR PEOPLE'S CAMPAIGN SETS UP "RESURRECTION CITY" IN D.C. TV DOCUMENTARY DRAMATIZES HUNGER AMONG AMERICAN CHILDREN. WARSAW PACT ARMIES IN CZECHOSLOVAKIA. "POLICE RIOT" MEETS PEACE DEMONSTRATORS AT CHICAGO CONVENTION. WOMENS LIBERATION PICKETS MISS AMERICA PAGEANT. N.Y. TEACHERS STRIKE AGAINST POLICIES OF BLACK COMMUNITY SCHOOL BOARD.

(U.S. RECORD SALES OVER A BILLION DOLLARS. CANDOR ON SEX, DRUGS AND POLITICS BANNED BY MANY ROCK STATIONS.)

January 1968

THE MOST continuously interesting folk song magazine is *Chapbook,* put out by Arthur Argo and friends in Scotland. The recent issue has a long article on Scottish Christmas customs, and discusses the continuous arguments between puritan and impuritan.

"It was the recognized policy of the Church to invest each pagan festival with a Christian significance, so that the customs of the people should be disturbed as little as possible. The Roman equivalent of Yule was the Saturnalia, when everybody downed tools and held high revelry. To the 25th of December the Romans gave the beautiful name, *dies natalis solis invicti,* the birthday of the unconquered sun. There is, of course, no historical justification for associating the day with the Nativity, but no date could have been more fitting to celebrate the birth of 'Him whom death could not conquer.'

" 'You may dance round your bonfires,' said the priests; 'you may eat, drink, and be merry; but it must be no longer in honour of Saturn or Thor, but of the King of Kings.'

"An apologia for the extravagance of the Fête des Fous is contained in a Lettre Circulaire de la Faculté de Paris of the fifteenth century. 'We do not do all these things seriously, but only for play, and to divert ourselves according to the old custom; in order that folly, which is natural to us, and which seems born with us, should escape and run away thereby at least once a year. Wine-barrels would burst if the bung or sluice were not sometimes opened to give them air. And we are old vessels, ill-bound barrels, which the wine of wisdom would burst if we were to let it boil constantly by incessantly addicting ourselves to devotion. We must give it some air and relaxation, for fear that it should be lost and spilt to no profit. It is for that that we give some days to games and buffooneries, that we may afterwards return with more joy and fervour to the study and exercise of religion.'

"After the Reformation the pendulum went full swing from licentiousness to a narrow puritanism. 'Popery' was taboo. Every religious rite and custom, however harmless in itself, if ordained by Rome and not expressly ordained in Holy Scripture, was ruthlessly condemned, in order to make the breach between the old Church and the new as wide as possible and thus check any tendency towards a return to Rome. . . .

"In 1574, on December 30th, certain persons were charged before the kirk-session at Aberdeen 'for playing, dancing and singing of filthy carols on Yule Day at even.' "

Anyone wanting to order *Scottish Chapbook* can send one shilling, sixpence, plus appropriate postage (you might as well simply send $1.00 and get two copies), to circulation manager James Dunnett, 114 Kirkhill Road, Aberdeen, Scotland.

March 1968

Memos for a year of crisis:

1. Some quotes from Thoreau, 1817(?)–1863. Old Henry was a cool and opinionated fellow. A friend said: "I like Henry but cannot love him . . . I would as soon lop my arm over the branch of a tree as to take his arm." But Thoreau was never more timely:

"There are thousands who are in *opinion* opposed to slavery and to the war, who yet in effect do nothing to put an end to them; who, esteeming themselves children of Washington and Franklin, sit down with their hands in their pockets and say that they know not what to do." (1846)

Or this: "Is there not a sort of bloodshed when the conscience is wounded? Through this wound a man's real manhood and immortality flow out and he bleeds to an everlasting death. I see this blood flowing now."

2. Some good friends of mine, including Dave Wilson of Boston's *Broadside*, feel that it is silly for me to try to get on TV. Here's a personal answer.

When I was fifteen, and in love with the out-of-doors (as I still am), I once got involved in a evening's argument with some older people about how to spend one's life. I brashly announced that, in view of mankind's all-consuming stupidity and hypocrisy, the only honest thing was to be a hermit. They jumped on me like a ton of bricks. "What kind of morality do you call that? You are going to be pure yourself, and let the rest of the world go to hell?"

I decided that they were right, and have since found no reason to change my mind. I've tried to sing to other human beings wherever I could, under all kinds of circumstances, honorable and ridiculous: Las Vegas hotels, churches, picket lines, classrooms, concert halls, vaudeville stages. Right now, I'm trying my damndest to get on network TV. There are 200 million American people out there, all sizes, shapes, and colors. It would be a crime not to try to reach them.

At various times, this policy can lead to working with people one highly disagrees with. But I wasn't born the truculent type. I think some of the editors of this magazine occasionally don't know their rear end from a hole in the ground. But that's all right: they probably hold a similar opinion of me. As long as we can agree on some main things, I'll keep writing this column.

3. Another quote, this time from William Pitt, England, 1776: "If I were an American, as I am an Englishman, while a foreign troop was landed in my country, I would never lay down my arms—never, never, never."

4. Banjo players: One of these days, I must put out a final, revised edition of that old five-string banjo manual of mine, written twenty years ago. Any suggestions that you can send me would be welcome.

5. On December 23, at Carnegie Hall, I was surprised to find that an almost improvised blues was what everyone remembered:

> When my songs . . . turn to ashes on my tongue,
> When I look in the mirror, and see I'm no longer young,
> Then I got to start the slow job of separating false from true
> And then I know, I know I need the love of you.*

(Separating false from true is not so easy. Our extraordinary English language is infected with racism: blackguard, blackhearted, blacklist, black day, etc.)

6. This year marks the one hundredth year since the birth of one of the great graphic artists of all time, Kaethe Kollwitz. She was born of an independent-minded, liberal Christian family in northern Germany. While a student, she became acquainted with socialism, married, and had two children. She tried to become a great sculptor—and (in her opinion) failed. She refused to flee the country when Hitler came to power, although her art was banned. Her favorite son was killed in World War I. Her favorite grandson was killed in World War II on the Russian front. Her home and all were destroyed by Allied bombing. A last lithograph, in 1944, shows a fierce mother shielding with her cloak several small children, one of whom has an impish smile. The caption: "Save

---

* By Peter Seeger. Copyright © 1968, Sanga Music, Inc. All rights reserved. Used by permission.

the Seed!" She died a month before the fall of Berlin. Do we understand the lessons she taught us?

7. *Life* Magazine showed a full-page photo of long-haired Bobbie Gentry walking across the Tallahatchie Bridge, which figured in her song, "Ode to Billie Joe." And some of us did a double take. The location is Money, Mississippi—a mile or two from where Emmett Till's body was found! Last year, there was an in joke among black Americans. They knew what was thrown off that bridge.

8. A friend of mine doesn't like folk festivals. "A carnival atmosphere is not the best way to present folk music." At the same time, I think that marketplaces, parties, and areas that one can call "fluxing places" (where different products and ideas can melt and flow in and around each other) have an important function. This magazine is a fluxing place where old and new music, pop music and art music, school music, and organized and disorganized music should probe each other.

9. As a whole, I like the music of amateurs. It's too easy to compromise professionals. Is this my definition of folk music? Mebbe. I wish this magazine had a masthead motto: "We are concerned with the homemade music of the American people, whether from their oldest traditions or adapted to the needs of the present." But more about this in the next issue. For now, as the chalked sign on the brick wall has it: STOP—IN THE NAME OF LOVE.

June 1968

"What good does it do to sing a song?"

A farmer once left a tall can of milk with the top off outside his door. Two frogs hopped into it and then found that they couldn't hop out. After thrashing around a bit, one of them says, "There's no hope." With one last gurgle he sank to the bottom. The other frog refused to give up. In the morning the farmer came out and found one live frog sitting on a big cake of butter.

It pays to kick.

Nevertheless, songs lie only halfway between thought and action, and too often substitute for both. "Verbal opposition is today in danger of becoming a harmless spectator sport, licensed, well regulated and, up to a point, even encouraged by the powerful" (Hans M. Enzenberger, in *New York Review of Books*).

Libba Cotten, seventy-two years old and black, got a standing ovation from 3,000 white students at Duke University in March. What she did broke all the rules of show business. She walked gravely to the microphone, sat down and started picking the guitar. It was a simple tune, and repeated itself over and over with only a few modest variations. But she did it superbly, effortlessly. Then she talked for a while, still strumming lightly. She told how, as a teenager, she had sneaked in to play her older brother's guitar. Because she was left-handed she had to learn everything backways around. Later in life she joined the church and gave up the guitar.

In Washington, D.C., she found a little yellow-curled girl wandering, lost, in a department store. The relieved mother, a piano teacher, got talking with her, and offered her a job as cook. The family had some folk music recordings, and a guitar in the house as well. Libba allowed as she used to be able to play a little.

Thereafter it was quite common for the two teen-age children, Michael and Peggy Seeger, to go into the kitchen and make a deal with her: they would wash the dishes if she would play the guitar. And one of the

Elizabeth Cotten

songs they learned from her has gone around the world. Libba Cotten had composed it when she was a twelve-year-old girl. Three thousand Duke students sang it with her.

> Freight train, freight train, going so fast,
> Freight train, freight train, going so fast,
> Please don't tell them what train I'm on
> So they won't know which way I have gone.
>
> When I die just bury me deep
> Down at the foot of Chestnut Street
> So I can hear old Number Nine
> As she goes roaring by.
>
> When I'm dead and in my grave
> No more good times do I crave.
> Place a stone at my head and feet;
> Tell my friends that I've gone to sleep.
>
> Freight train, freight train . . .

Printing presses are a great invention, but we have allowed them to cripple the art of amateur storytelling.

Béla Bartók claimed that a folk song was on as high a plane of art as a symphony. It was just a short form; a symphony is a long form.

Maybe, then, an anecdote can be on as high a plane of art as a novel? In any case, the art of anecdote is needed now: it's a great way to circumvent censors. But a truly great anecdote is as rare a thing as great art anywhere. Needed: lots of anecdotes, till we learn to make great ones. Needed: new tales for new times.

Harry Bloom, once a successful lawyer and author in Johannesburg, now in exile in London, told me a few stories about his former homeland.

An African friend told him of riding an escalator in a department store when he noticed a middle-aged woman ahead of him. She put her hand to her head and started to sway, as though she was going to faint. He made a move to catch her, but suddenly withdrew in fear. They were the only two people on the escalator. His skin was black, hers was white. What if she should scream? There would be no help for him. He shrank against the wall, and the woman tumbled past him to the bottom of the long stair.

On the beach a young man saved two people from drowning. A local citizens' group announced a standard reward for him, of $50 for each.

Then it was discovered that one of the persons saved was an African. One $50 reward was withdrawn. Then it was discovered that the other was an Indian. The other $50 reward was halved; the young man was sent a check for $25.

From the San Francisco *Chronicle* (Herb Caen's column, I think): "I don't think he meant it this way, but here's how it came out dept. (Sargent Shriver on Merv Griffin's show): 'The War on Poverty is doing a great job. We had hundreds of boys who couldn't even qualify for the army—now, with the help of the anti-poverty program we have been able to send 600 of these boys to Vietnam and six have been killed already.'"

Is any reader interested in ceramics? Within the last decade there has been an increasing interest in the simple shapes and muted earth colors of Japanese folk pottery. The story behind its revival parallels in many ways the revival of interest in folk music. Fifty years ago Bernard Leach, an Englishman, left the land of Wedgwood and abandoned Europe's intricately painted porcelains. He went to Japan and studied the art of the great Japanese potters. Came back home, wrote books, "threw" pots, lectured, taught students, and gradually got his ideas across. Modern designers in Europe and America realized that here also was someone striving for the beauty of the unadorned curve. If you want to know more, see *A Potter's Book*, by Leach. He's still going strong, age eighty plus.

If you'd like to get close to Mother Earth, the potter's craft is surely one of the earthiest. There's nothing quite like dunking your hands in water, and then slithering them around a wet hunk of clay, first centering it on the wheel (no easy thing to learn), and then, like God forming man and woman, drawing up the sides into a thing of beauty. It's an earthy miracle.

If you can't afford to buy a wheel and a kiln, there may be art centers in your town that you can join. Or you can club together with some friends to buy the necessary equipment. Then you, too, can have pot parties.

In Atlanta, Georgia, Bernice Reagon* puts on an annual "Penny Festival" in the black community. "I stay strictly away from the words 'folk music.' To my audience, that means some white college student with a

---

* Bernice Reagon, who was one of the original Freedom Singers, made a Folkways record in 1965, FA 2457. Her current LP is distributed by her directly: 207 Ashby Street SW, Atlanta, Ga. 30314; $4.30.

guitar standing on a stage. Our festival is about our roots, and our life."

The first year the Penny Festival related Afro-American music to old African music. The next year they related their songs to the life and writings of W. E. B. Du Bois.

NBC-TV was for a while interested in covering the festival. Someone had told them the Penny Festival was an important part of 1968 U.S.A. But when they heard the name W. E. B. Du Bois they backed off in a hurry.

Don't just shrug. This is something to get furious about.

Americans are surely some of the most mobile people in the world. From the dissenters and draft dodgers of Europe who came here in past centuries to the restless job seekers of today, we have been uprooted people. But there comes a time for nations as well as individuals to settle down and solve their problems right where they are. And I, too, feel like settling a little. In the past few years I've become ever more absorbed with the problem of pollution of the Hudson River, along whose shore I live.

It's an arm of the sea, deep and salty for half its length. Tides extend 150 miles, to the dam north of Albany. Once it teemed with fish. Huge sturgeon, 200 lbs, could be speared ten feet down in the clear water. A hundred years ago the catching and marketing of these fish was an important industry on the Hudson. They called it "Albany Beef." America used to export caviar to Europe in those days.

> Caviar comes from virgin sturgeon
> Virgin sturgeon's a very fine fish
> Virgin sturgeon needs no urgin'
> That's why caviar is my dish.
>
> (Tune, "Reuben, Reuben")

What has all this to do with a folk music magazine? Simply this: For the past year I've been helping to run folk music concerts up and down the valley, to raise money to build a full-size replica of a huge old-fashioned Hudson River sloop, 75 feet long, 25 feet wide, mast 105 feet, carrying the largest mainsail in the world.

Why? For What?

We figure that if the Hudson is going to be saved from being a perma-

The singing crew of the sloop "Clearwater"

nent sewer, people must learn to love it again, to come down to the water's edge and see it close. We plan to sail the boat up and down the river all nine ice-free months of the year, docking at every town, large and small. Schoolchildren can come down and climb on the rigging and get a whiff of Hudson history. Sailing buffs from all over can come aboard. Volunteer crews will raise the sail and anchor; a full-time captain will see that it doesn't run on the rocks. Every year it can take different exhibits to put up along shore. With an audience of townspeople on the banks, and with the sloop and the river as a backdrop, shows, concerts, movies can be put on.

Well, to many of you who read this, it may seem of no matter. But I bring it up because local projects such as this could spring up everywhere. The sloop shows have had fiddlers and ballad singers and blues guitar pickers, songwriters young and old. We've all been learning from each other, and what ties us all together is a love for this valley. There's a little of Don Quixote in everybody, and a good thing, too.

In 1952, at a party at Bob De Witt's, Topanga Canyon, California, I first heard Odetta sing. Someone told me that there was a young woman who really knew how to sing Leadbelly's songs. We had to hunt to find her, very shy, sitting in the farthest corner. But when she was persuaded to sing—Power, power, intensity and power! I told her she was the first person since Leadbelly had died to do justice to the song "Take This Hammer."

(The readers of this magazine should know: if *Sing Out* can dig itself out of its present financial hole, it will take the love and devotion of all. Some 12,000 bucks were lost in a misguided attempt to get the magazine sold on newsstands. Now we are smaller, broker, and perhaps have fewer illusions about the realities of American journalism. Maybe we are in a better position to move ahead and do some of the jobs that need doing.)

August 1968

ONE REASON I like Afro-American music* is that it is meant to be danced to. Modern life has chained too many human beings to desks and work benches; life consists of moving our rear ends from one seat to another. My personal regret is that my own music career has involved forcing thousands of people to stay seated for hours at a time. Automation, if used correctly, could free mankind from drudgery, but lest we get overconfident, here are a couple of stories to remember.

In West Germany a certain city designed a new electric power plant, completely automated. It even had a tape-recorded message which would be telephoned to the city engineer at his residence informing him of what was wrong at the plant in case of any breakdown.

The trouble was that the engineer moved his residence and left his own tape-recorded message at the old telephone number, notifying callers of his new number.

That very week the electricity went on the blink; the tape-recorded message was automatically telephoned to the engineer. His tape-recorded message automatically answered, giving his new number. But the first tape machine had already hung up, only to call again a few minutes later. For several hours the two tape machines talked to each other until finally someone in town got to wondering why it was taking so long to get the electricity fixed.

---

* Rock, jazz, Calypso, etc.

Here's another:

A technical-minded duck hunter who had been working on guided missiles worked out a rocket gun which would zero in on a flock of ducks. He persuaded a skeptical friend to come duck hunting with him early one morning and watch a demonstration. The sun had barely peeked over the horizon when far up the valley they saw a large flock.

"Watch this," said the inventor, and loosed his rocket.

"Hey, they're much too far away. Wait till they get closer, you're sure to get them," said his friend.

"Here, I'll make sure that they come closer." And out of his pocket he pulled an old-fashioned duck-calling device and blew on it, quacking away.

"Holy mackerel! Stop that immediately, you've ruined everything," the inventor screamed in alarm. "That rocket is set to hit anything that quacks like a duck. Look at it now, it's turning around! It's aiming right for us! Jump for your life!"

The two duck hunters leaped into the water as the rocket zeroed in and demolished the blind.

Last year when the folk festival at Fort Lauderdale was so viciously attacked by Birchers, a local man was unperturbed and chauffeured around some of the performers.

"Nope, I don't even bother replying to them. Never get in a pissing match with a skunk. One of the Birchers called me up on the phone and started to cuss me out. I asked her name. She wouldn't give it to me. I told her, 'Lady, my wife told me never to talk to strangers.' " Click!

For people who like the song "Wimoweh," here's an old Vietnamese prophecy: "When the hawk comes, the lion will rise, then peace will come to the world."

Worth quoting: "Analyzing wit is like dissecting a frog. When you take it apart you find what it's made of, but the subject is killed in the process." (André Maurois)

Sad but true: if you are in business as a professional singer, publicity is part of the business. When you are just getting started, it's hard to get publicity. Later on, you may get to the point where it's hard to avoid it.

Back in the 1940s there came out in English translation a remarkable little children's book by two Russian educators, *How Man Became a Giant.* It briefly recounted how mankind, by learning to work together, mastered problems and tasks that individuals could never solve. Canals, dams, and bridges all show Man taming nature. His accumulated knowledge and information make each of us able to do the work of a giant. I still have the little book on my shelf, and will pass it on to my grandchildren. But for accuracy's sake, a companion volume should be written, *How Man Nearly Became a Dwarf.*

On all sides nowadays, in all corners of the world, one can hear people saying: "But what can I do? I am just one small person."

In other words, the very existence of large machines, of large organizations, of mass media, make our individual efforts seem puny by comparison.

A young peace worker was standing in Times Square at midnight with a picket sign, protesting escalation of the war in Vietnam. A passerby asked, "Do you think you are going to change the world by standing here?"

"No . . . ," came the answer, "but I'm going to make sure that the world doesn't change me."

> This little light of mine
> I'm gonna let it shine
> Let it shine, let it shine, let it shine . . .

On West Forty-sixth Street, Manhattan, near Ninth Avenue, is what looks like a hippy church. Outside, in large colorful letters, is the sign, SMILE—GOD IS WATCHING YOU.

October 1968

"Hello! How are you?"

"Like a chicken with its head cut off," has been my standard rejoinder for years, meaning "lots of activity, but in too many directions at once." Nowadays I switch it to just answer, "Struggling." Here, too, one jerks from side to side, but there's a reason: trying to jerk loose.

Humorous signs pinned on office walls are a folk art. In a Denver hotel is this: "Sesquipedalian terminology obfuscates the rumination" (Long words confuse the thought).

For more than ten years the Ensemble of Centenarian Bards has been singing to overflow audiences in the Soviet Union. All members of the group are more than one hundred years old and come from villages in Abkhazia in Georgia, in the Caucasus. Their repertoire includes sixty songs which have been passed down through generations, and twelve Abkhazian dances which are centuries old. The Centenarians use a two-stringed apkhiartza with bow, a lyrelike ayuomaa with fourteen strings, and two other national instruments, known as the achongure and the akhmaa. (From *Tradition* Magazine, Australia.)

Pandora, in the *National Guardian,* sniped at Aretha Franklin for making a Coca-Cola commercial. Julius Lester, for whom Aretha is the greatest, sprang to her defense. I haven't heard the commerical, so I don't know who's right. But my guess is you'd have to be a great artist to get away with it.*

Mankind has an edifice complex. Experts like to plan and plan and get everything so neatly finished off that there is nothing for the rest of us amateurs to do but to sit around and admire them.

I once sat in a cathedral listening to the minister complain that the rank-and-file Christians were not taking more initiative in their lives. He said that they were too passive, that they were sitting back and waiting for their leaders to do everything.

The very surroundings contradicted his words. The huge Gothic edifice, the result of hundreds of thousands of hours of expert labor in planning and execution, left nothing for a rank-and-filer to do but gaze on it, admire it, and perhaps contribute money so that the roof can be repaired occasionally.

Same way with the choir's chorale. The notes were all written out with elaborate accompaniment and polyphony. What could the average churchgoer do but listen and feel humble? I think if I was a member of that church I would say, "Clear away the pews, let's have a dance, let's have some amateur contests. Let people bring their favorite pictures to put up all around the wall." The world does not need greater edifices, it needs the spirit of creativity spread more widely among the population. Thank God buildings eventually crumble.

---

* Later: I heard it. Lester's right. Aretha is great. The words are silly. But the real message is her magnificent singing.

Reverend Frederick Douglass Kirkpatrick

Resurrection City Reminiscences

JIMMY COLLIER was asked to lead the song "This Land Is Your Land" before a crowd of black and white people. He said, "I have been asked to sing this song several times, but I went over to our Indian friends first and checked if it was all right with them. They said it was all right now we are all down here together to try and get something done."

Rev. Kirkpatrick was leading a song session there when he shot a glance at my banjo and said, "See if you can hit Sally Goodin." And then he gave out with some of the best square-dance calling I had ever heard. Found out later that he helped raise money for the school athletic program in Louisiana by calling square dances.

It was later on in that same song session that I was flabbergasted by the athleticism of a seventy-year-old man who led—with his whole body —verse after verse of an old hymn, till the whole crowd was rocking (see p. 143 above).

It used to be said, "While there's life there's hope." After seeing that oldster give out, I decided that the reverse is more true: "While there's hope, there's life."

I guess it all depends on what and when your hopes are. Herbert Hoover in 1931 said, "Mr. Vallee, if you sing a song that will make people forget their troubles and the depression, I'll give you a medal."

And some musicians are still trying for that kind of prize.

December 1968

More of the problem of how to keep a good song from being co-opted. The song "This Land Is Your Land"* really needs some new verses to add to the old ones. Images should include red men talking to brown and black—and white. Need to show dissatisfaction with getting crumbs from the rich man's table. Clark Clifford, in March 1950, addressed wealthy businessmen at Chicago's Executive Club: "I believe the people have to feel that their small share of this country is just as much theirs as it is yours and mine . . ." (quoted in *Ramparts*, August 1968, p. 46). Without these extra verses, "TLIYL" falls right into Mr. Clifford's trap. I usually sing the verse mentioned in last month's issue:

> Was a great high wall there
> That tried to stop me.
> Was a great big sign that said Private Property;
> But on the other side
> It didn't say nothin'—
> This land was made for you and me.

---

* Words and music by Woody Guthrie. TRO-© copyright 1956, 1958, Ludlow Music, Inc., New York, New York. Used by permission.

Here's two more of Woody's old verses, now being sung:

> In the squares of the city,
> In the shadow of the steeple,
> By the relief office I saw my people.
> As they stood there hungry
> I stood there whistling
> This land was made for you and me.
>
> Nobody living
> Can ever stop me
> As I go walking my freedom highway.
> Nobody living
> Can make me turn back.
> This land was made for you and me.

And a verse of my own:

> Maybe you been working,
> Just as hard as you're able
> And you just got crumbs from the rich man's table.
> Maybe you been wondering,
> Is it truth or fable:
> This land was made for you and me.

Someone Should Write a Song #1: describing the difference between persistence and patience.

William Faulkner, after writing eloquently of the lives of black and white people in his home state, then stated for the public press that if it came to a shooting war between the government of the U.S.A. and the white government of Mississippi, he would take up arms for Mississippi. None of us may ever write or sing as eloquently as Faulkner, but at least we can take to heart, and state clearly for all to hear, the great verse of José Martí: "Con los pobres de la tierra/quiero yo me suerte echar." (With the poor people of this world I want to cast my lot—share my fate. This is the last verse of the song "Guantanamera.")

Letter from a student: "We believe school should not be a sweatshop for well-oiled thinking machines."

It has often been said, "Politics Is the Art of The Possible." This is not quite true. The real art of politics is to make what appears to be impossible, possible.

An official of an ETV station heard that the Ford Foundation was coming through with a huge grant for them. He confessed, "I feel like a plant in the desert that was dying of thirst and I heard there was a flood coming, and I didn't know whether it was better to die of thirst or be drowned."

Military generals have allowed enlisted men to bitch all they want as long as they are in the barracks. "Let them blow off steam." But when soldiers turn out for duty, then the lip must stay buttoned. Today in U.S.A. we enjoy great freedom of the press. "Let them blow off steam." But on TV you watch what you say . . . it can be snipped out of the tape before air time. What to do? Surround the station, capture it? Charm them with double talk? Get the story out, and surround them with ridicule—this they'll not break out of.

Words, words, words. Sometimes the most eloquent song I can sing is "Wimoweh," with no words at all. Just melody, rhythm, and great bass harmony.

Suggestion for name of new rock group: The Threshold of Pain.

1969

(N.Y. PANTHERS ACCUSED OF BOMB PLOT, HELD IN $100,000 BAIL EACH. N. IRISH CIVIL RIGHTS LEADER BERNADETTE DEVLIN ELECTED TO PARLIAMENT. STUDENT KILLED, CAMPUS GASSED, AFTER CREATION OF BERKELEY "PEOPLE'S PARK." ANTI-BALLISTIC MISSILES AUTHORIZED AGAINST ADVICE OF SCIENTISTS. MEN WALK ON MOON. "CONSPIRATORS" TRIED FOR '68 CHICAGO DEMONSTRATIONS. MASSACRE OF VIET VILLAGERS BY U.S. TROOPS ALLEGED. AGNEW DENOUNCES TV CRITICISM OF PRESIDENT. PEACE MARCH IN WASHINGTON ESTI-

MATED AT HALF MILLION. POLICE KILL CHICAGO PANTHER LEADER. INDIANS OCCUPY ABANDONED ALCATRAZ PRISON.
(GOSPEL CHOIR'S "OH HAPPY DAY" HIGH ON CHARTS. SOME WHITE PERFORMERS ADOPT "SOUL" LABEL. 300,000 PEACEFUL WOODSTOCK ROCK FANS JAM ROADS AND SWAMP FESTIVAL FACILITIES. BEATINGS AND MURDER BY HELL'S ANGELS "SECURITY GUARDS" AT CALIFORNIA ROLLING STONES CONCERT.)

February 1969

NEWS FOR BANJO PICKERS: Earl Scruggs's long-awaited big book on the banjo is finally out. Thirteen chapters plus autobiographical notes. Includes all details of picking, plus complete arrangements for thirty-two songs, and directions for how to build a banjo and making Scruggs's cam-type tuning pegs. A future issue of *Sing Out* will no doubt carry a detailed review, but why wait. Write Earl Scruggs & Songs, Inc., 201 Donna Drive, Madison, Tenn. 37115. $10.95 and worth it many times over.

At the same time appears another fine book: *Old Time Mountain Banjo,* by Art Rosenbaum (Oak Publications, 33 W. 60 St., New York, N.Y., $2.95). This has four chapters and three appendices, giving 23 (!) tunings, discussing What Kind of Banjo You Should Buy, and supplying a big discography. Thirty songs are notated, from the playing of such as Uncle Dave Macon, Charlie Poole, Doc Boggs, Hobart Smith, Wade Ward, and Roscoe Holcomb, using various styles of picking: frailing, up-and-down picking, etc. And beautiful illustrations by the author.

Fred Gerlach, who was a friend of Leadbelly and his family, got me started playing the twelve-string guitar. Fred mastered some of Leadbelly's techniques, and I decided maybe I could. Fred lives in California now. Good guitar picker. Good maker of guitars as well. He told me a story about Leadbelly, worth remembering:

At a crowded New York party in the forties, a young white man sat near Leadbelly saying things like "Negroes are so much better than white people at this, Negroes are so much better than white people at that." Leadbelly finally just stood up and said, "I'm proud of my race and I think everybody else ought to be proud of theirs." And then he sat down.

A book on the musical saw is being assembled by Jim Turner, 1026 Fifteenth Street, Denver, Col. 80302. He has sent out a call for information, "Are you a cutup? Have you ever sawed a musical scene? Or seen a musical saw? Please answer . . . if you have ever heard the sweet saw-chedelic sounds of the singing saw."

The above, and much other interesting information, from a refreshingly modest and useful journal: The *News-Letter* of the Folklore Society of Greater Washington ($5 a year, P.O. Box 19303, Twentieth Street Station, Washington, D.C. 20036).

In Ireland I was told that in the Middle Ages, Irish bards had great prestige. Even kings were afraid of their power of satire. It was said, "Never cast a spear at a satirist." Like a magician, he could do mysterious damage. A bard might walk through the thick of battle with nothing done to them.

Now, songwriters. That's status worth achieving.

My favorite new songbook: *Broadside, Vol.* 2 (Oak Publications, New York, $2.95)—has 100 more of the best from this lively topical song publication. You don't have to like all of the songs. But the average is still high, high.

Congratulations to Dick Reuss, one of the most competent of the young folk song researchers, on getting out a bibliography listing chronologically 124 articles, booklets, and several books written by Woody Guthrie, and another 350 or so more articles about Woody Guthrie. This bibliography can be bought ($5) from the Woody Guthrie Children's Trust Fund, Room 1304, 200 West 57 Street, New York, N.Y.

Someone Should Write a Song #2: A United Fruit Company plantation in French Guiana offered a bounty on rat snakes, which were slowing down the gathering of bananas. The drive was a tremendous success. To everyone's satisfaction, not a snake was left. But there was no banana crop next year. Normally controlled by the snakes, the rats had proliferated; they devoured the entire crop. Plantation owners were forced to import rat snakes from a Florida zoo supplier to restore the balance of nature (from *Time Is Short and the Water Rises*, by J. Walsh and R. Gannon, Dutton).

PART III

Making
Homemade
Music

5.Ways of Singing With and For People

Mass media doesn't have to control your musical life unless you want it to. And you don't have to invest a king's ransom in electronic gear. Here's a few ways music can be enjoyed whenever people feel like singing.

Most of these notes were written during the fifties; since then the Top Forty "folk boom" has come and gone. But do-it-yourself music is important now just as it was fifteen years ago—or fifteen centuries ago. And as it will be.

A Problem of Architecture

AN AUDITORIUM with semicircular seating is a more democratic auditorium than one where the seats are all in conventional straight lines. Why? Because the latter assumes that all wisdom and inspiration must come from the front, and that members of the audience have nothing to contribute to one another.

Most democratic of all were the council fires of early communal societies. Then, anyone could stand up in place and address his or her fellow citizens. When society became more autocratic, the lines of seats straightened out. The earliest churches in America were aware of this, and consciously faced pews in from the sides, even if squarely, so worshippers could see one another.

Similarly, folk music concerts and hootenannies should use a democratically semicircular seating. When everyone joins in on a chorus, there is a mutual lift from seeing each other.

How "Hootenanny" Came to Be

(1956 and 1963)

THE WORD "hootenanny" seems to have become part of the national vocabulary. (In 1947 a member of People's Songs, helping to compile Webster's *New World Dictionary of the American Language,* put the word in as "a gathering of folksingers." He was premature, but history caught up with him.)

For the record, and to settle some arguments, Grandpa would like here and now to give the plain, true, real, unvarnished and uninteresting facts of the case.

No, it has nothing to do with a girl nicknamed "Hootin' Annie," "famed among the lumber camps" according to Woody Guthrie's facetious report. Nor, I doubt, has the term anything to do with a French custom of shooing a bride and groom out into the fields the night before the wedding. (Two French students at Cornell were once shocked to hear that a hootenanny was to be held on campus.)

It is true that "hootenanny" can mean "Whatyoumaycallit." A mechanic might call to his assistant, "Fetch me that hootenanny in the corner, quick!" It is also a euphemism. "I have to visit the hootenanny [backyard privy]." But the folk song lover's meaning is not derived from these.

It is derived from another meaning of the word: a rip-roaring party, a wingding, a blowout.

In the summer of 1941 Woody Guthrie and myself, calling ourselves the Almanac Singers, toured into Seattle, Washington, and met some of the good people of the Washington Commonwealth Federation, the New Deal political club headed by Hugh DeLacy. They arranged for us to sing for trade unions in the Puget Sound area, and then proudly invited us to their next "hootenanny." It was the first time we had heard the term. It seems they had a vote to decide what they would call their monthly fund-raising parties. "Hootenanny" won out by a nose over "wingding."

The Seattle hootenannies were real community affairs. One family would bring a huge pot of some dish like crab gumbo. Others would bring cakes, salads. A drama group performed topical skits, a good 16-mm film might be shown, and there would be dancing, swing and folk, for those of sound limb. And, of course, there would be singing.

Woody and I returned to New York, where we rejoined the other Almanac Singers, and lived in a big house, pooling all our income. We ran Sunday-afternoon rent parties, and without a second's thought started calling them hootenannies, after the example of our west-coast friends. Seventy-five to one hundred Gothamites would pay 35 cents each to listen to an afternoon of varied folk songs, topical songs, and union songs, not only from the Almanacs but from Huddie Ledbetter, Josh White, the Mechau family, and many many others—including members of the audience.

After World War II the various members of the Almanac Singers were discharged from the Army and other wartime work, and helped to form the organization People's Songs. Of course, fund-raising was again needed, to pay for mimeographing a bulletin and for office rent. So the hoots started up again.

Within three months they grew in size till we had to rent Town Hall to accommodate the crowd.

When college students in the 1950s started using the term we didn't feel like stopping 'em. In the next ten years several hundred thousand Americans attended hootenannies in various cities and campuses of the Union.

In 1962 Ed McCurdy started Tuesday-evening hootenannies at The Bitter End, a New York coffee house, to bring old and new talent together. They were a great success. The owners of The Bitter End sold the idea and the name to ABC-TV.

Some of the big hootenannies have produced mighty thrilling music. But some of the smallest have also been the best.

People running hootenannies have always been beset by two complaints. One is: "The hoots are getting too big and formal. When they were small, and anyone could sing, and no one knew what was going to happen next, they were more exciting." Others say: "When on earth will the hootenannies grow up and put on a decently organized show? Some of the material is good, but some is amateurish, and the whole thing is so sloppy that it is painful to watch."

As a result it is usually the young people who throw themselves into the fun and become part of the hoots who enjoy them most. Someone who sits passively back and expects to be entertained is liable to be disappointed.

The best hoot, in my opinion, would have an audience of several hundred, jammed tight into a small hall, and seated semicircularwise, so that they face each other democratically. The singers and musicians would vary from amateur to professional, from young to old, and the music from square to hip, cool to hot, long-hair to short. Some songs might be quiet—like a pin drop. Others would shake the floor and rafters till the nails loosen. Something old and something new, something borrowed and something blue, as at a wedding.

The best hoots have had all this. Further, the hoots may rightly challenge all other music performances in the nation to present such variety as they have—Bach to bop; "Barbara Allen" to "Union Maid"; and, of course, the best singing audiences in the country.

Hoots are still young as an art form. They're growing. One of these years they will be a common phenomenon in all corners of our country. Here's a handclap for the young people who are starting them up.

1967 Footnote:

I never knew the real power of TV till 1963. For twenty years we had used the word "hootenanny" to describe a democratic kind of songfest where homemade music of many kinds could be swapped, where racism would receive short shrift, where the whole audience, young and old, could join in on union songs, old spirituals, and sharply pointed new songs.

But in six short months of ABC-TV's Hootenanny program, 99 percent of the nation received a whole new definition of the term. The old definition was almost obliterated. A hootenanny was now a gay variety show where nothing controversial would ever be presented.

The title "Sing Out!" used for the show produced by the Moral Rearmament people has produced similar confusion. Backed by the same razor company which backs the John Birchers, and by other millionaires, it has been touring the world with a comfortable cold-war picture of American music.

Moral: As Malvina Reynolds points out in the introduction to her great songbook, The Muse of Parker Street, *we have to be prepared to see any word distorted and misused. Any word in the world.*

Win Stracke, of the Old Town School of Folk Music in Chicago, worked out an interesting variant of the hootenanny which he calls the "gather-all."

He wrote me: "The word 'gather-all,' to the best of my knowledge, was coined by someone at Francis Parker School in Chicago to describe activities in which not only students participate but their families and teachers as well. At the Old Town School, students and teachers are encouraged to bring their entire families, regardless of age, or to bring one friend. We caution everyone that the gather-all should in no sense be considered a performance, and *that they should come dressed casually so that everyone can participate.*"

I don't imagine any two gather-alls would be exactly alike. They might start off with songs, go on to play-party games, then a half hour of folk tales, and conclude with a whole lot of singing of rounds. And maybe someone could demonstrate some folk toys or folk customs, then wind up with folk dancing, and after, some coffee and cake (and soda pop for the kids).

"We have also noticed difficulty in getting the students of the folk dance class interested in singing. Combining folk dancing with unaccompanied singing in the play-parties may achieve this. Since our singers enjoy folk dancing, I suspect that the dancers may be intimidated by the seeming indispensability of the instruments. In this regard, I feel that there is still far too much emphasis on the virtuosity of accompaniment.

"How many would make a good gather-all? Oh, not too many, perhaps a hundred, but it's important to have all ages and to overcome the usual stratification into neat age groups."

Singing Audiences

(1956)

THE REVIVAL of audience singing is an integral part of the whole revival of interest in folk songs. Consider the matter historically. It is only within recent human history that such emphasis has been put upon professional solo singers. In primitive tribes all songs, except for the long narratives, were sung by everyone. If a song had a chorus, everybody in the audience naturally sang it.

Modern civilization developed highly professional specialists in the arts as well as sciences. But comes the time when the intelligent person will say, "Hold on!" Just because we have cars is no reason to forget how to walk. Because we have books is no reason to forget how to tell a good story. Because we have cameras is no reason to forget the fun of wielding pencil and brush. And because we have the phonograph is no reason to forget how to make music.

The apex of a pyramid can be only as high as the base is broad. We cannot have great professionals unless we have also many amateur participants. How can one have big-league baseball teams unless there are many sandlot players?

If we really love folk music, we will get audiences singing with us. No matter that occasionally it may slow down a song. Tempos may drag, or we may have to abandon some beautiful harmony or spectacular effect.

Actually, the quality of audience singing has improved tremendously in the last twenty-five years. When I first started singing folk songs it was like pulling teeth to get anyone to sing with me. I had to use all sorts of tricks to coax a tune out of a crowd that had never sung together in its entire life. Today I can ask people to sing counterpoint or counterrhythms, softly or loudly, fast or slow, or revel in improvised harmony. Anybody can if they want to try.

This type of audience singing is a far cry from the raucus sound of "That Old Gang of Mine" on a Saturday night in Old Joe's Barroom. People are singing here because the songs are more than maudlin sentiment. This type of audience singing is different, too, from the average middle-class church where the congregation limps along half a beat behind the organ. Those who love folk songs can recall the warm feeling of a mass of people singing together. They can also remember the awkward times when a song leader, out of tune with the audience, tried unsuccessfully to get a group to loosen up and sing. One of the least appealing things in the field of music is the spectacle of someone trying to read the words off a song sheet, at the same time wheedling, "Come on, everybody, come on; let's sing now," followed by a waving of the arms like as not out of rhythm with the piano. It is a tribute to the lasting quality of folk music that such performances have not been able to kill it.

No two audiences are alike, and the leader must be prepared to improvise and feel his way until leader and audience are in tune with each other. At first, be wary of songs that are too strange and difficult. A song too familiar, stale or trite can be just as bad.

Take long enough to explain the part you want the audience to sing with you—but not too long. If the song is unfamiliar, take long enough to describe the background of the song, so that the words are meaningful. But too much talking is the death of music.

Often the main problem is how to loosen an audience up and make them lose self-consciousness. A good belly laugh is one of the best ways to do this, but don't risk the sour aftertaste of an unsuccessful attempt at humor. Perhaps, more than any trick or artifice, it is best simply to enjoy yourself completely and trust that it will be catching.

The song leader should be having so much fun that the audience joins in without being able to help itself.

Little things help. Pitch a song in a key everyone can sing. In the beginning, it is better to be too low than too high. Only low altos and basses can go below a G; only real tenors and sopranos can be counted on to be comfortable above C or D, an octave and a half higher. Certain songs need a warm and relaxed feeling and must be pitched as low as possible. Others have an occasional high note, which, to sound right, must be at the top of everyone's range. Small children can sing two or three tones higher than adults. As for teen-agers—no two voices are alike.

Accompaniment? A few songs need none, but we are so used to the rhythmic chords that some songs seem incomplete without them. Guitars and banjos are good because the sharp punctuation of the plucked string points out the rhythm without obscuring the melody.

Rhythm and pacing are most important. This is why it is such a help to play one's own accompaniment. It is more important than being in exact pitch or knowing the most appropriate harmonies, nice as these may be. Rhythm can be given to the singers not just by the sound of the accompaniment but by the sight of an arm or the whole body moving, or the feel of a foot tapping on the floor.

How to keep a large audience in rhythm? Main strength. Keep the tempo. But don't expect a large audience to be able to keep up with a fast hoedown.

Rhythm can be oppressive, too, so afford relief from it occasionally—vary it, and at times abandon strict time for free cadence.

Make the songs longer rather than shorter. It is as difficult to have a good two-minute songfest as it would be to have a good two-minute football game. Of course, if the music is of poor quality to begin with, even fifteen seconds is too long. But in many Negro churches the best congregational singing comes when the song has lasted not four or five minutes, but ten or fifteen minutes. It is not impossible to have good short songs, but better make them solos. The group sound steadily improves, even when the song is repeated twice all the way through. You get warmed up to the task. It's as simple as that.

Some day, perhaps in our lifetime, we will see an American population which can sing as readily and beautifully together as many "under-developed" peoples can today. We will sing together with harmony, rhythm, and good tone, which we do not always have at present. Meanwhile we song leaders have a long way to go in learning how to help audiences sing with us. Needed: not only songs with choruses, refrains and responses, not only rousing, spirited songs, but quiet and deeply moving songs as well. Composers! Can you compose for an audience?

Of course, a program of folk songs should not be all audience participation. Narrative songs, lullabies, often sound better sung by one person—just as they often sound better unaccompanied by any instrument. The art of programming is an art in itself; 99 percent depends on the particular needs of an audience, and the way a performer feels on that particular day. But if, between ballads and solos, we can help our neighbors in front of us realize some of their own potentialities as singers, we will be doing a service for our country.

Somehow, somewhere along the line, Americans must learn, as our grandparents knew, that it is fun to create for yourself. The problem: how to be a whole Human Being in a machine and monopoly age. Ultimately, rank-and-file participation in music goes hand in hand with creativity on other planes—arts, sciences, and yes, even politics.

Needed: A New Kind of Three-Part Song

WHEN A SINGER stands up before an audience and sings "Michael, Row the Boat Ashore" or "Passing Through," he is singing what amounts to a two-part song, in the sense that part of the song is for him to sing, and the other part is for the audience to join in on—the refrain or chorus.

When a trio or quartet or a chorus stands up before an audience and sings these same songs, the audience remains silent, since now both the solo and the refrain are being taken care of. This is a loss, no?

Why not develop a new kind of song which can provide for all three elements to have full play:

1) A solo part, to carry the verses (the words need to be clear).
2) A refrain with parts which could be handled by the trio, quartet, or chorus standing on the stage next to the soloist.
3) A unison chorus which can be handled by the audience.

These three elements might follow each other in sequence, or alternate, each clearly separate from the other. Or they might overlap or intertwine in many different ways. But songs built upon this three-part principle could make full use of: (1) the agile clarity of a solo voice, (2) the intricacy of a counterpoint from a rehearsed vocal group, and (3) the full-bodied power of sound which can be gotten from an audience when they are singing well.

Will we have to train a new generation of songwriters to do this?

Teaching African Choral Chants to an Audience

WHEN AN AUDIENCE is warmed up and singing well the bolder spirits can be encouraged to learn or improvise a harmonizing part. To involve the whole group in the excitement of harmony, a round is one obvious way. (Even a chestnut like "Frère Jacques" is impressive the first time you hear it surging around you with a few hundred voices on each part.) "Hine Ma Tov" and "Shalom Chaverim" can be enjoyed as unharmonized songs for their melodies and message, but once learned, it is even more satisfying, and not difficult, to do them as rounds.

The verse and chorus of a song like "Pick a Bale of Cotton," or the three parts of "Tzena Tzena," can also be put together with striking effect after they have been enjoyed separately.

The richest sonorities, the most dynamic interplay of rhythms, are found in the great choral chants of Africa. These are far more sophisticated than our familiar rounds, yet their effect is built up in essentially the same way: each voice has a short phrase that is repeated over and over. "Wimoweh"* has been enjoyed by every conceivable kind of audience since the Weavers learned it years ago. I have taught "Bayeza" and "Somagwaza" to audiences all over the country.

"Bayeza" has a more complicated lead part, but it is the easier of the two.

BAYEZA (OONOMOTHOTHOLO)

(The Nomothotholo was a local spirit who was supposed to be very mischievous. Among other doubtful habits, he hovers over the chimney tops cf houses and reports any useful conversation to the witch doctor, and is not above running down the chimney from time to time to steal tobacco if it is left lying about. The song is an invocation to this spirit to come with the dawn.)

The bass part is important to the total effect; it is best to get the low voices rolling first:

Ba - ye - za, ku - sa - sa, ba - ye - za.

---

* The Bells of Rhymney (Oak Publications, New York, 1964, p. 73). "Wimoweh" was adapted from an older Zulu song by the late Solomon Linda of Johannesburg, South Africa, and his popular quintet, The Evening Birds. The Weavers learned it from their record.

After they have done it two or three times, and are sure, the other voices are added one at a time:

When these parts are going well, over and over, add your solo part. Wait till the group is halfway through their phrase, then start:

When the lead tenor sings "ku-sa-sa" he should be singing it *at the same time* as everybody else.

When sung well, by singers who realize that they are building a mood, with a soloist who can improvise a bit, this song can go on for some minutes, getting better and better. But if it is not going well, you may want to end it after the short phrase has been repeated only ten or fifteen times. In any case, the leader can end it by simply adding one extra measure, with a ritard, and all will know this is the end.

Oo - no - mo - tho - tho - lo ba - ye - za, ku - sa - sa ba - ye - za.

Some parts, such as tenor or baritone, can be omitted (I usually do omit them). The song can be successfully performed by either men or women taking the "bass," "alto," and "soprano" parts.

"Somagwaza"* is a little more difficult, since no part starts at the same time. When all have sung it to their fill, the leader should give a signal, and then all end on the syllables "gwa-za" with a hold.

I Had a Rooster

THIS BARNYARD SONG has many familiar cousins, such as "Old MacDonald Had a Farm" and "I Had a Cat and the Cat Pleased Me." This version comes from country-music man Tex Ritter. Its advantage is a somewhat slower and more lyrical melodic line which does not suffer too much when I take a few seconds out between verses to draw a picture of the next bird, beast or bug about to be eulogized.

A teacher or song leader with little or no training in drawing can make quite a party out of this song.

---

* See p. 130, Chapter 3. These two chants are from the Joseph Maselwa–H. C. N. Williams collection, *Choral Folksongs of the Bantu,* published in this country by G. Schirmer (New York, 1960), and may be heard on Folkways FW 6912.

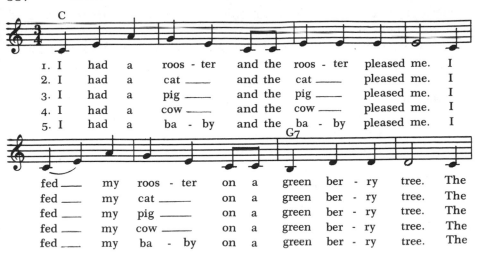

1. I	had	a	roos - ter	and the	roos - ter	pleased me.	I
2. I	had	a	cat ___	and the	cat ___	pleased me.	I
3. I	had	a	pig ___	and the	pig ___	pleased me.	I
4. I	had	a	cow ___	and the	cow ___	pleased me.	I
5. I	had	a	ba - by	and the	ba - by	pleased me.	I

fed ___	my	roos - ter	on a	green	ber - ry	tree.	The
fed ___	my	cat ___	on a	green	ber - ry	tree.	The
fed ___	my	pig ___	on a	green	ber - ry	tree.	The
fed ___	my	cow ___	on a	green	ber - ry	tree.	The
fed ___	my	ba - by	on a	green	ber - ry	tree.	The

(On first verse, omit the next four bars of music. In subsequent verses repeat these four bars as necessary.)

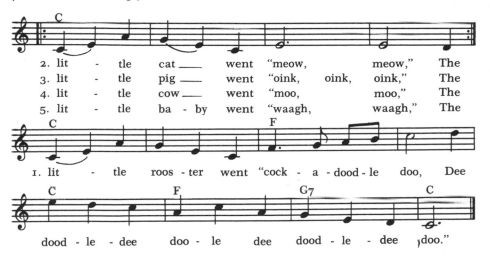

2. lit	-	tle	cat ___	went	"meow,	meow,"	The
3. lit	-	tle	pig ___	went	"oink,	oink, oink,"	The
4. lit	-	tle	cow ___	went	"moo,	moo,"	The
5. lit	-	tle	ba - by	went	"waagh,	waagh,"	The

1. lit - tle roos - ter went "cock - a - dood - le doo, Dee

dood - le - dee   doo - le   dee   dood - le - dee   ‚doo."

(That is—as usual in this type of song—you introduce a new animal and noise in each verse, then repeat the previous ones in reverse order; so the Baby verse will go:

I had a baby and the baby pleased me.
I fed my baby on a green berry tree.

The little baby went "waagh, waagh,"
The little cow went "moo, moo,"
The little pig went "oink, oink, oink,"
The little cat went "meow, meow,"

The little rooster went "cock-a-doddle doo,
   dee doodle-dee doodle-dee doodle-dee doo.")

For a group of children over three or four in number, the pictures had best be rather big, on large-size paper. Colored chalk or pastel usually shows better than crayon. Big Magic Markers are possible. Sometimes I use brushes and colored dyes; large sheets of newsprint, taken from the classified-advertising sections, present an even surface to the audience and absorb ink quickly.

I pin them to an improvised easel, or a wall, and make quick strokes with large Japanese brushes. Then the paper is torn down and handed to some child to hold, while we sing the new verse.

I do it somewhat as follows:

"Before we can sing this song, we have to have a picture of what we're going to sing about. Soon as you guess what it is, let me know."

"Anybody recognize it?"
> *(A few pauses make it more dramatic.)*

"How about it now?"

"Well, now you know what it is! Yes, a rooster!"

"There."

(Complete the sketch as quickly as possible. From beginning to end it shouldn't take more than twenty seconds.)

"Supposing you hold it up so we can all see it." (A child is selected to step forward and hold up the drawing.)

"Now here's the song." (Sing the first verse, and repeat the last line, with the "cock-a-doodle," so that everyone knows it.)

"Now, before we can sing another verse, we have to have another picture. This time I'm going to fool you for sure."

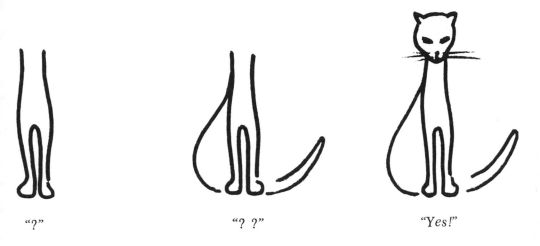

"?"   "? ?"   "Yes!"

(The exact order of the subsequent series of pictures does not matter.)

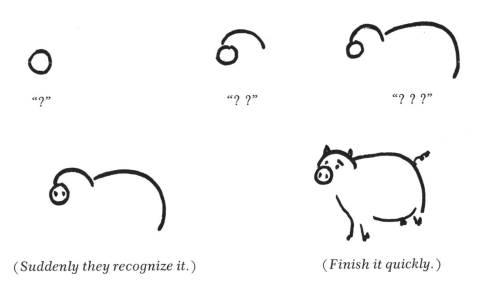

"?"   "? ?"   "? ? ?"

(*Suddenly they recognize it.*)   (*Finish it quickly.*)

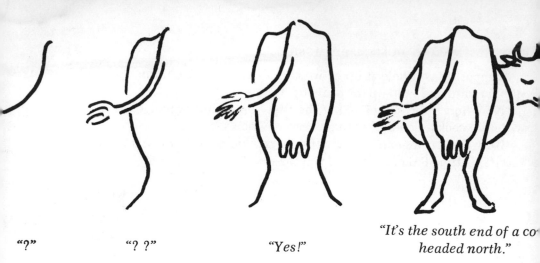

"?"   "? ?"   "Yes!"

"*It's the south end of a co
headed north.*"

I usually end with the baby.

"*One last picture. What's this?*"

"*Can you guess it now?*"

"*Now you must know it!*"

"*Yes . . . ?*"

"A baby!"

"Have you one at home?"

"How do they sound? ANHHH!!"

Infinite verses are possible: Bee ("buzz")

Lion ("roar")

Duck ("quack")

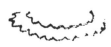  

Dog, mouse, horse, snake, etc. I usually find five or six verses are enough to make a four-minute song. Eventually we end up with a stage full of pictures.

A different color for each bird or animal is usually best—but do not get too ambitious. The entire picture should be completed in a few seconds, as anyone who has ever done chalk-talks knows. Practice for a few hours, and you can be an expert.

The Limbo

(1960)

THE LIMBO, a dance which is also a spectacular contest,* swept the West Indies in the 1950s. You need a long straight pole, a group of

---

* In Africa, music, singing and dancing are usually closely associated. (Translate "limbo" as "limber." There is a little song which often accompanies the dance: "Limbo, limbo, limbo like me; I want a woman who's limbo like me.")

energetic and adventuresome people, and strong rhythmic accompaniment—a steel band will do, or else simply some improvised hand-drumming on boxes or tables.

The pole is held by two responsible people, first at a height of four or five feet. The rhythm begins. The dancers line up on one side, their bodies swaying in time as they wait their turn. Each must go under it, bending over backward to avoid hitting the pole, but never touching the ground with any part of their body except their feet. When all have had their turn, the pole is lowered an inch or two and the process is repeated. The rhythm must never stop; it helps the dancers to do their best.

As the bar is lowered, dancers are eliminated; finally only the winner is left. An agile amateur can usually get below three feet. Only experts get below 18 inches. The champions make it down to 8 or 9 inches, believe it or not. I find it better not to talk of the experts, though, because it discourages the beginners from trying. (The trick is to spread your legs very far apart, and inch forward almost on the sides of your feet.)

Festivals

(1956)

EVER THINK OF organizing a local folk festival? Wherever you are this summer, in city or country, you could get one going if you have an idea of what you are looking for.

It need not be a big festival, with a heavy promotion budget, outside "stars" and an audience of thousands. It should not be. You can't expect some old grandmother with a store of wonderful ballads to project out across the footlights to three thousand spectators.

Rather, make it a community affair where neighbors, young and old, can exchange their traditions. To organize it, you need only two talents: a talent for persistent hard work in digging out the folklore that exists around you, and a talent for making friends with people, for drawing them out and making them feel that their own contribution is sincerely valued.

Oh, one other thing: you need the knowledge and the faith that in every community and people there remain heritages which have been ignored by our jukebox age.

Let me describe one such local festival which, for over fifteen years, brought much joy and happiness to those who started it, as well as to those who participated in it.

In the late 1930s a group of New York City schoolteachers started a children's camp in the Catskill Mountains in New York—Camp Woodland. They wanted it to be a democratic camp, thoroughly interracial. They also wanted to be on close terms with the country people in the surrounding villages. They wanted to avoid that situation, all too common, where a small island of city people is surrounded by a more or less hostile countryside. Think how often it occurs; the local folks look upon the campers as a gang of "city slickers," and the campers think the local folk are a bunch of "hicks." Not only with summer camps does this occur. Many a U.S. college remains a small island of intellectuality within a less-than-friendly community.

The founders of Camp Woodland energetically started to introduce their city kids to the history of the small towns of the Catskills. A station wagon full of twelve-year-olds, with the camp director, Norman Studer, would come unannounced to a crossroads country store inquiring if there was anyone around who could tell them what it was like when the tanneries were running fifty years ago. They met some of the senior citizens. In one house they might see a battered fiddle on the wall, and its owner would be invited to a camp square dance.

By the end of the summer they had arranged for several dozen local folks to participate in their first festival. A city musician who had scoffingly predicted that "all the folk songs have long vanished from the Catskills, leaving nothing but radios and billboards" was forced to eat his words.

Only half the program was provided by local talent. The children of the camp came up with their own contribution. Likewise, the audience was composed half of townspeople and half of campers and parents. Each gained a new appreciation of the other.

Each subsequent year brought new surprises. Ballad singers, square-dance callers, instrumentalists. One farmwife had the audience in stitches with her tall stories. A man who used to make wooden scoops brought a birch log on the stage. He split it, and with a few sure strokes of his home-forged tools roughed out a wooden bowl. He retired to the back of the stage while other things were going on, and an hour later brought it out for the finishing touches. It was old-time craftsmanship in action.

Townspeople, too, were introduced for the first time to the songs of the Jewish and Negro people, to songs of many lands that the children brought with them to camp.

Camp Woodland became a part of the Catskills. Local folk were as proud of it and its annual festival as the campers were proud of the Catskills. It was an example for the rest of the nation to follow. Other interracial camps followed Woodland into the Catskills. City and county folk both had an education in democracy.

No two such local festivals would be alike. They would differ as the national makeup of the population differs from community to community. Feel like starting a committee for such a festival in your community? It might be an education for you, too.

Caravans

(1955)

WHAT WILL YOU BE DOING this June, July and August? A summer camp job? A position on the staff of a resort, or a stopgap job in the city?

If you would like to get acquainted with this broad land, you might consider that there is a need for youth caravans to take songs, skits, movies, exhibits, from town to town. You could gather four or five friends and start one yourself.

In 1939, I and three others bought a twenty-five dollar car and took a puppet show through New York State. We played anywhere and everywhere—church socials, clambakes, children's camps, and from midsummer on for meetings of the Dairy Farmers' Union during their historic milk strike. We either charged five dollars or passed the hat. We were not great performers, and our repertoire was limited, but the skits were pointed and entertaining. We slept overnight with farm families or on folding cots in the summer fields. Though our total weekly income averaged $27, we returned home healthy and well fed, in debt to no one. It was an experience none of us will ever forget. (Similar experiences could be related by those who participated in the Caravans of 1948 or the touring theaters of the thirties.)

Want to try it? Here is what is needed for a successful caravan:

Personnel: four to six people of varied talents. At least one or two should be experienced. Others can be teen-agers. *Equipment:* a secondhand car, public-address system, and spotlights.

The Show? This would depend on the talents of the group. Any or all of the following could be useful: puppets, clowns, games for the kids, skits and plays, songs, dancing for teen-agers or square dancing for all ages, chalk-talks and other art work. A cheap silent-movie projector could show Charlie Chaplin films, or a more expensive machine for sound films. Exhibits of good prints can be displayed along the walls. Display a tableful of good books and phonograph records hard to obtain outside the big city. Prints, books and records can all be sold to make added income for the group.

All this, enumerated on handbills or posters, will make your program look like a three-ring circus. Your local friends can more easily get an audience for you.

Keep your expenses so low that you can afford to perform for small groups—in living rooms or backyards, or for a local organization with only a few dozen members. Rather than trying to line up big bookings in large cities, head for a limited geographical area and cover it intensively. (One might aim programs at a particular cultural or industrial group within an area.)

This way you can drive twenty or thirty miles away during the daytime, line up bookings for the following week, and return to perform at night. You can be your own advance agents.

In March you should be discussing the project. In April and May you should start rehearsing. In June you can be out on the road.

If the picture I paint sounds unrealistically rosy, I might point out that except for one or two semiprofessional leaders of such a group, there would be no salaries beyond spending money. But you would return rich in experience.

As a matter of fact, never again in your life may you have a chance to see the country so cheaply. Later on, you will have jobs you can't quit, families, homes, and responsibilities which have always made touring impractical for all but the well-to-do. Between the ages of eighteen and twenty-four is the average person's best time to travel.

Gather rosebuds while ye may.

Folk Choruses?

(*1956*)

WITH AN AMERICAN FOLK-SONG REVIVAL on in full force, with 500,000 guitars sold last year, and millions more having fun singing folk songs together, why is it that still there are comparatively few choruses in the country, and such as there are find themselves hard-pressed to keep up their membership?

I don't know the exact reason. Perhaps too few choruses sing short, manageable songs and concentrate too hard on long performance pieces. Perhaps the average singer remains unconvinced of the value of learning to read music in parts. Perhaps the average chorus director has an inadequate appreciation of what folk music is all about, an inadequate acquaintance with folk-song choral idioms, techniques and attitudes.

Perhaps a new concept of what a folk chorus can be is needed.

If this last conjecture is worth considering, take a look at the way a successful group in New York is organizing its program. In the first place, they call themselves the Latin American Song and Dance Group, and think of themselves less as a chorus than a club. It started with four or five people who wanted to sing together, with no thought of profit. One was a hand-drummer, another a guitarist. Now they number over thirty and include dancers as well. They include young and old, Negro and white, and former residents of over a dozen Latin American states and islands, as well as some Yankees who speak Spanish. Their aim is to present an honest picture of Latin culture to New Yorkers.

When they perform, they do not stumble on stage en masse, but each is introduced as an individual. "Next are Mr. and Mrs. ——, who hail originally from Honduras. We met them last May, and asked them to join our group when we heard how beautifully they could harmonize together." This regard for the individual and his personality is important. They say, in effect, to a new member: "Does society demand you be passive? With us you can express yourself and your own personal individuality." The chorus gives parties for any member who gets married, has a baby, or gets a job. Whole families attend.

Their programs alternate large choral numbers with solos, duets and trios, and dances. Use of costume makes the stage colorful, but it is not overdone, and they are careful to keep it authentic. Arrangements are rarely written down, and the two- or three-part harmony is usually worked out by trial and error during rehearsal.

They maintain a clubhouse for rehearsing, now that they have outgrown each other's parlors, and meet there often for social pleasure as well as for rehearsing. A member might bring a spouse or baby along. Everyone chips in for expenses of supper.

There is a certain resemblance here to the singing societies of the eighteenth century, whose members met regularly to harmonize on the latest rounds and catches. But this group has a larger perspective. They are eager to perform for outsiders, to present the true story of their Latin American lands so often misunderstood in the U.S.A.

If you are one who would like to sing with a large group of people, you might put down this page now and consider how such principles, applied to your own community, might turn out. No two groups would be exactly alike. It would call for much creative thinking. And for more, lots more, ordinary love and regard for our fellow men and women than we usually have time for in this workaday world. But might not the results be worth it—the love and friendship one would receive as well as the music?

If any reader is thinking of starting a chorus, here is another idea: try a family chorus, open only to two or more members of families. No adult allowed without a child, and vice versa. Keep the arrangements in two or three parts, so that they can be rehearsed over the supper dishes or driving home in the car. Mother might be alto, son or daughter a soprano, father a bass of some sort or else double on the melody.

(December 1962)
In spite of all the commercial hoopla, this is still a season for singing. In many corners of our country, readers of Sing Out *have tuned up their guitars and banjos, rehearsed briefly, and sallied forth into the cold air to bring songs of peace and good will, old and new, near and far, to their neighbors. Have you tried it? There's a sound to friendly, raw voices that no loudspeaker can ever match.*

"I had a voice like a bull, and I was as stupid as I was strong."

Harry Barnhart, a bearded old man, crusty and opinionated, was talking thus to me a few years ago, describing the extraordinary groups of community choruses he used to lead way back in the early years of this century.

He had them in New York, Buffalo, Philadelphia, and other cities. Fifteen hundred people would come in every week to rehearse his own rearrangements of operas, cantatas, and occasional pop songs from the nineteenth century, such as Stephen Foster's.

People would hestitate about joining. "But we can't read music."

"Good! I'm glad you can't," he would reply.

I asked him, "How did you teach them, then, by rote?"

"No, by inspiration!"

He would have whole sections sing solo arias, and, in 1915, had his then 2,000-voice chorus out in Central Park at a "Song and Light Festival." No less then 120,000 people were grouped around the Central Park lake, listening. This was in the days before microphones. He used his huge chorus as an amplified soloist, and got the whole 120,000 onlookers singing with him.

"But when I spoke to that crowd, they could hear me," the old man said defiantly. "I would stop them if they weren't singing right. I'd say, 'It has no tone, no spirit. Breathe deep. Let it flow.' You see, tone has to do with the soul of man. Nowadays? The microphone is a menace; it's killed the quality of sound."

Folk Song Clubs in the British Isles

(1967)

MANY AN AMERICAN CITY or college town has seen coffee houses come and go. We could learn from the English, Scottish and and Irish folk song clubs, a flourishing 400 or more.*

A club can be organized around any handful of people who like to sing. No two are exactly alike. Some concentrate on ballads, others on blues, others mix it up. It depends on the opinions of those who start it off, "the regulars." Certain standard procedures are common:

1. They meet once a week. Not once a month, not twice a week. Once. Always on the same night. Like church.

---

* At least 700 in 1969: it has become impossible to keep an accurate count.

2. Those who start it and run it, "the regulars," do not try to make a full-time income out of it, and often take little or no money from the kitty.

3. They usually rent a room above a pub, so visitors can send down for a mug of beer and make it a social evening. (But in parts of Ireland and Scotland where this is not legal, the singing seems just as festive.)

4. If a club gets too popular and too crowded (as often happens) it splits like an amoeba. British crowds prefer intimacy, the lack of microphones. Also, those in charge do not usually try to raise the low admission price just because a place gets popular.

The amateurs stay in control of the situation. American coffee houses, on the other hand, tend to get under control of the owner, and become straight commercial ventures.

(The Spinners, in Liverpool, have tried a combination: three nights a month they run a small folk club. On one night a month they rent a big hall and 2,000 people come.)

One of London's most popular folk song clubs is The Fox, started by singer Bob Davenport and friends. He says, "At The Fox we have our own band to play traditional English dance music, alternating with the songs. We never take money out of the kitty, so we have money to pay for outside entertainers more often. Once we invited some New Orleans jazz musicians.

"Once a group of West African drummers came. The same night the Stewart family was in town: Alex, Belle, and the two daughters. The drummers ended a session, then when Alex was playing the pipes, the drummers asked if they could accompany him on a number. Alex liked it so much that *he* asked *them* to accompany him more. For twenty minutes it was. 'Scotland the Brave'! The crowd went wild."

In New York, twenty-five years ago, the first Almanac Singers' hootenannies were very like the British folk song clubs. Every Sunday afternoon a hundred or more people crowded in to hear Woody and Lee Hays and me and the rest.

But then after the war, when we started them up again, they got too popular. We rented outside halls, getting bigger and bigger . . .

And some - day we all got to learn

That big - ger ain't bet - ter, ba - by.

Some critics sneer to hear a Kentucky miners' union song sung by a middle-class college student; but is it not just as strange to have a Carnegie Hall audience composed of Catholic, Jew, Protestant and atheist applauding Lutheran Bach chorales? Or city dwellers decorating their apartments with sculpture carved by distant tribesmen?

It would all be laughable, if we in the 1960s did not use these works of art of the faraway and long gone to help us in our own lives to create anew, to be more than mere spectators.

6.Voices

Sometimes I find a song in a songbook I think I'd like. I try it out; it seems stiff as a new shoe. But after a month of singing it, I get it broken in. It starts changing to shape itself to my individual bumps. After a time it's as comfortable as any old shoe.

A good song is like a many-faceted jewel. Or a woman of many moods. Or a tool of many uses. Try them out, turn them over, look at them from several angles. Taste 'em. On the page of a book they are in a state of suspended animation. It takes singers to bring them to life. And such is their magic, that they can bring fuller life to you.

The Singing Voice—Folk Style

IN TEL AVIV, a girl told me that she was taking voice lessons because she wanted to go into the profession of singing folk songs for a living. I told her I hoped her voice teacher knew what kind of songs she wanted to sing. Because vocal cords are muscles, just like any others in the human body, and they can be trained in a number of different ways. What's good training for one idiom may be bad training for another style. Swimming coaches don't allow their champion swimmers to go in for tennis; it tightens muscles in the wrong way.

My definition of a good vocal tone is the resonant rasp of a real country singer which has no vibrato to speak of and often strains the upper registers.* And with no such things as pear-shaped tones placed in the proper cavities. I have been as repelled by sterile imitations of folk music from effete, well-trained, middle-class musicians as by the worst commercializations on the jukeboxes.

I liked Woody Guthrie's style. Any singer in doubt about how to perform his songs should listen to such recordings of American folk music as the Carter Family, and the Folkways LP series *Anthology of American Folk Music*. This is the genre to which his music belongs.

But beware of trying to imitate Woody's own records too closely—it will sound fake and phony. Don't try and imitate his accent. Don't try and duplicate his individual vocal quality. In short, be yourself.

What any singer can learn from Woody's method of performance are such things as this:

1. A matter-of-fact, *un*melodramatic, *under*statement throughout.
2. Simplicity above all—and getting the words out clearly.
3. Irregularity.

This last perhaps needs explanation: to avoid a sing-song effect from repeating the same simple melody many times, Woody, like all American ballad singers, held out long notes in unexpected places, although his guitar strumming maintained an even tempo. Thus no two verses sounded alike. Extra beats were often added to measures. The melodies are usually changed rhythmically from verse to verse, to fit the words exactly.

Rarely if ever are ritards† used at the end of a song. Tempos of each song remain constant from first verse to last. Sudden crescendos and pianissimos are abjured. When the last verse is over, the song usually stops . . . without any extra vocal or instrumental flourishes.

Woody's songs, like many American folk songs, are easy to sing. They are difficult only in that they are often the essence of simplicity.

Many recordings made by the Carter Family in the twenties and thirties have been reissued. Folkways' *Anthology of American Folk Music* was the pioneer; now there are LPs on several labels.

---

* These comments refer to the *Anglo*-American singing tradition. The typical black country style, stemming mainly from Africa, is different in many ways—more relaxed, open-throated, emotionally expressive. Alan Lomax discussed these contrasts in the introduction to *Folk Songs of North America*. Since then he has carried out a major research project, with the help of linguists, anthropologists, psychologists, and even IBM computers, in which singing styles from every part of the world are systematically compared and related to every important aspect of the way of life of the societies. The results are published in *Folk Song Style and Culture*, published in 1968 by the American Association for the Advancement of Science, 1515 Massachusetts Ave., N.W., Washington, D.C. ($17.50)

† A fancy musician's word for slowing down the last few words of a song.

It would be well to become familiar with a number of authentic country voices
   while you are finding your own way of singing American songs. Consult the
   discography suggestions in the Appendix on pages 575–77.
One fascinating example of the variety which is possible is the Library of Congress
   disc AAFS L 54, on which thirty different singers are heard in their own
   versions of "Barbara Allen."

The Joy of Singing Unaccompanied*

A TRUTH I am reminded of when I visit Britain is how much
fun and how right it is to sing many folk songs without any accompaniment whatsoever. For some singers this is a shocking idea; accustomed
to that comforting strummed support, they would as soon walk out upon
a stage naked. Nevertheless, as any sculptor can tell you, the undraped
torso, be it ever so scrawny, is often more interesting than if wrapped or
overwrapped in the best our culture can offer.

Ewan MacColl and A. L. Lloyd led the way in singing unaccompanied.
Throughout the folk song clubs of England and Scotland dozens of fine
young singers have followed their example, and after an initial period of
imitation, found their own style.

I'll never forget seeing Bob Davenport lift his head with a huge shock
of bright red hair on it, in a fearfully crowded, hot and noisy London
coffee house, and start the slow love song "Will Ye Go, Lassie Go." A
capella. The place quieted as though by magic.

In the U.S.A. our traditions are somewhat different; perhaps we're
mainly influenced by the African tradition of tapping a drum while singing. A blues singer conducts a duet with his guitar. I love banjo picking
too much to abandon it except occasionally.

But many of our songs beg for no accompaniment, especially slow
songs like "Shenandoah," with free, irregular rhythm. Some work songs—
like "Another Man Done Gone"—and slow spirituals are taken out of
character when accompanied by pianos and orchestras, or guitars. Leadbelly never used his guitar when he sang field hollers like "Ain't Goin'
Down to the Well No More."

Some lonesome love songs seem just made for voice alone. Not so
long ago all the old English and Scottish ballads were sung without ac-

---
* Written in 1962.

companiment. Many of them still sound much better that way. And as for lullabies—I am sure many a child has been bedded "a capella."

If the idea is new to you, try it. You'll find, for one thing, your singing will improve. You can pay more attention to the story, pay more attention to the melody, without all that distracting string plucking. Freed of entangling alliances, the voice can soar, swoop, and turn. It can accent the irregular rhythms which best bring out the meanings of the words.

You see, it is with instruments as with many machines, devices, or skills. Human beings first have to learn how to use them. But subsequently it is just as important to learn when not to use them. A child first learns to talk, and then talks all the time. He has to learn when not to talk. A painter finds a new brush or paint and uses it too much, till he learns when not to. A bride is given a box of spices for her kitchen, and tries using all of them at once in the stew. Forbearance comes with maturity.

The Fun of Singing Folk Harmony

IN MANY Mediterranean countries—Italy, for example—there is a tradition of two singers harmonizing together on a melody. The lead voice is the higher of the two; the second voice sings a few notes lower, as an alto voice would support a soprano. This tradition is also strong in many Latin American countries, such as Mexico. Take the pop song known in U.S.A. as "Yours" (in Mexico "Quiere Me Mucho").

Music by Gonzalo Roig, Spanish words by Agustin Rodriguez.
Copyright © 1931, E. B. Marks Music Corp. Used by permission.

In North America we have a tradition of folk harmony where the melody is taken by the lower voice, and the harmony part is sung two or three notes higher by the second voice. One can hear this on many country music records. Does any reader remember the way the Carter Family sang "It Takes a Worried Man to Sing a Worried Song"?

The same technique can be used with "Go Tell Aunt Rhody"

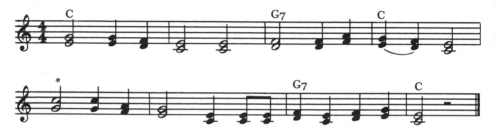

or "Skip to My Lou."

Or take a slower song, such as "Farther Along."

Traditional. Words and music adapted from W. P. Jay.

Far - ther a - long   we'll   know all   a - bout   it,

Far - ther a - long   we'll   un - der - stand why. _____

Cheer up   my   bro - thers,   live   in   the   sun - shine.

We'll un - der - stand   it   all   bye   and   bye. _____

Here you can note one of the strongest and most powerful aspects of American folk harmony: the strong open interval of four notes between the melody and the "high tenor," rather than the cloying and softer interval of a third. Check back to the notes which have an asterisk (*) over them to see what I mean.

Exactly how or when this style of harmony developed, I could not say. It is commonly known among both Negro and white folk musicians in the South. You can hear it (with more freedom and embellishment) in Negro work songs. And it is common in both Negro and white gospel singing, with the addition of a bass part, and occasionally an alto part.

Perhaps it had its origin in church music. The old shape-note hymn books, so popular throughout much of America a century ago, were full of this style of harmony. Bare fourths and fifths were often more common intervals than thirds or sixths. Furthermore, the melody was usually printed in the middle of the three staves. The top staff had a high part which might be sung by tenors as well as sopranos. The lower staff had a bass part which might be sung by older women as well as men. (In the choir of the St. Paul Baptist Church of Los Angeles I saw a group of older women standing in the bass section.) Until the twentieth century there were few alto parts in the shape-note hymn books.

Where did the shape-note hymn style come from? There's a disagreement here, too. The late George Pullen Jackson insisted it was all from Europe. Certainly older European harmony was full of bare fourths and fifths. But how can one explain that some of the oldest African folk music employs simple parallel harmony quite similar to American Negro spirituals and work songs? I think that, as in so much of American folk music, here too we have a mixture of European and African traditions.

As with learning any folk music, it is best to learn folk harmony not from notes and paper but by listening to a lot of it. Then experiment yourself in singing harmony while your friends take the melody. Try easy songs first, such as "Pharaoh's Army Got Drownded" or "Careless Love," "Deep Blue Sea," and "I Never Will Marry."

A friend reading this over says, "I still don't know what shape-note hymn singing is."* "And I still don't know the difference between a third and a fourth or fifth," says he.

Well, get with me and I'll show you. Let's both sing the first five notes of a scale. *Do, re, mi, fa, sol.* Got it? Now I'll sing *do* and hold it a long time. You sing *do, re, mi,* and hold *mi* a long time, while I'm still singing *do.* Those two notes, *do* and *mi,* are a "third" apart, and both of them sounding at once make the interval of a third. Try the same thing with *do* and *fa.* The two of them sounding at once are the interval of a "fourth." Likewise *re* and *sol* sounding at the same time are the interval of a fourth. *Do* and *sol* sounding together give the interval known as a "fifth." Lesson over. Any questions?

POSTSCRIPT: Of course, there's such a thing as having too much harmony. As with instrumental accompaniment, part of learning the technique is learning when *not* to use it. In each of the Decca recording studios there used to be a large photomural of a Central Park statue of an Indian maiden shading her eyes to scan the horizon. Underneath was Decca's caption: "Where's the melody?"

Folk harmony is heard in Folkways' *Anthology of American Folk Music* and on LPs of the Carter Family, J. E. Mainer's Mountaineers (Arhoolie X 106 and 107), Carter and Ralph Stanley (Nashville, Starday, Mercury and Melodeon records), Woody Guthrie and Cisco Houston (Stinson 32, 44, and 53, Folkways FA 2483 and 2485), Doc Watson (Folkways 2366 and other Folkways and Vanguard records)—and thousands of other country records.

For improvised harmony in Negro work songs:
> *Afro-American Spirituals, Work Song and Ballads,* Library of Congress AAFS L3
> *Negro Work Songs and Calls,* AAFS L8
> *Negro Prison Camp Work Songs,* Folkways FE 4475
> *Negro Prison Songs,* Tradition 1020
> (compiled by Alan Lomax)

---

* Instead of all round notes, shape-note hymn books used squares, triangles, semicircles, etc., so that, for example, whenever you saw a certain kind of triangular note you knew it was *do,* the first note of the major scale, no matter what key you were in. The system is explained in Richard Chase, *American Folk Tales and Songs* (Signet, 1956), pp. 13–14, and some of the history of this singing style is told in Alan Lomax, *Folk Songs of North America,* pp. 64–66 and 241. The complete story is in *White Spirituals of the Southern Uplands* (Dover) and other books by George Pullen Jackson, who did the basic scholarship in this field. Shape-note hymn singing may be heard on Library of Congress AAFS L 11, *Sacred Harp Singing,* edited by Jackson; and Atlantic 1349, *White Spirituals,* in the Lomax *Southern Folk Heritage* series.

How to Sing a Gospel Bass Part

BACK IN THE DAYS of the Almanac Singers Lee Hays taught
me what fun it was to improvise a bass part of some old hymn or spiritual, and I've been wishing I were a bass singer ever since. Your tried-and-
true bass does not envy the singer of the melody, or the tenor, or anyone
else. He knows he is the rock foundation of the musical edifice, the
firm support of all that glorious superstructure.

And do not think, either, that he is restricted rigidly to a few limited
notes. It is true that at certain crucial points he must give out with one
basic note and none other. But between these points he is free to roam,
to develop what is known as a "bass line." Examine the next two lines of
music. The melody is on the top stave. First I give an uninspired bass
part, sticking rigidly to the "root" of the appropriate chord at that point.

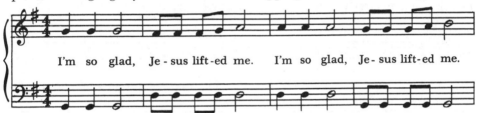

Here, to the same melody, you see how a good bass singer develops a
"bass line."

Of course, there is such a thing as a bass singer attempting to get too
fancy. I find myself objecting to too many chromaticisms (as bad as too
many witticisms). Again, two illustrations: the first has a nice bass part,
the second* has weakened the whole musical fabric by attempted
elegance.

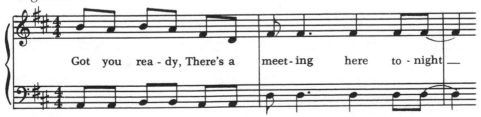

* See next page.

Sometimes the bass can bring out a musical point that would not have been noticed in a casual listening to the melody. For example, he can land on the relative minor (note arrow), and give a fine new coloration to that part of the song.

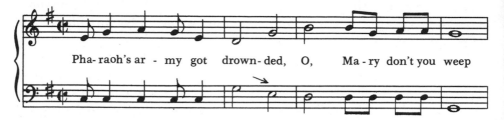

Sometimes a quartet or group with an exceptionally fine bass section develops bass parts which stand out in the clear, almost like solos.

Other times, it's good for the bass to stop singing completely for a moment. Then he returns to tie everything together.

For a last demonstration, try this:

---

* A traditional song I learned from SNCC members.
† Bass as sung by Lee Hays.

As usual in folk music, it would be better not to try to memorize note for note any one bass part, but rather get so familiar with the idiom that you can improvise within it. It is like a guitar picker getting used to the standard sequences of blues chords. Then even when making music with people you've never met before, you know how to fit into the picture. Many a bass singer has known the joy of being able to join in on a song he's never heard before. He can place the notes strongly and unerringly, like big stepping stones, not because he's familiar with the exact tune but because he's familiar with so many like it.

How low do you have to go to be able to sing bass?

While many bass singers pride themselves on their ability to go down to E or D or lower, if you can sing a strong low G (an octave and a half below middle C) you can usually get along all right. It helps if the song is pitched up high (perhaps in G instead of E). The altos may complain, but the tenors and sopranos will like it fine.

If a trained musician happens by accident to read this, he or she is probably wincing in pain by now. "Such oversimplification! You can't do this to the art of Bach and Handel."

Quite right. Don't try these precepts with the art of Bach and Handel. But do try them with a related but different musical language, namely, on some of the songs listed below. You'll sure have a lot of fun.

> We Shall Not Be Moved
> Study War No More
> This Little Light of Mine
> Every Time I Feel the Spirit
> Ezekiel Saw the Wheel
> Michael, Row the Boat Ashore
> Oh, Freedom
> Roll the Union On
> Kumbaya
> We Shall Overcome
> Amazing Grace
> Don't You Weep After Me
> Farther Along
> O Mary Don't You Weep
> Woke Up This Morning
>   (with My Mind Stayed on Freedom)
> I'm on My Way

Gospel singing can be heard in small churches in any sizable city of the U.S., and on recordings of the many church-based groups which have developed a national following.

For the old country tradition from which all of this flows, I suggest:
> *Afro-American Spirituals, Work Song, and Ballads*, AAFS L3
> *Negro Religious Songs and Services*, AAFS L10
> *Negro Church Music*, Atlantic 1351
> Records of the Clara Ward Singers (Vanguard, Savoy and others)

7.Some Instruments

What's the message of a virtuoso performer? "See what wonderful things a human can do if he practices."

What's the message of a singalong strummer? "See what fun it is to do something yourself, even if you're not expert."

Introductory

Is MUSICAL TALENT INHERITED? I bet most of it is developed by family and environment. Of course, some individuals are born with more or less, as some are born better athletes. But even a "natural athlete" would never develop if denied opportunity from birth. And as many found out in the Army, practically anyone can have a better physique, given proper exercise and training.

Similarly, if a child hears and *makes* music from birth, its rhythmic and tonal senses are sharpened, and its hands can coordinate so that learning an instrument later on is twice as easy.

Some may say: "All Russians can sing harmony," or "All Negroes have rhythm in their souls." Nonsense. Anthropologists have proved that growing up within deep folk traditions, which develop these abilities, produces adults who know how to make music as naturally as most of us know how to talk or walk.

Many Yankee Americans have a poorly developed sense of rhythm (compared to people in Asia, Africa, South America and Polynesia). Rhythmic ability can be taught and trained. Most people who have good rhythm have loved to dance, or participated in rhythmic music. Perhaps as babies their rhythmic education began with clapping games, and later the skip-rope and bounce-ball games known on a city sidewalk.

The rhythm of a banjo or guitar is more important than its harmony or melody.

The most important quality of a good steel band is perfect rhythm. (I have listened to Kim Loy Wong rehearse the same short tune for over twenty minutes without stopping, until he was satisfied that every member of the band played his own particular rhythm correctly.)

Did you ever see a drummer practicing on his little rubber pad? For hours on end he will beat the same patterns, first in one tempo and then another. He cannot be merely satisfied to know "how" a certain rhythm is to be played. He must know it so well that he can practically do it in his sleep. He must be able to hold if necessary the same tempo through a piece. No distractions, no inept fellow player, should be able to knock him off his course.

The banjo or guitar player's right hand must similarly learn each pattern of strumming and picking so well that he doesn't even need to think about it.

The best way to get rhythmic control is to play a lot, especially with other musicians. Curiously, I have often found that the students having the most difficulty learning rhythm are those with some formal musical training.

People sometimes ask, "What is the easiest folk instrument to learn?" What a question. Any instrument can be as difficult as you want to make it. It depends how far you want to go with it. A good craftsman will keep any tool as sharp as possible.

Some of the easiest to get started on, like the autoharp, are the hardest to continue with past kindergarten. Likewise the ukulele.

A banjo may be more difficult than a guitar, unless the learner has a good sense of rhythm to start with. But it might be easier than the guitar once you get over that first hurdle.

Chalils, fiddles, flutes take patience to start with. Once you get a good tone, they are as easy—and as difficult—as your artistry wishes.

Recorders are easy at first, harder later on to bring satisfaction, because of their limited tone. Harmonicas likewise, unless you have muscles to develop the blue notes, as does Sonny Terry.

The piano is a great instrument, but its usefulness to singers of folk music is limited. It may be fine for a square dance and other large gatherings where volume is needed and no amplification is provided. But to accompany a few average voices—too loud.

Further, unless under fingers of unusual talent, it tends to have a less expressive tone, and must rely, like the organ, on the effect of *many* notes, rather than on a few syllables well spoken.

Because so many notes are available to the player, it is a great temptation to modulate, to chromaticize. Not that such things are bad in themselves. But for a young person trying to work out accompaniment to simple folk tunes, nothing could be more dangerous. Think of the wonderful melodies which could have been written by . . . well, let's not mention any names . . . if he'd had no piano to help him compose.

Similarly, it is so easy to get a lot of noise out of an accordion that it is difficult to get music out of one. In the hands of an unfeeling person or a show-off, it can be a pain to listen to. But in the hands of a sensitive person with taste and restraint—and also with a good deal of strength and power in arms and shoulders—perhaps it can be just as beautiful as any instrument. Listen to the accordions accompanying the Piatnitsky chorus on Russian folk songs, or the Louisiana Cajun accordion ("windjammers" they called them—Leadbelly could play one).

The little octagonal concertina, with its limited rows of buttons, is an even better instrument to accompany quiet songs. It is not so loud as to drown out a voice, and has a sweeter tone than most big accordions. Sergei Matusewitch plays violin concertos on his concertina. In England, Alf Edwards plays some concertina music on the BBC folk music shows of Ewan MacColl and others. Sam Eskin told me he was learning the concertina to accompany sailor songs—and I think he is right. The roll and flow of the waves fit those reedy tones far better than they do a plucked string.

The guitar has proven itself perhaps the best all-around folk instrument we have handy. Its effects run from bass to treble, staccato to legato. But it's nice to see other American folk instrumental techniques being simultaneously revived: the dulcimer, for example.

The American dulcimer, the unique stringed instrument everybody assumed was dying out for good, is making a steady comeback.*

The charm of the instrument lies in its quiet, reserved tone and the ease of playing. Though it is limited harmonically, like the bagpipe, its

---

* Nearly every issue of *Sing Out* carries several ads of dulcimers and dulcimer books; Jean Ritchie, for example, has produced a book-and-record combination—*The Dulcimer Book* (Oak Publications, New York) and *Appalachian Dulcimer*, Folkways 8352.

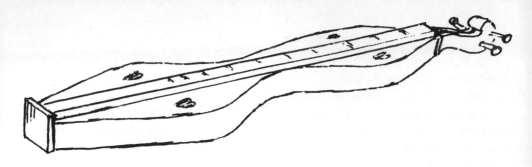

very limitations serve in the end to build a unique musical art. Is this not often a characteristic of folk music?

If the player can learn to live within the limitations of a folk instrument, exploring its subtleties can be a lifetime pastime. I have heard some songs ideally accompanied with a small drum, tastefully tapped by fingers.

(I am sometimes asked why in our songbooks and magazines we print only melodies and chord markings, but few complete accompaniments. Answer: partly because it's cheaper and easier. But partly because no one accompaniment, no matter how fine, can possibly be right for all the different situations when a song may be sung. People who love folk songs *must* learn to develop their own accompaniments, and shape them to the needs of the situation, the singer, the listeners, the instrument(s) available.)

There are dozens of instruction books available now. But I wouldn't depend on any one of them alone. There are many ways of playing. Any one teacher or book will give you mainly the technique of one person.

I'd rather put the student more on his own, anyway. It is as though a man asked me to teach him how to build a house, and all I have time to do is teach him how to mix and pour cement, hammer a nail, and saw on the square. From there on, I can only hope that he will have sense to go look at some houses, examine closely the ones he admires, and then construct likewise, adjusting the architecture to fit his own needs.

I hope you're the kind who keeps a banjo or guitar hung on the wall where it's handy. Don't think of yourself as "practicing" in the formal sense, but simply keep on playing a lot. Get together with others who like to sing and try running through various folk songs, ballads, blues and dance tunes.

I was teaching a housewife how to play guitar, near my home in the Hudson Valley, and she wasn't making any progress at all. I told her,

"Forget the dishes, forget the beds and the sweeping for a while." And, you know, next week she really had made some progress.

The Guitar

. . . has proven itself the most adaptable of accompanying instruments. Every nation has developed its own style of playing.

It started off in Asia thousands of years ago. An ancestor is the Persian "tar"; one of its illustrious cousins is the Indian sitar. The guitar itself, it is generally believed, was brought to Europe in the twelfth century by Gypsies.

Spaniards brought it across the Atlantic, and their part-Indian children developed it further. In Latin America you can find many wonderful methods of strumming. In Argentina alone there are eighteen common tunings.

During the nineteenth century the guitar and a lot of other cultural items—such as wide-brimmed hats, high-heeled boots, and cowboy lingo —filtered up to us from Mexico through Texas. The guitar spread through the South and then northern states. Afro-Americans developed a new style of plucking it. In the U.S.A. today we find "blues" guitar, "hillbilly" and "steel" guitar, and of course many jazz guitar styles.

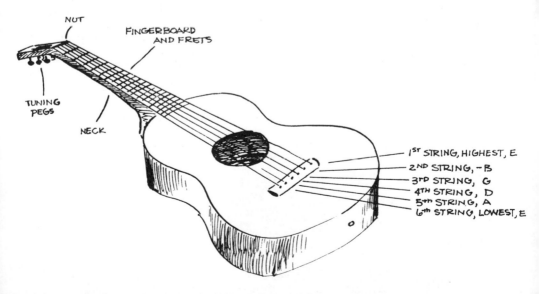

Among folk musicians you will find master technicians; but don't fail to notice also how much they can express with only a few chords and a few simple techniques. They have learned to discard ideas they don't like; you must also.

If you wanted to make like Andrés Segovia or Merle Travis, it would take a lifetime of training. But for most of us, playing a guitar can be about as simple as walking.

Remember, it took us all a couple of years to learn to walk.

Records:
Once you have learned a few simple things about folk guitar playing, your best guide will be hearing and seeing other performers, and listening to such records as those listed in the Appendix of this book. A few of the performers I think you will find rewarding are:
The Carter Family
Blind Lemon Jefferson
Woody Guthrie
Leadbelly
Merle Travis
Big Bill Broonzy
Brownie McGhee

Instruction books and records:
There are are hundreds of guitar instruction books on the market. Some are lousy. Here are some of my favorites:

Jerry Silverman, *Beginning the Folk Guitar* (Oak Publications, New York), $2.95; Folkways 8353, $5.79; record and book, $7.79.
(The Oak-Folkways series offers you three choices: you may buy the record, which includes a booklet; or the Oak instruction manual, giving instruction in tablature and music notation—coordinated with the record, but also complete in itself; or a combination of the two.)
Pete Seeger and Jerry Silverman, *The Folksinger's Guitar Guide* (Oak Publications, New York), $2.95; Folkways 8354, $5.79; record and book, $7.79.
Jerry Silverman, *The Folksinger's Guitar Guide, Vol. 2* (Oak Publications, New York), $2.95; Folkways 8356, $5.79; record and book, $7.79.
Jerry Silverman, *The Art of the Folk-Blues Guitar* (Oak Publications, New York), $2.95; Folkways 8355, $5.79; record and book, $7.79.
Alan Lomax and Peggy Seeger, *American Folk Guitar* (Robbins Music Corporation, New York, 1957), $1.25.
Harry A. Taussig, *Instrumental Techniques of American Folk Guitar* (Oak Publications, New York), $2.95.
Happy Traum, *Finger-Picking Styles for Guitar* (Oak Publications, New York), $2.95.

Group Playing of Guitars, and the Mexican Guitarron

ONE GUITAR can sound quite nice, even if not played expertly. Two guitars can sound even nicer occasionally. But have you ever tried to sing at a party with five or more guitars all whamming away at the same time? Oy.

Yankee folk guitarists could learn a lot from the Mexican Mariachi bands, the strolling musicians of the streets and saloons. They have developed a good technique of ensemble playing.

One guitarist may stick to playing the chords and nothing else—few runs or frills. Another guitarist will do nothing but bass runs. He will practically ignore the top strings of his instrument, but invent great flourishes and obbligatos on the lower strings, especially in the pauses between the melody. And a third guitarist will do nothing but filigree work on the top strings. He and the guitarist playing bass notes can answer each other, or chase each other all over the lot.

If there is a fourth guitar present, he might play chords higher up the neck, or with a differently accented rhythm.

Thus in a group of Mexican guitar players one rarely hears the monotonous throbbing of a number of guitars playing exactly the same chords at the same time, with no variation . . . and worst of all, being too loud to sing with comfortably. Why, it can get almost as bad as having to sing with a piano.

One other instrument commonly used by Mariachi bands is little known here, but should be introduced: it is a guitarron, a bass guitar, looking roughly like this.

It has a fat body, a short neck with no frets, and is tuned with cello strings. The strings are plucked one at a time or in octaves. The tone is not as full as a bass viol, but the instrument is far more portable and complements any group of guitarists. If you know someone visiting Mexico, get them to bring you back one. Price: about $20 to $50.*

A Footnote: The Tablature System of Writing Music for Fretted Instruments

TABLATURE was invented several hundred years ago by lute players. A modern, simplified version is used in many current manuals and articles. For accurate notation of a guitar or banjo accompaniment, it beats regular music writing. It not only shows every note played, but which string is sounded, at which fret, and, if necessary, which finger plucks the string.

The essentials are as follows:

Six lines represent the six strings of the guitar.

Numbers written on or above the lines represent the fret at which each string is pressed to the fingerboard by the left hand. (Zero means play the open string without fretting it at all.)

E major scale:

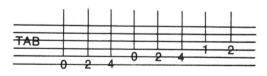

Chords:

* As of 1958.

—and so on.

Letters above or below the tablature may indicate what finger of the right hand plays each note (T = thumb, I = index finger, M = middle finger, R = ring finger). Basic guitar strum:

or:

Vertical bars divide the music into measures of two, three, or four beats, and each beat can be broken up into shorter notes—just as in regular music notation.

Quarter notes:

Eighth notes:

or:

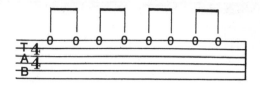

Sixteenth notes:

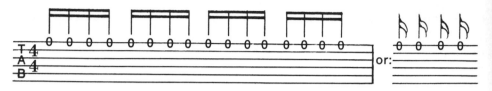

(Five-string banjo tablature, of course, has five lines instead of six.)

The Five-String Banjo*

> ". . . can I read notes? Hell, there are no notes to a
> banjo. You just play it."†

PLAYED by hundreds of thousands of Americans a century ago, by 1940 this instrument had nearly died out.

Some think the banjo an American invention. 'Tain't so. It's another U. S. development of an older idea.

The banjo was first brought here by a people enslaved because their skin color made it difficult for them to escape. They re-created the music of their lost homeland (where a distant cousin of the banjo is still played). Before that the origin is disputed.

The instrument is mainly known in Africa in the northern half, the area of Moslem influence. Possibly the Arabs brought it to the African west coast (the slave trade was most intensive along the west coast). Possibly the Arabs themselves picked it up from civilizations farther east.

---

* Written 1948–55.

† Reply made by an old-time banjo player, around 1850, when asked if he could read music. (Banjos in those days had no frets.)

Throughout all of the Near East and Far East, instruments like the banjo are common. While they might have independently developed on two continents, one is tempted to believe that there was some direct connection. The Japanese samisen is basically a banjo. Two instruments in India have short strings played by the thumb, just like the banjo: one is the sitar (cousin of the guitar), and the other is known as the sarod—and has a drumskin head!

Archaeologists tell us that the ancient Egyptians had orchestras of 600 instruments, and some of them were plucked and had skin-topped sound boxes. Perhaps it all came from Africa, the earliest probable homeland of the human race. No matter.

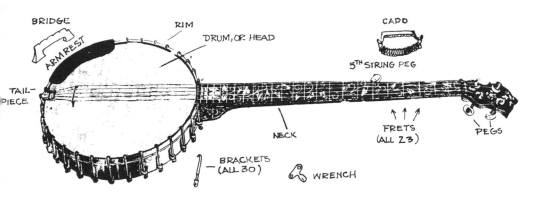

Thomas Jefferson, in his *Notes on Virginia* (1782), mentions the "banjar" as being the chief instrument of American Negroes. They developed African styles of playing the hoedowns, breakdowns, and other dance melodies learned here.

One hundred and fifty years ago the banjo consisted basically of three strings, with maybe just a possum hide stretched across a gourd for a drum. Then began a period of experimentation. Frets were added, various numbers of strings were tried out.

In 1831 a poor white farm boy in Virginia, Joel Walker Sweeney, learned the banjo from slaves near his home, and started putting on performances. The minstrel show was born. Within fifteen years the banjo conquered American pop music, the way rock and roll did 120 years later.

Joe Sweeney has been credited with inventing a little fifth string running from a peg halfway up the neck. But Paul Cadwell (New York lawyer and friend to all banjoists) quotes Judge Farrar of Virginia, who learned banjo from Sweeney in the 1840s: "I am confident that Sweeney added the *bass* string." In other words, it would now appear possible that the use of a higher-pitched thumb string was pre-Sweeney after all.

It was the five-string version that became so popular and was picked up by the country as a whole. It traveled west in the covered wagons. A banjo could be found hanging on the wall of any farmhouse or mining shack. Even trained singers, such as Patti, would play one for amusement.

Later, concert virtuosos, with phenomenal techniques, tried to take it out of the domain of the minstrel shows. I've heard of the William Tell Overture being attempted on a banjo.

With the advent of ragtime and jazz, around the turn of the century, the long-necked five-stringer was gradually abandoned in favor of the shorter, tenor banjo. This was tuned differently, and with heavier strings, to better compete with the loud brass instruments. The tenor banjo had its heyday in the 1920s, went around the world, and then in turn was left behind by modern dance bands.

For many years the five-string banjo was almost forgotten; instrument companies stopped making them; a hock shop was the most likely place to find one. Still, it was played by back-country people, especially in the South, to accompany ballads and play for square dances. And precisely because it is so excellently suited for such work, the old five-stringer has made a comeback.

In 1945 a young man named Earl Scruggs got a job with Bill Monroe and His Bluegrass Boys, playing on radio station WSM, Nashville, Tennessee. Scruggs had been playing the banjo since the age of six, and when he was a teen-ager he had worked out a syncopated variation on the old "clawhammer" finger-picking style.

Within three years he and Lester Flatt had a band of their own, playing on the Grand Old Opry. And soon the Gibson Company was back in the banjo business, supplying the thousands of young people wanting to learn Scruggs's style.

The people I learned banjo from were mostly old farmers, miners, or working people of one trade or another, who had played the instrument during their courting days, and later kept it hanging on the wall to pass away the time of an evening. Often they knew only a few tunes apiece, and maybe only one method of strumming, which they had picked up from their father or a neighbor.

Yet what they knew, they knew well, and the simple, rippling rhythm of their banjos had more art in it than many a hectic performance piece by a professional virtuoso. (The four-string tenor banjo was ruined, really, by exhibitionists who made an athletic exhibition out of each performance. After the piece was over, the audience was amazed, of course, as at the circus; but it was not music which moved or delighted one.)

The American folk style of playing seems to me to be basically non-European. A subtle rhythmic-melodic pattern is set up which repeats itself with no change in tempo, no matter what complex variations may be introduced. The sung melody may be quite free, at the same time. One can see a parallel in the playing of boogie-woogie piano.

The thing which gives this style of playing its distinctive flavor is the unusual function of the fifth string. It's the "ring" of "hear those banjos ringing." The fifth string comes in on an offbeat—kind of kicks off at the rear end of each beat. Like a triangle in an orchestra, it keeps on dinging away through a whole song, never changing in pitch, though strictly speaking it's not in harmony with some chords. (For some curious reason, probably because it is so high up, it never jars the ear. It's what composers call a "pedal point.")

> *As with tap dancing, banjo technique is nothing more than doing a few simple things over and over, till the whole procedure is fast and relaxed.*
> *Learn to play slowly as well as fast. It is the mark of an inexpert player that he is unable to slow down.*

As more Americans take hold again of their traditions of folk music, many also become acquainted with different kinds of songs from various corners of the world. And at the same time young musicians as far away as Europe and Asia are fascinated by our five-string banjo. Thus the unique qualities of this instrument, with its penetrating needlepoints of sound, are heard in many new forms.

Records:
It is from records that you can best learn the style and sweep of the banjo. Here are a few of my favorites among the many now available:

Anthology of American Folk Music, Folkways FA 2951, 2952, 2953.
   (Includes Clarence Ashley, Buell Kazee, Bascom Lamar Lunsford, Uncle Dave Macon, Stoneman Family, and others.)
Blue Ridge Mountain Music (Southern Folk Heritage Series), Atlantic 1347
   (Recorded by Alan Lomax in 1959.)

Banjo performances on Library of Congress records:
    Pete Steele on AAFS L 1
    Pete Steele, Thaddeus C. Willinghan, Wade Ward, Herbert Smoke on L 2
    Rufus Crisp on L 20
    Rufus Crisp, Bascom Lamar Lunsford, Pete Steele on L 21
Mountain Music of Kentucky, Folkways FA 2317
American Banjo Scruggs Style, Folkways FA 2314
The Stoneman Family, Folkways FA 2315
Smoky Mountain Ballads, Bascom Lamar Lunsford, Folkways FA 2040
Roscoe Holcomb and Wade Ward, Folkways FA 2363
Banjo Tunes and Songs, Pete Steele, Folkways FS 3828
Buell H. Kazee, Folkways FS 3810
Uncle Dave Macon, RBF 51
Grandpa Jones records—Decca and Monument labels

When Not to Play the Banjo

OBVIOUSLY, *when someone is trying to get the baby to sleep. Or when your neighbor, who has to be up at 5 A.M. to go to work, is trying to catch some much needed shut-eye.*

There are other times as well, in which a sensitive musical ear can tell you to lay aside the instrument. Some types of music, after all, were simply not made for it. This goes especially for certain types of slow songs, whose effect will be spoiled by the sharp punctuation of the banjo strings.

Furthermore, in accompanying yourself in a song, you will often find it desirable to stop playing for a whole phrase and let the voice stand alone. Then when the banjo rejoins you, it will be ever more welcome.

Instruction records and books:
How to Play the 5-String Banjo, by Pete Seeger (with booklet), Folkways 8303, $5.79.
Peter Seeger, *How to Play the 5-String Banjo* (Beacon, N.Y., 1961; distributed by Oak Publications), $2.00; record and book, $6.95.
Earl Scruggs and the 5-String Banjo (Earl Scruggs & Sons, Inc., 201 Donna Drive, Madison, Tenn. 37115), hardcover $12.95, paperback $10.95 (.75 postage). Record $3.95.
    (Picking instructions, 32 complete arrangements, how to build a banjo and make Scruggs pegs, autobiographical notes.)

Peggy Seeger, *The 5-String Banjo: American Folk Styles* (Hargail Music Press, New York, 1960), $1.95.

Art Rosenbaum, *Old-Time Mountain Banjo* (Oak Publications, New York, 1969), $2.95.

Peter Seeger, *The Goofing-Off Suite* (Hargail Music Press, New York), $1.50.
(Transcriptions mainly for banjo, from the Folkways record of the same name.)

Billy Faier, *Banjo Selections* (Hargail, New York), $1.00.
(Six pieces from his Riverside LP, *The Art of the 5-String Banjo.*)

A film:

The Five-String Banjo, produced by Pete and Toshi Seeger, distributed by Audio-Brandon Film Center, Inc., 34 MacQuesten Pkwy. So., Mount Vernon, N.Y. 10550.
(Demonstration of the techniques presented in the Pete Seeger manual, plus short scenes of several other banjo pickers.)

On the Subject of Banjo Cases

Under the hard usage of traveling, the average instrument case starts coming to pieces in a few years. I finally made my own case out of waterproof plywood, with steel corner guards. My brother Mike made a similar one, shaped slightly like a child's coffin, which he solemnly decorated with a large black cross.

These homemade jobs turned out to be pretty heavy, though, and about ten years ago I designed a padded leatherette banjo case, closed by a zipper and slung on the shoulder. My long-suffering wife, Toshi, sewed it up for me,* and it has worked out so well that I'm proud to pass on the design to anyone who'd like to use it, or improve upon it.

The key to its success is an inner sling, which carries the whole weight. Otherwise the seams on the lower end would split in no time.

The big advantage of such a case is the ease of carrying, leaving one's hands free for opening doors, carrying suitcases, etc. Because it is always nearby—in plane, train or car—the instrument actually gets more careful handling than it would from the usual baggage departments.

In cutting the pattern, make sure you not only make it large enough

---

* It broke the sewing machine. Subsequently I've had professional firms make them for me.

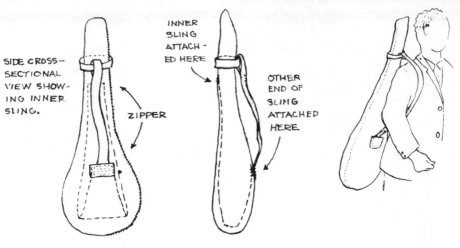

SIDE CROSS-
SECTIONAL
VIEW SHOW-
ING INNER
SLING.

ZIPPER

INNER
SLING
ATTACH-
ED HERE

OTHER
END OF
SLING
ATTACHED
HERE.

for side panels, seams, etc., but also leave a little extra room for spare shirts, socks, papers, whistles, and apples, cheese, or pastrami sandwiches.

The Twelve-String Guitar

Huddie Ledbetter, nicknamed Leadbelly, played a big twelve-string guitar. It has double strings, six pairs of them, usually tuned low. When the double strings are plucked together they give out one new tone. It is similar to the tone from an organ or accordion when several stops are pulled out. Or to the tone from a piano when a tune is played in octaves. A twelve-stringer tends to be bigger than a six-string guitar, probably to give deeper tone to the bass strings.

In the past, this instrument was rarely played in the U.S. Leadbelly was one of three or four old-time folk musicians I have ever heard play it. My guess is that it came to this country from Mexico, where it was played more commonly.

(Lutes usually had double strings; and the "Portuguese guitar" has five sets of double strings. Mandolins, and probably dozens or hundreds of other plucked stringed instruments of Europe, also use double strings.)

If you already play a six-string guitar, you can probably switch over to the twelve-stringer without too much trouble. It is tuned like a six-stringer (but usually two or three tones lower), and the chord patterns are about the same, with each finger of the left hand covering two strings at once.

It takes some muscle to push down those twelve strings onto the finger-board. The difference is roughly the same as that between driving a truck and driving a sports car. And unless you have unusual fingernails you will find it unsatisfactory to try and pick the strings with the bare fingers. In Mexico it is common to use a flat pick. Leadbelly used a thumb pick and a long steel finger pick. He never used a flat pick, so far as I know. Not enough oomph, I guess.

Relative advantages and disadvantages of the twelve-stringer:

The bass strings of the twelve-stringer can give impressive authority to a simple bass run which might sound inconsequential on a six-string. It is the difference between one violin playing a piece of music and a whole violin section playing the same passage.

But if that run is too complicated it may sound messy, mushy, and foolish, compared to the clarity of the more flexible and agile six-string playing the same run. It will be like an elephant trying to do a tap dance.

The top strings of the twelve-stringer, while they can have a warm, singing quality, also lack the crystal clarity of the single strings of the regular guitar.

Chords on the twelve-stringer can sound rich. Some chord positions, which on the six-stringer are undistinguished, become a brand new dis-covery on the twelve. But beware of becoming infatuated with them; sometimes they are *too* lush. It's like having too much fat in the gravy.

The twelve-stringer tends to lose that intimate feeling that a six-stringer can have.

After all, for everything you gain in this world, you lose something. Gain experience and you lose innocence.

In sum: the twelve-stringer lacks the clarity and precision of the regular guitar, but gives a rich, powerful body of tone which exactly suits some music. And for those that like this kind of music, it's exactly the kind of music they like.

Records:
Leadbelly's records (see Chapter 2, pp. 37–40).
    (The first step in becoming acquainted with this instrument.)
Jesse Fuller's records.
12-String Guitar, Fred Gerlach, Folkways FC 3529.
    (The first young city performer who seriously undertook to master Leadbelly's style.)

Instruction records and book:

What underlies Leadbelly's unique sound is basically the same type of country blues ("finger-picking") technique used by such musicians as Brownie McGhee, Merle Travis, and Big Bill Broonzy. The following offer some help in figuring out exactly how Leadbelly did it.

The 12-String Guitar as Played by Leadbelly, by Pete Seeger (with booklet), Folkways FI 8371 (2 LPs) $11.58.

(Based on excerpts from Leadbelly's performances; the techniques I have used with such songs as "Bells of Rhymney" and "The Water Is Wide" are also included.)

Julius Lester and Pete Seeger, *The Folksinger's Guide to the 12-String Guitar as Played by Leadbelly* (Oak Publications, New York), $2.95; record and book, $11.79.

The Autoharp

. . . is a sort of mechanized zither, invented in the late nineteenth century.

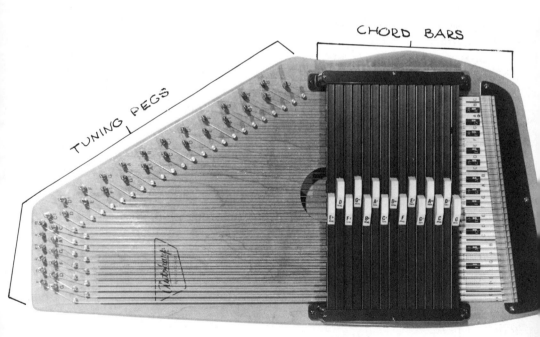

The strings run in a fairly complete chromatic scale from low F to high C, some three and a half octaves. Across them are thin wooden bars held up clear of the strings. Each bar has small felt pads on the bottom side, so arranged that when the bar is pressed down firmly, all the strings are damped out *except* those needed to sound a certain chord.

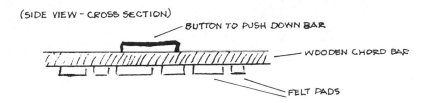

(SIDE VIEW - CROSS SECTION)

BUTTON TO PUSH DOWN BAR

WOODEN CHORD BAR

FELT PADS

Then one simply need scrape one's fingernail (or felt or plastic pick) over all 35 strings, and one hears a pure chord. The strings pressed by the felt pads do not ring out when the pick passes over them.

Each bar has felt pads arranged differently. The "Appalachian" autoharp introduced in the sixties provides fifteen possible chords (which make it more adaptable than older models for playing with guitar or other folk instruments):

A	G min	A⁷	D min	E⁷	A min	D⁷
E	D	B♭	C⁷	F	G⁷	C	G

For sixty years, the autoharp was used by music educators on a kindergarten level, and the standard way of playing it was to set it on a table and make graceful swoops across the strings to accompany singing—just an endless succession of arpeggios. It can get boring.

Then Mike Seeger, in his own wonderful brand of research, located the whereabouts of a number of musicians who made recordings of commercial country music back in the 1930s. Among the people he rediscovered were Ernest Stoneman and his musical family, still putting on weekend performances in Maryland. (Mike recorded a new LP of them in 1957.) In addition to the usual instruments such as fiddle, guitar, banjo, and mandolin, they also used the autoharp, but not in the kindergarten way; they played actual melodies on it, instead of just chords.

Subsequently Mike found that other southern musicians also played melodies on the instrument, including Maybelle Carter. Maybelle holds the autoharp up in her arms so she can move in and out of the microphone more easily when working with other musicians.

Mike learned these folk styles of autoharp playing and has spread the

techniques around the country. Here is the Carter manner of holding it.

You may not at first find it easy to hold it so, but it's a lot handier in the end than keeping it in your lap. More portable.

You put thumb picks and finger picks (plastic or metal) on the right hand, and play bass notes and melody, almost like a country guitar picker.

THUMB

FINGER

The thumb scrapes the general area of the lower strings, and then the area a little "north" of them. The result can either be alternating low and higher bass notes, or bass chords, depending on how extensive a scrape your thumb makes across the strings.

The finger pick (on either your index or middle finger) scrapes the general area where a melody note is located. As long as this melody note is not dampened out by the felt pads, it will be heard and the neighboring strings will not be.

Try to decipher the following two phrases from the old fiddle tune "Listen to the Mocking Bird":

(The letters refer to the correct chord bar to press down. The top staff contains the melody notes and other notes sounded by the finger pick. The lower staff contains bass notes and chords to be played by the thumb.)

If you try and play the above passage on an autoharp, don't be overly concerned with hitting the exact notes given for the thumb, but try and train your hand in the general strumming principles. When the thumb and finger play notes at the same time, as in the fourth-from-last measure, one's hand looks as though it were trying to pinch the strings. Other times, filling in after a melody note, as in the next-to-last measure, the thumb and forefinger simply alternate their strokes.

Some players like to put picks on three fingers and play a regular Merle Travis-guitar-style part, full of syncopated melody and countermelody notes. Mike Seeger feels the autoharp does not sound at its best when it gets too jazzy, though.

Note that in order to play the melody one has to change chords a lot more than would be usual on the guitar. See the third-from-last measure. Also, it is not always possible to get the best bass notes at the same time as the required melody notes. Some songs, especially pop songs that use a melody note purposely dissonant with the chord accompanying it (such as "September Song"), are impossible to play in this method.

On the other hand, ingenuity can conquer many obstacles. Mike Sherker, an art teacher in the Willow Run public-school system in Michigan, does Bach's "Jesu, Joy of Man's Desiring" superbly on the autoharp.

The old mechanical zither can graduate from the primary grades after all.

Some autoharp records:

The Stoneman Family, Folkways FA 2315

Mountain Music Played on the Autoharp (Neriah and Kenneth Benfield, Kilby and Jim Snow, Wade Ward, Mike Seeger), Folkways FA 2365

Several cuts of *The Anthology of American Folk Music,* Folkways FA 2951, 2952, 2953

Carter Family records

A book:

Once you grasp the basic idea and hear how this instrument sounds in mountain music, you'll probably find your own way. But if you want to study examples of varying difficulty, in music notation, this instruction manual provides them. Harry Taussig, *Folk Style Autoharp* (Oak Publications, New York), $2.95.

The Fiddle

. . . is one stringed instrument I've never been able to get more than a squeak out of. My mother is a good violin teacher, handing down the high art of European virtuosos. My younger brother Mike, however, taught himself quite a different style: old-time southern mountain fiddling. This calls for a steady left hand: no vibrato. And a powerful right arm which won't get tired through a long night of square dancing.

"Fiddler's green is two miles lower than Hell," according to the early churches of America. There were probably few things which were considered more sinful than the playing of a fiddle in early New England— unless it was dancing to the fiddle's tune.* (A young girl who had been

---

* A fascinating by-product of this outlook was the American play-party tradition, which, over the years, elaborated children's games as simple as "London Bridge" into an exciting teen-age form that included many typical square-dance figures. Play-parties were tolerated

seen attending a dance could be expelled from the church. "She danced herself right out of the church," the saying went.)

I became a Swedophile in the summer of '68, after hearing their own brand of folk fiddling. It's improvised, syncopated, and deeply moving. They use no accompaniment. In the old days two fiddlers would face each other and gaze at each other while trilling up and down the strings; one takes the melody, the other an alto part. Nowadays at the small-town fiddlers' gatherings in northern Sweden, one can hear groups of fiddlers ("Spelmanslage") playing together. It's like a choir of angels, or like starlings in a tree.

Ancient Swedish legends tell of fiddlers selling their souls to the devil. Churchmen inveighed against the instrument, banned it. More than any plucked instrument, I think fiddles seemed to be inspired by supernatural powers. Is it the physical act of stroking the string that seems so sinful? Is it the ability to mimic the voice? When the fiddle takes off and goes beyond this, to scream like a banshee in the swamp, then goodfolk worry for the safety of their daughters.

The country fiddler in the United States and Canada was generally a farmer or worker who played for occasional local square dances, but rarely made a living as a professional musician.

He inherited various North European traditions of country fiddling. In Quebec and Louisiana naturally the French idiom predominated. In isolated settlements perhaps Scandinavian or eastern European fiddling might be heard. But for the great majority of the population, it was Irish and Scottish fiddling.

Even today certain Irish tunes, such as "Devil's Dream," and "Miss McCleod's Reel," are among the favorite barn-dance melodies. But the way of playing them has often changed. They might be barely recognizable in Ireland.

In the American South a hard-driving, slurred and syncopated way of playing Irish fiddle tunes was worked out which during the last thirty years spread via radio and phonograph throughout the United States and

---

by the respectable because they used no "music" (i.e., instruments); they were accompanied only by the singing of the participants. "Skip to My Lou" belongs to this tradition. (Ben Botkin's classic 1937 collection, *The American Play-Party Song*, which gives a full account of the play-party's place in people's lives, was reprinted in 1963 by Frederick Ungar, New York, $7.50. A shorter introduction, if you are tempted to explore this lively and easily learned group activity, is *And Promenade All*, by Helen and Larry Eisenberg, 2403 Branch Street, Nashville, Tennessee, $1.00. Rev. Eisenberg also helped me and my eleven-year-old daughter some years ago to record a dozen of the songs, with dancing instructions, on Folkways FC 7604.)

Canada, almost obliterating local styles of playing. Recordings of Nashville fiddling sold well from Nova Scotia to Seattle.

The light and airy Irish style is not heard much nowadays. But there are still some regional variations. Jean Carignan, Montreal taxi driver, is master of the French-Canadian style. You can hear him on Folkways records.

If you'd like to learn the fiddle, and there is no fiddler near you, you can get records, movies, to help you. But sooner or later you will have to make a trip to visit some fiddlers and watch them closely, as in ancient days the Gypsies learned from each other. Keep the fiddle close and handy, stick with it, till it becomes a part of you. But one could say this of any folk instrument.

Fiddle records (a minute sample of those available):
Galax, Virginia: Old Fiddlers' Convention, Folkways FA 2435
The Legend of Clark Kessinger (of West Virginia), Folkways 5336
    (In his seventies, he is still one of the best.)
Old Time Fiddle Tunes, played by Jean Carignan (French-Canadian), Folkways FG
    3531

Fiddlers are included on:
Anglo-American Shanties, Lyric Songs, Dance Tunes, and Spirituals, Library of
    Congress AAFS L 2
Play and Dance Songs and Tunes, AAFS L 9
Anthology of American Folk Music, Vol. 2, Social Music, Folkways FA 2952

An instruction record:
Learn to Fiddle Country Style, by Tracy Schwartz, Folkways 8359
    (Tracy's own fiddling may be heard on recordings of the New Lost City Ramblers.)

A book:
Marion Thede, *The Fiddle Book* (Oak Publications, New York), $7.95
    (Embodies a lifetime of research by a member of an Oklahoma fiddling family;
    100-odd tunes transcribed from country fiddlers of Oklahoma and nearby states,
    with information on tuning and bowing.)

A film:
The Country Fiddle, filmed by Pete and Toshi Seeger, distributed by Audio-Brandon
    Film Center, Inc., 34 MacQuesten Pkwy. So., Mount Vernon, N.Y. 10550
    (The sound track of this film is included in Folkways' LP FS 3851.)

The Washboard Band

STYLES IN COUNTRY-DANCE MUSIC change from generation to generation. In Thomas Jefferson's day most dancers were accompanied by a solo fiddle. Later on in the nineteenth century banjos and guitars were added.

Just as there are many varieties of popular dance instrumentations using wind instruments, there are many regional varieties of country-dance orchestras. In the North the tendency is to the use of pianos; in the South, electrified string instruments, particularly the (electrified) Hawaiian guitar. Louisiana has a distinguishing feature in its country-dance music—the old-fashioned "windjammer" accordion, the kind that you push in to get one note and pull out to get another. In the Southwest, among Spanish-speaking people, whole orchestras are composed of nothing but guitars. One guitar will carry the melody, another guitar takes just the bass obbligatos, and a third guitar will only play the chords. In the north central states, such as Minnesota, you can hear the Scandinavian technique of several fiddlers playing at once.

Africans in America carried on the tradition that the "rhythm is the thing." "Plantation parties" often used nothing but clapping and the rattling of "bones" to accompany dancing. Today, in the streets of New York City you can hear teen-age rhythm bands composed of a bongo drum (taking the solo) and a Coke bottle and a wastebasket (taking the accompaniment).*

Who invented the first washboard rhythm band? We don't know. Probably in the nineteenth century some ingenious man or woman tried accompanying a dance with the rattling of tin pans and found that the rippling sound of thimbles on a washboard worked well with it.

In the 1920s a number of country-style commercial recordings were made of washboard bands using kazoos or harmonicas to take the melody. In this half of the twentieth century they can still be found in many corners of the country, but especially in the South. Various instruments will take the melody—fiddle, harmonica, guitar, mandolin—but note that the washboard, carrying the rhythm, still remains the central instrument.

---

* Tony Schwartz has recorded such groups on Folkways FC 7003 and FD 5558.

A well-equipped washboard is shown in this picture. Nailed to an ordinary tin washboard with wooden frame might be a tin pie plate or a cheap tin frying pan and a few tin cups or even a brass cowbell.

It is amazing how the "clickety, tick, pling, clunk, punk, clonk" can cut through all the noises of a crowded dance floor.

Unfortunately, at the present time there is no music school in the nation that gives instruction in washboard playing. All we can do is highly recommend the technique for anyone wishing to accompany square dances.

To assemble one, go to the local hardware store and buy an old-fashioned washboard. (If they don't have one, try an antique store.) Attach a few tin plates and cups of the right tone and pitch. Get a set of thimbles (metal, not the plastic kind). Be sure to buy some extra ones, since a night of hard playing will dent them considerably.

Every state in the union has people in it who can play the washboard and could give instruction. Conscientious searching would locate them. Advertise in the newspaper.

One nice thing about the homemade character of the washboard as an instrument is that it encourages other homemade instruments: the jug which will give off a bass throb when "beeped" into; tissue paper on a comb; penny whistles, and tablespoons rattled on the knee. And don't forget the washtub bass:

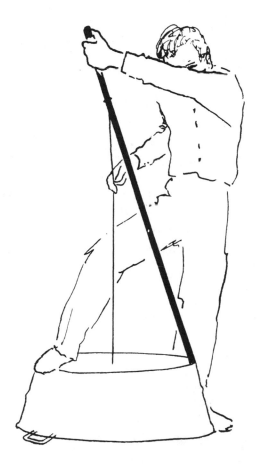

Vivat floreatque sympsalma trabe lavatorum rusticorum compacta!*

Records:
Washboard Country Band Dance Tunes, Folkways FA 2201
Sonny Terry's Washboard Band, Folkways FA 2006

---

* Long live the country washboard band! (Latin by courtesy of Moses Hadas.)

The Recorder*

IF YOU SEE someone blowing on what looks like a musical chair leg (the player will have a faraway, intent look in his eyes) you may become curious about the instrument he is playing. It's a recorder. Tom Jefferson played one; it was known as a flute in those days.

The instrument had its heyday during Shakespeare's time (you may have read of it in *Hamlet*), but in the nineteenth century it died out under the competition of the louder brasses and woodwinds. Revived some fifty or sixty years ago in England by the harpsichord specialist, Dolmetsch, it quickly spread throughout Europe, especially among youth groups. During the thirties, American students returning from the Continent brought recorders back with them, and today many schools teach it to children before they are ready for the more difficult orchestral instruments.

A good alto recorder will cost between $10 and $40. You can get a soprano recorder cheaper, but it's more shrill; tenors and basses are fun for quartet work but are more expensive.

Bach, Mozart and the baroque gang wrote extensively for the instrument. Dozens of small collections of folk songs, madrigals, and short classical selections have been published. If you want to buy some records which will give you an idea of how really beautiful the recorder can sound when played well, you might start with some of the albums of the Trapp Family choir. They played seven or eight at a time, and sang folk songs of Central Europe (not, in real life, Rodgers-Hammerstein tunes).

However, if you are an ear musician, like most folk artists, and nevertheless want to toot away on your tootin' cane, we suggest you pick out some of Burl Ives's melodies or those of John Jacob Niles. The old shape-note hymns sound well on the instrument, as do many Christmas carols.

If you are a boy you may find it advantageous to locate a pretty girl who sings a pretty tune, and start playing the alto part for her. Or let

---

* Written for the *People's Songs Bulletin,* September 1948.

your imagination and your instrument soar above her voice and play what's known as a "descant."

My daughters and I have found endless hours of fun playing what we call "nothing." Two players simply start playing improvised notes and let the dissonances fall where they may. As long as we play in the same key and keep the rhythm, it sounds remarkably harmonious. First one player, then another can lead, if they want to change key or rhythm. When you get good at it, add a third player, or a fourth.

Records:
The Trapp Family—half a dozen records issued by Decca (Schwann lists them under "Collections: Choral")
Some of my experiments in recorder improvisation may be heard on:
Nonesuch and Other Tunes (Pete Seeger and Frank Hamilton), Folkways FA 2439
Sound Track Music from Indian Summer, etc., Folkways FS 3851
Other kinds of flute playing are also of interest, such as Tommy Makem's tin whistle on the Clancy Brothers' records, or Ed Young's cane flute on *Roots of the Blues*, Atlantic 1398.

Books:
A fingering chart is usually supplied along with the recorder when you buy it. I suggest that you rely on this and your ear and bypass the books, at least temporarily. Strike out boldly on your own; find out how much you can do with only a few notes; add more as you need them.
Hargail, Oak, and most other music publishers issue recorder instruction manuals, many of which teach music reading along with the instrument.

The Chalil*

OF THE MANY TYPES of flutes and whistles played by the Family of Man, the chalil is one of the easiest to make. Less than an hour's work on a small piece of bamboo can often produce a satisfactory chalil.

---

* "Chalil" means "hollow" in Hebrew. Pronounce the *ch* as in Bach: "Kha*leel*."

It is not, however, the easiest to play. It has no slot built into it, as does the recorder, the flageolet, or penny whistle. It is simply a tube, open at both ends. Slowly one must train one's lip to direct a thin stream of air at one edge of one end. At first you get no musical tone at all. At the end of a day of frustrating attempts you may be able to get a few breathy notes. Only over the months will the quality of tone improve.

This very fact makes the chalil, in the end, more rewarding to play than a simple whistle. The tone can be flexible, warmer, softer, more human, faint or loud, as you require, even on the high notes. The chalil tends to have a more variable pitch than the recorder, and thus is less adaptable to playing in groups. But alone, or with a drum, it is almost unique in its effect.

Variations on this instrument are known throughout the Near East, Africa, and eastern Europe. Every language has a different name for it. Ilka Raveh of Israel, who taught me how to make chalils, learned the instrument from Arabs when he was a boy. The Arab version (called the nai) tends to be longer and more slender. The Arab tone usually tends to be somewhat higher in pitch.

Ilka gets a very pure soft tone out of it. An Arab friend of his was listening to him once and said, "That isn't music, that's talking to God."

Certain types of pastoral folk melodies, which sound well unaccompanied, are ideal for the chalil. Some other kinds of folk tunes, such as the blues, seem to fit it hardly at all. (But I may be wrong.)

When you can play some of your favorite melodies, you should learn to improvise upon them, and then to decorate them, as flutes can so well do. Sticking to the exact notes as sung by the voice would be a great waste of the capabilities of this instrument.

You will find your chalil able to say things which perhaps you have been unable to say any other way.

Records:
Shepherd and Other Folk Songs of Israel, sung by Hillel and Aviva, with pipe and
    drums, Folkways FW 6841
Songs from the Bible, Hillel and Aviva, Folkways FW 6842
    (The chalil at its best, played by Ilka Raveh—whose name was formerly
    Hillel Rabinadov.)

Book:
Peter Seeger, *How to Make a Chalil,* Sing Out, 33 W. 60 St., New York, N.Y.
    10012, $1.00
    (And how to play it)

Steel Drums and Steel Bands

THE SIXTY-FIVE-MILE-LONG ISLAND of Trinidad is the birth-place of one of the world's most unusual folk instruments, the steel drum. The drum is made by cutting off the end of a 55-gallon oil drum and working the disc until different sections of it emit distinct musical pitches when tapped with a rubber-tipped drumstick.

A steel band in Trinidad

No hi-fi system can duplicate the exciting tone of a live steel band. No other instrument known to this writer can make itself heard so clearly above the hubbub of a noisy crowd. The noisier the street, the more sweetly it sounds.

Steel drums were invented around World War II* because the Trinidad police put a ban on the traditional bamboo "stick bands," the "bam-

---

* See p. 164, Chapter 4.

boo tamboo," whose rhythm had been one of the joys of the year's great festival, a 42-hour spree known as Carnival.

During the 1950s Yankee tourists brought back home reports of a new musical instrument they had heard in the West Indies. A steel drum trio accompanied the dancer Geoffrey Holder briefly in the Broadway show "House of Flowers" in 1954. But the man who got most publicity for steel bands in the late fifties was Admiral Daniel V. Gallery, in charge of the Puerto Rican Naval Base. He fell in love with the music, and sent his whole Navy band to Trinidad for a week, with orders to buy a set of drums and come back knowing how to play them. Orders were orders, and they were well-trained musicians. Admiral Dan's Pandemoniacs soon became the hit of the island of Puerto Rico, and traveled to New York and Chicago to make television appearances.

A steel band has at least three instruments, and preferably eight or ten—or many more. The steel drums range from the soprano "ping pong" with a 25-note chromatic scale, second pan and cello pans, to the bass pans which give only five deep notes apiece and are used in groups of four.

There are other, odd sizes. And several nonmelodic instruments may add their counterrhythms to the total effect: maracas, called "shak-shak" in Trinidad, tapped with a finger or shaken up and down; a cowbell tapped with a stick; an automobile brake drum, sometimes called a "cutter," tapped with a long bolt; a "guiro," a foot-long gourd with parallel

grooves cut along one side and scratched with wires made from a coat hanger; claves; bongo and conga drums.

In the 1960s steel bands were formed in a number of New York settlement houses. But they have not swept the country as I was sure they would when, in 1956, I first learned to make and play the drums. Making them is a hard and exacting—and very noisy—job. Apparently it doesn't fit into the North American way of life as easily as into the Trinidadian. I hope that sooner or later a practicable method for mass-producing them may be developed.

I still feel the steel drum has great possibilities for us. I feel this way partly, of course, because I love the sound of the music. But there are other reasons.

Steel pans are inexpensive to make and hard to break. They are ideal for groups of amateurs who do not know how to read music. Everyone can participate on his or her own level.

It's the only instrument I know of that can be played outdoors in all kinds of weather, including rain or snow, heat or cold.

You can dance while playing it, or skate!

Nowadays all too often a parade is a cut-and-dried affair, a duty more than a pleasure, highly organized and humorless, with all floats created by a professional display firm. Steel bands could help American parades to once again take on the informality and enthusiasm that they had of old.

There is a kind of raucous democracy about a good street celebration like Carnival. People who, throughout the rest of the year, stay more or less politely out of each other's way, behind closed doors, find themselves in the streets rubbing shoulders and bottoms. Rich and poor, black and white, Catholic, Protestant, Jew and atheist find themselves irresistibly drawn by the rhythm out of their houses and into the street and enjoying themselves there together as fellow human beings on God's great green earth.

Records of steel drum music:

Steel bands are extremely difficult to record. They never sound as impressive over the loudspeaker as they do in the pulsating flesh. Some of the best records have been made by:

Cook Laboratories, 101 Second Street, Stamford, Conn.

OTHER LABELS:

Folkways: *Kim Loy Wong and His Wiltwyck Steel Band,* FS 3834

Monogram

Decca

Elektra

Instruction book and record:

Peter Seeger, *The Steel Drums of Kim Loy Wong* (Oak Publications, New York, 1961), $2.95; Folkways 8367, $5.79; record and book, $7.79

(How to make and play steel drums; suggestions of music to play.)

Film:

Music from Oil Drums, produced by Peter and Toshi Seeger, distributed by Audio-Brandon Film Center, Inc., 34 MacQuesten Pkwy. So., Mount Vernon, N.Y. 10550

(The Trinidad setting of steel band music, and detailed demonstration of making and playing the drums.)

Postscript:

SOME MAIN FOLK INSTRUMENTS got left out of this chapter because I don't know a darn thing about playing 'em.

For mandolin, listen to Bill Monroe recordings.

For harmonica ("French harp") listen to Sonny Terry's records (Folkways and Stinson), and see Tony Glover, *Blues Mouth Harp* (Oak Publications, New York), $2.95; with record $7.79.

For tambourines, visit your local gospel church.
For the instrument known as "Jew's harp" (formerly "jaw harp")—find
    someone who can play it and haunt him.
And the same goes for many and many another instrument.

There are still discoveries to be made. In your travels (or in your own family or neighborhood) you may come across a different instrument, or an instrument used in a different way, from anything you've heard before. And this might turn out to be the one kind of music that satisfies and inspires *you* more than any other. At the 1970 Berkeley Folk Festival I met a tall blond student who spent three years working in a leprosarium in East Africa. He learned how to make "thumb pianos" and now could play the instrument expertly, as though he'd been born to it.

8·Making New Songs

Ever wonder who makes up all the folk songs? Ordinary folks like you and me.

They didn't make up a song all together. They'd take over an old tune and change it. Some cowboy sang a sailor song called "Bury Me Not in the Deep Blue Sea." Of course, by the time he got through with it, it was called "Bury Me Not on the Lone Prairie."

You've probably done the same thing. You remember the old singing commercial:

> Pepsi Cola hits the spot,
> Twelve full ounces . . .

I was singing that to some kids in school, explaining that it came from an old English folk song,

> Do you ken John Peel at the break of day,
> Do you ken John Peel with his coat so gay,
> Do you ken John Peel when he's far, far away
> With his hounds and his horns in the morning?

"Oh," the kids said, "you're not singing it right. This is the way we sing it:

> Pepsi Cola hits the spot,
> Ties your belly in a knot,
> Tastes like vinegar, looks like ink;
> Pepsi Cola is a stinky drink.

You make them up all the time. Silly things that go on around you. If the song is good enough, someone will pick it up from you, and he'll hand it on to someone else, and maybe they'll change verses a little bit, change the tune a little bit. Hundreds of different people might have a hand in putting it together.

—Folk Songs for Young People, 1953
(Folkways FC 7532)

FOOTNOTE: *In 1968 a ten-year-old girl sang to my brother Mike the following, to the tune of "Frère Jacques": "May-ro-wa-na, may-ro-wa-na, Ell-ess-dee, ell-ess-dee. College kids are making it, high school kids are taking it. Why can't we? Why can't we?"*

Well, little girl, you see it's this way. . . . Back in 1920 they adopted Prohibition, and . . .

Folk Songs by You?

EVERY FOLK SINGER should consider himself or herself a song-writer on the side. If you love folk songs, consider how they have been changed and improved through the generations by singers who added their own home-grown genius.

For great songs to be written we must have an outpouring of topical song. What does it matter that most will be sung once and forgotten? The youthful Joe Hills, Tagores, Burnses and Shakespeares and Guthries can only thus get their training.

Time will sift the good from the bad. And perhaps centuries from now, when we are all crumbled to dust, some child in a world which has long since proceeded to tackle other problems besides how to ban the Bomb will be singing a verse which you tossed off in a moment of inspiration.

Many articles and books have been written on the subject "How to Write a Song." They tell the aspiring amateur to be simple, be clever, have a gimmick, be this and that—and I doubt have produced many new songwriters. Yet here we go again with another attempt.

A really outstanding song is rare. But it's easier than you think to write a "usable" song.

Your song must paint a picture or tell a story, to make your ideas come to life. Learn to make a rhyme, learn to create images, develop them, and hold your listeners in suspense. A rhymed editorial is worse than useless. It is not art. Phooey. Stinko. Underline this: *An editorial in rhyme does not make a song.*

Since it is harder to make a complete song than a fragment of one, first practice by writing verses to tunes you know, or writing new tunes for verses you hear. Try them out on your friends. If it isn't good enough for you to repeat to your friends, it probably isn't good enough to print, so try again. After a couple dozen successful but random verses you may be able to carry through a conception and create a complete song. Don't be afraid to make it specific. A song which hits home, goes right to the point, is worth more at that instant than any other song in your repertoire, and is worth, for that instant alone, the time it took to compose it, even though perhaps a week later it will be out of date and useless.

One California woman, Malvina Reynolds, is responsible for at least a dozen of my favorite songs* of the last two decades. Her creations have been eagerly listened to and sung (and modified) by thousands—some of them by millions—of people who found that she put into words and music exactly what they had been wanting to say.

When I meet a potentially good songwriter who is about to give up writing because his or her efforts meet with so little visible response, I tell them Malvina's story.

At age forty-five, with a Ph.D. in English Lit., but never having held a job as a teacher (blacklisted), but still full of ambition, she meets some guitar pickers and singers. "This is the kind of stuff I'd like to do," says she to herself.

The first thing she finds is, it's not so easy to write a simple song. Since others were not singing her songs enough, she bought a guitar and learned how to plunk on it in a rudimentary way. Many laughed at her amateurish efforts, but she would not give up. After several years, she had one or two mild successes.

She found herself handicapped by not knowing how to write down her tunes, so she went to school to learn music notation.

---

* Including "Little Boxes," "What Have They Done to the Rain?," "God Bless the Grass," "Where Are You Going, My Little One?" (Her Oak Publications songbooks are *Little Boxes and Other Handmade Songs* and *The Muse of Parker Street;* she sings her own songs on Folkways 2524 and *Malvina Reynolds Sings the Truth,* Columbia CL 2614.)

She tries writing every conceivable kind of a song: mad, glad, sad. Happy sappy, serious, curious. Loud-soft. She gets a home copying machine and sends copies to every singer she knows and to folk song publications here and abroad. With a scratchy voice she keeps on performing.

At age sixty-nine she is a good craftsman as a songwriter. She knows what she can do best and what she can't. She knows what a song can do and what it can't. She formed her own publishing company so as not to have to give 50 percent of royalties to someone else, and she makes a small steady income from it all.

But some of her best songs are made up for just one or two people. She spent a weekend with a family in Rhode Island and wrote a song for them describing the household. It was a great song—I wanted to sing it myself, but she said no, it was private and had best remain so.

Malvina is really one of my heroines. She refuses to give up on the human race. One of her best poems was sent out as a New Year's greeting a couple of years ago:

If this world survives—
And every other day I think it might—
In good part it will be
Because of the great souls in our Community.
There are a lot of them. I've seen them walk
In lonely thousands down a city's streets,
Or stand in vigils in the rain,
Or turn the handle of a print machine,
Or empty their purses as the box came by,
Or face into the camera's eye,
And answer the question:
Will the world survive?
And they have said,
We'll try,
We'll try.

Make it a practice to write one new song or verse a week, no matter how few ever hear it. Increase your knowledge of language, rhythm, and melody. Not only this; a deep and instinctive feeling for the hearts and minds of the people you sing to must develop in you. You must express for them what is in their hearts by expressing what is in your own. In this way you both lead and serve the people.

Of course it isn't easy. Whoever said it was?

The Song for Improvised Verses

IT MAY BE DIFFICULT to compose a song, but it is not difficult to compose a verse. "Hey Li Lee Li Lee Lo"* has become a vehicle for improvised stanzas. Originally a dance tune from the Bahamas with but one verse and a catchy chorus, it went thus:

HEY LI LEE LI LEE LO

Words and music by Alan Lomax and Elizabeth Austin. TRO-©
copyright 1941 (renewed 1969) and 1959, Ludlow Music, Inc.,
New York, New York. Used by permission.

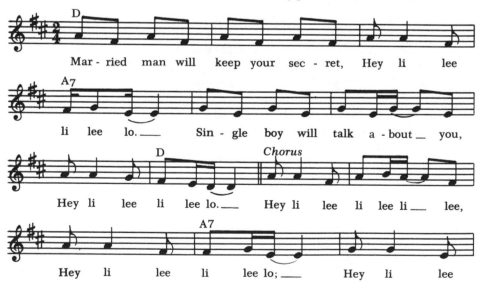

_____

* Thought by some to be spelled "Hay Lolly Lolly Low."

li   lee li ___   lee,   Hey   li   lee   li   lee lo. ___

Nowadays the balladeer is likely to start off by teaching everybody the chorus. Then he will sing:

> Lots of verses to this song—
>   Hey li lee li lee lo—
> Got to make 'em up as you go along—
>   Hey li lee li lee lo.

The audience joins in on the refrains and choruses and the session is off to a flying start. It may last from three to thirty minutes, depending on how the muse takes hold. The balladeer may need to take the first few verses if rhymesters in front of him are hesitant.

> Are there any poets in the house?
> I mean someone who can rhyme "house" with "mouse."

The melody adapts itself to many syllables being squeezed in, à la Calypso. Or as few as four or five syllables may artfully span the two musical measures. This type of song practically demands that the melody also change as needed. Further, the rhymes may fall on the last *two* syllables, depending on the accent. Compare this rhyme with the previous two:

> Sing it sweet or sing it raucous,
> But for God's sake, don't hold a caucus!

Let not the literati scorn your rhyming. Rhymes have been not just an embellishment but an integral part of some of the world's greatest poetry. According to Shaemas O'Sheel, meter may have been invented by the Greeks, but the Irish invented rhyme. Anyone want to argue?

Further, do not forget alliteration ("Five miles meandering with a mazy motion . . ."). Alliteration and "consonance" are more fundamental adjuncts of poetry than rhyme through much of Africa and Asia. The original folk verse had it:

> Married man will keep your secret,
> Single boy will talk about you.

Up to now we have discussed mostly form, not content. You may want to start with simple personal satires about people in the room, and graduate to more general themes.

> Or you may start off with generalities,
> And degenerate into personalities.

A whole series of verses will often develop around a certain subject: peace, love, jobs, civil rights, and so on. Verses may be taken whole cloth from other sources:

> Listen, folks, here is my thesis,
> Peace in the world or the world in pieces.

Best of all, arguments may develop in rhyme, giving a dramatic build to the whole session.

When the audience shows that it is tiring of singing and harmonizing the refrain and chorus, when the verses start dwindling, or the poets narrow down to one or two, then is the time for the balladeer to call a halt. "Always leave them wanting more" is good show business.

> Lots more verses to this song,
> But I guess we better be moving along.

Woody as a Folk Composer

WHY IS "So Long, It's Been Good to Know You," by Woody Guthrie, likely to last for centuries? Because it combines in a few short lines many, many good points:

1. A well-told, straightforward story about real events, symbolic for us all.
2. A good traditional melody for the verses.
3. A humdinger of a chorus, composed by Woody.
4. Humor and satire, aimed as usual at weakness and ignorance, and hypocrisy.
5. Hints of love and sentiment, and universal tragedy of all people.

Woody always claimed that he could not theorize, that he couldn't keep up with us and our book learning. He'd bow out of an argument rather than get tangled up in four-syllable words. But he had a number of sound theories about songwriting. I only wish we had been able to learn them better.

For one thing, he had outspoken contempt for mere cleverness. A joke was fine, a pun, a gag—he put plenty of humor into his songs. But humor was not enough by itself. There had to be some solid meat there. So in some of his most humorous songs, like "Talking Dustbowl," there's an undertone of bitter reality. In this respect Woody's songs are like the poems of Robert Burns.

Since he frankly agreed that he couldn't tell which of his songs would be good and which would be soon forgotten, he adopted a kind of scatteration technique—that is, he'd write a lot of songs, on the theory that at least some of them would be good. For example, as a "research consultant" for the Bonneville Power Administration he wrote several dozen songs. Nearly all of them have some special charm. One of them, "Roll On, Columbia," seems destined to last for generations.

Each "unsuccessful" song was not a waste of time. He could learn from it. Woody understood the old axiom: "There is no such thing as an unsuccessful experiment." (Reason: you get either a positive or a negative result. In either case you learn.) Hence, out of the many attempts he made, he learned enough to write good songs.

His method of composition was to pound out verse after verse on the typewriter, or in his precise, country-style handwriting, and try it out on his guitar as he went along. Later the song could be pruned down to usable size.

He put his rhymes to tunes which were, more often than not, amended versions of older folk melodies. Woody showed us all that folk music was not simply a group of old songs, no matter how nice, but rather was a process—which had been going on for centuries—in which ordinary people not only handed down traditional music but continually reshaped it to fit new situations.

Sometimes his new words would have nothing to do with the original words, sometimes they were just slightly changed. He took "Red Wing" and instead of singing, "There once was an Indian Maid," he had,

> There once was a union maid,*
> She never was afraid—

Sometimes I don't think he realized where he got the melody. When he was out making up songs for the Bonneville Power Administration in 1940–41, he sang:

Words by Woody Guthrie, music based on "Goodnight Irene" by Huddie Ledbetter and John Lomax. TRO-© copyright 1936 (renewed 1964) and 1963, Ludlow Music, Inc., New York, New York. Used by permission.

And he was surprised when I said, "Isn't that the tune of 'Goodnight Irene'? He said, "Why, sure 'nough!"

Of course, it wasn't *exactly* the same tune after Woody had shaped it to his new song.

Sometimes he would take a song he liked but wanted to add to. That was the case with a blues sung by Blind Lemon Jefferson. Blind Lemon used to sing—and he sang real high—

I'm broke and I ain't got a dime.
I'm broke and I ain't got a dime.
I'm broke and I ain't got a dime;
Well, everybody gets a little hard luck some time.*

When Blind Lemon used to sing it, it sounded like he was crying, very high up. With beautiful guitar work, of course. There was another verse:

Do you want your son to be bad like Jesse James?   (3 *times*)
Well, give him a six-shooter, let him highway some passenger train.

Woody liked the song, but he couldn't sing it in the same style. He was a different person. He had his own style. And, little by little, he changed that melody:

Words and music by Woody Guthrie. TRO-© copyright 1961, 1963, Ludlow Music, Inc., New York, New York. Used by permission.

I'm broke and I did not have a dime,
I'm broke and I did not have a dime,
I'm broke and I did not have a dime.
Singing hey, hey, hey, hey.

---

* "One Dime Blues."

In the next verse, you would get the line he missed:

> Well, every good man gets a little hard luck some time.
> Well, every good man gets a little hard luck some time.
> Well, every good man gets a little hard luck some time . . .
>   Hey, hey, hey, hey.

Woody made up a new verse for the song, which became the first verse, and gave a new title to the song:

> Standing down in New York town one day,
> Standing down in New York town one day,
> Standing down in New York town one day,
>   Singing hey, hey, hey, hey.*

Sometimes, as in "So Long" and "Reuben James," Woody created a complete chorus for a melody which originally had none; and the chorus became the high point of the whole song.

We can all learn from Woody's way of using words, and his subtle shaping of melodies. But perhaps the most impressive thing about his songs, and the hardest to learn, is their simplicity—the simplicity of genius. This, above all, is why the best of them live in people's memories while dozens of ingenious novelties come and go, and are forgotten.

Composing by Ear

UNTIL FAIRLY RECENTLY, most musicians trained in the European "fine art" tradition took it for granted that no music of real value (with the possible exception of unharmonized song tunes) could be created without notation. This view has been well refuted not only by jazz, but by hundreds of LPs bringing us, for example, the ancient, sophisticated styles of India; the gamelans of Java and Bali; the choral

---

* "New York Town."

and instrumental ensembles of Africa, Latin America, the Balkans (not to mention American country bands); as well as beautiful solo improvisations on everything from Arabic reeds to American banjos.

In 1959 Frank Hamilton and I, using banjo, guitar, harmonica and whistles, experimented with a series of instrumental pieces* influenced by folk traditions of the American South, popular music of the airways, ethnic recordings from several continents, and music of the symphony and concert hall. Later, in producing sound tracks for two films,† I worked out a more deliberate method of composing for several instruments at once, with the help of tape-recording.

I looked at the film dozens of times, with my banjo in hand and humming and whistling to myself. Then, watching one short section at a time, I improvised, rehearsed and recorded one instrumental part. As I worked out each additional part I listened through earphones to what was already recorded. The finished "score" of Lines, Vertical and Horizontal uses a chalil, two tenor recorders, a banjo, two guitars, a mandolin, drum, maracas, autoharp, and sound effects; as many as six instruments are heard at one time.

In this project I had the help of the Canadian National Film Board's expert engineers, with professional equipment. But elaborate technical facilities are not indispensable; the multi-dub score for the movie Many Colored Papers was produced with two ordinary home tape recorders.

Folk performers have always enriched and renewed their inherited music with their own vocal and instrumental inventiveness. Indeed, improvising, alone and especially with other musicians, is the only way to really master a folk technique. Today it is quite usual for young composer-performers (many of them largely self-taught by immersion in black and white American folk styles) to create their "sound," as the Weavers did, by the age-old method of improvising, listening, and improvising again.

With performers of genius from every part of the world available on his turntable, the contemporary ear musician is limited only by his own taste and good judgment. Current pop artists seem to draw on virtually everything that has been recorded as they develop their individual styles. Those who learn to be selective as well as eclectic are creating some wonderful music.

---

* Nonesuch, Folkways FA 2439.
† Lines, Vertical and Horizontal, distributed by Contemporary Films; Many Colored Papers, distributed by Audio-Brandon Film Center, Inc. Both sound tracks are reproduced on Folkways FS 3851.

9·Style, Standards and Responsibility

AMERICAN HERITAGE AND CONTEMPORARY SINGERS

The American cultural scene is littered with the corpses of talented cowards. . . .
It's not enough just to know the song. You've got to get the feel of the people behind the song. . . .

I never felt so much like kicking in the front of a TV set as one Saturday evening in the spring of 1963 when I heard a duo named Allan & Grier do a satirical song on the ABC "Hootenanny" show. I don't know the two personally and I've got nothing against them except the song. For all I know, they pay their bills promptly and honor thy father and mother. And I've got nothing against satire—but with all the things in the world that can be satirized, they decided they were going to do a take off on a Negro work song. In effect, what their song said was that Leadbelly was just a silly old man, and anybody who would give the song "Take This Hammer" more than a snicker was just plain naïve.

Tradition, Arrangements, and Personal Style

BÉLA BARTÓK, the modern Hungarian composer, said that a folk song might be on as high a plane of art as a symphony, only its range of expression was more limited, since it was a much shorter form.

In other words, a bagpipe or flageolet with seven simple holes nevertheless could use as much subtlety and complexity in a piece as a silver flute with its multitude of keys. (Some of the greatest melodies restrict themselves to a five-note scale.) And a six-stringed guitar, with its fine gradations of tone control, might play a melody with greater artistry than an organ with its multitude of stops.

Some songs sit in a book for years unused, until a talented arranger figures out a way to do them which brings them to life. But the very best arrangements are often the most inconspicuous. The greatest success is when the song itself overwhelms you, and you don't even think about the arrangement.

In a letter to *Sing Out,* Buzz Bodwell of Illinois wrote that he was bored by the "repetitive, dull three-chord" harmonies of most American folk banjo and guitar playing.

I think I know what you mean, Buzz. But before you jump to the conclusion that the alternative is a lot of snazzy augmented ninths and agitated double dominants, you should consider some of the classical music of India, as played on the sitar and sarod. It is perhaps the most highly sophisticated, complex, and sensitive music in all the world. And how many chords does it use? Not a one. Just the melody, and a drone bass (like a bagpipe), accompanied with a drum. The dulcimer player and the Scots bagpiper also restrict themselves to getting along without harmony.

When Woody Guthrie sang "Buffalo Skinners" he played one minor chord from first to last. And after twenty-five years I think I have finally learned to play "Old Joe Clark" halfway to my own satisfaction. One of the changes I made last year was to cut out the one chord change I used to have in it. It's now in solid G throughout.

(The American composer MacDowell wrote a popular piano piece based on an Indian theme. Some years later, he again met the Indian who had once played him the original melody on a cedar flute. MacDowell sat down and played the composition based on the melody. The Indian listened impassively. Afterward he said slowly, "You've ruined my song," and walked out, deeply hurt.)

So don't pretty up your harmony too much. It will distract from the words, and the melody too. It can destroy the music.

Of course, it all depends on the particular idiom the song is in. Some songs sound best sung by one person. Some sound best with no accompaniment whatsoever. But others, especially the spirituals and gospel songs, just beg for harmony.

Some, like the calypso "Money Is King"* by the Tiger, of Trinidad, can tolerate fancy harmony. Others, like "I Never Will Marry" or most of Woody Guthrie's songs, could be ruined.

Remember the aim of civilized man: to bring order and harmony—to simplify life. Any fool can get complicated. We are born in simplicity but die of complications.

> *You can run this simplicity bit into the ground, too, like anything else. There is a story about a cello player who was practicing in a large apartment house full of other music students. In neighboring apartments and floors above and below, one could hear singers, violinists, and flute players, all practicing their scales and arpeggios, going up and down. But this cello player just sat in his room sawing away on one note: A flat.*
>
> *When spring came and windows were opened, his fellow musicians couldn't help but notice it more and more. Day after day they heard him, still sawing away at A flat. Finally, they called a meeting and designated one of their fellow students to visit the cellist and find out what was the matter. The delegate knocked on the door; the cellist politely invited him in.*
>
> *They chatted a few minutes about the weather. The cellist seemed normal and sane.*
>
> *Then, the delegate asked him, "My friend, all of us are wondering why you continue to play, day after day, just one note, A flat."*
>
> *The cellist looked wise. "I suppose it does seem peculiar," he said at last. "But all the rest of you musicians are running up and down trying to find the right note. I've found it."*

Painting, as an art, would be similar to music, if one could imagine that it was impossible to make a permanent painting—all colors would fade in a few days. Thus a class of craftsmen would develop whose function in life would be to paint reproductions of great paintings of the past. Some schools of painting would believe in a close reproduction; others would encourage more improvising upon the old designs. They would place originality as their main aim.

In every art form known (writing, visual art, music) one can see two apparently opposing trends. One is a respect for tradition and the achievements of the past, and the other is an attempt to change these traditions

---

* See *The Bells of Rhymney*, p. 80.

in accordance with the needs of the artist and his times.

It would also appear that following either of these two trends too faithfully can be disastrous; either an artist can become sterile and imitative, or he can become so meaninglessly experimental that the audience is left behind.

The field of folk music is admirably suited to preserving a balance between the two. It would seem at first glance that maintaining a fine tradition is most important. But since folk music is a process that depends for its life upon the oral tradition, music is continually changed by folk performers, whether they intend it or not. Basic tradition is continually remolded to fit a new situation.

> "The cultural landscape is littered with magnificent fossils," wrote Bernard Shaw. I suppose he was thinking of Greek temples and Gothic cathedrals. But one could also list plays, novels, murals, and folk songs. The best of them have proved themselves triumphs of art, outlasting the ideology for which they were created.

The good folk musician is a creator as well as a re-creator, and when he creates he improvises within the idiom. Otherwise he could be like the scholar who sprinkles his work with phrases in a foreign language—he knows what he means, but nobody else does. There is always the need for experimentation, but don't expect people to want to listen to it.

Picasso has been the great experimenter in modern art. But in each of his forays he stuck around long enough to plumb some depths. Too many of his imitators were merely artistic Casanovas, thrusting here and there, but always infertile.

Anyway, experimentation is not the end goal and purpose of art. A teen-age girl came home from school with a gayly smeared canvas. "What on earth is that supposed to be?" asked her mother.

"Oh, mother, don't be old-fashioned. It's not supposed to be anything. I'm expressing myself. By the way, how soon is lunch?"

"Coming up in a moment," answered her mother, and shortly brought in a tray on which soup, salad, and dessert were strewn and mingled.

"Ugh, what's this supposed to be?" exclaimed the daughter in horror.

"Nothing. I'm just expressing myself."

(Maybe some anecdotes are needed to kid scientists who think that experimentation is the sole good of their disciplines. "All I did was invent the gas. Is it my fault if it was used to kill human beings?")

Many a young artist spends a lot of time trying to find his own style. "It ain't what you do, it's the way that you do it," went an old jazz song. And whether they arc singers, painters, or writers, they search hard and long.

Once, perhaps, in earlier societies, this was not such a problem. The young artist had little choice. He simply adopted the style of his country and his time without much question. It's still this way in many a folk community. It is natural for a folk musician to prefer to make all his music within one idiom. It is like a writer doing all of his writing in one language.

But in a modern city there are a thousand and one styles to choose from. The usual course of an artist is to imitate first one teacher, then another, till he matures. If he's lucky, one can finally say of him, "The style is the man."

Thus, for example, one can describe the style of Hemingway the writer and find in the end that one has described the character of Hemingway the man.

Those who search in vain for style are those who fall into the trap of thinking that style alone is sufficient. It's not entirely true that "it ain't what you do, it's the way that you do it." You still have to have something to say. Form and content go hand in hand. Inanities uttered in a pretty way are still inanities.

But the search for form *is* important. It is like a writer trying to decide on what language he will write in. Once he decides on it, and masters it (easier said than done), he can charge ahead and really say something. (It's helpful, of course, if he picks a language which others understand.)

If you love a song, you can make it your own by singing it; through the years it will become part of your life. Probably you will change the tune in subtle ways, little by little, or add or subtract verses. Someone else might like your changes or might probably not. In any case, the folk process over the years will sift the good from the bad. Think how many thousands of different ways the song "Barbara Allen" has been sung (and printed) over the last three hundred years. Today we have a handful of beautiful versions handed down to us, shining like gems.

If you don't feel like changing the song at all, don't be ashamed of that, either. Some of the first banjo tunes I learned, thirty years ago, I still play almost the same way I heard. I so admired them then, I thought they were the greatest American Music I ever listened to, and never since found any special way I wanted to improve them, except to play them better.

You'll find that after you have sung a song over and over, lived with it over a space of weeks or months, then you really know what you want to do with it. You'll know how you want to sing it. Over a period of years you'll get better at it, until the song is literally a part of yourself. And that's what folk music should be.

I-Don't-Know-Music-but-I-Know-What-I-Like Department

Seven ways to ruin an American folk song (for me):

Sing it in the kind of bel canto voice that says "Look what impressive pipes I have!"
Croon it as though it were just one more pretty pop song.
Change the words in order to take all the protesty quality out of it.
Change the words to take all the sex out of them, so as to make it proper for school songbooks.
Arrange it for symphony or orchestra, as if that automatically improved it.
Arrange it for jazz band, as if that automatically improved it.
Arrange it into a production number, such as for a finale on the Ed Sullivan show, with a grand "ta-ran-ta-ra" ending. (I can't think of a single folk song which could survive this manhandling.)

The Emasculation of Folk Music?

SAM HINTON, in his classes at the Idyllwild (California) Music Camp, cited a horrible example of what *can* happen to folk songs when they get printed in school songbooks. The sea chantey "Hanging Johnny" is presented in one widely printed school anthology as "Smiling Johnny." The original sailor's song went thus:

> Oh, they call me Hanging Johnny;
>   Away, boys, away!
> They says I hangs for money;
>   So hang, boys, hang.
>
> Oh, first I hanged my granny;
>   Away, boys, away!
> And then I hanged my daddy;
>   So hang, boys, hang.

The school version goes:

> Oh, they call me smiling Johnny;
> Away, boys, away!
> Because my smile is bonny;
> So smile, boys, smile.

As Sam points out, it would not be so reprehensible if the bowdlerized version were not presented as "an American sea chantey." Is it any wonder that generations of schoolchildren grew up thinking that a folk song was something that went "tra-la-la" and concerned skipping around a ring with birds and butterflies?

John Brunner once made a similar point in the magazine *Caravan*. John described being at a London skiffle club when Bert Lloyd, the English folklorist, and a fine singer, was introduced. Bert addressed the audience:

"Well, everyone seems to have been singing American songs so I'm going to sing some English songs. And they're going to be love songs."

John Brunner describes the reaction: "The audience composed itself to listen. One could see an attitude which indicated they were prepared to look politely interested but reserved the right to feel bored. And Bert sang about seven bawdy songs in a row—'My Husband's Got No Courage in Him' was the best—and the audience *loved* it."

The balance of John's column pointed out that in England most of the population was given a bowdlerized and emasculated version of English folk song. No wonder most working people laughed at it. How fortunate we were here that some of the folklorists in America were aware of this problem, and strove pointedly to present as realistic a picture of folk music as possible. I'm speaking of such people as Carl Sandburg and the Lomaxes. One result: their collections are rarely used in schools.*

Of course, teachers who must avoid the wrath of parents will have to make selections. Half the best sailor songs and cowboy songs (like soldier songs) were made up by and for an all-male audience and cannot be sung in mixed company without dropping some of the verses.

But at least we can insist, as Sam Hinton says, that a song is not changed from "Hanging Johnny" to "Smiling Johnny" and still be presented as "an American sailor song." Why not at least do what Tin Pan

---

* This article was written in 1958; in 1968 I peruse a widely advertised school songbook, and find:

> O have you heard tell of Sweet Betsy from Pike;
> She crossed the wide mountains with her *husband* Ike.

Alley does, and state in large letters: "New Words Composed by So-and-So"?

Let Tin Pan Alley show the path of honesty to our school system.

> *On the surface, at least, many a bawdy song reflects so much rank male supremacy that one wonders whether in an equalitarian age they will survive, at least in their present form. When are they sung mainly? In all-male situations, such as the Army, or in certain industries—such as sailing or logging. In former times the cowboy camp knew more unsingable songs than ones singable in polite company.*
>
> *But today there are few cowboy campfires, and loggers now mostly live with their families. Even ships are starting to see females among the working force. In many countries the armies are co-ed.*
>
> *So at the same time that frank sex language in many a song is now permissible in polite company, I rather think that certain of the bawdy repertoire (such as "The Bloody Great Wheel") will tend to be discarded. We may even see a rise in bawdy songs written from the woman's point of view. These seem to be rare at the moment. The U.S. Women's Army Corps (WAC) developed a few during World War II, but the tradition barely got started.*

> *When he's got you on your back*
> *Just remember you're a WAC . . .*

> *Considering that sex traditions already vary so much from country to country, it is conceivable that many a song which today is considered risqué and (until recently) unprintable will at some future time be considered merely quaint.*

> *Question: How does a "bawdy" song differ from a "dirty" song? My sister Peggy says there is a difference: the difference between seduction and rape.*

The Folklore of Prejudice*

IF FOLK MUSIC reflects all our life, it reflects our sins as well as our virtues. Therefore, when people talk of reviving folk music, they usually tend to revive what they like and censor what they don't like. If there is a folklore of bawdry, there is a folklore of prudery as well, for example. Causes and groups, mutually distrustful or antagonistic, contend to be heard.

At a lecture at Columbia University, during the question period, a slip of paper was handed me, asking, "Is there such a thing as a bad folk song?"

Surprised that anyone should have had to ask, I answered, "Of course. Many are uninteresting musically and poetically to all but a few who wrote them. If one considers that in folk music he can find reflections of all the life of working people, one can find songs expressing weakness as well as strength, injustice as well as generosity."

I did say that I felt there was a tendency for folk music to be more honest than popular music (because there was less money in it?), and that, furthermore, over the centuries, the folk process seems to weed out the bad and preserve the good.

In America, many prejudices have long been preserved in folk song. Because they are "folk," are we automatically interested in perpetuating them? I am referring to such common sayings as "Jews are avaricious," "Negroes (Indians, French-Canadians) are dishonest and lazy," "Irish are dirty," "Scottish are stingy," and so on ad nauseam.

That this is more than simple unfairness can be seen by the way it fits into the over-all picture of the chauvinism which, in a thousand billboards, magazines, and other cultural media, urges every one of us to distort the well-known melting pot theory into "You must melt into an Anglo-Saxon."

Emma Dusenberry, the blind folk singer of Arkansas, recognized the problem when she stopped singing the old ballad "The Jew's Daughter." "That song was made up a long time ago," she said, "and it just ain't true now." She knew it wasn't, because she had met Jewish youths at neighboring Commonwealth College. Not all ballad singers are so lucky.

---

* Written in 1962.

Many songs echo a past where the man of the household reigned supreme, and if his wife objected, she was labeled a nag or a shrew. In these days, when I sing at a college, looking at hundreds of eager, ambitious young women getting degrees (which I never got), how could I possibly sing "The Farmer's Curst Wife" without at least coupling it with "Equinoxial and Little Phoebe," the ballad about the man who foolishly claimed he could do more work in a day than his wife could do in three?* But male supremacy dies a hard death, and many put up with it simply because they are so used to it.

How can a well-known singer of folk songs stand up in New York's Town Hall (as I witnessed some years ago) and sing the verses of "I Am a Rebel Soldier":

> . . . I hate to see a nigger
> Dressed up in Yankee blue . . .

And this with young black people sitting in the audience! Some of them had risked their lives to save this country from fascism in World War II—fighting in segregated units because of the prevalence of the above-quoted opinion. "Tain't funny, McGee," as Fibber's wife Molly used to say.

Does not the folklorist who publishes a popular folk song collection owe it to the hundreds of thousands of American Indians, who are struggling against great odds to regain a sense of national dignity, to amend the way the words "Injun" and "squaw" are used in some pioneer songs? Remember, millions of American schoolchildren may be learning these songs, and parroting the slander.

The sad truth is that the folklore of prejudice runs deep, and infects the scholarly as well as the illiterate. The first task is to recognize its existence. Then what?

The vast treasuries of folk music encompass all life, kaleidoscopic, encyclopedic, universal. The librarian may be anxious to preserve all, the bad as well as the good, for future record. But the singer, the student, the editor of anthologies obviously has a more selective job.

Anyone with a normally contemporary bundle of opinions will have sharp tastes in selecting songs to sing with his or her friends. Young

---

* After a fair test—one day of trading jobs:
    Equinoxial swore by all the stars in heaven
    That she could do more work in a day than he could do in seven.

people will make their own selection, and old folks another one. Union folks will prefer what Woody Guthrie called "the protesty songs" more than the songs of wishful thinking.

If one "revives" folk songs for present-day performance and widespread singing, one is actually creating something new, not just a static repetition of the old. Do we not want to create our new traditions out of the *best* of the old?

Thoughts in 1968:

SAD BUT TRUE: some of the worst racism has come from organized working people who were trying to keep their jobs from being taken by another sector of the population that was willing to work for less pay.

It was the union workers of California who pushed through the Oriental Exclusion Act. The union workers of Australia keep the White Australia Policy on the books. My home community used to see waves of different races brought in to break strikes in the brickyards.

So once again the good and the bad in the world are wrapped so tight together it's hard to separate them. Here is a mid-nineteenth-century Irish longshoreman's song from New York City.

> I am a roving Irishman,
> I sailed from Greenland's shore
> To drive the hungry wolves away
> From the poor old landsman's door.
>
> O, give us pay for every day;
> That's all we ask of thee,
> For it's right that we're out upon a strike
> For the poor man's family.
>
> They'll bring their Eyetalians over here
> And Naygurs from the South,
> Thinking they can do our work,
> Take the bread from a poor man's mouth.   (*Etc.*)

The anthropologist looks for one kind of truth when he tape-records the songs of a people: does it truly reflect the culture he is studying, or is it an aberration, an import?

The average singer looks for a different kind of truth, the truth that he finds in the song, regardless of where it came from or how typical it is of what.

Most folklorists, and me too, waver a bit illogically between these two positions. We collect a song because it is typical of an idiom. But we also personally like the idiom. Sometimes the two kinds of truth obviously disagree with each other. Then a new truth emerges. As when camp or pop art turn meanings upside down.

Thus in singing songs of America's various wars ("Yankee Doodle," "John Brown's Body," etc.) I find myself unable to ignore a racist ditty of 1898:

> Damn damn damn the Filipinos,
> Cross-eyed kakiak ladrones,
> And beneath the starry flag
> Civilize 'em with a Krag*
> And go back to our own beloved homes.

Oy. No comment.

---

* Rifle.

PART IV

The World That Music Lives In

10·Races and Racism:
A Singer's View

This Paleface Does a Double Take—Confessions of an American History Buff

I SHOULD HAVE known better. As a kid I read the books of Ernest Thompson Seton, who quoted in detail the violence and treachery by which American Indians were forced off the broad face of this land and the survivors disarmed. But I made a fundamental mistake: "Well, that's all in the past." I put it out of my mind and read more encouraging stories.

The history of the sons and daughters of Europe on these shores is full of encouraging stories. I'm not just thinking of individual penniless immigrants who slipped the shackles of European feudalism, came here, and got rich quick. In 1736 John Peter Zenger fought for freedom of the press, and won. Quakers, Jews, Catholics, Mennonites fought for freedom of religion—and in a limited sense, they won. (Maybe all victories are limited.) American farmers and businessmen fought for independence from Britain, and won. Over a long period of years, American workers fought for the right to bargain collectively, and in a limited sense, won. Women struggled for the right to vote, and won.

In learning folk songs I found some little-known stories that were especially inspiring. Hudson Valley tenant farmers in the 1840s,* and Tennessee miners in the 1890s,† organized for violent struggle against conditions which made life unbearable. In both instances their organizations were crushed, their leaders jailed or killed. But because they

---

* See Chapter 3, pp. 92–93.
† See Chapter 3, pp. 79–84.

struggled they got publicity. In both instances the subsequent state elections were won by candidates pledged to abolish the oppressive institutions. So in the end they won their battles.

It seemed evident: the price of liberty is eternal publicity. When Rev. King and others started their sit-ins and marches in the early sixties, I counted on their eventually winning, if they could get enough publicity. I figured that within five or ten years the conscience of the country would be aroused; surely the next governor would be elected with a plank in his platform to end Jim Crow in jobs, schools, housing.

I should have known better. Rev. King got publicity all right, even on the TV screens of every American home. But I hadn't learned my American history accurately enough. Battles for democratic rights had been won by Americans with light skins. Battles for rights, when waged by Americans with dark skins, had more often been lost.

For example: In 1634, the Massachusetts colony determined publicly "to exterminate the Pequod race," and did just that—every squaw and papoose. In the next 334 years, Indian rights were consistently considered of less importance than the welfare and progress of the new large white population. It's still going on. In 1967 Dick Gregory and his wife went to jail in the Northwest helping to try and save the fishing rights of a small tribe.

Spanish Americans in Texas, New Mexico, Arizona and California found what it was like to be second-class citizens. When a man like Joaquin Murieta rebelled,* his Yankee captors operated on his body with the same sadistic fury which had mutilated the body of Nat Turner. (Yes, I know Pancho Villa once cut off the ears of his captives. So palefaces are now exonerated?)

In World War II there was no thought of jailing all Italian-Americans or German-Americans, but on the west coast anyone with a Japanese name and skin went behind barbed wire in "relocation camps."

And so on. The main evidence, of course, is the story of Africans in America. The history books all tell us of John Peter Zenger, 1736. Great victory for democracy. Yes! But has any reader read of what happened in that same little city of New York just five years later?

New York was at that time 10,000 souls; 2,000 were African slaves. The house of a municipal judge caught fire just after he had convicted two slaves for petty thievery! Through town swept the rumor that slaves were planning to revolt and kill their masters. A witch-hunt fol-

---

* A California Robin Hood, 1849.

lowed. Within five months 150 were arrested. Seventy were sold to slavery in the West Indies—life sentences. Fourteen were hung, seventeen were burned alive at the stake. Four white people were among these, including a Catholic priest. He was charged with gathering slaves in a circle and "reading them devilish incantations," which they would repeat. All this in a little city of 10,000, when Wall Street was "up town." What contemporary history book mentions the event?*

Of course, just as, in accuracy, one could say that all victories are limited, one might also say that no defeat is a complete defeat. And we know conditions have changed for black and tan as well as white. No struggle has ever been completely in vain. Even though northern whites, having defeated slaveocracy, then abandoned their black allies, nevertheless outright slavery was abolished. Some schools were started. But by and large, I think the foregoing paragraphs sketch out the correct picture.

That is why this paleface has done a double take and is reexamining his own study of U.S. history in a new light.

One judges the conduct of a nation, or of a group of people, not by what a few enlightened individuals say, but upon what the mass of people as a whole does. Ben Franklin spoke of the Indians of western Pennsylvania, "Savages, we call them, because their ways are different than ours." But this did not seem to affect future conduct of affairs between whites and Indians. Here are a few other examples.

In 1832 the intellectual community of the North was solidly in favor of the Cherokees being allowed to stay on their ancestral lands. Webster, Clay, and the Whigs also said as much. *But Andrew Jackson won the election.* Soon 15,000 Cherokees were forced at gunpoint to walk west on the Trail of Tears. Four thousand died on the way.

In 1860 white Appalachian farmers were against slavery, but how big a dent did they make in the Confederate war effort?

American writers from Mark Twain on down condemned McKinley's 1898 invasion of the Philippines, but the U.S. soldiers went right in, singing: "Damn, damn, damn the Filipinos."

Right now there are probably some shrewd American leaders who are counting on the same thing happening. What matter if every college in the U.S.A. protests? They can keep their three million votes.

But history doesn't repeat itself exactly. We have new mediums of

---

* I learned it from Valentine's *History of New York,* 1853. Out of print.

communication that never existed before. If we can force them open, masses of people can learn things they never learned from the printed page. There are millions of light-skinned Americans whose grandparents ate beans and scratched for pennies. Today the grandchildren have to take weight-watcher pills. You can't tell them this isn't the land of opportunity. But they have that magic screen sitting in their living rooms, too. It could be a window on the world, a window to look to the past and to the future. What will it tell them? The air belongs to *all* the people. This paleface did a double take. Perhaps others will.

The crucial question is: What action is going to be taken after the double take? There is a great human tendency to assume that because one's heart is in the right place that is all that is necessary. 'Tain't true. An old southern folk saying is, "I wish his do-so matched his say-so." Nowadays they say, "Put your money where your mouth is."

A couple of years ago David Susskind told me in great perplexity of interviewing two militant black nationalists on his television program. He asked them what in this world they hated the most. They had pointed their fingers right at him and said, "It's you white liberals. We hate you the most." Susskind said in surprise, "You mean you hate me more than George Wallace and the Ku Klux Klan?"

"Yes," they replied.

Susskind never was able to understand exactly why, but I explained it to him as follows: It's the same reason that April is the cruelest month, if you remember the poem by T. S. Eliot. It awakens hopes which are bound to be dashed. The black militants are trying to persuade the poor people of the world that freedom will not come unless they unite and struggle hard. The struggle will be dangerous, uncomfortable, but they are convinced that only through such united action will freedom come. Along comes the white liberal and cuts the ground out from under their feet by acting so nicely that many ordinary people are persuaded that they don't need to take the risk, that they don't need to struggle so hard, that surely freedom will come if they simply wait a little longer. And a little study of history will show the extent to which they are right or wrong.

No, it is not a little study of history that's needed, it's a lot of study, and very detailed study that is needed.

I rather guess that almost every part of the globe has known some form of race hate at some time. After all, in tribal days any member of another tribe was an enemy.

Today there are a million Koreans living in Japan who are treated like second-class citizens. I read in a Tokyo newspaper of a man who committed suicide because his daughter insisted on marrying a Korean.

And we all have read about Hindus and Moslems slaughtering each other in India. Ibos have more recently been slaughtered in Nigeria. Chileans ask Peruvians, "Why don't you treat your Indians better?" and the Peruvians reply, "You have no problems with your Indians because you killed them all."

In 1965 my wife and I were interested to visit a chain of cities in Soviet central Asia. We were curious to see how they had tried to solve the problem. These were all Moslem principalities 150 years ago. The czar sent his troops down to conquer them, to counter the British pushing up from India. When the Revolution came along Lenin said, "The czar's empire was a prison house of nations, but we want to build a soviet family of nations. You can leave or you can join us." At that time Finland left immediately. In Asia there were enough local Communists to swing the population in favor of staying in.

Alma Ata ("City of Apples") is a modern city of several hundred thousand, about a hundred miles from the Chinese border, directly north of Tibet. Its geography resembles Salt Lake City. A range of huge snow-capped peaks stands just south; a large salt desert is to the north. The whole town is on a slight slant, as is Salt Lake City. But imagine Salt Lake with Indians in Indian costume walking about, and Indian music on the radio.

Alma Ata is the capital of Kazakhstan, a huge agricultural area. On the streets we saw men in long robes and fur hats, side by side with girls in the latest fashions. The kiosk at the corner carried newspapers and magazines in Kazakh and in Russian. The radio had two kinds of music: wailing eastern melodies on one station, Tschaikovsky or Czech rock and roll, etc., came from another. The legislature and law courts spoke Kazakh. Public signs everywhere were in two languages. Children in school had to learn Russian as a second language. If a Russian came to work in the city he would send his kids to a school where Russian was the main language, but they had to study Kazakh as a second language as long as they lived there. From conversations, I gathered that while some of the old folks might complain that there were too many Russians around, "and in the old days women kept their place," nevertheless there was about as little friction as was possible between two peoples of different backgrounds.

The Soviets, with several hundred languages, really seemed to have solved the problem far better than most: a geographical area being set aside for each people. Perhaps they only failed to satisfy one group: Jews were given some land way out in Siberia, but few wanted to go there. Perhaps Gypsies, too, have some problems. In Czechoslovakia a man said, "Isn't it terrible the way Americans treat Negroes? I wouldn't mind living next to a Negro. But not a Gypsy."

It's easier to pass a law against race hate than to erase it from a man's mind. The way someone talks, or walks, or bargains in a store, or cracks a joke, or speaks too familiarly, or not familiarly enough—these all can rub neighbors the wrong way.

One neighbor sees the other walking down the street and thinks to himself, "Why do *those people* always have to walk so stiff and straight-backed, like they were stuck-up all the time. Why can't they be relaxed?" The other man is saying to himself, "Why do *those people* always slouch around so? Why don't they have some ambition?"

In Japan, my father-in-law visited the little village he had left fifty years before. "Tell me, brother," asked his sister, "is it true that in America people take baths in the same water that they wash in?"

"Yes," answered Takashi. (In Japan they carefully wash and rinse themselves before getting in the tub. After they are first well cleaned, then they may sit and soak in the steaming tub—sometimes with friends and neighbors of both sexes.)

"How can the Americans do such a disgusting thing," she went on, "to wash yourself in the same water that you sit in? It's hard to believe! You don't do that, do you, brother?"

"Oh, no, sister," said Takashi gravely, not wanting to shock her.

And did you ever hear of the wife of the Dutch governor of Bali who insisted that her husband decree that women must wear clothing on the upper half of their body? This was in the late nineteenth century. The following Sunday as the governor and his wife rode in their carriage to church, the populace lined up alongside the road. When the carriage approached, all the women raised their skirts and covered the upper half of their bodies.

Singing in Lebanon and Israel

(May 22, 1967)

THIS MONTH I managed to spend a week in Lebanon and a week in Israel, and got a two-week cram course in Arab-Jewish relations. There is still lots I don't know, but I know one thing: I met some wonderful people on both sides of the border, who sang along with me on the same songs and did not knock my block off when I asked them to repeat a chorus of "Guantanamera" and cried, "Let's dedicate this to all the exiles, of all countries, exiles of two thousand years and exiles of nineteen years!"

"Have you ever eaten Arab food, Mr. Seeger?"

"Why, yes, my family likes it a lot. We can buy Arabian bread on Atlantic Avenue in Brooklyn. We first got to know Arabian food three years ago when I had a concert in Jerusalem."

Pause.

"Was that Arab or Jewish Jerusalem?"

"I had a couple of weeks of concerts in Israel."

A few minutes later, when one of the men got out of the car for some cigarettes, the other leaned over and said, "Mr. Seeger, I myself am quite open-minded. But I think it would be best if, while you were here in Lebanon, you didn't mention that you were ever in Israel."

Sharif* is a doctor who studied in the United States. He knows English well and acted as my guide and interpreter for the whole week. As we drove past snowcapped mountains and ski slopes, visited Bedouin families and villages and Roman ruins, he and I talked of many things: world problems, war and peace, art and literature—and we talked about Israel.

"Pete, I don't want to see a war. No sensible man does. But I tell you that unless justice is given to the refugees, I think there will be a war.

"Actually, for myself, there are many things about the Jews which I like. Their music is great. They are bringing skills and talents and techniques which the Near East needs. . . . Of course, I can say this to

---

* Not his real name.

you here, but if I said it down at the refugee camp I would be shot."

There is no one quite so outraged as a farmer whose fields have been taken away from him. A farmer loves his land more than he does his wife.

And the Arab leaders consider Israel as a wedge of western colonialist power in their midst.

Sharif was thirteen years old when his family fled in terror from the city of Acca in northern Palestine.

I told him, "Can't you imagine what it is like for a man who is perhaps the only surviving member of his family after the rest have been sent to the gas chamber? He is desperate. He feels that the Jews have failed utterly to find a decent place for themselves in any country of the world. He is determined to build a place where Jews will never be discriminated against again."

"But two wrongs don't make a right," Sharif burst out. "We are not anti-Semitic here. Believe me, I am just as horrified as you at what Hitler did. Jews have always lived here in Lebanon and still do. But how can we make Israel admit the injustice that she has done?

"I attended a Friends Service Committee work camp in Europe and met a young man. We talked in English. 'Where are you from?' 'Acca,' says I. 'Acca, why I'm from Acca too,' and he rattles on, and I suddenly have a sinking feeling in my stomach that I can never explain to this young Israeli what it means to me that I can never go back to my home."

Returning from a visit to a refugee camp, I asked Sharif and the UN employee who guided us if there were any Palestinian refugees outside of the four neighboring Arab countries.

"Oh, yes. Some few have gone to America, to Canada and so on."

I said, half humorously, "Why, then, it would be possible for a Palestinian refugee to become a United States or Canadian citizen and go back to Israel if he wanted."

"Yes, I could do that myself," said Sharif, offhand.

"Don't; it would break your heart," said the UN man earnestly. He is a Palestinian refugee himself.

Just before leaving Lebanon, I was in a car with Sharif and two others.

"Now, when are you going to come back to visit us? We would like to have you give another concert here. There is much that we have still to show you about our country."

I could lie no longer. "I would love to come back. I would love to sing for you. I would like to do a benefit and have all the money go for vocational schools for the refugees. But it may not be possible. Next week I am singing in Israel."

I talked for about half an hour on how I, as a person of Yankee, Protestant-Christian background, had slowly come to know what it meant to be a Jew. I had learned this partly through their songs, partly through reading books, and of course largely through meeting American Jews who taught me things such as the saying, "If I am not for myself, who will be? If I am only for myself, what am I?"

Sitting in the car, we talked long and earnestly and soberly. Toward the end of our conversation one of the men turned to me abruptly and asked, "When you are in Israel will you tell them that you have been in Lebanon?" And I answered, "Yes."

At the airport the next day I embraced Sharif in the Arab fashion and we promised to continue writing.

"But please, Pete, when you write me, write carefully. Because, you know, the mail in some of the Arab states is censored. Just don't mention the name of the country you are visiting tomorrow."

> *A midnight dialogue overheard in the American Midwest:*
> *"Get off this estate."*
> *"What for?"*
> *"Because it's mine."*
> *"Where did you get it?"*
> *"From my father."*
> *"Where did he get it?"*
> *"From his father."*
> *"And where did he get it?"*
> *"He fought for it."*
> *"Well, I'll fight you for it."**

About two thousand years ago the Romans conquered most of the Near East. They had special trouble with one small kingdom and finally said to hell with it and deported and dispersed the entire population throughout their other colonies. "They'll soon be assimilated," said the Romans.

They reckoned without a Great Old Book which this people took with them and referred to regularly every week. It said, "I am the Lord thy God.

---

* From Carl Sandburg, *The People, Yes.*

Don't forget me and I won't forget you." So over two thousand years of being hounded from country to country, treated like second-class citizens at best, and tortured and murdered at worst, these people did not forget.

Meanwhile, what happened to the land they left? It was settled by other subjects of the Roman Empire, and when the great movement of Islam in the seventh century swept through, most of them became converts and learned the Arabic language.

A few of their cities were conquered around the twelfth century by the European Crusaders, but the latter made few friends and performed many massacres and were kicked out after about two hundred years. The Ottoman Turkish Empire then ruled the local Arab inhabitants—mostly farmers, with some nomadic shepherds—until World War I.

Arabs thought they were going to get their freedom when they helped the British and French to beat the Turks. But, to their outrage and fury, their land was divided up arbitrarily, between France (getting Lebanon and Syria) and England (getting Palestine and Transjordania). Even today, the biggest resentment among many Palestinian Arab refugees is not so much against the Jews as against "the treachery of the British."

Today, in Israel there's one Jewish village up near Galilee that was never evicted by the Romans. However, in the subsequent centuries, individual families filtered back and managed to live amicably with the rulers of the country, whoever they were. (One exception: when the Crusaders captured Jerusalem, they herded all the Jews into their synagogue and burned the building down.) By the eighteenth century there were perhaps four thousand Jews living in Palestine. Around the end of the nineteenth century, more European Jews started coming down. The failure of revolutionary hopes in Europe led many to think that the only thing to do was to try to build a life, difficult as it may be, down in Palestine. Around the turn of the century, a Viennese journalist named Herzl formalized these hopes and called it Zionism: the determination to build a Jewish national homeland in Palestine.

Some of the early Zionist literature proclaimed, "The Holy Land is a desert, waiting for you to come and bring it to life." When the new arrivals came, they saw Arab farmers all around. (When the British mandate ended in 1948, the Arab population of Palestine was close to a million—in a territory not much larger than Vermont.)

But Herzl, in *AltNeuLand*, had envisioned Arabs and Jews getting along well together.

A magazine editor who had been born and raised in the Bronx invited us to visit the kibbutz he lives in, some thirty-five miles from Tel-Aviv.

On a slight rise of ground, there was a cluster of trees, with a few large buildings in the center containing workshops, dining room, and kitchen. Surrounding them were the smaller dwelling houses, and at the far end, schools and dormitories for children. We drove up the winding blacktop road and got out, almost speechless with amazement. Whoever had landscaped it was an artist! The curving paths, the green lawns, the shrubs and trees, the profusion of flower beds around every little house. . . . Why a millionaire's resort couldn't have looked more beautiful. We stood on the terrace outside the dining room and gazed over twenty miles of fertile plains with fields and rows of trees, and in the distance the hills of ancient Judea. It was so beautiful we almost felt like crying.

Nobody earns any money. No, not one penny. If you need cigarettes or books or any luxury, you simply discuss it with the appropriate committee and money is taken out of the fund for it, unless it is disapproved. It's like one big family. Everybody works hard, but they all insist that each other take time to play as well, whether it is in sports or cultural activities or simply taking time off by yourself to read or gather flowers or swim in the big, new pool.

In addition to running a huge farm with a variety of crops, they have a machine shop making pipe fittings which are sold in many countries of the world. Twenty years ago they were close to starvation and lived a very Spartan life. Now, though no one wastes money, they can have luxuries, such as awarding some of their members an occasional trip to Europe or even to the United States. Many of the kibbutzniks are former Americans.

Husbands and wives share small one-and-a-half room apartments, but children, from the time they are babies, live separately in dormitories. Marriages usually take place around twenty-one years of age, after everyone's compulsory two years' army service is over.

I found that it was customary for boys and girls to marry outside the kibbutz or at least outside their own age group, which they had been living with since birth. I kidded them: "That's because you have no illusions about each other. For romance, you need a few illusions." They admitted: "After living with a girl all your life, she is more like a sister." At any rate, they were the healthiest, happiest young people I had seen in a long time and reminded me of young people I met in a cooperative religious colony called the Society of Brothers back in the States. I think that it is a clear example of what happens when you live a cooperative life without the intense competitive pressures which most city people live under.

Before leaving Israel, I spent one very moving and exciting evening. There is a group in Tel-Aviv, started by intellectuals both Arab and Jewish, called the Israeli Movement for Arab-Jewish Cooperation. I agreed to appear for them. And on twenty-four hours' notice, telegrams were sent out to members and friends, and over one thousand people showed up at the Hilton ballroom. And all this with daily mounting headlines about the threat of war with Egypt and harassments on the Syrian border. I sang for about half an hour and talked for about twenty minutes, telling them about people I had met in Lebanon. (Everything I said was translated first into Hebrew and then into Arabic.)

Before I sang the song "Walking Down Death Row," I said, "I think there's been too much talk about crime and guilt. When it comes down to it, I have been as much a criminal as anyone else in the world. My ancestors landed on the shores of North America and with their guns and written language pushed out the previous inhabitants in the most heartless way. And my country was built, in large part, on the sweat of millions of black slaves. The problem for me now is not to try to figure out how to atone for crimes that were done years past but simply to acknowledge that they were crimes and take steps to see that such things will never happen again. To see, for example, that first-class citizenship is granted to American Indians, American Negroes, Mexican Americans, and other citizens of minority descent."

Both Arabs and Jews got up to speak on the stand. Warm, earnest, searching talks. One very extraordinary man who was a member of Parliament spoke: "I am glad Pete Seeger has sung to us about Vietnam, because a meeting like this should not exist if we do not mention the horror of Vietnam. When Jews were being killed by the Nazis we asked why did the rest of the world remain silent. Now it is up to us to ask each other how we can remain silent while crematoriums are being rained from the skies upon a helpless population."

This man was one of a number of Jews who threw themselves down on the highway in front of army trucks in order to present a protest against mistreatment of Arabs.

I started to play the chalil: the song, in Yiddish, by Hirsch Glick, the partisan in Poland, then I broke down and started weeping in the middle of it at the tragedy of the whole situation. Ilka Raveh (who years ago taught me to make and play this instrument) came up with his own chalil and played it so beautifully that he helped me pull myself together, and then, with him standing at my side, I stood up and played the piece bravely . . . as it should be.

One of the founding leaders of this organization is the wife of an extraordinary writer, a survivor of Auschwitz. She was meeting with a group of

Arab women when one of them suddenly asked her, "Tell us about your husband—what is he like?" They did not know that her husband was a writer. They were simply curious to know the relationship between Jewish women and Jewish men. She hesitated and then started slowly, "My husband has a number burned into the flesh of his left arm . . ." Before she was finished, the Arab women were in tears.

Something like this is really what has to be done. The Arab people are basically very sympathetic, emotional people. If they could only realize the desperation and horror in the family history of practically all the Israeli Jews, how the situation might change! And if Israeli Jews could realize the desperation and hopelessness of a man who has little education but only his love of the land and his Arab heritage, then too the situation might change.

I have played my little Israeli chalil in twenty-five countries of the world, and I always introduce it: "I learned this from an Israeli Jew, who learned to play it from Arabs. I hope they will get back together again one of these years."

11·Money and Music

OBSERVATIONS ON THE COMMERCIAL BIG TIME
AND ITS ATTEMPT
TO MAKE MONEY OUT OF FOLK MUSIC

*I'm told that someone once asked Doc Watson for advice
on whether or not he should become a professional singer
of folk songs. Doc is reported to have answered in his
usual grave way:*

*"Do it as a last resort, when you've failed in every other
way to make a living."*

Who Killed Norma Jean?

I ONCE HAD a vision of a beast with hollow fangs. I first saw it
when my mother-in-law, whom I loved very much, died of cancer. This
beast came and fastened itself upon her back. It had a hundred hollow
claws and fangs which it sunk into her neck and shoulders, into her
upper arms and up and down her spine. Its two huge eyes glared at us
silently as if to say, "You'll never unfasten me till I have drunk my fill."
For each fang was hollow and sucked the juices of life from her body till
it was left a lifeless shell.

The vision of hollow claws and fangs has come back to me more than
once when I have seen a friend in the clutches of the "culture" industry,
which values creative human beings only for what profit can be sucked

from them. This destruction goes on all the time, though it seldom is dramatically visible to the general public.

Words by Norman Rosten,* music by Pete Seeger. TRO-© copyright 1963, 1964, Ludlow Music, Inc., New York, New York.

1. Who killed _____ Nor-ma Jean? I, said the ci - ty, As a ci-vic du-ty, I killed Nor-ma Jean.

Tune to verses 3 & 8

3. Who caught her blood? I, said the Fan, With my lit-tle pan. I caught her blood.

2. Who saw her die?
   I, said the Night,
   And a bedroom light,
   We saw her die.

4. Who'll make her shroud?
   I, said the Lover
   My guilt to cover,
   I'll make her shroud.

5. Who'll dig her grave?
   The tourist will come
   To join in the fun,
   He'll dig her grave.

6. Who'll be chief mourners?
   We who represent
   And lose our ten percent,
   We'll be chief mourners.

7. Who'll bear the pall?
   We, said the Press
   In pain and distress,
   We'll bear the pall.

8. Who'll toll the bell?
   I, screamed the Mother,
   Locked in her tower,
   I'll pull the bell.

9. Who'll soon forget?
   I, said the Page
   Beginning to fade,
   I'm first to forget.

---

* Norman Rosten was a close friend of Marilyn Monroe, who committed suicide in August 1962.

January 1958

LAST WEEK, for the first time in eight years, I got a transcription job in the New York radio field. Replayed over many stations, it should end up making for a profitable recording session. But if another such job ever comes along I don't think I'll take it.

It was a singing commercial. For a cigarette company. Maybe if it had been for Vega banjos, or stone-ground whole wheat bread, I could have put my heart into it. But as it was, the job was pure prostitution. Now, prostitution may be all right for professionals ("Honey," said the veteran to the neophyte, "you're making good money, you might as well lay back and enjoy it")—but it's a risky business for amateurs.

If you start doing solely for money something which you would normally do for love, you're liable to find that it makes it difficult or perhaps impossible to do it for love any more.

Do you remember the plot of the Broadway comedy a few years ago, *Three Men on a Horse*? Some professional gamblers find a mild little man whose hobby is picking winners in horse races. And he's right every time! They latch on to him and start to clean up. Comes a day and he picks a real long shot. They stake all they have, and are set to make a killing, when the little man becomes uncertain of his choice. The gamblers, wild with alarm, grab him by the neck.

"Are you trying to doublecross us? How come you ain't betting?"

"Oh, I never bet myself."

They force him to bet all he has, to prove he's on the level. The race starts. It's a photo finish. Finally, after a wrong announcement, his choice is declared winner. All is elation, and the gamblers get together and ask the little man for his tips on the next race.

"Oh, I've lost my power, my sixth sense. I'm no better than you are now to try and pick a winner, now that I've gambled." End of story.

Well, of course, there is no such thing as absolute purity, as everyone knows, and some say you are compromised with the world if you decide to live in it. Lord knows I can't criticize anybody for making a living as best they can. But maybe everyone has to decide for themselves what they are going to do for money and what for love. Fortunate are they who can make a living at what they love to do.

P. S. The company didn't accept our commercial anyway.

Stay Small and Stay Alive

1959

"Bigger does not mean better." Many a small U. S. company has found it advisable to stay small rather than risk direct competition with a larger firm. An example of this is Folkways Records.

Moe Asch went bankrupt with an earlier firm, Disc Records, in 1948, and decided that the reason was that he tried to produce records which the bigger companies could sell cheaper. In his new firm he concentrated on folk music. His present catalogue lists about 500 LPs,* covering nearly every corner of the globe. Many of these records do not sell more than a hundred copies. A larger firm would go broke with such small sales. But Folkways keeps costs down by not going in for three-color pictures on the jackets, and by spending practically nothing on advertising. By charging relatively high prices, it can break even.

Through the years the reputation of the firm spread till folklorists and anthropologists throughout the world depend on it to supply out-of-the-way items which are unavailable from any other source. Do you want a record of the religious music of northern Afghanistan? Folkways will have it.

The experience of Folkways points up the existence of a marginal area on the edge of every mass market, which the large firms supplying the mass market cannot afford to satisfy. General Motors and Ford could not afford to experiment in the small-car field. It took the small European companies to do it. Victor and Columbia could not afford to experiment widely in the folk music field. So it was wide open for a small outfit like Folkways.

As long as the small producer will stay within his clearly prescribed limits, he can have the field more or less to himself. Of course, there is always the possibility that his efforts will create a mass market where there was none before. The bigger companies will move in. But this is one of the most valuable functions of the small company: to feel out marginal areas in a way that the more inflexible large company cannot

---

* In 1968, about 1300 LPs, plus a growing repertoire on three new pioneering labels: Asch and RBF (mainly reissues of important older records) and Broadside (mainly topical).

afford to do. Instead of a high-production/low-cost policy, the small firm must use its opposite, a low-production/high-cost principle. When and if the larger firm moves into the field, the small one need not go out of business. It can move on and explore the frontier, which will be a little further out than before.*

How Come You Got a Clean Banjo Head for a Change?

Spring 1960

WELL, it's like this. It was payola. About four or five years ago the Vega banjo company of Boston called me to say they'd received several requests to make banjos with especially long necks (an idea I got in 1942 when trying to play "Viva la Quince Brigada" in the C minor position, which was a bit too high to sing).

Vega asked, "Could we officially call it 'the Pete Seeger Model'?"

"It would be an honor," says I.

"Would you like us to pay you a royalty on each one sold?"

"No, I'd rather not get involved." (After all, how many such requests could there be, at $295.00 apiece?)

However, in 1959 Vega called again. "We thought you'd be interested to know that we've sold over three hundred of the Pete Seeger models."

Holy mackerel. I did some rapid arithmetic and began to wonder if I shouldn't have asked for a royalty.

"By the way, which model of our banjos do you yourself play?" asked Vega.

"Oh, I have an old Tubaphone rim with a homemade neck."

"Good heavens, that will never do. Could we present you with a Pete Seeger model?"

"I'd be delighted."

Thus so easily is the human race corrupted. The banjo arrived last week, and is a beaut—quite the nicest I ever had.

---

* 1969: The above was too complacent. The pattern rarely works out so neatly. Too often the small outfit which creates the trend is steamrollered by the big outfit, which appropriates the name but provides an ersatz product. It is as though someone says, "Here, let me help you carry the ball," and then carries it in another direction.

1962

It is good practice for any singer to try singing in a saloon occasionally. The difficulties are instructive. The danger comes when you get to like it too much.

Once upon a time folk songs in nightclubs were considered too, too esoteric. However, the folk song revival has now developed to the point where nightclubs have been founded precisely upon the growing city audience for folk music of various sorts, rather than, as in the past, upon jazz, or dancing, or comedy and girl shows. (I do not include liquor; there are cheaper places to get drunk.)

The result now is that when I sing folk songs in a nightclub, I no longer have to battle the noise, the drunks, the consternation and perplexity that I faced fifteen years ago. Then, patrons of nightclubs were totally unprepared for listening to "Come All Ye Fair and Tender Ladies."

And in 1951, when the Weavers tried singing "Follow the Drinking Gourd" in Ciro's of Hollywood, the manager bustled over to us. "Here, here," said he, "people come in this place to forget their troubles. They don't want to hear those old slave songs. Sing 'Good Night Irene.'"

We were trying to sing songs to deepen people's consciousness of life; this just ran counter to the purposes of his nightclub.

Nowadays, at least in certain clubs, the audience will be intent and still, and request numbers ranging from "Barbara Allen" to "Talking Union" and "Die Gedanken Sind Frei."

Nightclub work has another advantage: the audience is smaller than in a concert hall. They are usually grouped more informally around the mike and the atmosphere is more relaxed, thus more conducive to good singing.

There are disadvantages too: most nightclubs cost an arm and a leg to get out of. Many working people cannot afford to come. Furthermore, they are all too hot, smoky, and one still has to compete with noise from the kitchen. But all this is petty carping. I repeat: it is good practice for a singer to try singing in a saloon occasionally.

Summer 1962

A GOOD PERFORMER can make almost any fragment of a melody sound wonderful. The following story was told to me by a friend in the music business. He couldn't say whether it happened more than once:

When Fats Waller was broke he visited the music publishers at 1619 Broadway. He would start on one floor and work his way down, going in each door. Fats would say hello, then he'd sit down at the piano.

"There's a little idea I got recently—I wonder if you're interested in it," he'd say.

He'd start improvising, and before you knew it he would have some fine little theme going. The publisher would say, "Why, that sounds wonderful, Fats. Will you go ahead and finish it?" "Yes, if you like it, I'll go ahead and finish it for you," Fats would say. "Can you give me a little advance?"

By the end of the day Fats had worked his way down to the bottom of the building and collected advances from a dozen publishers.

For months afterward publishers would ask, "Say, Fats, when are you going to finish that song you started for me?" And Fats would answer, "Well, it just didn't turn out the way I hoped it would. I'll try." Finally the episode would fade into the dim past.

One couldn't really call it larceny. Fats probably just felt he was getting even with some publishers.

December 1962

YOURS TRULY has made a lot of records I can't bear listening to—some by myself, some with others. But one of the worst is one which Decca just released, entitled *Weavers' Gold*. It causes me and the Weavers many a wince. A couple of the songs on it are not too bad, but many are awful. They were done in 1951, under pressure from Decca to turn out "hits" with big-band accompaniment. Some were never supposed to be released. Nothing we can do about them now. Decca owns them.

Summer 1963

TRYING TO PRESENT genuine folk music on a stage before 5,000 people is like trying to present an exhibit of miniature paintings in Madison Square Garden. From the back rows no one can see the twinkle in the eyes of the old ballad singer. But TV cameras can come in close. The first U. S. TV producer who really learns how to present folk music is going to find a gold mine of material available to him. So far it's been unused because of the following reasons:

1. The TV producers didn't understand the material and its meaning.

2. They tended to try and get trained professional performers of folk music instead of getting the real thing.

3. They treated folk music like any other variety act; it should have been treated as "situation music" instead of "stand-up" music.

The sad state of American TV is as much a national outrage as the pollution of our rivers or the slums of our cities. It's something all of us should be ashamed of and which we should figure must sooner or later be changed. It's not enough to simply say, "Well, I don't have to look at it. I prefer to read books anyway, or see a good play." Tens of millions of Americans are enslaved by that tyrannical little box. If we have any patriotism in us we ought to try our best to improve American TV.

You might as well view a polluted river flowing past your town and say, "Well, I don't have to swim in it. I've got a swimming pool." Meanwhile all the poor kids in town have no other swimming hole.

I've filmed enough folk music in the field, and I've watched enough other people try to film in the field, to know the difficulties of it. But I know, and am positive, that only in "the field" can folk music be filmed right. The best folk performers in the world, brought onto a nice stage with the lights bright upon them, are not going to be able to do the kind of program you want. Would you film a wild-animal picture in a zoo?

The fact that folk music has proved a big hit on the stages of Carnegie Hall and other big auditoriums shows that it's just so good you can't keep it down. But it's not the right kind of music to be on such big stages. Folk music is an art form developed for small rooms—kitchens, living rooms, back porches. And the only time somebody hollered was if he was away out in the field or at a noisy square dance.

There is drama here—drama far greater than most script writers ever get into their scripts. The drama of hardworking persons who still can make music and bring love and laughter into the lives of family, friends and neighbors.

We have some fine professional performers of folk music in the country today. They've learned how to project to the back balcony and they can crack a gag at the right time. But frankly, it won't go over on TV. No more than Jack Benny and his stand-up comedy really went over on TV.

The reason stand-up comedy didn't go well on TV was that the viewer no longer had a chance to build up a mental image of the joke which the comedian was telling. On radio, Jack Benny could tell a joke, and while you were hearing his voice telling it your mind's eye was full of whatever image he was describing. On TV this didn't happen—you just saw Benny standing there telling the joke. And because you were concentrating on the picture of him on the screen, you didn't get such a good image of the funny incidents he talked about. Therefore, TV found that situation comedy was the best. "I Love Lucy," "The Honeymooners," the Sid Caesar skits—here you got right into the middle of the situation, and joke after joke flowed out of it.

Similarly, a man standing up before a TV mike and trying to recreate "John Henry" is at a disadvantage. The visual images are all wrong: there's a curtain in back of him—there's a studio audience in front of him. Almost anything would be better than that. It could be a coffee house, it could be any house; preferably it would be a shack by the railroad, I guess. But whatever it is, it should not be the TV studio. Or supposing he's singing a Negro spiritual. How much better it would be if the person singing it is in that little church where they are used to singing these songs, and everything you see relates to the song rather than conflicts with it.

You needed to have situation comedy on TV. And you need situation music on TV. That is, you go to the place where the music normally takes place and film it as it normally takes place. It doesn't matter whether it's a Baptist church in Alabama, a freedom rally in Mississippi, a square dance in Ohio, a group of Maine fishermen swapping stories in a waterside shack, a group of college students in the basement of a fraternity house, some Slovakians getting together over beer in Pittsburgh, a fiddlers' convention in Idaho, a sociable evening in a 'dobe hut of Mexican Americans in Arizona, or aboard a boat off the coast of Virginia where the menhaden fishermen are hollering their wild spirituals to the waves. Get where the music normally is, film the people who normally sing it and invariably sing it better than anybody else in the world. Then you'll have the world's greatest drama. There'll be humor as well as tragedy—all kinds of meanings will be flickering back and forth.

Another big mistake made by the people who try to put folk music on TV is in not letting the music have time to really tell its story. They think that a song is just two minutes and then it's all over. Now, let me draw a parallel here: did you ever notice how unsatisfactory it is to view the movie newsreels of the highlights of a football or baseball game? They are almost meaningless. Here are these great dramatic moments of a two-hour game, and we are seeing them in a few seconds, disconnected from all that has gone before. Why are they almost meaningless? Because we have not had the long, built-up suspense preceding the fleeting instant. Yet a full-length football game or baseball game is some of the best TV fare. There's great drama, great suspense, great excitement—you may have to wait ten minutes for a high point to develop, but then it is all the more worth it. In a baseball game, you might become restless that no runs or hits are being made, when suddenly you realize it has turned into an exciting pitchers' duel—maybe even a no-hitter for one of the hurlers. And fifteen minutes packed with highlights of fifteen football games, with touchdowns galore, is not as dramatic, or half as satisfactory to the viewer, as a live game where the Giants and Packers slug it out to a scoreless tie.

Similarly, in presenting folk music, it must be presented with the chance to build up to the climaxes. If, for example, you are filming a session in a Baptist church, don't expect it to suddenly start off with the high points of the music. You have to have the people drifting into the church, saying hello to each other; the tuning up by the musicians, if there are any instrumentalists present; the hemming and hawing; lots of waiting around. When the singing finally comes along—whoops! It'll take you by storm. But if you cut out all those preliminaries, you might as well try to put on a baseball game and cut out all the preliminary pitches. It would be ridiculous.

Set up the situation the way you set up a baseball game—you've got the contestants, you know they're good performers, you've got them where they feel at home, where they know they're in the right place. Then simply turn on your cameras and let the music roll. Take it for what it is—the drama of hardworking American people having fun, telling their stories, whether they are sassy or sad, mad or glad.

TV is *the* great medium for the live presentation of folk music. Here we've got the greatest live music in the world. It's a godamned shame that nobody is presenting it right.

Summer 1963

Bess Hawes writes from Santa Monica:

". . . I am currently all involved with Bessie Jones and the four other singers she has with her. They were brought out here by a cafe owner in San Diego who thought all he had to do was sign them to a contract, write all the college concert people, and sit back and watch the dollars roll in. The result, of course, is that they are all sitting here broke, with no work except sporadic jobs here and there, and the rent piling up back home. Why in the dickens do people think that managing is such a snap? I am so tired of coping with this sort of thing. Ed Pearl has come through like a trouper, though, and we may be able to salvage some of the wreckage and at least not send them back home completely bitter. The group itself is marvelous; I come away from hearing them with a new appreciation of the dignity of man."

The Copyright Hassle

December 1963

THE SECRETARY at Columbia Records was taking down over the phone the names of the authors and publishers of various songs I had recorded on a recent album. When I came to the title "Barbara Allen" I said, "Public domain."

"Oh, thanks," was her surprised and pleased voice.

I told a friend about it afterward. "Of course Columbia's happy," he said. "You just gave them a thousand dollars by not claiming copyright control for your arrangement and adaptation of 'Barbara Allen.' I not only think you're a fool, I think you're wrong. Columbia has no right to that money. Columbia didn't write 'Barbara Allen.' "

Here we get right down to the nitty-gritty.

Face it: the reason so many arguments come now about the pros and cons of copyrighting folk songs is that money *is* being made from them. "If he gets all that money, why shouldn't I?" Back in the thirties, when no one was making money out of folk music, this argument never came up.

It has often weighed on my conscience that I could make money singing at a concert, while the people who taught me the songs, or perhaps arranged or even wrote them, were as broke as ever. From time to time I have sent money, unsolicited, to some person whose song I have used a great deal. But charity is never a solution to the problem.

I have also referred publishers to the collector whenever I know of the original collector. But sometimes it is difficult to determine who collected what and with which and from whom.

The International Folk Music Council has an established principle that folk songs should be copyrighted by the collector and the informant. But the IFMC failed to set rules to decide who is the collector and who the informant, and what to do if two collectors collect the same song from two different informants.

Let's examine the roots of this term "ownership." "We *have* what we enjoy," wrote Emerson. And a child who uses a rattle calls it "*my* rattle." Lincoln has been quoted to the effect that the product of a man's mind should be his to control as much as any solid property. And even the communistic American Indian considered the deer he'd killed to be his property till he later shared it with the rest of the tribe. A booking agent or manager says, "This is my singer. I discovered him. You cannot hire him unless I get a 20 percent cut." Why can't a collector of folk songs say, "This is my song. I discovered it. You can't use it without giving me a 2 percent cut."

The rub is that the agent's contract runs out in 5 years. The copyright law permits ownership to last for 56 years. Another rub: two folklorists can collect the same song.

Last year I wrote to a number of leading folk song collectors to get their opinion on the copyright situation. Most of them passed the buck to their publishers, or threw up their hands, saying it was impossible of solution. One collector, more forthright than the rest, came right out and compared the situation to that of a national park being abandoned by the government and sold to the first claimers. If he didn't get in there and claim ownership of a song he collected, it would be only a matter of time before a New York performer of folk music, his manager, and publisher stepped in to copyright it and begin collecting "author's royalties" from record companies. There's gold in them hills. "We might as well get ours."

An idea I once had was to set up a "Folk Song Research Fund," to which could be given money received for songs I've copyrighted* to which I've added but a small amount. For example, I made an English translation of the Norwegian song "Oleanna." After I sang it through the country, a number of others started singing it. One quartet made a Decca recording and claimed all royalties. Since Decca was going to hand out royalties to someone (and why let Decca keep the money?), my publisher undertook to collect them for me.

However, less than half the song is my work (the rest being a traditional tune and words composed in 1843). Over the years I've tried as best I could to channel such income back to the original folk performers, or in some other direction which might help keep folk music alive and growing.

Of course, the problem is fundamentally insoluble under free enterprise. All one can hope for is that the situation may be improved slightly. Consider: one wrong word or note can ruin a song. Also, one right word or note can change a poor song to a good one. The person who adds that one note can claim that his contribution gives him the right to receive all royalties from his version of the song. Perhaps he is right. Who is to say? My father, Charles Seeger, wrote this:

Perhaps the Russians have done the right thing, after all, in abolishing copyright. It is well known that conscious and unconscious appropriation, borrowing, adapting, plagiarizing, and plain stealing are variously, and always have been, part and parcel of the process of artistic creation. The attempt to make sense out of copyright law reaches its limit in folk song. For here is the illustration par excellence of the Law of Plagiarism. The folk song is, by definition and, as far as we can tell, by reality, entirely a product of plagiarism.

(I usually figure a song that I compose is like a child: mine to control only as long as it sticks around the house. When it goes out into the world, it grows and has a life of its own, or maybe dies. I'm glad to collect royalties when someone records it, of course, and I'll fight to prevent it from being bowdlerized or emasculated. But in the long run, it is those who listen to the song throughout the world who will decide which version will last, and which will be forgotten.

---

* Sometimes songs have been copyrighted in my name without my knowing it. For example, "On Top of Old Smoky" appeared in sheet music with the by-line, "New words and music by Pete Seeger"—quite untrue. The Weavers' publisher was responsible. I wrote to the Library of Congress to try and erase the mistake. No soap.

(But let's get back to talking about public-domain folk songs.)

Face it: even with all the money being made out of folk music now, there is less collecting being done than before. And it's very much needed. The sporadic amateurs with tape machines can't do the job adequately. We need trained folklorists who know what they are looking for and where to look for it. But the government is no longer paying for collecting (even in the thirties this was ridiculed as "boondoggling"). University grants for collecting are few and far between. Recording companies are no longer sending equipment into small towns and advertising for country singers, as they did in the 20s. No publisher I know of is spending the kind of money needed for field trips. Collectors should get money from the songs they collect until the day they get it elsewhere.

The copyright hassle is not too different from a lot of problems we face in our modern world. Many, confronted with a bad situation, will throw up their hands and say it's unsolvable unless you change the whole system of society. But this attitude often results in nothing being done.

Meanwhile you have to be a practicing schizophrenic in this world. You have to work to lay the foundations for a better world, because you know that only in a more just society can some of these problems really be solved. But you also have to make do as best you can in the present world. I kidded a New York City settlement-house worker once with the famous quote, "Social work is a Band-Aid on the festered ass of democracy." But he seriously countered: "I'll agree. But I'm not going to throw up my hands. I'm going to keep putting on Band-Aids and putting on Band-Aids. I don't refuse to sweep the floor even if I do live in a tenement where the dirt seeps out of every crack."

I'd like to suggest here a couple of measures which I think would help keep down such things as New Yorkers changing five words in an old Alabama song and then collecting royalties on it based on "New words and music by . . . ," etc.

1. Pass a law saying that all recording companies should pay two cents per song per record into a PD (public domain) fund for any PD song on the record (to be used, say, for the Library of Congress to finance collecting). This way someone who unjustly claims copyright is not taking from Columbia Records; he's stealing from the PD fund which is being used to collect new folk songs.

2. Someone who copyrights a version of a folk song after making slight changes in it can keep others from making further changes in his version for only 5 years instead of 56.

3. The PD fund should have a right to sue people who unjustly claim copyright control over folk songs.

In the absence of such a law, record companies, publishers, and performers who copyright folk songs, or otherwise make money from them, should contribute some very small percentage to a fund (possibly sponsored by the American Folklore Society) to finance research and, in general, help keep folk music alive. A "seal of contribution" could be awarded to appear on record labels, sheet music, concert programs, etc., in recognition of this contribution. The aim should be to put firms and individuals on the defensive if they are not able to display the seal. Like the union label.

Some day human beings will not need to scrabble so meanly over pennies, and then we can simply say, "A good song is the precious possession of the people; a poor song is not worth the paper it is written on."

Regulations of the Copyright Office of the Library of Congress concerning "new versions" of public domain and/or previously copyrighted works.

1. New Versions

Under the copyright law (Title 17 of the United States Code) a new version of a work in the public domain, or a new version of a copyrighted work which has been produced by the copyright owner or with his consent, shall be copyrightable as a "new work." Copyrightable "new works" include compilations, abridgments, adaptations, arrangements, dramatizations, translations, and works republished with new matter.

The copyright in a new version covers only the additions, changes, or other new material appearing for the first time in the work. There is no way to restore copyright protection for a work in the public domain, such as including it in a new version. Likewise, protection for a copyrighted work cannot be lengthened by republishing the work with new matter.

2. Reprints

The Copyright Office has no authority to register claims to copyrights in mere reprints. In order to be copyrightable, a new version must either be so different in substance from the original as to be regarded as a "new work" or it must contain an appreciable amount of new material. This new material must also be original and copyrightable in itself. When only a few slight variations or minor additions of no substance have been made, or when the revisions or added material consist solely of uncopyrightable elements, registration is not possible.

The Copyright Office considers the information contained on the application form in determining registrability, and makes no attempt to compare the version submitted with any earlier version of the work.

3. Compilations and Abridgments

Any work, to be copyrightable, must be the "writing of an author." Thus, compilations and abridgments may be copyrighted only if authorship is involved in their preparation. When the assembling of a "compilation" is a purely mechanical task without any element of editorial selection or when the preparation of an "abridgment" involves only a few minor changes or deletions, registration would not be authorized.

Is There a Blacklist in U. S. Television?

1963

MOST PERFORMERS do not go out of their way to tell of their blacklist problem, if they have one. It doesn't help their careers any. Also, they may be accused of trying to make martyrs of themselves. However, I'm convinced that the over-all situation is one that ought to be better known by the American people.

About 1955 a young friend of mine told me he was going to get a job in the casting department of one of the big television networks.

"See if you can find out something of how the blacklist operates," I asked him.

"Oh, don't be ridiculous," he replied. "I'm sure there's no such thing as a blacklist in TV. It would be illegal."

A couple of months later I met him again, and with a somewhat crestfallen face he said, "I'm afraid you're absolutely right. When I select the actors I want to have in a dramatic show there is an extension number I'm supposed to call to find out if the actors are 'available.' I don't know where in the building this telephone is that I'm calling. It may not even be in the building. But at any rate, after a few hours I get word back from the extension letting me know which actors, if any, are 'unavailable'—and I know perfectly well what that means."

Of course, that was eight years ago. My guess is that things have gotten considerably better since then. For one thing, a man named John Henry Faulk won a $3,000,000 damage suit against a professional blacklisting outfit known as "Aware, Incorporated." And since then the networks have been eager to insist that there is no such thing as a blacklist in existence.

The origin of the term "blacklisting" I don't know. I first read of it being used in the labor-union struggles of the late nineteenth century, such as those of the Molly Maguires in the Pennsylvania mining areas. It seems to have been common practice for employers to circulate among each other a list of known "agitators," to insure that they would not get a job in any similar mine or factory after they had been discharged from one. But the practice must be far older.

The emotions behind the practice of blacklisting certainly are ancient: people do not like to buy the product or labor of someone whose activities or opinions they despise. My grandmother would not keep a book by Owen Johnson in the house ("That man has had *five* wives!"), and a Jewish community center director told me he had wanted to buy a Volkswagen for a staff car, but too many members would have felt uncomfortable riding in this product of Nazi engineering.

This kind of boycotting may be spontaneous or organized—principled or purely emotional. But when we speak of a blacklist we usually mean that substantial economic power is being wielded by a few people to attempt to control the actions and thoughts of many.

Today the term is used mainly in our part of the world to describe the difficulties in gaining employment for persons suspected of having "Communist" sympathies. It is most common in the radio-TV-movie field. Even here there is probably not one list, but many lists, of varying effectiveness. Those having only mild trouble with them are called "gray-listed."

The situation is full of illogical surprises, contradictions, paradoxes, and considerable humor. The work of European authors and artists such as Sean O'Casey, Picasso, or even G. B. Shaw, is not banned here—though if they were American citizens their sympathies or affiliations would have had them up before the HUAC long ago. Jules Dassin was blacklisted from Hollywood, but *Never on Sunday* becomes a hit in U. S. movie theaters. The Broadway and off-Broadway theater is full of authors blacklisted from Hollywood or radio. Often it seems as though the right hand doesn't know what the left hand is doing: *The New Yorker* Magazine has occasionally given me favorable reviews over the years, but in 1960 its advertising department told Folkways Records that it would not accept advertisements for my records.

Perhaps TV actually has no such thing as a "list." But it is a fact that anybody who participates in what might be called "controversial" activities, whether political or otherwise, will find himself kept off the U. S. television networks. Frank Lloyd Wright once said that there is nothing so timid as a million dollars. I guess the only thing more timid would be ten million dollars. And the TV networks have got hundreds of millions tied up in their operations, and naturally they don't want to endanger a cent of it.

American TV today is 99 percent white;* hardly ever are Negroes presented or is Negro life presented. Nor do we see other minorities fairly presented, whether American Indian, or the Mexican American of the Southwest. Or the Italians, or Ukrainians, or one hundred and one other minority groups. On the contrary, comedy shows and dramatic shows usually have clean, white Anglo-Saxons speaking "good" English. Only one or two different kinds of music get onto TV, only one or two different kinds of comedy, only one or two different kinds of melodrama. There are hundreds, yes, thousands, of minority tastes, whether in music or art or drama or sports, that never get a hearing on TV. Why not? Because the available hours are preempted by the highest bidder.

This is as big an outrage as if Yosemite Park was sold to the highest bidder, to put a big fence around the beautiful waterfalls and charge $4 for a ticket to come in and look at them, and sell hot dogs around the base.

Well, some will say that's neither here nor there, that this was supposed to be a story about blacklisting in TV. But it's all related. The fact is that there are lots of good people who are kept off of TV not because there's a blacklist but just because the sponsor figures that's not the way to make the most money. Nat King Cole was one of America's greatest singers, but he was never able to get his own TV show. Once, after a tremendous amount of pressure was put on the networks, he got a show. The network carried it unsponsored for a few weeks in the hopes that they would get a sponsor. When they were unable to get a national sponsor they dropped the show. Why did he get no national sponsor? The advertisers felt that if he had a national show they would lose some business in the southern states.†

As for me, I'm considerably luckier than most musicians. First of all, I make a good living from personal appearances. I would like to get on TV because I think folk music as an art form is well suited to that little screen. But I have yet to get any network jobs, at least in the States.** I've

---

* In 1970, 95 percent.
† Same for Dick Gregory in '68.
** As of 1963, when this article was written; in 1967 I started getting brief network guest appearances. The Smothers Brothers even fought for, and in the second round won, my chance to sing "Waist Deep in the Big Muddy" (*"and the Big Fool says to push on"*) to the TV audience. This song got the most explosive approval of any I have ever sung.

done some network TV in Canada, and I've done some local appearances in the States.

In Boston, in June 1963, I did a concert in the city park. Since it was free and well advertised in advance, they had somewhere between 35,000 and 45,000 people in the audience. And the local educational television station carried the whole two hours, from start to finish. So far as I know, they had only a few crank phone calls insulting them, and most of the people figured these calls came from the John Birch Society. They got a whale of a lot of phone calls and letters congratulating them for having such a long music program.

So I am confident that sooner or later I will be able to get on network television. I don't look upon the blacklist as an impregnable brick wall, but more like an old-fashioned stone wall. I'm poking around trying to find a chink in the wall, a loose stone, and I'm going to pry it out and get through somehow. It's a shame that the ABC-TV "Hootenanny" show is not better.* There are all kinds of wonderful traditional folk musicians who are being pointedly excluded from it—people like Doc Watson, Sonny Terry, Memphis Slim, Horton Barker, and many, many more. Real wonderful country traditional musicians, Negro and white. Instead, the program is using only a succession of well-polished city performers. Maybe the best thing you can say about them, though, is that they have broken the ice. Now the way is wide open for a decent folk music show to be put on American TV.

(*A 1968 footnote:*) After all is said and done, I suppose the blacklist is closely related to the problem of censorship, and is probably wrassled with in every corner of the globe. One is freest in talking to oneself or one or two others. One is less free if one rents a hall to speak to thousands or can afford to print words which will be read by thousands. And in the States today, if you are doing a TV show for an estimated 40-million audience they are damn careful to put the whole thing on video tape so it can be carefully screened first.

Back in the thirties, before tape recording was known, I heard a story about some Mississippi plantation owners as they sipped their mint

---

At all my concerts in 1968 it was a top request; I wasn't asked to sing it a second time on TV, though.

(The network didn't take long to lose patience with the Brothers' obstinate efforts to give their guests a free rein. In less than two years CBS exiled Tom and Dick—and slapped their 33 million listeners in the face—as cynically as any dictator.)

* 1963–64.

juleps. "You know," said one, "those Yankees wouldn't cause us so much trouble down here if they really knew how well we get along with our nigras. Take Uncle Mose. He's been with our family all his life. I love him and he loves me. You know what we ought to do? Let's raise some money and buy time on the radio network, and let those Yankees hear about it straight from his own mouth."

They made some phone calls to friends, raised the necessary cash, and arranged for a remote hookup. Uncle Mose was brought up to the big white house and shown the microphone.

"Uncle Mose, we've known each other fo'ty years, haven't we?"

"Yassuh, boss."

"And we've always gotten along together well, haven't we?"

"Oh, yassuh, boss. You know me."

"Well, Uncle Mose, we've got this microphone here, and people around the country are listening on their radios. You just step up and tell 'em in your own words what it's like here in Mississippi."

"You mean if I speak into that thing they'll hear me in California?"

"Yes!"

"Will they hear me in Washington?"

"Yes!"

Uncle Mose hesitantly shuffled over to the microphone and grasped it in his hand. He opened his old lips, took a breath.

"HEEEEELLLP! ! !"

December 1964

THE COUNTRY seems to be full of ambitious young people with guitars in their hands. I get letters every week asking, "How can I get started as a folk singer?"

I used to beg off, protesting that I was no one to hand out advice. I was singing for the fun of it for twenty years before anyone paid me for singing. And then, I sang for another ten years for five- and ten-dollar bills, and, very occasionally, for a big fee like fifty dollars.

Only in the last five years have I been able to turn down work, during summer vacation, for example, so I can spend more time with my family.

I guess I feel like urging people who would like to spend their lives making music not to be in too much of a hurry to make money from it.

It is true that artists must eat, but if you are in too great a hurry about eating, sometimes the art isn't so good. You can make the same kind of mistakes as the girl of sixteen who is overanxious to marry.

Consider, also, that if you really enjoy making music, you are liable to enjoy it for many years longer if you keep it for a hobby and do not make it your profession.

But, if you love people as well as love music, okay. 1964 is a good time to start. It's an expanding market, and there are jobs. Get a friend with a tape recorder to help you make a few small audition tapes, and start mailing them around. Ask for honest criticism, rather than a polite turndown.

Meanwhile, sing for as many different kinds of audiences as you can. Experiment widely. Duck down a dozen blind alleys and duck back out again. Sing for hospitals and veterans' homes, orphanages, golden-age clubs, indoors, outdoors, in small and big places, for rich and poor, drunk and sober. Summer camps are often good for a job. The pay is not astronomical, but it is sometimes adequate. The worst hazard here is that you can very easily get hoarse. But learning how to pace yourself so you don't strain your voice is one of the most important things a singer can learn. So, in this respect, a summer camp is as good a training ground as a saloon. (Saloons are good experiences, too; Woody Guthrie used to advise young singers to try them.)

All this will force you to experiment with different kinds of songs and different kinds of idioms and approaches. How can you decide what path you want to follow if you can't poke around a bit and see what the various paths are like? After a few years, you'll have a couple of hundred songs stored in your memory, and will have the know-how to fit the right song to the right occasion. (Is it hard? It's always hard to do something well, and that goes for baking a cake or teaching a class. Any fool can do something sloppily, and some can even get away with it for a few years and make a living at it.)

The biggest mistake you could make would be to think you have to "make it" quick while you're young, while the fad is on. Quick fame can be one of the headiest of poisons, and the aftereffects are rough, to say the least.

I hope you don't take all this as an attempt to discourage you from being a musician. On the contrary, I feel like urging every talented person I know to take up the profession. The world is full of human beings who live in little boxes and don't know about each other, and you can teach them and encourage them more freely than perhaps with any other art form. Novelists need publishers, actors need theaters, composers need orchestras, and painters need galleries, sculptors need warehouses—but all you need are some songs in your head, a guitar in your hands, and people with ears to listen.

True, it's a rough life. Like a gambler, you'll not be sure from month to month what your future will bring. It's hell on trying to raise a family. It is so hard on the health (irregular sleep, irregular food) that a person in poor health usually can't keep up with it.

But the things you'll see! The people and places, and most of all, the warm feeling that you've raised somebody's spirits and helped them "keep on keeping on" (see Len Chandler's song). Go to it.

February 1966

The Arrival of "Folk Rock"

POPULAR MUSIC did not start "borrowing from folk music" with the Weavers. The Andrews Sisters sang "Bei Mir Bist Du Sheyn" in the 1940s. W. C. Handy wrote "St. Louis Blues" in the twenties. Minstrel-show banjo tunes of the nineteenth century were mostly imitations of the older, more honest, plantation music. The topical broadsides of eighteenth-century London swiped older folk melodies to carry their verses. Commercial musicians in the marketplaces of medieval cities swiped ideas from peasant music of the countryside as well as from the orchestra in the duke's castle.

Because most of these pop musicians were concerned with making a buck, of course they turned out a lot of hack work. They were neither worried by the "high artistic aims" of the trained composers, nor had they the simple honesty of the country musicians who only made music for the fun of it and the love of it. But pop musicians have also created some fine music: witness "Greensleeves," "Old Dan Tucker," and the works of Duke Ellington. This is all pop music—and great stuff, too.

We should not be surprised that the pop process is still going on. Now the word "folk" is being taken over for whatever money it can make. What should we do, we who over the years have come to realize the variety, the artistry, the honesty of the many kinds of folk music in our land?

1. Fight to see that the many "minority" forms of music are not stamped out just because any one idiom becomes suddenly popular and saturates the airwaves.

2. Strive that local people are not ashamed of their local traditions, and different national and racial groups are not ashamed of their national and racial traditions.

3. Don't waste time fighting pop music *per se*. Who knows—the electrified guitar may prove to be the most typical folk instrument of the twenty-first century. But we can continue to ridicule the worthless hack songs, and if we want, continue to sing the occasional good ones.

4. Fight to see that any idiom, when and if it is suddenly popularized, is not debased or prostituted, as often happens.

5. Above all, strive to persuade the average citizens that they can like what they like, and that they can ignore the fashions of the day—which usually change for no better reason than rapid obsolescence is profitable. We don't have to be swamped by mass-manufactured culture if we don't want to. We can make our own music, new or old, loud or soft, electric or unamplified, plain or fancy, sad or silly. It may not be profitable, but it will be our own.

June 1967

SOMEONE SAID to me after a concert, "I'm so glad you haven't gone commercial." I had to disillusion her. "I've been commercial for a long time. In fact, you probably would never have heard me sing if I hadn't been." Still, I know how she felt. But you have to work out a balance.

I'll admit that once upon a time I was highly against the idea of "building up a career." Sang anywhere and everywhere for all sorts of causes. Never expected, nor particularly wanted to try and get jobs or publicity in the mass media.

In 1949 I was helping edit the *People's Songs Bulletin* when Irwin Silber, in the same office, received a phone call from the American Labor Party in Brooklyn. They needed his help in locating a friend of mine, a well-known performer of folk songs. They wanted to run a concert series to raise some money for the organization.

"Well, perhaps I can help you get him," says Irwin. "But in case he can't make it, how about getting Pete Seeger to do the concert for you?" "Oh, we know Pete," came the answer, "he's sung on our soundtrucks and parties for years. But we need someone who can bring in a mass audience. We need to raise money."

When Irwin put down the phone and told me the conversation, I started doing some hard rethinking about my own work. Here I'd been knocking myself out all these years, congratulating myself on not "going commercial," and the result was that I was not as much use to the Brooklyn ALP as was my friend, a highly conscientious and hardworking artist, but one who also set out in a more conventional fashion to build a Career. He could bring in a big audience for them. I couldn't.

Later that year I started working hard with the Weavers, and we took the drastic step of getting a job in a nightclub, and the following spring had a hit record, "Goodnight Irene," selling two million copies. (We also got ourselves saddled at first with a manager who wouldn't *let* me sing for the Brooklyn ALP.) During the next two years we saw the glorious and the seamy sides of the commercial music business: the promotions, the phony advertising, with the artist as a highly publicized but obedient employee of people who really have very little interest in music.

Fortunately, now I'm more or less my own boss, and I can decide for myself how I've got to tack or jibe through this world. As my sister Peggy once remarked, there's a difference between going commercial and selling out. I hope, with help, I'll be able to draw that line myself. In a sense, the task is made easier these days by my being attacked by the John Birch Society and by Billy Hargis' self-styled Christian Crusade. Of course, it's no fun to be lied about and know that ignorant people are actually being taken in by their lies. But one learns things one might not learn any other way. Benjamin Franklin said: "Love your enemies, for they point out to you your faults."

1968

In ancient Arabia it was customary for poets to comment upon events of the day. If a king put a gifted poet on his payroll and attached him to the court, it was called "cutting off the tongue of the poet." I think of this now I'm being offered occasional jobs on TV.

12·A Question of Patriotism

Definition of a left extremist:

Someone who stands up to defend the Bill of Rights, the Declaration of Independence, and the Sixth Commandment (Thou Shalt Not Kill).

THIS CHAPTER really must start with a plug for an extraordinary book published in 1967, *Rhythm, Riots, and Revolution* by Rev. David A. Noebel. It can be ordered for $1.00 from Christian Crusade Publications, Box 977, Tulsa, Oklahoma.

The gist of the book is: The international Communist conspiracy is out to conquer America by any means it can. Rhythm is hypnotic. People can be hypnotized into supporting communism. Many songwriters and performers, including one Pete Seeger, have "performed for Communist causes." Therefore it follows: Rhythmic folk music, rock and roll, etc., including the Beatles, are all part of a devilishly organized international Communist plot to brainwash the U.S.A.

You'd have to read the book to believe it. Sad to say, some people do believe it, word for word. On the cover I saw,

Workingmen of all tongues unite—you have nothing to lose but your chains— you have a world to win. Vive la Revolution Sociale.—Pete Seeger

I read the lines with amazement. It's just not my style. When did I write or say that? Finally on page 127 I find the sentence, "In Seeger's book *American Favorite Ballads* we are boldly confronted with, 'Workingmen . . .'"

Still I was mystified. I pulled the songbook from the shelf, leafed through it. Suddenly, on the page with the old union song "We Shall Not

Be Moved," I see that my publisher picked an appropriate illustration, a line drawing of a pre-World War 1 Socialist banner carrying the slogan quoted.

And the rest of the quotes in the book, all footnoted, are just about as accurate.

"GO BACK TO RUSSIA! KIKES! NIGGER-LOVERS!" shouted the crowd at Peekskill, New York, in 1949.

In 1967, outside the concert hall in New Haven, picket signs proclaimed: "Don't Support Commie Singers," and "Seeger Is Khrushchev's Songbird." The leaflets they handed out used identical phrases I had seen in leaflets passed out in San Diego and in Palm Beach—". . . identified Communist in sworn testimony . . ."

I don't usually bother arguing. I'd rather just go on making the best music I know how. Sensible people will draw their own conclusions, and all the breast beating is a waste of time. But perhaps this chapter will give some needed information.

I

IN 1948, liberals and left wingers, wanting to put an end to the Cold War and return to Franklin Roosevelt's policies, tried to get Henry Wallace elected President. The People's Songs organization did its best to help them. Some of the ex-New Dealers staffing the office of the Progressive party in New York arranged to have me sing for the convention and before the speeches at a string of large rallies. Some of the crowds ranged up to 50,000. The whole campaign has been written up by Curtis McDougall in his book *Gideon's Army*. I'll just mention one rather exciting trip.

Wallace set aside a week to speak in southern states. At Winston-Salem, North Carolina, the police let some people get away with throwing eggs at him. As soon as they found they could get away with it, Ku Kluxers showed up at each rally, armed for business. Wallace was in real physical danger, but refused to consider canceling the tour.

Our motorcade came to a small country town. Four hundred angry white men were waiting for him. Not a black face was to be seen. Somehow the main police guard and most of the motorcade had got separated from us. Wallace bravely tried to speak, but couldn't be heard for the booing. The lone policeman said, "Mr. Wallace, I can't hold this crowd; you better leave."

Wallace got in his car with his aides and moved off. I and some newspaper reporters were in the only other car, trying to push through the crowd. One reporter almost got left behind. He was no friend of Wallace, but the crowd considered him another damyankee. "Wait for me!" he screamed with fear, and got in the car, white-faced.

In November the votes were counted. It was obvious: many people had found themselves in the booth reluctantly choosing the lesser of two evils. Truman beat Dewey. Wallace got only a million votes.

A few weeks later I was to be on a small New York TV children's show, my first commercial TV job. A sharp-faced man glanced at me as I waited in the lobby. In a few minutes the director came out and said he was sorry but plans had been changed and there was no room for me on the program. I found out months later that the sharp-faced man had been the owner of the station. "What's that young fellow doing in the lobby? He's the sonofabitch who was singing at the Wallace convention. Get him out of here."

"The Peekskill riot?" asked the young New Zealander in 1968. "I think I once heard about that. Wasn't there a recording about it, or a book?"

In September 1949 the baritone Paul Robeson was asked to give an outdoor concert near Peekskill, about forty miles north of New York City. Although he was an internationally famous star, he had been under attack because of his outspoken opinions. In Paris he had said that American Negroes would refuse to fight against the USSR, as it was the one nation which had outlawed race discrimination. In Peekskill there had been talk of opposition to his concert.

Pianist Leonid Hambro and I had been asked to do a few numbers in the first half of the concert. But when I and my mother drove up that evening, the roads near the concert area were impossibly jammed with cars and we could not get near. I hailed a state trooper: "I'm one of the performers on tonight—can you help me get through?"

He gave me a peculiar look, but only said, "The concert has been called off. It's impossible for anyone to get through." After vainly trying to get ahead, I managed to make a U-turn on the narrow road and drove home. Next day we learned that an American Legion mob had got to the site early, had overturned stage and equipment, had beaten up some of the young people preparing things, including a pregnant woman.

Robeson and those arranging the concert said that this is America and the concert would be put on the next week. They would not be intimidated. Next Saturday afternoon, a lovely sunny day, several thousand cars were parked in the large field, and a huge audience listened to a great concert. Bodyguards stood close by Robeson, as there had been threats on his life. A crowd of 300 ignorant people stood near the entrance to the field shouting epithets: "Go back to Russia! Kikes! Nigger-lovers!" But they were not allowed on the field. A thousand staunch union members from Local 65, New York, stood shoulder to shoulder around the entire field, to make sure no one broke in to cause a disturbance.

When the concert was over, we all congratulated ourselves that things had gone smoothly. But the cars seemed to leave very slowly. When our car—a station wagon, carrying my wife, two babies, their grandfather, and two friends—pulled out of the gate, the policeman would not let us turn left or go straight ahead. He directed all traffic down one narrow road, several miles to a parkway. The crowd of 300 was still shouting insults, but we breathed easier and turned right and picked up speed.

Suddenly we saw a lot of broken glass on the road. "Uh-oh. Watch out," said I. Sure enough, up ahead were young men with piles of fist-sized stones heaving them at every car that passed. "Crash, klunk!"—we got it. Only a hundred feet away was a policeman. "Officer, aren't you going to do something about this?"

"Move on! Keep moving!" he shouted angrily. Our car was holding up traffic and the cars in back of us were getting it worse.

I started up again, but in the next two miles ten or fifteen rocks hit us. Every window in the car was broken. Being tall, I sat as straight and high as possible; the glass flew around below my eye level. Everyone else ducked low. Fortunately no one was more than slightly cut. Only three stones actually came through the plate glass. (I cemented them into a fireplace for mementos.)

We were told later that down near New York, gangs of men threw more rocks at any cars passing with smashed windows. And a bus full of Negroes who had not even been to Peekskill but had been visiting Roosevelt's home at Hyde Park, was stoned as it drove through Westchester County on the way back to the city.

Many of my friends assumed that American fascists were ready to take over the country. Signs were put in car windows throughout Peekskill: "Wake Up America, Peekskill Did!"

But here's the interesting thing. After about three weeks these signs disappeared. I rather suspect that in many homes there were arguments. "You mean you threw rocks at women and children? Well, I don't like Commies any more than you do, but still you don't throw rocks at women and children."

Years later I met a young man who had become a popular guitar picker in coffee houses. When he knew me well, he said, "You know, that riot was all arranged by the Ku Klux Klan and the police. I was living in Peekskill; my father was a police official. They had walkie-talkies all through the woods. They had that place surrounded like a battlefield."

II

IT IS A FACT well known to old-timers that the U.S. folk song revival was spearheaded in the Dirty Thirties by New Dealers and left-wingers. (Leadbelly sang for $10 at houseparties raising money for loyalist Spain when no one else would hire him.) This fact has seemed very confusing to young people who came along in a rush of enthusiasm for this favorite new music of theirs and then heard it accused of being subtle Communist propaganda.

As the years went by, some individual performers made their peace with the Congressional committees. Others managed to ignore the situation, or dodge. In 1955 yours truly, after a family conference, decided the best thing was to meet the House Un-American Activities Committee head on.

The HUAC and similar inquisitions hurt America a great deal.* Our

---

* The Un-Americans, by Frank J. Donner (Ballantine Books, New York, 1961), documents HUAC's almost total failure to serve a legislative function—or any function except that of stifling free speech and free opinion. Unfortunately this book is out of print; but it may be consulted in libraries.

If anyone is interested in the legal intricacies of my own experience, the documentation is as follows:

Hearings before the Committee on Un-American Activities, House of Representatives, 84th Congress, 1st Session: Investigation of Communist Activities, New York Area (Entertainment), August 15–18, 1955.

United States District Court, Southern District of New York: USA vs. Peter Seeger, March 27, 1961.

United States Court of Appeals for the Second Circuit, No. 27, 101, USA vs. Peter Seeger; Defendant-Appellant's Brief.

United States Court of Appeals for the Second Circuit: No. 293 September Term, 1961 (Argued April 9, 1962, Decided May 18, 1962) Docket No. 27101.

EINSTEIN RALLIES DEFENSE OF RIGHTS

In Replies on Eve of His 75th Birthday He Advocates Resistance to 'Inquisition'

By WILLIAM L. LAURENCE
Special to THE NEW YORK TIMES.

PRINCETON, N. J., March 13—Prof. Albert Einstein today urged all intellectuals "to refuse to cooperate in any undertaking that violates the constitutional rights of the individual."

This, he said, "holds in particular for all inquisitions that are concerned with the private life and the political affiliations of the citizens." He added a warning that "whoever cooperates in such a case becomes an accessory to acts of violation or invalidation of the Constitution."

Professor Einstein made these declarations of his beliefs in written replies to five questions on civil liberties and academic freedom submitted to him by the Emergency Civil Liberties Committee. The questions and answers were made public here today at a conference on "the meaning of academic freedom,"

held under the auspices of the committee in honor of Dr. Einstein's seventy-fifth birthday anniversary tomorrow.

Two hundred persons attended the all-day conference. The speakers included Corliss Lamont, who was denied a passport in 1951 as an alleged member of Communist-front organizations; Mary Van Kleeck, former director of studies, Russell Sage Foundation, who has been cited by Congressional committees as an alleged member of sixty Communist-front groups; I. F. Stone, former columnist for The Daily Compass; Prof. Dirk Struik, mathematician, who was accused by witnesses before the House Un-American Activities Committee of having been a member of a Communist "cell" at the Massachusetts Institute of Technology, and Harvey O'Connor, author, who last year was indicted for contempt of Congress for having invoked the First Amendment when asked by the Senate Investigating subcommittee if he were a member of the Communist conspiracy.

Although Professor Einstein agreed to answer questions, he declined to appear in person and refused to allow a delegation to deliver flowers to his door on his birthday tomorrow. He was quoted as saying: "You may bring flowers to my door when the last witch-hunter is silenced, but not before."

One of the questions was: "What in your opinion are the special obligations of an intellectual in a free society?"

"In principle," Dr. Einstein replied, "everybody is equally involved in defending the constitutional rights. The 'intellectuals,' in the widest sense of the word, are, however, in a special position since they have, thanks to their special training, a particularly strong influence on the formation of public opinion.

"This is the reason why those who are about to lead us toward an authoritarian government are particularly concerned with intimidating and muzzling that group. It is, therefore, in this situation especially important for the intellectuals to do their duty.

"I see this duty in refusing to cooperate in any undertaking that violates the constitutional rights of the individual."

Another question was: "What in your view are the particular responsibilities of a citizen at this time in the defense of our traditional freedoms as expressed in our Bill of Rights?"

"The strength of the Constitution," Dr. Einstein replied, "lies entirely in the determination of each citizen to defend it. Only if every single citizen feels duty bound to do his share in this defense are the constitutional rights secure. Thus, a duty is imposed on everyone which no one must evade, notwithstanding the risks and dangers to him and his family."

The New York Times, *March 14, 1954*

reputation throughout the world suffers when citizens in other countries read in their papers about Americans being pilloried or jailed for their opinions. If one truly loves America, one should try to put inquisitors out of business.

To explain why these committees harm America can't be done in two or three words. The newspaper headlines of decades have to be rebutted. Perhaps one of the best ways they can be rebutted is to tell a detailed and specific story about one person.

The Committee on Un-American Activities of the U. S. House of Representatives subpoenaed me in 1955. I answered some questions—such as my name and address—but refused to answer other questions, such as who did I know, and where and when did I ever sing. I didn't use the Fifth Amendment.

I stated that I didn't want to cast any aspersions on people who had used the Fifth Amendment. I simply did not feel that I wanted to use it myself. As my lawyer explained it to me, using the Fifth Amendment is in effect saying, "you have no right to ask *me* this question"; but using the First Amendment means in effect, "you have no right to ask *any* American *such* questions." Since I felt I was in a strong enough position to make a broader attack upon the committee, I chose the second course. *

From testimony before the Committee on Un-American Activities, August 18, 1955, pp. 2448–49, 2452–53, 2457–58:

MR. TAVENNER: The committee has information obtained in part from the *Daily Worker* indicating that over a period of time, especially since December of 1945, you took part in numerous entertainment features . . .

MR. SEEGER: Sir, I refuse to answer that question whether it is a quote from *The New York Times* or the Vegetarian Journal . . . I am not going to answer any questions as to my associations, my philosophical or religious beliefs or my political beliefs, or how I voted in any election or any of these private affairs. I think these are very improper questions for any American to be asked, especially under such compulsion as this.

I would be very glad to tell you my life if you want to hear of it.

CHAIRMAN WALTER: What is your answer?

MR. SEEGER: I will tell you what my answer is. I feel that in my whole life I have never done anything of any conspiratorial nature, and I resent very much and very deeply the implication of being called before this committee that in some way, because my opinions may be different from yours, or yours, Mr. Willis, or yours, Mr. Scherer, that I am any less of an American than anybody else. I love my country very deeply, sir.

CHAIRMAN WALTER: Why don't you make a little contribution toward preserving its institutions?

MR. SEEGER: I feel that my whole life is a contribution, that is why I would like to tell you about it.

CHAIRMAN WALTER: I don't want to hear about it.

---

* The Fifth Amendment prohibits forcing anyone to testify against himself. (The times when torture for this purpose was customary were fresh in the memory of our Founding Fathers; they believed that to sanction any kind of pressure for confession meant risking a return of those tyrannical times.)

The First Amendment protects (in addition to freedom of religion, speech, and press) the right to assemble and to petition the government—in other words, to form political associations without asking anyone's approval.

MR. TAVENNER: I want to know whether or not you were engaged in a . . . service to the Communist party in entertaining. . . .

MR. SEEGER: I have sung for Americans of every political persuasion, and I am proud that I never refuse to sing to an audience, no matter what religion or color of their skin, or situation of life. I have sung in hobo jungles, and I have sung for the Rockefellers, and I am proud that I have never refused to sing for anybody . . . because I disagreed with their political opinion, and I am proud of the fact that my songs seem to cut across and find perhaps a unifying thing, basic humanity.

MR. TAVENNER: There are various peace groups in the country which have utilized your services, are there not?

MR. SEEGER: I have sung for pacifists and I have sung for soldiers. I would be curious to know what you think of a song like this very great Negro spiritual, "I'm Gonna Lay Down My Sword and Shield, Down by the Riverside."

MR. TAVENNER: That is not at all responsive to my question.

A year later I was cited for contempt of Congress (along with playwright Arthur Miller and economist Otto Nathan). A year after that I was indicted. In 1961 I finally was tried.

From Defendant's Opening Statement, U. S. District Court, March 27, 1961, pp. 45a, 47a–48a.

What was the nature of this investigation? . . . They said that it was Communist infiltration into the entertainment industry in New York. But they never defined what they meant by Communist infiltration. . . . A struggle took place in this AFTRA union between the people who favored blacklisting . . . and those who opposed the blacklist.

In the course of this struggle within this union this committee came to New York and went into this question of whether or not any of the witnesses whom it called were part of what they called a Communist caucus who were fighting blacklisting within the union.

Now, it is our contention that this had absolutely nothing to do with any question or any subject with which the Committee was concerned . . . but had merely to do with different sides of the union issue, and the Committee couldn't pass any legislation on this question, and, in fact, never proposed any legislation dealing with this question.

Peter Seeger was not charged at this hearing with being a member of the Communist party . . . Peter Seeger was asked where he sang, and what songs he sang, and three of the songs were mentioned. . . .

And Peter Seeger said, in answer to all these questions, "I have sung before all kinds of people, of all religions, of all political faiths. I have never tried to propagandize for Communism, or for anything else, and I challenge your rights. These questions are improper."

At the end of the trial the jury found me guilty of refusing to answer ten of HUAC's questions.

United States District Court, Southern District of New York, April 4, 1961, before Thomas F. Murphy, District Judge, pp. 279a–280a:

THE COURT: Mr. Seeger, do you have anything to say before I pass sentence on you?

DEFENDANT SEEGER: I do.

THE COURT: You may.

DEFENDANT SEEGER: Thank you very much, Your Honor. After having heard myself talked about pro and con for three days I am very grateful for the opportunity to say a few words, unrestricted words, myself.

Firstly, I want to thank my lawyer deeply for his masterly preparation and presentation of my defense. He has worked over long weeks and months, and done all this knowing that it is beyond my power to pay him adequately for his work.

I believe that he and great legal minds like Justice Hugo Black and Dr. Alexander Meiklejohn, and others, have stated far better than I can the reasons that they believe that the First Amendment gives an American citizen the right to refuse to speak upon certain occasions.

Secondly, I should like to state before this court, much as I stated before Congressman Walter's committee, my conviction that I have never in my life said or supported or done anything in any way subversive to my country.

Congressman Walter stated that he was investigating a conspiracy. I stated under oath that I had never done anything conspiratorial. If he doubted my word, why didn't he even question it? Why didn't he have me indicted for perjury? Because I believe even he knew that I was speaking the truth.

Some of my ancestors were religious dissenters who came to America over 300 years ago. Others more recently were abolitionists in New England in the 1840s and '50s, and I believe that in choosing my present course I do no dishonor to either them or to the people who may follow me.

I will be 42 years old next month and I count myself a very lucky man. I have a wife and three healthy children. We live in the house we built with our own hands on the bank of the Hudson River, a very beautiful place.

For over 20 years I have been singing folk songs of the American people and people of other lands to people everywhere. I am proud that I never refused to sing for any group of people because I might disagree with some of the opinions held by some of them.

I have sung for rich and poor, for Americans of every political and religious opinion and persuasion, for every race, color and creed.

The House Committee wanted to pillory me because it didn't like some few of the many thousands of places that I have sung. Now, it so happens that the specific song whose title was mentioned in this trial, "Wasn't That a Time," was not permitted to be sung at the time. It is one of my favorites. The song is apropos to this trial, and I wondered if I might have your permission to sing it here before I close.

THE COURT: You may not.

DEFENDANT SEEGER: Well, perhaps you will hear it some other time. A good song can only do good, and I am proud of the songs that I have sung. I hope to be able to continue to sing them for all who want to listen to me, Republicans, Democrats, or Independents, for as long as I live.

Do I have a right to sing these songs? Do I have a right to sing them anywhere?

WASN'T THAT A TIME

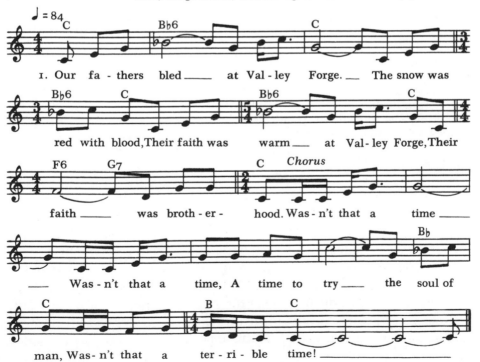

2. Brave men who died at Gettysburg
   Now lie in soldiers' graves,
   But there they stemmed the slavery tide,
   And there . . . the faith was saved.   (*Chorus*)

3. The fascists came with chains and war
   To prison us in hate,
   And many a good man fought and died
   To save the stricken faith.   (*Chorus*)

4. And once again the madmen came,
   And should our vict'ry fail?
   There is no vict'ry in a land
   When free men go to jail.

   Chorus:

   Isn't this a time!
   Isn't this a time!
   A time to try the soul of man,
   Isn't this a terrible time!

5. Our faith cries out, we have no fear,
   We dare to reach our hand
   To other neighbors far and near,
   To friends in every land.

   Chorus:

   Isn't this a time!
   Isn't this a time!
   A time to free the soul of man!
   Isn't this a wonderful time!

At the very beginning of my trial Irving Younger, the prosecuting attorney, had carefully pointed out that I was charged with contempt of Congress, *not* with being a Communist. Nevertheless, Judge Murphy invited me to say whether I was or not before he pronounced sentence.

Of course, my whole reason for being there was to contend that the Constitution stops *any* official from probing, under pressure, an American's private beliefs. I did not accept the judge's invitation.

He disagreed with my Statement to the Court and sentenced me to a year in jail; I was granted bail pending appeal.

The following year turned out to be a hectic one for our family. My wife assumed that because of my being convicted and sentenced to a year in jail, I would have many concert engagements canceled. So she accepted every booking that came in. As it turned out, not a single one was canceled. I was never so busy.

"Never again," said Toshi. "I was counting on you going to jail and getting some peace and quiet around here. Instead, all my plans for getting some of my own projects done had to be canceled. Next time I'll know better. No appeal."

A year later three judges of the U.S. Court of Appeals *did* agree with me and reversed the decision. They found that instead of a "clear, accurate, and unambiguous definition" of the subcommittee's authority, the indictment "contained a wholly misleading and incorrect statement of the basis of that authority. This not only runs afoul of the accepted notions of fair notice, but goes to the very substance of whether or not any crime has been shown."

Judge Irving R. Kaufman, who wrote this decision, added:

We are not inclined to dismiss lightly claims of constitutional stature because they are asserted by one who may appear unworthy of sympathy. Once we embark on shortcuts by creating a category of the "obviously guilty" whose rights are denied, we run the risk that the circle of the unprotected will grow.

(I remember these words sometimes, when I read complaints about the courts "coddling criminals," "shackling police," and so on. Do the complainers realize that what's at stake is *their* right to be treated as innocent till proven guilty—not just the rights of some wretched ghetto dweller? Hitler got his start by attacking Jews and Communists—there weren't enough Negroes around—but ended up turning Germany into a prison for most of the golden-haired "Nordics.")

I was disappointed that the decision dealt only with the defects of the indictment, and not specifically with the First Amendment rights of witnesses.* The Government attorneys complained that the reversal of my conviction was based on a "technicality." So I waited for them to seek a new indictment which would correct this technical slip-up and "properly allege" HUAC's right to conduct such hearings and ask Americans such questions.

But instead, after many months, the Department of Justice announced that my case was closed—leaving me free to deduce that in the end even they felt unable to justify these proceedings under what Judge Kaufman called "the transcending principles embodied in our Constitution and protected by our law."

III

OF COURSE, acquittal in open court does not greatly impress the groups who share HUAC's view of "Americanism"† (a word, by the way, which the thirty-year-old committee never got around to defining). To quote Donner:

The committee cannot afford to leave the fate of its victims to chance. . . . To this end, it has perfected a system of collaboration with the Network of rightist organizations. Among the most prominent of these are: the American Legion, the Veterans of Foreign Wars, AWARE, Inc., the Christian Anti-Communist Crusade, the Daughters of the American Revolution, and the American Council of Christian Churches. . . .

The Network's members get access to the committee's files and dossiers. . . . Members of the Network visit the local newspapers to develop pressure

---

* "Seeger contends that his conviction should be reversed on several grounds. . . . Some of these contentions pertain to claimed violations of appellant's rights under the First and Fifth Amendments to the Constitution. However, we find it unnecessary to consider the merits of any of these arguments, except one: that the indictment was defective. . . ." (As we have seen in a number of Supreme Court decisions, the courts traditionally prefer not to rule on major questions of constitutionality if the particular case can be settled on lesser grounds.)

† Or "Security," the word that in 1969 has been borrowed from the Senate's less flamboyant investigators to rename the House committee and try to patch up its ragged reputation. (Security from what? New ideas? Free speech? Or—could it be—from the danger of not re-electing the Northern machine politicians, and the Southerners, chosen by a tiny fraction of their fellow citizens, who man this committee and keep it alive?

on employers. They personally write, call and visit private and public employers. They . . . write letters to the newspapers demanding the discharge of the unfriendly witnesses, pack board of education meetings called to discuss the fate of the teachers who were unfriendly witnesses, and organize telephone campaigns to force sponsors to fire performers and writers.*

I am far more lucky than most. The HUAC ruined the careers of many people. But my income comes from so many sources that they were not able to cut it off. From time to time, the hate groups do campaign to keep me out of an auditorium—sometimes successfully. But I have learned that many an American town has other citizens—whether liberals or authentic conservatives—who will indignantly insist on their right to think for themselves—to hear this music in person before judging how dangerous it might be.

In my home town of Beacon, New York, a campaign against me in 1965 was spearheaded by a local Catholic priest; but some lay Catholics did not agree with him and weren't afraid to say so. They were average working people who knew Toshi and me from the PTA or because we shop in their stores.

In the first week of the campaign, several Birch types took a petition against the concert up and down Main Street, and got 700 signatures. If someone balked at signing, they'd look at him as though to say, "Well, what kind of a Commie are you?" If the person was a businessman, they'd threaten him with loss of business to force him to sign.

But since a few people were brave enough to speak up, a few more spoke up and by the third week a flow of support came toward me, including finally some of the most respected people in town.

The local school board and the teachers' association (which was sponsoring me) refused to cancel the concert. It was a case of simple civil liberties. They wanted to hear a concert and refused to pass judgment on my politics, whatever they might be.

By the night of the concert, the opposition admitted that they were not going to have a picket line. The high school auditorium was packed, and several hundred had to be turned away. It was a real singing crowd, all ages from little kids to octogenerians.

The battle was won not by any organized campaign but by the simple democratic traditions of a few ordinary Americans, both Republicans and Democrats.

---

* Frank J. Donner, *The Un-Americans*, pp. 30–31, 62–63. (Donner's description of the "Network" is substantiated by many pages of specific documented facts.)

Harry M. Allred, president of the Beacon Board of Education, wrote:

"It appears obvious from statements that have been made to the Board of Education and in the press that certain members of our community are asking the Board of Education to sit as a tribunal to judge an individaul within the community on the basis of ideas he has expressed or statements he has made. It is implied that the Board of Education should determine the right to use the public school facilities on the basis of whether or not an individual expresses opinions with which all other members of the community agree. The inherent danger of such an assumption is so obvious that it needs very little discussion. It is sufficient to say that those who are now petitioning the Board of Education would not be willing to have the Board determine their access to the public schools on the basis of whether their past opinions were in agreement with the opinions held by the Board of Education or with the opinions held by some particular group or segment of the community.

"Our legal and judicial structures—the laws and the courts—establish clear criteria and legal agencies for trying an individual and detrmining his right to participate in society. **The Board of Education should not and must not substitute itself for these legally established agencies.**

The Evening News (*Beacon*), *November 19, 1965*

A more long-drawn-out controversy, involving court action, took place in East Meadow, Long Island. (The concert was finally held a year after its originally scheduled date.)

Newsday (*Long Island*), *May 21, 1966* (My emphasis.)

Rabbi Raps Bar on Seeger Concert

By Arnold Abrams

Westbury — Westbury rabbi conducting sabbath services criticized the East Meadow school board last night for barring a Pete Seeger concert and suggested that the board probably would have banned Jesus and the prophet Isaiah because they, too, were controversial figures.

"If Pete Seeger is too controversial for East Meadow," said Rabbi Charles Kroloff of the Westbury Community Reform Temple, "then so was Isaiah and so is Jesus." If Jesus and Isaiah were alive today, he said, "they would probably try to preach in Moscow and Hanoi, and their utterances might resemble Seeger's."

In a departure from the usual services, cantor David Ferro sang four folk songs associated with Seeger and ended with the theme song of the civil rights movement. "We Shall Overcome." The 150 worshippers present joined enthusiastically in the singing.

The rabbi, noting the school board's claim that it feared the scheduled March 12 concert of the folk singer would result in disturbances, scored the group for advocating what he described as "a monolithic standard of education which is afraid of passion, yes, even of discord."

He added: "I do not send my children to school to learn how to be tranquil. I reject the philosophy of a school board that revokes permits because 'people may be disturbed.' " Seeger has been accused of harboring left wing sympathies.

When informed of the rabbi's sermon, Owen Walsh, president of the East Meadow school board, said that the board "has squared up to its moral responsibilities." He said that the board banned the Seeger concert because "we are responsible to 60,000 East Meadow residents and to the $32,000,000 plant we have." He said board members had feared the concert might lead to protest demonstrations that would result in property destruction. He added that the community had supported the board's action by reelecting the incumbent board members in recent school elections.

In an interview afterward at the temple at 275 Ellison Ave., Rabbi Kroloff said he had devoted his sermon to the Seeger issue because a portion of the services were dedicated to a group of youths about to be confirmed. "It is the children I am concerned about," he said. "This issue has broad implications for the intellectual climate of the community and the type of education the children receive. I do not believe that tranquility is a primary goal of our society. Communities have committed atrocities while their citizens remained tranquil."

E. Meadow Can't Ban Seeger: Top NY Court

Special to Newsday

Albany—The state's highest court ruled yesterday that in barring a performance last year by controversial folk singer Pete Seeger at W. Tresper Clarke High School, the East Meadow School Board acted unconstitutionally and improperly.

By a 6-1 margin, the Court of Appeals held that "The expression of controversial and unpopular views . . . is precisely what is protected by both the federal and state constitutions." The judges said that "there is no showing that Seeger's expression of his views would 'immediately and irreparably create injury to the public weal,'" and that the board's unlawful restriction of the constitutional right of free speech and expression."

The Court of Appeals decision affirmed a ruling of the Appellate Division last Oct. 7 giving the school board 20 days to reschedule the Seeger performance, which had been sponsored by the East Meadow Community Concert Association. On the 20th day, the board appealed to the Court of Appeals.

In yesterday's decision, the Court of Appeals said: "The record before us clearly establishes that the plaintiff (association) qualifies under the Education Law as an organization entitled to use the school facilities during out-of-school hours and that it was unconstitutional and improper for the defendant (school board) to deny the use of these facilities to the plaintiff solely because of the controversial views that had previously been expressed by the scheduled performer, Pete Seeger."

Newsday, *January 20, 1967*

It does not make me happy to be the occasion of rancor within any community; I have always sung in hopes of unifying people, not dividing them. But I don't mind being controversial, or being accused of singing controversial songs. The human race benefits when there is controversy and suffers when there is none.

It seems to me that any singer who values the future of his work and his children would want to feel that his work was helping to build world peace, and an early dismantling of all atom bombs, the burning of all military uniforms (or maybe weave 'em into rag rugs). Surely they must assume that this must come sooner or later. Are they willing to imagine closely the alternative?

A lullaby, a love song, a rip-roaring hoedown—these all tremble with love of life. Can we be so careless as not to try and figure out steps to insure Life's continuation?

IV

MARK SPOELSTRA has a song "Don't Label Me," and I go along with it. It's too easy and too untrue to call anyone these days some kind of an "ist."

Some labels I accept. I'm a musician. I'm married. I'm a U.S. citizen.

But in 1965 when I sang for 4,000 young Lutherans in California, and a group of ministers asked me, in the friendliest way, about myself, my philosophy, I was hard put to answer. I didn't want to hedge. But neither did I want to mislead by giving an oversimplified answer.*

"Mr. Seeger," one Lutheran said, "we have fought hard for you to come and sing for us; people said you were a Communist and that you should not be allowed to come. We heard your program and we liked it. But we are still curious. What, exactly, do you think of communism?"

Says I (if I can remember my words), "It all depends on what you call communism. Anthropologists say the first Americans—Indians—all lived in a state of tribal communism. The Birchers say Eisenhower is a Communist. There are groups of religious communists in Canada and America today."

"But we are asking about the Marxist communism of Russia and China, the world subversive conspiracy . . ."

I said I thought they would still have to be more clear. Not only the Russians and Chinese disagree violently on the definitions. There are a considerable number of people who call themselves Marxists who don't go along with either China or Russia.

"In general, I can't help thinking of the famous quote from H. L. Mencken: 'The only thing wrong with communism is the Communists, just as the only thing wrong with Christianity is the Christians.' It is one thing to write down an idealistic plan for world order, and another thing to try and put it into practice. My guess is that there is a lot that Russia and China can learn from the U.S.A., and a lot that the U.S.A. can learn from Russia and China. And all of us can learn from Africa."

"Mr. Seeger," says another, a little plaintively, "on Monday we found that our first speaker, Ann Landers, was Jewish. Our speaker on Tuesday,

---

* "No one should speak more clearly than he thinks." (Alfred North Whitehead)

we knew, was Catholic. Would you be able to tell us just *what* you are?"

"It is true I am not a Lutheran," says I, "although I have found during these last three days many points of agreement with what I have heard here at your convention. My family background is mostly Episcopalian, Unitarian, Quaker, etc. I am not a Catholic, although I enjoy singing for Catholics and I have also found many areas of agreement with them, as also I have found when I have sung for Jews.

"If I had to accept any kind of label, I'd call myself some kind of Naturalist, perhaps like the Swedenborgians—although I haven't read enough about it to know for sure. But I so admired the man Johnny Apple-seed, who was a Swedenborgian, that I named my magazine column after him. I'm not a vegetarian, but I do believe that Man must learn to live in harmony with nature or we shall destroy this earth and ourselves. I guess I'm about as Communist as the average American Indian was."

Beyond this, I can only say that whatever I believe in can be easily de-duced from my songs. Darn near a thousand different ones, during the last twenty-five years or more. My songs can't help but reflect my feelings about people, the world, peace, freedom, etc. I'm about as much a Communist as my songs are. I'm about as anti-Communist as my songs are. I am as right as my songs are. And as wrong.

I'm an ordinary person who has made many mistakes and will probably make more. But they have all been my own mistakes. Nobody has ever ordered me what I should think, or speak, or sing. But I have learned from all of you.

V

REREADING this chapter in 1968, I feel I was too damn polite. I wish I had stood up and shouted at that HUAC, as did Paul Robeson, "YOU ARE THE UNAMERICANS!"

It now is quite clear to millions that the America which Tom Paine and Jefferson fought to build, which Thoreau, Lincoln, Frederick Douglass, Mark Twain, and W. E. B. Du Bois tried to develop, is steadily being destroyed. Not only are the rivers, the air and streets polluted, but the gulf between rich and poor becomes wider, the gulfs between different sections of the population become wider.

MY DIRTY STREAM

By Peter Seeger. Copyright © 1964, 1965, Fall River Music, Inc.
All rights reserved. Used by permission.

2. At Glens Falls, five thousand honest hands
Work at the Consolidated Paper Plant
Five million gallons of waste a day—
Why should we do it any other way?
Down the valley one million toilet chains
Find my Hudson so convenient a place to drain
And each little city says, "Who, me?
Do you think that sewage plants come free?"

3. Out in the ocean they say the water's clear
But I live at Beacon here.
Halfway between the mountains and the sea,
Tacking to and fro, this thought returns to me:
Sailing up my dirty stream
Still I love it and I'll dream
That some day, though maybe not this year,
My Hudson River and my country will run clear.

And all the time the world's greatest medium of communication, that little magic screen, is preempted for irrelevance, is for sale only to the highest bidder.

For thirty years I assumed that the kind of songs I sang would be black-listed from the mass media. I was resigned to it. I am no longer. America does not have "all the time in the world" to solve its problems. The rulers of all our mass media must be blasted loose from their tight control; genuine controversy (not fake controversy) must be heard or there will be hell to pay.

These days I carry an egg-sized stone in my banjo case. Here's why. In April 1968, I got a phone call from a white-haired poet friend, John Beecher. He has a job as a consultant of some sort at Duke University in North Carolina, one of the richest and most respectable colleges in the nation.

"Pete, you've got to come down here. I've never seen anything like it on any southern campus. After King's assassination about two hundred white students decided they must do something, not just talk. They went to the million-dollar home of the president, demanded he resign from his white-only country club, that he bargain collectively with the Negro employees' union, and several other things.

"He refused to talk further with them. They refused to leave. After two days he went to the hospital with a breakdown. They moved their vigil to the quadrangle. Their numbers grew to five hundred, to a thousand, to fifteen hundred. I've been reading poems to them. Will you come down and sing for them?"

I hurriedly consulted the family schedule. "How about this Wednesday?" "Fine," said John. A couple days later I found myself facing some two thousand pure and honest young people seated on the grass in the center of their campus. There was an improvised PA system; a bare electric light bulb hung from a small tree.

I sang a few songs. John Beecher read some of his powerful free-verse poems from his book *To Live and Die in Dixie*. A well-dressed older man, president of the union of Negro maintenance employees, gave a short speech.

"I wish I could speak to you like Dr. King. But I'm not an educated man. I've been a janitor here for seventeen years. Dr. King had a dream. I can't give a long talk about it as he did. But I have a vision. I have a vision that I'd like to be able to pick up after black boys here, as well as white boys."

I whispered to one of the students, "Why hasn't there been more publicity about this nationally?" He replied, "Oh, the local papers have been full of it, but the wire services have hardly mentioned it. When we called up the TV networks they said they didn't have any cameramen to spare, 'but let us know if there is any violence—we'll send someone down.' "

I felt a deep rage boil in me, as though all the experiences with TV censorship and misrule had suddenly come to a head. When my turn came to sing again, I found myself speechifying—probably a dangerous thing for any singer.

"You read today about crime in the streets! I say there's crime in the New York offices of CBS and NBC! Crime! I'd like to make a pledge to you here tonight. I'll have to explain. I've never carried a gun since I got out of the Army twenty-two years ago. I've never thrown a stone at any person, and I don't intend to. I've had stones thrown at me, and it's no fun."

I told them briefly about the Peekskill concert of 1949, then went on. "So I don't intend to throw stones at a person. But I'll make this pledge to you. Before I leave Duke I'm going to take a stone with me, and put it in my banjo case, and if I ever meet a TV man up there who says he won't cover a story like this because there's no violence, some*thing* is going to get hurt."

Afterward a student came up and gave me a small stone.

At the time this book goes to press it hasn't been used yet. In the deepest sense, I'd love to say that I hope I never have to use it. I've remembered from childhood the old Chinese maxim, "He who starts to use his fists has demonstrated the failure of his argument." But what are you going to do when some people don't pay any attention to your words? I rather suspect I shall have to make that little rock sound sometime, or confess my cowardice. You have to put up or shut up.

ANGER IN THE LAND

(Years ago a southern white poet, Don West, picked up a black hitchhiker. Later he put the man's story down in verse, and years later his daughter, Hedy West, set them to a melody. And I picked up the song from Bernice Reagon, who may have changed it still slightly further.*)

By Hedy and Don West. Copyright © 1962, 1967, M. Witmark & Sons. All rights reserved. Used by permission of Warner Bros. Music.

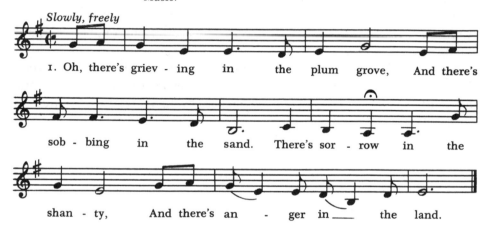

Slowly, freely

1. Oh, there's griev - ing in the plum grove, And there's sob - bing in the sand. There's sor - row in the shan - ty, And there's an - ger in __ the land.

2. There's been another lynching,
And another grain of sand
Swells the mountain of resentment;
Oh, there's anger in the land.

3. A woman sits in silence
Close beside an open door.
Flung, flimsy, on her doorstep
Lies a corpse upon the floor.

4. You'll not ask me why I'm silent
The woman said to me.
But her eyes blazed with anger
And her heart cried agony.

5. Once my heart could cry in sorrow;
Now it lies there on the floor
In the ashes by the hearthstone.
They can't hurt him any more.

6. Let the wind come crying softly
In the treetops by the spring;
Let its voice be low and feeling
Like it was a living thing.

7. Oh, there's grieving in the plum grove
And there's sobbing in the sand.
There's sorrow in the shanty
And there's anger in the land.

* You can hear Hedy sing it on *Hedy West Vol. 2*, Vanguard 79162.

Julius Lester has come in for a lot of hard words as a result of his frank letter about "destroying this country," but I find him about as constructive a person as I know.* When it comes to the subject of destruction, *Fortune* Magazine entitled a whole issue "New York City, a City Destroying Itself." And a well-reviewed book by a member of the Sierra Club was entitled *The Destruction of California*. Will a future historian write a chapter, "The Destruction of America"? If so, I doubt that he'll pin total blame on revolutionists.

Remember Patrick Henry? "Caesar had his Brutus, King Charles his Cromwell, and George the Third . . ." Cries of "Treason! Treason!" interrupted him. Patrick continued, ". . . may profit by their example. If that be treason, make the most of it."

Napoleon and Hitler united the world against them. The empires of Alexander, of Rome, of Genghis Khan, and of Spain all crumbled from within as much as from without. And those who glory in the power of America . . . may profit by their example. If that be unpatriotic, make the most of it.

And the Puritan revolution had its witchcraft trials, the French Revolution its guillotine epidemic, the Russian Revolution its purges, and present-day revolutionists . . . may profit by their example. If that be revisionism, make the most of it.

The Torn Flag

MALCOLM X once got into an argument with another black man as to whether they could call themselves Americans. "I'm not an American," said Malcolm. "Why do you think you are?"

"I'm an American because I was born here," said the other.

---

* It is probably unfair to quote any writer out of context, but the following sentences occur in a long and beautiful letter in which this young black singer and writer resigned from the editorial board of *Broadside* (N.Y.): ". . . I don't sing much now because nothing short of destroying this country will satisfy me. I hate what happened to Peter LaFarge and what's happening to Mr. Fink's daughter so much that I have to destroy everything in this country. Or to put it another way, I love so intensely the beauty of humanity that I hate everything that frustrates, stifles, and destroys that beauty, and I hate it so much that I will kill to see that it comes into being. . . ."

Any reader wanting to look up Julius's complete letter should get *Broadside* No. 84 (215 W. 98 St., New York, N.Y.). A longer article by him appeared in *Sing Out*, Vol. 17, No. 5 (1967). And read his book, *Look Out, Whitey! Black Power Gon' Get Your Mama*.

"Well, you could put a shoe in an oven but that wouldn't make it a biscuit," was Malcolm's retort.

I'm afraid I have no such easy answer. My own light-skinned ancestors participated in the good and bad decisions which formed this country. I had a poet uncle who wrote "I have a rendezvous with death, at midnight in some flaming town." So I swiped his line and used it for a new verse.

At midnight in a flaming angry town
I saw my country's flag lying torn upon the ground.
I ran in and dodged among the crowd
And scooped it up, and scampered out to safety.

And then I took this striped old piece of cloth
And tried my best to wash the garbage off,
But I found it had been used for wrapping lies.
It smelled and stank, and attracted all the flies.

While I was feverishly at my task
I heard a husky voice that seemed to ask
"Do you think you could change me just a bit?
Mrs. Ross did her best, but she made a few mistakes.

"My blue is good, the color of the sky.
The stars are good, for ideals, Oh, so high.
Seven stripes of red are strong to face all danger.
But those white stripes, they, they need some changing.

"I need also some stripes of deep rich brown;
And some of tan and black; then all around,
A border of God's gracious green would look good there.
Maybe you could slant the stripes; then I'd not be so square."

I woke and said, "What a ridiculous story.
Don't let anyone say I suggested tampering with Old Glory."
But tonight it's near midnight, and in another flaming town.
Once again I hear my country's flag lies torn upon the ground.

Who really owns America? The chief of a northwestern Indian tribe, fighting for its fishing rights, said, "We are the stewards of this land. Notice that we did not say we are the owners. The Great Spirit owns all this earth. We are but his stewards."

And so I'd say also, take it from an old blacklisted singer who has had to fight most of his life against people who wanted to make him an outcast in his own home: this land belongs to the hardworking people who love freedom. Woody Guthrie had a great verse which should be sung now:

> Was a great high wall there
> That tried to stop me.
> Was a great big sign that said Private Property;
> But on the other side
> It didn't say nothin'—
> This land was made for you and me.
>
> This land is your land,
> This land is my land,
> From California to the New York Island,
> From the redwood forest
> To the Gulf Stream waters,
> This land was made for you and me.*

13·Other Folk

SONGS AND CELEBRATIONS
IN SEVERAL PARTS OF THE WORLD

Most of the items in this chapter are excerpts from letters home, 1963–64, when Toshi and I and three children tripped around the world, visiting some 23 countries during ten months. By now some of these countries have new governments; some are richer, some are broker. Each item is dated to help keep things straight.

Republic of Western Samoa
August 27, 1963

A SAMOAN "welcome song": One leader stands up in front of the group, which is seated in a tight semicircle on the floor around him. He suddenly crouches and rubs his hands, flat-palmed, vigorously in front of him. They all do likewise. Then comes a thunderous unison handclap, and the song begins: rich sonority, three or four parts, and soft drumming on a rush mat by one man. The leader would put most of our choral directors to shame. He was a dancer, lithe and graceful. His dance was part of the welcoming song. At times he made vigorous arm motions which, I was told later, cued certain kinds of handclaps. The faces of the singers remained impassive, but the leader's was animated—a flashing smile and sparkling eyes darting from right to left.

The Welcome Song

Chet Williams, formerly the UNESCO adviser to the school system of Western Samoa, sent me this quotation:

"Music is the pulse of Island life. It is taken for granted and is a part of everyday living. The people sing when they work on land, they sing when they are on the sea, they even sing when traveling by bus from village to village. They sing as old men and women or as babes in arms. The Islanders compose extempore songs in praise of a person or as a 'permanent' record of a brave deed or a successful village undertaking; they compose songs when they are in love, when they wish to ridicule their enemies, or when they want to tell a story with a 'moral.' They sing at weddings and farewells and also at funerals. They even have songs about tuberculosis and leprosy. Singing is vital to their whole being. It is taken for granted, yet it is the one thing that has the power of bringing out the 'Island' in one, wherever one may be. Long before an Island child learns how to read or even to speak properly, he already knows a few of the popular songs of the day. Nothing is more incongruous than to hear an Island child of three years or more expressing in song a very 'grown-up' philosophy of life."*

Izumi, Japan
October 18, 1963

AT OSAKA, a huge city of three million, we got on a modern steamer for the 200-mile trip through the Inland Sea to Matsuyama ("Matsu" means pine, and "Yama" is mountain). As the boat pulled away from the dock, several hundred paper streamers unrolled between passengers on board and their friends or relatives waving goodbye on the dock. The loudspeaker gave forth with "Auld Lang Syne" (a popular tune in Japan). The streamers got longer and longer as the space between boat and dock widened. Each streamer was about a quarter of an inch wide, and sold in rolls about 4 inches in diameter. The passenger on the boat holds one end, and the person on the dock gradually lets the other end unroll in his hands. When there was no more, he would give the end one last squeeze and then let go. The streamers were by now all about 100 feet long, and the air caught them and twirled them in great sweeping curls alongside the boat as we pulled away from the dock, and then the people on the boat let go, and the streamers sank in the water. A beautiful custom.

And the Inland Sea is a fabulously beautiful body of water. One is never out of sight of land. It is dotted with small islands. One sees terraced rice fields, a cluster of neat houses near a beach, and wooden fishing boats pulled up. In the evening we arrived at a small floating dock, near Matsuyama, 100,000 population, where we banqueted with several dozen relatives.

Izumi, the town where my father-in-law, Takashi Ohta, was born and spent much of his childhood, is a village about thirty miles down the coast. We took a train, then a five-mile taxi ride down there.

It was one of the—no, it was *the* most hair-raising ride any of us ever took. The road, once just a path for horses or walking, clings to the edge of steep cliffs along the sea. Still unpaved, about ten feet wide, it had no guard rails. The smoothest part of the road was often along the outer edge, and the driver would cling there, with two wheels a few inches from

---

* From "A Study of the Developing Pattern of Education and the Factors Influencing That Development in New Zealand's Pacific Dependencies," by Fanaafi Ma'la'i (Master's Thesis, Victoria University of Wellington, New Zealand, 1957).

a sheer drop of about thirty or forty feet to the rocks and surf below. We careened madly along, all of us holding our breath, closing our eyes, gritting our teeth, tense all over.

The driver honked his horn continuously, because of the blind corners. Sure enough, on one of them we met another car. Screams. Brakes. Then we inch past slowly, not daring to look down.

Well, after twenty minutes we get to Izumi, still alive.

It is a beautiful town of about 100 houses, about 600 people. The valley is terraced with rice fields, the hillsides with orange groves. The high ridges are planted with pine. A little brook of clear water bubbles over stones through the center of town to a pebbly beach. A breakwater protects a dozen small wooden fishing boats.

The roofs are tile, except for a few with thatch. The walls are mostly mud, plastered on bamboo lattice. The architecture, even of the poorest houses, shows taste and design.

The town is almost unchanged since Takashi left it 50 years ago. We were the first foreigners *ever* to have visited it, within anyone's memory.

Takashi's grandfather had been a wealthy and respected man, the local Daimyo, or feudal lord. He built the breakwater; he supplied soldiers from time to time to put at the service of his feudal superior, the Lord of

The shrine goes down to the sea

The dragon peers into a house

Matsuyama, 30 miles away; and his large manor house and 20 outbuildings stood at the edge of town.

But in the late 1860s Takashi's father went to study in Europe. He witnessed the Paris Commune, and came home a radical. Over a period of 40 years all the family's fortune was stripped away. Economic and political reprisals included the banishment of one son, Takashi. Only one sister still lives in Izumi.

We visited the family shrine. Our visit coincided with an annual festival day (each village in Japan has at least one). We all went to the temple, and then followed the procession. The gilded, elaborately carved shrines were lifted out of the small temple and carried down to a carved stone platform by the sea, where for about an hour a Shinto priest and some village elders prayed over them, made small food offerings, and the rest of the town stood around—not solemnly. It was a festive day.

A man in a blue kimono, with a fearsome red mask and a stick, was making everyone laugh by chasing and scaring small children. Twelve teen-agers, dressed in white shirts, pants, and sneakers, carried a "dragon." A frame of bamboo about ten feet long, covered over with dark cloth, had a head of carved wood, with a movable jaw. The head could be shot out five or six feet on a long pole, from inside. Cloth for the neck hid the pole from sight. The twelve young men, shouting and chanting, charged around the town, visiting every house, poking the dragon's head into windows, and into the faces of bystanders.

Four children inside a sort of palanquin were banging on a big drum. Altogether much shouting and fun.

The town is very, very poor. There is a steady drain of ambitious young people, away, to get good jobs in the big cities (Tokyo is now 12 million!). The few who stay in town do so because they have to, or because they love the place too much, or for a combination of those two reasons. There is a poor living to be made from farming, and a poor living to be made from fishing.

But here, too, are 600 honest hardworking people, full of hopes for the future, who would like to hold onto what they can of their ancient traditions, while getting more of the advantages of the modern world. And their ancient traditions *are* very beautiful. I have never seen any town in the U. S. A. as lovely in its architecture, for example. Nothing fancy. But lovely shaped roofs, and carefully arranged gardens in even very

The little drummers ride through Izumi

poor homes, with a pool of water and some goldfish. At their back the lovely green mountains climbing up into the clouds. At their doorstep one of the world's most beautiful seas—clear blue waters dotted with distant islands. And that's Izumi.

Tokyo
November 7, 1963

BILL MALM, a Michigan musicologist, came to Tokyo for a year to study intensively an ancient art: the singing and samisen playing which accompany the Bunraku, traditional puppets.

He took us to a recital of this art, which by itself is called Joruri. Up an alley, off a side street, we entered a door, took off our shoes downstairs, and went up to a large room. About eighty men were seated on the floor in front of a small stage. Most were middle-aged or older, but there were a few in their early thirties. Tea and other refreshment were passed around occasionally. When the curtain went up, a small stage was revealed, with two women kneeling formally, facing the audience.

One recited all dialogues and sang all songs. The other played the samisen, whose melody occasionally roughly paralleled or preceded the melody of the singer, or occasionally fell silent while the singer went into some long prose passage. The samisen player's face was impassive. But at crucial points she released a sort of yelp; these were of two kinds, mouth open or closed. Like the temple dogs, one of whose mouths is closed, the other open.

The other spoke and sang scenes from famous plays of two hundred years ago. She was younger, and rather good-looking, but when she voiced a man's part she growled and roared. When she voiced a girl's part, her voice squeaked high.

We could stay only two hours, and saw three different scenes, which Bill was kind enough to translate for us. To me it was fascinating. The singer's face was highly mobile and passionate, but her body was controlled and kneeling. Here is one scene:

A man traveling on business stops at an inn, and is surprised to see written on a fan a poem he had composed years before. He asks who put the verse there; the innkeeper says it is a blind woman who sometimes plays music for guests. The traveler realizes it must be an old girl friend, for whom he once wrote the poem. He asks if she can come to perform for him. The innkeeper says he thinks so; the woman is found and is led into the room. Sure enough, it is her. The two men listen; she sings, not knowing that one of her listeners is her former lover. After, they ask her to tell her story. It is completely tragic. She went blind because of weeping over her lover's disappearance. She did not want to marry the man her parents picked for her.

The traveler can't bring himself to disclose his identity. He gives her some money, and medicine which can cure her blindness, and leaves the inn. Then she discovers who he was. Hysterically she demands to know which direction he has gone. She dashes out into the night. But the river is swollen and flooded, and at the bank, blind, she realizes she is unable to follow him. Her screams go unanswered into the night.

The audience followed every word avidly, as if they knew it by heart. Hoarse shouts at exactly the right times could be heard, and clapping often *preceded* an important point.

Bill said there were in all Toyko only a few thousand devotees of this particular genre. It was as though we had witnessed a London recital of favorite scenes from Shakespeare. And how many were in the professional performers' guild for this art form? Fifteen, said Bill. Wouldn't it die out soon? Not necessarily; two were younger men, aged twenty.

The next day I accompanied Bill when he went to take a lesson from one of the older ones, a delightful seventy-year-old man. They kneeled facing each other across a small table. Bill sang and recited long passages, and the teacher played the samisen. He would stop Bill from time to time to make a criticism, friendly but firm, about his pronunciation, intonation or rhythm. Afterward for three-quarters of an hour the old man philosophized to us on what he felt were differences between western and Japanese music and culture: "The simple is most difficult. . . . Japan, in isolation, developed deeply along its own unique lines."

Next day I described the old samisen player to our regular interpreter, a fine young political-science student. He remarked briefly that many young Japanese were fed up with this "looking backward." I realized that one of my main jobs here is to explain our feeling that folk music is not simply a collection of old songs, however good, but rather that it is a good old language (perhaps you would rather say "approach" since the basic approach is what remains most constant, while the stylistic language changes faster) in which there could be many songs, both new and old.

At the moment, it seems to me that people here assume that the old styles of singing are strictly for old songs, and new songs will normally be written in a western style. Perhaps they are right. I hope not.

New Delhi, India
December 1963

A FRIEND OF OURS here is an American working for the Asia Foundation. Last year while partridge hunting he came across a small village inhabited entirely by snake charmers and their families. He took us out there today.

We bumped over miles of dusty wagon tracks, through one muddy village after another. Just past the carcass of a water buffalo, being devoured by several dozen huge vultures, we find it. About one hundred people living in a couple dozen small mud huts with thatched roofs, clustered tight together on a couple acres of land.

They have been living in this spot for generations, we were told, but at some time in the past, perhaps a few hundred years back, they had migrated from a province 400 miles northwest. Here they were casteless, and hence outcasts. A neighboring village allowed them to get water from the village well, but social intercourse between the villages was unthinkable. Only a couple children in the village attend school, "because it is so expensive": 60 cents per month. Each household has a few chickens and goats, but they have no tillable land, and have to buy their grain from neighboring villages. They have petitioned the government for land, but have not the money to pay for it.

About 25 men, and their snakes, are out breadwinning at any time of year. They take the train to distant places where money is not too scarce, and play for tips in the marketplaces . . . and can earn maybe 75 cents a day. Big pay. Then they come here after half a year and spend a few months at home. It is the only way anyone in this village has ever earned a living. Our interpreter says he has met snake-charmer families before, but never a whole village full of them.

Well, of course, they put on a show for us. We got out the tape recorder and cameras. A couple of men produced instruments sounding like bagpipes, except that the only bags were their cheeks, which puffed in and out, keeping a steady stream of pressure on the pipes. While his cheeks expelled air, his nose breathed in quickly. The pipers were accompanied by a couple drums, one of snakeskin, and two others of large earthenware pots with rubber inner tubes stretched over their mouths—they had a deep thumping tone, similar to American Indian water drums. Then some small boys came out and danced in the dust. Beautiful anklets around their bare feet gave a tinkling rhythm as they stamped and swayed.

Now came the snakes. We saw two flat circular baskets with covers. Whoops, up came two big hooded heads, three feet in front of mc. Smiling faces indicated that it was quite safe; I was pushed back into my seat.

The man kept moving his hand rhythmically. I'm told that snakes really can't hear, and that it's the motion that hypnotizes them. However, these dopes appeared to be brainwashed. They darted their heads aimlessly, but didn't try to bite anyone . . . and a whole village full of children and adults were standing around. Including us. Toshi clicked on the movie camera.

These two six-footers were just the aperitif. Suddenly out of another basket a man brings the biggest doggone cobra I ever hope to see. At least ten or eleven feet. And out of another basket another just as big. I lift my legs and start to move, but the man next to me smiles and motions that it's all right. Our interpreter says the fangs have been removed. I hope he's right. He may know it, but does the snake know it?

After ten minutes we run out of film, just as the snake is slithering over to Toshi and the camera. The man picks up the biggest cobra, and with a smile beckons to our 15-year-old daughter, Mika; she approaches, and he loops it around her neck. She smiles nervously. We all take pictures. Nothing much else we can do. The pipes and drums are still filling the air with wild music.

After 45 minutes all the snakes are put back. We pack our cameras, etc. Our American friend bargains with the village leaders about the tip —great Oriental custom, it seems. Finally, it is set, and we roll off in a cloud of dust. The rich Americans have departed.

Calcutta, India
December 1963

I WISH I knew Bengali, or some other Indian language, well enough to learn a couple of their folk songs. They are charming, and would appeal immediately to most Americans. The vocal tone is not strange or strained, as in traditional Japanese and Chinese music. The harmony is simply that of the drone bass, as in a bagpipe. My ears don't mind this a bit. I prefer not being distracted by tonic-dominant progressions. The beautiful melodies are subtle and quick, and the rhythms too.

Watching the snake charmers

Some polyphony is used, such as when a group of singers repeats a strong rhythmic phrase over and over, and the soloist holds a high flowing descant, usually on the fifth of the scale, and descending from it.

Western music has hardly made a dent here. It's no wonder. Their own music is so good. Folk songs: my God, 57 hundred varieties. Each province has got its own style. (There are three hundred languages in India.) Solo songs, group songs, work songs, love songs, religious songs. (Especially religious songs. This is a most God-conscious land. More of that later.) Great rhythms, great melodies, and great sense of poetry in all the people. Here are a couple of themes from some of the songs:

"O people, don't get involved in love . . . that sticky stuff. . . . Like glue, it will never let you go."

A man says: "I can tame the wild elements, but not a wild girl like you."

A woman's protest, whose husband is taken off to war.

The god Shiva arguing with his wife. Humorous song.

And boatmen's songs. Hundreds of 'em. Mostly with the general theme of comparing the soul to a boat tossing on the waves.

Man's song (by Tagore): "In town they call you just another black girl. I call you a black flower. Like the beautiful black clouds which bring the sweet rain to my land, you also . . . Now, whether this black girl ever looked at me, and whether I ever returned her glance, is known only to me and that girl."

The favorite Indian instruments are distant cousins of the banjo and guitar, the sarod and the sitar. Village folk have simple versions; trained classical virtuosos have elegant masterpieces. Usually accompanied by drums, tapped by hand. Many varieties of them. The most common seems to be the tabla: two drums used together, with a black rubber spot near the center to deepen the tone.

Flutes are popular too. Small cymbals, and bells, and jingles around the ankles. I saw also in a village a neat one-stringed instrument I'll draw a sketch of here.

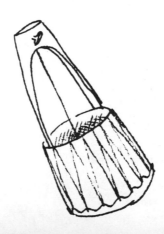

The one string can be tightened with the peg. The other end goes through a hole in the center of the skin drumhead. If a song is in the key of C, the one string is tuned to a C, but the player can lower it from time to time by squeezing the two sides. Called an ektara (*ek*, "one"; *tar*, "string"). The string is kept taut simply by the pressure of the player's left hand. He holds the drum tight under his left arm, and strums with a wooden pick over the knuckles of his right hand. By varying the pressure with the left hand, great "quong quong" sounds come from it.

We saw this instrument played by a relligous group known as Bauls, in a small village a hundred miles north of Calcutta. Bauls rarely own their own homes, but travel from place to place. Unlike most religious orders in India, they are not ascetics. They marry and raise children to follow their line of business. Women are more equal to men than in most of India. The Bauls have their own songs and styles, usually singing in a group of three to eight people. One soloist, and the rest joining in from time to time, and then as they get the spirit, dancing and whirling, like the Jewish Chassidim. They sing in the marketplace for tips, and serve God and keep alive that way.

One of their songs again said, "O Lord, my boat is tossing on the waters of life. Please see me safely to where I am going—wherever that is." Within the next three days I heard no less than seven other songs, both classical songs and folk songs, which had the same essential theme. And in conversation with different persons I found that this was India's main tradition: God rules the world. Our fate is in his hands. The best we can do is pray that he shows us how to act.

The city intellectuals tell me that this is just because India is a very poor country. When people have so little, they have to have faith in God. But I've seen other poor countries that didn't have it so intensely as here. And Tagore, the poet, was an aristocrat, and deeply religious too. His song "Jana Gana Mana" is the national anthem and translates roughly as follows: "O Thou who leads the minds of the people, unite us now from the Himalayas to the Ganges . . ." It is a fine song—along with "The Marseillaise" the best national anthem I know. I sang it with 10,000 people in Calcutta's Park Maidan last Sunday.

But I'm afraid I have my doubts—at least concerning this definition of God. God helps those who help themselves.

I wish our movie film could return some day and be shown on Indian TV. India needs TV more than it needs new industries, hospitals, hydroelectric dams. After twenty years of "independence" they are still prison-

ers of poverty and ignorance. Only 20 percent can read and write. The average peasant does not know if his nation is square or round. But a battery-operated TV set in each village could have all 500 million Indians learn one common language in a year, could unite its disunited and demoralized population.

Of course the crucial problem would be: who would control what goes on that magic little screen? If it is to be sold to the highest bidder, as in the U.S.A., you might as well forget the whole idea.

In Calcutta an economist described to me India's plans for economic expansion. I interrupted to ask what India was doing about the population problem. His face suddenly sagged. "Last year we had a 5 percent increase in productivity. We also had a 5 percent increase in population. If something is not done soon, we will have to have forcible sterilization of millions."

November 1969:

What I have learned now about population problems is that it is the rich nations of the world who must FIRST limit their (our) numbers— we who burn up most of the world's oil, use up most of the world's raw materials, and are mostly responsible for polluting the world's air and water.

(Remember, it was Hitler who thought he could decide which people are the surplus people.)

Nairobi, Kenya
December 12, 1963

THE PLANE LANDS at Nairobi. We see green grass, human beings who are not half starved. Kenya seems like an affluent nation compared to India.

The greatest politicians have a strong sense of poetry. Premier Kenyatta's slogan, emblazoned on the new national coat of arms, is pure genius. It is one Swahili word: Haram*bay*. Roughly translated, Harambay means "all together now" or "heave ho." But this isn't all. The term originated on the docks at Mombassa, ancient Kenya port for the Arab ships of a thousand years ago. The dock workers used the term in lifting loads; it was also used for hauling on ropes.

It means that English and African must haul together, country and city, illiterate and Ph.D., and turbaned Indian. There are several hundred thousand of the latter here, originally brought sixty years ago to build railroads, and now comprising the large class of shopkeepers. Those who think it is impossible to have a multiracial democratic country are leaving, or keeping their thoughts to themselves now. Those who hope and think this can be a prosperous, booming nation know there is only one way:

"Harammm-bay!"

Nairobi population is about 300,000. Population of all Kenya is about 8.5 million—small for such huge acreage. About a couple of dozen main tribal groups. Biggest are the Kikuyu, a million and a half—agricultural. The Masai, half a million, are nomadic herders. All speak different languages, but many understand Swahili, the language of the old Arab traders with many African words in it. Only in Nairobi do many understand English, but it is likely that as education becomes more universal, much of the country will know it as a second language.

Few Kenyans realize quite the variety of cultures in their own country, and so it was a stroke of genius to put a lot of tribal dancing in the Independence Day Celebration. Let me describe the evening of Wednesday, December 11, 1963. At midnight Kenya ceased being a colony and became a member of the British Commonwealth.

For miles the highways were clogged with cars, buses, and trucks. Along the grass hurried thousands of eager people, some of whom had walked for days to get here. Finally our taxi parked and we walked the last mile over a muddy field to a huge football stadium. 250,000 people —no fooling—were there for the ceremony. Were there speeches? Not a one! Dozens of groups of tribal dancers, no two alike, came on at one end of the field, and gradually circled in front of the stands.

Each would pause in front of the stand, and perform their dance for five or ten minutes, then move on a couple hundred feet and do it for the next section. Another group closely followed them. At one time I counted thirty different groups on the field, with twenty to eighty dancers or musicians in each group. The color, variety, rhythms, and movements were staggering.

> Here is one group of women, hips swishing, and singing. A soft undulating feeling.
> Here are tall Masai warriors, with twelve-foot spears glistening, and hair plastered down with red ocher. A shuffling ominous phalanx.
> Here are fifty wildly painted drummers, each with a narrow

drum, five feet long, hung between his legs. A thunderous precision, and then suddenly half of them jump on the shoulders of the others and continue the rhythm unbroken.

Here come a troupe of tall thin dancers, whose white plumed headdresses reach two or three feet above their heads. In their hands are huge rattles which swish and thump as they toss their plumes.

Here are twenty little men whose armor contains so much metal that they sound like the contents of twenty kitchen cupboards being shaken in syncopation.

Next come more women in brilliant dyed gowns.

By 10 P.M., spotlights wave, and in comes a motorcade. Third in line is a white convertible. The crowd roars, "Jomo, Jomo," and standing up in the back is the powerful figure of Kenyatta, waving his famous fly whisk, as his car slowly circles the field and ends at the canopied stand.

More cars. Then some cheers. It's the Duke of Edinburgh, here to formally relinquish control.

Twenty minutes later the scene takes a new turn. A precision-drilled group of English soldiers, the Gordon Highlanders, appears. Trumpets. Drums. A brass band of about 600 takes the center of the stage. Scenes of ancient barbaric splendor give way to modern barbaric splendor. For an hour the Queen's African Rifles, famous crack infantry troops, do close-order drill, up and down, back and forth, to a succession of march tunes.

So far not a word has been said over the loudspeakers. The people have been treated to a breathtaking pageant of the past and present powers controlling the destinies of Kenya.

It is nearing midnight. Three religious leaders ascend the rostrum and intone short prayers in three languages. The band stands poised at attention. Kenyatta and the Queen's governor walk out on the center of the now-empty field, alone and unattended. All lights go off. The band plays "God Save the Queen." In starlight the Union Jack slowly comes down on a flagpole at the end of the field. The lights go on. The national anthem of Kenya is begun. Only the opening two notes are heard, because the roar of the crowd drowns out everything as the black-green-and-red new flag slowly goes up. Deafening cheers as Kenyatta and the governor walk back to the rostrum.

Now comes 40 minutes of the most spectacular fireworks we have ever seen. At the end, the crowd streams happily across the field to the exits.

A Scotsman near us (about 5 percent of the crowd near us are white) says with a smile, "I came dressed in my tribal costume too," and displays his kilts.

We slowly make our way across the muddy field to our car. It is the most orderly and happy crowd. No drunks. No pushing or shoving. And even when some stumbled in water and mud over a foot deep, no cursing. At the cars are crowds of people helping to push each other's vehicles out of mud holes. Along the roadway in the distance we can hear singing.

Next day we met some Americans who told us that some white Kenyans may have been at the Uhuru celebrations, but others stayed home and barred their doors, certain that there was to be a riot. And another friend, who came up from Tanganyika to the celebration, was asked by shocked white farmers: "You going up there? Oh, I'd be scared to. All those Mau Mau!"

The Mau Mau, granted amnesty by Kenyatta, are now coming out of the woods. One of their leaders came to see the English flag go down at the football stadium. He walked up and identified himself to Kenyatta, and the photographers clustered about recording the scene. Kenyatta went back and asked the Duke of Edinburgh if he would like to meet him, but the Duke shook his head.

The Mau Mau general had long hair in ringlets below his shoulder. "Samson lost his strength when his hair was cut, and we vowed not to cut our hair till Kenya was free."

Ede, Nigeria
January 3, 1964

Up EARLY. A wild ride for fifty miles over a one-lane road to the town of Ede. The Timi (chief) of Ede is famous as an expert on the talking drums. He himself has to be away for an official conference today, but he has asked his brother to explain them to us.

We drove into Ede, a town of small tin-roofed buildings like Oshogbo, and to the Timi's "palace" (the home of the chief of Ede), a large two-story affair with a big courtyard. As we drove through the gate, five drummers sitting near the doorway under a porch drummed a thunderous announcement of our arrival.

The Babakekere, as the chief's brother is known, was a charming host. A short, stocky man, in beautiful embroidered robes and cap, speaking excellent English, he asked the court drummers to stand around while he explained the various drums and their duties.

Some of the drums were only used as accompaniment. One drum could only speak two sentences (farm information, like "Father, come in from the field"). But the master drum could say anything which could be spoken in the Yoruba language.

Yoruba is a tonal language, like Chinese. The same syllables can mean completely different things, depending on whether the voice inflects them on a high, medium, or low pitch, ascending or descending.

So the way the drum "talks" is to imitate the high or low pitch of the syllables, together with the rhythm of the words. Then with a little experience, anyone who understands the Yoruba language can understand the talking drums.

The Babakekere showed us how he could alter the pitch of the drum by pressure of his arms upon the thongs which tighten the drumhead. The drum itself has an hourglass shape. Wasp-waisted. But the thongs (several dozen in all) go straight from the one end to the other, in parallel lines. Squeezing the drum around its waist tightens all the thongs, thus tightening the skin upon each end. As much as one octave difference in pitch can be achieved on one drum, and it can of course be changed slowly or fast, and before or during or just after the head is struck by the drumstick, a curved affair. Quite a variety of sounds can come from one drum.

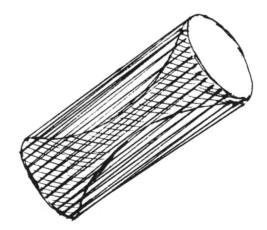

The six court drummers now demonstrated how they would wake the chief up in the morning. "Get up, put on your trousers, the people are arriving and the day's business will begin." One drum "talked"; the other five accompanied him with rhythms. Then the drummers demonstrated how they might play for a dance, with the master drummer giving directions to the dancers, such as, "Now bend low . . . now straighten up . . . now lift your feet high."

Lastly, to prove the ability of the master drum to transmit any message, the Babakekere sent a servant to the other side of the courtyard, and asked me in a low voice what message I would like to send to the servant. I suggested, "Ask him to pick up the umbrella leaning against the wall and bring it to me."

This request he now whispered in Yoruba to the master drummer. For about six seconds the drummer tapped and pounded in staccato syncopation. The servant promptly went to the umbrella, picked it up and brought it to me.

We were overcome with amazement. Fortunately Toshi and Danny caught the whole scene on sound-movie film, so when we get home we hope we can prove we're not liars. I asked the Babakekere a few more questions. It seems the drums were used in the old days for military messages—from the front to the rear, for example. The sounds can carry for a mile or two or three. Nowadays their main function is for official functions, announcements and dances. Radio Nigeria starts every day with them. The Ghana parliament opens with talking drums.

Before going we all shook hands gravely with a dozen or more chiefs now seated under the porch. These were heads of various important

Street in Nigeria; Toshi and Tinya listen to a drummer

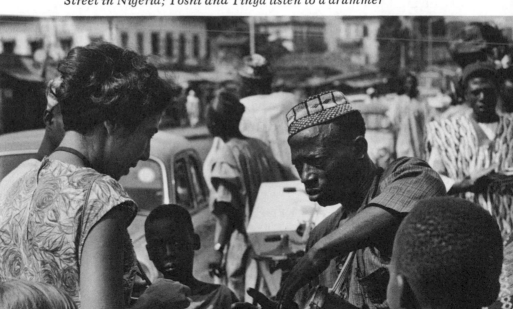

families of Ede who regularly gathered at the palace for consultation. The Babakekere bid us a warm farewell, and added: "If you ever go to Kentucky, look up my son. He's studying in college at Louisville."

Ghana
January 7, 1964

GHANA HAS a vigorous program of research and collecting, *and,* equally important, publicizing and distributing its own folk music. Their university has an Institute of African Studies, headed by Professor J. N. Nketia, author of several collections of folkmusic, and a composer. Folklore collecting is done throughout Ghana. But what is rare in universities: African dance and music is also *taught.* Some first-rate African drummers and dancers are on full salary, teaching intensively to students who are studying for degrees.

One of the teachers in the Institute said we might be able to find some fishermen singing at a spot forty miles up the coast. We zipped along a modern blacktop highway, traveled a half mile off of it down to the beach, and had hardly parked when we heard singing. A long rope stretched endlessly out into the blue Atlantic. Thirty cheerful people sang as they slowly pulled it up into the palm trees, cinched it, and walked down for a fresh grip. One man did no pulling but accompanied the singing with a sort of metal castanet held in his hand. He wore a papier-mâché mask!*

In the distance were large dugout canoes taking fishermen out through the surf. We rope the camera tripod to the front seat of one of these boats, lash the tape recorder and battery pack next to it, cover them all with plastic against the surf, and push off. Crowds of children help us get it afloat, and then six paddlers get us through the surf. Danny and I and an interpreter sit crouched in the stern, helping by staying out of the way till the boat is safe beyond the breakers.

Finally we're out there, bobbing easily upon the swelling brine. We take the plastic off the camera, get ready to roll. The paddlers wait, however, till the drummer is ready.†

---

* We never discovered the reason for the mask. Carnival spirit? Ancient religion?
† This is a characteristic of African work songs, it seems. They must have accompaniment. We passed a group of men cutting grass with long knives yesterday. Our driver hopped out for us to see if they knew any work songs, which are often sung by grass cutters. Oh yes, they knew many. But they couldn't sing them now, because they didn't have their

Drumming, singing and paddling

Now start the drums in the canoe. Metal castanets pick up a syncopated pattern. The singing starts. Very ragged at first. No one seems to know exactly what to do. But by now I realize this is a typical folk music method. They are not a rehearsed chorus coming in on cue. They have to sound each other out, see how they feel.

Mika comes alongside with another translator in another canoe. She is taking short bursts of film with a hand-held camera to cover mistakes that I may make with the main camera. The men in her boat start clapping in rhythm. Gradually the harmony and quality of singing become richer and stronger. The solos and choruses follow each other right on cue. Different paddlers take turns on the short solo lines. I am not an experienced cameraman, and I am praying that it all comes out well when developed. The sunlight glints on the strong dark muscles; the melody, harmony and rhythm all fit together. Since the camera is locked to the boat, the singers will stay in focus and not bob around too much, but the horizon tips back and forth as the boat is rocked on the waves.

Finally we run out of film, and come ashore. I suppose within a generation fishing around here, too, will all be done with machines. Fisher-

---

music with them. Their "music" was a calabash rattle and metal castanets. (Played by an expert, these become quite fantastic instruments.) One might as soon play tennis without a net as try and sing without one's "music."

men will be paid more, fish will be cheaper. But for everything you gain in this world, you lose something; and if these songs are lost, I for one will regret it. The world is full of many skills which are outmoded economically, but which deserve to live because they are beautiful. I have a suspicion that Ghanaians, because they love their country and their culture, will find ways to keep some of these traditions alive. Maybe they'll have canoe races every year, for the young men of the town to show off.

Israel
January 1964

WE VISITED a Yemenite village. About 60,000 Jews emigrated from Yemen, the Arab state down on the Red Sea, and still maintain much of their ancient Oriental culture. They had lived in comparative isolation from the European Jewish communities for two thousand years, and in their own way are very orthodox.

We drove down a muddy village street, pulled up at a plain white-washed bungalow, and there was the whole family standing on the porch waiting for us. Old Grandpa with a long beard and black cap. Younger people put on traditional Yemenite costumes for the occasion, although now they usually wear store-bought clothes.

First we had to sit down to a meal. In comes the bottle of wine, with a ceremonial song to accompany it. We sit down to eat, but first a long chanted prayer while salt is sprinkled on the bread. Then the soup, a delicious chicken broth. More songs.

It seems that 90 percent of the Yemenite songs are folk tunes using the famous poems of a certain Shalom Shabazi, a Yemenite Jew of the sixteenth century, who wrote a vast number of religious poems in Hebrew. Some of them are now among Israel's most popular songs.

At one point in the dinner the old man got into a heated discussion; the translator laughingly told me: "He's complaining that in Yemen old men are allowed to marry young girls if they want to, but that here in Israel they won't allow it. You see, European Jews abandoned polygamy around the eleventh century, and monogamy was enforced by the rabbis, but the Yemen Jews never heard of the rule, or didn't want to hear of it, so polygamy has been practiced by them right up to the time they emigrated to Israel. Now he wants to marry a fourteen-year-old girl, but isn't allowed to."

After lunch we went out to the porch, where there was sufficient light for the cameras, and filmed song after song. The songs were mainly of two kinds: men's songs, of longing for the return to Israel, and women's songs, about love. And most of them could be danced to. Two or three people at a time would get up and, side by side, perform graceful and dipping steps in unison. The motions were flowing and remarkably similar to the dances of the Bauls, the religious dancers whom we filmed in India. The songs were all quite rhythmic, and sung in strong, high voices, accompanied by the rhythm of the ceramic drum or, occasionally, a large oil can.

After we had run out of film, we packed up the cameras, and we went down with the old man to admire his goat and sheep herd. He used to be a jeweler in Yemen, but now he wants to work out of doors, and proudly showed us his flock. He was a colorful figure with his long beard, and we waved to him as he went down the road. An afternoon of smiles and good feeling.

Singing and dancing together

Prague, Czechoslovokia
March 19, 1964

THE NEW SYNAGOGUE in Prague was built in the year 1269 but is still called new because it was built to replace a previous one destroyed by fire. Outside, on a neighboring building is an ancient clock with Hebrew letters on it. The hands turn counterclockwise. The Germans, for their own perverted reasons, didn't destroy this building, but kept it as an anti-Semitic museum. Inside, the old Gothic structure was dark and dank. Slits through the massive inner walls allowed women to view the service. A cloth over one chair signified the seat that the famous Rabbi Lev used centuries ago, and which must never be sat in again. He it was who made the golem.

And who was the golem? According to folk legend, Rabbi Lev was so smart he made a servant out of clay, and, placing a holy stone between its lips, brought it to life. It did all necessary work for Rabbi Lev, but on Friday night the holy stone was always removed, because no one must work on the Sabbath. One Friday evening by some error the stone was not removed. The golem ran amok all Saturday, killing people, until he was at last destroyed. Folk legend adds a nice coda: The golem's ghost is supposed to be still sitting in the high stone arches of this old synagogue. In an anteroom of the synagogue was a counting room, where every week gold was weighed and paid out to the king for permission for Jews to live in the city. The surrounding blocks were the ghetto. One block away is the most extraordinary cemetery I have ever seen. It was for centuries the only cemetery Jews were allowed to be buried in, and thus so crowded that some graves have the remains fifteen deep, on top of each other. A symbol of overcrowded ghetto life as well as overcrowded death.

Just to stand in the middle of the graveyard and look around is an experience. The weather-beaten stones stand, stacked inches apart, tipping slightly, like giant playing cards of stone. Trees grow up between some of the stones. The whole silent scene has an overpowering eloquence. We walked down the path to the other end, and there in a small stucco synagogue, restored after the war, we saw something which was most unforgettable of all.

Inside, it is almost empty. On every wall, from floor to twelve feet high, are painstakingly lettered the names, birth dates and death dates of 75,000 Jews of Prague who were shipped off to death camps by Nazis during World War II. Men, women, children, infants—their names are there. People come from all over the world, peering down the alphabetized list, to find relatives or friends. A couple of names were erased when by some miracle it was found they had survived. We studied the walls in shocked silence for some time. You have no idea how impressive it is to see 75,-000 names, realizing that each was a separate, breathing, hoping, human individual.

At one end of the room is a simple stone altar of sorts, covered with flowers and wreaths. I noted on the ribbons that several came from Germany. Most were from East Germany, but one said "Junge Christen aus Hamburg." Another was in Polish: "Union of Anti-Fascist Fighters."

If any of you reading these words ever find yourself in Prague, will you go to see this? Ask for the Pincus Synagogue.

Brno, Czechoslovakia
March 21, 1964

DANNY AND I were invited to a rehearsal of a big "folk orchestra." "What do you mean?" we asked. "It's made up of folk instruments. Thirty musicians. You'll see," they replied.

With some misgivings we set out. I have had disastrous encounters with massed guitars; I was once a member of a tenor banjo "club."

Well! There in the rehearsal room were two shining cymbalons (a trapezoid-shaped table, with a couple dozen strings that are struck with hammers; in the U.S.A., it would be called a hammer dulcimer). Around them were lots of fiddles, a cello and two bass viols, a few reeds. Stacked near were some strange wooden whistles, including one about five feet long. The average age of the performers was thirty or thirty-five. Some oldsters of forty and fifty, and a few youths. One girl.

Danny and I were bowled over. They played half a dozen numbers for us. Expertness! They used no conductor, but a lead fiddler or shepherd's flute would start off, and keep the rest with him. It was very arranged folk music—a shepherd's tune starting off unaccompanied, and then the rest filling in with full harmony, and then the whole band breaking into a breakneck dance, including stamping and whistling.

Some of the fiddlers showed conservatory training, others were obviously folk originals. The soloists, especially a flute player-singer-dancer, were amazing.

When the cymbalon hammers got going at breakneck speed, Zbynek

Macha, a Czech friend who has studied both European and American folk music, whispered to me, "The cymbalon was brought to this country half a century ago, from Rumania. What you are hearing now is Czech bluegrass music."

Afterward I asked Macha if they played on the radio and gave concerts. "Oh yes, they are completely professional musicians. But this kind of thing is not so popular as it was fifteen years ago. The trouble is, the government sponsored it, and it was all you could hear on the radio. Young people started listening to American popular music on Radio Luxembourg. Finally, five years ago, the government gave in, and now Czech radio has three kinds of popular music: our old folk music, which is mainly popular with older people, and jazz, which has a small but intense following, and Big Beat music, which you call rock-and-roll or twist. Big Beat is the main thing with Czech teenagers now. There are two hundred amateur groups playing it in Prague. Electric guitars and all. Some of it is quite good. The singing is in Czech."

Prague
March 26, 1964

A SYMPOSIUM was arranged in Prague to discuss folk music. In a big hall were seated about a thousand people with tables in front of them. Looked like a convention. People were taking notes. The chairman gave a five-minute introductory speech, and then the whole rest of the evening consisted of me trying to answer questions that were written on notepaper and passed up.

"What is the relationship of American folk music to Big Beat rock-and-roll?" "What is bluegrass music?" "Are the blues considered folk music?" I was on the spot, knowing that I wasn't an authority, but trying my best to answer.

Too many questions came in asking my personal artistic judgment. "What do you think of Czech music?" "What do you think of Chuck Berry?" "What do you think of Hank Snow?" I protested. In the first place, I don't know enough about these musicians to express an opinion. Second, I don't like to hand out opinions off the cuff. Third, it would be wrong to do so. "Every one of you must make up your own mind whether you think an artist is good or bad. These are crucial decisions, and only you can decide."

At the end I asked *them* a question: "Do you think it possible that my

American style of banjo picking might be used to accompany Czech folk songs?" I picked up the five-stringer and scrugged off a rhythm behind a little ditty that every person in the audience knew from childhood. I had to whistle it, because my voice was shot.

A ripple of surprise went through the audience, then shy laughter and applause. Afterward a Czech friend said to me: "It was the best thing you could have done. They've forgotten how good their own music is."

I have a suspicion that when folk music appeared here on a stage, it often may have been formalized, arranged or costumed. This is similar to what bogged down Cecil Sharp's attempt to encourage a folk song revival in England fifty years ago. The music was neatly arranged for piano and chorus. All the bawdiness and protest were taken from the lyrics so that they would be "proper" for schoolchildren. No wonder many an adult Briton said to himself, "They can keep their folk music."

Well, experience has shown in Britain and elsewhere that folk music can even survive its revivalists. And I'm willing to bet that a few years from now young Czechs will realize that they have a helluva lot of fine tunes and rhythms and poetry that they can use to make their lives more musical, to understand where they came from and where they want to go, and to use as a basis for their own imagination and creativity.

Well, well, look who's talking. An American who has tried to sing songs in a dozen other languages. A Yankee who decided that southern folk songs were his favorite kind of music, and has been making a living singing them ever since. Okay, I'm guilty.

Road sign in the Crimea

Dzhankoy, USSR
April 21, 1964

THE CRIMEA is a diamond-shaped peninsula on the north side of the Black Sea. It is famous for grapes and wine, and also as a favorite resort area for the USSR. The small range of mountains on the southern edge drops sharply into the sea. In the old days castles and villas of the nobility nestled among the crags. Now there are hundreds of workers' resorts. The central area of the Crimea is flat—only slightly rolling. Treeless but for hundreds of thousands of fruit trees and vineyards.

Simferopol, in this center section, is a city of about 200,000. I learned this from a man who stopped me in the street and in slow but good English told me that he and his wife had seen me sing in Moscow. How come? They had been on their honeymoon. He was a medical student. The medical school here has 2,000 students.

We drive to a town labeled on the map Джанкой. It is pronounced John-*koy* and usually anglicized as Dzhankoy. Dzhankoy is really a lovely town. We were all in good spirits, with the warm weather and sunshine. And because they don't need to burn vast quantities of soft coal, the air is clean and the streets too. Main streets were of cobblestone, and the smaller streets unpaved. Dan took lots of pictures, including one charming one of a man sleeping in the railroad station waiting room, with his head resting on his wife's broad bottom.

This was an exploratory trip. I didn't know who we were going to see.

I aimed for the newspaper office first, and explained my problem to a very nice man sitting behind a desk.

"Thirty years ago there was a song written here. It was collected by a folklorist and published in a book in the U.S.A. I and other people learned it, and through us, many hundreds of thousands of Americans have heard the song. It gives us a little glimpse of Soviet life. It was all in Yiddish and described life on a collective farm. I have been told that in 1942 this whole area was destroyed by the Nazis, and many people killed, but do you think it would be possible to find anyone who knows the song and, perhaps, who or when or where it was made up?"

I sang him a verse of the song. The editor was a man in his thirties. He shook his head. "I wasn't living here then, and I don't know the song. But you go get some lunch with your family. I'll make some phone calls, and perhaps in an hour I'll be able to help you."

When we returned I found myself being interviewed by a reporter on the paper. I gave him all the verses as best I knew them from Ruth Rubin's book, *A Treasury of Jewish Folksong*.

DZHANKOYE*

(*words on next page*)

---

* From p. 94 (under the title "Az Men Fort Kayn Sevastopol") in Ruth Rubin, *A Treasury of Jewish Folksong* (Schocken Books, New York, 1951; paperback edition, Oak Publications)—where you will also find Ruth's singing translation. (Mine is in *The Bells of Rhymney*, p. 70.)

	Literal translation: *
Az men fort kayn Sevastopol,	As one travels to Sevastopol—
Iz nit vayt fun Simferopol,	It's not far from Simferopol—
Dortn iz a stantsiye faran.	There is a railroad station:
Ver darf zuchn naye glikn?	Who wants to look for new glory?
S'iz a stantsiye an antikl,	This is a station, a beauty,
In Dzhankoye, Dzhan, Dzhan, Dzhan.	In Dzhankoy, Dzhan, Dzhan, Dzhan.

Chorus:

Hey Dzhan, hey Dzhankoye,	Hey Dzhan, hey Dzhankoy,
Hey Dzhanvili, hey Dzhankoye,	Hey Dzhan-village, hey Dzhankoy,
Hey Dzhankoye, Dzhan, Dzhan, Dzhan.	Hey Dzhanoky, Dzhan, Dzhan, Dzhan.

Entfert Yidn oyf mayn kashe,	Answer my question, Jews:
Vu'z mayn bruder, vu'z Abrasha?	Where's my brother, where's Abrasha?
S'geyt bay im der trakter vi a ban.	His tractor is going like a locomotive.
Di mume Leye bay der kosilke,	Aunt Leye is at the butter churn,
Beyle bay der molotilke,	Beyle at the thresher,
In Dzhankoye, Dzhan, Dzhan, Dzhan.	In Dzhankoy, Dzhan, Dzhan, Dzhan.

Ver zogt az Yidn konen nor handlen,	Who says Jews can only buy and sell,
Esn fete yoych mit mandlen,	Only eat fat chicken soup with soup nuts,
Nor nit zayn kayn arbetsman?	Just so as not to be workingmen?
Dos konen zogn nor di sonim!	This can be said only by our enemies!
Yidn! Shpayt zey on in ponim!	Jews! Spit in their faces!
Tut a kuk oyf Dzhan, Dzhan, Dzhan!	Take a look at Dzhan, Dzhan, Dzhan!

(*ey*—as in "they"; *ay*—long *i* as in "mine")

Then I learned a lot.

The town had built up to a population of about 5,000 when the war came. Some young people and children were saved by being shipped further east, but for most it meant slaughter. Thousands of Jews were killed outright and dumped in mass graves. Only the railroad station was still upright as a building when, three years later, the Nazis were forced to retreat.

But the whole town was rebuilt and now numbers about 50,000. It would not be thought a wealthy city by U.S.A. standards, but it is clean and neat, with tree-lined streets, and parks and suburbs with thousands of little houses with fruit trees blooming in the yards. There is an airfield; construction workers stream through, working on a giant canal to bring Dnieper River waters to the sunny and fertile Crimean plains.

And the collective farm? "There's been some consolidation of the

* Thanks to Mrs. Ida Goodman for helping us with the translation.

farms since the war. More efficient. The nearest one, called Rossiya,* combines what were formerly several different farms. It's one of the leading farms in the whole country and quite famous."

"How big?" I asked. "Oh, more than five thousand."

"Did any Jews come back here after the war?"

"Why, 55 or 60 percent of Rossiya Collective Farm is Jewish, though they also have Russians and Ukrainians."

"I'm interested to hear that," says I, "because when the stories came out about some of the things that had happened under Stalin, some people said to me, 'See, there is anti-Semitism in the Soviet Union, and the song is a lie.' "

There was a roar of laughter from my listeners, who numbered now about six men of the staff of the newspaper. "The assistant manager of Rossiya is Jewish, and the woman who is the head agronomist is also Jewish. She writes poems, some of which we have printed in our paper."

Now drifted into the room about twenty people, in their smocks, from the printing rooms below. Over half were women. All ages, from youthful to gray-haired. One man with a wooden leg. They sat down in chairs, and I took out my banjo and gave a short concert, including "Dzhankoye." Some of the older workers nodded. "Yes, we remember it. There was even a recording of it you could buy." Another said, "I think it was made up by someone from the Sholem Aleichem Kolkhoz. That's part of Rossiya now."

We posed for photos. The room was hung with banners and slogans and mottoes of the Communist party. It was a conference room. Portraits of Lenin and Khrushchev. And fifty or more photos of prizewinning workers from the farms and factories. I noticed several names like Lerner and Feigin.

We packed up, said goodbye, and went to the doorway outside, when one of the women came after us: "Wouldn't you like to see where we work?" And there were women running big power presses, and tall linotype machines, and in another room a woman cutting paper.† Big piles and rolls of various kinds of paper all through the room. Our interpreter says: "Pete has been trying to find some extra-thin typewriting paper . . ." Without hesitation they pick up a big hunk of a thousand sheets of it and insist we take it as a present.

---

* Pronounced Rosseeya.
† Next to her was a tall potted plant, something quite common in Soviet factories where women work.

April 22, 1964

Today we visited Rossiya Collective Farm itself. We drove again over the gently rolling Crimean plains, down a straight avenue lined with flowering cherry, apple and plum trees, till we came to a sign: Россия (Rossiya), and near it a cast cement statue of a girl athlete with a volleyball (such statues are not uncommon near gates and entrances).

We drove down a smooth dirt road for about five miles and then turned in at a neat village. There were many straight unpaved streets, with young trees planted along them, and little white or buff houses with tile roofs or roofs of corrugated composition. Then we turned a corner and found ourselves on a broad avenue with a grand fountain, and at the end of it a neo-Greek building being put up!

We pulled up in front of an office, and the manager of the farm came out to greet us—a tall muscular man in his fifties, who looked like a successful midwestern farmer. Even in a business suit, shirt and tie, his tanned face, creased neck, and pale forehead told me his profession. A firm jaw and a shrewd eye. Altogether, one could see, a practiced administrator, and experienced judge of people, cows, grapes, financial affairs and a thousand other details.

We sat down with him in his office, and within a half hour, learned the main outlines. The farm is about half Jewish, the rest Russians and Ukrainians. The assistant manager is Jewish. The manager is not, but must speak all three languages. (Russian and Ukrainian are very similar.)

Rossiya is a combination of some eleven small collective farms that existed before the war. The Germans conquered the region in October, 1941, and were driven out in April 1944. The region was utterly devastated.

Now the farm is composed of about 1,000 families, over 4,000 people in all (those who survived the slaughter were added to by many who come from other districts), and is one of the most prosperous farms in the Crimea.

They have 13,000 hectares* of land:

---

* 13,000 hectares is approximately 32,500 acres.

5,000 in wheat,
1,500 in grapes,
900 in fruit trees,
300 in vegetables,
200 for corn.

The rest is grass for 7,000 head of cattle. They also have 6,000 pigs and 25,000 chickens, ducks, etc.

And to help to do the work, 120 tractors, 54 combines, 70 vehicles (trucks and cars); and in addition, they run their own milk and butter plant, winery, meat-packing and pickle factory, as well as a technical repair center for farm machinery, also used by other farms around.

Members get paid for the work they do. If the farm has a successful year, all share in the good fortune. If it has a bad year, they all have to take a cut. The standard minimum for a day's work is about $3, but it is usual for quotas to be overfulfilled, so average daily pay on the farm as a whole is about $6.50 a day—higher than average USSR city wages. Some skilled workers, such as tractor drivers, can earn $10 a day or more. This is, of course, in addition to free rent, schooling, complete medical care, including childbirth care for women, two weeks vacation per year (usually at the seashore), pensions for older people. About 5 percent of the youth go on to college (also free). Anyone can resign and leave the farm if they wish, but this does not happen so much as new people join it, either marrying into it or for any other reason. The farm has its own store where members can buy their own produce at lower prices than in town, and everyone eats (and drinks) exceedingly well.

About 100 families have private cars. Many more would, but the USSR purposely is not producing enough cars for its citizens, preferring to put the time and materials into more urgent projects. Cars are extremely hard to get. Many at Rossiya get motorcycles of some sort. No great shortage of them. Members can add rooms to their houses at their own expense if they wish, also toolsheds, etc. And when I looked closely at their homes I realized that hardly any two houses were exactly alike, though all were similar. All were built with big blocks of a porous coral rock which is quarried nearby, then plastered over smooth, and painted. In the Ukraine, it is traditional to paint houses at least once a year.

Well, now, after all these details, what about the song? By luck, a man passing nearby was one of the older settlers, Mosseyevitch Shapiro. He'd come here as a child in 1924. Had he ever heard the song? Oh yes, but he could only remember the first verse. He'd first heard it back in 1926. There were many young people who liked to sing and make up songs. Who composed the song? Oh, it must be like so many folk songs: different people contribute to them.

I took out the tape recorder and he without hestitation sang a first verse and chorus. Somewhat slower than I have been doing it, and slightly different words and melody. We got talking about life on the farm. "This is a very good farm. . . . Russians, Ukrainians, Jews . . . we all get along well together. . . . No, no anti-Semitism! . . . We have many things in our houses; I have a television set. . . ."

And since it was only his lunch hour, and he had to get back to work, we thanked him, and went on to look about the town. In back of the manager's office was a park. The shade trees were all newly planted and not very tall yet, but walks were laid out, with occasional benches. A big, ornate fountain at one end, and at the other, a tall statue of Lenin, freshly painted with gilt paint. By coincidence, today was Lenin's birthday, and a hundred schoolchildren were gathered about for a brief ceremony. A teen-age girl seemed to be in charge, and introduced a few short recitations, three-minute speeches, exchange of gifts, and a song. Altogether it was astonishingly like what might have been done for a Lincoln's birthday celebration in the U.S.A., including the fact that the teen-age boys sang hardly at all, but let the others do the work.

Then we went to a large neo-Greek building at one side of the park. "This is our Palace of Culture." Inside was an auditorium with crystal chandelier, and plaster wreaths all around it, a stage with a red plush curtain. "It is too small, only 700 seats." Upstairs was a music school: three teen-agers studying accordion, and next door two girls at a piano trying to learn something that sounded like Tchaikovsky to me, and a very little girl standing next to them, singing earnestly in a loud, clear voice, under the watchful eye of a teacher. Across the hall was a large reading room, with political literature, and also books and pamphlets on farm matters. These are exchanged between different farms, it seems. I picked up one, written by a collective-farm worker some place, titled "How I Was Able to Raise 128 Lambs in a Year." Around the walls were mottoes such as one sees on every public building here: "Peace, truth, fraternity, labor," and so on. Also some quotes from Lenin.

After this we were asked, "Would you like to see our school?" Sure, we said. A long two-story building, very neat, clean, light and airy. Thirty teachers for about 350 students, in this particular one. (Our school near

Tchaikovsky at Dzhankoy

Beacon has 18 for 250 students.) Even allowing for administrative personnel and specialists, this means classes would be on the whole smaller than U. S. average. In the biology room we went into, there were desks for about 20. Hung high on the walls over the charts and exhibits were portraits of famous biologists . . . all Russian. Place of honor went to Michurin, the Russian who showed how new varieties of fruit could be produced. On another wall, a portrait of Lysenko, the contemporary biologist who got into such hot arguments with the traditional geneticists over what was possible and what they said was impossible to do to genes.

Down the hall a small gym equipped for basketball and tumbling. We poked our head into other classrooms. Girls all wear white aprons. Both boys and girls wear bright red neckerchiefs. On the wall in the hall is a series of faded reproductions of paintings by Russian landscape painters. Here is a poster put up by the German-language circle, with a quote (in German) from Lenin: "A foreign language is a weapon in the battle for Life."

And after this, lunch. (Am I boring you with all this? I figure that if I am to be honest, I must present as many dry facts as I know of. The editorializing can come later. I am full of mixed feelings about Rossiya.)

In one of the member's homes we all sat down at a long table. Everything spotless clean. A big white tablecloth. (In all the USSR we have never eaten on a bare tabletop except once at a quick lunch counter.) The two bedrooms leading off of the dining room were light and airy, and not too small.

Wonderful bread, big plates of butter. First course: fish, pickled tomatoes and pickled cucumbers. Second course: pot roast beef and potatoes. Third course: braised steak. And white wine, red wine, and pop!, a bottle of Soviet champagne. Then my glass is filled with about four shots of cognac. I know we are being treated like VIPs, nevertheless, we are bowled over. I am facing a rather personal problem now. For the past year I have found my system growing so increasingly sensitive to alcohol that I almost have to stay off it completely. But I am on the spot.

The manager of the farm stands and fixes me with an intent glance. "To peace and friendship between the Soviet peoples and the people of America!" He empties his four shots of cognac in one gulp. I pretend to sip at mine. He is clearly disappointed. The other members of the Seeger family do somewhat better than I. Mika and Toshi sip at their champagne, Danny at his wine. I ask Lisa, our pretty interpreter, to explain that I can't drink, but she says, "You must try, it is the custom."

A damn foolish custom, I think to myself.

The manager goes around the table filling up everyone's glasses. I swipe some of Tinya's pink soda pop and try to toast with this, but the manager is even more grim looking. I am humiliated and can't look him in the eye. He asks if there are not any more questions I would like to ask. I try, but somehow the words will not come out. After lunch, out in the sunshine, he asks again if there is anything else he can do for us. It is really very nice of him, because this is one of the busiest seasons of the year.

The one thing I would like seems to be an impossibility: I would like to meet some members of the farm who like to sing, and just sit around and exchange some songs with them. But they are all out working. And they are all working overtime, as hard as they can, this month. In the evening they will return dead tired and anxious to hit the hay, since early next morning comes another hard working day. We have come at the wrong season of the year for folklore collecting, at the wrong day of the week even. So we realize the impossibility of our request. We shake hands all around, with our hostess, a short cheery Jewish woman, and with the other men, and the manager. They all wave their hands till we are out of sight down the road.

Just before lunch I had been sitting by the big fountain near the manager's office, trying to sort out my confused mind. The handsome young driver of our car was listening to some Czech rock-and-roll on the car radio. Out of a distant window I could still hear the two little girls practicing Tchaikovsky. I thought of the forty-year-old Jewish song which I felt was more beautiful than either, which was remembered only by some of the old-timers. The youngsters speak Russian now more than Yiddish.

The fountain seemed to sum up many of Rossiya's qualities: It was pretentious in a way, but very humble, too. The whole thing was of cement. The pool was about 30 feet long. An iron pipe sprayed thin streams of water over four central figures: four children—one skipping rope, one kicking a football, one holding a model of a sputnik, and another holding some books, and all striding purposefully into a happy future.

The figures were painted with white-enamel paint. Above their heads a kind of cement mushroom shape had a flat top on which were eight or ten white-enameled doves of peace, and in the center the top end of a neo-Greek column, with some kind of flowers coming out of the top of it. Only it wasn't in the center, but slightly askew.

I know artists in the States who would laugh at such an attempt to beautify a town, but I could not laugh. These people were hoping and striving as best they knew how. And they really mean it when they keep reiterating that word "Mir" (peace). Each family here lost loved ones a generation ago. And should I criticize what I think is their poor taste in architecture and sculpture? Parks too. (All their parks are laid out in neat geometric squares, circles, and triangles, just like the gardens of the Russian aristocrats who were trying to imitate Versailles.)

On the contrary, I think I'll go along with Mao Tse-tung, who wrote: "If you want to lift a pail of water from the ground, you can't extend your arm horizontally and expect to find the pail there. You have to bend down to the ground where it is and start lifting."

These people here are lifting steadily. Their standard of living is way higher than ever before. I asked at the winery how prices were set by the government for their produce. "According to the quality." In other words, prices didn't fluctuate wildly with market whims, as in the U.S.—the kind of quick market drops which wiped out some farmers overnight are unknown here.

At the rate they are going, I wouldn't be surprised to see all kinds of prosperity here in another twenty-five years. And perhaps a symphony orchestra composed of members of the farm. But maybe there will be rock-and-roll bands. And, who knows, perhaps within twenty years a folk song revival such as inundated U. S. popular music this year; and their young people may rediscover an old Yiddish song made by their grandparents.

These few pages don't do justice to the tremendous musical life in the socialist countries. There are huge country folk festivals and many small intimate ones. People in small villages hang on tenaciously to their deeply loved traditions.

In 1965, two years after most of this chapter was written, Toshi and I toured six central Asian Soviet republics. On the corner newsstands one could see magazines and books in two languages: Russian and the local language. One might see also the magazine Ogonyok (*Soviet equivalent of* Life *or* Look *magazine), printed in the local language. Ogonyok is printed in* eighty *languages. In Tashkent, capital of Uzbekistan, I spent an hour talking with a local musician, an expert performer on a type of Uzbek lute.*

"Where do you perform, mostly?" I ask him. "At weddings, parties?"
"Oh no. Like you. Radio, TV."

I found he also taught at the Tashkent institute of traditional music— such institutes are maintained throughout the Soviet Union.

But in the big cities young people here also tended to think of folk music as representing the past. When they look forward, many of them seem more interested in jazz and cabaret music.

Clones, Ireland
May 1964

HEREWITH, a report on one of the world's most interesting folk festivals, an Irish Fleadh Cheoil. That's pronounced Fla' Kyol, and it means "Festival of Music" in Gaelic. It is sponsored by an all-Ireland society to promote traditional music. Each year, they hold it in a different town (like the Olympic Games).

The first was held twelve years ago, with only a few hundred people attending. Now, there are hundreds of local parish Fleadh Cheoils and dozens of county Fleadhs. The big annual Fleadh attracts such large crowds that the sponsors are trying to find ways to cut it down. In 1963, when it was held near Dublin, about 100,000 came. This year, by holding it farther away from the big city, they hoped to keep the crowd down to

60,000. This year's Fleadh was held at Clones, a town of about 4,000 up on the border between the Free State and British-held North Ireland. Of course, the music was not the only attraction. The strong beer flowed in dozens of pubs (and dozens of improvised pubs) throughout the town. More on this later.

"Where does the crowd all sleep?" I asked Tommy Makem, who, with the Clancy Brothers, first told me about the Fleadh. "Who sleeps?" says he.

When we drove into Clones (pronounced Clo-ness) a day early, the fields outside the town were already filling up with cars and pup tents. At the Fleadh office, a cordial local committeeman found us a nearby farm where we could park our van and use a bathroom. Next day, when we came back to town, police were stopping all but a few cars from entering. All the roads for three miles away were lined with parked cars and, in town, the streets were filled with milling thousands.

The Fleadh lasted Saturday, Sunday, and Monday. There were no big performances such as we are used to in Stateside folk festivals. During the first two days, there were elimination contests in five or ten small auditoriums around town—church halls, schoolrooms, tents. On the final day, the winners performed again. No audience was bigger than a few hundred, and many contests had only a few dozen watching, mainly performers and their families. The contests were in ballad singing (in Gaelic and in English), lilting (rhythmic mouth music), fiddling, accordion playing, tin whistling, and bagpiping (bagpiping of two kinds: one type of pipe was the Scottish-style "warpipes"; the other, the Irish Uillean pipes, had the wind forced into the bag from a bellows strapped under the player's right arm—drones were held in the lap, where occasional chords could also be played on them).

There were also contests for harmonica, ceilidh bands (ten players, including fiddler, accordionist, pianist, and snare drummer), plain whistling, and harp playing. Sadly, there were no entries for the latter two classes.

But, for many of the thousands coming to Clones, the real music was in the pubs and homes—and in the dozens of little groups gathered in the streets. Here, there were no contests, just good fellowship and lots of singing and beer. The most popular instruments were fiddle, accordion, tin whistle, and a large flat drum called a boron (I don't know the exact spelling). The disc is about twenty inches across, and the frame is thin wood, about three and a half inches wide. The left hand holds it up vertically, and the right hand holds a short, thick drumstick pointing toward the stomach. The right wrist is curved, and the hand shakes al-

Street in Clones: a boron player

most as in frailing a banjo. The loose sheepskin gives out a deep throbbing rhythm, a perfect foil for the shrill penny whistle. And often someone nearby would be rattling a pair of spoons on their knee.

Many of the young people wandering into town with knapsacks on their backs also had guitars with them. This instrument was not really approved by the Fleadh committee, since it had been the vehicle for so much imported American folk music. And the traditionalists felt emphatically that ballads should be unaccompanied. But I have a suspicion that, twenty-five years from now, the guitar, too, may be considered kosher. After all, when did the accordion make its appearance?

The great hit song of the Fleadh, an old sailor's song called "The Holy Ground," was a song not featured in the contests. Like most sailors' ballads about shore life, its early meanings were purely scandalous, but now it seems to be proper to sing it everywhere; it has romantic words, a brisk march tempo, and a startling shouted phrase at unexpected points:

> For the secrets of my mind
> (FINE GIRL YOU ARE!)
> You're the girl that I adore
> And still I live in hopes to see
> The Holy Ground once more
> (FINE GIRL YOU ARE!)

We heard it roared out by groups of young men careening arm in arm down the street. In the pubs one heard it too, but inside, one would also hear more of the quiet songs, from the popular and even mawkish "Molly Malone" to "She Moved Through the Fair" and the McPeakes' "Will Ye Go, Lassie, Go?"

The visitors to Clones were mostly young people from local and surrounding counties, plus a few folk buffs from the cities. During the daytime, we saw a number of older people and families with children, but in the evening the shy and conservative ones tended to leave (perhaps, sensibly, to get some needed sleep). It was daylight until near 10 P.M. At 3 A.M. the evening was in full swing when the next morning was just beginning; then, the streets were full of roving young men and fewer hardy girls—roaming, singing, dancing, listening, and beering. This was the first time that Clones had such an invasion, and, on the whole, the community seemed most cooperative and warm to the thousands on their doorsteps. But there were occasional disapproving faces looking from front doorways, probably wondering about the outcome nine months from now.

By and large, it was not a rowdy crowd. We only saw one fight ourselves. (One year, in Mullingar, there were many, we were told, and two men were killed in one.) The Fleadh committee was, of course, trying to keep it from getting out of hand. But the beer must still flow; it is an essential part of "the Fla'."

Also in the streets—besides ice-cream vendors (4 cents)—were gambling tables with roulette wheels and barkers, and in open lots, there were carnival attractions such as merry-go-rounds and whizzer-loops.

We took a movie camera into Protestant Hall, where the fiddle competition was being held. As families and friends drifted in, six fiddlers were tuning up and playing in different corners of the hall. Cacaphony! Half an hour later, three judges arrived and sat at a table in front of the stage. Over the next hour the hall gradually filled up. Each contestant played three or four pieces: jigs, reels, hornpipes, and at least one slow air. All were unaccompanied. When the judges' decision was handed out, the speaker gave a serious dissertation on the reasons for the decisions: this one used too heavy a bow, another ended with two strokes when he should have used one. "This is nice fireside playin'. But if he'd keep the bow nearer the bridge, he'd get more bite. Now, here's the hard part. I'll announce the winner. I hate to hurt the other fellows' feelin's."

Most of the fiddlers were men, but some of the younger ones were girls. Competition was in three sections: Junior (children), Novice (any beginner), and Senior (experienced older performers).

Summary: the big problem with these contests (a problem faced by all contests including Olympic boxing and U. S. elections) is that rarely do the best players participate in them. Many of the best traditional players in Ireland came to the Fleadh, but would rather have died than appear on a competition platform. Others were too shy to come to Clones, or couldn't afford the trip for the sake of winning a silver cup.

I came to the conclusion that Clones should have had a few invitational programs in which specific, good traditional performers could come and be paid a nominal fee, as at Newport. This would make a three-cornered balance for the weekend: the pubs, the competitions, and the invitational programs.

But, as is, there was no doubt that some of the competitors were damn good. Only one man competed in the Senior class for Uillean pipes, one Felix Doran, from Manchester, England ("there are more Irish living in England than in Ireland"). But Doran was generous and gave a private concert for half an hour for the hundred people present. There was great applause from a group of rawboned farmers in the back, their faces ruddy and their foreheads pale from wearing hats in the fields.

The best thing about the Fleadh was the rank-and-file spirit and the hundreds of little gatherings. The comparative lack of famous traditional musicians didn't matter much. Attending the Fleadh was cheap; if you wanted to hitchhike there and camp out, 35 cents covered all daytime events, and the music was free in the pubs and streets. And holding the Fleadh in a different town each year gives the audience of local working people a glimpse of traditional music and a sense of its importance when thousands of visitors stream in.

Tuesday morning, we packed up our van and trundled off. Clones looked deserted except for some men sweeping up huge piles of paper in the streets. Everybody else must have been catching up on sleep, after not having gotten much for 72 hours. A day later, fifty miles away, we were crossing the border and I overheard a young woman in the car ahead of us joshing with the customs inspector, a portly older man who seemed to be an old friend.

"Did you make it to the Fla'?" she asked him. "No? Oh, it was fine. We were there on Sunday. Next year, there'll be one at 'Blaney. It's not far. I'll come take you myself." And she gave him a squeeze about the waist.

If you like unaccompanied ballad singing in English or Gaelic, or you like good traditional fiddling or flute playing, and you find yourself in Dublin, Ireland, stop in at the O'Donaghues' pub. Any night of the week.

Up near the front of the pub might be a handful of men exchanging ballads with a dozen or more listening to them. Thirty feet down the bar might be two men playing jigs and reels on silver flutes, fluttering up and down in unison. And in the back room, twenty-five feet further on, might be Barney McKenna and some friends giving out with some Dublin street songs.

There is no MC, no planned program, but it's all under the firm and watchful eye of Maureen O'Donaghue and her husband. When it comes to music, they know what they like. In the old days, they would promptly toss out on his ear any fellow who raised his voice in song, because it was usually of the "Irish Eyes Are Smiling" variety. But in March of 1963 some of their regular customers came in, bubbling with enthusiasm over a concert they'd just given of traditional Irish ballads. They started singing the concert through again, with the help of some of O'Donaghue's dark beer. "Ah, ha," said the O'Donaghues, "this is the kind of music we like." And the tradition was born.

Their only problem now is that as the word spreads quickly of O'Donaghue's being a musical sort of place, not everyone realizes what kind of music is appropriate there. Tommy Makem tells me that last year a fellow came in with an electric guitar and plugged it into a wall socket.

"What in the name of God is that!" says Maureen.

"It's an electric guitar," says he.

"And whose electricity are you using?"

"I'm just plugging it into the wall."

"If you can't play it by yourself, you're not going to play it with my electricity."

And out he went.

In Dublin the newspapers carried advertisements of American movies, and rock-and-roll bands (Chubby Checker was a huge hit on his tour here last year), and concert performers. But, by and large, I feel there are enough Irish who really love their own music to hold onto it for a long time.

My concert was in an arena usually used for prizefights. I could imagine next day one of my audience recounting:

"I was at the stadium last night."

"Really? Who was on?"

"Seeger and folk songs."

"Oh. Who won?"

> *June 5, 1964: Home again. The United States seems very big, very rich, the cars huge. The Hudson Valley still seems like one of the most beautiful spots on earth, even if the river does stink with sewage. It's good to be home.*

14·Languages, Translations and Mixtures

SOME COMMENTS ON THE MANY VOCABULARIES OF MUSIC, SPEECH AND OTHER WAYS OF HUMAN EXPRESSION

> *George Bernard Shaw once said, "A man cannot write well in more than one language."*
>
> *Mahalia Jackson once told me: "I love to hear people sing their own songs, because they can sing 'em so much better than anyone else."*
>
> *But Rockwell Kent wrote me: "If you learn another man's language, you learn something of the soul of his people."*

UNDERNEATH everyone's surface layers of politeness, underneath deeper layers of disagreement between individuals and classes, there are still further layers of agreement. One reason musicians are suspect is that it is often these layers we appeal to. (The conservation issue, I have found, also reaches these layers; it's bringing together people who normally wouldn't speak to each other. After all, there is only one ocean of air we all breathe, one ocean of water lapping every shore. If these become poisoned, of what use to inherit the earth?)

So I and my fellow musicians tromp over the globe, suspected by many, attractive to many. Fascists say, "Better dead than red." The Wobblies said, "The working class and the employing class have nothing in common." I sing "A Hard Rain Is Gonna Fall" to humans and inhumans alike.

A young man wrote me from Tokyo in 1965, when he was just entering college:

". . . Japan today is crowded with many musics from overseas countries. . . . We Japanese are also influenced by standardization, as supermarkets, buying the same foods, dress, and living in the same houses and the same living style. . . . I believe these people are not human beings but goods. . . . But I love Japan.

". . . The nature of folk songs is that everyone from children to adults can sing easily and naturally. But it is difficult for youth who are very interested in European musics to turn their eyes to Japanese folk songs. Further, as a vocalization of Japanese songs is somewhat difficult, they dislike it.

"I think it would be a nice way to add a modern element to Japanese folk songs, following the example of the folk song revival movement in America. . . . It will be occurred the loss of its purity, but we will conquer it by spreading it to a great many people.

"In this decadent world, we need folk music. . . . The expression of folk songs with the joy, sorrow, and resistance of men is more stronger than that of literature and also classical or popular music. It is said generally that music is a element comforting us. Surely this point of view is important, but another view is that music is something to inspire us.

"I think the latter, that inspiring men with courage, and let us contact with each other for creating a new world is more important."

Kiyohide Kunizaki
Tokyo, Japan

Translating or Not Translating Songs

IF YOU RUN ACROSS a beautiful song in a foreign language do one of three things: learn to sing it well in the original, pronouncing the words right, or else locate or compose really poetic English lyrics for it, or leave the song for someone else to sing. *What not to do:* ruin it for young ears by singing a second-rate English translation.

In the old *People's Songs Bulletin* we once had a hot argument on whether or not to try and sing English translations of songs from other countries. Ruth Rubin felt that my attempt to translate "Dzhankoye" missed too much of the original meaning. I must agree that one thing that repels me from the folk songs printed in many school songbooks is the poor quality of the translations. It's an almost impossible job, of course. Remember Robert Frost's famous definition of poetry? "Poetry is what gets lost in the translation."

Furthermore, the rewards of learning even a little bit of another language are many.* Edgar Snow said he felt he began to understand China when he started learning the written language as well as the spoken language.

Often there is no exact equivalent for a word in another language. It is as though different human beings have faced the varying phenomena of the world—all shades of colors, from light to dark, all kinds of musical sounds, from high to low—and picked out what they considered key locations to be identified with a word.

But different cultures consider different key locations to be important.

Thus one language may describe: loping, trotting, running, galloping, racing. Another language (an Australian aborigine one) has fifty different words to pinpoint different kinds of running, including running scared and running angry.

In Japan one of the big problems in translation is Japanese politeness vs. Yankee bluntness. Their word for "you" literally means "my dear, precious you." Even if you hate someone, you use this word: "I hate my-dear-precious you."

I've never yet heard a first-rate translation of some of my favorite songs, like "Tumbalalaika," "Guantanamera," "Suliram," or "Meadowland." And songs in some dialects of English are similarly unsingable if "translated" into another brand of English.

I heard a lot of beautiful songs when I was in Scotland. Some I could sing in Americanese. But others were impossible to translate adequately. Too much of the poetry was lost. I finally decided it was worth learning Scottish so as to sing Hamish Henderson's "Freedom Come-All-Ye," one of the songs that came out of the anti-Polaris movement there. It's one of the world's greatest songs, it's worth your taking a half hour to decipher the following verses.

---

* You ought not to try and pick up a song in a language you don't know just from a book. Get someone who knows the language to help you with the subtleties, or at least listen carefully to phonograph records. Otherwise you run the risk of butchering the poor song (something I have done too often myself).

FREEDOM COME-ALL-YE

Words by Hamish Henderson; music adapted by Hamish Henderson from "The Bloody Field of Flanders." Copyright © 1964 by Hamish Henderson.

1. Roch the wind in the clear day's dawin' (roch—rough; dawin'—dawning)

   Blaws the cloods heelster gowdie ow'r the bay. (cloods—clouds; heelster gowdie—helter skelter)

   But there's mair nor a roch wind blawin' (mair nor—more than)

   Through the great glen o' the warld the day. (glen—valley; the day—today)

   It's a thocht that will gar oor rattans, (thocht—thought; gar—make; oor—our; rattans—vermin)

   Aa they rogues that gang gallus, fresh and gay, (gang—go; gallus—reckless)

   Tak the road an' seek ither loanin's (ither—other; loanin's—lanes, avenues)

   For their ill ploys tae sport and play. (ill ploys—evil games; tae—to)

2. Nae mair will the bonnie callants (bonnie callants—fine young men)

   Mairch tae war, when oor braggarts crusely craw, (crusely craw—crow boastfully)

   Nor wee weans frae pit-heid an' clachan (weans—little children; pit-heid—head of the mine; clachan—valley)

   Mourn the ships sailin' doon the Broomielaw; (Broomielaw—a Scottish naval channel)

   Broken faimlies, in lands we herriet (herriet—harried)

   Will curse Scotland the Brave nae mair, nae mair;

   Black an' white, ane til ither mairriet, (mairriet—married)

   Mak the vile barracks o' their maisters bare. (mak—make; maisters—masters)

3. O come all ye at hame wi' freedom, (hame—home)

   Never heed whit the hoodies croak for doom; (whit—what; hoodies—crows or buzzards)

   In your hoose aa the bairns o' Adam (hoose—house; bairns—children)

   Can find breid, barley bree, an' painted room. (breid—bread; barley bree—beer)

   When MacLean meets wi's freens in Springburn (MacLean—great Scottish radical leader of 50 years ago; Springburn—Glasgow working-class district)

   All the roses an' geans will turn tae bloom, (geans—flowers)

   An' a black boy frae yont Nyanga (yont—yonder)

   Dings the fell gallows o' the burghers doon. (dings—knocks; burghers—businessmen) (doon—down)

The person who tries to sing a song in dialect runs two dangers: one is that he (or she) will make a fool of himself; the other is that he will unintentionally insult someone in the audience.

The first danger will be recognized by anyone who ever saw an English movie where the English actors try to affect a Brooklyn accent. It's laughable. Imagine, then, the reaction of West Indians hearing some of the North American attempts at Calypso music. Or the amazement of a Scotsman to hear Americans attempt his accent in "The Ball of Bellamuir." If you are going to try much singing in dialect, you damn well better do it expertly or not at all.

> *There was once an actor who had to play the part of the father of Anna Christie in O'Neill's play. The part requires a Swedish-American accent. The actor found that the newspaperman at the corner was of Swedish background, and engaged him in conversation regularly until after several weeks, he had the accent down perfect. Came the performance. Afterward, the actor found himself talking to a Swede. "Tell me," he asked, "what did you think of my accent?"*
>
> *"Why, yes, quite well done. But tell me, why do you lisp?"*

The other danger is more subtle, but more dangerous, too. For over a century Americans have chauvinistically laughed at exaggerated dialects given out by a succession of blackface comedians, "Irish," "German," "Jewish," "Mexican," "Italian," "Chinese," and other stereotypes. Now such humor is less common, but still anyone who sings a song, however innocently, with the so-called dialect of a racial or national minority, must pay for the sins of others; someone in the audience is bound to be deeply insulted.

Oh yes, perhaps one can say that theoretically there is such a thing as being over-sensitive. But supposing your skin has been rubbed and rubbed until the flesh is raw. I come along then and just touch you. You leap with the pain. "But I only touched you," say I. No matter. Others had rubbed the skin raw, and now, if I have any sense, I will be careful where I touch.

Mimicking other people's "peculiar" way of speaking is such a natural form of humor—children do it easily—that surely it must be an ancient art, known even in prehistoric times. Aristophanes, in his antiwar play *Lysistrata*, poked fun at the Spartans' pronunciation of Greek.

Perhaps five hundred years from now, Americans of any shade of skin will be able to read Uncle Remus and laugh with pleasure, but now . . .

But now . . . let us realize that no word is good or bad except by what it means to the person who is listening; and that unfortunately many a folk song has helped perpetuate a racist lie which has destroyed innocent lives.

I find people of non-English-speaking groups like it when I try to sing a song in their language, be it Yiddish, Spanish, or Hindustani. (I'm always careful to apologize for my amateurish pronunciation.)

Nevertheless, translation, difficult though it is, can be done, and has to be attempted continually. The Irish people over a period of centuries composed English words for hundreds of their best Gaelic melodies. Medieval minstrels, going from castle to castle, rewrote the best ballad plots into every language of Europe. The Bible got translated—eventually pretty darn poetically too.* Several songs I know would not be sung were it not for adequate translations: "Oleanna" and "Peat Bog Soldiers." The best of all is Art Kevess' translation of "Die Gedanken Sind Frei." It is a landmark, a great achievement.

---

* While we are about it, let's give a vote of thanks to the group of scholars at Cambridge University who accepted responsibility for translating the Book of Ecclesiastes (circa 1610 C.E.): Roger Andrews, Andrew Bing, Laurence Chaderton, Francis Dillingham,

> *"But at all cost, a thing must live, with a transfusion of one's own worse life if one can't retain the original's better. Better a live sparrow than a dead eagle"* (*Edward Fitzgerald, translator of the* Rubaiyat of Omar Khayyam).

If one believes, as I do, that the folk process tends to improve songs, one could conclude that the translations of some works might be better poetry than the originals.

In a broad sense, every human being has to undertake translation of sorts. We translate the precepts of our parents to fit new times. We translate ideas and inventions from other countries to fit our climate and culture. A woman learns a recipe and translates it to fit new stomachs.

And every singer is faced with a job of translation: how to make an old song meaningful to a new audience.

James Thurber met a woman in France; "Mr. Thurber, I first read your books in French translations. I think they are better in French than in English."

"Yes," said Thurber gravely. "My work suffers in the original."

The Crisis in Communication

To MEET today's worldwide communications crisis, the printed page is inadequate. For one thing, there is not enough pulpwood in the world; if other nations used paper as fast as the U.S.A., there would be no more forests. Second, the language barrier is a very real one, even within one nation.

Many scientists are desperately pessimistic about the future of the human race. They see the Information Gap growing as fast as the gap between rich and poor. They write books like *Silent Spring, The Population Bomb,* and *Is There Intelligent Life on Earth?* I tell them, "Stop

---

Thomas Harrison, Edward Lively, John Richardson, Robert Spaulding, John Bois, William Branthwaite, Andrew Downes, John DuPort, Jeremy Radcliffe, Samuel Ward, Robert Ward, Thomas Bilson, Editor.

"To every thing there is a season, and a time to every purpose under the heaven."

wasting your time writing books. Learn to speak in the vernacular. Demand the right to get on TV."

Too many professionals in all fields still talk only to each other. The language they use is unintelligible to 90 percent of the American people; at its rare best, you can call it academese; at its common worst I call it scholargok.* Scholargok uses long, impressive Latin-based words in preference to short and forceful Anglo-Saxon ones, passive verbs in preference to active verbs, and in a hundred ways obstructs clear and simple meanings. I sometimes feel that it is ruining the American language.

In Mississippi during the summer of 1964, I met college students from the North who were teaching history, mathematics and other subjects to thousands of young people in the Freedom Schools. But when they talked, I noticed that their ability to communicate in beautiful and accurate language was often inferior to the abilities of their pupils. A teen-ager would stand up and in resonant and rhythmic tones, with fine imagery and choice of expressions, put his teacher's voice to shame.

The teen-ager had probably led a life of talking, not reading. In church he had been called upon to testify and had got used to speaking on his feet. And the rich heritage of Afro-American story and song had taught him more about language than college English courses had taught his teachers.

I told one of the northern students: "You ought to work out a swap. You-all come down here to teach history and geography; get some Mississippi people to go up to your college and teach elocution." The world's great political leaders—consider Jesus, Churchill, Lincoln, Lenin, Martin Luther King—have all drawn upon the beautiful rhythms, sounds and expressions found in everyday speech. So did Shakespeare, Mark Twain, Will Rogers, Woody Guthrie, Langston Hughes.

For a scholar accustomed to the luxury of a 20,000-word vocabulary it may not be easy to omit polysyllables and learn to talk as directly and vividly as a black Mississippian—or an Irish-American New Yorker. Whenever was learning a language easy? But it is possible. If honest and intelligent men are not willing to enter the general marketplace of ideas, to talk with laymen in laymen's language, they leave the field wide open for the prostitutes of communication, the hired press, the dishonest politicians, the hucksters of escapism.

Rome's emperors had a slick trick. While their armies were out con-

---

* First cousin to gobbledygook, the word coined a generation ago by Congressman Maury Maverick to express his feelings about bureaucratic double-talk.

quering the world, and while they enjoyed the pleasures of their villas, they kept the Roman populace from revolting by giving them free bread and circuses.

America has TV. Turn on the magic screen; you'll find an assortment of diverting comedy, fairy stories, and shoot-em-ups. Where is the real richness and variety of American life, with its hundreds of ethnic groups, with its thousands of conflicting opinions? Where is the exciting controversy that Jefferson looked forward to? ("We have nothing to fear from error so long as reason is free to oppose it.")

I used to be snobbish about TV; I am no longer. The world at present is on a crash course, and the printed page has failed to get people together. TV is a much more powerful means of communication.

The air belongs to everyone, but we have foolishly sold it to the highest bidders. They tell us, "The programs that are on TV are there because the majority wants them."

Not true. How many does the most popular comedy show reach? Forty million? That's not a majority of 200,000,000 Americans.

If TV were really to satisfy a majority of the American people, in any week in any big city there would be room for programs of jazz and classical music, and for a dozen kinds of folk and traditional ethnic music. There would be room for the searing and biting new songs that are coming from the younger generation. There would be room on TV not just for the two major parties, but for George Wallace, for Eldridge Cleaver, yes, and the Birchers and socialists and communists. There would be room for the Seventh Day Adventists and the Mormons, and room for Madalyn Murray, and room for the Evergreen Press.* If a viewer objects he can turn to the best censor of all, that little knob, and switch it off.

Vital—though often unpalatable—facts would have a chance to reach the ordinary people who are entitled to know them. (At present, scientific information is, in effect, often blacklisted. "It's not entertaining.")

In the United States of North America in 1969, communicating is like trying to talk at a crowded cocktail party. There is so much irrelevant communication going on that getting a sensible word in edgewise is difficult. Many of our fellow citizens have concluded that to act is the most definitive communication.

Not only peace and freedom workers have become actionists. Con-

---

* In the Harvard Alumni Bulletin of April 28, 1969, I proposed that Congress require each TV station to donate 20 percent of its time—including production staff and facilities —for "public sector" broadcasting. I also outlined a democratic method of allocating that time, in each region, according to the tastes and real needs of various groups of viewers.

servationists have also. Near San Francisco a young man swiped a bulldozer and rammed it into a PG&E powerline near a proposed nuclear power plant. Then he turned himself in and took a five-year sentence, to publicize his protest. And a troubador friend of mind was driving through the western desert, admiring the scenery, when he came upon a huge billboard. Ten miles later, still seething, he turned his car around, came back and chopped it down.

If America explodes in the next few years, or if it goes the way of Hitler's Germany, it will be largely the fault of TV, because TV had the chance to do something about it. Mankind faces three great crises: the biological crisis (population explosion, pollution, diminishing resources); the social-cultural crisis (alienation); and the economic crisis (the rich get richer and the poor get poorer). Overall is the military crisis, the violence crisis. Essential to solving any one of these crises is communication.

Part of this will be communication between experts. But, as Will Rogers used to say, "There's nothing more ignorant than an educated man when you get him outside the field he is educated in." It is also essential that we have communication between experts and laymen. It is essential to have communication between laymen and laymen.

TV, if used right, may be able to save this world. The greatest entertainers have always been more than "mere entertainers." Look at Shakespeare, G. B. Shaw, François Villon, Bob Dylan. The best folk songs in a thousand idioms also probe reality: "Where do we come from; where do we go?"

Entertainment is communication. TV could open up people's hearts and minds to each other. We could learn about each other's troubles. We could learn about each other's beauties.

Otherwise, one of these years, the stones will not be going through liquor store windows, but down at the offices of NBC and CBS. There is a lot of plate glass there. "Too little and too late" has been the epitaph of many an establishment.

> *A man is driving down a narrow one-lane country road. He sees a car come round the corner toward him. As it came closer, he saw it was a woman driver. So he's gallant; he goes in the ditch with two wheels, stops. As the other car passed, the woman stuck her head out the window and shouted, "PIG!"*
>
> *The man was shocked. Adrenalin shot through his body. He angrily jammed his foot on the gas, zoomed out the ditch, down the road, around the corner. And ran into the pig.*

ALL MIXED UP

1. You know, this lan - guage that we speak, Is part

Ger - man, part Lat - in and part Greek, With some

Cel - tic and Ar - a - bic all in the heap,

Well a - mend - ed by the man in the street.__

Choc - taw gave us the word "o - kay,"__ "Va -

moose" is a word from Mex - i - co way, __

And all of this is a hint, I sus - pect,

Of what comes next. I think __ that this whole world

Soon,— ma - ma, my whole wide world, Soon,— ma - ma, my whole world Soon— gon - na be get mixed up.

2. I like Polish sausage, I like Spanish rice,
   Pizza pie is also nice.
   Corn and beans from the Indians here,
   Washed down by some German beer.
   Marco Polo traveled by camel and pony,
   Brought to Italy the first macaroni.
   And you and I, as well as we're able,
   Put it all on the table.   (*Chorus*)

3. There were no redheaded Irishmen
   Before the Vikings landed in Ireland.
   How many Romans had dark curly hair
   Before they brought slaves from Africa?
   No race of man is completely pure,
   Nor is any man's mind and that's for sure.
   The winds mix the dust of every land,
   And so will man.   (*Chorus*)

4. This doesn't mean we will all be the same;
   We'll have different faces and different names.
   Long live many different kinds of races!
   And difference of opinion that makes horse races!
   Just remember the "Rule About Rules," brother:
   "What's right with one is wrong with another,"
   And take a tip from La Belle France,
   "Vive la Difference."   (*Chorus*)

The most American story I know: A man asked where he could find a restaurant serving pizza. He was directed down the street, and when he got there, it was a Chinese restaurant. He went in anyway, and sure enough, they had very good pizza. He asked the waiter, "How come a Chinese restaurant serves pizza?"

The waiter replied, "Well, you see, we have a large Jewish clientele."

You and I are descended from a lot of people who spoke many beautiful languages, who had many magnificent folk traditions, brought to these shores from other lands. There's no reason we should forget them completely.

But with the radio and television, the slick magazines, the jukeboxes, there seem overwhelming pressures on all sides to forget and forego these old traditions and accept the commercialized culture which is handed out to us so cheaply. That is, they say it is cheap. Often the price of accepting it is to abandon some of the most wonderful things in the world—the traditions which our parents and grandparents have handed on to us. We sell our birthright for a mess of pottage.

Do some traditions have to be attacked? Look how Matt McGinn does it.

MANYURA MANYAH

I've heard men complain
O' the jobs that they're dain'   (doing)
While houkin' the coal   (digging)
Or diggin' the drain.
But whoever they are
There is non that compar'
Wi' a man that sets shovelin'
Manyura manyah!

    Chorus:
    Wi' manyura manyah,
    Wi' manyura manyah,
    Wi' manyura, manyura,
    Manyura manyah!

Aa the streets o' the toon   (town)
Were aa covered aroon   (around)
Wi' stuff that was beautiful
Golden and broon.   (brown)
It was put there, o' course,
By a big Clydesdale horse,
And its name was manyura,
Manyura manyah!   (*Chorus*)

I follered its track
Wi' a shovel and sack
And as often as no
Wi' a pain in me back.
It was aa for the rent
And the beoooooootiful scent
O' manyura, manyura,
Manyura manyah!   (*Chorus*)

But I'm feelin' sae sore,   (so)
For me job's been took o'er
And everythin' noo   (now)
Is mechanical power.
And there's nought left fer me
But the sweet memory
O' manyura, manyura,
Manyura manyah!   (*Chorus, once more with feeling!*)

(Same tune for chorus)

A sociologist once told me, "Usually the first generation tries to retain what it can of the old country. The second generation usually tries to forget as much as it can. The third generation doesn't know anything about it. The fourth generation tries to recapture it, but it is too late." Perhaps he was overly cynical, but I think he had a measure of truth. I can see it in my own family: I am several generations away from whatever folk traditions my great-grandparents had. Now, suddenly I come along and realize my paucity and try and recapture a few traditions.

My own solution has been to try and learn from other people. I have learned from Negro people, from Jewish people, from Ukrainian people and many others.

Future centuries may recognize that one of America's chief claims to fame has been the ability to form hybrids. The ability to develop and exploit the ideas given us by others. I'm not just talking about music, and thinking of jazz, banjos, and bluegrass. It's true in cooking, architecture, and technologies of many kinds.

The reason we can form hybrids easily is that we are an uprooted people. You can see a parallel in horticulture. If a nurseryman wants to raise a shrub to be transplanted, he first transplants it several times within his own nursery. It loses a deep root system but develops many short roots and a physique which can withstand transplantings. Thus when the shrub is sold, it stands a much better chance of surviving violent changes in soil and climate.

Similarly, in America we have a population transplanted several times, across 3,000 miles of ocean, 1,000 miles of prairie, from country to city and from one city to another. And our roots may not be very deep anywhere, but we've developed the ability to absorb and use traditions from many places. Thus our American cuisine includes traditions from Italy, Germany, Mexico, and China, as well as England; from American Indian tribal life as well as Le Cordon Bleu. Thus, also, our folk music makes use of Spanish guitars, African banjos, Irish fiddles, Italian mandolins, German harmonicas, as well as Lord knows what else.

This mixing is still going on. Five hundred thousand Puerto Ricans in New York have introduced a new popularity for the bongo drum within the past twenty years.

Some hybrids (like the English language) arc supremely successful. Others (like the attempt to play Tchaikovsky with a swing band) seem less so. Some hybrids flourish so like weeds that one fears for the very existence of other forms, just as the English sparrow has driven other birds from our parks. In many countries American popular music is looked upon in this way.

Cocacolonization and the Need for Barriers

IN 1963 AMERICAN FOLK MUSIC became so commercially successful that we threatened to flood the world with it.

Flood the world—the idea gives me a chill. I now wonder whether I was doing right, traveling around the world singing American songs. Much though I love Kentucky-style banjo picking, I would hate to see it sweep into the gardens of the world like a weed, pushing out the flowers already in those gardens. (You know the gardener's definition: "A weed is a plant that is out of place.")

Perhaps in some countries a bricf experience with American music was a good jolt for their own musical life; after they learned that music can be informal and improvisatory, that the words can have bite and reality, they went back and found how good their own music could be. This happened in England.

But the tremendous power of mass-produced culture from the United States of America is liable to swamp the rest of the world, for good or bad, unless people consciously and systematically sit down and decide what they want to do about it.

Australia's 11 million people have no movie industry of their own. Sweden, with only 8 million, produces fine movies. But

Australia has no language barrier to keep out the flood from Hollywood.

In Nigeria I found a TV station playing reruns of "I Love Lucy" because it was cheaper than trying to put on new shows using African authors and actors.

If I lived in Nigeria or Australia, I'd slap a tariff on all the incoming American movies, TV shows, hit records, and visiting folk singers.

Some people will probably say, "Why do anything about it? If I want a good song or want to see a good movie, I shouldn't have to pay extra for it simply because it comes from outside our political borders."

I used to feel this same way. I used to think, Down with all barriers, all national borders! One world!

But then I saw the terraced rice fields of Indonesia, and I saw how a wall is necessary at times. Without these thousands of little barriers holding the water on the side of the mountain, the available rainfall would fall kerplunk down to the bottom of each valley and rush away to the ocean. But by holding the water on the terraces for a short while, they are able to grow rice crops on the steep mountainsides.

Similarly, without tariff barriers and other border controls, no nation in the world will be safe from the floods to and from the modern industrial centers of the world. All the money will fall, kerplunk, *into New York*.

The Australians don't have to actually keep out our mass-produced culture, but they should take the tariff money and use it to encourage their own creative artists. Only the Australian creative artists—the writers, the songwriters and the playwrights—can make Australians proud of their own heritage. Songwriters who are writing good songs about Australia should be encouraged; their songs should be recorded, printed, and they themselves should be given some money to go and sing. This money could come out of the tariff on performances by foreigners.

Every nation, every people, every region, deserves to be able to have pride in their own language and customs, to have their own art and industry. They will not have it if they don't erect an occasional barrier.

Some barriers can be blamed for preserving inequalities. But other barriers are needed in the present world to *prevent* inequalities. Britons have been worrying about the "Brain Drain." Over 50,000 valuable scientific workers from Britain and western Europe are working in the U.S.A., attracted by higher U.S. wages. In India and Africa I heard also the complaint that their good students were sent away for training, but then they didn't all come home. Some preferred to take the higher pay and more comfortable living conditions in other lands.

So now I can't really blame East Germany and other socialist countries for closing their borders to emigration. I hope soon it will be possible to open them up. But at present it would mean a disastrous drain of their most valuable personnel at the very time they need them most.

The Brain Drain goes on also *within* every country. In Nova Scotia I was told, "Our biggest export is brains"; the graduates from Dalhousie University, Halifax, tended to head straight for good-paying jobs in Toronto. And small-town life in the U.S.A. for the last hundred years has lost the most ambitious and talented of each generation, leaving the towns increasingly in the hands of an Old Guard. During the flowering of New England in the 1840s the small towns were full of nonconformist thought, but today many of them are stagnant pools of conformity. The Midwest and the South are continually being drained of ambitious people who run off to New York or California.

Granted: The problem can't be solved just by barriers. Each nation, each region, must make its own people *want* to stick around and improve the home pastures rather than seek greener pastures elsewhere.

The U.S.A. was largely settled by people who were seeking greener pastures—many of them fleeing jails and executioners' axes. And during one of my recent trips abroad an American expatriate couple told me: "We feel that a country which does not respect the rights of its citizens does not deserve support." Late that night, alone and grinding my teeth, I thought: If we won't stay to try and set our country straight we don't deserve to have a country.

To emigrate or not to emigrate? Hard-pressed individuals in many countries face this question nowadays. Some refuse to leave home even under threat of death or inhuman, fascist-type imprisonment. For others, discomfort and shame are the only risks.

I've sung a lot of songs of exiles: "Guantanamera," "Follow the Drinking Gourd," "Oleanna." But (with very few exceptions) I think the time for exiles is over. Sinner man—poor immigrant—where you gonna run to? If the hard rain threatens to fall, perhaps we who live in the lair of the monster can do something about it.

Here I am, here I am, here I'll stand, _____

_____ Though I'm told it's stol-en land. _____ Too

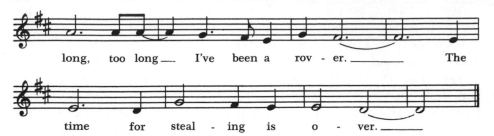

long,   too long ___ I've   been a   rov - er. _____   The

time   for   steal - ing   is   o - ver. _____

How Multilingual Can You Get

. . . and still be yourself?

Let's ask three questions:

Is it possible to learn a language one was not born into?

Is it possible to learn several languages?

Is it possible to combine several languages without producing meaning-less gibberish?

In the field of music, I would answer the first question, "Yes, but don't expect to learn it overnight." After thirty years of playing a certain little mountain banjo tune, I only recently feel that I am playing it right.

I would answer the second question, "Yes, but don't expect to be able to learn all of them equally well."

And to the third question I'd say, "Maybe! But combining different idioms is one of the world's most difficult tasks. It is worth attempting, but it usually takes a generation of musicians to achieve a new idiom combining several old ones."

Everywhere in the world, it seems, there are people trying to learn the music of another country. One isn't surprised to know that in Dubuque, Iowa, a chorus is earnestly rehearsing a chorale written by a German named Bach. But I confess to still being startled to find Tennessee-style fiddlers in Tokyo, spiritual singers in Prague, and kids on an Israeli kib-butz practicing bluegrass banjo. I guess the whole world is busy trying to learn someone else's music.

In each country I am asked, "What do you think of it?" They hope I am an expert whose judgment will encourage or discourage them. I usually evade a direct answer and describe a young fellow I know in Omaha who is playing flamenco guitar.

He is talented and, with a year's study, can play well. The only trouble is, he's working from a few books and records, and all by himself. If he lived in Spain, where he could have constant interchange with other guitarists, he might become one of the best. But in Omaha he can only go so far. Then he is stopped, wondering: "Am I doing right? What do I do now? I have imitated as far as I can. But, if I step out and create on my own, am I still in the tradition?"

One solution for him is to say frankly, "Okay, I can't be authentically in the tradition, but I'll be myself." In Africa, I met a man who had fallen in love with the saxophone. He was experimenting enthusiastically with tones and phrases and figures, and not giving a damn about trying to sound like Coltrane or any other jazz great.

Another solution is to listen so widely to dozens and hundreds of records (not just two or three) that you have a real knowledge of the good and bad in the idiom you are trying to learn.

Isn't it true that what many of us find so attractive in the life of a real folk community is its homogeneity? Their lives seem "all of a piece." Their streets do not reflect a history of waves of fashions and fads coming and going with the seasons, as our American streets do. Their art, music, dancing, stories—everything harmonizes.

Evidently many Americans have questioned the Japanese along these lines. In a Japanese magazine I found a lead article trying to defend their position: "A Question of Identity: A Modern Nation Disillusions Foreigners." The author says: do not confuse "Westernization" with "Modernization." We are simply becoming a modern nation, learning from Europe as centuries ago we learned from China or Korea.

Does a Japanese lose his identity by donning a white shirt and suit and tie? Does a Tennessee farmer lose his identity by donning a white shirt, suit and tie?

Yes, I think in both cases there is a danger of it. The mask becomes the face.

Some musicians, therefore, who try to pretend that they are equally familiar with many idioms may end up sounding like a perpetual tourist who has a dilettante's knowledge of many parts of the world but does not know his own home.

I found out when we were traveling that millions of people are becoming multilingual in a hurry. In Indonesia everyone knows at least two languages—their local language (of which there exist over a hundred) and the Indonesian national language, a former Malay traders' language now taught in all schools from kindergarten up. In high school they all study some European language, usually English. In East Africa, the driver of our car knew seven languages: English, French, Swahili, and four local languages—all this with no more than a grade-school education.

I'm not experienced enough to know which language I would think best. The language with fifty words for the verb "to run" might be more accurate for scientific work; but English, with its great generalized and unspecific meanings, leaves lots of room for poetry. (At the same time, I didn't find a single person around the world who thought English a beautiful language.)

In the one world which we are working for it is very possible that there will eventually be one language. However, meanwhile we are faced with the need to preserve the many beautiful languages of the world. I am, of course, speaking not just of the language of words but of the language of music and art and dance and of all the traditions which we hold dear. If we are to build one world and one language, we have to build them out of many old worlds, languages and communities. How can we if we let this inheritance die, simply because mass production and standardized mass entertainment are cheap and profitable?

Ideally, each nation of the world should, in this period of history, jealously preserve its own languages. Words, music, food, costume, living and sleeping. But learn something of other languages. And gradually add to the vocabulary of your own language with what you learn. One improves a language by adding words from other languages. We can try to make our music better by listening to music of Asia, Africa, South America, etc. It is possible to build a new folk music out of older folk music, combining idioms and styles.

But one must start on a firm basis of one's own music.

For better or worse, this century seems to be mixing up the human race more than ever before. Today's citizens are being thrown in contact with not one or two or three, but dozens and hundreds of traditions. Which to follow? "A hunter cannot chase two rabbits at once," says a Japanese proverb.

But young people are combining various traditions together at a faster rate than the world has ever seen. It's not a smooth and easy thing. There's lots of confusion, hardship and misunderstanding.

Perhaps the solution for nations as well as individuals is to realize that in this vast and confusing world we can and must make our own brave choices as to what we think *is best* (avoiding both the fear of being nonconformist and fear of being conformist) and then coolly temper our action with a shrewd estimate of what is expected of us and what is possible.

If we can make honest choices of what we think is best, then we will end up being ourselves, though we may borrow from a dozen or a hundred different sources. Then, when you are fairly certain that you know what you like and dislike, you can live at peace with your neighbor, who probably has quite different likes and dislikes. You can hear his songs and be interested, but not insulted by them.

One thing I'm sure we could all agree on: if there is going to be a mixture, it cannot be forced. Not now. If anyone thinks the world can be bombed into a Pax Americana, it's up to us to tell him, "You go commit suicide by yourself. Don't drag us with you."

> This old humanly race
> 2 million years
> up from the ape
> tooth and claw
> stick and stone
> sword, gun and bomb
> What will happen now?
>
> But still we have babies, love, laughter, song

Our clothing? Once we were a herd of brown fur.
Now a kaleidoscope of color—and will be more.
Our diet? Once unvarying,
    now see the varied menus.
Our houses? Once all alike,
    now . . . ugh. "Fashion is a form of ugliness—etc."
Once we knew all the same music.
    Now: LPs.
    My complaint: TV is too *much* alike.
    Let the individual choose.

As a tourist, I like the homogeneous folk village.
   But do *they*?
What if one of them wants to Express his Personality?
I guess each nation needs an area of its life to be traditional,
   and an area to be individual and different.

  If only people didn't imitate the ugly.
  Does the good always drive out the bad?

You've got to compromise: every family knows this.
If you all agree to speak one language occasionally, at least
   you can understand each other.
If you agree to the same rules, you at least can play
   the same game together—occasionally.
What's needed are cultural zoning laws.
A time and a place for conformity
And a time and place to not conform.

  This old humanly race
  Up from the ape
  Tooth, claw, stone, bomb
  What will happen now?

15·The Incompleat Folksinger

SOME SUPPLEMENTARY MEMORIES, ACKNOWLEDGMENTS AND GENERALIZATIONS

This man is advertised as a singer—but he obviously hasn't much voice.

He is a Yankee but sings southern songs.

He sings old songs, but somehow his meanings are contemporary.

He tries to talk simply, but obviously has a good education and has read widely.

He sings about poor people, though I doubt he is poor himself.

Altogether, he is a very professional amateur.

I would call him a phony, except that I think he is just another modern paradox.

Dear Fellow Humans: *

I USUALLY MISTRUST older people's giving advice to younger, because while often their advice is very good (the values of foresight, temperance, persistence, etc.), they forget that younger people usually know one of the most important things of all: the value of enthusiasm and enjoyment of life.

Twenty-five years ago Franklin Roosevelt spoke to my generation. "Youth: Hold fast to your dream," he said. In other words, don't give up your ideals of peace, freedom, justice, truth—the way so many adults do.

When you come down to it, more people die from discouragement than any disease. And why do people get discouraged? Because they feel that life's a joyless struggle; because they feel they're on a dead-end street.

So here are a few of my own recipes for avoiding this kind of discouragement. They may or may not apply to you. Only you can decide.

1. It's better to take a job you want at less pay than a job you don't want for more pay. But you can learn from any job.

2. It's okay to suffer intense temporary discomforts in order to reach a longer-range goal. But make sure it is only temporary.

3. Debts can be chains, best used when they can haul you to new heights, rather than entangle your legs. It's the same with possessions: "Man doesn't possess possessions; they possess us."

4. Travel while you are young, and still are free of responsibilities. See what a big, broad, beautiful land we have here, then maybe a foreign land or two. See that there are honest, hard-working people in every corner of the globe, all quite certain that their own way of living, their local geography, their music, etc., is most beautiful.

5. Keep your health. It's easy while you are young. But our fine, tempting, modern civilization can erode it easily too. Many a woman or man has finally worked himself into a position where he could do something, and then found he no longer had the health to do it or enjoy it.

5½. In view of the fact that good health and energy don't last forever, it's worth doing some things earlier than late. When my wife and I were about thirty and very broke, we built our own house, inch by inch, on a mountainside. Glad we did; doubt we'd have energy enough

---

* From the "Talks to Teens" series, *Seventeen* Magazine (November 1963).

to do it now. And I've known too many people who put off such projects "until we have the money" or "until we have the time"—and if they eventually did get the money or the time, they no longer had the energy.

6. A happy sex life may take years to achieve, but it's worth it in the long run. Worth the time, the thought—or rather, the thoughtfulness— and, often, the waiting.

7. A few short ones: Prestige is much overrated. The celebrity business is for the birds. Respectability is nice, but consider: who do you most want to respect you? Money is like air or water. You need a certain amount to live. Beyond that, who wants to be a dog in the manger?

And now I'll stop before I rattle on any longer, like any old graybeard. All the foregoing applies to the one central thing I mentioned at the beginning: how to keep discouragement from withering the priceless enthusiasm which most young people have.

So far I've quoted F.D.R. and Ralph Waldo Emerson. Here are a few more favorite quotes. (Note: When you steal from one person it's plagiarism. When you steal from ten, it's scholarship. When you steal from a hundred, it's original research.)

First, a story about the late comedian Fred Allen. He once saw a small boy toddle in front of a truck and snatched him to safety just in time. On the sidewalk again, he said, "S'matter kid, don't you want to grow up and have troubles?"

Next, a fragment from the German poet Bertolt Brecht.

> . . . For we know only too well:
> Even the hatred of squalor
> Makes the brow grow stern;
> Even anger against injustice
> Makes the voice grow hard. Alas, we
> Who wished to lay the foundations of kindness
> Could not ourselves be kind.

Here's a famous line credited to Gandhi: "To the millions who have to go without two meals a day, the only form in which God dare appear is food." A line from a Harvard graduate back from Africa: "Nigerians are a proud people who don't want tourists, don't want heroes, don't want saviors. They just want schoolteachers."

Now, a paragraph from Woody Guthrie, the Dust Bowl balladeer, who taught me much not only about music but about my country and life in general: "The worst thing that can happen to you is to cut yourself loose from people. And the best thing is to sort of vaccinate yourself right into the big streams and blood of the people . . . to feel that you know the best and the worst of folks that you see everywhere, and never to feel weak, or lost, or even lonesome anywhere. . . . There is just one thing that can cut you to drifting from the people, and that's any brand or style of greed. . . . There is just one way to save yourself and that's to get together and work and fight for everybody."

Lastly, I quote the words of a song I put together using words from the Book of Ecclesiastes.

To everything (turn, turn, turn)
There is a season (turn, turn, turn)
And a time for every purpose
Under heaven.

A time to be born, a time to die,
A time to plant, a time to reap,
A time to kill, a time to heal,
A time to laugh, a time to weep.

A time to build up, a time to break down,
A time to dance, a time to mourn,
A time to cast away stones,
A time to gather stones together.

A time of love, a time of hate,
A time of war, a time of peace,
A time you may embrace,
A time to refrain from embracing.

A time to gain, a time to lose,
A time to rend, a time to sew,
A time to love, a time to hate,
A time for peace—I swear, it's not too late!

To everything (turn, turn, turn)
There is a season (turn, turn, turn)
And a time for every purpose
Under heaven.*

* Words from the Book of Ecclesiastes. Adaptation and music by Pete Seeger. TRO-© copyright 1962, Melody Trails, Inc., New York, New York. Used by permission.

Well, here's hoping all the foregoing will help you avoid a few dead-end streets (we all hit some), and here's hoping enough of your dreams come true to keep you optimistic about the rest. We've got a big world to learn how to tie together. We've all got a lot to learn. And don't let your studies interfere with your education.

Sincerely,
Pete Seeger

"Author! Author!"

. . . is the cry heard at the end of a play. Like any singer, I am indebted to songwriters, I take off my hat to the whole race and genius of songmakers. Some of their names we know: Woody Guthrie, Bob Dylan, Tom Paxton, Malvina Reynolds, Ernie Marrs, Peter LaFarge, Joe Hill, Ed McCurdy, Oscar Brand, Florence Reece, Jim Garland, Stephen Foster, Dan Emmett, Huddie Ledbetter, Lee Hays, Fred Hellerman, Dr. Alex Comfort, Sis Cunningham, Les Rice, Thurso Berwyck, Phil Ochs, Mark Spoelstra, Matt McGinn, Ewan MacColl, Bertha Gober, Bill Oliver, Guy Carawan, John Brunner, Banjo Patterson, Earl Robinson, Dave Arkin, Big Bill Broonzy, Leroy Carr, Blind Lemon Jefferson, George Gershwin, Irving Berlin, J. S. Bach, Paul Dessau, Bertolt Brecht, Julia Ward Howe, Don West, Oscar Brown, Jr., Hy Zaret, Aunt Molly Jackson, Solomon Linda, T-Bone Slim, Norman Rosten, Hirsh Glick, Idris Davies, Len Chandler, Brother Fred Kirkpatrick, Don McLean, and lots, lots more.

If all the people who have contributed to the making up of the words and tunes we sing were known, it would be a list of thousands upon thousands, and stretch back thousands of years.

I thank them one and all—the ballad makers long dead and nameless; the jokey boys whose smiles are dust; the singing grandparents; the singers in lumber camps and cattle trails and chain gangs and kitchens; the fiddlers in buckskin, the banjo pickers, and guitar whammers, and lonesome harmonica blowers; the horny-handed, hospitable, generous, honest and inspired folk artists.

I thank the people who taught me music: Leadbelly, Woody Guthrie, Alan Lomax. My parents: Charles Seeger, and Constance Seeger Dowding.

Bless their laissez-faire styles of child-raising. Ditto Spring Hill School and Avon Old Farms, Connecticut. Thanks also to many who never knew they helped me: music teachers in schools, chorus directors, jazz musicians, "classical" musicians, folk musicians: Aunt Molly Jackson, Bess Hawes, Sam Hinton, Libba Cotten, Sonny Terry, Big Bill Broonzy, Paul Robeson, Brownie McGhee, Pete Steele, Ruth Rubin, Ruth Crawford Seeger, Mike, Peggy, and John Seeger, Rufus Crisp, Wade Ward, Jean Ritchie, Eric Darling, Cordell Reagon, Charles Sherrod, Bernice Reagon, Amar Sanyal, Carlos Montoya, Sandy Bull, O. J. Abbott, Jean Caragnan, Hélène Baillargeon, Kim Loy Wong, Moses Asch, Tony Schwartz, Sara Ogan and Jim Garland. Some I learned from their recordings: Uncle Dave Macon, William Hinton, Walter Williams, Frank Profitt, Yankee John Galusha, Mrs. Texas Gladden, Ironhead Baker, Dock Boggs, A. P. Carter & family, Lily DeLorme, Lily May Pearson, and lots, lots more. If I really took the time to sit down and count, the list would run into hundreds, at the very least.

Thanks to the folk song collectors, underpaid, unsung, whose books I have pored through: John and Alan Lomax, Carl Sandburg, Cecil Sharp, Ruth Rubin, Francis James Child, Bertrand Bronson, Waldemar Hille, Joanna Colcord, A. L. Lloyd, Ewan MacColl, Hamish Henderson, Bascom Lunsford, Marius Barbeau, Helen Creighton, Sam Eskin, Stan Hugill, Margaret Larkin, Zilphia Horton, Bill Wolff, Hugh Tracey, Maude Karpeles, Edith Fowke, Norman Cazden, Herbert Halpert, Norman Studer, Lynn Rohrbough, Norman Buchan, Paul Arma. And lots more.

Last but not least: thanks to my wife Toshi, without whom the world would not turn nor the sun shine.

I SAID I had a laissez-faire upbringing. I'm forever grateful for it. From age eight I was away at boarding school. It was the decade when the term "progressive education" first flowered. Our class would take up a "project" (ancient Egypt, the Middle Ages, etc.). We'd write a play about some event in those times, stage it and act in it. Shop class, English class, even math would be drawn into it. The main thing we all got from it: learning, real learning, is fun.

And summers at home we were forever building things. One summer it was model boats, another summer model airplanes. Music? We made music for the fun of it. My parents, bless them, decided to let me find out for myself what kind of music I liked.

I did get one strict lesson at school, which I'll not forget. At age fourteen I started a school newspaper, just for the hell of it. It was in competition with the official school paper, which was dull, respectable, and always late. Mine was pure Free Enterprise, a mimeographed weekly; I gathered the news, typed it up, sold it for a nickel, and kept the money.

But after a few months I'd had my kicks and decided to quit it. The headmaster called me in. "Peter, I think you ought to continue the paper." He explained that the wealthy old woman who paid the school's deficit liked reading it; its informal tone made her feel closer to the school. Her journalist friends, the young Alsop brothers, had complimented her on it.

I demurred. It's a lot of work, says I, and doesn't leave me as much free time as I'd like. But the headmaster was firm. "Better get your copy for next week's issue."

My favorite teacher sided with the headmaster. "You can't be a butterfly all your life, Peter." So for two more years I brought it out on schedule. Years later I discovered that this was why I got a complete scholarship to an otherwise rather expensive school. But just as valuable was what I learned, while running the Avon Weekly Newsletter: typing, writing, editing, cartooning, and learning how to walk up to a stranger and try to ask the right questions. The goofs I made! Edna St. Vincent Millay visited the school when we put on her play *Aria da Capo,* an antiwar allegory. (With my hair in curls, I'd played the female lead—Avon was not co-ed.)

The English teacher said I should take the opportunity to get an interview with her. "She's an important modern poet."

"What the heck will I ask her?"

"Don't be silly."

So I found myself seated awkwardly before this demure and beautiful woman, blurting out, "What do you think of Shakespeare?"

When I was a boy, the world seemed to me like a big cafeteria, but my eyes were bigger than my stomach, and sooner or later I had to realize that one couldn't do everything. So I stopped painting, stopped trying to be a writer, stopped trying to be an organizer of this or that. But I still have a tendency to attempt more projects than I have time to finish, and my files are full of ideas for songs that never get written; the barn is full of half-finished constructions.

Nevertheless there are advantages to being a jack of many trades, even if master of none. For example:

I am no great shakes as an artist, but one summer I made a living painting watercolors of people's houses in return for whatever they would give me. It was in New England, and I traveled by bicycle with camping equipment so I could sleep out in haystacks.

One thing I learned was a whole new set of artistic values. I sat down in one field to paint a long yellow barn, and the owner, an old Polish farmer who could hardly speak English, came to look over my shoulder. "You're not doing it correctly," he insisted. "That barn, I just build it. It's over a hundred twenty feet long, and you make it look less than a hundred." However, after corrections, his family did very well by me. I got a quart of milk, half a dozen eggs and a fresh-killed chicken which I managed to roast over the fire, although some of it was burned and some of it pretty darned near raw.

Another example: because I went to a progressive school I learned how to chop trees. As a result my three children have grown up in a mortgage-free log cabin—however anachronistic.

When I first got out of school, I worked as cook and general house-keeper for a small household consisting of my brothers and some friends, and since we lived on the lower East Side, I did all my shopping in the local Jewish groceries, where the marvels of sour cream, pumpernickel, bagels, blintzes, etc., were revealed.

I don't do so much cooking nowadays. My wife and daughters are too good at it; I've backslid into the role of a typical male. But come spring, Pop uses the oven. He may not be the best banjo picker in the world, but no one has ever bested his

Traditional American Strawberry Shortcake*

Use about two quarts of strawberries for six people to make sure that there is enough to go around. There's nothing worse than having something good to eat and not having enough of it. I put half of the strawberries in a bowl and cut them up into small pieces with two knives. Don't mash them; that would make them too juicy. Simply slice them up well and pour, say, a quarter cup of sugar on top. The funny thing is, though I've made this shortcake so often,

---

* From a letter to Leslie Haworth, an English strawberry farmer and folk singer (see his "Here's to Cheshire," p. 222).

I couldn't tell exactly how much sugar to use. Try it for yourself and decide whether it is too sweet or not.

The other half of the strawberries I simply hull, and then put it all in the ice box. Maybe you could sprinkle a little sugar on the other strawberries, too. Some people like it, some don't. It depends on how sweet the strawberries are naturally.

I make my shortcake by mixing about two and a half cups of flour with about a half of a pound of butter. I knead the butter into the flour with my finger tips. Oh—also three teaspoonfuls of baking powder and perhaps a quarter teaspoonful of salt and a tablespoonful of sugar. This all gets kneaded together, dry.

Now you shouldn't actually put the shortcake in the oven until you're half-way through the meal. When you figure that dessert time is only 20 or 25 minutes away, then you excuse yourself from the table, go into the kitchen, pour just enough milk into the flour-butter mixture to make a very thick batter—it doesn't need to be so thick that it has to be rolled, but thick enough that when you pick up a lump of it on a tablespoon you have to use your finger to get it off the tablespoon into a greased tin. However, this all needs to be done very quickly so that only about thirty seconds has elapsed from the time you put in the milk to the time you are spooning it out into the tin and putting it into a hot oven.

Then, while the shortcake is cooking, you get about a pint, or two pints at most, of heavy whipping cream. I put it in the icebox to get very cold just be-fore I whip it, so that it whips quickly and easily. I don't whip it too stiff— just stiff enough to come off the spoon without being forced off. Whip the cream and add maybe a half a teaspoonful of vanilla, quarter of a cup of sugar, or even a half a cup, depending again on how sweet you like your whipped cream. Put it back in the icebox, and take out some butter.

Then go back and finish your meal.

A couple of peeks into the oven will tell you when to take out the short-bread. It should be tinged with brown and crisp on the outside—big separate lumps all over your baking tin—and soft in the center, of course. Take it out of the oven and to the table.

The final process now should be done with lightning-like rapidity. You slit the piece of shortbread open, put a pat of butter inside it and pour over it the sliced-up strawberries and clap on the top of the shortbread and spoon on a great blob of whipped cream and then a handful of whole ripe red straw-berries on top, and serve it. It shouldn't take you more than a couple of minutes to prepare all six servings. If you delay too long you will lose one of the best things, namely the contrast between the steaming hot, crusty short-bread and the icy-cold, sweet strawberries and the cold, bland whipped cream.

I realize that the above directions are very vague. I can only suggest that you try it out several times with varying amounts of sugar and varying types of cream and even varying proportions of butter in the shortbread. The shortbread is basically, of course, nothing more or less than what we call in America "baking-powder biscuit," with an extra amount of butter in it.

If you think of any good variations on the recipe I hope you'll get in touch with me. Best of luck.

One of the big disadvantages of notoriety is that the little common courtesies, which help one remain a human being, become almost impossible to maintain. Mail piles up. One has to start using a secretary to answer it even hastily. An acquaintance in my home town has composed something for the piano; would I listen to it? It's a simple request and I say I'd be glad to. But the weeks roll by, each with a new, urgent deadline. Finally the guy probably decides that I'm one more show biz figure who doesn't have time for his friends any more.

I've been accused of being a Communist front for so many years that I've grown immune to the charges. But now I must confess. I really am front man for an organization: my wife, my agent, plus secretaries and publishers' staffs. They see that letters are answered, appointments kept, and business attended to. Mostly what I gotta do is sing. This paragraph was thunk up while in bed with a bad cold.

Why do you want to be a mathematician? I argued with a young friend in 1952. You are otherwise a very sensible fellow and a good banjo player.

What's wrong with mathematics? (he countered). It is the purest and most exact science.

On the contrary, it's most inexact. Mathematics is a glittering but flimsy edifice reared for human convenience. It rests on the world's shakiest foundation.

Quit your kidding. What could be more certain than two and two equal four?

That's just it. Two and two do not equal four. In fact, not even does one equal one. In this whole world, in all our universe, we have never been able to find even two raindrops equal in size and shape, or two snowflakes of exactly the same design. Scientists assume for convenience that all hydrogen atoms look alike, but if they do, they are the only things in the universe which do. It is logical to suspect that if and when we ever get a microscope to examine them more closely they, too, will differ among themselves. So how can you say that one of anything equals another? Two and two do not equal four, because there are not two of anything.

    Enough sophistry. I know two apples when I see them.
You think you do—sometimes. But what is that apple—just the weight and form? Isn't the smell part of the apple, and memory of it that lives on after it is eaten? And when is an apple? How soon after the blossom can you call that nubbin an apple? And at what exact point can you say that an apple fallen to the ground has turned to brown mush and is no longer an apple? This isn't sophistry, or idle semantics. No mathematician has been clear when asked "two *what* equal two *how*?"

        I'm sorry, but neither I nor you nor anyone else we know bases life
        on such exactitudes. The approximation seems to suit us all,
        whether we pay the grocery bill or sign a salary check.
Oh, have it your own way then. Be a mathematician. There certainly is no living to be made playing the banjo. It's funny, but the majority of banjo players I know these days have turned out to also be attracted to the physical sciences. Perhaps the same spirit that causes them to wistfully long for mathematical exactitude makes them delight in the precise rhythms a banjo can give, when you can pinpoint a beat right on the nose . . .

    You mean approximately on the nose. . . .
(At this point the subject was changed.)

    I like to start off a program with a song that is mostly instrumental on banjo or guitar. Why? I guess because the music says more about who I am and what I want to do than a whole string of words.

    Where do you come from, where do you go?
    Where do you come from, Cotton-eye Joe?

So ran the old song, and so goes the unspoken thought in the girl's mind to the new boy. And so the audience wonders about the person they see on the stage in the spotlight. If he or she sang only a lot of translations from different places, their questions remain unanswered: "This translator—where is his home?"

In 1962 I wrote to the *Times* of London (after they published an article on folk music which included a critique of my singing):

"When I sing in America some of the beautiful songs which I learned in Britain I will try and keep the spirit, the strength and the truth of the songs. But it would not be authentic of me to try and sing them in an English accent. I am an American. It would not be authentically me if you want to come down to that. And for me to sing one of these songs in Britain with my American accent might sound as silly to an English audience as it would be occasionally when American audiences see English actors trying to put on Brooklyn accents.

"Furthermore, it seems to me that the first duty of any artist is to produce good art. The only artists who are exempt from this first commandment are those who are in a very specialized field of creating historical reproductions. The first commandment for these, of course, is to be authentic to what they are trying to reproduce, as in a museum restoration of an eighteenth-century drawing room. As far as those people are concerned, they can only hope that the original was good art.

"Since in the field of folk songs the authentic original is best captured on an authentic field recording I think it would not only be futile but completely wrong of a singer such as myself to try and produce exact imitations. Rather it is my duty to be authentically myself and to make as good music as I possibly can, and to transmit the truth as well as I am humanly able to those whom I am fortunate to sing for. Do you feel that I am incorrect in this?"

Any artist must be highly discriminatory, highly intolerant, in his own work. As a painter is concerned over the slightest degree of shading in his colors, a good musician is concerned for his notes, sounds, rhythms.

But I am also a practicing schizophrenic, as perhaps we all must be in this world. I use a completely different scale of values when I am asked what I think of others' music. Here I must be highly tolerant. This other musician has a right to be different from me. I must wryly admit he probably thinks as much of my noise as I do of his.

It sometimes seems as if we let machinery run our life. We have automobiles, and forget how to walk. We have books, and forget how to improvise a good story. In millions of homes stands the tyrannical little box, saying in effect, "Don't participate in sport; sit back and watch a professional athlete. Don't try to hold a witty conversation; sit back and watch a professional wit. Don't lead an adventurous life; watch others be adventurous."

Most ridiculous of all: in millions of homes husband and wife sit there like sticks of wood watching a professional actor pretend to kiss another actor on the little magic screen.

But since World War II millions of people have also tried to build a more creative life for themselves. They see that it is not enough to simply have a job and come back and spend the money you have earned in buying some cheap product. It is not enough to come home and simply switch on the TV. On all sides we have seen ordinary working people try to once again do something creative.

Sometimes the attempts are pitiful; we have been uprooted from whatever folk traditions our grandparents had. The Sunday painters try to fill in little squares on the canvas. Some man with a do-it-yourself kit in the basement painstakingly copies the trite designs for furniture which *Popular Mechanics* gives him. Somebody with a guitar painfully gropes for "the G chord, the C chord, the G chord," and so on.

> *George Bernard Shaw, the old snob, said, "The only thing wrong with amateur musicians is that they expect other people to listen to them."*
> *I don't really have any sure fire retort to him, except you might consider this:*
> *A poor fiddler is better than a bad violinist.*

But as I said earlier, if you want to lift a pail of water from the ground, you have to bend down to the ground first and start there to pick it up. If we want to have a creative life, we have to start wherever we can.

If we can continue to nurture creativity in one corner of American life—such as making one's own music—perhaps the habit might spread. Let's attack the tyranny of mass media in any way possible. Who knows, it might even lead to more independent political thinking.

It would be disingenuous of me to claim that I am not happy if you buy my records or come to hear me sing. But I'll tell you what would give me a helluva lot more pleasure: the knowledge that you like to sing yourself, not only occasional songs you learned from me, but the solid kind of music which expresses You and Your Own Traditions, whatever they are. It's fine to sing some songs of our brothers and sisters in far-away lands; it's fine to sing songs out of American history, or from some little-known nook or cranny of our country, but in the end you have to be yourself. Yourself, here and now.

It calls for a good deal of self-censorship. You don't like the word "censorship"? All right, be your own editor. In this confusing, all-mixed-up world, every individual has a difficult and important task: to decide what he or she thinks is good or bad, and not to take anybody else's word for it.

If you are not certain who You are, you should realize that finding this out is one of the most important jobs of your life.

Extroduction

A social worker brought some little girls to my concert in Los Angeles, and later on wrote me what one of her little girls had said. This girl had spent one year in the psychiatric unit of the Los Angeles General Hospital. She had been badly beaten, had refused to speak or eat, and had to be fed through tubes for three weeks.

"You know what, Miss Glaser, maybe nobody knows how it feels to be me, but music knows me pretty good.

"And if it's your mother, she could hit you, but music will never hurt you."

"All your songs, your stories—do you think they are going to influence history? THEY ARE NOT WORTH BEANS." We've all had that thrown in our face at one time or another. So here's a little story about beans. A true story; my father-in-law says it happened in Japan when he was a boy.

A big steel cargo ship carried a load of soy beans. There was a leak in the boat, but the captain didn't know about it. When they checked, the bilge was dry. The water was being absorbed by the beans as it came in.

One day the ship just split in half and sank. Those beans had gradually swelled and swelled until the pressure was too much, and the steel plates cracked, just like that. Snap!

What can a song do?

It depends who you are and where you are. And when.

If you can cheer yourself up, you perhaps can cheer up others. You can make them proud of themselves, of their land, their people. You can help them understand who they are, and where they came from, and perhaps where they might be going, and why. In olden times a singer just knew the songs of his own home town. Nowadays we have the heritages of the world to draw on if we have the skill and persistence to stick with something long enough to do it well.

The message of a virtuoso is, "Look what wonderful things a human can do if he practices." The message of a sing-along song leader might be, "Look what fun you can have even if you don't practice." The message of many entertainers is, "Eat, drink, and be merry, because you don't know what is going to happen tomorrow and you can't do anything about it anyway." I suppose the message of this particular writer and singer could be summed up in the titles of some of my favorite songs.

> Where Do You Come From, Cotton-eye Joe?
> Come All You Bold Fellers and Listen to Me
> Come All Ye Fair and Tender Ladies
> Round and Round Old Joe Clark
> The Water Is Wide
> O Mary Don't You Weep
> We Shall Overcome
> A Hard Rain's Gonna Fall
> Which Side Are You On?
> Twelve Gates to the City, Halleloo!

But there's thousands of other songs. You pick out the ones *you* like best. No one else can do it for you.

TWELVE GATES TO THE CITY

> As learned from Marion Hicks, Brooklyn, N.Y., 1955 (with foot-
> notes for the scholarly)

Oh, what a beautiful city,[1]
Oh, what a beautiful city,
Oh, what a beautiful city.
Twelve gates to the city, halleloooooya.[2]

    Three gates in the East[3]
    Three gates in the West[4]
    Three gates in the North[5]
    Three gates in the South[6]
    Twelve gates to the city, halleloooya.

Oh, what a beautiful city, *etc.*

    Who are those children there, dressed in red?[7]
        Twelve gates to the city, halleloooya.
    Must be the children that Moses led.[8]
        Twelve gates to the city, hallelooooya.

Oh, what a beautiful city, *etc.*

    When I get to Heaven,[9] gonna sing and shout.[10]
        Twelve gates to the city, halleloooya!
    Ain't nobody there gonna keep me out![11]
        Twelve gates to the city, hallelooooya!

Oh, what a beautiful city, *etc.*

(Repeat verses; borrow verses from other songs; sing till the Spirit[12] suffuses all
   within earshot and they are singing too.)

---

1 The City of Heaven? The world of the future? A dream?
2 Ancient Hebrew word, now part of many languages. Great for singing.
3 Hello, Peking.
4 Hello, Chicago.
5 Hello, Stockholm.
6 Hello, Nairobi; hello, Havana.
7 All human blood is red.
8 The black slave lighted on this chapter and memorized it.
9 Where? When? Each singer knows; that's most important.
10 The Africanization of U. S. folkways?
11 No more Jim Crow, no more blacklist, no more scared dogmatics.
12 No need to argue definitions again. If you have it, you know it.

IN EACH of my concerts there are some old songs which you and I have sung together many times before, but which can always stand another singing. Like another sunrise, or another kiss, this also is an act of reaffirmation.

Our songs are, like you and me, the product of a long, long human chain, and even the strangest ones are distantly related to each other, as are we all. Each of us can be proud to be a link in this chain. Let's hope there are many more links to come.

No: Let's make damn sure there are more links to come.

Appendix
Where to Find Songs?

There's Gold in Them Thar Hills—and Streets
Learning from Folks

"There was no folk music in this town before we got this club started."

This was said to me by some good people in a western city where I sang. And they really believed it, and were rather taken aback when I pointed out that there had been Mexican Americans living in that town for a century, and more recently Filipino Americans, not to speak of southern white and Negro migrant laborers. And all of them had some music, and pretty damn good music, too.

Joan O'Bryant, when teaching folklore at the University of Wichita, used to require each student in her class to collect a song and sing it for the class. Bravo. (This reminds me of the anthropology professor who started off his course on primitive man by announcing to the class that there was one requirement which every student must fulfill in order to get a passing grade. His assistants then went up and down the aisles of the huge lecture hall handing a small stone to each student. The professor announced: "In your hands each of you now has a piece of flint. You must make an arrowhead out of it and bring it to me before you can pass this course.")

There is not a corner of the U.S.A. in which you can find folk music easily and obviously. North, south, east, and west, in all of the fifty states the only music which will be apparent will come out of a jukebox or a television set, or a few semi-professional musicians in local dance halls.

However, in all of the fifty states there *is* folk music. You have to dig for it. There is gold in them thar hills, but it's not lying around on the surface for anyone to pick up.

The secret is to get acquainted with people, and hear the music that they play in their homes. And you don't necessarily have to go to the backwoods for it, either. A neighbor of mine in the city of Beacon, a worker in the local rubber factory, is a fine blues guitar picker (and his wife sings "Just a Closer Walk with Thee" so beautifully that Mahalia Jackson would applaud). But you wouldn't find out about him if you just drove through the city of Beacon in a car.

Tony Schwartz proved that he could find a lot of folk music right in the center of the biggest and most cosmopolitan city of the country. The records he has put together for Folkways* have been a revelation to New Yorkers themselves, who didn't even know the many kinds of musics in their own city. Jacob A. Evanson, former school music supervisor in Pittsburgh, has collected hundreds of songs there, in several languages.†

Would that there were others doing a similar job for Chicago and Los Angeles and Detroit and Houston and Seattle.

The folk music available today in record stores is like the jewelry in a store window. It's concentrated and refined there, to buy if you have the money. But the gold in the hills is scattered, and takes many a weary tramp and long days of patient searching to find. And when you find it you may only find a little, and have to tramp on long days to find more. What you find might be rough and crude and unusable in the form in which you find it. But the search is worth it, if you can spare the time. It might be the most beautiful of all.

---

* *New York 19,* Folkways FD 5558; *Nueva York,* FD 5559; *Millions of Musicians,* 5560; *One, Two, Three and a Zing Zing Zing,* FC 7003.
† See "He Lies in the American Land," p. 101.

Too Many People Listen to Me—
and Not to the People I Learned From
Learning from Records

WHEN AN AUDIENCE applauds me for some little banjo piece like "Arkansas Traveler" I get a funny feeling inside me. I feel like telling them: "You should have heard Hobart Smith of Virginia play that; he made great music out of it." Or when someone writes that they like the way I play "Coal Creek March," I write them and suggest they listen to a man who really knows how to play it: Pete Steele, of Hamilton, Ohio. He recorded it for the Library of Congress over thirty years ago, and I can't imagine it ever being done better by the greatest musician on earth.

It's embarrassing to think of the number of people listening to me; they should be listening to the kind of people I learned from. Perhaps the role of performers such as myself should best be thought of as that of an intermediary. We can introduce music to audiences to whom the straight stuff would seem raw, crude, unintelligible. We also have the advantage of being able to present a broader picture of folk music than any true folk musician could. A true folk musician may be a genius at his or her own kind of music—but that one kind may be all he knows.

After having been introduced to folk music by someone like me, the listener should go on and hear it done by people who have been raised on it since they were knee-high, who have it in their bones, whose music blends in with their lives, the way music always ought to be.

I've been privileged to learn some songs directly from the lips and hands of folk performers (some of them superb artists with large repertoires, some of them everyday people who cherished one or two beautiful songs). But phonograph records have also taught me some of my favorites—for example:

PETE STEELE
    "Coal Creek March"*: *Anglo-American Shanties, Lyric Songs, Dance Tunes and Spirituals,* Library of Congress AAFS L 2

VERA HALL
"Another Man Done Gone"*: *Afro-American Blues and Game Songs*, Library of Congress AAFS L 4
"What Month Was Jesus Born?"*: *Spirituals*, Folkways FA 2038
THE BENTLY BOYS
"Down on Penny's Farm": *Anthology of American Folk Music*, Vol. I, Folkways FA 2951
SOLOMON LINDA AND THE EVENING BIRDS
"Mbube" ("Wimoweh")*: *New York 19*, Folkways FD 5558 (reproduced from a South African tape)
BASCOM LAMAR LUNSFORD
"Little Margaret"* (Lady Margaret): *Smoky Mountain Ballads*, Folkways FA 2040
UNCLE DAVE MACON
"Buddy Won't You Roll Down the Line": *Anthology of American Folk Music*, Vol. III, Folkways FA 2953
COON CREEK GIRLS
"Little Birdie"*: *Lily May, Rosie and Susie*, Country 712
THE CARTER FAMILY
"Worried Man Blues": *The Famous Carter Family*, Harmony 7280 (also Woody Guthrie, *Library of Congress Recordings*, Elektra 271–272)
"Sinking in the Lonesome Sea" (The Golden Vanity)*: *Carter Family Favorites*, Sunset 1153, also *Carter Family Sounds*, Harmony 7422
AUNT MOLLY JACKSON
Several ballads.* (Aunt Molly is included in Library of Congress records *Anglo-American Shanties, Lyric Songs, Dance Tunes*, and *Spirituals*, L 2; *Versions and Variants of "Barbara Allen,"* L 54; and *Child Ballads Traditional in the United States*, L 57. She recorded numerous other songs for the Archive of American Folk Song which have not as yet been published.)
B. F. SHELTON
"Darling Corey"*
"Pretty Polly"*
CLARA WARD
"This Little Light"*
JIMMIE RODGERS
"T for Texas"*
SONNY TERRY
"Go Where I Send Thee"*
WOODY GUTHRIE†
"This Land Is Your Land" and "Pastures of Plenty": *Bound for Glory*, Folkways FA 2481
"Pretty Boy Floyd": *Library of Congress Recordings*, Electra 271–2
"Buffalo Skinners"*
"Keep My Skillet Good and Greasy": *Woody Guthrie Sings Folksongs, Vol. I*, Folkways FA 2483
LEADBELLY†
"Bring Me a Little Water, Silvy," "Good Night Irene," "Grey Goose," "Pick a Bale of Cotton": *Take This Hammer*, Folkways FA 2004

---

* Songs which I play almost as I learned them.
† I learned most of these (and many more) from Woody and Leadbelly in person. They are gone; but we have their records to learn from.

"Rock Island Line": *Rock Island Line*, Folkways FA 2014
"Bourgeois Blues": *Easy Rider*, Folkways FA 2034
"Alabama Bound": *Leadbelly Sings Folk Songs*, Folkways FA 2488
"Midnight Special": *Leadbelly's Last Sessions* Vol. 2, Folkways FA 2942
"If It Wasn't for Dicky,"* *Leadbelly Library of Congress Recordings*, Elektra EKL 301/2

A bewildering abundance of authentic folk recordings is now available. It is not surprising if the novice wonders where to begin—and perhaps for that very reason decides to rely instead on the preselected, and modified, material which city professionals offer.

Fortunately, you can become acquainted with a large proportion of the (English-language) varieties of folk music in the U.S. from just two sets of LPs:

Anthology of American Folk Music, Folkways
   FA 2951 Vol. 1, *Early Ballads*
   FA 2952 Vol. 2, *Social Music* (dance music and religious songs)
   FA 2953 Vol. 3, *Songs*
      Reissues of commercial records made in the 20s. $11.50 for each two-disc volume (list price)

Library of Congress records:
   AAFS L 1 *Anglo-American Ballads*
   AAFS L 2 *Anglo-American Shanties, Lyric Songs, Dance Tunes and Spirituals*
   AAFS L 3 *Afro-American Spirituals, Work Songs, and Ballads*
   AAFS L 4 *Afro-American Blues and Game Songs*
      Selected by Alan Lomax from hundreds of field recordings made by folklorists for the Archive of Folk Song in the 30s and early 40s. $5.40 for each LP (order direct from Recording Laboratory, Library of Congress, Washington, D.C. 20540)

When you have heard all or most of these you will probably know what you want more of. Consult selected discographies like the one in Lomax's *The Folk Songs of North America*. Visit your public library's record department. Listen to folk programs on FM radio. Watch the record reviews in folk song, folklore, and record magazines.

Send for the complete Library of Congress catalogue (40 cents),* and Folkways' Comprehensive Catalogue (write Pioneer Records, 701 7th Avenue, New York, N. Y. 10036).

Folkways has by far the largest and most representative collection of any commercial firm, and has never discontinued any record—as most other companies do if sales are low. But many other firms now issue excellent folk records. The following are a few of the smaller and more specialized labels, together with some of the jazz labels which also offer basic blues and/or gospel music. They may not be well represented in your local record shop; but most of them will send you a catalogue and accept mail orders.

Arhoolie Records, Box 9195, Berkeley, Calif. 94719
Asch, RBF and Broadside Records: Pioneer Record Sales Corp., 701 7th Ave., New York, N. Y. 10036

---

* This catalogue lists several dozen LPs (including several hundred songs) selected from more than 16,000 records which constitute the Archive of Folk Song. Scholars can also arrange to obtain tapes of material which has not been issued on LPs.

Biograph Records Inc., P.O. Box 109, Canaan, N. Y. 12029
Blue Thumb, 427 N. Canyon Drive, Beverly Hills, Calif. 90210
Buddah Records, Inc., 1650 Broadway, New York, N. Y.
Chess Records, 320 E. 21st St., Chicago, Ill. 60616
Cook Laboratories, 101 Second St., Stamford, Conn.
County Sales, 309 E. 37 St., New York, N. Y. 10016
Delmark Records: Jazz Record Mart, 7 N. Grand Ave., Chicago, Ill. 60610
The Everest Record Group (including Archive of Folk and Jazz Music, Archive of
    Gospel Music, and Tradition), 10920 Wilshire Blvd., Los Angeles, Calif. 90024
Folk-Legacy Records, Inc., Sharon, Conn. 06069
Historical Records, Inc., Box 4204, Bergen Sta., Jersey City, N. J. 07304
Milestone Records, Inc., 119 W. 57th St., New York, N. Y. 10019
Origin Jazz Library, P. O. Box 863, Berkeley, Calif. 94701
Paredon, P. O. Box 889, Brooklyn, N. Y. 11202
Savoy Records, Inc., 56 Ferry St., Newark, N. J. 07105 (mainly for gospel singers)
Sire Records, 146 W. 54th St., New York, N. Y. 10019
Starday Records, P. O. Box 115, Madison, Tenn.
Stinson Records, P. O. Box 3415, Granada Hills, Calif. 91344
Vanguard Recording Society, 71 W. 23 St., New York, N. Y. 10010
Yazoo Records, Inc., 54 King St., New York, N. Y. 10014

The aim is to build a singing and listening repertoire which fits your own unique
needs and tastes.

(For other languages: the Folkways list is a goldmine; Library of Congress has
Texas Spanish, Louisiana French, Latin American, and a large selection of American
Indian music. Consult folklore journals, and general periodicals serving the language
group you are interested in. And don't forget your bilingual neighbors.)

"Can You Read Music?"
"Not Enough to Hurt My Playing."

Learning from Books

EVERY PERSON who ever tried to transcribe American folk
songs into music notation was faced with some almost insoluble
problems:

1. It is impossible to write down all the slurs between the notes, and
impossible to write down the way that good singers purposely sing cer-

tain notes sharp or flat. If you have listened to Negro folk singers you will have noticed that, whether it is a blues or a work song or a spiritual, the third and seventh notes of the scale tend to be flatted, and the fourth is sometimes sharpened.

Also, no two verses are sung exactly alike. It would be *wrong* to sing them alike. The words are different. The melody changes as the words require. (Of course, you better stay within the general idiom of the song.)

2. It is also impossible to write down the exact rhythm of many songs. If you wrote down all the syncopation of a blues, it would be impossible to read. Furthermore, folk singers often throw in extra beats to break up the sing-song character of a simple four-line verse. Woody Guthrie did it in every ballad he ever sang. Banjo pickers do it. Are such songs as "East Virgina" or "Little Birdie" in 4/4 time or 3/4 time? Actually they are in strict *1/4* time, with odd notes in every verse being held for long numbers of beats. The number of times you repeat the chorus is also optional.

No piece of paper can ever teach you how to play and sing a folk song. You have to listen to folk musicians—not just their urban interpreters —and teach yourself.

Books:

IT WOULD BE a brave person who would undertake to list the ten or twenty best books among hundreds of folk song collections now available. I suggest that you start with Alan Lomax, *The Folk Songs of North America in the English Language*, Doubleday & Co., Garden City, N.Y., 1960, $7.50.

Alan has personally collected more different kinds of music than any other individual; he also has encyclopedic familiarity with the work of other scholars. He was a pioneer in making folk music accessible to the general public, and in this book he tries to provide virtually everything the beginning amateur needs. Besides the 317 songs he chose as representative, there are background chapters giving a full, documented picture of the ways of life within which the songs flourished; guitar chords, edited by Peggy Seeger, for all the songs (and piano arrangements for many); capsule instruction manuals (again with Peggy's collaboration) on American guitar and banjo playing; bibliography and discography.

Alan's annotated bibliography will guide you to all the additional books you are likely to want for quite a while.

Hard-cover music books are not cheap. (Don't forget to use libraries.) If you want a less costly and more portable collection, there are:

Alan Lomax, *The Penguin Book of American Folk Songs,** Penguin Books, Baltimore, 1965, $1.95. (The British edition, if you can get hold of it, will fit your coat pocket; on the other hand, the folio-sized American version is easier to read.)

Pete Seeger, *American Favorite Ballads,* Oak Publications, New York, 1961, $1.95 (with a page of guitar-chord diagrams).

————, *The Bells of Rhymney and Other Songs,* Oak Publications, New York, 1964, $2.95 (both American and foreign songs, including many recently composed).

It can be rewarding to browse in the catalogues of publishers who issue folk music paperbacks (including reprints of important out-of-print works); for example:

Oak Publications, 33 W. 60 St., New York, N. Y. 10023
Hargail Music, Inc., 28 W. 38 St., New York, N. Y. 10018
Dover Publications, Inc., 180 Varick St., New York, N. Y. 10014

Mail-order catalogues including old and new folk music books of many publishers are issued by:

Legacy Book Sellers (formerly Folklore Associates), Box 155, Haverford, Pa. 19041
The Folklore Center, 321 Sixth Ave., New York, N. Y. 10014

Magazines:

Sing Out!, 33 W. 60 St., New York, N. Y. 10023, bimonthly, $5.00 per year. Traditional folk music and related kinds of new songs. Each issue includes a dozen or more songs, plus articles, news and comment, book and record reviews.

Broadside, 215 W. 98 St., New York, N. Y. 10025, monthly, $5.00 per year. Concentrates on publishing as many topical songs as possible as soon as possible after the events they deal with. Varying amounts of comment, news of concerts and other relevant matters, occasional reviews.

In recent years there have been numerous local publications for folk singers, of varying longevity. *Sing Out* and *Broadside* provide frequent information about them. For a different approach:

Ethnomusicology, the journal of the Society for Ethnomusicology, Room 513, 201 S. Main St., Ann Arbor, Mich. 48108. Three issues a year. Membership, $12.50 (members receive 33⅓ percent discount on Folkways records). Music from an anthropological point of view; the world-wide horizon is stimulating. Excellent coverage of books, records and films.

Journal of the American Folklore Society, University of Texas Press, Austin, Texas 78712. Membership $10.00 (includes also *Abstracts of Folklore Studies*). Scholarly articles, with music only one among several folklore branches. Book and record reviews.

There are also state and regional folklore journals covering most parts of the country.

A number of other countries have folk singers' magazines similar in outlook and content to *Sing Out.* Some of my favorites:

---
* See Chapter 4, p. 275.

Australian Tradition magazine, 36 Westbourne St., Prahan, Victoria 3181, Australia
Chapbook, James Dunnett, 114 Kirkhill Road, Aberdeen, Scotland
Spin, 34 Thirlmere Drive, Wallasey, Cheshire, England
Journal of the African Music Society, P. O. Box 138, Roodeport (near Johannesburg), South Africa
Sing Out itself frequently publishes and discusses songs from abroad.

On the scholarly side, one might start with: *Journal of the International Folk Music Council*, Messrs. Heffer and Sons, Ltd., Cambridge, England

Folk Music Films

A NEARLY IDEAL WAY to learn about folk music would be from sound films of authentic performers in their normal home environments. A good many such films have been made; but few are readily available, chiefly because prints are expensive to make and wear out rapidly. I have wrestled with this problem for years without finding a good solution; at present my best hope is that TV tape machines will come down in price enough to be practical, if not for the average family, at least for schools and organizations.

The following rental films on American folk music have been listed in *Ethnomusicology*. (Not all of them give the music its actual native setting, but all present genuine folk musicians.)

From Indiana University Audio-Visual Center (Bloomington, Ind. 47401):

High Lonesome Sound
    Roscoe Holcomb, Bill Monroe and other Kentuckians
To Hear Your Banjo Play
    Mrs. Texas Gladden, Horton Barker, Woody Guthrie, Brownie McGhee, Sonny Terry, Pete Seeger (all except the last are country musicians)
Music Makers of the Blue Ridge
    Bascom Lamar Lunsford and other North Carolinians
Music of Williamsburg
    Hobart Smith of Virginia, Bessie Jones and Georgia Sea Island Singers, Ed Young of Mississippi
The Search
    Booth Campbell, Mary Jo Davis, Doney Hamontree, Fred High, of the Ozark Mountains
Lyrics and Legends (films from an educational TV series)
    1. *Mexican-American Border Songs*
    2. *The Roots of Hillbilly Music*
        Clarence Ashley, Maybelle Carter, Mose Ranger, the Walker Family
    3. *Sea Songs*

Frank Warner, Sam Eskin, E. G. Huntington (only Huntington is a former windjammer seaman)
4. *Square Dance Play-Party*
The Ritchie Family, Corbett Grigsby, Marion Sumner (Kentucky)
Songs of Nova Scotia
(Helen Creighton collects from traditional singers)
Music from Oil Drums
Kim Loy Wong and other Trinidadians

(Also films on the music of various American Indian tribes)

From C.C.M. Films, Inc. (34 So. MacQuesten Parkway South, Mount Vernon, N. Y. 10550. The former Brandon Films, Inc. is now part of C.C.M.):

The Blues
J. B. Short, Pink Anderson, Furry Lewis, Baby Tate, Memphis Willie B., Gus Cannon, Sleepy John Estes
The Country Fiddle
Jean Caragnan of Canada, Mrs. Marion Unger Thede of Oklahoma, and others

From Contemporary Films (Princeton Rd., Hightstown, N. J. 08520):
Blind Gary Davis
(Southern-born Harlem street singer)

(C.C.M. and Contemporary also handle some of the films listed under Indiana University.)

From Folklore Research Films (Box 431, Beacon, N. Y. 12508):
Afro-American Work Song in a Texas Prison
(Groups of prisoners singing while chopping trees and hoeing)

The following are available for sale only:
From Educational Services, University of Washington Press, Ott H. Hyatt, Manager (Seattle, Washington 98105):
A Program of Songs by Lightnin' Sam Hopkins
(Texas blues singer)

From The Housing Foundation, Inc. (255 Center St., Box 349, Manchester, Conn. 06040):
Instruments for Folk Songs
Jimmy Driftwood of Arkansas

A recently completed film is available from John Cohen (Rte. 1, Tompkins Corners, Putnam Valley, N. Y.):
The End of an Old Song
Dillard Chandler and other North Carolina ballad singers

(John also handles *The High Lonesome Sound*.)

Films from a number of countries are available at Indiana University. One of special interest to Anglo-Americans is *'Oss 'Oss Wee 'Oss*, a village festival in Cornwall, England, filmed by Peter Kennedy, Alan Lomax and George Pickow.

The Picture Makers

Sometimes a photographer seems nearly as impossible to trace as the very first singer of an old song. We've tried hard to identify and credit all of them, but still have to list several "unknowns."

Continued from page iv

Index